BRITISH ANTIQUE REPLICAS

Over 50 dining tables on display in our showrooms made by master craftsmen to a standard unsurpassed this century, together with 100 styles of Chairs, also sideboards, Desks, Filling Cabinets, Cocktail Cabinets, TV & Video Cabinets, Leather Chairs, Chesterfields & Looking Glasses. All available in three separate ranges to suit all life styles & income groups.

Specialist export packing & shipping worldwide

BRITISH ANTIQUE REPLICA HANDMADE
Cabinet Furniture is Guaranteed for 50 YEARS

Visit our factory & Showrooms to see the world's largest
display of English Antique Replica Furniture
Mon-Sat 9am-5.30pm
SCHOOL CLOSE, QUEEN ELIZABETH AVE, BURGESS HILL
(BETWEEN GATWICK & BRIGHTON) WEST SUSSEX RH15 9RX
TEL 01444 245577

INTERNATIONAL
Antiques
PRICE GUIDE

INTERNATIONAL
Antiques
PRICE GUIDE

Consultant
Judith Miller

Associate Editors

Ian McKay

Elizabeth Norfolk

Introduction by
Lita Solis-Cohen

1997
Volume XVIII

MILLER'S INTERNATIONAL ANTIQUES PRICE GUIDE 1997

Created and designed by
Miller's
The Cellars, High Street,
Tenterden, Kent, TN30 6BN
Tel: 01580 766411

Consultant: Judith Miller

Associate Editors: Ian McKay, Elizabeth Norfolk
Editorial and Production Co-ordinator: Sue Boyd
Editorial Assistants: Marion Rickman, Jo Wood, Gillian Judd
Production Assistants: Gillian Charles, Karen Taylor
Advertising Executive: Elizabeth Smith
Advertising Assistants: Melinda Williams, Liz Warwick
Index compiled by: Hilary Bird, Goudhurst, Kent
Design: Jody Taylor, Kari Reeves, Shirley Reeves, Matthew Leppard
Additional photography: Ian Booth, Roy Farthing, Dennis O'Reilly, Robin Saker

First published in Great Britain in 1996
by Miller's, an imprint of
Reed Books Limited,
Michelin House, 81 Fulham Road,
London SW3 6RB
and Auckland, Melbourne, Singapore and Toronto

This edition distributed in the US
by
Antique Collectors' Club Ltd
Market Street Industrial Park
Wappingers' Falls
New York 12590

© 1996 Reed International Books Limited

A CIP catalogue record for this book is
available from the British Library

ISBN 1-85732-892-2

Bromide output by Perfect Image, Hurst Green, E. Sussex
Illustrations by G.H. Graphics, St. Leonard's-on-Sea
Colour origination by Scantrans, Singapore
Printed and bound in England by William Clowes Ltd.,
Beccles and London

Front cover illustrations:
top l. *A Tiffany Favrile glass and bronze Dragonfly Lamp, on a mosaic Dragonfly base,
c1910, 16½in (42cm) high. S(NY)*
r. *A Regency mahogany quarter-striking longcase clock, altered and restored, 102in (260cm) high. C*
bottom l. *A pair of George I figured walnut side chairs. C*

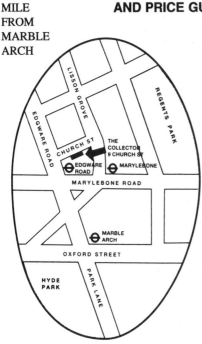

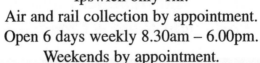

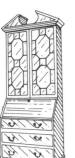
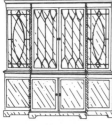

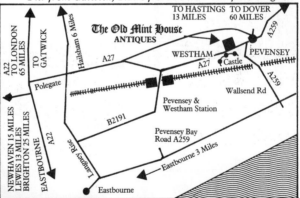

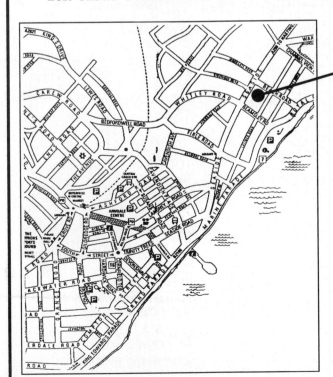

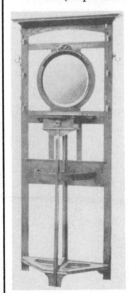

The Collectors' Service

"As a collector, The Collectors' Service is the answer to a dream. I often wonder how I ever managed before I found out about this service, and at such a reasonable price too."

A private collector

The service provides information gathered from over 450 salerooms, holding regular auctions of interest to the enthusiastic amateur or serious collector. Most are general sales and include a mixture of antiques and collectables that may contain the treasure you have been seeking. You can also find all sorts of varied items at these auctions - a Victorian cheese wagon, a Regency sideboard, a family portrait or a pair of Staffordshire dogs.

The service allows you to discover where an item is appearing at auction, without consuming endless hours reading sale catalogues, and yet still provides the excitement of participating on sale day!

An unrivalled source of information delivered to you via a weekly report, will give details of sale viewing times and place, lot number and the text description for the item you are seeking. Checking, viewing and placing the bid is up to you.

"I used to pride myself that I had my field covered very thoroughly. That is until I subscribed to the service! Now I realise that I was barely scratching the surface. Many of the treasures that I have been able to add to my collection have only been possible because the system unearthed them for me."

A private collector

Subscription to "The Collectors' Service" is **£34.99** for a period of three months or 13 weekly reports. Bonus months are available if we are unable to locate the item during your subscription.

To subscribe, please send your name and address details, with the description of the item that you wish us to locate, together with a cheque for £34.99 to:
The Collectors' Service, 76 Gloucester Place, LONDON W1H 4DQ.
Phone 01983 826199, or Fax your details with your credit card number to 0171 487 4211.

Your interest should be described as laid out in reference books such as Miller's Antiques Price Guide, ie furniture, Mahogany wine cooler, Longcase clock by maker, Ceramics by factory type and particular figure/group or pattern and set description. For artist please include name and alternative spellings and if possible date of birth.

CONTENTS

1997

KEY TO ILLUSTRATIONS

Each illustration and descriptive caption is accompanied by a letter code. By referring to the following list of Auctioneers (denoted by *) and Dealers (•) the source of any item may be immediately determined. Inclusion in this edition in no way constitutes or implies a contract or binding offer on the part of any of our contributors to supply or sell the goods illustrated, or similar articles, at the prices stated. Advertisers in this year's directory are denoted by †.

If you require a valuation for an item, it is advisable to check whether the dealer or specialist will carry out this service and if there is a charge. Please mention Miller's when making an enquiry. Having found a specialist who will carry out your valuation it is best to send a photograph and description of the item to the specialist together with a stamped addressed envelope for the reply. A valuation by telephone is not possible. Most dealers are only too happy to help you with your enquiry, however, they are very busy people and consideration of the above points would be appreciated.

AAV	*	Academy Auctioneers & Valuers, Northcote House, Northcote Avenue, Ealing, London W5 3UR Tel: 0181 579 7466
AEF	•	A & E Foster, Little Heysham, Naphill, Bucks HP14 4SU Tel: 01494 562024
AF	•†	Albert Forsythe, Mill House, 66 Carsontown Road, Saintfield, Co Down, Ireland BT24 7EB Tel: 01238 510398
AG	*	Anderson & Garland (Auctioneers), Marlborough House, Marlborough Crescent, Newcastle-upon-Tyne, Tyne & Wear NE1 4EE Tel: 0191 232 6278
AH	*†	Andrew Hartley, Victoria Salerooms, Little Lane, Ilkley, Yorkshire LS29 8EA Tel: 01943 816363
AHO	•†	Amanda House, The Barns, Twigworth Court, Twigworth, Glos GL2 9PG Tel: 01452 731296
AL	•†	Ann Lingard, Ropewalk Antiques, Ropewalk, Rye, Sussex TN31 7NA Tel: 01797 223486
ALS	•†	Allan Smith Clocks, Amity Cottage, 162 Beechcroft Road, Upper Stratton, Swindon, Wiltshire SN2 6QE Tel: 01793 822977
AMH	•	Amherst Antiques, 23 London Road, Riverhead, Sevenoaks, Kent TN13 2BU Tel: 01732 455047
ANG	•†	Ancient & Gothic, PO Box 356, Christchurch, Dorset BH23 2YD Tel: 01202 478592
ANT	•†	Anthemion Antiques, Bridge Street, Cartmel, Grange Over Sands, Cumbria LA11 7SH Tel: 015395 36295/36362
APa	•	Angela Page Antiques, 15 Cumberland Walk, Tunbridge Wells, Kent TN1 1VT Tel: 01892 522217
APO	•†	Apollo Antiques Ltd, The Saltisford, Birmingham Road, Warwick, Warwickshire CV34 4TD Tel: 01926 494746
ASA	•†	A. S. Antiques, 26 Broad Street, Pendleton, Salford, Gt. Manchester M6 5BY Tel: 0161 737 5938
ASH	•†	Ashburton Marbles, Grate Hall, North Street, Ashburton, Devon TQ13 7QD Tel: 01364 653189
ASP	•	John Aspleys Antiques.
B	*	Boardman Fine Art Auctioneers, Station Road Corner, Haverhill, Suffolk CB9 0EY Tel: 01440 730414
B&B	*	Butterfield & Butterfield, 220 San Bruno Avenue, San Francisco, USA CA 94103 Tel: 415 861 7500
BaH	•	Calamus, The Shambles, Sevenoaks, Kent TN13 1AL Tel: 01732 740603
BaN	•	Weald Antiques Gallery
Bar	•†	Chris Barge Antiques, 5 Southside Place, Inverness, Scotland IV2 3JF Tel: 01463 230128
BAS	•†	Brighton Architectural Salvage, 33 Gloucester Road, Brighton, Sussex BN1 4AQ Tel: 01273 681656
Bea	*	Bearnes, Avenue Road, Torquay, Devon TQ2 5TG Tel: 01803 296277
BEV	•	Beverley, 30 Church Street, London NW8 8EP Tel: 0171 262 1576
BHa	•†	Judy & Brian Harden Antiques, Glos. Tel: 01451 810684
BKK	•†	Bona Arts Decorative Ltd, 19 Princes Mead Shopping Centre, Farnborough, Hampshire GU14 7TJ Tel: 01252 372188
Bon	*†	Bonhams, Montpelier Street, Knightsbridge, London SW7 1HH Tel: 0171 584 9161
BOR	•	Bed of Roses, 12 Prestbury Road, Cheltenham, Glos GL52 2PW Tel: 01242 231918
BRA	•†	Billiard Room Antiques, The Old School, Church Lane, Chilcompton, Bath, Somerset BA3 4HP Tel: 01761 232839

Bri	*†	Bristol Auction Rooms, St John's Place, Apsley Road, Clifton, Bristol, Avon BS8 2ST Tel: 0117 973 7201
BS	•	Below Stairs, 103 High Street, Hungerford, Berkshire RG17 0NB Tel: 01488 682317
BUT	•†	Butchoff Antiques, 233 Westbourne Grove, London W11 2SE Tel: 0171 221 8174
BWC	•	British Watch and Clock Collectors Association, 5 Cathedral Lane, Truro, Cornwall TR1 2QS Tel: 01872 41953
BWe	*	Biddle and Webb Ltd, Ladywood Middleway, Birmingham, West Midlands B16 0PP Tel: 0121 455 8042
ByI	•	Bygones of Ireland, Westport Antiques Centre, Lodge Road, Westport, County Mayo, Ireland Tel: 00 353 98 26132
C	*	Christie, Manson & Woods Ltd, 8 King Street, St James's, London SW1Y 6QT Tel: 0171 839 9060
C(G)	*	Christie's (International) S.A., 8 Place de la Taconnerie, 1204 Geneva, Switzerland Tel: 00 4122 311 17 66
C(S)	*	Christie's Scotland Ltd, 164-166 Bath Street, Glasgow, Scotland G2 4TG Tel: 0141 332 8134
C(SP)	*	Christie's, 501 Orchard Road, 15-02 Lane Crawford Place, Singapore 0923 Tel: (65) 737 3884
CAG	*†	Canterbury Auction Galleries, 40 Station Road West, Canterbury, Kent CT2 8AN Tel: 01227 763337
CB	•	Bridge Antiques, Christine, 78 Castelnau, London SW13 9EX Tel: 0181 741 5501
CBu	•	Buck Antiques, Christopher, 56-60 Sandgate High Street, Folkestone Kent CT20 3AP Tel: 01303 221229
CCC	•†	Crested China Co, The Station House, Driffield, Yorkshire YO25 7PY Tel: 01377 257042
CCP	•†	Campden Country Pine Antiques, High Street, Chipping Campden, Glos GL55 6HN Tel: 01386 840315
CDC	*	Capes Dunn & Co, The Auction Galleries, 38 Charles Street, Off Princess Street, Gt Manchester M1 7DB Tel: 0161 273 6060/1911
CHR	•	Charnwood Antiques, 'Greystones', Coalville, Leicester, Leicestershire LE67 4RN Tel: 0116 283 8530
CLC	•†	The Clock Clinic Ltd, 85 Lower Richmond Road, London SW5 1EU Tel: 0181 788 1407
CMF	•	Childhood Memories, The Farnham Antique Centre, 27 South Street, Farnham, Surrey GU9 7QU Tel: 01252 724475
CNY	*	Christie, Manson & Woods International Inc, 502 Park Avenue, (including Christie's East), New York, USA NY 10022 Tel: 001 212 546 1000
COT	•	Cottage Antiques, Bakewell & Woburn Antiques Centres, Bucks Tel: 01283 562670
COW	•†	Clive Cowell, Glassenbury Timber Yard, Iden Green, Goudhurst, Cranbrook, Kent TN17 2PA Tel: 01580 212022
CS	•†	Christopher Sykes Antiques, The Old Parsonage, Woburn, Bucks MK17 9QM Tel: 01525 290259
CSA	•	Church Street Antiques, 10 Church Street, Godalming, Surrey GU7 1EL Tel: 01483 860894
CSK	*	Christie's South Kensington Ltd, 85 Old Brompton Road, London SW7 3LD Tel: 0171 581 7611
CTO	•†	Collector's Corner (Tudor House), 29–31 Lower Bridge Road, Bridge Road, Chester, Cheshire CH1 1RS Tel: 01244 346736
DA	*†	Dee, Atkinson & Harrison, The Exchange Saleroom, Driffield, Yorkshire, YO25 7LJ Tel: 01377 253151

DaD   *   David Dockree, 224 Moss Lane, Bramhall, Stockport, Cheshire SK7 1BD Tel: 0161 485 1258

DAF   •†   Arts Decoratifs, 18–20 Suffolk Parade, Cheltenham, Glos GL50 2AE Tel: 01242 512774

DBA   •†   Old Bakery Antiques, St Davids Bridge, Cranbrook, Kent TN17 3HN Tel: 01580 713103

DeG   •   Denzil Grant, Hubbards Corner, Bradfield St George, Bury St Edmunds, Suffolk IP30 0AQ Tel: 01449 736576

DN   *†   Dreweatt Neate, Donnington Priory, Donnington, Newbury, Berkshire RG13 2JE Tel: 01635 31234

DOL   •   Dollectable, 53 Lower Bridge Street, Chester, Cheshire CH1 1RS Tel: 01244 344888/679195

DOR   •†   Dorset Reclamation, Cow Drove, Bere Regis, Wareham, Dorset BH20 7JZ Tel: 01929 472200

DRA   •†   Derek Roberts, 24-25 Shipbourne Road, Tonbridge, Kent TN10 3DN Tel: 01732 358986

DSP   •   David & Sarah Pullen, PO Box 24, Bexhill-on-Sea, Sussex TN40 1EF Tel: 01424 222035

DW   *†   Dominic Winter Book Auctions, The Old School, Maxwell Street, Swindon, Wiltshire, SN1 5DR Tel: 01793 611340

E   *   Ewbank Auctioneers, Burnt Common Auction Rooms, London Road, Send, Woking, Surrey GU23 7LN Tel: 01483 223101

EB   *   Escritt & Barrell, 24 St Peter's Hill, Grantham, Lincolnshire NG31 6QF Tel: 01476 65371

ED   •   Elite Designs, Sussex Tel: 01424 434856

EL   *   Eldred's, Robert C Eldred Co Inc, 1475 Route 6A, East Dennis, Massachusetts 0796, USA 02641 Tel: 001 508 385 3116

EP   *†   Evans & Partridge, Agriculture House, High Street, Stockbridge, Hampshire SO20 6HF Tel: 01264 810702

ERA   •   English Rose Antiques, 7 Church Street, Coggeshall, Essex CO6 1TU Tel: 01376 562683

ET   •†   Early Technology, 84 West Bow, Edinburgh, Scotland EH1 2HH Tel: 0131 226 1132

EUR   •   Eureka Antiques, Cheshire Tel: 0161 941 5453 (Appointment only)

FD   •   Frank Dux Antiques, 33 Belvedere, Bath, Avon BA1 5HR Tel: 01225 312367

FOX   •   Foxhole Antiques, High Street, Goudhurst, Kent TN17 1AE Tel: 01580 212025

G&CC   •†   Goss & Crested China Ltd, 62 Murray Road, Horndean, Hampshire PO8 9JL Tel: 01705 597440

Gam   *   Clarke & Gammon, The Guildford Auction Rooms, Bedford Road, Guildford, Surrey GU1 4SJ Tel: 01483 66458

GAS   •   Gasson Antiques, PO Box 11, Cranleigh, Surrey GU6 8YY Tel: 01483 277476

GeC   •†   Gerard Campbell, Maple House, Market Place, Lechlade, Glos GL7 3AB Tel: 01367 252267

GH   *   Giles Haywood, The Auction House, St John's Road, Stourbridge, West Midlands DY8 1EW Tel: 01384 370891

Gle   *   Glendinings & Co, 101 New Bond Street, London W1Y 9LG Tel: 0171 493 2445

GN   •†   Gillian Neale Antiques, PO Box 247, Aylesbury, Bucks HP20 1JZ Tel: 01296 23754

GOO   •†   Gooday Gallery, 20 Richmond Hill, Richmond, Surrey TW10 6Q Tel: 0181 940 8652

GUN   •†   Gaby Gunst, Antique Clocks & Barometers, 140 High Street, Tenterden, Kent TN30 6HT Tel: 01580 765818

GV   •†   GarthVincent, The Old Manor House, Allington, Nr Grantham, Lincolnshire NG32 2HD Tel: 01400 281358

HAB   •†   Hamilton Games Co, Park Lane, Knebworth, Hertfordshire SG3 6PJ Tel: 01438 811995

HAL   •†   John & Simon Haley, 89 Northgate, Halifax, Yorkshire HX6 4NG Tel: 01422 822148/360434

Hal   *   Halls Fine Art Auctions, Welsh Bridge, Shrewsbury, Shropshire SY3 8LA Tel: 01743 231212

HAM   *†   Hamptons Antique & Fine Art Auctioneers, 93 High Street, Godalming, Surrey GU7 1AL Tel: 01483 423567

HAR   *   William Hardie Ltd, 15a Blythswood Square, Glasgow, G2 4EW Tel: 0141 221 6780

Har   •   Patricia Harbottle, Geoffrey Vann Arcade, 107 Portobello Road, London W11 2QB Tel: 0171 731 1972

HCC   *†   H C Chapman & Son, The Auction Mart, North Street, Scarborough, Yorkshire YO11 1DL Tel: 01723 372424

HCH   *   Hobbs & Chambers, Market Place, Cirencester, Glos GL7 1QQ Tel: 01285 654736

HDS   *   HY Duke & Son, Dorchester Fine Art Salerooms, Dorchester, Dorset DT1 1QS Tel: 01305 265080

HEA   •   Peter Hearnden, Tel: 01634 374132 (Appointment only)

HEI   •†   Heirloom Antiques, 68 High Street, Tenterden, Kent TN30 6AU Tel: 01580 765535

HEM   •†   Hemswell Antique Centre, Caenby Corner Estate, Hemswell Cliff, Gainsborough, Lincolnshire DN21 5TJ Tel: 01427 668389

HIS   •   Hiscock & Hiscock Antiques, 47 High Street, New Romney, Kent TN28 8AH Tel: 01797 364023

HOA   •†   Bob Hoare, Pine Antiques, Unit Q, Phoenix Place, North Street, Lewes, Sussex BN7 2DQ Tel: 01273 480557

HOLL   *†   Dreweatt Neate Holloways, 49 Parsons Street, Banbury, Oxfordshire OX16 8PF Tel: 01295 253197

HOW   •   Howards Antiques, 10 Alexandra Road, Aberystwyth, Dyfed, Wales SY23 1LE Tel: 01970 624973

IW   •†   Islwyn Watkins, 1 High Street, Knighton, Powys, Wales LD7 1AT Tel: 01547 520145

J&L   •   James & Lister Lea, 1741 Warwick Road, Knowle, Birmingham, West Midlands B93 0LX Tel: 01564 779187

JAd   *   James Adam & Sons, 26 St Stephen's Green, Dublin 2, Ireland Tel: 00 3531 676 0261/661 3655

JC   •   J Collins & Son, 28 High Street, Bideford, Devon EX39 2AN Tel: 01237 473103

JES   •   John Jesse, 160 Kensington Church Street, London W8 4BN Tel: 0171 229 0312

JH   *   Jacobs & Hunt, Lavant Street, Petersfield, Hampshire GU32 3EF Tel: 01730 262744/5

JHo   •†   Jonathan Horne (Antiques) Ltd, 66C Kensington Church Street, London W8 4BY Tel: 0171 221 5658

JL   •   Joy Luke, The Gallery, 300E Grove Street, Bloomington, USA IL 61701 Tel: 001 309 828 5533

JNic   *   John Nicholson, The Auction Rooms, Longfield, Midhurst Road, Fernhurst, Surrey GU27 3HA Tel: 01428 653727

JO   •†   Jacqueline Oosthuizen, 23 Cale Street, Chelsea, London SW3 3QR Tel: 0171 352 6071

JP   •†   Janice Paull, Beehive House, 125 Warwick Road, Kenilworth, Warwickshire CV8 1HY Tel: 01926 855253/0831 691254

JRe   •   John Read, 29 Lark Rise, Martlesham Heath, Ipswich, Suffolk IP5 7SA Tel: 01473 624897

JSH   *   Jack Shaw & Co, The Old Grammar School, Skipton Road, Ilkley, Yorks LS29 9EJ Tel: 01943 609467

KEY   •†   Key Antiques, 11 Horse Fair, Chipping Norton, Oxfordshire OX7 5AL Tel: 01608 643777

KID   *†   George Kidner, The Old School, The Square, Pennington, Lymington, Hampshire SO41 8GN Tel: 01590 670070

L   *   Lawrence Fine Art Auctioneers, South Street, Crewkerne, Somerset TA18 8AB Tel: 01460 73041

L&E   *†   Locke & England, Black Horse Agencies, 18 Guy Street, Leamington Spa, Warwickshire CV34 4RT Tel: 01926 889100

LCA   •†   La Chaise Antiques, 30 London Street, Faringdon, Oxfordshire SN7 7AA Tel: 01367 240427

LEN   •   Lennox Catto, Coombe House Antiques, 121 Malling Street, Lewes, Sussex BN7 2RJ Tel: 01273 473862/0836 233473

LHA   *   Lesley Hindman Auctioneers, 215 West Ohio Street, Chicago, Illinois, USA IL 60610 Tel: 001 312 670 0010

LHB   •   Gallery 'Les Hommes Bleus', Bartlett Street, Bath, Avon BA1 2QZ Tel: 01225 316606

M   *   Morphets of Harrogate, 4-6 Albert Street, Harrogate, Yorkshire HG1 1JL Tel: 01423 502282

MAT   *   Christopher Matthews, 23 Mount Street, Harrogate, Yorkshire HG2 8DQ Tel: 01423 871756

MB   •   Marilynn Brass, 205 Walden Street - 45 Cambridge, USA, MA 02140 Tel: 617 492 2777 Ex 2413

MBr *† Morris Bricknell, Stuart House, 18 Gloucester Road, Ross-on-Wye, Hereford & Worcs HR9 5BU Tel: 01989 768320

MCA * Mervyn Carey, Twysden Cottage, Benenden, Cranbrook, Kent TN17 4LD Tel: 01580 240283

McC * McCartneys, Ox Pasture, Overture Road, Ludlow, Shropshire SY8 4AA Tel: 01584 872251

MER •† Mere Antiques, 13 Fore Street, Topsham, Exeter, Devon EX3 0HF Tel: 01392 874224

Mit * Mitchells, Fairfield House, Station Road, Cockermouth, Cumbria CA13 9PY Tel: 01900 827800

MJB * Michael J Bowman, 6 Haccombe House, Netherton, Newton Abbot, Devon TQ12 4SJ Tel: 01626 872890

MJW • Mark J West, Cobb Antiques Ltd, 39a High Street, Wimbledon Village, London SW19 5YX Tel: 0181 946 2811

MLa •† Marion Langham, London Tel: 0171 730 1002

MM • Michael Marriott, 588 Fulham Road, London SW6 5NT Tel: 0171 736 3110

MMo • Maureen Morris, Essex Tel: 01799 521338 (Appointment only)

MofC • Millers of Chelsea Antiques Ltd, Netherbrook House, 86 Christchurch Road, Ringwood, Hampshire BH24 1DR Tel: 01425 472062

MR *† Martyn Rowe, Truro Auction Centre, Calenick Street, Truro, Cornwall TR1 2SG Tel: 01872 260020

MSh • Manfred Schotten, The Crypt Antiques, 109 High Street, Burford, Oxon OX18 4RG Tel: 01993 822302

MSW *† Marilyn Swain Auctions, The Old Barracks, Sandon Road, Grantham, Lincolnshire NG31 9AS Tel: 01476 568861

N *† Neales, 192-194 Mansfield Road, Nottingham, Notts NG1 3HU Tel: 0115 962 4141

ND *† Nock Deighton, Livestock & Auction Centre, Tasley, Bridgnorth, Shropshire WV16 4QR Tel: 01746 762666

Nor •† Sue Norman, L4 Antiquarius, 135 King's Road, London SW3 5ST Tel: 0171 352 7217

OD • Offa's Dyke Antique Centre, 4 High Street, Knighton, Powys, Wales LD7 1AT Tel: 01547 528635/528940

Oli *† Olivers, Olivers Rooms, Burkitts Lane, Sudbury, Suffolk CO10 6HB Tel: 01787 880305

OLM •† Old Mill, The, High Street, Lamberhurst, Kent TN3 8EQ Tel: 01892 891196

OO •† Pieter Oosthuizen, 1st Floor, Georgian Village, Camden Passage, London N1 8DU Tel: 0171 359 3322/376 3852

OPH •† Old Pine House, 16 Warwick Street, Royal Leamington Spa, Warwickshire CV32 5LL Tel: 01926 470477

ORI • Oriental Gallery, The Malthouse, Digbeth St, Stow-on-the-Wold, Glos GL54 1BN Tel: 01451 830944

P *† Phillips, 101 New Bond Street, London W1Y 0AS Tel: 0171 629 6602

P(B) * Phillips, 1 Old King Street, Bath, Avon BA1 2JT Tel: 01225 310609

P(Ba) * Phillips Bayswater, 10 Salem Road, London W2 4DL Tel: 0171 229 9090

P(C) * Phillips Cardiff, 9-10 Westgate Street, Cardiff, Wales CF1 1DA Tel: 01222 396453

P(Ch) * Phillips Chichester, Baffins Hall, Baffins Lane, Chichester, Sussex PO19 1UA Tel: 01243 787548

P(E) * Phillips Exeter, Alphin Brook Road, Alphington, Exeter, Devon EX2 8TH Tel: 01392 439025

P(F) * Phillips Folkestone, 11 Bayle Parade, Folkestone, Kent CT20 1SG Tel: 01303 245555

P(G) * Phillips Fine Art Auctioneers, Millmead, Guildford, Surrey GU2 5BE Tel: 01483 504030

P(H) * Phillips, 1 Princes Square, Harrogate, Yorkshire HG1 1ND Tel: 01423 500566

P(HSS)* Henry Spencer & Son (Phillips), 20 The Square, Retford, Notts DN22 6BX Tel: 01777 708633

P(NE) * Phillips North East, St Mary's, Oakwellgate, Gateshead, Tyne & Wear NE8 2AX Tel: 0191 477 6688

P(O) * Phillips, 39 Park End Street, Oxford Oxfordshire OX1 1JD Tel: 01865 723524

P(S) * Phillips Fine Art Auctioneers, 49 London Road, Sevenoaks, Kent TN13 1AR Tel: 01732 740310

P(Sc) * Phillips Scotland, 65 George Street, Edinburgh, EH2 2JL Tel: 0131 225 2266 and 207 Bath Street, Glasgow G2 4HD Tel: 0141 221 8377

PAO •† P A Oxley, The Old Rectory, Cherhill, Nr Calne, Wilts SN11 8UX Tel: 01249 816227

PBi • Peter Bird, 811 Christchurch Road, Boscombe, Dorset BH21 1TZ Tel: 01202 429111

PC Private Collection

PCh *† Peter Cheney, Western Road Auction Rooms, Western Road, Littlehampton, Sussex BN17 5NP Tel: 01903 722264/713418

PEx •† Piano Export, Bridge Road, Kingswood, Bristol, Avon BS15 4PW Tel: 0117 956 8300

PGH • Paris, 42A High Street, Tenterden, Kent TN30 6AR Tel: 01580 765328

PHA •† Paul Hopwell Antiques, 30 High Street, West Haddon, Northants NN6 7AP Tel: 01788 510636

PNF •† Pinfold Antiques, 3 Pinfold Lane, Ruskington, Lincolnshire NG34 9EU Tel: 01526 832057

POT • Potboard, 30 King Street, Carmarthen, Dyfed, Wales SA31 1BS Tel: 01267 236623

POW • Sylvia Powell, 18 The Mall, Camden Passage, London N1 0PD Tel: 0171 354 2977

PP • Poole Pottery, The Quay, Poole, Dorset BH15 1RF Tel: 01202 666200

PSA • Pantiles Spa Antiques, 4-6 Union House, The Pantiles, Tunbridge Wells, Kent TN4 8HE Tel: 01892 541377

PT •† Pieces of Time, 1-7 Davies Mews, London W1Y 1AR Tel: 0171 629 2422

RA • Roberts Antiques, Lancashire Tel: 01253 827798

RAF •† Raffety, 34 Kensington Church Street, London W8 4HA Tel: 0171 938 1100

RAR *† Romsey Auction Rooms, 86 The Hundred, Romsey, Hampshire SO51 8BX Tel: 01794 513331

RAY •† Derek & Tina Rayment Antiques, Orchard House, Barton Road, Barton, Nr Farndon, Cheshire SY14 7HT Tel: 01829 270429

RBB *† Russell, Baldwin & Bright, Ryelands Road, Leominster, Hereford & Worcs HR6 8NZ Tel: 01568 611166

RCh • Rayner & Chamberlain, London Tel: 0181 293 9439

RdeR •† Rogers de Rin, 76 Royal Hospital Road, London SW3 4HN Tel: 0171 352 9007

REN • Paul & Karen Rennie, 13 Rugby Street, London WC1N 3QT Tel: 0171 405 0220

RHa • Robert Hall, 15c Clifford Street, London W1X 1RF Tel: 0171 734 4008

RHE * R H Ellis & Sons, 44-46 High Street, Worthing, Sussex BN11 1LL Tel: 01903 238999

RIC •† Rich Designs, 1 Shakespeare Street, Stratford-upon-Avon, Warwickshire CV37 6RN Tel: 01789 261612

ROD •† Roderick Antiques Clocks, 23 Vicarage Gate, London W8 4AA Tel: 0171 937 8517

RP • Robert Pugh, Avon Tel: 01225 314713

RPI * Raymond P Inman, The Auction Galleries, 35 & 40 Temple Street, Brighton, Sussex BN1 3BH Tel: 01273 774777

RTw • Richard Twort, Avon Tel: 01934 641900

RUM • Rumours Decorative Arts, 10 The Mall, Upper Street, Camden Passage, Islington, London N1 0PD Tel: 0171 704 6549/01582 873561

RWB •† Roy W Bunn, Antiques, 34/36 Church Street, Barnoldswick, Colne, Lancashire BB8 5UT Tel: 01282 813703

RYA • Robert Young Antiques, 68 Battersea Bridge Road, London SW11 3AG Tel: 0171 228 7847

S * Sotheby's, 34-35 New Bond Street, London W1A 2AA Tel: 0171 493 8080

S(Am)* Sotheby's Amsterdam, Rokin 102, Amsterdam, Netherlands 1012 KZ Tel: 31 (20) 627 5656

S(G) * Sotheby's, 13 Quai du Mont Blanc, Geneva, Switzerland CH-1201 Tel: 41 (22) 732 8585

S(HK)* Sotheby's, 502-503 Exchange Square Two, 8 Connaught Place Central, Hong Kong Tel: 00 852 2524 8121

S(NY) * Sotheby's, 1334 York Avenue, New York USA NY 10021 Tel: 212 606 7000

S(S) * Sotheby's Sussex, Summers Place, Billingshurst, Sussex RH14 9AD Tel: 01403 783933

S(Sc) * Sotheby's, 112 George Street, Edinburgh, Scotland EH2 4LH Tel: 0131 226 7201

SA • Somerville Antiques & Country Furniture Ltd, Moysdale, Killanley, Ballina, Co Mayo, Ireland Tel: 00 353 963 6275

SAS •† Special Auction Services, The Coach House, Midgham Park, Reading, Berkshire RG7 5UG Tel: 01734 712949

SAU • Pine Furniture, 6 Station Street, Lewes, Sussex BN7 2DA Tel: 01273 474842

SCO • Peter Scott, Stand 26, Bartlett Street Antique Centre, Bath, Avon BA1 2QZ Tel: 0117 986 8468

SeH •† Seventh Heaven, Chirk Mill, Chirk, Wrexham, Clwyd, Wales LL14 5BU Tel: 01691 772622/773563

SEL • M & D Seligmann, 37 Kensington Church Street, London W8 4LL Tel: 0171 937 0400

SEM *† Semley Auctioneers, Station Road Semley, Shaftesbury, Dorset SP7 9AN Tel: 01747 855122

SER •† Serendipity, 168 High Street, Deal, Kent CT14 6BQ Tel: 01304 369165

SHa •† Shapiro & Co, Stand 380, Gray's Antique Market, 58 Davies Street, London W1Y 1LB Tel: 0171 491 2710

Sim *† Simmons & Sons, 32 Bell Street, Henley-on-Thames, Oxfordshire RG9 2BH Tel: 01491 571111

SK * Skinner Inc, The Heritage on the Garden, 63 Park Plaza, Boston, USA MA 01740 Tel: 001 617 350 5400

SK(B) * Skinner Inc, 357 Main Street, Bolton, USA, MA 01740 Tel: 0101 508 779 6241

SLN * Sloan's, C G Sloan & Company Inc, 4920 Wyaconda Road , North Bethesda, USA, MD 20852 Tel: 0101 301 468 4911/669 5066

Som •† Somervale Antiques, 6 Radstock Road, Midsommer Norton, Bath, Avon BA3 2AJ Tel: 01761 412686

Sp * Spink & Son Ltd, 5 Kings Street, St James's, London SW1Y 6QS Tel: 0171 930 7888

SPa •† Sparks Antiques, 106 High Street, Tenterden, Kent TN30 6HT Tel: 01580 762939

STH • Steppes Hill Farm Antiques, Steppes Hill Farm, Stockbury, Nr. Sittingbourne, Kent ME9 7RB Tel: 01795 842205

SUC •† Succession, 18 Richmond Hill, Richmond, Surrey TW10 6QX Tel: 0181 940 6774

SWA •† S.W. Antiques, Abbey Showrooms Newlands, Pershore, Hereford & Worcs WR10 1BP Tel: 01386 555580

SWB •† Sweetbriar Gallery, Robin Hood Lane, Helsby, Cheshire WA6 9NH Tel: 01928 723851

SWO *† G E Sworder & Sons, 14 Cambridge Road, Stansted Mountfitchet, Essex CM24 8BZ Tel: 01279 817778

TED •† Teddy Bears of Witney, 99 High Street, Witney, Oxfordshire OX8 6LY Tel: 01993 702616

Tem •† Great Western Antiques, Torre Station, Newton Road, Torquay, Devon TQ2 5DD Tel: 01803 200551

TGa •† Thames Gallery, Thamside, Henley-on-Thames, Oxfordshire RG9 2LT Tel: 01491 572449

TK • Timothy Kendrew, Ravenshead, Notts NG15 9AL Tel: 01623 798924

TMA *† Brown & Merry Tring Market Auctions, Brook Street, Tring, Hertfordshire HP23 5EF Tel: 01442 826446

TMe •† Thomas Mercer (Chronometers) Ltd, 32 Bury Street, St James's, London SW1Y 6AU Tel: 0171 930 9300

TP •† The Collector, 9 Church Street, Marylebone, London NW8 8EE Tel: 0171 706 4586

TUR • W.F. Turk, London Tel: 0181 543 3231 (Appointment only)

TVA •† Teme Valley Antiques, 1 The Bull Ring, Ludlow, Shropshire SY8 1AD Tel: 01584 874686

VCL • Vintage Cameras Ltd, 254 & 256 Kirkdale, Sydenham, London SE26 4NL Tel: 0181 778 5416

VF • The Victorian Fireplace, Thanet House, 92 Broad Street, Canterbury, Kent CT1 2LU Tel: 01227 767723/01227 767743

VS *† T Vennett-Smith, 11 Nottingham Road, Gotham, Notts NG11 0HE Tel: 0115 983 0541

VSt • Vera Strange, 811 Christchurch Road, Boscombe, Dorset BH21 1TZ Tel: 01202 429111

W * Walter's, No 1 Mint Lane, Lincoln, Lincolnshire LN1 1UD Tel: 01522 525454

W&W •† Walker & Walker, Halfway Manor, Halfway, Nr Newbury, Berkshire RG16 8NR Tel: 01488 658693

WAL *† Wallis & Wallis, West Street Auction Galleries, Lewes, Sussex BN7 2NJ Tel: 01273 480208

WeA • Wenderton Antiques, Kent Tel: 01227 720295 (Appointment only)

WIL • Peter Wilson, Victoria Gallery, Market Street, Nantwich, Cheshire CW5 5DG Tel: 01270 623878

WL *† Wintertons Ltd, Lichfield Auction Centre, Wood End Lane, Fradley, Lichfield, Staffordshire WS13 8NF Tel: 01543 263256

WLD • The Old Mill, High Street, Lamberhurst, Kent TN3 8EQ Tel: 01892 891400/784315

WLi • Wakelin & Linfield, PO Box 48, Billingshurst, Sussex RH14 OYZ Tel: 01403 700004

WN • What Now, Cavendish Arcade, The Crescent, Buxton, Derbyshire SK17 6BQ Tel: 01298 27178/23417

WRe • Walcot Reclamations, 108 Walcot Street, Bath, Avon BA1 5BG Tel: 01225 444404

WTA •† Witney and Airault, Prinny's Gallery, 3 Meeting House Lane, The Lanes, Brighton, Sussex BN1 1HB Tel: 01273 735479

WV •† Westville House Antiques, Littleton, Somerton, Somerset TA11 6NP Tel: 01458 273376

WW * Woolley & Wallis, Salisbury Salerooms, 51-61 Castle Street, Salisbury, Wiltshire SP1 3SU Tel: 01722 411422

YC • Yesterday Child, Angel Arcade, 118 Islington High Street, London N1 8EG Tel: 0171 354 1601

YY • Yesteryear, 24D Magdalen Street, Norwich, Norfolk NR3 1HU Tel: 01603 622908

ZAR • Zarins, 12 Victoria Street, Southwold, Suffolk IP18 6JF Tel: 01502 724569

ACKNOWLEDGEMENTS

The publishers would like to acknowledge the great assistance given
by our consultants:

OAK & COUNTRY FURNITURE & FOLK ART

Robert Young, 68 Battersea Bridge Road, London SW11 3AG

FURNITURE:

Sparks Antiques, 4 Manor Row, Tenterden, Kent TN30 6HP

Neil Lanham, Boardmans, Station Road Corner, Haverhill, Suffolk CB9 OEY

POTTERY & PORCELAIN:

Christopher Spencer, Greystones, 29 Mostyn Road, Merton Park, London SW19 3LL

STAFFORDSHIRE FIGURES:

John Sandon, 15 Bathurst Close, Staplehurst, Kent TN12 ONA

POT LIDS:

Brian Harden, Gloucestershire. Tel/Fax 01451 810684

WEMYSS WARE:

Rogers de Rin, 76 Royal Hospital Road, London SW3 4HN

CORKSCREWS:

Sally Lloyd, Christopher Sykes, The Old Parsonage, Woburn, Bedfordshire MK17 9QM

SILVER:

Richard Came, Sotheby's, 34–35 New Bond Street, London W1A 2AA

CLOCKS:

John Mighell, 48 Balcombe Street, London NW1 6ND

Derek Roberts, 24–25 Shipbourne Road, Tonbridge, Kent TN10 3DN

BAROMETERS:

Walker & Walker, Halfway Manor, Halfway, Nr. Newbury, Berks RG20 8NR

SCIENTIFIC INSTRUMENTS:

John Baddeley, Sotheby's, 34–35 New Bond Street, London W1A 2AA

CAMERAS:

David Larkin, 38 High Street, Tenterden, Kent TN30 6AR

ORIENTAL SNUFF BOTTLES:

Robert Hall, 15 Clifford Street, London W1X 1RF

PORTRAIT MINIATURES:

Claudia Hill, Bonhams, Montpelier Street, Knightsbridge, London SW7 1HH

METALWARE:

Danny Robinson, Key Antiques, 11 Horsefair, Chipping Norton, Oxfordshire OX7 5AL

CARD CASES:

Isobel Ward, Bonhams, Montpelier Street, Knightsbridge, London SW7 1HH

DECORATIVE ARTS:

Audrey Sternshine, 26 Broad Street, Pendleton, Salford, Manchester M6 5BY

ART NOUVEAU & ART DECO GLASS:

Patrick & Susan Gould, Stand L17, Grays Mews Antique Market, Davies Mews, Davies Street, London W1Y 1LL

TWENTIETH CENTURY DESIGN:

Paul I. Rennie, 13 Rugby Street, London W1X 1RF

FABERGÉ:

Sheldon Shapiro, Stand 380, Grays Antique Market, London W1Y 1LB

TEDDY BEARS:

Richard Tatham, Bears Galore, 8 The Fairings, High Street, Tenterden, Kent TN30 6QX

We would like to extend our thanks to all auction houses and dealers who have assisted us in the production of this book.

HOW TO USE THIS BOOK

It is our aim to make the Guide easy to use. In order to find a particular item, consult the contents list on page 19 to find the main heading, for example, Furniture. Having located your area of interest, you will find that larger sections have been sub-divided. If you are looking for a particular factory, designer or craftsman, consult the index which starts on page 796.

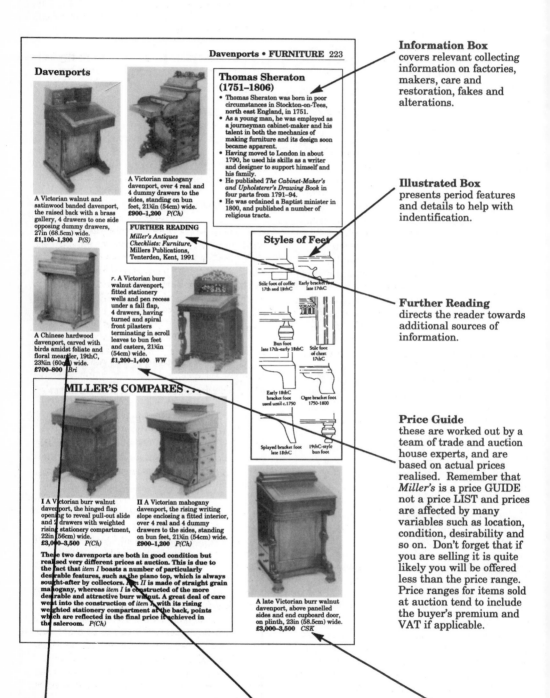

Davenports • FURNITURE 223

Davenports

A Victorian walnut and satinwood banded davenport, the raised back with a brass gallery, 4 drawers to one side opposing dummy drawers, 27in (68.5cm) wide.
£1,100–1,300 *P(S)*

A Victorian mahogany davenport, over 4 real and 4 dummy drawers to the sides, standing on bun feet, 21¼in (54cm) wide.
£900–1,200 *P(Ch)*

Thomas Sheraton (1751–1806)

* Thomas Sheraton was born in poor circumstances in Stockton-on-Tees, north east England, in 1751.
* As a young man, he was employed as a journeyman cabinet-maker and his talent in both the mechanics of making furniture and its design soon became apparent.
* Having moved to London in about 1790, he used his skills as a writer and designer to support himself and his family.
* He published *The Cabinet-Maker's and Upholsterer's Drawing Book* in four parts from 1791–94.
* He was ordained a Baptist minister in 1800, and published a number of religious tracts.

FURTHER READING
Miller's Antiques Checklists: Furniture, Millers Publications, Tenderden, Kent, 1991

A Chinese hardwood davenport, carved with birds amidst foliate and floral meander, 19thC, 23¼in (60cm) wide.
£700–800 *Bri*

r. A Victorian burr walnut davenport, fitted stationery wells and pen recess under a fall flap, 4 drawers, having turned and spiral front pilasters terminating in scroll leaves to bun feet and casters, 21¼in (54cm) wide.
£1,200–1,400 *WW*

Styles of Feet

Stile foot of coffer
17th and 18thC

Early bracket foot
late 17thC

Bun foot
late 17th–early 18thC

Stile foot of chest
17thC

Early 18thC bracket foot
used until c.1750

Ogee bracket foot
1750–1800

Splayed bracket foot
late 18thC

19thC-style bun foot

MILLER'S COMPARES . . .

I A Victorian burr walnut davenport, the hinged flap opening to reveal pull-out slide and 2 drawers with weighted rising stationery compartment, 22in (56cm) wide.
£3,000–3,500 *P(Ch)*

II A Victorian mahogany davenport, the rising writing slope enclosing a fitted interior, over 4 real and 4 dummy drawers to the sides, standing on bun feet, 21¼in (54cm) wide.
£900–1,200 *P(Ch)*

These two davenports are both in good condition but realised very different prices at auction. This is due to the fact that *item I* boasts a number of particularly desirable features, such as the piano top, which is always sought-after by collectors. *Item II* is made of straight grain mahogany, whereas *item I* is constructed of the more desirable and attractive burr walnut. A great deal of care went into the construction of *item I*, with its rising weighted stationery compartment at the back, points which are reflected in the final price it achieved in the saleroom. *P(Ch)*

A late Victorian burr walnut davenport, above panelled sides and end cupboard door, on plinth, 23in (58.5cm) wide.
£3,000–3,500 *CSK*

Information Box
covers relevant collecting information on factories, makers, care and restoration, fakes and alterations.

Illustrated Box
presents period features and details to help with indentification.

Further Reading
directs the reader towards additional sources of information.

Price Guide
these are worked out by a team of trade and auction house experts, and are based on actual prices realised. Remember that *Miller's* is a price GUIDE not a price LIST and prices are affected by many variables such as location, condition, desirability and so on. Don't forget that if you are selling it is quite likely you will be offered less than the price range. Price ranges for items sold at auction tend to include the buyer's premium and VAT if applicable.

Caption
provides a brief description of the item including the maker's name, medium, year it was made and in some cases condition.

Miller's Compares . . .
explains why two items which look similar have realised very different prices.

Source Code
refers to the 'Key to Illustrations' on page 20 that lists the details of where the item was photographed.

INTRODUCTION

*M*iller's International Antiques Price Guide is just as useful to a dealer in Exeter, New Hampshire, as it is to a dealer in Exeter, England. The antiques market is linked worldwide by computers, faxes, telephones, the internet and the worldwide web.

New technology using images on a computer disc or 'on-line' has made it possible to preview auctions in many parts of the world without leaving home. In time, electronic bidding will make it possible to buy at auction from your living room, although it cannot equal the excitement of being in the saleroom or the fun of shopping at a fair.

In this new world Miller's British-based publication provides a picture of the worldwide antiques market the old-fashioned way, between the covers of a book. Relaxed in a hammock, flipping through its pages you can get an idea of the value of a broad range of antiques from Aalto to Zsolnay, carpets to wristwatches, cameras to violins and not get cross-eyed from staring at a small screen.

There is no denying that a lot of people know what is happening in the antiques business the world over. For example, recently a George I footstool sold for $49,500 at Ken Farmer's auction in a large warehouse space in the remote college town of Radford, Virginia. Advertised in 'as found condition' with its upholstery off and one corner tied on with a red ribbon, its exuberantly carved shells, grasses and the lions' masks on each knee attracted attention. It was bought on the telephone by a British collector underbid in the salesroom by a dealer who had come from Dublin to bid on it after seeing it advertised in an American trade paper.

'A very special piece will bring a big price but it is hard to put a value on ordinary antique furniture these days,' said Ken Farmer. 'The middle market is soft; unless a piece of furniture has a lot of decorative appeal it is hard to get much competition, and any repairs or replacements hurt the value a lot.'

Marketing plays an important role in the final price. Prices at an on-site house sale or for items owned by a celebrity can be as much as three, ten or one hundred times higher than prices for similar objects owned by ordinary people.

Take the sale of leftovers from Jacqueline Kennedy Onassis' estate held at Sotheby's in New York, 23rd–26th April, 1996, recorded by television cameras and the international press. The association with an American President and First Lady caused the tape measure in a Tiffany silver case mongrammed 'JBK' to sell for $48,875. Jackie's three-strand fake pearl necklace was knocked down for $211,500 to the president of a company planning to reproduce it to sell for $200. The publisher of *Cigar Aficionado* magazine paid $574,500 for President Kennedy's walnut humidor, a present from the comedian Milton Berle, with a plaque on it dated '1/20/61'. Collecting such modern-day relics is a strong segment of the marketplace hyped by major auction houses.

Documentation increases value. For example, the pair of George II silver soup tureens, designed in 1774 by Robert Adam, doubled their estimate, selling for $464,500, at Christie's recently because they were so well documented.

'We know the designer, Robert Adam, whose original drawings survive in the Soane Museum in London', said Jeanne Sloan of Christie's silver department in New York. 'We know the original owner, a major art patron of the period, Sir Watkin Williams-Wynn, the retailer, Joseph Cresswell, and the silversmith, John Carter.'

On the other hand the market for ordinary Georgian silver without a history rarely goes up or down. Like the middle market for furniture, condition and decorative appeal determines the value.

Miller's International Antiques Price Guide illustrates some record-setting items along with hundreds of less expensive objects like ones you have inherited or may want to collect. After studying each illustration carefully you will begin to understand why one piece sells for $3,000–5,000 and another for $30,000–50,000.

You will notice a great disparity in price between the finest and the ordinary, and between American examples and British ones. Take needlework for example. A large framed canvas-work chimney piece stitched c1753 by Hannah Otis at a Boston dame's school sold at Sotheby's recently to the Museum of Fine Arts, Boston, for $1,157,500, an all-time record for needlework and schoolgirl art. 'If it had been British it may have sold for $50,000,' said Amy Finkel a specialist dealer in American and British needlework in Philadelphia.

This record price has brought to the market needlework that has been in families or was bought by collectors years ago and it has caused much interest in this collecting area. There is still a short supply of American needlework and, therefore, more interest in British embroideries of the late 18th and early 19th centuries. 'They are plentiful, so condition is very important, and the brightness of the colours can determine the price,' observed Amy Finkel. These are priced well below American examples of the same period which are bolder, freer and can be more easily documented because American scholarship has focused on regional studies, and genealogies are available.

We are always anxious to improve the Guide. If we have left out something or if you have other comments about the book, please let us know. We want people who use this Guide to tell us how to make it even better.

Lita Solis-Cohen

Dates	British Monarch	British Period	French Period
1558–1603	Elizabeth I	Elizabethan	Renaissance
1603–1625	James I	Jacobean	
1625–1649	Charles I	Carolean	Louis XIII (1610–1643)
1649–1660	Commonwealth	Cromwellian	Louis XIV (1643–1715)
1660–1685	Charles II	Restoration	
1685–1689	James II	Restoration	
1689–1694	William & Mary	William & Mary	
1694–1702	William III	William III	
1702–1714	Anne	Queen Anne	
1714–1727	George I	Early Georgian	Régence (1715–1723)
1727–1760	George II	Early Georgian	Louis XV (1723–1774)
1760–1811	George III	Late Georgian	Louis XVI (1774–1793) Directoire (1793–1799) Empire (1799–1815)
1812–1820	George III	Regency	Restauration (1815–1830)
1820–1830	George IV	Regency	
1830–1837	William IV	William IV	Louis Philippe (1830–1848)
1837–1901	Victoria	Victorian	2nd Empire (1848–1870) 3rd Republic (1871–1940)
1901–1910	Edward VII	Edwardian	

German Period	U.S. Period	Style	Woods
Renaissance	Early Colonial	Gothic	Oak Period (to c1670)
		Baroque (c1620–1700)	
Renaissance/ Baroque (c1650–1700)			Walnut period (c1670–1735)
	William & Mary		
	Dutch Colonial	Rococo (c1695–1760)	
Baroque (c1700–1730)	Queen Anne		
			Early mahogany period (c1735–1770)
Rococo (c1730–1760)	Chippendale (from 1750)		
Neo–classicism (c1760–1800)		Neo–classical (c1755–1805)	Late mahogany period (c1770–1810)
	Early Federal (1790–1810)		
Empire (c1800–1815	American Directoire (1798–1804)	Empire (c1799–1815)	
	American Empire (1804–1815)		
Biedermeier (c1815–1848)	Late Federal (1810–1830)	Regency (c1812–1830)	
Revivale (c1830–1880)		Eclectic (c1830–1880)	
	Victorian		
Jugendstil (c1880–1920)		Arts & Crafts (c1880–1900)	
	Art Nouveau (c1900–1920)	Art Nouveau (c1900–1920)	

FURNITURE

I t is possible to look into this guide and see just objects and sums of money, but money is about people; more especially, what people are doing with their money, and why. In considering the price potential of a piece of furniture we have to take into account not just the what, but the where, the who, the why and the when as well.

In the 1950s and 1960s every small town had at least one dealer who bought for stock and for the auctioneer this meant that almost everything in the saleroom was covered, and would find a buyer. That is not the case nowadays. Private buyers, once a novelty, have come to play a much larger and more influential part in the auction room. From the trade point of view, few dealers now carry large stocks; instead they target a few pieces that they know they can sell quickly and often completely ignore an equally fine piece, regardless of price.

This approach has resulted in the occasional unpredictability of saleroom prices. There could be twenty or thirty people wanting one article; after all, what the dealer perceives as readily re-saleable will, by definition, appeal to those collectors who buy at auction. Demand in the auction room comes from the private sector, overseas dealers and dealers from the home country buying for stock, to sell at fairs or, to a much lesser extent these days, to trade on.

As far as the private sector is concerned, and by extension the home trade, English oak continues to be much sought-after by buyers more interested in good furnishing pieces than in earlier pieces of academic interest alone. We have, therefore, seen a rise in the value of 17th and 18th century tables, chests and, most significantly, dressers.

The American market remains strong for country items and perhaps the biggest rise in the past year, driven by both English and American tastes, has been in the area of naive but honest country furniture, particularly for items in the different fruitwoods. Elm sells well because of its colour, and period painted furniture has been in ever increasing demand.

There has been a noticeable change in buying patterns among overseas dealers. The large numbers who once came from Belgium, Holland and Germany have dwindled and we have seen a decline in the price of the Continental 16th and 17th century carved oak furniture. However, new markets have opened up in Portugal and Spain and despite the fall in the Italian lire, demand for 18th century Italian furniture has been strong. In the 1960s and '70s the Spanish dealer in the UK was virtually unknown but one sale that I conducted last year saw a quarter of the lots sold to Spain.

An Italian kingwood and marquetry commode, in the manner of Guiseppe Magolini, 18thC, 49in (124.5cm) wide.
$20,250–22,500 *B*

For the auctioneer and dealer it is important to identify what the overseas buyer wants. It is also useful to the private buyer to recognise those areas in which strong competition and high prices might be expected.

The Spanish dealers are buying good furnishing pieces and require Georgian mahogany, Regency rosewood, Victorian and 18th century walnut furniture starting at $750 and rising to $15,000. There has, however, been a decline in their interest in furniture of the 16th and 17th centuries, even if it is Spanish.

To get back to the question 'What is it worth?', I think it is important to discount either very high or very low prices, not just because of the problems of condition and restoration – and people are more than ever demanding untouched, original pieces with good colour – but to make allowance for particular circumstances in the saleroom.

A piece may move from saleroom to saleroom, from London to the country or vice versa, and double or even treble in price for reasons that may be peculiar to the moment. Many factors, major and minor, can affect prices. For example, where an object stands in the room, its position in the sale catalogue – something offered immediately after a major lot can easily be eclipsed – whether it is a private house sale – where prices may sometimes be out of all reason – or the presence of two buyers who are either unaware or unconcerned about worth and value, and are determined to buy regardless.

In projecting past prices into an opinion of present worth, one may heed and adapt with care Disraeli's observation: 'The greater a man's knowledge of the past, the greater his ability to cope with the future'.

Neil Lanham, FRICS

OAK & COUNTRY FURNITURE
Beds

l. A Flemish oak half tester bed, the foliate carved panelled canopy dated '1642', with winged female masks to the corners, the panelled head-board decorated with foliate scrolls, angels and grotesque masks, the panelled front with ribbon tied foliate swags, the block feet carved with lion masks, 78in (198cm) wide. **$4,500-5,250** *Bon*

An oak tester bed, the panelled top above 2 turned uprights at the foot end and carved panelling to the head end, with central architectural arched panel with 'H.K. 1635' etched above, basically 17thC with later alterations, 85in (216cm) long. **$5,250-6,000** *P(Sc)*

Bookcases

A George III mahogany crossbanded oak bureau bookcase, the cabinet with cavetto moulded cornice above a pair of shaped headed panelled doors, enclosing shelves and pigeonholes, the sloping fall enclosing a fitted interior, above 2 short and 2 long drawers, on bracket feet, poor condition, later handles, part of cornice missing, 37½in (95.5cm) wide. **$3,000-3,750** *P(Ch)*

A Regency inlaid oak bookcase, the moulded cornice above a chequer and line-inlaid frieze, 2 panelled doors with central shell marquetry enclosing shelves, above 2 short and 3 long drawers, on bracket feet, restored, 52in (132cm) wide. **$1,300-1,800** *CSK*

r. An oak bureau bookcase, with moulded cornice and a pair of arched fielded panelled doors, above 2 candle slides, the sloping fall enclosing a fitted interior, above 2 short dummy and 3 long drawers, on pierced bracket feet, mid-18thC, 39in (99cm) wide. **$3,300-4,500** *CSK*

Boxes

A Spanish walnut *vargueno*, the foliate carved moulded fall front enclosing 8 foliate carved drawers and a central deep drawer with biblical painted panel, the sides with carrying handles, the interior re-fitted, 17thC, 41½in (105.5cm) long. **$2,700-3,000** *CSK*

r. An oak box, c1671, 11in (28cm) long. **$2,250-2,650** *DBA*

An elm box, with original hinges and lock, c1790, 30in (76cm) wide. **$150-230** *APa*

Buffets

A James I oak buffet, with guilloche frieze above a cupboard with central arcaded door, flanked by 2 canted arcaded panels behind fluted turned supports, above a frieze and 2 front cup-and-cover turned legs united by a stretcher at the base, 45in (114.5cm) wide.
$4,200–4,800 *B*

An oak buffet, the frieze decorated with thumb moulding concealing a single drawer, turned vase-shaped columns, 17thC, 45in (114.5cm) wide.
$3,000–3,750 *WIL*

A Flemish oak buffet, the upper section with projecting cornice and frieze above a pair of panelled doors carved with foliage and strapwork and flanked by split mouldings, above a gadrooned frieze drawer carved with lion masks, a pair of cupboard doors below with central bosses and flanked by strapwork and split moulding uprights, on moulded plinth, part 17thC, 54in (137cm) wide.
$3,300–4,500 *CSK*

A French fruitwood buffet, c1790, 66in (167.5cm) wide.
$5,000–5,800 *DeG*

A Flemish oak buffet, with cleated top and 2 projecting frieze drawers carved with swags and fruit, above a pair of twin-panelled cupboard doors carved with strapwork, flanked by part fluted uprights applied with split mouldings, 19thC, 63in (160cm) wide.
$2,250–3,000 *CSK*

Bureaux

A George I oak fall-front bureau, the shaped and fitted interior with a well, 2 short and 2 long drawers below with brass loop handles, applied rail mouldings, on bracket feet, c1725, 30in (76cm) wide.
$1,350–1,850 *N*

An oak bureau, the fall-front enclosing small drawers, pigeonholes, an apron drawer and a well, above 2 short and 3 long cockbeaded drawers, on bracket feet, 18thC, 35in (89cm) wide.
$1,800–2,200 *P(S)*

An early Georgian oak bureau, the interior with pigeonholes, door, drawers and well, the 2 short and 2 long drawers with scratch cockbeading, on bracket feet, 36in (91.5cm) wide.
$1,700–2,300 *Bri*

r. An early Georgian oak bureau, the fall-front enclosing a stepped fitted interior with drawers, pigeonholes and well, over 2 short and 2 long drawers, with brass drop handles, on bracket feet, 36in (91.5cm) wide.
$2,000–2,400 *AH*

A George III oak bureau, the shell inlaid fall-front enclosing a series of drawers and pigeonholes above a central inlaid cupboard, above 2 short and 3 long graduated drawers, with oval stamped brass handles, on shaped bracket feet, 41¾in (106cm) wide.
$1,350–1,850 *WL*

Candlestands

r. A Welsh ash and sycamore stool-based rushlight and candleholder lighting device, c1860, 36½in (93cm) high.
$1,500–1,900 *RYA*

l. A French solid walnut tripod candlestand, on baluster turned stem, c1830, 31in (79cm) high.
$750–830 *RYA*

An oak stool-based candlestand, with lipped top and original paint, c1750, 13in (33cm) wide.
$1,500–1,800 *RYA*

Chairs

r. A set of 3 joined oak chairs, the panelled-backs with carved stylised floral decoration, above later solid seats, on ring-turned column supports tied by block stretchers, south Yorkshire/Derbyshire, late 17thC.
$2,000–2,250 *Bon*

An oak panelled-back side chair, in original condition, Lancashire c1680, 45in (114.5cm) high.
$1,300–1,500 *KEY*

A joined oak armchair, c1660, 45in (114.5cm) high.
$4,500–5,250 *DBA*

An oak side chair, with arched panelled-back, c1710 45in (114.5cm) high.
$1,100–1,300 *KEY*

An oak side chair, with panelled-back and carved cresting rail, Lancashire, c1695, 45in (114.5cm) high.
$1,200–1,300 *KEY*

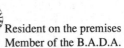
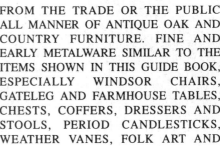

Chair Backs

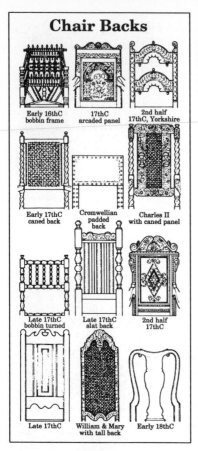

Early 16thC bobbin frame

17thC arcaded panel

2nd half 17thC, Yorkshire

Early 17thC caned back

Cromwellian padded back

Charles II with caned panel

Late 17thC bobbin turned

Late 17thC slat back

2nd half 17thC

Late 17thC

William & Mary with tall back

Early 18thC

A set of 6 oak dining chairs, the backs with scroll-carved crestings and fielded panelled splats, solid seats, baluster-turned front legs, fascia stretchers, c1700.
$3,000–4,500 *P(S)*

A primitive elm bobbin chair, early 18thC.
$1,650–1,950 *MBr*

An elm and yew Gothic style Windsor armchair, damaged, mid-18thC.
$2,700–3,000 *MR*

A George III fruitwood armchair, in original condition, c1795.
$1,500–1,800 *PHA*

A set of 6 elm and fruitwood comb-backed Windsor dining chairs, c1780.
$5,250–6,000 *RYA*

A cherrywood turned and carved side chair, with pierced splat and Spanish feet, Connecticut, c1780.
$825–900 *SK(B)*

r. A set of 4 oak and ash spindle-back chairs, c1790.
$750–900 *OLM*

l. Two similar crescent-back single chairs, with solid seats and turned stretchers, Yorkshire, c1750.
$950–1,150 *WIL*

Chests of Drawers

An oak chest of drawers, the moulded top above 3 moulded drawers, on stile feet, 17thC, 34¾in (88cm) wide. **$1,300–1,800** *P(B)*

An oak and walnut chest of drawers, in 2 parts, with 4 moulded long drawers and panelled sides, on later bun feet, late 17thC, 14½in (37cm) wide. **$1,500–1,800** *P(S)*

A joined oak and fruitwood chest of drawers, with moulded top, dentil frieze and 4 long drawers, on bracket feet, c1680, 47in (119.5cm) wide. **$1,800–2,250** *Bon*

A walnut chest of drawers, the moulded top above 3 fielded panelled long drawers with applied split baluster mouldings, on bracket feet, c1695, 42in (106.5cm) wide. **$5,000–5,250** *Bon*

r. A Queen Anne oak chest-on-stand, the moulded cornice above a cushion-moulded frieze drawer, with 2 short and 2 long graduated drawers below, the stand with a long frieze drawer, on baluster turned legs and bun feet, tied by curved X-shaped stretchers, c1700, 41in (104cm) wide. **$4,500–6,000** *Bon*

An oak chest of drawers, in 2 parts, with 4 long moulded panelled drawers with later brass drop handles, late 17thC, 40½in (103cm) wide.
$1,200–1,800 *DN*

An oak chest of drawers, the top with a moulded edge, above 4 long drawers with later brass handles, divided by spiral split turnings, on later bun feet, 17thC, 36in (91.5cm) wide.
$2,500–3,000 *DN*

A George II oak chest of drawers, fitted with 2 short and 2 long graduated and cockbeaded drawers beneath a brushing slide, brass handles, on bracket feet, c1760, 35in (89cm) wide.
$1,400–1,800 *N*

An oak chest-on-stand, the top with moulded edge above 3 long graduated drawers, each with brass handles, above a shallow central drawer, flanked by 2 deeper drawers, with shaped skirt below, standing on cabriole legs with pad feet, early 18thC, 29in (73.5cm) wide.
$4,000–5,000 *Mit*

A George II oak chest-on-stand, the upper part with 2 short and 3 long graduated drawers flanked by rounded corners, on a raised stand, with a central shallow drawer flanked by 2 deeper drawers, on cabriole legs with pad feet, 41½in (105.5cm) wide.
$2,700–3,300 *Bon*

A George III oak chest of drawers, the moulded top above 2 short and 3 long graduated drawers, on shaped bracket feet, 36¾in (93.5cm) wide.
$600–750 *Hal*

l. An oak chest of drawers, with panelled sides, c1740, 40in (101.5cm) wide.
$975–1,275 *WLD*

A George II oak chest of drawers, the moulded top with canted corners above 2 short and 3 long graduated drawers, flanked by canted split column pilasters, on ogee bracket feet, mid-18thC, 32½in (82.5cm) wide.
$3,750–4,500 *Bon*

An oak chest-on-stand, the upper part with moulded cornice over a drawer in a cushion frieze, 2 short and 3 long drawers below with brass handles, the base with 3 drawers, shaped apron and cabriole legs with pointed pad feet, 18thC and later, 41½in (105.5cm) wide.
$1,800–2,300 *AH*

Coffers & Chests

An oak planked coffer, with panelled front, c1620, 30in (76cm) wide.
$2,700–3,300 *DBA*

A William and Mary oak panelled coffer, with drawer, c1690, 48in (122cm) wide.
$2,650–3,750 *PHA*

An oak chest, the twin panelled top inlaid with chequered banding and the initials 'I. G.', above a banded front with 2 stop-fluted carved panels, on moulded stile feet, mid-17thC, 43½in (110.5cm) wide.
$2,250–3,000 *Bon*

An oak boarded chest, c1650, 39in (99cm) long.
$3,000–3,750 *DBA*

An oak coffer, the two-plank hinged lid with moulded edge above a carved triple panel front, raised on brackets, mid-17thC, 54in (137cm) wide.
$900–1,200 *Bon*

l. An oak coffer, with original ironwork, c1660, 33in (84cm) wide.
$2,250–2,700 *KEY*

An oak panelled coffer, with original hinges, mid-17thC, 52in (132cm) wide.
$1,800–1,950 *KEY*

An oak panelled coffer, with original carving and hinges, c1680, 41in (104cm) wide.
$1,800–2,000 *KEY*

An oak coffer, the plank lid revealing a candlebox, carved panelled front, on panel legs, late 17thC, 53in (134.5cm) wide.
$675–975 *WW*

An oak coffer, with triple plank top, lunette carved frieze, triple panelled front carved with stars, chip and stop-fluted muntins, 17thC, 51in (129.5cm) wide.
$2,250–3,000 *L*

A George II elm coffer, the hinged lid above a panelled front bearing the initials 'EH' and dated '1754', with a drawer to the base, 48in (122cm) wide.
$500–750 *Bon*

An oak lift-top chest, with 3 carved panels, above a single carved drawer, previous conversion to a fall-front, 18thC, 47in (119.5cm) wide.
$1,200–1,800 *EL*

An oak mule chest, the moulded top above a front with 3 fielded panels above 2 drawers, on bracket feet, restored, mid-18thC, 55in (139.5cm) wide.
$300–380 *Hal*

An oak coffer, with 4 carved panels, 18thC, 56½in (143.5cm) wide.
$1,000–1,200 *TMA*

An oak and iron-bound chest, with hinged top, on foliate carved stile feet, 17thC, Westphalian, 73in (185.5cm) wide.
$8,600–9,000 *CSK*

A Spanish walnut chest, with hinged top, above a carved front centred by an arcade, on ribbed feet, the feet re-supported, c1690, parts later, 64in (162.5cm) wide.
$1,800–2,300 *CSK*

A German oak and ironwork chest, with domed hinged lid, above egg-and-dart moulding, with carrying handles to the sides, marked 'IMCSOH anno 1791', 18thC, 51in (129.5cm) wide.
$2,500–3,000 *CSK*

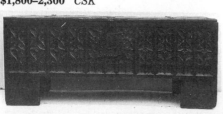

l. An oak planked coffer, with stiles, the lid with iron strap hinges, the front with incised decoration of arcaded Gothic tracery flanking the shaped iron hasp, 16thC, Westphalian, 67in (170cm) wide.
$7,500–8,250 *B*

Cupboards

An oak cupboard, with a moulded cornice, 3 doors with 2 doors below, inset with carved panels of roundels centred by male and female figure masks, the foliate spandrels with stylised crowns, drapery and masks, linen-fold panels with iron lock-plates and hinges, on block feet, 16thC and later, 66in (167.5cm) wide.
$15,000–18,000 *CSK*

An elm boarded mural cupboard, with original paintwork and hinges, repaired, 16thC, backboard later, 15½in (39.5cm) wide.
$4,500–6,000 *DBA*

A Charles I oak standing cupboard, with original hinges, c1640, 48in (122cm) wide.
$11,250–12,750 *PHA*

A Charles II joined oak carved court cupboard, c1660, 47in (119.5cm) wide.
$10,500–12,000 *DBA*

A joined oak press cupboard, c1670, dated '1722', 55in (139.5cm) wide.
$8,250–9,750 *PHA*

An oak press cupboard, the upper section with inlaid muntin and panelled doors, inscribed 'John Lingard' and 'Mary Lingard 1667', over panelled doors, on stile supports, 61in (155cm) wide.
$5,400–6,000 *Sim*

r. An oak cupboard, with moulded cornice above 3 doors, on stile feet, some mouldings replaced, 17thC, 58in (147.5cm) wide.
$3,000–3,750 *CSK*

A joined oak press cupboard, the upper section with a fluted projecting cornice and turned finials, above a pair of panelled cupboard doors flanking a central panel, the base with a pair of panelled doors, on stile feet, late 17thC, 57½in (146cm) wide.
$1,125–1,500 *Bon*

An oak press cupboard, in 2 sections, with moulded cornice and a pair of geometrically moulded panel doors centred with diamond bosses, above 2 further panels and one long frieze drawer, on stile feet, early 18thC, 48in (122cm) wide.
$4,000–5,000 *CSK*

A George II oak hanging corner cupboard, with sunburst inlay to the door, c1735, 20in (51cm) wide.
$1,800–2,200 *PHA*

A George III oak standing corner cupboard, with a moulded cornice above 2 pairs of panelled doors, crossbanded in mahogany, enclosing shaped shelves and flanked by canted pilaster corners, 44in (112cm) wide.
$2,900–3,300 *DN*

A George II oak deuddarn, the triple ogee arched panelled doors above 3 frieze drawers, above a central panel flanked by a larger pair of panel doors, mid-18th, 73in (185.5cm) wide.
$6,300–6,800 *S(S)*

A George III oak food cupboard, with drawers, c1770, 38in (96.5cm) wide.
$3,300–3,800 *PHA*

A George III oak bowfronted corner cupboard, with moulded cornice, mahogany veneered frieze decorated with whitewood shell inlay, 2 doors crossbanded in mahogany and black stringing, the interior with 3 shelves and single spice drawer, 40in (101.5cm) high.
$1,200–1,300 *WIL*

An oak tridarn, the back with an open shelf beneath a canopy and 3 cupboards, the centre with 2 short drawers and pigeonholes, the other 2 with a single shelf, above 3 frieze drawers and cupboard with shelf enclosed by a pair of arched fielded panelled doors, 18thC, 59in (150cm) wide.
$14,250–15,000 *Oli*

A George III oak deuddarn, the cornice with twin pendents above triple ogee arched and fielded recessed panel doors, with 3 drawers and a pair of panelled doors below, on stem feet, late 18thC, 57in (145cm) wide.
$3,150–3,750 *S(S)*

A housekeeper's oak cupboard, the cavetto cornice above 5 panelled doors, the central door enclosing an arrangement of 12 spice drawers, the lower part with 9 drawers and a central panelled door, on turned bun feet, early 19thC, 85½in (217cm) wide.
$2,500–3,000 *Hal*

An oak clothes press, the cavetto-moulded cornice above a broad frieze, the pair of shaped ogee head panelled doors enclosing hanging space, the lower body with moulded waist above 2 pairs of faux and a pair of actual drawers, on plain stile feet, early 19thC, 46¾in (119cm) wide.
$2,000–2,400 *P(Ch)*

A George III oak wall cupboard, with fitted interior, c1785, 24in (61cm) wide.
$2,250–3,000 *PHA*

A Victorian carved oak court cupboard, with a stop-fluted cornice above a scrolling foliate frieze, the central cupboard carved with foliage within an arch and flanked by 2 canted doors, each centred by a portrait oval, flanked by foliate and reeded bulbous supports, the lower part with 3 foliate carved panel doors, on turned stile feet, late 19thC, 62½in (159cm) wide.
$600–900 *Hal*

A Flemish oak and ebony inlaid cupboard, the later moulded top above a fielded panelled door enclosing a shelf, above a frieze drawer, the sides with geometric moulded panels, late 17thC, 26¼in (66.5cm) wide.
$1,800–2,300 *Bon*

Clothes Presses

- Clothes presses were introduced c1750, until 1780 many were mahogany.
- Some Victorian presses are veneered in satinwood or walnut.
- Essentially practical bedroom pieces rather than decorative drawing room ones, and made for all types of households.
- The quality varies: some are highly sophisticated with fine carving or, from the end of the 18thC, inlaid; others are simply constructed and unadorned.

A Continental oak cupboard, with guilloche carved carcass and 4 panelled doors separated by 2 drawers, on stile feet, 17thC, 53in (134.5cm) wide.
$2,000–2,400 *Bea*

A Dutch oak glazed hanging cupboard, c1790, 30in (76cm) wide.
$2,250–2,750 *PHA*

A Flemish carved oak cupboard, the strapwork frieze centred and flanked by masks, with a pair of panelled doors with foliate and figure carving interspersed by guilloche bands, the lower part with a central mask carved door, flanked by a pair of panels, on turned feet, 19thC but with some 17thC components, 52½in (133.5cm) wide.
$975–1,175 *Hal*

Dressers

A William and Mary oak dresser base, the moulded top above 3 geometrically panelled frieze drawers, flanked by split bobbin-turned mouldings, on baluster turned and square legs joined by stretchers, late 17thC, 73½in (186.5cm) wide.
$11,250–12,750 *S(S)*

An oak dresser base, the raised back above a moulded top, with 3 block-fronted drawers, on turned and square legs, restored and altered, late 17thC, 77¼in (196cm) wide.
$2,250–3,000 *Hal*

A George I oak pot board dresser base, the drawers decorated with panels of pollard oak and inlaid with ash, mid-Wales, c1725, 60in (152.5cm) wide.
$12,750–14,250 *PHA*

An early Georgian oak dresser base, the moulded top above 4 crossbanded drawers, on ring-turned and block legs, formerly with superstructure, early 18thC, 90½in (230cm) wide.
$3,750–4,500 *CNY*

r. An oak Welsh dresser, with lattice-patterned pot board, c1770, 70in (178cm) wide.
$7,500–9,000 *KEY*

An oak pot board dresser, the rack with shaped sides and a lower shelf with spoon holes, above 3 drawers, the 6 turned legs supporting a deep shaped apron returned at the sides, south Wales, c1740, 63in (160cm) wide.
$10,500–12,000 *DBA*

An oak two-part dresser, with moulded and scrolled cornice, the upper section with 3 shelves, the base with 3 drawers, pierced apron and cabriole legs with padded slipper feet, restored, 18thC, 84in (213.5cm) wide.
$3,000–3,750 *EL*

A George III oak dresser base, the moulded top above 3 frieze drawers and a pair of panelled cupboard doors, flanking a central panel, on block feet, mid-18thC, 56¼in (143cm) wide.
$6,300–7,000 *Bon*

A George III oak and mahogany crossbanded dresser base, the moulded top above 3 frieze drawers, on cabriole legs with pad feet, c1760, 74in (188cm) wide.
$3,300–4,000 *Hal*

A Welsh oak pot board dresser base, with patinated top, 5 boxwood-inlaid drawers in a deep frieze, on 6 baluster legs, c1740, 62in (157.5cm) wide.
$13,500–15,000 *DBA*

An oak dresser, the enclosed rack with cavetto cornice above a broad frieze, with 3 shelves, the lower part with 3 cockbeaded frieze drawers above a further 3 central cockbeaded doors, flanked by a pair of enclosed cupboards, on plain stile feet, north Wales, early 19thC, 63in (160cm) wide.
$4,500–5,250 *P(Ch)*

An oak dresser base, the plank top with moulded edge, above 3 crossbanded drawers with black and white stringing, with turned front legs, restored, 18thC, 75in (190.5cm) wide.
$2,250–3,000 *WIL*

A Georgian oak dresser, with mahogany banding, the moulded cornice with shaped frieze and boarded back, with shelves and cupboards, the base with 3 drawers and shaped frieze, on cabriole legs, 69¼in (176cm) wide.
$3,750–4,500 *Bri*

A late George III oak Welsh dresser, outlined with mahogany banding and boxwood stringing, the upper section with a pierced frieze and 3 open shelves flanked by panelled doors, the base with an arrangement of 7 drawers and 2 doors, on a plinth base, 73in (185.5cm) wide.
$5,000–6,000 *Bea*

An elm dresser, with moulded top and 3 frieze drawers, on ring-turned tapering legs, one back leg with woodworm damage, early 19thC, 72in (183cm) wide.
$5,000–5,700 *CSK*

l. An oak 'dog kennel' dresser, the base in original condition, 18thC, with later plate rack, 53in (134.5cm) wide.
$3,750–4,500 *SWO*

A George III oak and mahogany crossbanded dresser base, the moulded top above 3 frieze drawers, on cabriole legs with pad feet, late 18thC, 67in (170cm) wide.
$2,800–3,300 *Hal*

An oak dresser base, with 3 central drawers flanked by 2 cupboards, late 18thC, 70in (178cm) wide.
$3,100–3,750 *JH*

Settees

A turned and painted settee, the shaped back above 33 tapered spindles, the arms ending in flared hand holds, with plank seat, on vase and reel-turned legs joined by bulbous stretchers, now painted salmon over grey, signed 'John Wire', Philadelphia, Pennsylvania, damaged, c1800, 79in (201cm) long.
$8,250–8,700 *S(NY)*

A turned sack-back Windsor settee, the arched crest above tapering spindles, with oblong dished and incised plank seat and ring and vase-turned legs joined by bulbous stretcher, New England, c1795, 42¾in (108.5cm) long.
$23,250–24,750 *S(NY)*

Settles

An oak box settle, the back with picture panel depicting figures in period costume operating a still, rail inscribed 'Robert Gough' with monogram crest and date '1685', seat with hinged lid and three-panelled base, restored, 17thC, 38in (96.5cm) wide.
$3,100–4,500 *WIL*

An oak bacon settle, with moulded cornice, 2 panelled doors, reeded arms on baluster supports, panelled base with hinged seat, on moulded plinth, 18thC, 61½in (156cm) long.
$2,700–3,700 *AH*

An early 18thC style oak settle, the high panelled back decorated with lozenge motifs, foliated scrolls and fruiting vines, above open arms and box seat, the carved frieze on square legs, 78½in (199.5cm) long.
$1,000–1,200 *AG*

> ### Did you know?
> *MILLER'S* Antiques Price Guide *builds up year-by-year to form the most comprehensive antiques photo-reference library available.*

An oak and pine concave-shaped settle, with moulded cornice and a pair of twin fielded panelled doors, flanked by similar side sections, the outswept arms on ring-turned supports, the reeded solid seat above 4 fielded panels, the centre 2 as doors, on plinth base, 19thC, 74in (188cm) long.
$3,000–3,750 *CSK*

A George III elm settle, c1790, 40in (101.5cm) wide.
$3,000–3,750 *PHA*

A fruitwood high-backed settle, with plank back and angled top with shaped ends, the box seat with twin lids, restored, West Country, early 19thC, 66in (167.5cm) long.
$1,800–2,250 *CSK*

Stools

A child's oak stool, 17thC, 14in (35.5cm) high.
$3,000–3,750 *DBA*

An oak joint stool, with lunette carved frieze, c1640, 20in (51cm) high.
$1,800–2,250 *KEY*

A pair of oak joint stools, the thumbnail moulded tops above lunette carved friezes, with cannon barrel ring-turned legs united by an all-round stretcher, 17thC, 22in (56cm) high.
$3,500–3,750 *B*

An oak joint stool, the top above a moulded frieze, on slightly splayed baluster supports and stretcher rails, 17thC, 18½in (47cm) high.
$1,800–2,250 *WW*

A William and Mary turned and painted birchwood joint stool, the oval top above a joined base on vase-turned legs joined by stretchers ending in flattened ball feet, New England, c1720, 19thC paint, some removed, 22in (56cm) high.
$6,750–7,500 *S(NY)*

A joined oak box stool, 17thC, 16½in (42cm) high.
$3,750–4,500 *DBA*

A joined oak refectory table, the three-plank top above a plain frieze, on ring-turned column supports tied by later block stretchers, mid-17thC, 80¾in (205cm) long.
$4,000–4,500 *Bon*

Tables

A joined oak and fruitwood gateleg table, the top with elliptical leaves above an end frieze drawer, on baluster turned legs and peg feet tied by block stretchers, c1690, 47¾in (121.5cm) long.
$2,700–3,300 *Bon*

A Charles II oak bobbin-turned side table, c1680, 36in (91.5cm) long.
$12,000–13,500 *PHA*

A joined oak refectory table, with plank top, on turned legs with stretchers, late 17thC, 79½in (202cm) long.
$5,250–6,000 *DN*

A Jacobean oak refectory table, restored, 29¾in (75.5cm) long.
$3,750–4,500 *SK*

An oak refectory table, with rounded corners to top, above a floral carved frieze, the turned uprights united by moulded square section stretchers, early 17thC, 89in (226cm) long.
$5,250–6,000 *P(Sc)*

Tables

The earliest 'tables' were simply boards placed on trestles, but during the 15thC the improvement in joinery techniques made possible the development of 'table boards' with permanent sub-frames. The first table to be made by a joiner was a standing low cupboard on extended legs, or stiles, and was used for serving food and for storage. Gradually, the space below the table top was reduced to a shallow frieze which enabled the table to be sat at in relative comfort. The legs were united by stretchers.

Until the beginning of the 18thC most tables, apart from those specifically intended for dining, were small, multi-purpose side tables. Until the mid-17thC these were made mainly in oak. Designs were straightforward and solid, with Gothic carving. After the Restoration in 1660, walnut was also used, with styles becoming more adventurous and ornate, reflecting French and Dutch tastes, with a greater emphasis on decorative features.

An oak side table, good patination and colour, late 17thC, 36in (91.5cm) long.
$3,750–5,250 *DBA*

A William and Mary fruitwood and oak side table, the top with moulded edge, one long drawer, supported on turned legs with box stretchers, 29½in (75cm) long.
$1,350–1,500 *TMA*

An oak side table, the moulded top above a single panelled drawer, on baluster turned and square legs joined by stretchers, some 17thC components, 36in (91.5cm) long.
$750–900 *Hal*

A George III oak dressing table, the top fitted with 3 drawers, above shaped skirt, on straight chamfered legs, late 18thC, 32in (81.5cm) wide.
$3,500–3,750 *S(NY)*

A George III oak tripod table, the two-plank top on a baluster turned stem and 3 downcurved legs, 18thC, 33¾in (86cm) diam.
$450–600 *Hal*

A George III elm lowboy, c1760, 32in (81.5cm) wide.
$15,000–18,000 *PHA*

l. A refectory table, the mahogany top with a moulded edge, on an ash trestle frame with X-end supports, iron reinforcing plate to one end, and a central braced stretcher, early 19thC, 73¾in (187.5cm) long.
$3,000–3,750 *DN*

A George III oak tripod table, c1760, 18in (46cm) diam.
$1,500–1,800 *PHA*

An oak refectory table, the plank top on 6 baluster turned legs linked by a shaped and channel-moulded underfrieze and foot stretchers, part-17thC, 93¼in (237cm) long.
$5,250–6,000 *P(Ch)*

An oak refectory table, with single plank top, moulded frieze, on turned legs joined by square section moulded stretchers, one cleat replaced, associated, late 17thC and later, 87in (221cm) long.
$4,800–6,000 *CSK*

A Welsh side table, with sycamore top and drawer front, on original painted ash legs and frame, c1800, 36in (91.5cm) long.
$370–550 *APa*

An oak washstand, with 2 drawers and tapered legs, c1835, 36in (91.5cm) wide.
$300–360 *OD*

An oak dish-topped cricket table, 1830, 25in (63.5cm) high.
$600–670 *KEY*

A painted and grained stand, the top and drawer façade with brown and yellow vinegar painting outlined in black, the stand painted yellow with black striping, old surface, original turned handle, slight damage, New England, c1825, 18in (46cm) wide.
$4,500–5,250 *SK*

A William and Mary turned maple and pine tavern table, the top above a single frieze drawer, on vase and ring-turned legs with flattened ball feet, joined by stretchers, probably New England, c1730, 40in (101.5cm) long.
$3,750–4,500 *S(NY)*

A William and Mary painted tavern table with drawer, old red paint, Newbury, Massachusetts, adapted, early 18thC, 39in (99cm) long.
$9,300–10,500 *SK*

A Flemish/German oak refectory table, with cleated plank top and 2 end frieze drawers, on baluster turned legs joined by a central flattened stretcher, 18thC, 88in (223.5cm) long.
$5,250–6,000 *CSK*

A French oak refectory table, on square tapering legs, 19thC, 124in (315cm) long.
$4,500–5,250 *CSK*

Shaker Furniture

A pine lidded chest and cupboard, with old varnish finish, the cupboard with 2 doors each with brass sliding spring latch and original lock, 2 different size keys, both brackets missing from front legs, salmon wash on the back, red wash to the interior, the exterior probably old refinish, Canterbury, New Hampshire, c1840, 81in (205.5cm) long.
$3,750–4,500 *SK(B)*

An ash and maple laundry basket, Enfield, New Hampshire, c1850, 29¼in (74.5cm) high, with a Shaker laundry list, in pen and ink on ruled paper, dated '1888', mounted in the original butternut frame, Mount Lebanon, New York.
$1,800–2,250 *S(NY)*

A maple rocking chair, with rush seat, refinished, Harvard Community, Massachusetts, c1840.
$2,250–2,500 *S(NY)*

A pine sewing desk, with fruitwood handles, the 4 graduated drawers of nailed construction, the bottoms chamfered in at the front, drawer blades set in with half dovetails, salmon paint, repaired, Sabbathday Lake, Maine, c1840, 26in (66cm) wide.
$7,800–8,800 *SK(B)*

A red stained butternut sewing table, the 3 drawers with bone pegs on the dies, appears to retain its original finish, New Lebanon Community, New York, c1840, 28in (71cm) wide.
$13,500–15,000 *S(NY)*

Only a very few New Lebanon sewing tables have survived with their rare bone pegs on the apron.

l. A maple and pine box, the top painted with a geometric grid in black on a brown ground, probably Maine, mid-19thC, 10in (25.5cm) wide.
$1,000–1,100 *S(NY)*

A pine double cupboard-on-chest, in 2 sections, with original brown paint, the 5 drawers dovetailed with thumbnail moulded lips, extensive use of glue blocks, replaced handles, slight damage, Groveland, New York, c1840, 36½in (92.5cm) wide.
$25,500–27,000 *SK(B)*

Shaker Furniture

The Shakers are a Christian communal sect which was first set up in New Lebanon, New York, USA, in the late 18thC. They produced a wide range of simple, functional furniture which immediately became popular in neighbouring towns and villages due to its sound craftsmanship. As a result the Shakers soon began manufacturing furniture on a commercial basis in communal workshops, and by the end of the 19thC it had become so highly prized that many pieces were being faked. The Shaker chair is probably the best known of all their furniture and can be described as a more elegant version of English farmhouse style.

A pine table, with 2 plank top and single drawer, morticed case, painted red, repaired, Canterbury, New Hampshire, c1850, 60¾in (154.5cm) wide.
$1,800–2,250 *SK(B)*

FURNITURE
Beds

A mahogany cradle, with cane Gothic-shaped canopy and turned finials, 19thC, 36in (91.5cm) long.
$670–750 *DN*

A Victorian white painted cast iron cot, with brass top rail and knobs, on original porcelain casters, 48in (122cm) long.
$450–550 *GH*

A 'crown and canopy' four-poster bedstead, with brass decoration enclosing a hand painted floral design plaque on the foot panel, and a cast brass crown, c1860, 54in (137cm) long.
$2,250–2,600 *SeH*

l. A bleached mahogany tester bed, the moulded cornice hung with swagged drapes, with arched headboard and reeded front posts, adapted, the front posts probably 18thC and Colonial, 67in (170cm) wide.
$12,000–13,500 *C*

A Regency mahogany full tester bed, the tester with cream gesso and green and pink foliate design, turned, lobed and gadrooned foot posts, on short lobed feet, 71in (180.5cm) wide.
$12,750–14,200 *WL*

A pair of Victorian single brass bedsteads, with circular head and footboards decorated with foliate and ribbon drapes, 42in (106.5cm) wide.
$1,700–2,250 *M*

A Victorian brass and red walnut bed, 54in (137cm) wide.
$1,600–1,800 *SWA*

A wrought and cast iron bedstead, with central cast brass plaques, c1875, 54in (137cm) wide.
$1,100–1,500 *SeH*

A mahogany tester bed, with pierced and carved canopy, on reeded columns decorated with carved acanthus leaves, 19thC, 54in (137cm) wide.
$3,750–4,500 *AG*

A Victorian mahogany full tester bed, the front posts with turned twisting and tulip decoration, original iron support for the pelmet, 57in (145cm) wide.
$1,900–2,200 *B*

An Edwardian double bed, with mahogany and floral inlaid head and footboards, probably Waring & Gillow, 60in (152.5cm) wide.
$1,200–1,500 *AAV*

A French elm country four-poster bedstead, with a panelled backboard and tester, c1830, 52in (132cm) wide.
$1,800–2,400 *SeH*

l. An Edwardian brass and cast iron bedstead, with a mother-of-pearl plaque in the foot panel, and brass Art Nouveau style peacock design rosettes in both panels, c1910, 54in (137cm) wide.
$1,200–1,350 *SeH*

r. A Napoleon III mahogany and brass-mounted bed, applied with tablets inlaid in brass, with urns and ribbon hung swags of flowers, the panelled head and footboard flanked by fluted columns, with a modern 'box' base, 48¾in (124cm) wide.
$1,200–1,500 *P*

An Edwardian mahogany bedroom suite, the bedstead with shaped panels inlaid with swags of flowers and ribbon bows in coloured woods, backed by satinwood, on cabriole legs, together with a triple wardrobe, dressing table, washstand, bedside cupboard, a pair of bedroom chairs with cane seats, and a mahogany towel rail.
$3,750–4,000 *P(HSS)*

A Louis XVI white painted and parcel gilt bed, the canopy with domed centre and guilloche frieze with flowerhead angles and ribbon-tied laurel centres, redecorated, mattress supports replaced, possibly previously with a dome, stamped twice 'Tilliard', 75½in (192cm) wide.
$127,500–135,000 *C*

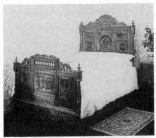

A Breton oak wedding bed, with original side rails, 19thC, 60in (152.5cm) wide.
$4,000–4,500 *SWA*

A Breton style fruitwood bed, of Arts & Crafts influence, with original side rails, late 19thC, 60in (152.5cm) wide.
$3,300–3,600 *SWA*

l. A Louis XV style walnut bed, with original side rails, late 19thC, 54in (137cm) wide.
$1,800–2,000 *SWA*

A French walnut double bedstead, the head and footboards of shaped fluted outline, carved with a pair of amorini, shellwork and flowersprays, on leaf scroll legs, late 19thC, 61in (155cm) wide.
$670–820 *N*

A Louis Philippe mahogany *lit en bateau*, the shaped uprights decorated with paterae and U-shaped centre, on split roundel feet, 51in (129.5cm) wide.
$1,350–1,800 *CSK*

l. An American Empire tester bed, the overhanging cornice above 4 columnar posts, hung with draperies, adapted, c1830, 85in (216cm) wide.
$33,000–37,500 *S(NY)*

Day Beds & Chaises Longues

A Regency rosewood day bed, with gilt-bronze mounts, padded scroll ends, on shaped and turned legs with gilt-brass mouldings, anthemion mounts and collars, c1810, 90½in (230cm) long.
$7,800–8,800 *S*

A French walnut *lit de coin* day bed, with carved mahogany floral decoration, c1880, 42in (106.5cm) long.
$1,800–2,700 *SeH*

A Louis XV giltwood and painted chaise longue, the caned back and seat with loose cushion, on cabriole legs carved with flowers and leaves, mid-18thC, 68in (173cm) long.
$15,000–16,500 *S*

A Victorian walnut chaise longue, the chair back with buttoned upholstery, on cabochon carved cabriole legs with scroll feet, c1860, 61½in (156cm) long.
$750–900 *Hal*

A mid-Victorian rosewood chaise longue, the buttoned padded back with scroll arm terminals, serpentine seat, on cabriole legs with scroll feet, 75in (190.5cm) long.
$1,500–2,250 *CSK*

A Louis XV beechwood chaise longue, the moulded, arched top rail carved with flowerheads and leaf tips, upholstered in brown leather, repaired, mid-18thC, 77in (195.5cm) long.
$30,000–32,000 *S(NY)*

l. A Victorian mahogany patent folding day bed, with 3 cane panels, each supported on a ratchet, on turned baluster legs, 69in (175.5cm) long.
$600–670 *HCC*

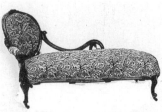

r. A Victorian walnut framed single chair back chaise longue, with carved floral decorated frame, with serpentine front and cabriole legs, 60in (152.5cm) long.
$1,250–1,450 *WIL*

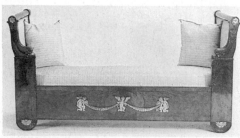

An Empire mahogany and ormolu-mounted day bed, with stylised dolphin arms, the frieze applied with an ormolu figure of a cherub and swags, on reeded feet, 67in (170cm) long.
$2,600–2,800 *P(B)*

A Regency mahogany and gilt day bed, with over-scrolled end and down-curved back, squab cushion and reeded frame, on down-swept reeded legs with claw feet, 81in (205.5cm) long.
$2,700–3,300 *CSK*

Bookcases

l. A mahogany bookcase, in the manner of
A. W. N. Pugin, with a
castellated cornice above a
pair of glazed doors with
Gothic arch and quatrefoil
glazing bars, on plinth base,
19thC, 63¼in (160.5cm) wide.
$4,000–4,800 *HDS*

A George III mahogany
bookcase, the dentil cornice
above a pair of astragal
glazed doors, the later base
fitted with a pair of
panelled doors, on bracket
feet, 49in (124.5cm) wide.
$3,300–3,750 *CSK*

r. A Regency mahogany open
bookcase, with 4 graduated
open shelves, a pair of gilt and
lattice wire panel doors below
and 2 drawers to the base, on
turned feet, 41in (104cm) wide.
$3,750–4,500 *P(C)*

A George III inlaid mahogany
bookcase, some damage, adapted,
49½in (125.5cm) wide.
$3,300–4,000 *S(NY)*

A George I walnut
bookcase, with cavetto
cornice above 2 glazed
doors outlined with a
narrow herringbone
band with upper re-
entrant corners, above
2 candle slides and
flanked by fluted
pilasters, the base with
a slide above 5 long
herringbone
and crossbanded
drawers, with original
brass handles and
escutcheons, restored,
39in (99cm) wide.
$6,500–7,500 *DN*

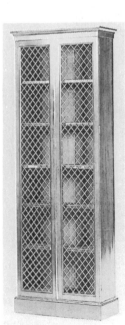

A Regency mahogany
bookcase, the moulded
cornice above a pair of
brass grille doors,
enclosing adjustable
shelves, on a plinth
base, 33in (84cm) wide.
$5,000–5,500 *CSK*

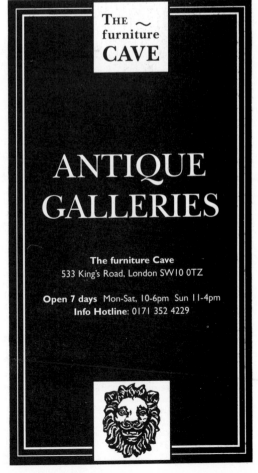

An early Victorian mahogany bookcase, the open shelves flanked by reeded pilasters headed by carved paterae, reduced in height, 53½in (136cm) wide.
$1,500–2,250 *P(B)*

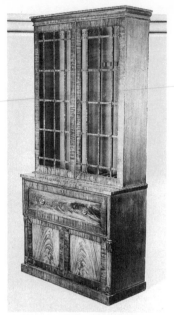

A William IV mahogany bookcase, adapted for guns and fishing tackle, with 2 glazed astragal doors, above a deep panelled drawer and 2 panelled doors, 48in (122cm) wide.
$2,000–2,700 *DN*

A Victorian mahogany bookcase, with 2 arched glazed doors enclosing adjustable shelves, the base with a shallow frieze drawer above 2 panelled doors, 39in (99cm) wide.
$4,000–4,500 *DN*

A Victorian mahogany glazed bookcase, on cupboard base, 46in (117cm) wide.
$1,650–2,250 *BWe*

A Dutch mahogany bookcase-on-stand, with a fret-carved gallery above the dentil cornice, the glazed door mounted with gilt-brass classical motifs and flanked by Corinthian columns, on a fluted stand with tapering legs, early 19thC, 34in (86.5cm) wide.
$2,000–2,500 *Bea*

A Biedermeier satin birch bookcase, with an arched dentil cornice, above a pair of astragal glazed doors with a pair of drawers beneath, flanked by turned pilasters, on block feet, c1830, 59¾in (152cm) wide.
$4,000–4,800 *Bon*

Biedermeier

Biedermeier furniture was made in Germany, Austria and Scandinavia from the 1820s to the 1840s. It has a simple, unpretentious elegance, and is typically made of blond woods, such as ash, maple and cherrywood. Fruitwoods were also very popular, particularly for less sophisticated pieces.

An Edwardian mahogany bookcase, the swan neck pediment with satinwood fan medallion inlay, the frieze with a chequer band above arcaded mahogany and satinwood mouldings, 2 glazed doors enclosing adjustable shelves, the lower part with 2 panelled doors of inlaid satinwood bands and string lines, enclosing adjustable shelves, on bracket feet, 38in (96.5cm) wide.
$2,400–2,800 *P(S)*

Bureau Bookcases

l. A Queen Anne walnut bureau bookcase, the concave cornice above a pair of arched panelled doors opening to a fitted interior, above a slant-front opening to a leather-lined writing surface with a fitted interior, 2 short and 2 long graduated feather-banded drawers below, damaged, 42in (106.5cm) wide.
$12,750–14,250   *S(NY)*

A George III mahogany bureau bookcase, with adjustable shelves enclosed by 2 glazed astragal doors, the base with a fall-front enclosing a fitted interior of small drawers and pigeonholes, above 2 short and 3 long drawers, with later brass handles, on bracket feet, 50in (127cm) wide.
$4,500–5,250   *DN*

A mahogany and marquetry bureau bookcase, the foliate inlaid cornice with broken swan neck cresting above a pair of astragal doors, the inlaid sloping fall-front enclosing a fitted interior, above 4 long graduated drawers, on bracket feet, the bureau late 18thC, later inlaid, the bookcase top late 19thC, 42½in (108cm) wide.
$3,000–3,750   *CSK*

l. A mahogany bureau bookcase, the associated upper part with a moulded cornice, fitted with adjustable shelves enclosed by a pair of glazed astragal panel doors with 2 candle slides below, the sloping fall-front enclosing a fitted interior, 4 long drawers below, on ogee bracket feet, restored, 18thC, 45in (114.5cm) wide.
$6,750–7,500   *CSK*

A mahogany bureau bookcase, with neo-classical style painted decoration, the moulded cornice with a swan neck pediment above adjustable shelves, enclosed by a pair of glazed doors, the fall-front with a Kauffman design panel, the interior with a cupboard door, drawers and pigeonholes, above 4 long oak-lined graduated drawers, with brass swan neck handles, on bracket feet, one drawer stamped 'Edwards & Roberts', 19thC, 42in (106.5cm) wide.
$6,750–7,500 WW

A Victorian Sheraton revival satinwood and marquetry bureau bookcase, in the style of Edwards & Roberts, crossbanded, mostly in tulipwood and strung in ebony and boxwood, the moulded cornice with Gothic pendent frieze, a marquetry inlaid and pen work fall-front with fitted interior, above one long, 2 short and 2 further long graduated and cockbeaded drawers, with brass drop handles, on bracket feet, 37¾in (96cm) wide.
$8,200–9,750 HAM

A mahogany bureau bookcase, the associated top with glazed doors, the base with a fall-front enclosing a fitted interior, above 4 long drawers, with chased brass handles, on ogee bracket feet, 19thC, 43in (109cm) wide.
$3,300–3,750 DN

A late Victorian mahogany cylinder bureau bookcase, with arched pediment above a pair of glazed panelled doors, enclosing 3 adjustable shelves, the base with a fitted interior above a pull-out writing surface, with a shelf enclosed by a pair of panel doors, on plinth base, 48½in (123cm) wide.
$1,800–2,250 P(NE)

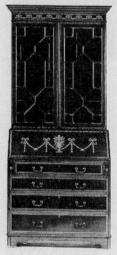

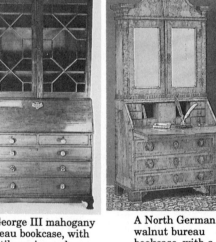

An Edwardian mahogany and marquetry bureau bookcase, the moulded cornice above a swag decorated frieze and a pair of astragal glazed doors, enclosing 3 adjustable shelves, the fall-front decorated with central urn and hairbell swags, with fitted interior, above 4 graduated crossbanded drawers, on bracket feet, 38in (96.5cm) wide.
$2,500–3,000 CSK

A mahogany bureau bookcase, in 2 parts, the upper part with moulded swan neck pediment centred with 3 urn and spirally-carved finials, a pair of arched doors opening to a fitted interior and a pair of candle slides, the lower section with hinged moulded fall-front with fitted interior above 4 graduated blocked long drawers, on bracket feet, Boston, Massachusetts, c1750, 40in (101.5cm) wide.
$255,000–270,000 S(NY)

A George III mahogany bureau bookcase, with dentil cornice and glazed doors, the fall-front with 2 short and 3 long drawers below, 49¼in (125cm) wide.
$2,400–3,000 P(G)

A North German walnut bureau bookcase, with a raised cornice above a pair of mirrored panelled doors, enclosing shelves and small drawers, the fall-front decorated with crossbanding and ornate moulded brass lock escutcheon, on bracket feet, mid-18thC, 40in (101.5cm) wide.
$17,250–18,750 AG

l. A South German baroque burr-walnut bureau bookcase, early 18thC, 52½in (133.5cm) wide.
$9,750–11,250 SK

Library Bookcases

A William IV mahogany breakfront bookcase, with moulded cornice above a panelled frieze with draught-turned bosses, above 4 astragal glazed doors, the base with 4 panelled doors, 92¼in (234cm) wide.
$11,250–12,750 *HAM*

A Victorian mahogany breakfront bookcase, decorated with applied scrolling brackets, 105in (266.5cm) high.
$7,500–8,250 *AG*

r. A George IV mahogany breakfront library bookcase, the upper part with a moulded cornice, above 4 glazed doors, the lower part with 3 frieze drawers, above 4 panelled doors, on a plinth base, 84in (213.5cm) wide.
$7,500–8,250 *P(S)*

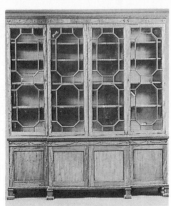

A mahogany breakfront library bookcase, in Adam style, restored, 19thC, 91in (231cm) wide.
$10,500–12,000 *DN*

l. A George III mahogany library bookcase, with moulded cornice, 3 pairs of astragal glazed doors, 3 pairs of panelled doors below, on a plinth base, reconstructed, 118in (300cm) wide.
$5,250–6,000 *Bea*

r. A mahogany breakfront secrétaire library bookcase, the upper section with glazed doors, late 18thC, the base 19thC, 97⅜in (248cm) high.
$7,800–8,800 *HAM*

l. A mahogany breakfront library bookcase, with moulded and dentil cornice, 4 glazed astragal doors with carved paterae, above 4 panelled doors with chequer strung ovals and roundels at the corners, on a plinth base, 19thC, 116in (294.5cm) wide.
$12,000–13,500 *DN*

Low Bookcases

A French kingwood veneeered double book rack, with ormolu mounts and casters, c1900, 30in (76cm) wide.
$2,700–3,000 *GAS*

A Regency rosewood and cut-brass inlaid dwarf bookcase, with bobbin-moulded frieze and a pair of glazed doors, replacement top, 31in (79cm) wide.
$3,000–4,500 *J&L*

A mid-Victorian rosewood veneeered serpentine-fronted open bookcase, 52in (132cm) wide.
$4,000–4,500 *Bea*

r. A Victorian rosewood bookcase, with a raised mirror back on moulded curvilinear supports, the marble top above a beaded frieze and adjustable shelves, c1850, 61¾in (157cm) wide.
$1,200–1,800 *Hal*

A William IV rosewood open bookcase, the *scagliola* top on lotus carved columnar supports, the 3 shelves on turned supports, on a plinth base, 44in (112cm) wide.
$3,750–4,500 *Bea*

A Victorian mahogany breakfront bookcase, the ebonised moulded top with three-quarter gallery, leather trimmed adjustable shelves and on a plinth base, by Marsh Jones and Cribb, 74in (188cm) wide.
$2,700–3,000 *AH*

Revolving Bookcases

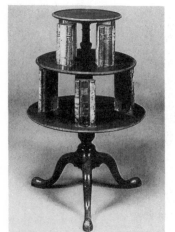

A George III mahogany two-tier revolving bookstand, raised on a baluster standard, on splayed legs ending in pad feet, late 18thC, 24½in (62cm) diam.
$3,500–4,200 *S(NY)*

An Edwardian mahogany revolving bookcase, the top inlaid with circular motif and satinwood banding, 19in (48.5cm) wide.
$900–1,200 *CAG*

r. An Edwardian mahogany two-tier revolving bookcase, with brass balustraded gallery, label for Maple & Co, 19½in (49.5cm) wide.
$1,800–2,250 *MCA*

An Edwardian mahogany revolving bookcase, with banded inlay, 19¼in (49cm) wide.
$900–1,200 *WL*

Secrétaire Bookcases

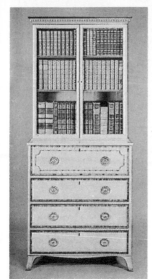

A George III satinwood and rosewood crossbanded secrétaire bookcase, the moulded cornice above a pair of glazed doors, the secrétaire drawer enclosing an arrangement of drawers and pigeonholes, above 3 further drawers, on outswept bracket feet, attributed to Gillows, c1780, 34in (86.5cm) wide.
$12,000–13,500 *Bon*

A Regency mahogany secrétaire bookcase, the line inlaid hinged fall enclosing baize-lined writing surface and fitted interior, restored, 42in (106.5cm) wide.
$4,000–4,800 *CSK*

r. A George IV mahogany secrétaire bookcase, the upper part with arched pediment inlaid in ebony with star motif, a pair of astragal glazed doors, a secrétaire drawer with fitted pigeonholes and 3 short drawers, 3 long graduated drawers below, with shaped apron, on splayed bracket feet, some damage, 42in (106.5cm) wide.
$5,500–6,500 *CAG*

r. A George III mahogany, tulipwood crossbanded and marquetry inlaid secrétaire bookcase, with swan neck pediment, a pair of astragal glazed doors above a baize-lined fall, 3 long drawers below enclosed by a pair of panel doors, 46⅜in (119cm) wide.
$9,000–10,500 *P*

A George IV mahogany secrétaire bookcase, the scrolled cresting above a pair of astragal glazed doors, the hinged fall enclosing a leather-lined surface and fitted interior above 2 cupboard doors, flanked by reeded pilasters, on turned feet, 33in (84cm) wide.
$2,700–3,300 *CSK*

A George III mahogany secrétaire bookcase, with a pair of astragal glazed doors, secrétaire drawer above 3 graduated long drawers, on bracket feet, the 2 parts associated, 34in (86.5cm) wide.
$2,250–3,000 *Bon*

A George III mahogany secrétaire bookcase, the arched cornice with 4 urn finials above a lancet moulding and a pair of doors with plumed arched glazing bars enclosing 3 adjustable shelves, the fitted secrétaire drawer and the pair of panelled doors below inlaid with ovals, on splayed bracket feet, c1795, 48in (122cm) wide.
$52,500–60,000 *S*

The pattern of the glazing bars, with the Prince of Wales' feathers and festooned drapery, corresponds exactly to a design by the cabinet-maker William Casement which was published in 1793 in The Cabinet-Maker's London Book of Prices, and reissued in 1803 in a subsequent edition of the same publication.

A Regency ebony inlaid mahogany secrétaire bookcase, associated, 42½in (108cm) wide.
$2,500–3,000 *SK(B)*

A Regency mahogany secrétaire bookcase, decorated with ebony lines, the lower part with pull-out writing surface and fitted interior, 35¼in (89.5cm) wide.
$3,500–4,000 *P(C)*

A George IV mahogany secrétaire bookcase, with ebony strung borders, the base with a double fronted secrétaire drawer, 48in (122cm) wide. **$3,000–3,750** *DN*

A Victorian mahogany kneehole secrétaire bookcase, the base with a long frieze drawer with fitted interior and writing slide, a shaped frieze drawer below and 3 short drawers to each side, on a plinth base with bracket feet, 42in (106.5cm) wide. **$3,000–3,750** *CSK*

An early Victorian mahogany secrétaire bookcase, the drop pendent moulded cornice above a pair of astragal glazed doors, a secrétaire hinged drawer, enclosing a fitted interior and 3 drawers, on outswept bracket feet, 55½in (141cm) wide. **$3,400–4,000** *CSK*

A late Victorian mahogany secrétaire bookcase, the galleried surmount above a moulded cornice and 2 glazed panelled doors, the lower section fitted with bird's-eye maple veneered and leather-lined secrétaire drawer above 2 cupboard doors, on shaped bracket feet, 45¾in (116cm) wide. **$1,200–1,800** *P(Sc)*

A Victorian mahogany secrétaire bookcase, 40in (101.5cm) wide. **$2,250–3,000** *Bon*

r. An Edwardian mahogany secrétaire bookcase, with kingwood crossbanding and boxwood and ebony stringing, 49in (124.5cm) wide. **$2,700–3,500** *Bea*

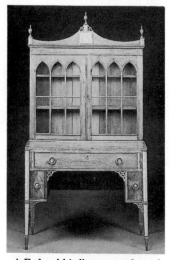

A Federal bird's-eye maple and flame-birch inlaid mahogany desk and bookcase, in 2 parts, original brass pulls fitted with spring mechanism, Northeastern Shore, New England, c1815, pierced fretwork possibly of a later date, 41in (104cm) wide. **$10,500–12,000** *S(NY)*

Buckets

A mahogany coopered and brass-bound plate bucket, with brass carrying handle, early 19thC, 15in (38cm) diam. **$1,800–2,250** *S*

A George III mahogany and brass-bound bucket, with brass handles and liner, c1780, 17¼in (44cm) diam. **$6,000–6,750** *S*

r. A George III mahogany and brass-bound bucket, with brass liner and handles, c1780, 13¾in (35cm) diam. **$7,500–8,250** *S*

Bureaux

A walnut and crossbanded bureau, inlaid with feather banding, with fitted interior, damaged, c1710, 35¾in (91cm) wide.
$3,300–4,000   S(S)

A George I walnut-veneered bureau, outlined with boxwood and ebony stringing, with false frieze drawer, restoration and alteration, 36in (91.5cm) wide.
$3,750–4,500   Bea

A George I walnut fall-front bureau, in 2 sections, restored, 42½in (108cm) wide.
$3,300–3,750   SK

A George II walnut bureau, with fitted interior, with trade label 'Henry Bell', 30in (76cm) wide.
$8,250–9,000   C

A George II mahogany bureau, c1755, 41in (104cm) wide.
$6.750–7,500   S

A George I walnut bureau, the fall-front enclosing a fitted interior, above 2 short and 3 long drawers, 30in (76cm) wide.
$6,000–6,750   L

Bureaux

In the 17thC bureaux were made in two parts – a bureau top and chest base, with a 'waist' moulding to cover the join. This moulding was retained even after bureaux began to be made in one piece at the beginning of the 18thC, but was finally dropped c1720. Thereafter, designs varied very little, but the type of wood, handles and decoration will provide clues for dating.

A George III mahogany bureau, with fitted interior above 4 graduated drawers, on bracket feet, 42in (106.5cm) wide.
$2,700–3,300   MR

A George III mahogany bureau, 28¼in (72cm) wide.
$2,250–3,000   P(S)

A George III mahogany bureau, the crossbanded fall-front enclosing a fitted interior, with 2 short and 2 long drawers below, on bracket feet, 36in (91.5cm) wide.
$2,700–3,700   CSK

A George III mahogany bureau, the fall-front enclosing a fitted interior, 2 short and 3 long graduated drawers, handles replaced, 45½in (115.5cm) wide.
$1,350–1,800   Mit

A George III mahogany
bureau, with fall-front
enclosing a fitted interior,
above 4 long graduated
drawers, on bracket feet,
40in (101.5cm) wide.
$3,000–3,750 *C(S)*

A Dutch walnut bureau, the fall-
front enclosing a fitted interior
above a well and with 2 small
loper drawers, on later bun feet,
c1735, 37in (94cm) wide.
$12,000–13,500 *S*

A Victorian burr walnut and
foliate marquetry bureau,
the raised back with a
shaped mirror, a drawer,
2 glazed doors and chased
brass galleries, above a
rosewood fitted interior with
a well enclosed by the fall, on
cabriole legs, chased brass
mounts, 32in (81.5cm) wide.
$3,000–3,750 *DN*

r. A Louis XIV red
tortoiseshell boulle
bureau mazarin,
the kneehole with
a concave drawer
above a cupboard
with 3 drawers on
each side, partly
inlaid in mother-of-
pearl and copper,
c1700, 41in
(104cm) wide.
$67,500–75,000 *S*

l. A George IV mahogany cylinder bureau,
crossbanded in satinwood, the cylinder
inlaid with an oval, opening to reveal a
fitted interior, 48in (122cm) wide.
$3,750–4,500 *L*

A French kingwood and
ormolu-mounted cylinder
bureau de dame, c1870,
36in (91.5cm) wide.
$8,250–9,750 *BUT*

A Transitional kingwood *bureau
en pente,* the parquetry inlaid
fall enclosing a stepped interior
of drawers above a well, with
2 frieze drawers below, on gilt-
metal mounted cabriole legs,
stamped 'J. Popsel, Jme',
c1760, 32in (81cm) wide.
$4,500–5,250 *Bon*

A late Victorian rosewood and
inlaid *bureau de dame,* decorated
with scrolling foliage, the arched
shelved surmount supported on
turned uprights above 2 drawers
and a folding hinged writing
surface over a frieze drawer,
on square tapering legs, 31in
(78.5cm) wide.
$2,250–3,000 *P(Sc)*

A George II mahogany bureau, the
fall-front enclosing a stepped and
concave interior, with 4 graduated
long drawers below, on ogee
bracket feet, probably New
England, 38¼in (97cm) wide.
$6,750–7,500 *P*

A French mahogany *bureau à cylindre*, with brass inlay, the marble top with pierced gallery above 3 small drawers, the tambour with further drawers behind, hinged writing surface and a frieze drawer, on tapered brass fluted supports, c1890, 31¾in (80.5cm) wide.
$3,000–3,750 *Bri*

A German walnut and marquetry bureau, on associated stand, with foliate inlaid central door enclosing compartments and drawers flanked by 8 drawers above fall-front, on bulbous turned and reeded legs, joined by an X-stretcher, 18thC, 39½in (100cm) wide.
$6,000–6,750 *P(Sc)*

A south German walnut and crossbanded bureau, 18thC, 44in (112cm) wide.
$14,250–15,750 *P(O)*

r. A Dutch marquetry bombé-fronted bureau, inlaid with vases of flowers and floral meander on an oak ground, 18thC, 30¾in (78cm) wide.
$4,500–5,250 *Oli*

A Dutch walnut feather banded bureau, the sloping front with a book rest enclosing a stepped fitted interior and a well, 18thC, 41in (104cm) wide.
$4,800–6,000 *L*

r. A Dutch oak and marquetry bombé-fronted bureau, the panels with sprays of flowers within boxwood strung borders, 18thC, 42in (106.5cm) wide.
$5,250–6,000 *DN*

l. A Dutch oak bombé-fronted bureau, decorated with foliate scrolls with meandering tendrils, the sloping fall with a ribbon-tied basket of flowers and enclosing a fitted interior and well with slide, restored, 19thC, 44in (112cm) wide.
$6,400–7,000 *CSK*

A central Italian walnut parquetry bureau, mid-18thC, 46½in (118cm) wide.
$6,000–6,750 *S*

An Italian burr walnut and ebonised bureau, the moulded top concealing a drawer, the fall-front enclosing a fitted interior and a sliding surface, above 3 serpentine drawers, on carved feet, 18thC, 67in (170cm) high.
$67,500–72,000 *S*

This bureau stands out from the recorded group of Lombard ribalte for its unusual design. It bears two inscriptions written in brown ink, practically illegible, which may refer to the maker of the piece. Only two very fine Lombard bureau cabinets are recorded inscribed with the name of the maker and the date of their execution.

A north Italian walnut and kingwood bureau, with crossbanded and strapwork inlaid fall, c1750, 44½in (113cm) wide.
$11,250–12,750 *Bon*

A north Italian walnut fall-front bureau, with engraved inlaid ivory figural and leaf decoration, a fitted interior, above 3 long graduated drawers, on bracket feet, 18thC 43¼in (110.5cm) wide.
$13,500–15,000 *JAd*

A north European walnut and crossbanded bureau, the fall-front opening to reveal a fitted interior, above 4 graduated drawers, with a shaped apron below, c1740, 36in (91.5cm) wide.
$7,500–8,250 *S*

A walnut and burr walnut marquetry bureau, possibly Swiss, mid-18thC, 41¾in (106cm) wide.
$5,250–6,000 *S*

A north Italian bureau, japanned in Chinese style with flowers and fruit, figures and landscapes, 18thC, 43in (109cm) wide.
$2,250–3,000 *DN*

A Chippendale curly maple bureau, with fitted interior, 4 long drawers, raised on ogee bracket feet, probably some alteration to writing interior, New England, c1765, 35¾in (91cm) wide.
$6,800–7,500 *S(NY)*

A Chippendale maple bureau, restored, Connecticut, late 18thC, 39¼in (99.5cm) wide.
$2,400–3,000 *SK(B)*

l. A Chippendale mahogany bureau, with fall-front writing surface, above 4 graduated reverse serpentine drawers, on ball-and-claw feet, Massachusetts, late 19thC, 43¼in (110.5cm) wide.
$1,800–2,700 *LHA*

A carved oak tester bed, together with needlework curtains and bed cover, 17thC and later, 54in (137cm) wide. **$6,800–7,800** *S(S)*

A George III oak food cupboard, in good condition, c1770, 36in (91.5cm) wide. **$3,000–3,750** *PHA*

An oak hall cupboard, with a pair of fielded panelled doors over 3 dummy and 4 real drawers, 18thC, 51in (129.5cm) wide. **$3,750–4,500** *RBB*

A maple pencil-post bedstead, with pine headboard, 4 tapering octagonal posts, original paint, New England, c1800, 55½in (141cm) wide. **$6,800–7,800** *S(NY)*

A Dutch oak, ebony and ebonised side cabinet, restored, late 17thC, 64¼in (163cm) wide. **$12,000–14,250** *C*

A French Provincial oak and pine buffet, the overhanging moulded cornice above a pair of grille-inset doors, the lower part with 2 drawers and a pair of cupboard doors, repaired, c1800, 49in (124.5cm) wide. **$6,750–7,500** *S(NY)*

A two-sectional oak chest, the 4 long drawers with beaded borders, late 17thC, stand later, 41in (104cm) wide. **$1,800–2,000** *HOLL*

An Elizabethan oak press cupboard, inlaid with holly and bog oak, c1580, 61in (155cm) wide. **$11,250–12,750** *Bon*

A James I carved joined oak press cupboard, c1630, 84in (213.5cm) wide. **$19,500–22,500** *PHA*

A Charles II oak chest, with 4 drawers, split baluster decoration, on original bun feet, c1670, 38in (96.5cm) wide. **$9,750–11,250** *PHA*

A George II oak corner cupboard, c1800, 36in (91.5cm) wide. **$6,500–7,500** *PHA*

A joined oak chest of drawers, the 3 drawers veneered with ivory and ebonised parquetry, on block feet, c1680, 39½in (100.5cm) wide.
$12,750–14,250 *Bon*

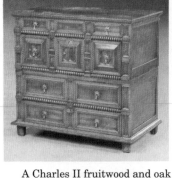

A Charles II fruitwood and oak chest of drawers, in 2 sections, the 4 drawers with applied mouldings, on stile feet, late 17thC, 38in (96.5cm) wide.
$4,000–5,000 *S(S)*

An oak, pine and birchwood chest of drawers, the 3 drawers with geometric mouldings, on turnip feet, Massachusetts, 1660–1700, 37in (94cm) wide.
$13,500–15,000 *S(NY)*

A George III oak and mahogany crossbanded chest of drawers, with 2 short and 4 long graduated drawers, on shaped bracket feet, restored, early 19thC, 39in (99cm) wide.
$1,200–1,350 *Hal*

An oak chest-on-stand, the moulded cornice above 2 short and 4 long graduated drawers, the stand with 3 frieze drawers, mid-18thC, 37in (94cm) wide.
$2,250–2,750 *Bon*

A William and Mary oak side table, with a drawer, shaped apron and 4 front legs, joined by shaped stretchers, c1690, 32in (81.5cm) wide.
$7,500–9,000 *DBA*

A narrow oak chest, with moulded top, 2 short and 3 long graduated drawers, on bracket feet, restored, early 18thC, 21½in (54.5cm) wide.
$1,200–1,500 *Bon*

A William and Mary oak side table, the shaped apron with one drawer, the legs with cross-shaped stretcher, dated '1690', 31in (78.5cm) wide.
$5,000–6,000 *DBA*

A George I oak lowboy, with one long above 2 short drawers, the apron decoratively shaped, on 4 cabriole legs, brasses replaced, c1720, 31in (78.5cm) wide.
$6,750–8,250 *DBA*

A George I oak lowboy, with 3 frieze drawers and a shaped apron, on cabriole legs with pointed pad feet, c1725, 30¼in (77cm) wide.
$3,000–3,750 *Bon*

A figured maple tavern table, with a single drawer, on cabriole legs with pad feet, New England, 1740–80, 22in (56cm) wide.
$8,250–9,750 *S(NY)*

An oak side table, the shaped friezes decorated with winged heads of angels and foliage, on carved, turned and square legs joined by stretchers, 19thC, 43in (109cm) wide.
$450–550 *Hal*

An oak coffer, the panelled top above a triple panel front carved with strapwork and foliage, on stile feet, restored, c1680, 56½in (143.5cm) long.
$600–720 *Hal*

A joined oak coffer, the 2 front carved panels divided by an incised carving of the Tree of Life, lockplate repaired, c1680, 39in (99cm) wide.
$3,000–3,750 *DBA*

An oak and mahogany crossbanded dresser base, with two-plank top, 3 frieze drawers, a shaped apron centred by a pointed star inlay, on cabriole legs to the front, early 18thC, 69¾in (177cm) long.
$6,750–7,500 *P*

An oak coffer, with lunette carved frieze above a pair of arched panels, flanked by stylised foliate stile feet, later top, mid-17thC, 49½in (125.5cm) long.
$675–825 *Hal*

A French oak low dresser, the top with a moulded border, 2 moulded frieze drawers, above 2 doors and a central carved panel, on turned feet, late 17thC, 71in (180.5cm) wide.
$4,000–5,000 *DN*

An oak Welsh dresser, with shelf back, 3 frieze drawers above an open recess, early 18thC, 68½in (174cm) wide.
$4,000–4,500 *S(S)*

An oak tridarn, with open recess above 2 small and 2 large panelled doors, dated '1725', 51in (130cm) wide.
$5,250–6,000 *S(S)*

An oak low dresser, with 3 frieze drawers, undulating apron, on turned columnar front legs, early 18thC, 79¾in (202.5cm) wide.
$4,500–5,250 *Bea*

An oak dresser, the top with moulded cornice, with 4 central drawers, frieze drawers and panelled cupboard doors, restored, mid-18thC, 105in (266.5cm) wide.
$10,500–12,000 *Bon*

Paul Hopwell Antiques

Early English Oak

Dressers, tables and chairs always in stock

A set of eight (four showing) early C19th ash and alder spindle back dining chairs. Excellent colour, condition and patina. English c1820.

A set of eight (four showing) Georgian ash wavyline ladderback dining chairs. Excellent colour, condition and patination. English c1800.

A small Charles II oak cupboard dresser base.
Excellent colour, condition and patina. Lake District. c1680

Paul Hopwell Antiques

A superb George III oak potboard
dresser and rack. Excellent colour,
condition and patina.
Wales. c1780

A small C17th oak tridarn with original
spoon rack. Excellent colour,
condition and patina.
North Wales. c1690

A small George III oak cupboard
dresser and rack. Excellent colour,
condition and patina
North Wales. c1760

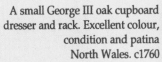

An oak refectory table, the single plank top with cleated ends, on waisted standard end supports, early 17thC, 138in (350.5cm) long.
$12,750–14,250 *CSK*

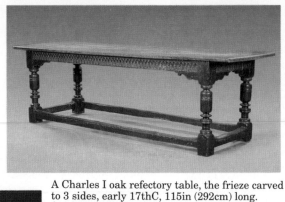

A Charles I oak refectory table, the frieze carved to 3 sides, early 17thC, 115in (292cm) long.
$13,000–15,000 *S(S)*

An Italian walnut centre table, with 2 drawers and trestle supports, 17thC, 72in (183cm) long.
$10,000–11,250 *S(S)*

A French fruitwood draw-leaf table, on square tapering legs, 19thC, 139in (353cm) extended.
$7,000–8,250 *CSK*

An oak settle, the back carved with 3 panels, c1695, 98in (249cm) wide.
$3,750–4,250 *PHA*

A William and Mary red stained figured maple and birchwood fall-front desk-on-stand, c1730, repaired, 27½in (70cm) wide.
$27,500–37,500 *S(NY)*

An oak box settle, with 6 panels to the back and 2 below the seat, 17thC, 54in (137cm) wide.
$6,000–7,000 *PHA*

An oak box settle, the back carved with many panels and 3 below the seat, c1690, 60in (152.5cm) wide.
$6,500–7,500 *PHA*

A joined oak armchair,
West Country, c1660.
$5,250–6,000 *DBA*

A joined oak side chair,
with chequerboard
carving, repaired, c1680.
$1,800–2,200 *DBA*

A Carolean joined oak
framed chair, upholstered
in leather, c1670.
$1,800–2,600 *DBA*

A pair of fruitwood
dining chairs,
early 19thC.
$250–300 *OD*

A Charles II joined oak
armchair, c1660.
$5,250–6,500 *DBA*

A Victorian oak hall settee, the splats
carved with Elizabethan female portraits,
late 19thC, 47½in (120.5cm) wide.
$600–750 *Hal*

A pair of Charles II panelled-
back side chairs, restored.
$1,300–1,700 *Hal*

A 17thC style oak wainscot
armchair, with a carved apron.
$825–975 *Gam*

A walnut side chair,
with cane back and
seat, restored, c1680.
$750–900 *Hal*

A fruitwood correction
chair, with reed carved
splat, 18thC.
$900–1,100 *TMA*

A pair of George III oak
side chairs, c1800.
$850–1,000 *PHA*

A joined oak wainscot
armchair, with carved
back, 17thC.
$3,000–3,500 *KEY*

A harlequin set of 8 yew and fruitwood
Mendlesham chairs, comprising 2 pairs,
a single and a set of 3 chairs, c1820.
$4,500–5,250 *Bon*

An oak dining chair,
with carved back and
ornate stretchers, 17thC.
$1,800–2,000 *DBA*

A heavily carved oak bed, from
the Alsace region of France,
19thC, 62in (157.5cm) long.
$5,000–6,500 *SWA*

A George IV mahogany
tester bedstead, with
acanthus carving, on
faceted footposts with
foliate capitals, c1825,
89½in (226cm) wide.
$6,000–6,750 *CNY*

A George III mahogany tester bed,
the arched canopy with moulded
painted cornice, the reeded front
posts with stiff-leaf carving, restored,
c1790, 75½in (192cm) wide.
$37,500–42,000 *S*

A Regency mahogany four-poster bedstead, with
twist-fluted footposts and dentil cornice, plain
backposts and sprung box base, 60in (152.5cm) wide.
$2,300–2,700 *Bri*

An American Empire mahogany bedstead,
with hanging canopy and pendent finials,
leather upholstered headboard, and
panelled footboard with spherical finials,
c1845, 59in (150cm) wide.
$7,500–8,250 *S(NY)*

A Regency oak chaise longue, with padded scroll
ends and half back, with ebonised moulding and
inlay, on sabre legs, c1810, 87in (221cm) long.
$7,500–8,250 *S*

A Louis XVI fruitwood *duchesse brisée*, with padded
back, scrolled arms, the channelled seat rail with
bowfronted section, on rosette-headed turned tapering
fluted legs, restored, remains of previous paint.
$3,750–4,500 *C*

A Louis XV walnut *duchesse brisée*, the arched
padded back and sides within a moulded frame,
on fan-carved cabriole legs ending in scrolled
feet, restored, ottoman later.
$12,750–14,250 *S(NY)*

A mahogany breakfront
library bookcase, restored,
c1760, 70in (178cm) wide.
$27,750–33,000 *S*

A mahogany breakfront secrétaire
bookcase, c1760, 97½in (248cm) wide.
$39,000–47,000 *S*

A Regency thuyawood and
brass-mounted bonheur du jour,
40in (101.5cm) wide.
$27,750–33,000 *S*

A mahogany and parcel gilt
breakfront bookcase, parts 18thC,
100½in (255.5cm) wide.
$12,750–14,250 *S(NY)*

A George III mahogany breakfront
bookcase, later cornice carving,
restored, c1780, 95¾in (243cm) wide.
$19,500–22,500 *S*

A rosewood and marquetry bonheur
du jour, c1780, 25½in (65cm) wide.
$6,750–8,250 *S*

A George III inlaid mahogany
breakfront bookcase, restored,
74in (188cm) wide.
$19,500–22,500 *S(NY)*

A mahogany breakfront bookcase,
with Gothic fretwork cornice,
226in (574cm) wide.
$33,000–37,500 *C*

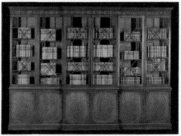

A mahogany breakfront bookcase, c1775, 150in (381cm) wide.
$40,000–45,000 *S*

An oak breakfront bookcase, with
ebonised mouldings and paterae,
c1810, 85in (216cm) wide.
$6,750–8,250 *S*

A George III mahogany breakfront
bookcase, altered, c1780, parts
later, 90in (228.5cm) wide.
$9,000–10,500 *S*

A Regency mahogany and ebony
lined breakfront bookcase, by
Wyman, 90½in (230cm) wide.
$13,500–15,000 *P(Sc)*

A Regency mahogany bureau bookcase, with fitted interior, 30in (76cm) wide.
$8,250–9,000 *DN*

An Edwardian inlaid mahogany breakfront bookcase, on bracket feet, c1890, 81in (205.5cm) wide.
$22,500–24,750 *S(NY)*

A Dutch walnut and floral marquetry bombé bureau bookcase, inlaid with birds, flowers and figures, with moulded cornice, the fall-front enclosing a fitted interior, on carved claw-and-ball feet, 18thC, 49½in (126cm) wide.
$26,250–29,250 *P*

A Victorian figured walnut bookcase, 91in (232cm) wide.
$14,250–15,750 *S(S)*

A Queen Anne inlaid burr walnut bureau bookcase, in 2 parts, with arched cresting above a pair of mirror-inset doors flanked by pilasters, fitted interior to both upper and lower parts, 3 long and 3 short drawers to lower section, brass carrying handles, on bracket feet, restored, c1710, 41in (104cm) wide.
$50,000–55,000 *S(NY)*

An Edwardian mahogany and inlaid library bookcase, the base with 2 drawers above 2 panel doors, 46¼in (117.5cm) wide.
$3,750–4,500 *Bri*

A rosewood library bookcase, probably Scottish, altered, c1840, 124in (315cm) wide.
$6,000–6,750 *S(S)*

An Edwardian mahogany breakfront dwarf open-front bookcase, by Edwards & Roberts, the top and frieze inlaid, banded in satinwood, 72in (183cm) wide.
$3,750–4,500 *CAG*

A George III mahogany revolving bookcase, with an urn finial, c1810, 72in (183cm) high.
$24,750–27,750 *S*

A mahogany revolving bookcase, by Mack, Williams & Gibton, c1825, 49½in (126cm) high.
$19,500–22,500 *S*

A George III mahogany secrétaire bookcase, the lower part with oval panelled doors enclosing drawers and a cellaret drawer, c1780, 43in (109cm) wide.
$15,750–18,750 *S*

A George III mahogany and boxwood strung secrétaire bookcase, with 2 astragal glazed doors, on ogee bracket feet, 49¼in (125cm) wide.
$7,500–9,000 *P(Sc)*

A George III mahogany secrétaire bookcase, by George Simson, with inlaid boxwood lines, paper label, 34in (86cm) wide.
$24,750–27,750 *C*

A Regency brass inlaid mahogany secrétaire bookcase, raised on curved feet, some damage, late 19thC, 46in (117cm) wide.
$12,000–13,500 *S(NY)*

A George III inlaid mahogany secrétaire bookcase, in 2 sections, on bracket feet, late 18thC, 42½in (108cm) wide.
$8,250–9,750 *S(NY)*

A mahogany secrétaire bookcase, raised on a plinth, signed and dated 'William Cawthron, Golden Square London, March 1816', 47in (119cm) wide.
$9,750–11,250 *S*

A Georgian Irish mahogany brass-bound turf bucket, c1800, 15in (38cm) high.
$3,500–4,000 *S*

An Irish Georgian mahogany brass-bound turf bucket, c1775, 18½in (47cm) high.
$6,000–6,750 *S*

A pair of Regency rosewood bookcases, each with 4 open adjustable bookshelves divided by moulded panels, on a moulded plinth and casters, c1815, 24in (61cm) diam.
$33,000–37,500 *S*

A burr walnut bureau, the fall-front with fitted interior, some repairs, later bun feet, c1700, 38½in (98cm) wide.
$12,000–13,500 *S(NY)*

A George I burr walnut bureau, the fall-front with fitted interior, restored, c1720, 38in (96.5cm) wide.
$9,750–11,250 *S*

A Queen Anne field maple bureau, crossbanded in walnut, the fall-front above 2 short and 2 long drawers, on later bun feet, 38in (96.5cm) wide.
$33,500–37,500 *C*

A George II walnut bureau, the fall-front with fitted interior, above 2 small, one short and 3 long drawers, 37½in (95.5cm) wide.
$3,750–4,500 *Gam*

A George I walnut bureau, with a dummy drawer above 3 short and 2 long drawers, 37in (95cm) wide.
$6,000–6,750 *P*

A George III red walnut bureau, with fall-front, above 2 short and 2 long drawers, 39in (99cm) wide.
$2,250–2,750 *DN*

A mahogany bureau, the fall-front with fitted interior, above 4 long drawers, on ogee bracket feet, c1765, 39½in (100.5cm) wide.
$3,000–3,750 *Bon*

A fruitwood and chevron banded bureau, with frieze drawer and 2 short and 2 long drawers, early 18thC, 36¼in (92cm) wide.
$6,750–8,250 *P*

A mahogany bureau, with fall-front, above 3 long drawers, c1790, 38in (96.5cm) wide.
$975–1,125 *Hal*

A George II mahogany bureau, the cleated fall-front with fitted interior, above 4 long graduated drawers, on ogee bracket feet, c1755, 38½in (98cm) wide.
$5,250–6,000 *S*

A mahogany cylinder bureau, with galleried superstructure above a fitted interior and a frieze drawer, restored, c1795, 24½in (62cm) wide.
$7,000–8,250 *S*

A Queen Anne burr walnut bureau, with fitted interior and 3 long drawers, 30in (76cm) wide.
$6,000–6,750 *HAM*

An Empire mahogany cylinder bureau, with ormolu mounts, fitted interior and 8 drawers, 48in (122cm) wide.
$15,750–18,000 *JNic*

A Dutch walnut and marquetry bombé bureau, with fitted interior, 2 short and 3 long drawers, late 18thC, 42in (106.5cm) wide.
$8,250–9,750 *DN*

An Austrian walnut marquetry bureau, with fitted interior, above 3 long drawers, on later feet, c1740, 41¼in (105cm) wide.
$8,000–8,500 *S*

An Italian walnut bureau, the fall-front with fitted interior, above 3 long drawers, on later bun feet, mid-18thC, 51¼in (130cm) wide.
$21,000–23,250 *C*

A burr walnut bureau cabinet, decorated in rosewood and sycamore, with shaped panels of marquetry scrolling leaves with chevron borders, shaped mirror plate doors with fitted interior, above a fall-front, 5 short and 2 long drawers, c1730, 43in (109cm) wide.
$15,000–16,500 *DN*

A Hungarian ash cylinder bureau, inlaid with ebonised lines, with fitted interior, above a frieze drawer, c1800, 26in (66cm) wide.
$4,500–5,250 *P*

An Italian child's walnut bureau, with fall-front and 3 drawers, late 18thC, 19½in (49.5cm) wide.
$9,000–10,500 *Bon*

An Italian walnut crossbanded bureau, the fall-front with fitted interior, above 2 long drawers, shaped apron, late 18thC, 30in (76cm) wide.
$3,000–3,750 *Bon*

A North European walnut bureau cabinet, with brass-engraved mounts, the fall-front with fitted interior, above 4 serpentine drawers, c1740, 37in (94cm) wide.
$12,500–14,250 *S*

A pair of Regency mahogany bureau cabinets, inlaid with fruitwood, each with roll tops, fitted interiors, above 2 short drawers and 2 tambour shutters, 30½in (77.5cm) wide.
$45,000–52,500 *C*

A William and Mary style oyster veneered and marquetry cabinet, with 2 doors, 2 short and 2 long drawers, 48¾in (124cm) wide.
$24,000–27,000   *P(B)*

A William and Mary escritoire, veneered with olivewood oysters, with fitted interior, on a stand with one drawer, on later legs, 36in (91.5cm) wide.
$6,000–6,750   *DN*

A black and gilt japanned cabinet, early 18thC, 40in (101.5cm) wide.
$4,500–5,250   *DN*

A Dutch marquetry cabinet, with arched astragel glazed doors, early 19thC, 66½in (169cm) wide.
$7,500–9,000   *Bon*

A Dutch mahogany and marquetry display cabinet-on-stand, with a glazed panel door, and 4 drawers, 19thC, 37in (94cm) wide.
$6,000–7,000   *CSK*

A pair of Japanese gilt-copper mounted black and gilt lacquer cabinets-on-stands, cabinets late 17thC, stands 19thC, 29in (73.5cm) wide.
$33,000–37,500   *C*

r. A French Louis XVI style marquetry pedestal cabinet, with marble top, 34in (86.5cm) wide.
$4,500–5,250   *AG*

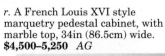

A Victorian boulle marquetry and ebonised side cabinet, with foliate inlaid frieze above a panelled door, flanked by canted fluted columns, on toupie feet, 40¼in (102cm) wide.
$1,200–1,400   *Hal*

A serpentine credenza, inlaid with tortoiseshell and brass, with gilt-bronze mounts, central door flanked by a pair of glazed doors, on a plinth base, mid-19thC, 82in (208cm) wide.
$3,000–3,750   *P*

A pair of Victorian mahogany hall chairs, on octagonal and turned tapering legs, c1850. **$600–900** *Hal*

A set of 8 Regency dining chairs, with cane back and seat, later decorated. **$4,500–5,250** *CSK*

A pair of Louis XVI giltwood chairs, the backs with associated Aubusson tapestry, originally caned, late 19thC gilding, tapestry and some decoration. **$7,500–8,250** *C*

A pair of Regency mahogany hall chairs, in the manner of Gillows, the backs with painted and parcel gilt coats-of-arms flanked by columns. **$3,800–4,500** *P*

A set of 4 Chippendale style mahogany dining chairs, with 'S. & H. Jewell' ivory labels, late 19thC. **$1,800–2,700** *P*

A pair of Dutch walnut chairs, in the French manner, the backs and seats covered in tapestry depicting figures from Europe and Africa, mid-18thC. **$9,000–10,500** *DN*

A pair of Louis XV walnut *fauteuils*, each with acanthus-wrapped channelled frame, with cartouche-shaped padded backs, covered in floral needlework, on foliate-trailed channelled cabriole legs, restored.
$9,000–10,500 *C*

A carved mahogany wing armchair, with cabriole legs and hairy paw feet, c1750.
$4,600–5,000 *S*

A figured walnut corner armchair, with a cabriole front leg and pad foot, Massachusetts, c1750.
$10,500–12,000 *S(NY)*

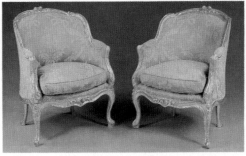

An Empire *marquise*, the armrests carved with dolphins, on sabre legs, now painted white, early 19thC.
$6,750–7,500 *S(NY)*

A Louis XV open armchair, with carved and gilded beech frame, seat rail stamped 'J. B. Boulard', 19thC wool and beadwork covers.
$8,250–9,250 *DN*

A pair of George III giltwood and gesso bergères, with carved moulded frames, on cabriole legs, re-gilded and repaired.
$7,500–9,000 *P*

A pair of Second Empire mahogany bergères, the bowed caned seats flanked by caryatids, on tapering legs with lotus leaf sabots and casters, upholstery distressed.
$8,250–9,750 *P*

A Louis XVI walnut bergère, by Pierre-Elois Langlois, on turned tapering fluted legs and toupie feet, restored.
$4,500–5,250 *C*

A Sheraton style bergère, with carved and painted decoration, c1880.
$750–900 *APO*

An Empire mahogany library armchair, with carved knees and paw feet.
$4,500–5,250 *P*

A pair of Louis XVI painted *fauteuils*, with carved frames, stamped 'I. B. Sené'.
$9,000–10,500 *S*

A pair of Louis Philippe giltwood *fauteuils*, carved with flowerheads, leaves and scrolls, with Aubusson or Beauvais tapestry, on cabriole legs.
$7,500–9,000 *P*

An Italian rococo painted serpentine commode, the faux marble top above 2 drawers, with cabriole legs on hoof feet, c1800, decoration restored, 32½in (82.5cm) wide.
$4,500–5,250 *S(NY)*

A Dutch rosewood marquetry serpentine and bombé-shaped commode, with inlaid floral decoration and ebony and boxwood stringing, 19thC, 41¾in (106cm) wide.
$5,250–6,000 *Gam*

A Swedish walnut parquetry commode, of serpentine bombé form, with gilt-bronze mounts, mid-18thC, 43¼in (110cm) wide.
$7,500–8,250 *S*

A painted satinwood commode, with a panelled cupboard door, late 19thC, 41¾in (106cm) wide.
$5,250–6,000 *P(Sc)*

A Louis XV kingwood and purple-wood serpentine commode, with marble top, 38¼in (97cm) wide.
$8,000–8,500 *P*

A Louis XV Provincial marquetry serpentine commode, mid-18thC, 36in (91.5cm) wide.
$8,500–9,500 *S*

An early Georgian crossbanded walnut chest of drawers, on shaped bracket feet, restored, chalk mark 'CAC69', 31¾in (80.5cm) wide.
$16,500–19,500 *C*

A George I walnut secrétaire chest-on-chest, the bottom drawer with an inlaid sunburst, on bracket feet, c1720, 41¾in (106cm) wide.
$30,000–33,000 *S*

An oyster laburnum and olivewood chest of 5 drawers, original brasses, feet repaired, 38in (96.5cm) wide.
$15,000–18,000 *PHA*

A George III mahogany serpentine commode, the 4 cockbeaded drawers flanked by scroll and foliate carved stiles, 43in (109cm) wide.
$36,000–42,000 *S(NY)*

A Maltese orange and olivewood marquetry chest of drawers, 18thC, 61½in (156cm) wide.
$15,000–18,000 *P*

A George II walnut and oak-sided inlaid and crossbanded tallboy, the top with moulded cornice, 3 short and 3 long drawers, the lower part with 3 long drawers, 40in (101.5cm) wide.
$8,250–9,750 *CAG*

A George II mahogany crossbanded serpentine chest of drawers, with a slide and 4 graduated drawers, on ogee bracket feet, c1755, 42¼in (107cm) wide.
$12,000–13,500 *S*

A Dutch walnut bombé chest of 4 long drawers, chequer-banded and inlaid with motifs, c1900, 39½in (100cm) wide.
$2,500–3,000 *WL*

A Regency Gothic parcel gilt and painted mahogany coffer, attributed to John Nash, c1815, 43¼in (110cm) wide.
$9,750–11,250 *Bon*

A Chippendale walnut carved chest-on-chest, late 18thC, 41in (104cm) wide.
$14,250–15,750 *SK*

A George III mahogany tallboy, with gilt brass swan neck handles, 42in (106.5cm) wide.
$1,800–2,000 *J&L*

A painted satinwood Carlton House desk, with drawers and cupboards above a gilt tooled leather inset writing slide, 3 frieze drawers, on acanthus carved fluted tapering legs, c1900, 51in (130cm) wide.
$6,000–6,750 *Bon*

A Georgian walnut crossbanded kneehole desk, restored, 30in (76cm) wide.
$5,250–6,000 *C*

A satinwood Carlton House desk, painted with neoclassical foliage and figural scenes, c1900, 41in (104cm) wide.
$9,000–9,750 *S(NY)*

A Dutch walnut and floral marquetry lowboy, on cabriole legs, 18thC, 30in (77cm) wide.
$3,800–4,500 *P*

A Regency mahogany two-tier dumb waiter, with raised galleries and reeded borders, 24in (61cm) diam.
$3,200–3,800 *DN*

A Victorian mahogany and ivory inlaid writing desk, with satinwood veneer, with raised stepped back, 39in (99cm) wide.
$4,500–5,250 *S(S)*

A George IV mahogany two-tier dumb waiter, 24in (61cm) diam.
$3,000–3,600 *CSK*

A north German or Dutch rosewood parquetry cupboard, with a moulded cornice above a pair of panelled doors and a long drawer, faced by carved pendants and swags, c1680, 80in (205cm) wide.
$8,250–9,750 *S*

A Dutch oak bombé cupboard, the panelled doors flanked by ebonised columns, early 19thC, 60in (152.5cm) wide.
$3,750–4,500 *CSK*

A German carved oak cupboard, with 2 panelled doors above 2 drawers, on cabriole feet, early 19thC, 60in (152.5cm) wide.
$3,750–4,500 *CSK*

A German ash cupboard, the moulded cornice above a pair of rocaille carved doors with cartouche-shaped panels between canted angles, on block feet, late 18thC, 65in (165cm) wide.
$4,500–5,250 *CSK*

A Dutch brown painted corner cupboard, with 4 cupboard doors decorated with sailing ships and trailing foliage, restored, 19thC, 38¼in (97cm) wide.
$2,500–3,000 *CSK*

A Dutch walnut and floral marquetry cupboard, with bombé lower section, on turned feet, 18thC and later, 74¾in (190cm) wide.
$17,250–19,500 *S*

A George III mahogany linen press, the dentilled cornice with Gothic tracery, c1770, later shelved interior, 52in (132cm) wide.
$1,900–2,300 *CNY*

A Victorian painted simulated bamboo wardrobe, the top with doors simulated as drawers, on ring-turned feet, 39in (99cm) wide.
$3,500–4,000 *C*

A William IV mahogany clothes press, the pediment with lion masks and key-shaped stringing, 48in (122cm) wide.
$2,200–2,700 *DN*

A George III giltwood mirror, the frame carved with scrolls, leaves and flowers, with leaf-scroll cresting, c1760, 67¾in (172cm) high. **$21,000–24,000** *S*

A pair of George III carved giltwood mirrors, the gadroon-carved frames surrounded by ribbon-tied palm fronds, c1770, 39in (99cm) high. **$13,500–15,000** *S*

A Venetian glass and cobalt mirror, etched with foliage and composed of mirrored leaf and scroll-shaped segments, 19thC, 56in (142cm) high. **$8,250–9,750** *S(NY)*

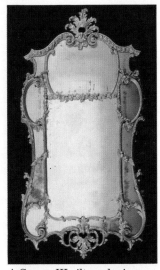

A Flemish giltwood mirror, the carved frame surmounted by Minerva and martial trophies, with scrolling foliage and other figures, late 17thC, 78¼in (199cm) high. **$27,750–33,000** *S*

A George III giltwood mirror, the frame and apron carved with acanthus leaves, wheat, pineapples and C-scrolls, c1760, 78in (198cm) high. **$30,000–33,000** *S(NY)*

A George III giltwood mirror, with scrolled egg-and-dart cornice and later foliate finial, restored, 66in (167.5cm) high. **$12,500–14,000** *C*

A George III carved giltwood mirror, possibly Continental, restored, 71in (180cm) high. **$12,000–13,500** *S(NY)*

A gilt gesso mirror-framed mirror, with a shaped pendant fitted for candle arms, restored, c1770, 74in (188cm) high. **$20,250–22,500** *S(NY)*

A set of 4 Venetian giltwood girandôles, each with a two-branch candelabrum, mirrors later engraved with allegorical figures, c1740, 39½in (100cm) high. **$19,500–23,250** *S*

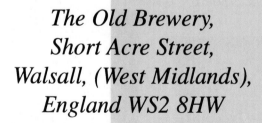

Bureau Cabinets

A William and Mary figured-walnut bureau cabinet, in 3 sections, the double-domed upper section enclosing a fitted interior above 2 candle slides, with feather banded slope enclosing a fitted interior, above 2 short and 2 long drawers, on shaped bracket feet, restored and the feet probably replaced, 39⅜in (101cm) wide.
$15,750–18,000 *C*

A Queen Anne walnut bureau cabinet, in 3 parts, with a moulded cornice, fitted with shelves enclosed by a pair of bevelled mirror panel doors, sloping fall enclosing a fitted interior, the lower part containing 3 long drawers, on bracket feet, 35¾in (91cm) wide.
$18,000–21,000 *P*

A walnut bureau cabinet, with feather banding and crossbanding, inscribed paper labels, restored, c1720, 3 brass finials and 2 later glazed doors, 41in (104cm) wide.
$55,500–60,000 *CNY*

A red and gilt japanned bureau cabinet, with fitted interior, above 2 short and 2 long drawers, on a shaped moulded plinth, c1725, 39¾in (101cm) wide.
$60,000–67,500 *S*

A mahogany bureau cabinet, with a pair of cartouche-shaped fielded panelled doors enclosing adjustable shelves with candle slides below, the fall revealing a fitted interior, above 3 long graduated drawers, now on acanthus carved cabriole legs, with claw-and-ball feet, c1755, 44in (112cm) wide.
$9,750–11,250 *S*

l. An Austrian walnut parquetry bureau cabinet, inscribed in ink with the marks of the restorer 'GZE Berlin', c1730, 39¼in (100cm) wide.
$7,500–8,250 *S*

r. A German walnut parquetry bureau cabinet, with a pierced carved cresting, 2 doors inlaid with 2 female figures under canopies, the fall-front inlaid with strapwork, c1740, 47¼in (120cm) wide.
$7,800–8,800 *S*

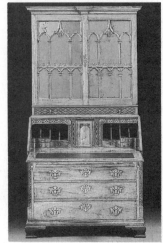

A George III mahogany bureau cabinet, with a pair of mirror inset doors with Gothic arched mullions enclosing a shelved interior, the fall enclosing a fitted interior over 4 long drawers, on later ogee bracket feet, 47½in (120.5cm) wide.
$37,500–45,000 *CNY*

Cabinets

A walnut cabinet, restored, 17thC, 56in (142cm) wide.
$7,500–9,000 *CSK*

A Queen Anne walnut cabinet-on-chest, with moulded cornice, single glazed door enclosing shelving, the base with slide above 2 short and 3 long drawers, brass ring handles, on bracket feet, possible marriage, 29in (73.5cm) wide.
$4,500–5,250 *AH*

A inlaid burr walnut cabinet-on-chest, the moulded top above a cushion-moulded drawer over a pair of feather banded doors, etched brass lock plates, keyhole escutcheons and brass drop pulls, raised on later bun feet, restored, c1710, 43in (109cm) wide.
$17,250–19,500 *S(NY)*

An early Georgian mahogany secrétaire cabinet, attributed to William Strickland, with central secrétaire/dressing drawer and baized brushing slide, 50in (127cm) wide.
$20,250–21,750 *B*

A Louis XIV ebony and boulle cabinet, in 2 sections, inlaid in *contre-partie* marquetry with brass, pewter and brown tortoiseshell, possibly German, 57in (145cm) wide.
$78,000–87,000 *C*

A mahogany serpentine-fronted library cabinet, early 19thC, 88in (223.5cm) wide.
$25,500–28,500 *S(NY)*

A mahogany cabinet-on-chest, the breakfront upper part with a broken pediment above a parcel gilt glazed door, flanked by a pair of shorter doors, the lower part with a slide and a pair of doors, c1755, 37¾in (96cm) wide.
$5,250–6,000 *S*

A French walnut cabinet, with a moulded cornice centred by a carved eagle, late 17thC, 62½in (159cm) wide.
$6,000–6,750 *DN*

A brass-bound mahogany cabinet, the mottled salmon marble top above 5 graduated drawers and 2 concave panelled doors, on outswept bracket feet, Baltic, early 19thC, 34¾in (88cm) wide.
$1,500–2,250 *CSK*

Dutch Marquetry Cabinets

- The cabinet was an important piece of Dutch furniture, indicating status – the larger and more impressive the cabinet, the wealthier and more important its owner was deemed to be.
- Marquetry decoration was popular with Dutch cabinet makers from the early 17thC through to the 19thC.
- Marquetry is a decorative veneer applied mainly to walnut furniture, and consists of a mosaic formed from shaped pieces of wood or other suitable materials, such as bone or ivory.

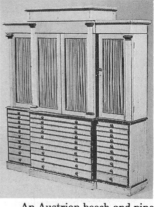

An Austrian beech and pine breakfront cabinet, in the style of Biedermeier, with ebonised borders, 19thC, 68in (172.5cm) wide. $1,200–1,800 *DN*

A German pewter-inlaid walnut and ebonised cabinet, the arched upper part containing a door, the lower section also with a panelled door, all inset with panels incorporating the devices of Duke August Wilhelm of Brunswick-Wolfenbüttel, amidst drapery, eagles and strapwork, inscribed 'C. L. Kiel' twice on the carcass, Braunschweig, c1740 and later, 45½in (115.5cm) wide. $14,250–15,750 *S*

This cabinet was given as a wedding present to Mr Frederic Hostrup-Schultz and Mrs Marie Rönchendoff in 1861.

l. A Dutch mahogany and marquetry cabinet-on-chest, with fitted interior, enclosed by a pair of panelled doors with central floral, urn and bird decoration, door frame also with floral designs, the lower section with 3 long drawers, c1800, 58in (147.5cm) wide. $4,500–6,000 *RBB*

Cabinets-on-Stands

A William and Mary lacquered brass-mounted black and gilt japanned cabinet-on-stand, in the manner of John Stalker, on a giltwood stand, the stand re-gilt, the stretcher possibly later, 34in (86.5cm) wide.
$10,500–12,000 *C*

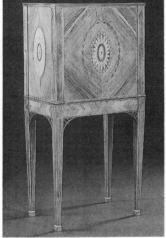

A William and Mary walnut and seaweed marquetry cabinet-on-stand, with a cushion drawer above a pair of doors enclosing a fitted interior, the later stand containing a frieze drawer, on later square legs with pierced spandrels, 43¼in (110cm) wide.
$7,500–9,000 *P*

l. A rosewood and marquetry cabinet-on-stand, in the manner of Thomas Chippendale, the banded top with outset corners centred by a satinwood panel, the quarter-veneered door inlaid with paterae within ribbon-tied husks flanked by chevron-veneered panels, veneered brackets and block feet, c1775, 24¾in (63cm) wide.
$5,250–6,000 *S*

A Flemish baroque ebony and polychrome painted cabinet-on-stand, the inverted top with hinged lid enclosing a painted panel, the front with 2 panelled doors and painted panels to the fitted interior, with a central door surmounted by a gallery and flanked by half columns, enclosing a mirrored interior with ivory and ebony floor, the stand with spiral twist legs, joined by a tier, on bun feet, 17thC, stand later, 34¼in (87cm) wide.
$42,000–45,000 *S(Am)*

A William and Mary walnut and marquetry cabinet-on-stand, inlaid with scrolling acanthus and flowers, restorations to the marquetry, stand 19thC, 49in (124.5cm) wide.
$30,000–33,000 *C*

Display Cabinets

A late Georgian mahogany display cabinet, the dentil cornice above astragal glazed doors enclosing adjustable shelves, the base with pair of panelled doors, on bracket feet, inscribed to top of base 'Colonel Clarke, Rl. Scots Grays, 1845', 47¼in (120cm) wide.
$4,200–4,800 *Bri*

A George III mahogany display cabinet-on-stand, the cornice with an arched pierced trellis-cresting centred by strapwork, with later gilt finials, above a pair of glazed doors enclosing 2 shelves, the lower section with 3 drawers around a trellis filled kneehole, on canted square legs, one pane cracked, 32¾in (83cm) wide.
$10,500–12,000 *C*

The cabinet, with its exotic urn capped and pagoda crest, is richly fretted in the mid-18thC manner popularised by Thomas Chippendale's Gentleman and Cabinet-Maker's Director, *1754-63, which featured this pattern of glazing-bar.*

A concave-fronted mahogany display cabinet, with moulded cornice and a pair of glazed doors enclosing 3 adjustable shelves, the panelled lower doors enclosing an adjustable shelf, base c1780, top later, 46½in (118cm) wide.
$5,400–6,400 *S*

A walnut display cabinet, with a cushion drawer and a pair of two-panelled glazed doors, enclosing adjustable glass shelves, with a pair of panelled doors below enclosing a shelf, on bracket feet, associated, 18thC, 44in (112cm) wide.
$6,900–7,800 *S*

A burr walnut display cabinet, with tulipwood crossbanding, inlaid and with gilt metal mounts, bordered with boxwood lines, applied with paterae and foliate bandings, mid-19thC, 36in (91.5cm) wide.
$3,900–4,800 *P(E)*

A mahogany breakfront display cabinet, the cornice with moulded, foliate and egg-and-tongue ornament, with a beaded frieze, a central glazed astragal door with foliate scroll and rocaille mouldings, flanked by 2 glazed cupboards, with cavetto and gadrooned base raised on claw-on-ball feet, 19thC, 99in (251.5cm) wide.
$8,250–9,750 *P(E)*

Display Cabinets

Display cabinets were not made in England to any extent until the mid-18thC, when decorative objects such as porcelain figurines began to be made in Europe. Even then, they were not plentiful until the 19thC.

A burr yew cabinet, inlaid with ivory and ebony, with ormolu mounts, c1870, 39in (99cm) wide.
$900–1,200 *BUT*

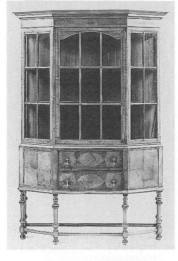

l. A late Victorian line-inlaid mahogany display cabinet, the moulded cornice above a glazed door and sides enclosing shelves, above 2 drawers and 2 panelled cupboard doors, on turned tapering baluster legs, joined by stretchers, 57in (145cm) wide.
$2,000–2,700 *CSK*

A late Victorian mahogany display cabinet, the central section with shaped bevelled mirror, 2 display cabinets with pierced and moulded decoration, 54in (137cm) wide.
$1,200–1,500 *WIL*

An Edwardian mahogany bowfronted display cabinet, with satinwood banding, a pair of glazed doors enclosing plush-lined interior, one long drawer below, on square tapering legs and spade feet, 38in (96.5cm) wide.
$2,000–2,700 *RBB*

A late Victorian inlaid mahogany display cabinet, the shaped pediment with swept edge above the central bowfronted glazed panel, the inlaid panel below flanked on either side by a glazed door with wooden astragals and inlaid panel below with a shaped skirt, standing on tapered legs and spade feet, 45in (114.5cm) wide.
$1,800–2,400 *Mit*

An Edwardian mahogany corner display cabinet, crossbanded in satinwood and strung with ebony and box, raised on bracket feet, 30½in (77.5cm) wide.
$2,700–3,700   P(HSS)

An Edwardian floral marquetry display cabinet, the mirror-back above a frieze drawer and panelled door flanked by 2 glazed doors, with pierced brass galleries, on square tapering legs with spade feet, 54½in (138.5cm) wide.
$2,000–2,700   CSK

An Edwardian mahogany cabinet, the top inlaid with boxwood lines, the lower section with inlaid frieze and inlaid panelled doors, trade plate 'Edwards & Roberts', 60in (152.5cm) wide.
$4,800–5,800   E

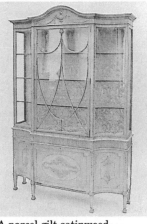

A George III style painted satinwood display cabinet, the kingwood crossbanded top painted with scrolling foliate tendrils and husks, the 2 bowed glazed doors flanked by serpentine doors, on square tapering legs with spade feet, early 20thC, 60¼in (153cm) wide.
$4,000–4,500   Bea

An Edwardian satinwood and decorated display cabinet, with moulded cornice, painted with swags of flowers and classical figures, enclosed by a central glazed door, turned and tapering legs joined by arched stretchers, 37¾in (96cm) wide.
$2,400–3,000   P(B)

A parcel gilt satinwood-veneered display cabinet, in the manner of Sheraton, the arched pediment centred by an urn and husk swags, the base with crossbanded panels, outlined with kingwood banding and ebonised stringing, on tapering square legs with block feet, early 20thC, 57½in (146cm) wide.
$8,250–9,750   Bea

A Louis XVI style gilt-bronze mounted mahogany vitrine, with marble top above a single glazed cupboard door, flanked by glazed panels, raised on toupie feet, early 20thC, 50in (127cm) wide.
$4,500–5,250   S(NY)

A Louis XIV olivewood parquetry cabinet, inlaid with motifs, on bracket feet, with later glass panels, c1720, 34¾in (88.5cm) wide.
$6,750–7,500   S

A Dutch marquetry display cabinet, inlaid with floral sprays and flower-filled vases, the arched cornice above a pair of astragal glazed doors flanked by canted glazed panels, the base with a central pair of arched cupboard doors flanked by 2 pairs of drawers and canted corners with arched cupboard doors, on octagonal tapering legs and bun feet, tied by a shaped stretcher, alterations, 86¼in (219cm) wide.
$21,000–23,250   Bon

Secrétaire Cabinets

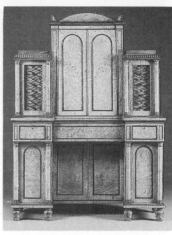

A walnut secrétaire, inlaid with feather banding, the moulded cornice above a cushion frieze drawer, the quarter-veneered fall-front revealing a fitted interior, the lower part with 2 short and 2 long graduated drawers, on later bun feet, c1700, 63¼in (160.5cm) wide. **$14,250–15,750** *S*

A William and Mary walnut and inlaid *escritoire*, the moulded cornice above a cushion frieze drawer, the inlaid fall enclosing a fitted interior, the projecting base with 3 long graduated drawers, on bun feet, 41¼in (105cm) wide. **$6,750–7,500** *P(B)*

A Regency oak and rosewood secrétaire cabinet, attributed to George Bullock, the upper section with an arched pediment and a pair of panelled doors enclosing 3 shelves, flanked by a pair of doors with pierced columns and pierced bronzed trellis enclosing mahogany lined drawers, the lower section with central secrétaire drawer enclosing a fitted interior with leather-lined writing surface and cedar and mahogany-lined drawers, a pair of central kneehole doors and flanking doors enclosing shelves, on lotus-leaf cut feet, 61½in (156cm) wide. **$15,750–17,250** *C*

A walnut secrétaire, with feather banded moulded doors enclosing adjustable shelves, the secrétaire drawer with fitted interior above 2 long drawers, on bracket feet, c1720, 43¼in (110cm) wide. **$5,750–6,750** *S*

A mahogany secrétaire cabinet, the pierced swan neck moulded cornice with dentil moulding and fret-carved panels above an astragal moulded glazed door, the lower part with secrétaire drawer, above 3 long drawers, on bracket feet, c1775, 33in (84cm) wide. **$33,000–36,000** *S*

l. A Regency brass-inlaid and ormolu-mounted rosewood secrétaire cabinet, the cornice with ball finials above a pair of mirror-backed Gothic glazed doors enclosing 2 shelves, the lower section with overhanging frieze above a foliate and scroll-inlaid frieze drawer enclosing a green leather-lined writing surface and fitted interior, above a further pair of panelled doors, on paw feet, 36¼in (92cm) wide. **$10,500–12,000** *C*

A Regency brass-mounted and inlaid rosewood secrétaire cabinet, with brass supports and grille-inset sides, above a secrétaire drawer with fitted interior, 2 oval-inset cupboard doors below, raised on block feet, 32½in (82.5cm) wide.
$9,000–9,750 *S(NY)*

A Charles X ormolu-mounted birchwood *secrétaire à abattant*, with black fossilised marble top above a drawer, the fall-front opening to a fitted interior, over 3 long drawers with freestanding columns continuing to circular feet, restored, c1820, 38½in (98cm) wide.
$8,400–9,000 *S(NY)*

An Empire mahogany *secrétaire à abattant*, the top above a long drawer with a fall-front opening to a fitted interior, over 3 long drawers flanked by freestanding columns, on turned circular feet, restored, early 19thC, 43⅛in (110.5cm) wide.
$9,750–11,250 *S(NY)*

A Louis XVI style gilt-bronze mounted tulipwood parquetry *secrétaire à abattant*, with a single frieze drawer above a fall-front, and a pair of cupboard doors, raised on toupie feet, 28in (71cm) wide.
$4,500–5,250 *S(NY)*

A Dutch marquetry *secrétaire à abattant*, walnut veneered, the top crossbanded in tulipwood, the front inlaid with flowers to the parquetry veneered drawer, oak lined, the fall inlaid with birds and an urn of flowers, revealing a fitted interior above a pair of doors, gilt-brass mounts to the canted corners, inlaid sides, on front brass-mounted scroll legs, damaged, late 18thC, 35in (89cm) wide.
$6,000–7,500 *WW*

A German mahogany *secrétaire à abattant*, with a foliate scrolling arched cornice flanked by turned finials above a cushion-moulded frieze drawer, the oval panelled fall-front enclosing a fitted interior with drawers around a central recess, with 3 cushion-moulded drawers below, on foliate capped downswept feet, 19thC, 41½in (105.5cm) wide.
$2,000–2,700 *CSK*

l. A Dutch neo-classical style mahogany and marquetry secrétaire, the top over a drawer, above a fall-front enclosing a fitted interior, over cupboard doors enclosing drawers, late 19thC, 35¼in (89.5cm) wide.
$4,800–5,300 *SK(B)*

Writing Furniture

Until the mid-17th century items of furniture used for writing were often extremely primitive. The first writing furniture specifically designed as such was derived from French and Italian furniture of the 16th century, and took the form of a fall-front cabinet on a chest or stand, with drawers, known today as a secrétaire cabinet, *escritoire*, or *secrétaire à abattant*. The *escritoire* was popular in Europe throughout the 18th and well into the 19th century.

Side Cabinets

A harewood and marquetry D-shaped side cabinet, attributed to Mayhew & Ince, the top with a half-fan medallion with baskets, urns and chains of tinted ribboned flowers and satinwood crossbanding with lion masks, the satinwood frieze with loops of inlaid beads, the door with a painted oval of Apollo, flanked by a pair of griffins, the side panels each with an urn on a ram's-headed table enclosed by leaf sprays, the turned legs with gilt feet, with brass mouldings, damaged, c1775, 43in (109cm) wide.
$210,000–225,000 *S*

A George III satinwood and marquetry chiffonier, crossbanded in kingwood, inlaid with boxwood and amaranth lines, the moulded top above a pair of inlaid doors enclosing a mahogany lined interior, above 5 mahogany-lined drawers, on later rosewood inlaid square tapering feet with caps, metal inventory tag to the reverse '1248', 36in (91.5cm) wide.
$7,500–9,000 *C*

A pair of brass inlaid rosewood side cabinets, each with inset mottled grey, white and rust marble top, the frieze panelled as 2 drawers above a door, on turned feet, possibly made from a larger cabinet, c1815, 23in (58.5cm) wide.
$3,000–3,750 *S*

A Regency rosewood chiffonier, decorated with inlaid brass stringing, foliate banding and motifs, the pair of panelled doors with brass trelliswork decoration, raised on paw feet, 42in (106.5cm) wide.
$4,500–5,250 *AG*

A William IV rosewood chiffonier, with pierced brass three-quarter gallery to a shelf above mirror-back, the base with 2 shaped top panel doors enclosing adjustable slides, on a plinth base, 47¼in (120cm) wide.
$1,800–2,300 *Bri*

A pair of rosewood chiffoniers, with mirror-backed brass gallery and pilasters, above a brass inlaid mirror-backed base with brass-mounted scrolled legs, on a plinth, c1820, 37¾in (96cm) wide.
$19,000–21,000 *S*

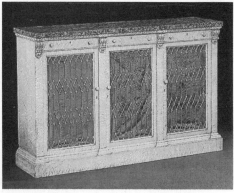

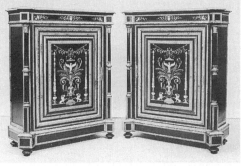

An early Victorian bird's-eye maple side cabinet, with mottled brown and grey marble top, 3 drawers and 3 doors with brass trellis enclosing adjustable shelves, with parcel gilt moulding, 62½in (159cm) wide.
$6,300–7,300 *S*

A pair of mid-Victorian ebonised and amboyna-banded side cabinets, applied with gilt-brass foliate mouldings and with freestanding columns to the canted corners, each panelled door inlaid in the Mannerist style, with an urn of foliage with griffins flanked by columns and on a plinth with turned feet, 38½in (98cm) wide.
$9,000–10,500 *Bea*

A rosewood chiffonier, the arched mirror-back carved and pierced with leaf scrolls, rosettes and lotus, centred by a gadrooned shelf on lobed lotus scroll pillars, the breakfront base with a white marble top, the frieze fitted with 3 drawers, above 3 glazed doors, divided by lobed turned free-standing pillars, on a deep moulded plinth, c1850, 58in (147.5cm) wide.
$2,600–3,300 *N*

A Victorian walnut breakfront credenza, satinwood inlaid with floral sprays and ormolu mounts, 3 glazed compartments with shelves, on later feet, 66in (167.5cm) wide.
$3,000–3,750 *M*

A late Victorian walnut and burr walnut credenza, gilt-metal mounted and inlaid, the bowed top above a decorative frieze over a cupboard door with central urn inlay surrounded by scrolling foliage, flanked by fluted columns, on a plinth base and bun feet, 60¼in (153cm) wide.
$6,300–7,300 *P(Sc)*

r. A pair of Burmese hardwood chiffoniers, with gadrooned and foliate decoration, each with associated graduated shelves, with a pierced foliate scroll back, the lower part enclosed by a pair of pierced panelled doors, on bun feet, 19thC, 54in (137cm) wide.
$1,800–2,600 *CSK*

A walnut and thuyawood banded credenza, the frieze inlaid with satinwood panels, the pair of central doors now with mirror panels, flanked by gilt metal corbels and curved glazed doors, on a plinth base, damaged, c1860, 71¾in (182.5cm) wide.
$4,500–5,250 *S(S)*

A Victorian walnut credenza, marquetry inlaid and gilt-metal mounted, with central panel door flanked by glazed bowed doors, on a shaped plinth, 67¾in (172cm) wide.
$3,300–4,200 *Bri*

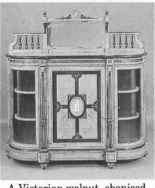

A Victorian walnut, ebonised and inlaid credenza, with gilt-metal, incised and 'Wedgwood' style applied plaques, the shelved superstructure with mirrored spindle-back, above a panelled door between enclosed bowed compartments and projecting fluted columns, on spool feet, 60¼in (153cm) wide.
$3,300–4,200 *P*

A Victorian walnut floral marquetry and ormolu-mounted credenza, the frieze, stiles and enclosing panel door with ebonised panels of flowers heightened in harewood between bowed enclosed glazed compartments, on a plinth base, 69¼in (176cm) wide.
$6,750–7,500 *P*

l. A gilt and silvered ebonised side cabinet, the top above a frieze centred with a plaque flanked by chandelles, above a central cupboard door with an oval medallion, inscribed 'Diehl, Paris, 19r., Michelle Conrte', mid-19thC, 47in (119.5cm) wide.
$7,200–8,600 *S(NY)*

A Napoleon III gilt-bronze and porcelain mounted tulipwood parquetry side cabinet, with a marble top, above a single frieze drawer and glazed cupboard doors, c1860, 36½in (92.5cm) wide.
$5,200–5,700 *S(NY)*

A Napoleon III gilt-metal mounted scarlet boulle inlaid ebonised side cabinet, the eared slate top above a frieze drawer and 2 panelled doors, flanked by caryatids, on shaped plinth base, 42½in (108cm) wide.
$2,200–2,500 *CSK*

A Louis XV/Transitional style rosewood parquetry side cabinet, the moulded Brescia marble top above a pair of panelled doors enclosing 2 shelves, on short cabriole legs with sabots, stencilled on the back and under the marble 'Meubles Bronzes Anciens Hopilliart, Leroy, Paris, 12 Rue Des St Peres', mid-19thC, 49¼in (125cm) wide.
$3,000–3,500 *P*

r. A French brass-mounted ebonised breakfront side cabinet, with mottled marble top, panelled cupboard door flanked by uprights, on plinth, with toupie feet, stamped '2522', late 19thC, 30in (76cm) wide.
$1,500–2,000 *CSK*

A Louis XVI style gilt-bronze mounted mahogany side cabinet, with black marble top, above a single cupboard door decorated with a medallion, on feet formed as quivers of arrows, late 19thC, 35in (89cm) wide.
$7,500–8,000 *S(NY)*

A north European mahogany side cabinet, with stepped rectangular top, the frieze drawer above an acorn key fob and bowed door, enclosing 2 shaped shelves, with deeper drawer below, on block feet, mid-19thC, 26in (66cm) wide.
$950–1,100 *CSK*

r. An Italian giltwood low cabinet, the shaped moulded top above a frieze carved with arching flowers and leaves and 2 arched panelled doors, each set with a carved and painted figure and flanked by fluted pilasters headed by painted masks, on a shaped plinth base, 19thC, 54¼in (138cm) wide.
$3,700–4,200 *DN*

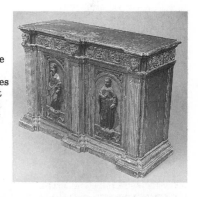

A mahogany and satinwood breakfront side cabinet, incorporating an early 19thC Dutch side cabinet with lacquered panels as its centre section, flanked by cupboards, on square tapering legs, 75½in (192cm) wide.
$1,800–2,200 *P*

A Napoleon III gilt-metal mounted ebonised wood and boulle credenza, late 19thC, 90in (228.5cm) long.
$3,500–4,000 *SK*

Open Armchairs

A George II mahogany open armchair, of Gainsborough design, in the French style, with stuff-over serpentine back and seat, padded fluted arm supports with acanthus leaf ornament, on cabriole legs with similar foliate decoration, terminating in scroll feet and leather casters.
$5,500–7,000 *P*

A George II mahogany library open armchair, the acanthus-carved arms with cabochon terminals, the scrolled apron centred by a foliate cartouche, on cabriole legs headed by flowerheads and foliate feet, restored.
$6,300–7,000 *C*

A late George II walnut open armchair, with pierced vase-shaped splat, scroll arms, stuffed seat and straight legs.
$600–750 *DN*

A George II walnut corner chair, the bowed crest rail with 2 pierced splats and 3 turned and fluted supports, drop-in seat, leaf-carved cabriole front leg.
$1,000–1,200 *DN*

A pair of George II mahogany library open armchairs, covered in their original gros and petit point wool and silk needlework, with scrolled padded arms with out-turned acanthus cabochon terminals, with a foliate carved scroll running down and back without a break into the side rail and back leg, the cabriole legs headed by confronting C-scrolls centred by a berry, one repaired, one inscribed in ink 'A24', the other with paper label.
$375,000 + *C*

A mahogany corner armchair, the shell-carved top rail continuing to scroll-carved terminals, above 2 pierced floral and tassel-carved back splats, the flame-stitch needlework seat on chamfered square legs headed by pierced brackets and joined by an X-shaped stretcher, repaired, late 18thC.
$4,000–4,800 *S(NY)*

A matched pair of walnut library armchairs, the outscrolled arms with foliate carved handholds and trailing foliate supports, on cabriole legs and hairy paw-and-ball feet, with recessed casters, mid-18thC.
$129,000–138,000 *CNY*

An Irish mahogany armchair, the serpentine-back with central foliate cartouche and shell-carved ears above a pierced splat, the upholstered drop-in seat above a shell-carved seat rail, on hipped cabriole legs headed by shells with paw feet joined by stretchers, late 18thC.
$15,000–17,250 *CNY*

A pair of giltwood armchairs, in the manner of John Linnell, each padded back within a guilloche-carved surround, on down-curved supports terminating in a Greek key, carved serpentine seat, on leaf-carved fluted tapering circular legs, restored, c1770.
$12,000–13,500 *S(NY)*

John Linnell was the son of William Linnell who owned a large and prosperous cabinet-making and upholstery business in London. John took over the showrooms in 1763 and one of his biggest commissions was to furnish the Buckinghamshire home of William Drake from 1763–68. Many items were supplied including settees, sideboards and 'French' chairs. The Victoria & Albert Museum has a number of designs for furniture by Linnell, from the period 1773–81. He died in 1799.

A pair of giltwood armchairs, with serpentine upholstered backs, padded arms and upholstered serpentine seats, on moulded cabriole legs with scroll feet, distressed, c1760.
$13,500–15,000 *S*

A carved mahogany armchair, the pierced serpentine carved top rail with C-scrolls and acanthus leaves above a pierced trellis splat, drop-in floral tapestry seat, carved cabriole legs, on claw-and-ball feet, minor restorations, c1755.
$5,250–6,000 *S*

r. A pair of painted and parcel gilt armchairs, in Louis XVI style, the oval padded backs with carved flowerhead crestings, the bowed stuffed seats with paterae-carved seat rails, on fluted turned legs, c1775.
$6,750–7,500 *S*

A pair of George III carved giltwood armchairs, the moulded cartouche-shaped backs with paterae-carved corners, the padded arms leaf-carved and with downswept moulded supports, the serpentine seats carved with guilloche, on husk-carved tapering moulded legs, c1775.
$15,000–17,250 *S*

The legs of these chairs closely relate to those of a set in the Victoria & Albert Museum attributed to John Linnell.

A set of 4 mahogany armchairs, the arched backs, arm caps and seats covered in green leather, restored, c1785.
$13,500–15,000 *S*

l. A pair of mahogany armchairs, in the manner of Gillows, the shield-shaped backs carved with Prince of Wales' feather plumes and drapery swags, the upholstered seats on square tapering legs with spade feet, arms replaced, c1790.
$7,500–8,250 *S*

A George III beechwood armchair, the oval panel-back later upholstered in floral gros point needlework, with padded scroll arms and serpentine seat, on square fluted tapering gaitered legs.
$1,800–2,250 *CSK*

A set of 4 Queen Anne style rosewood open armchairs, the shepherd's crook arms terminating in eagles' heads, early 19thC.
$15,750–18,000 *P*

A set of 4 George III green painted and decorated open armchairs, minor repairs.
$8,250–9,750 *C*

A late Regency carved mahogany armchair frame, the arched bowed top rail with flowerhead motifs flanking the armorial bearings of the City and County of Newcastle-upon-Tyne, above a horizontal mid-rail, scroll arm supports, on sabre legs.
$1,800–2,250 *P(NE)*

A pair of George III green painted open armchairs, the pierced entrelac table top rail above a caned back, the outscrolled baluster arms above a caned seat, on ring-turned tapering legs and toupie feet.
$3,300–3,750 *C*

A set of 4 late George III giltwood armchairs, with bead decoration, caned panelled backs, foliate scroll arms, bowed seats with squabs, on reduced turned fluted tapering legs, 3 with label 'Drawing Room'.
$9,000–10,500 *CSK*

l. A Regency mahogany metamorphic library armchair, in the manner of Morgan and Sanders, the reeded frame with horizontal splat, upholstered seat, on sabre legs, the steps baize-lined, the seat rails strengthened.
$5,250–6,000 *C*

r. A carved walnut armchair, the padded back above a pierced and scroll-carved panel, with similar scrolled arms, the padded seat raised on flower-carved cabriole legs with scroll feet and casters, c1860.
$450–600 *Hal*

A Gainsborough chair, with carved mahogany frame, original leather upholstery, c1860.
$2,250–2,700 *WLi*

A Gainsborough chair is a deep armchair with an upholstered seat and back, padded open arms, usually with carved decoration.

A George II style mahogany armchair, the acanthus-carved serpentine cresting rail above a conforming carved, pierced vase-shaped splat, the padded seat upholstered in nailed red hide, with a gadrooned apron moulding, on cabriole legs with acanthus-carved knees and claw-and-ball feet, partially re-railed, late 19thC.
$2,500–3,500 *S*

A pair of walnut armchairs, with foliate crestings above a padded panel, flanked by carved foliate panels and spiral supports, padded scroll arms, on turned tapered legs with brass caps and ceramic casters, c1860.
$900–1,000 *Hal*

A pair of giltwood armchairs, carved with flowerheads and leaves, early 18thC.
$19,500–21,750 *S*

l. A set of 4 mahogany armchairs, the buttoned leather-covered backs with padded arms and turned tapered fluted spindles with carved supports, the buttoned leather seats on turned tapered fluted legs, c1870.
$18,000–20,250 *S*

A pair of open armchairs, now covered in brass nailed Rexine, the padded arms with leaf and scroll-carved supports, on turned and fluted legs, 19thC.
$670–750 *DN*

An Edwardian satinwood armchair, with pierced scroll lyre splat, husk and foliate-decorated arm supports, padded seat, on square tapering legs.
$2,250–2,700 *CSK*

Make the most of Miller's

Unless otherwise stated, any description which refers to 'a set' or 'a pair' includes a price guide for the entire set or the pair, even though the illustration may show only a single item.

l. An Edwardian satinwood and decorated armchair, the shield-shaped back with foliate and drapery swag splat, padded seat, on square tapered gaitered legs.
$1,800–2,250 *CSK*

A pair of Victorian walnut open armchairs, with cartouche-shaped padded backs, padded arm rests, overstuffed seats with shaped rails, on cabriole front legs with brass caps and china casters.
$1,200–1,350 *AH*

A set of 10 painted armchairs, with padded square backs, arms and seats, on fluted tapering legs, stamped 'G. Jacob', c1770.
$52,500–60,000 *S*

A set of 4 giltwood armchairs, with padded medallion backs, curved arms and seats, carved with a ribbon motif, on spirally-turned legs, stamped 'Delanois', c1780.
$39,000–45,000 *S*

A set of giltwood armchairs, carved with flowers and scrolling leaves, covered with contemporary Aubusson tapestry, mid-18thC.
$33,000–37,500 *S*

A Dutch mahogany and floral marquetry armchair, the arms with dolphin supports, on sabre legs with paw feet, early 19thC.
$1,800–2,250 *CSK*

A pair of French rosewood framed open arm *fauteuils,* and a pair of matching single chairs, 19thC.
$900–1,200 *CAG*

A set of 4 giltwood armchairs, with padded backs, arms and seats, spiralling fluted arm rests and legs, carved with leaves and rosettes, stamped 'J. B. Demay', c1780.
$19,500–21,750 *S*

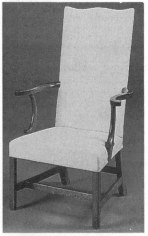

A Chippendale carved mahogany chair, with upholstered back, serpentine arms ending in outscrolled hand holds, down-curving and volute-carved arm supports, on moulded square legs joined by stretchers, old repair, Portsmouth Area, New Hampshire, c1785.
$37,500–42,000 *S(NY)*

A pair of German walnut armchairs, the cartouche-shaped backs carved with leaves, drop-in seats, on serpentine legs carved with scrolling leaves, mid-18thC.
$13,500–15,000 *S*

A pair of Italian giltwood armchairs, the top rails carved with a shell and husks, the frames carved with a guilloche motif, with scrolled arms and fluted tapering legs, Genoa, late 18thC.
$13,500–15,000 *S*

r. A set of 4 French giltwood *fauteuils,* each with stiff-leaf mouldings, the backs, scroll arms and bowed seats upholstered with tapestry, c1900.
$7,800–8,800 *CSK*

Upholstered Armchairs

A William and Mary walnut wing armchair, covered in flame stitched coloured cotton, on hipped cabriole legs joined by a waved part baluster H-shaped stretcher, restored.
$2,500–3,500 *CSK*

A walnut lady's chair, with carved top rail and legs, the open arms supported on cabriole legs, c1845.
$1,500–1,800 *LCA*

A George III mahogany wing armchair, upholstered in green leather.
$4,000–4,800 *TMA*

A pair of Edwardian white painted wing armchairs, with ivory floral cotton loose covering, on fluted square tapering legs with brass casters.
$1,300–1,500 *C(S)*

r. A George III style mahogany wing back armchair, with button upholstered back and squab cushion, scroll arms, on cabriole legs, with pad feet and inset casters, the casters inscribed 'Cope's patent' and a registration mark dated 'January 1877'.
$1,200–1,400 *Hal*

An occasional or bedroom chair, with turned front legs, reupholstered, 1890s.
$1,100–1,450 *LCA*

A walnut armchair, with serpentine front, on carved cabriole legs, c1850.
$1,100–1,500 *LCA*

A pair of Victorian walnut-framed spoon back easy chairs.
$3,000–3,750 *CAG*

Bergère Chairs

A mahogany desk bergère, the moulded tub-shaped cane back above a bowed cane seat, on ring-turned legs headed by rectangular capitals, on brass feet and casters, c1810.
$12,200–13,200 *S*

A late Regency mahogany bergère, the curved cane panel-back with stylised gadrooned bar top rail, scroll arms and cane seat with gros point needlework floral squab, on ring-turned tapering legs with brass caps and casters.
$1,800–2,250 *CSK*

A mahogany bergère, the reeded and moulded frame with cane back, sides and seat, with leather cushions, scrolled arms, on reeded sabre legs with brass casters, c1800.
$8,250–9,750 *S*

A George IV beechwood bergère, with a cane panel curved arched back with a husk and paterae decorated top rail, cane sides and seat with squab, on turned, reeded tapering legs with brass caps and casters.
$3,000–3,750 *CSK*

r. A mahogany library bergère, the cane back and sides with red leather arm caps and cushion seat, on sabre legs with brass casters, c1820.
$6,000–6,750 *S*

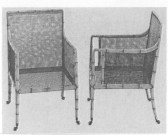

A pair of Regency painted bamboo pattern bergère armchairs, on turned legs and brass casters, paintwork chipped and refreshed.
$6,000–6,750 *CAG*

A set of 4 Russian Karelian birch bergères, each with curved back above a bowed drop-in seat upholstered in flowerhead-filled trellis-patterned black horsehair, on tapering sabre legs, 19thC.
$14,250–15,750 *C*

A pair of George IV brass-inlaid rosewood bergères, each with scrolled backs, outscrolled arms and squab upholstered cushions, the arms terminating in acanthus volutes and centred on the seat rail by a plaque of scrolling foliage, on spirally-turned reeded and gadrooned turned legs with brass casters, attributed to Gillows of Lancaster.
$33,000–37,500 *C*

A matched pair of library bergères, the cane scoop backs with shaped top rails and scroll arms, cushion seats, on turned tapered legs with brass casters, c1840.
$12,750–14,250 *S*

Children's Chairs

r. An early Victorian mahogany child's highchair-on-stand, with balloon variant back, foliate ladder rail, downscrolled arms with restraining bar, loose seat, on turned supports with footrest, the square stand on turned supports. **$450–600** *CDC*

l. A French Louis XV style gilt painted child's armchair, the back with 2 flowerheads carved at the top, drop-in seat, cabriole legs with carved scroll and floral motif, small amount of woodworm, frame repaired, 19thC. **$1,000–1,100** *S*

Dining Chairs

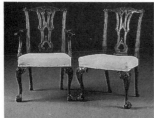

Five George II mahogany dining chairs and a later open armchair, each with a pierced splat with foliate Gothic arches flanked by reeded uprights, serpentine padded seats, above cabriole legs headed by a foliate cartouche with central cabochon and foliate angle brackets, on claw-and-ball feet, 3 with later brackets, the front legs possibly later. **$11,250–12,750** *C*

A set of 10 mahogany dining chairs, including a pair of armchairs, the shield-shaped backs with pierced splats and curved upholstered seats, on square tapering legs joined by H-shaped stretchers, c1790, one armchair and 2 side chairs modern. **$10,500–12,000** *S*

> ## Make the most of Miller's
> *Unless otherwise stated, any description which refers to 'a set' or 'a pair' includes a price guide for the entire set or the pair, even though the illustration may show only a single item.*

l. A set of 8 mahogany dining chairs, possibly Irish, the shaped scrolled top rails carved with paterae and husks above a pierced scrolled splat, within double scrolled moulded uprights carved with icicles, the drop-in seats on leaf-carved hipped and moulded cabriole legs, carved with icicles, H-shaped stretchers, restored, c1765. **$16,500–18,750** *S*

A set of 4 mahogany dining chairs, the acanthus-carved serpentine cresting rails above pierced trellis splats, the drop-in seats on chamfered square legs joined by H-shaped stretchers, c1760. **$1,800–2,250** *S*

A set of 8 mahogany dining chairs, including a pair of armchairs, the arched crested rails with bellflower carving above stick splats, the stuffed seats on square tapering legs with spade feet, old restorations, c1790. **$14,250–15,750** *S*

One armchair bears the trade label of Edwards & Roberts indicating that it was sold or restored by them some time during the second half of the 19thC.

A set of 8 George III mahogany dining chairs, comprising 2 carvers and 6 standard chairs, each with shaped arched backs and pierced splat, overstuffed dropped seats covered in gold damask, supported on square moulded legs united by square stretchers. **$4,000–4,800** *L&E*

A set of 14 George III mahogany dining chairs, including a pair of armchairs, each with a curved bar top rail and vertical splats, with padded seats, on square tapering legs.
$9,000–9,750 *CSK*

A set of 4 Hepplewhite period mahogany dining chairs, with pierced splats, c1790.
$3,000–3,500 *ANT*

A set of 10 mahogany dining chairs, the moulded shield-shaped backs pierced and carved with Prince of Wales' feathers and swags, the red leather covered sprung seats on square tapering moulded legs, with H-shaped stretchers, some with legs cut or repaired, c1790.
$14,250–15,750 *S*

A set of 8 Georgian mahogany dining chairs, comprising 2 carvers and 6 single chairs, with reeded bar backs, reeded uprights and splats, lift-out velvet upholstered seats, on square tapering legs joined by H-shaped stretchers.
$5,250–6,750 *B*

A set of 6 mahogany dining chairs, each with rope-shaped top rail and crossbar, a carved scroll centre panel, the drop-in seats on sabre legs, c1810.
$5,250–6,000 *S*

l. A set of 8 mahogany dining chairs, comprising 2 armchairs and 6 side chairs, with turned legs, c1810.
$10,500–11,250 *BUT*

A set of 6 mahogany dining chairs, each with serpentine top rail, pierced vase splat, leather-covered drop-in seat, on moulded square legs with stretchers, 5 chairs George III, one of later date.
$3,300–4,000 *Bea*

r. A set of 6 Sheraton period mahogany dining chairs, with H-shaped stretchers, c1800.
$4,500–5,250 *ANT*

A harlequin set of 8 mahogany dining chairs, comprising 2 armchairs and 6 side chairs, each with a yoke top rail above a pierced splat, with drop-in seat, on moulded square legs joined by stretchers, late 18thC.
$2,300–3,000 *Hal*

A set of 6 bar-back dining chairs, with brass inlay, cane seats and sabre legs, 19thC.
$3,000–3,750 *JH*

A set of 6 mahogany
dining chairs, including a
pair of carvers, with
stylised leaf decoration to
the back rails, c1825.
$6,000–6,500 *ANT*

A set of 14 mahogany dining
chairs, including 2 armchairs,
the rail backs with brass strung
carved mid-bars, green damask
upholstered drop-in seats, on
sabre legs, re-finished, one
armchair modern, c1820.
$10,800–11,250 *S*

A set of 6 Regency mahogany
dining chairs, the backs with
reeded curved bar top rails inlaid
with brass lines and pierced scroll
incised panel horizontal splats,
upholstered stuff-over seats, on
ring-turned tapered legs.
$3,000–3,750 *P(E)*

Miller's is a price GUIDE
not a price LIST

A set of 8 William IV mahogany
dining chairs, including one
armchair, each having a bar-
back with horizontal splat,
drop-in seats, on turned and
reeded tapering legs.
$3,000–3,500 *P(E)*

A set of 6 early Victorian
mahogany dining chairs, the
balloon-backs carved with leaf
scroll decoration, drop-in seats,
on turned fluted tapering legs.
$2,500–3,000 *JAd*

l. A set of 12 painted
dining chairs, with applied
gilt-metal mounts and
curved bar top rails,
c1820, painted green later.
$6,750–7,500 *S*

A set of 10 William IV mahogany balloon-back
dining chairs, including 2 armchairs.
$10,500–12,000 *CAG*

A set of 12 walnut dining chairs, with leather
upholstery, each stamped 'Gillows Lancaster',
two with paper labels and inked inscription
'Small chairs', c1835.
$45,000–48,000 *S(NY)*

A set of 8 Hepplewhite design mahogany dining chairs, including 2 armchairs, the backs with shaped and pierced splats carved with paterae, drapes, husk chains and anthemions, upholstered seats, moulded square section tapering legs with spade feet, one chair stamped 'T. Willson, 68 Great Queen Street, London', mid-19thC.
$6,750–7,500 *P(S)*

A set of 8 Victorian rosewood dining chairs, with balloon backs.
$4,500–5,250 *SWO*

A set of 12 late Victorian mahogany dining chairs, including a pair of open armchairs, each with arched foliate carved top rail above the pierced splat, the out-turned arms with acanthus scroll ends, red leather covered seats, on square tapering legs headed by husk-trailed and bead-and-reel angles, with pad feet, incised and inscribed, all side chairs twice stamped 'Gillows'.
$19,500–21,750 *C*

A set of 12 Regency style mahogany dining chairs, comprising 2 armchairs and 10 side chairs, each with turned horizontal splats, drop-in seats and sabre legs, late 19thC.
$15,000–17,250 *S(NY)*

A set of 6 Edwardian inlaid mahogany chairs, with acanthus carved cresting, stuff-over seats, on square tapering block legs and spade feet.
$2,000–2,700 *WL*

Miller's is a price GUIDE not a price LIST

A set of 10 Chippendale style mahogany dining chairs, the serpentine acanthus-carved crestings centred by shell motifs, above pierced vase-shaped splats, upholstered seats, on cabriole legs with acanthus knees and claw-and-ball feet, early 20thC.
$7,500–8,250 *S*

A set of 12 Victorian oak dining chairs, including 2 carvers, with arched crests, with maker's label 'Charles Mills and Co, Bradford'.
$3,750–4,500 *AH*

A set of 8 Franco-Flemish dining chairs, with gilt leather upholstery, restored, late 17thC.
$10,500–12,000 *S(Am)*

r. A set of 8 mahogany dining chairs, including a pair of armchairs, each with a rocaille and foliate scroll top rail, ogee arched splat with foliate scrolls, arms with foliate-scroll terminals, drop-in serpentine seat, on cabriole legs headed with cabochon ornament and claw-and-ball feet, restored, late 19thC.
$9,000–10,500 *CSK*

A set of 6 Empire/Biedermeier mahogany dining chairs, the curved backs with moulded top rails, upholstered with beige striped fabric, on sabre legs, early 19thC.
$5,250–6,750 *S(Am)*

A set of 10 mahogany dining chairs, the line-inlaid trellis backs above upholstered seats, the armchairs with serpentine arms and scrolled hand holds, above bellflower-inlaid down-curving arm supports, each on line-inlaid square tapering legs ending in crossbanded cuffs, minor repairs, attributed to Elbert Anderson, New York, c1800.
$52,500–60,000 *S(NY)*

> **Miller's is a price GUIDE not a price LIST**

r. A set of 6 Anglo-Dutch walnut chairs, in the manner of Daniel Marot, each with a shaped open back carved with a fish-scale pattern, the pierced splat carved with floral motifs, the drop-in serpentine seat on cabriole legs carved with shell motifs and pad feet, joined by a carved stretcher, c1720.
$14,250–15,750 *S*

A set of 6 North Italian walnut and bone marquetry chairs, each with a squared open carved back with a ribboned profile medallion, the pierced splat back inlaid with standing figures of warriors, the drop-in seat with frieze carved similarly to the top rail, on square fluted tapering legs, late 18thC, possibly inlaid in the 19thC.
$9,000–10,500 *S*

A set of 12 American rococo laminated rosewood dining chairs, each with a pierced scroll-back topped with an upholstered crest, attributed to John Henry Belter, c1855.
$7,500–9,000 *S(NY)*

l. A set of 6 North European fruitwood dining chairs, the shield-shaped backs with pierced slats, drop-in seats and square tapering legs, late 18thC.
$2,250–3,000 *DN*

Hall Chairs

A pair of early George III mahogany hall chairs, the balloon-shaped backs with re-entrant corners, similar moulded recessed panel seats, on X-shaped front and back supports, joined by curved stretchers.
$1,200–1,500 *P*

A pair of mahogany and ebonised hall chairs, the waisted backs with a central shield flanked by scrolls, c1820.
$1,800–2,250 *S*

A pair of early George III mahogany hall chairs, the backs carved with eagles' heads and dolphins, pineapple leaves and shells, the shaped seats with gadroon carved edges, on rope-twist carved legs, one chair damaged.
$5,500–6,300 *TMA*

A pair of mahogany hall chairs, the scroll-carved backs centred by vacant cartouches, with solid seats, on turned tapered legs, c1855.
$600–900 *Hal*

A set of 3 mahogany hall chairs, with oval backs inset with a roundel, serpentine solid seats, on square tapering legs with stretchers, c1780.
$2,500–2,700 *S*

A pair of Victorian oak hall chairs, of Carolean design.
$1,200–1,350 *C(S)*

Nursing Chairs

A Victorian ebonised spoon-back nursing chair, the padded back with carved crest and leaf-carved supports, with floral beadwork upholstery, on fluted and turned tapering supports and brass casters.
$600–750 *AH*

A Victorian walnut framed nursing chair, the buttoned back with show wood frame decorated with floral carving, on carved cabriole legs.
$530–600 *WIL*

A maple nursing chair, with floral and scroll-carved top rail, the needlework upholstered back and seat depicting a tinker, on carved and turned legs, c1850.
$2,000–2,400 *S*

Side Chairs

A pair of burr walnut side chairs, each slightly curved cresting carved with a central scallop shell, the solid baluster back splat flanked by curved uprights terminating in roundels, with drop-in compass-shaped seat, the apron carved with a stylised fan and foliage, on shell and bellflower carved cabriole legs ending in claw-and-ball feet, c1715.
$135,000–150,000 *S(NY)*

A late George II walnut side chair, the shaped scrolling back and seat covered in brass nailed leather, on cabriole legs with scroll toes, the front legs carved with acanthus leaves, the back legs angled backwards.
$3,000–3,750 *DN*

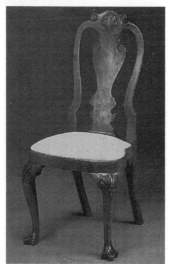

A carved walnut side chair, the serpentine volute and shell-carved crest above a vase-form splat and compass seat, on cabriole legs, minor repairs, Philadelphia, Pennsylvania, c1730.
$87,000–93,000 *S(NY)*

l. A pair of Louis XIV style carved giltwood and gesso side chairs, on square channelled legs carved with husk chains, joined by arched X-shaped stretchers, upholstery distressed, 19thC.
$975–1,125 *P*

A pair of George III mahogany side chairs, the backs with upright splats carved with flowers and drapery, with stuffed seats and square tapering moulded legs, on spade feet.
$420–480 *DN*

A Victorian maple side chair, with shell-carved cresting rail, needlework back on twist supports, with tapestry seat on turned legs, damaged, c1850.
$420–480 *S*

A set of 4 George IV mahogany side chairs, with reeded crests and rosette-carved centre rails, drop-in seats and sabre legs.
$1,100–1,300 *DN*

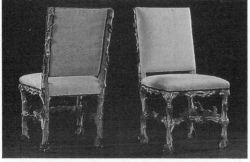

A pair of Italian giltwood and painted chairs, each with a square padded back and seat, the seat rails, legs and stretchers in the form of leafy branches, early 18thC.
$15,000–17,250 *S*

A set of 4 Chippendale manogany side chairs, minor damage, Boston, Massachusetts, c1755.
$9,300–10,300 *SK(B)*

Two Louis XV beech side chairs, each with a foliate carved top rail and cane back, on flower-carved cabriole legs, restored.
$220–300 *Hal*

l. A pair of Second Empire mahogany side chairs, with gilt-bronze classical mounts, the backs with panelled splats and top rails above bowed padded seats, on sabre legs with bronze paw feet.
$900–1,200 *P*

A set of 6 Dutch ash and walnut side chairs, decorated in floral marquetry, repaired, 18thC.
$6,750–7,500 *DN*

Miscellaneous Chairs

A mahogany reading chair, in the manner of Morgan & Sanders, the horseshoe-shaped back fitted with a sliding book rest, flanked by 2 small drawers and brass candleholders, the back with vertical stick splats and scroll supports, the saddle-shaped seat on turned and tapering front legs with brass casters, c1815.
$12,300–13,500 *S*

A Louis XVI beech *voyeuse,* the padded top rail, back and bowed seat covered in green trellis-patterned cut velvet, on stop-fluted turned tapering legs headed by flowerheads, previously decorated, restored.
$2,250–2,700 *C*

A Victorian carved walnut conversation seat, the detachable superstructure with 4 domed arch upholstered panels with spiral ribbon, husk and foliate crestings centred by an urn, the padded arm supports with pierced foliate scroll terminals, upholstered serpentine seats, on beaded, turned and fluted tapered legs, headed with paterae and terminating in casters.
$4,000–4,800 *P(E)*

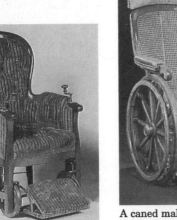

A Victorian mahogany invalid's chair, with 2 handle-driven wheels and a folding footrest, labelled 'Dupont Lits Et Fauteuils Mechaniques Rue Hautefeuille 10, Paris'.
$530–630 *CSK*

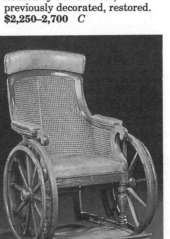

A caned mahogany wheelchair, the back with detachable headrest, padded arms and seat, turned front legs and sliding footrest, the brass-rimmed ten-spoked wheels with wooden handgrip and central smaller wheel at the back, c1840.
$5,500–6,300 *S*

An Aesthetic Movement ebony inlaid maple slipper chair, attributed to Herter Brothers, New York, with India Rubber Co casters, restored, c1875.
$750–900 *SK*

Chests of Drawers

A William and Mary laburnum oyster-veneered chest of drawers, restored, 34in (86.5cm) wide.
$5,800–6,300 *MR*

A walnut chest of drawers, with moulded top, a brushing slide and 3 graduated drawers, on shaped bracket feet, mid-18thC, 42¼in (107.5cm) wide.
$750–900 *Hal*

A Queen Anne oyster-veneered chest of drawers, the moulded top inlaid with interlocking circles, above 2 short and 2 long drawers, the base with a single drawer, on shaped bracket feet, altered and restored, c1705 and later, 41in (104cm) wide.
$4,200–4,800 *Hal*

A George I walnut and crossbanded chest of drawers, with a brushing slide and 4 graduated drawers, brass drop handles and escutcheons, on bracket feet, 30in (76cm) wide.
$4,500–5,250 *L&E*

A mahogany bowfront chest of drawers, with original brass handles, c1800, 43in (109cm) wide.
$3,000–3,750 *ANT*

18th Century Drawers

- Drawer linings oak until mid-18thC.
- Good quality drawers had oak sides, with top edges rounded.
- Bottom boards made from 2 or 3 pieces of same wood, and grooved to form bottom runners.
- Until 1770 grain in bottom boards ran from front to back; after 1770 from side to side, often with central bearer for extra support.
- No 18thC drawer exactly fitted space between front and back, a space always being left for ventilation.

r. A George I walnut and feather-strung chest of drawers, with crossbanded top, a brushing slide and 4 long drawers below, on later bracket feet, restored, 36in (91.5cm) wide.
$6,750–7,500 *CSK*

A George III mahogany metamorphic chest of drawers, the leather-lined moulded hinged top above dummy drawers, with an end cupboard, the top opens to reveal 4 leather-lined library steps, c1800, 29½in (75cm) high when closed.
$12,000–12,750 *S*

A George III mahogany chest of drawers, with brushing slide above 2 short and 2 long drawers, on bracket feet, 36in (91.5cm) wide.
$1,400–1,500 *RBB*

A George III yew chest of drawers, with 4 long graduated drawers, on shaped bracket feet, 37in (94cm) wide.
$2,400–3,000 *HOLL*

A George III mahogany bowfront chest of drawers, the 4 graduated long drawers with cockbeaded edges and turned knob handles, triple reed edge and advanced segmental forecorners with tapering reeded pilasters, on turned feet, 47in (119.5cm) wide.
$2,250–3,000 *CDC*

19th Century Drawers

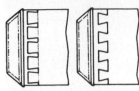

Hand-made   *Machine-made*

- Corner mouldings on drawers introduced by Sheraton, so giving date after 1799.
- Victorians made bottom boards from one piece of wood, usually screwed to sides.
- Machine-made dovetails indicate piece was made after 1880s.

A Regency mahogany bowfront chest of drawers, with 4 graduated drawers, on turned and reeded tapering feet, 33in (84cm) wide.
$1,000–1,100 *Bon*

A mahogany chest of drawers, with 2 short and 3 long graduated drawers, above a shaped apron, on splayed bracket feet, alterations, 19thC, 29¼in (74.5cm) wide.
$1,000–1,100 *Hal*

A mahogany bowfront chest of drawers, with 2 short and 3 long graduated drawers, above a shaped apron, on bracket feet, mid-19thC, 42¼in (107.5cm) wide.
$830–900 *Hal*

A Dutch mahogany chest of drawers, with a secret frieze drawer, above 5 graduated and chequered inlaid drawers, a stepped plinth, on sabre legs, early 19thC, 44in (112cm) wide.
$1,800–2,250 *Hal*

A Victorian walnut chest of drawers, with 2 short and 2 long drawers, c1860, 37½in (95.5cm) wide.
$530–600 *OD*

A German walnut serpentine chest of drawers, with moulded top, 2 drawers and a shaped apron, on cabriole legs, metal mounts and handles, c1900, 25¾in (65.5cm) wide.
$600–670 *Hal*

l. A mahogany Biedermeier secrétaire chest of drawers, the moulded edged top with protruding corners, the secrétaire drawer with leather writing surface and sliding compartments, 3 moulded edged drawers below flanked by wrythen leaf-carved pilasters, on plinth base with wave pattern frieze, 19thC, 42in (106.5cm) wide.
$1,400–1,500 *AH*

A Dutch marquetry tallboy chest, the 6 graduated drawers with floral and scroll decoration to fronts, moulded marquetry decorated cornice, urn and floral marquetry to the sides in coloured woods, on splay supports, c1810, 42in (106.5cm) wide.
$2,700–3,300 *RBB*

Chests-on-Chests

A feather banded walnut and oak tallboy, the moulded cornice above 3 short and 6 long drawers, on bracket feet, restored, early 18thC, 41in (104cm) wide.
$4,500–5,250 *CSK*

A George III mahogany chest-on-chest, the upper section with a moulded cornice above a blind fret decorated frieze, 2 short and 3 long graduated drawers, flanked by fluted canted corners, the base with 3 long graduated drawers, on ogee bracket feet, c1760, 46in (117cm) wide.
$3,750–4,500 *Bon*

A George II mahogany tallboy, the dentilled swan neck cresting with central blank cartouche and grotesque mask, the upper section with 2 short and 3 long drawers between canted fluted angles headed by composite capitals, the lower section with 3 long drawers between fluted angles, on shaped bracket feet, 47in (119.5cm) wide.
$10,500–12,000 *C*

A George I walnut tallboy, the upper section with a cavetto cornice fitted with 2 short and 3 long drawers, each with a moulded edge and feather stringing, the lower section with 3 long drawers, on bracket feet, 42½in (108cm) wide.
$4,800–5,800 *L*

l. A Welsh George II pollard oak tallboy, with brushing slide, good colour, condition and patina, original brasses, c1745, 34in (86.5cm) wide.
$22,500–25,500 *PHA*

r. A George II walnut chest-on-chest, the upper section with a moulded cornice above 3 short and 3 long drawers, flanked by reeded angles, the base with fitted secrétaire drawer above 3 long drawers, the lower drawer inlaid with a concave compass star, on bracket feet, c1730, 43in (109cm) wide.
$10,500–12,000 *CNY*

A George I walnut secrétaire chest-on-chest, with canted and fluted corners to the top and bottom sections, an inlaid sunburst and pierced bracket feet, the secrétaire drawer probably a later addition, the sides re-veneered and the cornice re-built, 41in (104cm) wide.
$13,500–15,000 *SWO*

A George I inlaid walnut chest-on-chest, damaged and restored, c1720, 43½in (110.5cm) wide.
$9,300–10,300 *S(NY)*

MILLER'S COMPARES . . .

I A George III mahogany chest-on-chest, the cavetto cornice above 2 short and 6 long graduated drawers, on ogee bracket feet, c1775, 43in (109cm) wide. **$3,750–4,500** *Hal*

II A George III mahogany chest-on-chest, the cavetto cornice above 2 short and 5 long graduated drawers, on shaped bracket feet, with alterations, 41in (104cm) wide. **$1,300–1,450** *Hal*

Although these 2 chests look very similar, *item I* fetched considerably more at auction than *item II*. The most obvious difference between the 2 pieces is that *item II* has 2 drawers rather than 3 in the lower chest, the third having been removed at some stage. This greatly detracts from its value, as does the fact that the timber it is made from is not of the highest quality, and the handles and escutcheons are unlikely to be original. *Item I* on the other hand, has all its original features, an excellent colour, superb linings and ogee feet, which are more popular than the square feet of *item II*. *Hal*

A George III mahogany tallboy, the upper section with moulded and dentil cornice, 2 short and 3 long drawers with fluted canted corners, the base with 3 long drawers, on bracket feet, 37in (94cm) wide. **$4,000–4,800** *CAG*

A George III mahogany chest-on-chest, the upper section with a solid dentil cornice, blind fret carved canted corners, 2 short and 3 long drawers, the base with a brushing slide above 3 graduated drawers, on moulded ogee bracket feet, 43¼in (110cm) wide. **$3,000–3,700** *WL*

A George III mahogany chest-on-chest, the upper section with cornice above 2 short and 3 graduated long drawers, the base with 3 long graduated drawers, all cockbeaded, with original brass swan neck handles, on shaped bracket feet, 46½in (118cm) wide. **$2,700–3,700** *BWe*

A Georgian walnut chest-on-chest, with cross and herringbone banding, the upper section with 2 short and 3 long drawers with fluted canted angles, the base with 2 short and 2 long drawers, on bracket feet, altered and damaged, 39½in (100cm) wide. **$4,000–4,800** *Bri*

r. A George III mahogany secrétaire tallboy, the drop-flap enclosing drawers and pigeonholes, with 6 other graduated drawers, on bracket feet, 40¼in (102cm) wide. **$1,300–1,800** *P(Ch)*

Miller's is a price GUIDE not a price LIST

Chests-on-Stands

A japanned chest-on-stand, decorated with gilt chinoiserie on a black ground, now on a stand with squared legs and pierced brackets, mid-18thC, 32in (81cm) wide.
$4,500–5,250 *S*

A William & Mary burr yew and yew chest-on-stand, the top centrally inlaid with a burr yew diamond above 3 short and 3 long graduated drawers, the stand with 3 frieze drawers and a shaped apron, on later inverted baluster turned legs and bun feet, tied by shaped solid stretchers, c1700, 39½in (100.5cm) wide.
$5,700–6,300 *Bon*

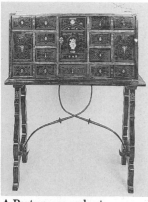

A Portuguese walnut *vargueño*, inlaid with brass stringing and a central architectural arch, gilt metal mounts, 19thC, 41in (104cm) wide, associated table stand.
$3,000–3,750 *P(S)*

A William III walnut chest-on-stand, restored and alterations to base, c1700 and later, 41½in (105.5cm) wide.
$1,500–1,800 *Hal*

A William and Mary oyster olivewood chest-on-stand, with kingwood crossbanding and rosewood mouldings, the hinged top revealing a well, the 2 long drawers above spiral-twist rosewood supports joined by waved stretchers, c1690, 39½in (100.5cm) wide.
$4,800–5,300 *S*

Beware!

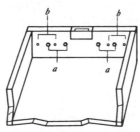

Check inside drawer front for (a) new holes, (b) old, filled-in holes where width reduced.

- If the dovetailing in all drawers in a piece do not match.
- If handles have been moved or changed: drawer may have been reduced in width. Check reverse of front for filled holes. If no corresponding holes on front, veneer almost certainly later than drawer.
- If dovetails at back of drawer show signs of alteration: drawer has probably been reduced in depth.
- If wood of carcass is not same age as base and back of drawer: look closely at rest of piece.
- If you find one replacement, alteration or restoration: look for others!

A Louis XIV pewter and ivory inlaid floral marquetry and ebony *coffre de mariage*, attributed to Pierre Gole, minor replacements to marquetry, c1665, 29¼in (74.5cm) wide.
$45,000–52,500 *C*

The use of this particular type of coffer is difficult to determine. It is believed that the coffer was moved morning and evening from its stand in order to be placed on the master's bed and was frequently covered with velvet, occasionally with Savonnerie and, from 1685, in tortoiseshell.

> **Did you know?**
> *MILLER'S* Antiques Price Guide *builds up year-by-year to form the most comprehensive antiques photo-reference library available.*

A veneered burr walnut and maple tallboy, in 2 sections, the upper section with moulded cornice above 2 short and 3 long graduated crossbanded drawers, the lower section with projecting moulding above 3 short drawers, the shaped skirt below on trumpet and vase turned legs joined by a shaped stretcher, on ball feet, Boston-Ipswich area, Massachusetts, c1700, 39in (99cm) wide.
$172,000–180,000 *S(NY)*

Dressing Chests

A George II mahogany enclosed kneehole dressing chest, the moulded re-entrant corner hinged top enclosing a central lined panel between lidded compartments, with a fitted twin arched apron drawer flanked by 6 short drawers to either side of a central enclosed recessed cupboard, on bracket feet, 32¼in (82cm) wide.
$6,000–6,750 *P*

An early George III mahogany dressing chest, with a brushing slide to the frieze above 3 long graduated and cockbeaded drawers, with brass swan neck handles and bead oval lock plates, on bracket feet, 30in (76cm) wide.
$2,700–3,300 *HAM*

r. A George III mahogany dressing chest, after Thomas Sheraton, the satinwood banded top above a fitted drawer with adjustable writing slide and enclosing a mirror, boxes and trays, above 3 long drawers, flanked by inlaid satinwood panels, on square tapering feet, c1795, 40in (101.5cm) wide.
$7,200–7,800 *S*

A George III mahogany dressing table, the serpentine crossbanded top with a moulded edge above a conforming drawer, the recessed lower part fitted with 2 small and 2 long drawers, on bracket feet, repairs to rear feet, late 18thC, 35in (89cm) wide.
$7,500–8,250 *S(NY)*

Linen & Blanket Chests

An Irish blanket chest, the well-figured cleated hinged top with moulded edge and a pair of drawers, the stand with shaped apron and applied with central scallop shell, the shell-carved cabriole legs with claw feet, c1750, 51in (129.5cm) wide.
$5,250–6,000 *S*

A mahogany chest-on-stand, the moulded hinged top with gradrooned edge, the case fitted with a gilt-bronze keyhole escutcheon and carrying handles, on a conforming stand raised on shell-carved cabriole legs, ending in claw-and-ball feet, 19thC, on a later stand, 46in (117cm) wide.
$3,300–3,800 *S(NY)*

A Spanish walnut vestment chest, the bevelled top above a moulded front with one long and 2 short frieze drawers above a fall inlaid with the initials 'I.H.S.' within a sunburst, the front also inlaid with a Latin inscription, on later bracket feet, late 17thC, 51in (129.5cm) wide.
$1,500–1,800 *Bon*

A George II mahogany linen chest, the hinged top and straight sides with moulded corners, on shaped bracket feet, restored, c1755, 50½in (128.5cm) wide.
$750–900 *Hal*

l. A George II Irish mahogany and banded mule chest-on-stand, the moulded hinged top above 2 frieze drawers, the carved stand with a shaped apron and central shell, floral and leaf-carved cabriole legs and claw feet, 49¼in (125cm) wide.
$3,000–3,750 *P*

Military Chests

A mahogany and brass bound military chest, in 2 sections, with 2 short and 3 long drawers, on turned feet, with a label 'Army & Navy c.s.l Makers', 19thC, 45in (114cm) wide.
$1,000–1,300 *CSK*

A burr walnut secrétaire military chest, in 2 sections with brass corners, by Hill and Millward, 7 Duncannon Street, London, patented 1873, 19thC, 39in (99cm) wide.
$4,500–5,000 *B*

A camphorwood and brass inlaid military chest and writing desk, in 2 sections, bordered with lines and decorated with stylised foliate designs, the upper part with a hinged fall enclosing a fitted interior, the lower part fitted with 2 long drawers, with recessed brass handles, raised on bracket feet, 19thC, 36in (91.5cm) wide.
$3,000–3,700 *P(E)*

Wellington Chests

l. A Victorian mahogany Wellington chest, with 7 drawers flanked by corbelled pilasters, one pilaster hinged and with a lock, on a plinth base, 24in (61cm) wide.
$1,800–2,250 *S(S)*

A Victorian mahogany secrétaire Wellington chest, with 7 small drawers surrounding the central secrétaire drawer, with fall-front and fitted interior, 54in (137cm) high.
$3,300–3,700 *B*

A mid-Victorian walnut secrétaire Wellington chest of drawers, the centre with 2 dummy drawers revealing a secrétaire front and fitted interior, 60in (152.5cm) high.
$3,300–3,750 *MR*

r. A Victorian walnut secrétaire Wellington chest, with 5 graduated drawers above and beneath the secrétaire drawer fitted with satinwood-faced small drawers, the locking bar and opposing style with carved fruit and foliate mouldings, 22in (56cm) wide.
$2,250–2,700 *P(S)*

Commodes

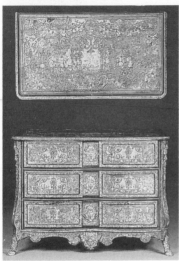

A Louis XIV ormolu-mounted boulle brass inlaid ebony and red tortoiseshell commode, originally with a further small central drawer between the 2 flanking small drawers and with a filled keyhole to the top, the marquetry distressed, restored, 19thC, 47in (119.5cm) wide.
$60,000–63,000 C

A George III mahogany commode, the serpentine top crossbanded and with boxwood lines, above a green baize-lined brushing slide and 3 graduated drawers, the serpentine apron between splayed legs, the underside inscribed 'Gallie', 39½in (100.5cm) wide.
$16,500–18,000 C

A Louis XV ormolu-mounted kingwood commode, by François Lieutaud, the associated serpentine-fronted moulded marble top above 3 long drawers with quarter-veneered panels within crossbanding and separated by brass lines, on bracket feet with pierced scrolling foliate sabots, the marble top repaired, re-mounted, inscribed in blank ink 'U' and stamped twice 'FL', 34in (86.5cm) wide.
$10,800–12,000 C

A Louis XV ormolu-mounted fruitwood commode, with 2 long drawers *san traverse*, above the serpentine apron centrally carved with a shell, raised on cabriole legs, with scrolled toes, mid-18thC, 45½in (115.5cm) wide.
$9,750–11,250 S(NY)

A Louis XV red and black lacquered and gilt-bronze mounted commode, the serpentine form with a moulded mottled grey and green marble top, the front with 2 drawers, painted with chinoiseries including figures, birds and trees, the mounts cast with scrolling foliated motifs, with sabre legs, label of 'Muller, Ebéniste à Nancy', stamped twice 'Dubois', mid-18thC, 28in (71cm) wide.
$150,000–165,000 S

A Louis XV/XVI Transitional floral marquetry commode, with mottled grey and rust marble top, the front with 2 long drawers, inlaid similarly to the sides with baskets and sprays of flowers, raised on cabriole legs, c1780, 51½in (131cm) wide.
$21,000–23,250 S

A Louis XVI fruitwood commode, the grey and white marble top above one frieze drawer and 2 long drawers flanked by fluted columnar supports, raised on 2 toupie feet, now fitted with later brass handles and keyhole escutcheons, late 18thC, 50½in (128cm) wide.
$3,750–4,500 S(NY)

Miller's is a price GUIDE not a price LIST

An Italian seaweed marquetry commode, inlaid with walnut, mahogany and ivory panels, late 18thC, 61½in (156cm) wide.
$28,500–31,500 AAV

An Italian walnut marquetry commode, fitted with 2 shallow drawers flanking a deep drawer, the top with ribbon, branches and berries, the front and sides with rosettes and floral scrolls, on fluted and turned tapering feet, late 18thC, 50in (127cm) wide.
$18,000–20,250 RBB

Cupboards

A mahogany veneered standing corner cupboard, the moulded cornice above a painted interior with serpentine front shelves, the pair of doors with figured panels banded with stringing, above a girdle moulding, the base fitted with a shelf enclosed by a further pair of doors with ivory escutcheons, angled sides on bracket feet, 18thC, 38in (96.5cm) wide.
$5,000–5,500 *WW*

A George I japanned hanging corner cabinet, the moulded cornice centred by a finial above a bevelled mirror-panelled cupboard, decorated in gold on a black ground, c1720, triangular pediment possibly of a later date, 28¾in (73cm) wide.
$4,500–5,250 *S*

FURTHER READING
Miller's Antiques Checklists: Furniture, Miller's Publications, Tenterden, Kent, 1991

A George III mahogany corner cupboard, in 2 sections, with swan neck pediment above a blind fretwork frieze over a panelled crossbanded door enclosing 3 shaped shelves, flanked by fluted, canted sides, the lower section of similar design, on ogee feet, 33½in (85cm) wide.
$3,750–4,500 *P(Sc)*

A late Georgian mahogany corner cupboard, in 2 sections, the top half with a swan neck pediment above a moulded cornice, a pair of panelled doors enclosing a series of green painted shaped shelves, the base fitted with a pair of panelled cupboard doors enclosing shaped shelves, on bracket feet, 43in (109cm) wide.
$2,400–2,700 *Mit*

r. A mahogany hanging corner cupboard, the dentil cornice above a frieze and arched fielded panelled door enclosing shaped shelves and flanked by canted corners, 18thC, 31½in (80cm) wide.
$450–600 *Hal*

l. A George III mahogany standing corner cupboard, the later shaped moulded cornice above a pair of double banded doors, enclosing a painted interior, above similar doors and on shaped bracket feet, c1790, 42¼in (107cm) wide.
$10,500–11,250 *S*

A black japanned and decorated corner cupboard, restored, early 19thC, 43in (109cm) wide.
$4,500–5,250 *CSK*

A George III inlaid mahogany hanging corner cupboard, the moulded cornice above a panel inlaid frieze, the single panelled door with chequered stringing and a central cartouche inlaid with a shell, above one real and 2 dummy drawers, with canted corners, c1800, 34½in (87.5cm) wide.
$825–975 *Hal*

A George III mahogany linen press, the moulded cornice above a pair of quarter-veneered doors with inset oval panels outlined with crossbanding and stringing, the interior containing sliding trays, the base with 2 short and 2 long graduated drawers, on splayed feet, c1790, 51¼in (130cm) wide.
$5,500–6,500 *S*

A William IV mahogany bowfront corner cupboard, the drop pendent cornice above 2 pairs of panelled doors with beaded edges, on bracket feet, 41in (104cm) wide.
$2,000–2,500 *CSK*

l. A mahogany standing corner cabinet, the dentil cornice above a pair of astragal glazed doors enclosing shaped shelves, the lower part with a pair of panelled doors and on a plinth base, with canted corners, 19thC, 44in (112cm) wide.
$3,500–4,000 *Hal*

A late Victorian satinwood bowfront corner cupboard, in the neo-classical revival style, crossbanded in rosewood and inlaid with stringing, with brass mouldings, the upper part fitted with 2 graduated shelves with bevelled mirror-back panels, on square tapering legs, 25½in (65cm) wide.
$7,000–8,000 *CAG*

A George III mahogany clothes press, with a dentil cornice above 2 panelled doors enclosing sliding trays, the base with 2 short and 2 long drawers, with chased brass handles, on panelled bracket feet, 50in (127cm) wide.
$2,500–3,000 *DN*

A George III mahogany clothes press, in 2 sections, the top half with a moulded dentil cornice above a pair of panelled doors enclosing a series of oak trays, the base fitted with 4 drawers, brass drop handles and cockbeading, on shaped bracket feet, 49in (124.5cm) wide.
$1,900–2,200 *Mit*

A George III mahogany linen press, the top with moulded edge above a frieze and a pair of oval panelled doors enclosing slides with 2 short drawers below, raised on bracket feet, 56in (142cm) wide.
$1,800–2,200 *Bon*

A George III Sheraton breakfront wardrobe, raised on 6 turned and reeded legs, 39¼in (100cm) wide.
$6,000–6,750 *B*

A George III mahogany linen press, the moulded cornice above a pair of panelled doors enclosing a shelved interior, on a lower section of 2 short and 2 long drawers, with splayed bracket feet, damaged, 53in (134.5cm) wide.
$1,500–1,800 *Bon*

A late George III mahogany clothes press, with moulded cornice and 2 oval panelled doors with boxwood and ebony strung borders enclosing sliding trays, above 2 short and 2 long drawers, on splayed bracket feet, 50in (127cm) wide.
$3,800–4,200 *DN*

A George III mahogany and string inlaid linen press, with moulded and dentil cornice, panelled doors enclosing slides, over 2 short and 2 long drawers with brass drop handles, on bracket feet, 49in (124.5cm) wide.
$1,800–2,200 *AH*

A mahogany linen press, married, early 19thC, 44in (112cm) wide.
$2,000–2,500 *P(HSS)*

A late George III mahogany clothes press, with a moulded cornice above 2 panelled doors enclosing sliding trays, the base with 2 short and 2 long drawers, on splayed bracket feet, 50in (127cm) wide.
$3,600–4,400 *DN*

A mahogany linen press, with reeded cornice, above 2 panelled doors enclosing trays, over 2 short and 2 graduated long drawers below, on splayed bracket feet, early 19thC, 48½in (123cm) wide.
$1,900–2,200 *Bea*

A William IV mahogany breakfront wardrobe, the central panelled doors enclosing sliding trays above 2 drawers, flanked by pilasters with lappet-carved capitals, 7 graduated drawers to one side and dummy drawer door to the other, turned handles, on stepped plinth base, 98½in (250cm) wide.
$1,900–2,200 *DN*

A Regency mahogany linen press, the domed cornice with a central reeded panel, above a pair of panelled doors, the lower part with 4 short and one long drawer, on turned feet, c1815, 53in (134.5cm) wide.
$1,200–1,500 *Hal*

A veneered oval and quartered satinwood gentleman's wardrobe, with swan neck pediment, c1860, 45in (114.5cm) wide.
$8,250–9,000 *WLi*

A Victorian bird's-eye maple breakfront wardrobe, stamped 'Holland & Sons', c1860, 113in (287cm) wide.
$3,500–4,000 *Hal*

A painted satinwood serpentine-fronted wardrobe, decorated with lovers in landscapes, floral swags, urns and scrolling foliage, early 20thC, 58in (147cm) wide.
$3,750–4,500 *Bea*

A walnut cupboard, with stepped top and concave frieze above 2 doors with shaped panels, flanked by stiles, with panelled sides, above a concave shaped base, on bun feet carved with stylised leaves, Frankfurt, 18thC, 78¾in (200cm) wide.
$20,250–22,500 *S(Am)*

l. A German walnut and crossbanded cupboard, with shaped moulded arched cornice enclosed by a pair of fielded panelled doors, on ebonised bun feet, 18thC, 85in (216cm) wide.
$7,000–8,000 *CSK*

A Victorian marquetry inlaid satinwood wardrobe, stamped 'Wilkinson & Son, 8 Old Bond Street 20400', the locks stamped 'Cope & Collinson', late 19thC, 101in (256.5cm) wide.
$4,600–5,400 *Bon*

A mahogany linen press, with dentil moulded cornice, 2 short above 2 long drawers, on shaped bracket feet, 19thC, 47½in (121cm) wide.
$2,000–2,500 *WL*

A rococo oak cupboard, possibly associated, carved with scrolls, rocailles and flowers, the shaped apron with flower twigs, on scrolled feet, Liègeois, early 18thC, 37½in (95cm) wide.
$5,500–6,500 *S(Am)*

An Italian walnut cupboard, with a moulded cornice enclosed by a pair of fielded panelled doors and stiles, on bracket feet, early 18thC, 70in (178cm) wide.
$6,750–7,500 *CSK*

A Chippendale gumwood linen press, New Jersey, c1795, 49in (124.5cm) wide.
$6,000–6,750 *S(NY)*

A rococo oak cupboard, carved with rocailles, scrolling foliage and flowers, on bun feet, Liègeois, c1730, 72½in (184cm) wide.
$168,000–172,000 *S(Am)*

A Dutch rosewood and ebony cupboard, with moulded cornice, enclosed by a pair of raised panelled doors, 18thC, 86in (218.5cm) wide.
$18,750–21,000 *CSK*

A Dutch neo-classical mahogany linen press, the pediment with border of leaf tips centring a cartouche with garlands, each door with rope-twist border, opening to slides and drawers, similarly carved, raised on bracket feet, late 18thC, 69½in (176.5cm) wide.
$33,000–36,000 *S(NY)*

A pair of Italian walnut cupboards, each with panelled sides, carved corners and a central door, possibly originally used together as a centrepiece, possibly Emilian or Tuscan, early 17thC, 58¼in (148cm) wide.
$36,750–39,000 *S*

A Dutch neo-classical inlaid mahogany linen press, the dentil moulded broken pediment centred by a leaf-carved plateau above a pair of doors, the lower section with fluted canted corners, 3 long drawers, on fluted feet, damaged and restored, late 18thC, 73in (185.5cm) wide.
$21,000–23,250 *S(NY)*

A Chippendale gumwood linen press, in 2 sections, New Jersey, c1785, 51in (129.5cm) wide.
$6,750–7,500 *S(NY)*

An American mahogany wardrobe, the cornice with egg-and-dart border above a mirrored door, flanked by panelled doors with columns at each side, opening to shelves and drawers, raised on a conforming plinth with bun feet, c1840, 66in (167.5cm) wide.
$7,500–8,250 *S(NY)*

Davenports

A George IV mahogany davenport, the sliding top with hinged writing surface, enclosing fitted interior, the lower section with 2 slides and 2 panelled doors, on reeded bun feet, c1820, 19¾in (50cm) wide.
$2,000–2,500 *Hal*

A William IV rosewood davenport, with a spindle gallery above a leather inset slope, enclosing 2 small drawers, above a frieze drawer, on plain end supports with a turned stretcher, 21in (53cm) wide.
$1,000–1,200 *DN*

r. A Victorian walnut davenport, the stationery compartment with a hinged lid, writing slope and red leather inset, base fitted with 4 true and 4 false drawers, all with turned handles, interior missing, 20½in (52cm) wide.
$825–1,125 *WIL*

An early Victorian figured walnut davenport, with pierced fret-carved decoration, the right side with 4 drawers, dummies to the left side, on china casters, 22½in (57cm) wide.
$4,000–4,500 *P(O)*

A Victorian rosewood davenport, with raised stationery compartment, tooled leather insert to the writing slope, 4 real and 4 false side drawers, on spiral turned front supports to a shaped plinth and bun feet with casters, 22¼in (56.5cm) wide.
$1,500–1,800 *Bea*

A Victorian walnut davenport, with a lidded stationery well above a fall enclosing an adjustable writing slide and drawers, with a panelled cupboard door below enclosing 4 drawers, with floral carved scrolled front supports, the locks stamped 'Nettlefolds, Patent', 22½in (57cm) wide.
$3,000–3,750 *Bon*

> **Miller's is a price GUIDE not a price LIST**

l. A walnut davenport, the gallery-back with raised section, inset leather writing surface revealing a maple-lined fitted interior, 4 side drawers opposed by 4 dummy drawers, turned knob handles, supported on turned columns, c1870, 21in (53.5cm) wide.
$2,300–2,700 *L&E*

A Victorian walnut veneered harlequin davenport, the rising stationery compartment with a gallery, the fitted interior with leather inset writing slope, pierced and carved brackets to base, fitted with 4 true and 4 false drawers at each side, 22in (56cm) wide.
$3,600–4,400 *WIL*

A Victorian burr walnut harlequin davenport, the rising top with brass galleried back, the cylinder flap with fitted interior, fitted on either side with 4 drawers and 4 dummy drawers, on 2 foliate moulded and C-scrolled columns with dolphin mounts, on 4 bun feet, 19thC, 22in (56cm) wide.
$4,000–5,000 *GAK*

MILLER'S COMPARES . . .

I A Victorian burr walnut davenport, the hinged flap opening to reveal pull-out slide and 2 drawers with weighted rising stationery compartment, with 4 real side drawers and 4 dummy drawers to the reverse side, with scroll-shaped front supports, 22in (56cm) wide.
$4,500–5,250 *P(Ch)*

II A Victorian mahogany davenport, the rising writing slope enclosing a fitted interior, over 4 real and 4 dummy drawers to the sides, standing on bun feet, 21¼in (54cm) wide.
$1,300–1,800 *P(Ch)*

These two davenports are both in good condition but realised very different prices at auction. This is due to the fact that *item I* boasts a number of particularly desirable features, such as the piano top, which is always sought-after by collectors. *Item II* is made of straight grain mahogany, whereas *item I* is constructed of the more desirable and attractive burr walnut. A great deal of care went into the construction of *item I*, with its rising weighted stationery compartment at the back, the adjustable writing slope in the pull-out slide and the cabriole scrolls at the front, points which are reflected in the final price it achieved in the saleroom. *P(Ch)*

A Victorian burr walnut davenport, with banded borders, fitted stationery wells and pen recess under a fall flap, having maple-lined fitted interior, leather inset, 4 false drawers, 4 drawers, having turned and spiral front pilasters terminating in scroll leaves to bun feet and casters, 21¼in (54cm) wide.
$1,800–2,000 *WW*

l. A late Victorian oak davenport, the superstructure with 4 short drawers above an embossed leather writing fall, on turned supports, with 2 base side drawers, 23in (58.5cm) wide.
$525–675 *Bon*

l. A late Victorian burr walnut davenport, the projecting lid enclosing a pull-out leather lined interior with compartment and drawers, the domed pop-up superstructure with fret carved gallery and letter rack, above panelled sides and end cupboard door, on plinth, 23in (58.5cm) wide.
$4,500–5,250 *CSK*

A Chinese hardwood davenport, the top with galleried open shelf above hinged fall, carved with birds amidst foliate and floral meander, 19thC, 23¾in (60cm) wide.
$1,000–1,200 *Bri*

Desks

A fruitwood and oak kneehole desk, with burr walnut veneer, crossbanded and feather strung, with a single long and 6 short drawers, central enclosed cupboard, with shaped apron drawer above, on bracket feet, early 18thC, 33in (84cm) wide.
$8,500–9,500 *P(E)*

A George III inlaid satinwood writing desk, the shelved superstructure fitted with 7 small drawers, the hinged writing surface above a drawer, on foliate inlaid straight tapering legs, restored, 28in (71cm) wide.
$3,000–3,750 *S(NY)*

A George III mahogany pedestal partners' desk, with green leather-lined writing surface, later moulded plinth and wooden casters, one shelf lacking, restored, 54½in (138.5cm) wide.
$26,250–27,000 *C*

An early George III mahogany kneehole desk, the moulded top above a crenellated frieze and 9 drawers surrounding a recessed cupboard door, on ogee bracket feet, restored, c1760, 35in (89cm) wide.
$5,250–6,000 *S*

A George III mahogany and crossbanded roll-top desk, the tambour fall enclosing a fitted interior, a pair of candle slides, tooled leather inset panel and adjustable ratcheted slope, on square tapering legs with brass cappings and casters, 43¼in (110cm) wide.
$9,000–9,750 *P*

A mahogany pedestal desk, the leather inset top above 3 frieze drawers, raised on a pair of pedestals each with 3 graduated drawers and on plinth bases, the reverse with dummy drawers to match, c1820, 53in (134.5cm) wide.
$3,750–4,500 *Hal*

A walnut kneehole desk, inlaid throughout with feather banding, the quarter-veneered moulded top with cusped corners, above 7 drawers surrounding a shaped apron and a recessed cupboard door, on bracket feet, c1725, 30in (76cm) wide.
$7,500–8,250 *S*

A George II mahogany kneehole desk, the moulded top above a frieze drawer with central hinged reading slope flanked by lidded wells, lacking one interior lid, 32½in (82.5cm) wide.
$10,500–12,000 *C*

A George III mahogany kneehole desk, the top with embossed leather, above 7 drawers to the kneehole, with inset cupboard and letter slide, raised on bracket feet, restored, 35in (89cm) wide.
$1,900–2,500 *Bon*

l. A George III style mahogany pedestal partners' desk, 19thC, 60in (152.5cm) wide.
$6,000–6,750 *S(NY)*

A mid-Victorian mahogany pedestal desk, the superstructure with 4 small drawers flanking a stationery compartment and sloping flap enclosing a well, the frieze with 2 side drawers and a panelled door and plinth base to each pedestal, 48in (122cm) wide.
$4,000–5,000 *Bea*

An early Victorian mahogany pedestal desk, the leather-lined top above 3 frieze drawers, each pedestal fitted with 3 drawers, on a plinth base, stamped 'I. Waterer & Son, Chertsey, 54½in (138.5cm) wide.
$4,000–5,000 *CSK*

A Victorian oak writing desk, the raised back with a galleried shelf flanked by 4 drawers, lift-up writing slope and 2 frieze drawers above 3 graduated drawers to each pedestal, plinth bases, 53½in (136cm) wide.
$1,500–1,800 *WL*

A Victorian mahogany pedestal desk, on shaped bracket feet, late 19thC, 54½in (138.5cm) wide.
$750–1,000 *Hal*

A George III mahogany pedestal partners' desk, with leather-lined top, restored, 72in (183cm) wide.
$6,750–7,500 *S(NY)*

A Victorian mahogany breakfront pedestal desk, the tooled leather inset top above a central frieze drawer, flanked by a pair of pedestals, each containing 4 graduated drawers flanked by canted corners and moulded corbels, on plinth bases, late 19thC, 53½in (136cm) wide.
$1,500–1,800 *Hal*

l. A mahogany pedestal desk, the top with a superstructure of 2 mahogany shelves each with a brass three-quarter gallery, on slender turned brass columns, brown gilt tooled leather-lined writing surface, 19thC, 44in (112cm) wide.
$2,700–3,000 *L*

A George III style mahogany pedestal partners'
desk, late 19thC, 82½in (209.5cm) wide.
$6,750–7,500 *S(NY)*

A late Victorian mahogany pedestal desk, the
raised back including a pair of drawers above a
leather inset top, with 6 drawers and a
cupboard, on a plinth base, labelled 'Goodall,
Lamb & Heighway Ltd, Cabinetmakers and
Upholsterers Manchester', 59¾in (152cm) wide.
$1,500–2,250 *S(S)*

l. A late Victorian walnut pedestal partners'
desk, with moulded leather-lined top and
6 frieze drawers, each pedestal with 3 drawers
and opposing panelled cupboard door, on
plinth bases, 60in (152.5cm) wide.
$3,250–3,750 *CSK*

A Victorian mahogany reverse
breakfront desk, by H. Goertz
of Windsor, the top with
thumb-moulded edge and
rounded corners, 9 graduated
short panelled drawers with
knob handles, the reverse
with a panelled door to each
pedestal enclosing shelves,
57in (145cm) wide.
$3,200–3,800 *HAM*

A walnut enclosed writing desk,
the adjustable top inset with a
panel of tooled leather, hinged
panelled sides and fitted interior
with an arrangement of drawers
and pigeonholes, with carpet
tread foot rests, raised on a
plinth base with casters, late
19thC, 28½in (72.5cm) wide.
$3,000–3,750 *P(E)*

A mahogany veneered cylinder
desk, with inlaid stringing and
satinwood banding, the fall with
brass lion mask knob handles,
interior with satinwood veneered
drawers, oak-lined with
pigeonholes and a pull-out
writing slide, square tapering
legs on brass casters, 19thC,
36½in (93cm) wide.
$2,600–3,000 *WW*

An Edwardian satinwood and
floral painted cylinder desk,
with three-quarter pierced
brass gallery, the cylinder flap
enclosing a fitted interior with
morocco writing slide, 35½in
(90cm) wide.
$3,750–4,500 *C(S)*

An Edwardian mahogany writing
desk, decorated with satinwood
crossbanding and stringing, with
brown leather-inset top, central
frieze drawer, stamped
'BESSANT, 2 Berners St, W',
54in (137cm) wide.
$4,000–4,500 *WIL*

An Edwardian light oak twin
pedestal desk, with brown
leather-inset top, each pedestal
fitted with 4 graduated drawers
with brass handles, central
drawer above kneehole, side
panels decorated with linenfold
decoration, 64in (162.5cm) wide.
$1,500–1,800 *WIL*

A Louis XV style gilt-bronze mounted tulipwood lady's desk, the superstructure with 4 drawers around an open recess surmounted by a clock dial, signed 'Le Faucheux, Paris', late 19thC, 50in (127cm) wide. **$18,000–20,250** *S(NY)*

A Louis XV style gilt bronze and lacquer tulipwood lady's desk, the upper section with 6 drawers surmounted by a three-quarter gallery centred by a clock with patinated putti, the sides fitted with a pair of foliate-scrolled candelabra, the lower section with an inset leather writing top above 2 frieze drawers raised on cabriole legs, lacquer panels depicting Chinese landscape scenes, late 19thC, 67in (170cm) wide. **$45,000–52,500** *S(NY)*

A Chinese export black lacquer and parcel gilt kneehole dressing table, decorated with Chinese figures, the moulded top with serpentine edge above one long over 6 small drawers, with recessed small drawers in the kneehole, raised on bracket feet, shrinkage crack to top, mid-19thC, 42in (107cm) wide. **$7,000–8,000** *S(NY)*

l. An American ormolu-mounted mahogany writing desk, the upper section with brass gallery above a pair of leather-covered drawers, the writing section with leather panel and frieze drawer, on scrolled legs ending in paw feet joined by a stretcher, damaged, c1825, 38in (96.5cm) wide. **$3,750–4,500** *S(NY)*

An inlaid mahogany shaped front lady's writing desk, early 20thC, 27in (68.5cm) wide. **$525–675** *JH*

An Edwardian inlaid mahogany kneehole music desk, the top with tooled leather inset, with boxwood stringing, ebony and satinwood feather veneer above the frieze, each drawer being fall-front for music, on square tapering legs terminating in brass casters, 48in (122cm) wide. **$825–975** *Mit*

A Russian neo-classical brass-mounted mahogany pedestal desk, the leather inset top with brass inset border, restored, 57in (145cm) wide. **$9,500–10,000** *S(NY)*

Dumb Waiters

A William IV mahogany dumb waiter, the telescopic top opening to reveal 3 shelves, on panelled end supports with turned crossbar and bun feet, 43¾in (111cm) high when open.
$5,600–6,000 *S*

A satinwood three-tier oval étagère, with removable glass tray, c1900, 28in (71cm) wide.
$2,600–3,000 *GAS*

A George IV two-tier dumb waiter, joined by 3 turned supports, on a turned column with 3 leaf-carved splayed legs with brass casters, 25in (63.5cm) wide.
$1,000–1,200 *DN*

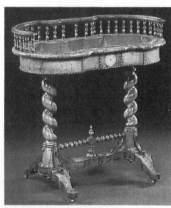

l. A Victorian mahogany three-tier buffet, each tier with a raised gallery and on baluster turned supports with ball finials, on tapered legs with brass cappings and casters, c1850, 48in (122cm) wide.
$750–900 *Hal*

An early Victorian mahogany three-tier dumb waiter, with an angled arched three-quarter ledge gallery, the tops with moulded edges, on turned uprights terminating in brass cappings and wheel casters, 48½in (123cm) wide.
$1,800–2,300 *P(E)*

Jardinières

A French kingwood veneered jardinière, with ormolu mounts and Sèvres style plaques, metal liner, c1880, 14in (35.5cm) wide.
$1,500–2,250 *GAS*

An early Victorian rosewood jardinière, with three-quarter spindle gallery and zinc liner, c1840, 39in (99cm) wide.
$3,250–3,750 *S*

A Regency rosewood jardinière table, with winter lid and replacement metal liner, c1810, 30in (76cm) wide.
$2,700–3,000 *GAS*

In Regency times there were no flowers available in winter and so a lid was used to cover up the gravel to show a normal table.

A French kingwood veneered and walnut jardinière, with ormolu mounts and metal liner, c1880, 13in (33cm) wide.
$900–1,000 *GAS*

A satinwood jardinière stand and metal liner, with painted urns and flowers, floral festoons and chains, on turned legs with curved stretchers, 19thC, 31in (79cm) wide.
$1,800–2,200 *P(S)*

The Tenterden Galleries

FLOWER HOUSE ANTIQUES

Flower House Antiques

FINE ENGLISH & CONTINENTAL FURNITURE,
COLLECTABLES,
VALUATIONS, RESTORATION,
ITEMS PURCHASED

90 High Street, Tenterden,
Kent TN30 6JB

Telephone: 01580 763764

Jan Byhurst

Heirloom Antiques

68 High Street,
Tenterden, Kent

We buy and sell quality
furniture, collectables,
jewellery, porcelain, silver.
A wide range of antique
and interesting items
always available.

Open 7 days a week

Full or part house
clearances undertaken,
sound advice given

01580 765535

GABY GUNST
ANTIQUE CLOCKS & BAROMETERS

George Prior London 1793-1830
3 train musical bracket clock with 4 tunes
on 12 bells, 62cm high, red lacquered case.

140 High Street, Tenterden, Kent
Tel: 01580 765818

3 showrooms of antique Longcase,
Grandmother, Skeleton, Bracket & Wall
clocks all restored in our own workshop.

Trading for 25 years. Closed Sundays

Sparks Antiques

English &
Continental
furniture,
objects
&
collectors'
items.

4, Manor Row,
Tenterden, Kent.
TN30 6HP

Tel: 01580 766696

Lowboys

A Chippendale figured walnut lowboy, with carving attributed to Bernard and Jugiez, Philadelphia, Pennsylvania, the centre drawer carved with a shell flanked by acanthus leaves, on cabriole legs ending in claw-and-ball feet, repaired, impressed stamp on the backboard 'I.S.', c1765, 34½in (87.5cm) wide.
$30,000–33,000 *S(NY)*

A George II walnut lowboy, the top crossbanded and chequer strung with re-entrant corners, on scroll-carved cabriole legs with pad feet, damaged, 31in (78.5cm) wide.
$3,000–3,750 *P*

r. An oak and mahogany crossbanded lowboy, with shaped top above one long and 2 small drawers, shaped apron, on cabriole legs and pad feet, 18thC, 31in (78.5cm) wide.
$2,250–3,000 *L&E*

A Dutch marquetry lowboy, the top inlaid with vases, floral sprays, mythical birds and scrolls, the frieze fitted with a single long drawer with brass handles, a shaped skirt below, on cabriole legs with heart-shaped feet, 18thC, 33in (84cm) wide.
$3,300–4,200 *Mit*

Miniature Furniture

A satinwood and rosewood banded miniature bowfronted chest of drawers, c1820, 16in (40.5cm) wide.
$1,500–1,800 *CBu*

A mahogany miniature display cabinet, the moulded cornice above an astragal glazed door enclosing a single mahogany shelf, on swept feet, c1820, 8in (20.5cm) wide.
$700–1,000 *JC*

A Victorian miniature sideboard, c1870, 25in (63.5cm) wide.
$300–450 *WLD*

> ### Miniature Furniture
> Small scale models of furniture were made in the 18th and 19thC by cabinet-makers as travelling samples or for window displays.

A miniature centre table, with marquetry decoration, c1860, 4in (10cm) diam.
$450–550 *WLi*

A French flame-figured mahogany miniature wardrobe, c1830, 24in (61cm) high.
$650–850 *MM*

A French miniature display table, veneered in red tortoiseshell, with ormolu mounts and original lining, c1870, 11in (28cm) wide.
$2,300–2,700 *GAS*

Mirrors

A George I gilt gesso mirror, the associated shaped plate within a foliate trailed slip with pounced ground, restored, later back inscribed 'Top' and '3', 40¼in (102cm) high.
$2,550–3,000 *C*

A George II parcel gilt walnut veneered wall mirror, c1755, 50in (127cm) high.
$15,000–17,250 *S(NY)*

A George III giltwood overmantel mirror, the divided mirror plate within a surround carved with a beaded border, C-scrolls and acanthus leaves, the cresting with a floral spray, some mirror plates replaced, slight damage, c1765, 54in (137cm) high.
$33,000–36,000 *S(NY)*

A George I giltwood mirror, c1715, cartouche and masks later, 54in (137cm) high.
$2,700–3,300 *S*

A pair of George II style giltwood pier mirrors, each pedimented cresting with a shell-shaped cartouche, the frieze with a female mask, foliage and scrolls, the mirror plate within a frame with egg-and-dart border and oak leaves, the shaped pendent with a lion's mask and a pair of eagles' heads, 19thC, 75in (190.5cm) high.
$23,250–24,750 *S(NY)*

An early George III giltwood mirror, with projecting pagoda canopy with columns, icicles and foliate urns, the plate flanked by columns with entwined foliage, icicles and C-scrolls with rocaille and cabochon ornament and swan below, 53¼in (135cm) high.
$6,000–6,750 *P*

A George II giltwood mirror, the frame carved with roses and ribbons and overlaid with leaves and scrolls, the double pierced shell cresting flanked by acorns and oak leaves, the apron centred by a mask, c1730, 50in (127cm) high.
$3,300–4,000 *S*

A George III mirror, with a giltwood carved frame, later mirror plate, 31in (78.5cm) high.
$1,800–2,200 *DN*

A George III giltwood mirror, 48¾in (124cm) high.
$6,000–6,750 *P*

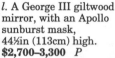

r. A mahogany adjustable zograscope, inlaid with boxwood and ivory chequered stringing, 18thC, 25in (63.5cm) high.
$450–530 *LCA*
This was originally a device for magnifying engravings, which could be converted to use as a shaving mirror.

l. A George III giltwood mirror, with an Apollo sunburst mask, 44½in (113cm) high.
$2,700–3,300 *P*

A George III giltwood mirror, the mirror plate within a beaded, moulded frame surmounted by a cresting in the form of a Prince of Wales' plume encircled by a coronet with ribbons at the sides, c1780, 20½in (52cm) high.
$4,500–5,250 *S(NY)*

A pair of George III style giltwood and gilt gesso girandôles, 19thC, 60in (152.5cm) high.
$52,500–55,500 *S(NY)*

An early Victorian giltwood overmantel mirror, by William Thrale Wright, restored, backboard inscribed, trade label, all mirror plates later, 78½in (199.5cm) high.
$3,750–4,500 *C*

A Regency mahogany cheval mirror, the swing plate within a ring-turned frame, on hipped splayed legs joined by a stretcher, 26½in (67.5cm) wide.
$2,250–3,000 *CSK*

A pair of George III style giltwood mirrors, in Chinese Chippendale style, 19thC, 51in (129.5cm) high.
$8,250–9,000 *S(NY)*

A Chippendale parcel gilt mahogany wall mirror, the shaped scrolled crest centring a phoenix flanked by incised gilt decorated scrolling vines, c1780, 41in (104cm) high.
$12,750–14,250 *S(NY)*

A George IV mahogany cheval mirror, the turned frame with ebonised mouldings, c1825, 61½in (156cm) high.
$2,000–2,500 *S*

A George III mahogany swing toilet mirror, with a bowfronted base, c1810, 20in (51cm) wide.
$850–1,000 *CBu*

A Victorian burr walnut dressing table mirror, raised on columns, standing on a base with 3 shaped drawers, 35in (89cm) high.
$650–750 *WIL*

A Victorian carved walnut console and mirror, applied with gilt-metal swivel hinged candle sconces, white marble top with C-scroll decorated apron, on cabriole legs with scroll feet, 96½in (245cm) high.
$5,250–6,000 *P*

A Victorian mahogany shaving mirror, the later plate hinged on turned supports, with a knopped turned stem and circular base, c1860, 29in (73.5cm) high.
$250–300 *Hal*

A gilt composition rococo style pier mirror, the shaped divided plate with an arched frame moulded with a flower stem, rocaille, C-scrolls and foliage, late 19thC, 89½in (227cm) high.
$950–1,000 *P*

A giltwood and composition mirror, with leafy cresting, tied with ribbon and hung with swags of husks, late 19thC, 68½in (174cm) high.
$3,000–3,750 *P*

A giltwood mirror, late 19thC, 45¼in (115cm) high.
$1,500–1,800 *P*

A giltwood overmantel mirror, late 19thC, 65½in (166cm) high.
$450–530 *P*

A Flemish ebonised and brass repoussé wall mirror, 19thC, 42½in (108cm) high.
$750–900 *P*

A Louis XV giltwood mirror, c1730, 80¼in (204cm) high.
$6,300–7,200 *S*

A north European giltwood mirror, the later plate within a bevelled mirrored outer border with foliate spray, with trade label of 'Messrs Stair & Andrew Ltd', regilt, restored, mid-18thC, 50¾in (129cm) high.
$10,500–12,000 *C*

A Second Empire style gilt-gesso pier glass, the triple arched plates with acanthus cresting, diaper and fluted column framework, surmounted by 2 cherub figures, 84in (213cm) high.
$1,000–1,200 *WL*

A Louis XV style gilt-plaster overmantel mirror, with scrolling foliate scrolls surmounted by a rocaille crest moulded on a grey painted ground, 19thC, 32¼in (82cm) high.
$600–700 *S(Am)*

Regilding

The original gilding on a very old mirror is likely to be in a poor state because of the effects of age and damp. Good professional regilding is acceptable, showing contrasts of burnished and matt areas, although the carved decoration beneath the gilding should be original.

A French giltwood mirror, the plate within a rope-carved frame, late 19thC, 57in (145cm) high.
$3,750–4,500 *S(NY)*

l. A repoussé gilt-metal, cut and moulded glass and semi-precious stone mounted mirror, replacements and losses, restored, one bracket later, possibly Venetian, c1700, 60in (152.5cm) high.
$30,000–33,000 *C*

A south Italian moulded glass and gilt gesso girandôle, glass restored, 18thC, 36in (91.5cm) high.
$4,500–5,250 *C*

A set of 4 Italian giltwood mirrors, one finial restored, 19thC, 19in (48.5cm) high.
$10,500–12,000 *C*

A Florentine wall mirror, the giltwood frame with scrolling acanthus, 18thC, 16¾in (42.5cm) high.
$350–550 *Bea*

Pedestals

A pair of George IV Irish mahogany pedestals, with printed paper label of 'P Ceppi & Sons', back feet replaced, restored, 45¾in (116cm) high.
$7,500–8,250 *C*

A pair of George III mahogany dining room urns and pedestals, the urns with lead-lined interiors, the plinths with plain friezes carved with gadrooned bosses, each with an inlaid cupboard door, restored, one stamped '105062', 72in (183cm) high.
$11,250–12,750 *C*

A George III mahogany dining room pedestal, with hinged top, later galleried interior, a hinged door to the base enclosing a plain part-lined interior, altered and restored, 16in (40.5cm) wide.
$1,800–2,300 *C*

A pair of George III mahogany dining room pedestals, attributed to Thomas Chippendale, each with stepped top above a plain frieze and panelled door, one with a metal-lined warming interior, the other with 2 mahogany lined drawers and a cupboard, the upper drawer fitted with a tap, the central drawer with a lead-lined removable well, on bracket feet, 38½in (98cm) high.
$27,750–29,250 *C*

Night Commodes

A George III mahogany night commode with pierced gallery and 2 doors, above a pull-out fitted slide with a shaped apron and brass handle, on straight legs, 21½in (54.5cm) wide.
$850–1,000 *DN*

A George III mahogany night commode, with a shaped tray top above a recess and a shaped pull-out fitting, tambour missing, 23¾in (60.5cm) wide.
$1,000–1,200 *DN*

A mahogany bowfronted night commode, with hinged top section, false drawer and doors, on bracket feet, 19thC, 25in (63.5cm) wide.
$350–550 *DN*

A George IV mahogany night commode, in the manner of Gillows, with hinged reeded top, hinged sides, and moulded supports, the commode section on turned tapered reeded legs, c1820, 21in (53.5cm) wide.
$4,500–5,250 *S*

A mahogany tray top commode, with shaped three-quarter gallery, pierced handles, a pair of panel doors and pull-out drawer, on square moulded legs, adapted, 19thC, 24½in (62cm) wide.
$750–900 *CSK*

Screens

A William IV mahogany fire screen, with a tapestry panel, 22½in (57cm) wide.
$550–700 *Bon*

A six-panel coromandel screen, decorated with Japanese scenes, c1900, 72in (183cm) high.
$3,750–4,500 *ORI*

l. A Victorian mahogany pole screen, inset with petit point needlework crest, on turned and lobed adjustable brass column with tripod base, 59in (150cm) high.
$450–520 *WL*

l. A Victorian faded rosewood pole screen, with a floral needlepoint woolwork panel in a carved frame, 60in (152.5cm) high.
$450–550 *WIL*

r. A Chippendale carved mahogany fire screen, fitted with an adjustable octagonal needlepoint panel depicting a shepherdess tending her flock, raised on acanthus leaf-carved cabriole legs on claw-and-ball feet, Boston-Salem, Massachusetts, c1760, 55¾in (141.5cm) high.
$82,500–90,000 *S(NY)*

A mid-Victorian simulated rosewood pole screen, the finial capped pole with a floral needlework screen, within a carved frame, on outswept legs, 60in (152.5cm) high.
$400–450 *Bon*

Sideboards

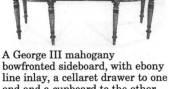

A George III mahogany bowfronted sideboard, with ebony line inlay, a cellaret drawer to one end and a cupboard to the other, 2 central drawers, one with an arched pull, brass lions' mask ring-pull handles, on turned tapering legs, 66in (167.5cm) wide.
$2,000–2,700 *TMA*

A George III mahogany sideboard, crossbanded in satinwood and inlaid with stringing, 46in (116.5cm) wide.
$2,500–3,000 *Bri*

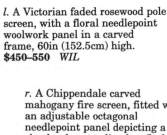

A George III mahogany sideboard, c1800, 44in (112cm) wide.
$1,400–1,800 *JH*

r. A Regency mahogany and ebony strung breakfront sideboard, with a frieze drawer and arched apron flanked by 2 deep drawers, on turned tapering legs, 74in (188cm) wide.
$2,250–3,000 *CSK*

l. A George III mahogany broken D-shaped sideboard, on ring turned legs, c1800, 48in (122cm) wide.
$6,000–6,750 *WLi*

A George III mahogany
breakfront sideboard, c1800,
59½in (151cm) wide.
$6,300–7,500 S

A Regency mahogany bowfront sideboard,
70in (178cm) wide.
$3,000–3,750 CSK

A George III mahogany sideboard, the double
crossbanded top above a frieze drawer with a
tambour cupboard below, flanked by deep cellaret
drawers, on square tapering moulded legs and
block feet, c1790, 60¼in (153cm) wide.
$8,700–9,300 S

Thomas Sheraton (1751–1806)

- Thomas Sheraton was born in poor
  circumstances in Stockton-on-Tees, north
  east England, in 1751.
- As a young man, he was employed as a
  journeyman cabinet-maker and his talent
  in both the mechanics of making furniture
  and its design soon became apparent.
- Having moved to London in about 1790, he
  used his skills as a writer and designer to
  support himself and his family.
- He published *The Cabinet-Maker's and
  Upholsterer's Drawing Book* in four parts
  from 1791–94.
- He was ordained a Baptist minister in
  1800, and published a number of
  religious tracts.
- His second book of designs, the *Cabinet
  Dictionary*, published in 1803, was less
  successful than his first.
- The last project he embarked on, *The
  Cabinet-Maker, Upholsterer and General
  Artist's Encyclopaedia*, was published
  incompletely in 1805, a year after his death
  in 1804.
- The term 'Sheraton style' is loosely applied
  to mahogany and satinwood furniture made
  c1790-1810.

A George III mahogany bowfront sideboard,
inlaid throughout with stringing, with
3 frieze drawers and a cellaret drawer,
c1790, 53¼in (135cm) wide.
$6,750–8,250 S

A Sheraton period crossbanded mahogany
breakfront bowed sideboard, inlaid with satinwood
bands and boxwood stringing, 60in (152.5cm) wide.
$4,200–4,800 MCA

l. A George III mahogany sideboard, the
crossbanded bowed top above a frieze drawer
and a recessed napery drawer, flanked by a
deep cellaret drawer and a pair of drawers,
on square tapering legs, formerly fitted with
a brass rail, c1790, 72½in (184cm) wide.
$5,250–6,750 S

A Regency mahogany sideboard, with ebonised line inlay, the breakfront top above a frieze drawer with an arched panelled drawer below, flanked by a pair of bowed cellaret drawers, on square chamfered legs and block feet, 72in (183cm) wide.
$1,500–2,250 *CSK*

An inlaid mahogany sideboard, some alterations, probably Scottish, c1830, 78½in (199.5cm) wide.
$10,500–11,250 *S(NY)*

A Regency mahogany sideboard, the top with wide crossbanding, above 4 frieze drawers, on tapered pedestal cupboards, one with cellaret drawer, each enclosed by a panelled door, on spayed feet, 77¾in (197.5cm) wide.
$1,200–1,300 *Oli*

A late Regency mahogany and rosewood sideboard, with a scroll and foliate crested back above 3 frieze drawers with crossbanding and quarter reel mouldings, above a single recessed panelled door enclosed by 2 further panelled doors, on flattened bun feet, 57¾in (146.5cm) wide.
$1,300–1,400 *P(C)*

A Regency mahogany twin pedestal sideboard, with brass rail back and 2 frieze drawers, each pedestal with a drawer above and a panelled door, one enclosing a cellaret, on bracket feet, 73in (185.5cm) wide.
$1,500–2,250 *Bri*

> **Use the Index!**
> *Because certain items might fit easily into any number of categories, the quickest and surest method of locating any entry is by reference to the index at the back of the book.*

A Victorian walnut sideboard, with mirrored back, a drop centre with grey marble shelf, all decorated with whitewood floral inlay, 60in (152.5cm) wide.
$800–1,000 *WIL*

A mahogany serpentine-fronted pedestal sideboard, with moulded arched mirrored backboard, the moulded frieze with a drawer and flanked by a pair of curved cupboards each faced with carving and enclosing a revolving container for bottles, drawer stamped 'Wilkinson & Son', c1850, 89in (226cm) wide.
$2,000–2,700 *S*

A Gothic revival oak side cabinet, with marble inset top, late 19thC, 32½in (82.5cm) wide.
$650–850 *Bon*

The revival in the popularity of medieval style began in the mid-18thC and continued well into the 19thC with such famous exponents as A. W. N. Pugin and Bruce Talbert.

l. A Sheraton style mahogany sideboard, with a single bowfront drawer flanked by drawers and a cellaret, on moulded block legs and spade feet, the whole with applied garlands and classical motifs, stamped oval brass handles, 19thC, 82¾in (210cm) wide.
$2,200–2,700 *WL*

Sofas

A Queen Anne walnut upholstered settee, repaired, early 18thC, 60in (152.5cm) wide.
$4,000–4,500 *S(NY)*

A pair of Queen Anne walnut settees, upholstered in tapestry, repaired, c1710, 37in (94cm) wide.
$55,000–60,000 *S(NY)*

A George II mahogany double chair-back settee, each yoke-shaped back with solid splat, the drop-in seat upholstered in velvet flanked by downscrolled arms, on hipped cabriole legs headed by shells and joined by stretchers, with pad feet, mid-18thC, 58in (147.5cm) wide.
$8,250–9,000 *CNY*

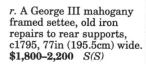

A George III sofa, with arched and rounded back, moulded swept arms and serpentine seat, on square tapering fluted legs with spade feet, one seat bearer replaced, 76½in (194.5cm) wide.
$4,000–5,000 *DN*

r. A George III mahogany framed settee, old iron repairs to rear supports, c1795, 77in (195.5cm) wide.
$1,800–2,200 *S(S)*

l. A George III mahogany framed settee, 72in (183cm) wide.
$3,000–3,750 *Bea*

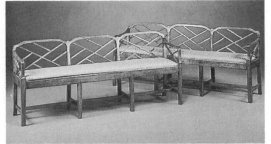

A pair of George III mahogany triple chair-back settees, each with pierced cockpen back rest and sides above a drop-in seat, raised on square legs joined by stretchers, repaired, each with a brass plaque on the top rail, 'ROUT SETTEE FROM THE BATH ASSEMBLY ROOMS/1771–1899', the underside of one with a brass plaque, 'W. Williamson & Sons UPHOLSTERERS, . . . GUILDFORD', 73¼in (186cm) wide.
$12,750–14,250 *S(NY)*

A Regency sofa, with mahogany show frame, 86in (218.5cm) wide.
$1,800–2,200 *DN*

A Regency mahogany settee,
76½in (194.5cm) wide.
$6,500–7,000 *C*

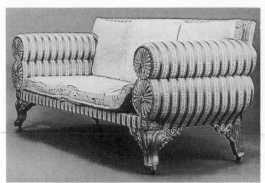

A Regency sofa, on giltwood moulded squat
cabriole legs, 91in (231cm) wide.
$5,000–5,750 *CSK*

A George IV mahogany sofa, attributed to Gillows
of Lancaster, later under-support,
79in (200.5cm) wide.
$5,250–6,000 *C*

A mahogany framed sofa, with overscrolled arms
carved with foliage and on reeded supports,
early 19thC and later, 72in (183cm) wide.
$825–975 *CSK*

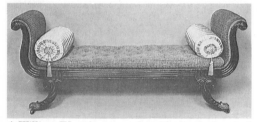

A William IV mahogany sofa, with classical arched
open roll arms, 78in (198cm) wide.
$1,500–1,800 *M*

Condition of Sofas

A sofa should be in basically good condition,
however, certain signs of wear are to be
expected. Sofas of any age will almost certainly
have been reupholstered, preferably with
webbing rather than springs. Prone surfaces
and carving will show evidence of wear,
especially along the seat rail.

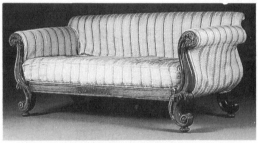

A William IV brass inlaid rosewood sofa, attributed
to Gillows of Lancaster, with pressed metal label
stamped 'ROBSON & SONS/MAKERS/
NEWCASTLE-ON-TYNE', 79in (200.5cm) wide.
$6,000–6,750 *C*

A William IV rosewood sofa, with a scroll, gadroon
and fan-carved crest rail, the arms faced with
carved foliate scrolls above a reel-turned border,
the turned and lobed legs with brass leaf terminals
and casters, 66in (167.5cm) wide.
$2,400–3,000 *DN*

A Victorian walnut sofa, the double-ended buttoned
padded back with foliate carved top rails flanking a
pierced foliate central panel above padded arms and
a serpentine seat, on acanthus-carved moulded
cabriole legs, c1860, 74in (188cm) wide.
$1,800–2,200 *Bon*

A Victorian carved walnut and upholstered settee, with a pierced arched cresting, the sprung seat flanked by crescent-shaped arms, on cabriole legs and ceramic casters, c1860, 64¼in (163cm) wide.
$1,200–1,500 *S(S)*

A Victorian double-ended buttoned back settee, in a simulated rosewood frame, the arms with moulded scroll uprights, on slender cabriole legs carved at the knees with shells, 68in (172.5cm) wide.
$1,300–1,500 *Oli*

A Victorian walnut settee, with twin upholstered high back ends, pierced and scrolled central splat, downswept arms with scrolled ends, on barley-twist legs with brass toes and casters, 34in (162.5cm) wide.
$1,400–1,800 *AH*

A Victorian sofa, in a rosewood show-frame, 69in (175.5cm) wide.
$1,500–2,200 *DN*

A walnut and caned sofa, the reeded frame carved with leaves and child mask terminals, with double cane-filled back and sides and serpentine seat, carved with rosettes and drapery, on square tapering fluted legs, 66in (167.5cm) wide.
$1,800–2,200 *DN*

An Edwardian mahogany framed settee, with caned panels and seat, cane damaged, 72in (183cm) wide..
$900–1,000 *WL*

A Chippendale mahogany camel-back sofa, repaired, New England, c1785, 90in (228.5cm) wide.
$9,500–10,000 *S(NY)*

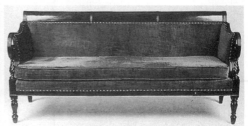

A carved mahogany veneered settee, probably Philadelphia, damaged, c1810, 74in (188cm) wide.
$2,000–2,500 *SK(B)*

Stands

A William IV walnut folio stand, c1830, 43in (109.5cm) high.
$6,000–6,750 *BUT*

A carved walnut duet music stand, the music rests with pierced lyre-shaped splats, the adjustable telescopic brass stem rising from a fluted and petal-carved turned stem, on tripod cabriole legs, c1860, 54¾in (139cm) high.
$2,250–2,500 *S(S)*

A mahogany coat stand, with reeded baluster stem, the central drawer carved with an armorial, on reeded pillar and down-curved legs, c1825, 85in (216cm) high.
$5,500–6,000 *S*

Steps

A set of Victorian mahogany library steps, the top 2 leather-lined bowfronted steps with hinged tops, above turned uprights, on turned tapering legs, 27in (68.5cm) high.
$1,200–1,400 *CSK*

A mahogany metamorphic side table/library steps, the hinged top enclosing collapsible treads, on square tapering legs with casters, casters impressed 'Cope's Patent', late 18thC, 34½in (87.5cm) high.
$7,500–8,250 *CNY*

A set of Victorian walnut metamorphic library steps, with 4 steps condensing to 2 table tops, on barley-twist supports with china casters and squared stretchers, 36in (91.5cm) high.
$1,800–2,200 *RBB*

Stools

A walnut stool, c1720, 30in (76cm) wide.
$1,800–2,200 *DeG*

A mahogany stool, with padded seat, on turned tapering fluted legs, c1785, 23in (58.5cm) wide.
$9,000–10,500 *S*

A mahogany hall stool, with dipped seat, on X-shaped legs with carved stylised flowerhead paterae, c1800, 21¾in (55cm) wide.
$5,000–5,750 *S*

A pair of carved giltwood stools, in the manner of William Kent, each with damask-covered seats, on turned tapering legs with leaf-carved lappets, guilloche carved collars and egg-and-dart carved feet, c1735, 25in (63.5cm) wide.
$22,500–24,000 *S*

A pair of mahogany stools, with brown hide drop-in seats, chamfered square legs joined by H-shaped stretchers, on leather casters, c1770, 19¾in (50cm) wide.
$4,500–5,250 *S*

A George III mahogany revolving piano stool, c1800, 15in (38cm) diam.
$875–975 *ANT*

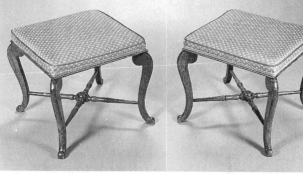

A pair of stools, on beech cabriole legs painted to simulate rosewood, with turned X-shaped stretchers centred with roundels, early 19thC, 18in (45.5cm) wide.
$1,125–1,275 *DN*

Miller's is a price GUIDE not a price LIST

A Regency mahogany stool, after the designs of Tatham, the seat with a reeded border and scroll ends, plain seat rails with central recessed panels, on tapering column legs, each with 3 flutes headed by roundels, with rounded feet, 33in (84cm) wide.
$6,750–7,500 *DN*

A mahogany gout stool, the adjustable angled foot rest with green leather upholstery, hinged to plain frame, on turned legs with brass caps and casters, restored, c1825, 21in (53.5cm) long.
$825–975 *Hal*

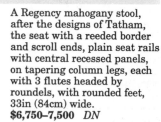

A Victorian beechwood stool, on turned sabre legs joined by stretchers, with geometric needlework seat, c1840, 18in (45.5cm) square.
$640–700 *S*

l. A pair of early Victorian rosewood stools, each with a drop-in seat on a moulded frieze, with canted scroll legs joined by turned X-shaped stretchers, c1840, 39in (99cm) wide.
$8,250–9,000 *S*

A needlework box frame stool, covered in grand point geometric needlework, c1850, 17in (43cm) wide.
$400–500 *S*

A mid-Victorian walnut stool, on shell-carved cabriole legs with scrolling feet, 23½in (59.5cm) wide.
$525-400 *CSK*

A maple stool, with needlework seat and flower carved scroll legs, c1860, 18in (45.5cm) square.
$1,000-1,200 *S*

A Louis XV giltwood footstool, carved with scrolled motifs, on cabriole legs, stamped 'I. Boucault', mid-18thC, 24in (61cm) wide.
$3,250-3,750 *S*

A Victorian rosewood duet stool, with individually adjustable padded seats and panelled seat rail, on turned and fluted legs with casters, stamped beneath 'H. Brooks and Co', and '94444', 43in (109cm) long.
$1,000-1,200 *DN*

A Victorian walnut stool, with upholstered seat, on cabriole legs with scroll feet, 33in (84cm) wide.
$1,250-1,350 *CSK*

A Victorian stool, the padded top on scrolling X-shaped frame supports joined by a turned stretcher, 16½in (42cm) wide.
$525-675 *CSK*

A Louis XVI style giltwood dressing stool, the beaded top rail with foliate terminals, above baluster turned uprights, with an oval padded seat, on gadrooned, turned and fluted legs, 19thC, 21in (53cm) wide.
$300-375 *CSK*

A Victorian rosewood stool, with padded seat in green cord material, on U-shaped end supports and splayed feet carved with leaf designs, 49½in (125.5cm) long.
$1,125-1,275 *DN*

A Louis XVI giltwood foot stool, the frieze carved with musical trophies and swags, on tapering feet, possibly Piedmontese, late 18thC, 19¼in (49cm) wide.
$3,250-3,750 *S*

Did you know?
MILLER'S Antiques Price Guide *builds up year-by-year to form the most comprehensive antiques photo-reference library available.*

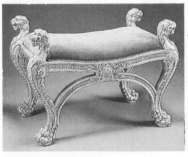

l. An Italian baroque style giltwood stool, the green velvet upholstered dipped seat on lion monopodia carved with leaves and ending in lion paw feet, the frame carved with foliage and a guilloche border, 19thC, 38in (96.5cm) wide.
$19,500-21,000 *S(NY)*

A pair of Italian giltwood stools, each with bowfront padded seat, the waved, channelled seat rail centred by a C-scroll and scallop shell clasp, on foliate trailed cabriole legs joined by a waved X-shaped stretcher, on claw feet, regilt, restored, mid-18thC, 19in (48.5cm) wide.
$7,000-8,000 *C*

Suites

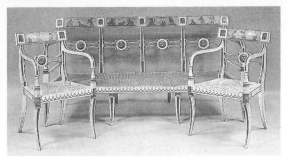

A Regency painted drawing room suite, comprising
a settee and a pair of armchairs, the top rails with
putti in grisaille between Egyptian masks and
C-scroll splats centred by lion masks, cane seats
and seat rails with interlaced ornament, on
polygonal sabre legs, restored, stamped 'J. G.'.
$5,250–6,000 *P*

A Victorian mahogany show frame sofa
and a pair of matching chairs, the sofa
with a shaped and scroll carved back,
scroll arms, serpentine seat and cabriole
legs, 76in (193cm) long.
$3,000–3,500 *DN*

A Victorian nine-piece walnut suite, with buttoned
green dralon upholstery, on turned and fluted legs,
restored, c1870, settee 72in (183cm) long.
$2,500–3,000 *S(S)*

A late Victorian walnut three-piece salon suite,
the button upholstered show frame backs with
carving, sprung seats and carved turned legs,
sofa 71¾in (182cm) long.
$2,250–2,750 *Bri*

A Victorian walnut-framed scroll-end
settee, the buttoned end with floral carved
cresting, on dwarf cabriole legs, carved at
the knees with shells, upholstered in gold
dralon, 72in (183cm) long, and a matching
gentleman's armchair upholstered in
crimson sculptured velvet.
$2,700–3,000 *Oli*

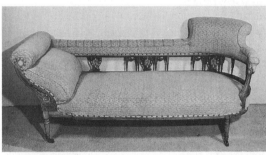

An inlaid rosewood three-piece suite, comprising a
chaise longue and a pair of armchairs, each with
padded backs above spindle and pierced panel
galleries, inlaid with strapwork and foliage, on
turned tapered legs with brass caps and ceramic
casters, c1895, chaise longue 73½in (186.5cm) long.
$1,125–1,275 *Hal*

A north Italian walnut suite, comprising
a settee and 2 matching armchairs, with
shaped top rails, padded backs, arms
and seats, on turned tapering legs, late
19thC, settee 74in (188cm) long.
$1,000–1,200 *CSK*

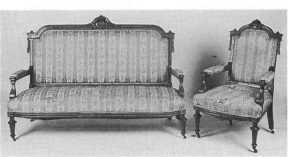

A Renaissance revival rosewood, marquetry and
gilt-incised four-piece suite, late 19thC, settee
64in (162.5cm) long.
$1,500–2,250 *SK*

Architects' Tables

A George III mahogany architect's table, the top with beaded edge above a shallow frieze and a frieze drawer concealed as 5 separate drawers enclosing a green baize-lined writing surface with adjustable reading slide, concealing a central well, 6 hinged lids with the letters of the alphabet, 2 containing sunken wells and concealing 2 further hidden wells, above a central kneehole with panelled door enclosing 2 compartments, flanked by 3 drawers on either side, lock stamped 'I. Bramah Patent', attributed to Gillows of Lancaster, 49in (124.5cm) wide.
$14,250–15,750 *C*

A George III mahogany architect's table, the top dividing to provide a ledge, the drawer front with brass drop handle, fitted interior with baize-lined writing surface concealing fitted compartment, 42in (106.5cm) wide.
$4,500–5,250 *L&E*

r. A mahogany architect's table, with ratchet top and adjustable candleholders, restored, late 18thC, 35¾in (91cm) wide.
$3,000–3,750 *SK*

A George III style mahogany architect's/artist's table, c1860, 24½in (62cm) wide.
$6,000–6,750 *S(NY)*

Breakfast Tables

A late Georgian mahogany breakfast table, with moulded edged hinged top, on carved raised column supported on 4 reeded and splayed legs with brass caps and casters, by Gillows of Lancaster, 48in (122cm) wide.
$2,300–2,600 *TMA*

A Regency mahogany breakfast table, the tilt-top with reeded edge, on a turned support with 4 downswept legs with brass claw feet and casters, re-railed, 55in (139.5cm) wide.
$1,000–1,200 *Bon*

A mahogany breakfast table, with crossbanded tilt-top above a turned stem with gadrooned collar, the tricorn base on anthemion carved scroll feet and casters, c1825, 47¼in (120cm) diam.
$6,000–6,750 *S*

A Regency rosewood breakfast table, with satinwood banded tilt-top, on a ring turned stem above a gadrooned platform, on hipped splayed legs with anthemion cast feet and casters, early 19thC, 47½in (120.5cm) diam.
$7,000–7,500 *CNY*

A George IV mahogany breakfast table, with tilt-top, on a turned tapering column with 3 reeded splayed legs, brass feet and casters, 56½in (143.5cm) wide.
$1,000–1,200 *DN*

r. A Regency brass inlaid rosewood and simulated rosewood breakfast table, the feet possibly replaced, restored, 54in (137cm) diam.
$8,750–9,500 *C*

A Regency rosewood breakfast table, with moulded rim tilt-top, above a tapering column with foliate lappeted platform below, on carved claw feet, with brass plaque stamped 'Improv.d Circular Loo table', 51in (129.5cm) diam.
$3,250–4,000 *CSK*

A Victorian walnut and floral marquetry breakfast table, bordered with lines, the crossbanded and quarter-veneered top with a moulded edge, centred by a panel with a spray of flowers and foliage, on a carved foliate baluster column with quadruped splayed supports and scroll feet, 55½in (141cm) diam.
$1,600–2,200 *P(E)*

A mid-Victorian burr walnut breakfast table, the top with inlaid border and moulded edge, on 4 turned supports and downswept legs, with acanthus carved feet and casters, 54in (137cm) diam.
$2,000–2,500 *Bon*

A William IV rosewood breakfast table, the tilt-top on a square column with gadrooned moulding, on a quadripartite plinth, with scrolled feet and casters, 52in (132cm) diam.
$1,800–2,200 *Bon*

A Victorian mahogany breakfast table, the tilt-top on baluster stem, with triple moulded cabriole legs and scroll feet, 48in (122cm) diam.
$1,000–1,400 *Oli*

An Anglo-Indian padouk breakfast table, the tilt-top with a carved border, on a turned column, with 4 leaf carved splayed legs and brass paw feet, 19thC, 63in (160cm) diam.
$1,000–1,400 *DN*

A brass-inlaid rosewood breakfast table, with tilt-top above a square standard on conforming plinth, on hipped downswept legs with brass casters, slight damage, c1830, 51in (129.5cm) diam.
$8,500–10,000 *S(NY)*

An early Victorian mahogany breakfast table, the rounded cornered tilt-top on turned column and splayed cabriole legs, 48½in (123cm) wide.
$1,850–2,250 *CSK*

An inlaid walnut breakfast table, the quarter-veneered top with band and string inlay, on 4 turned and geometrically carved supports, panelled and inlaid downswept legs, scroll feet and casters, c1870, 45¼in (115cm) wide.
$1,200–1,500 *Hal*

r. A mahogany breakfast table, the crossbanded top on a turned tapered pedestal, with downswept tripod base, brass caps and casters, c1790, 63in (160cm) wide.
$7,500–9,000 *S*

Card Tables

A George II walnut and burr walnut veneered card table, the divided hinged top inlaid with feather banding, the frieze with a drawer, on acanthus carved cabriole legs with claw-and-ball feet, 30¼in (77cm) wide.
$7,100–7,800 *Bea*

A serpentine mahogany card table, in the French style, with moulded top and cabriole legs with fan panels, c1770, 33in (84cm) wide.
$4,500–5,250 *S*

A rosewood card table, the top double banded in satinwood, with an engraved banding centred by a fan patera, the square tapering legs headed by oval paterae, the back 2 hinged, c1780, 38in (96.5cm) wide.
$6,000–6,750 *S*

A mahogany card table, the foldover-top with outset candle stand corners, on lappet carved turned tapered legs on pad feet, c1735, 34in (86.5cm) wide.
$4,100–4,800 *S*

A George III satinwood and marquetry foldover-top card table, with serpentine outline, the top inlaid with a fan medallion, rosewood bands and pendent husk chains, the frieze inlaid with a neo-classical urn and husk chain panel, tapering legs with inlaid husk chains, on block feet, 36¼in (92cm) wide.
$8,250–9,000 *P(S)*

A semi-eliptical mahogany card table, with boxwood stringing, c1790, 42in (106.5cm) wide.
$4,500–5,250 *MM*

r. A George III mahogany card table, the top with kingwood crossbanding and corded lines, the frieze similarly inlaid, the tapering moulded square legs headed by oval medallions ending in spade feet, 36¼in (92cm) wide.
$2,600–3,000 *Bea*

l. A George III mahogany card table, crossbanded and string inlaid, with folding D-shaped baize-lined top and panelled frieze, on 4 square tapering legs, 36in (91.5cm) wide.
$750–1,000 *AH*

A pair of serpentine-fronted mahogany tables, one for cards, the other for tea, with moulded tops, conforming friezes and square chamfered legs with pierced fret brackets, one c1765 the other later, 32⅜in (83cm) wide.
$10,500–12,000 *S*

A George III mahogany card table, the top centred by an inlaid patera, narrowly crossbanded and moulded edge, serpentine frieze, on moulded slender cabriole legs, 32in (81.5cm) wide.
$2,250–2,500 *L*

A veneered satinwood demi-lune card table, the frieze with crossbanded panels in rosewood, c1790, 36in (91.5cm) wide.
$4,500–5,250 *WLi*

A George III mahogany card table, with a shaped breakfront folding top and apron, crossbanded in satinwood with boxwood and ebony stringing, on square tapering legs headed by satinwood panels, 36in (91.5cm) wide.
$1,400–1,800 *DN*

A satinwood foldover D-shaped card table, banded and strung on double-action support, with narrow ring turned legs, in the manner of Gillows, c1800, 35½in (90cm) wide.
$2,000–2,500 *WL*

A walnut foldover-top card table, on plain column, with scroll feet, early 19thC, 36in (91.5cm) wide.
$2,000–2,400 *MR*

A mahogany veneered foldover card table, with beadwork decoration, c1800, 36in (91.5cm) wide.
$3,750–4,500 *WLi*

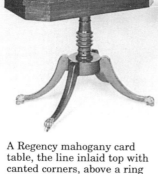

A Regency mahogany card table, the line inlaid top with canted corners, above a ring turned shaft on a platform, with 4 downswept legs, on claw feet, 36in (91.5cm) wide.
$1,500–1,800 *CSK*

An early Victorian rosewood card table, with folding swivel top, on a turned tapering column carved at the base with stylised leaves, on a circular base with 4 carved paw feet, 36½in (92.5cm) wide.
$820–1,000 *DN*

A William IV rosewood card table, with rounded edge top, column support with lotus carved collar, on a concave-sided platform with scroll toes, 36¼in (92cm) wide.
$1,250–1,500 *Bea*

A Victorian burr walnut card table, the shaped top with a moulded edge, on acanthus carved moulded cabriole legs, 38¼in (97cm) wide.
$1,800–2,000 *Bon*

A pair of rosewood card tables, each swivel top with rounded corners, on a tapering octagonal column, carved base and 4 scroll feet, c1840, 36in (91.5cm) wide.
$6,750–7,500 *S*

l. A pair of Regency fruitwood inlaid rosewood card tables, each hinged top with foliate inlaid borders, the frieze inlaid with a pair of mythical beasts and a lyre, on baluster supports and plinth with 4 down-swept inlaid legs, with brass feet and casters, damaged, early 19thC, 36in (91.5cm) wide.
$18,750–22,500 *S(NY)*

A George III inlaid mahogany D-shaped card table, on square tapering legs, 36in (91.5cm) wide.
$1,500–1,800 *MR*

A walnut serpentine card table, the hinged moulded top above a flower and foliate carved frieze, on flower-carved cabriole legs, restored, c1855, 33in (84cm) wide.
$750–1,000 *Hal*

A Victorian burr walnut serpentine-shaped card table, with lined folding swivel top, on turned and carved end supports, with splayed legs and a turned stretcher, 36¼in (92cm) wide.
$1,800–2,000 *DN*

An Edwardian satinwood card table, with divided top, each panel with a large oval, fitted with frieze drawer, on slender square tapering legs, 18¾in (47.5cm) wide.
$1,100–1,300 *L*

A Victorian rosewood card table, with a lined folding swivel top, above a shaped scroll-carved apron, on octagonal baluster column, concave-sided base with carved paw feet, 35⅜in (91cm) wide.
$900–1,000 *DN*

A brass inlaid and scarlet tortoiseshell card table, with serpentine outline, applied with gilt-metal mounts, the hinged top above a mask centred frieze, on cabriole legs with sabots, 19thC, 34in (86.5cm) wide.
$1,000–1,200 *CSK*

An inlaid satinwood card table, in the Sheraton style, with kingwood crossbanding and various stringing throughout, the breakfront D-shaped top centred by ovals, the frieze with trellis work and ovals, on square tapering legs joined by arched stretchers, early 20thC, 34¼in (87cm) wide.
$2,500–3,000 *Bea*

A Chippendale figured mahogany card table, with stop fluted serpentine front, Goddard-Townsend School, Newport, Rhode Island, c1780, 32in (81.5cm) wide.
$42,000–48,000 *S(NY)*

An Anglo-Chinese padouk card table, the foldover-top opening to reveal counter wells, the frieze with a drawer to either side, on shell carved cabriole legs with claw-and-ball feet, late 18thC, 33in (84cm) wide.
$3,600–4,200 *P(O)*

l. An Edwardian mahogany envelope card table, the quartered hinged top above a fretwork frieze drawer, on cabriole legs tied by a pierced stretcher, 21in (53.5cm) wide.
$600–750 *Bon*

A mahogany card table, with turret-like corners, thumb moulded drawer, cabriole legs and high pad feet, slight damage, replaced drawer handle, Boston, Massachusetts, c1740, 26¼in (66.5cm) wide.
$135,000–150,000 *SK(B)*

Centre Tables

A marble-topped and painted centre table, with fluted frieze, on turned and fluted legs, c1780, 47½in (120.5cm) wide. $4,200–4,800 S

A Regency mahogany centre table, the top with reeded edge above a frieze fitted with a drawer to either end, the centre support with 4 downswept reeded legs, with brass paw feet and casters, 36in (91.5cm) wide. $2,000–2,500 Mit

A veneered rosewood centre table, with brass stringing and star decoration to the base, c1815, 48in (122cm) diam. $10,500–12,000 WLi

A marquetry-inlaid walnut centre table, the gilt-tooled leather-inset serpentine top inlaid with C-scrolls and flowerheads, above a frieze drawer inlaid with foliate sprays and centred with a gilt metal mask, on cabriole legs with female mask espagnolettes and foliate sabots, c1860, 42in (106.5cm) wide. $4,000–4,500 Bon

A slate inset centre table, the top painted with flowers and exotic birds, on a hexagonal standard, with a concave-sided plinth, on lions' paw feet with casters, c1840, 48in (122cm) diam. $19,500–22,500 S(NY)

A micro-mosaic centre table, the black marble top inlaid with Pliny's doves and views of Rome, on an ebonised and parcel gilt base, with turned legs joined by an X-shaped stretcher and toupie feet, mid-19thC, 23¼in (59cm) diam. $4,000–4,500 P

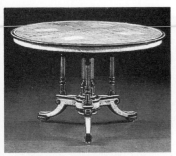

An amboyna centre table, with crossbanded and beaded top, on an ebonised and parcel gilt column, flanked by further columns, on 3 downswept legs, c1860, 45in (114cm) diam. $5,600–6,750 S

A marquetry-inlaid centre table, the top inlaid in various woods and mother-of-pearl with floral sprays, C-scrolls, butterflies and birds, on pierced lyre-shaped end supports, scrolled feet tied by a barley-twist stretcher, with paper label from 'F. Danbys upholstery and cabinet works, Leeds', inscribed 'No. 31073, workman's name J. Spence', c1860, 51½in (131cm) wide. $4,100–4,800 Bon

A Victorian figured walnut centre table, 59½in (151cm) wide. $2,700–3,000 P(O)

A Victorian carved oak centre table, the octagonal tilt-top with leaf-carved edge, deep frieze with trailing vine divided by protruding panels carved with masks in low relief, faceted stem, on spreading octagonal base, 48in (122cm) diam. $2,000–2,500 AH

l. A William and Mary style walnut parquetry centre table, the top with geometric panels, on barley-twist legs joined by an X-shaped stretcher, on bun feet, 19thC, 46½in (118cm) wide. $1,800–2,000 S(NY)

A Louis XVI brass-mounted and marble inset mahogany centre table, altered and damaged, 28in (71cm) diam.
$3,750–4,500 *S(NY)*

An Italian walnut centre table, the associated moulded top above a dentilled frieze with inset panels and one drawer, on ring-turned baluster legs joined by stretchers, basically 17thC, restored, 60½in 153.5cm) wide.
$7,000–8,250 *C*

A Louis XV/XVI style gilt-bronze and porcelain-mounted centre table, the marble top above a frieze fitted with Wedgwood medallions and foliate scrolls, on scrolled legs headed by rams' heads, late 19thC, 28½in (72.5cm) diam.
$12,000–13,500 *S(NY)*

A Dutch marquetry centre table, the top inlaid with an urn of flowers and birds and scrolling foliage, above a frieze drawer, on square tapering legs joined by a crossed platform stretcher, with bun feet, restored, 19thC, 42½in (108cm) wide.
$4,500–5,250 *S(NY)*

An Italian rococo painted and parcel gilt centre table, with *faux marbre* top above the serpentine apron centred by a shell, on cabriole legs with acanthus scrolled knees and hoof feet, mid-18thC, 29½in (75cm) high.
$4,800–5,700 *S(NY)*

A French Louis XV style kingwood and marquetry centre table, with serpentine outline and frieze drawer, on cabriole legs applied with brass mounts, early 20thC, 39in (99cm) wide.
$1,650–2,000 *WIL*

An Italian walnut centre table, with 2 frieze drawers and panelled sides, the lyre-shaped legs joined by a shaped stretcher, 17thC and later, 49½in (125.5cm) wide.
$14,250–16,500 *S*

A Russian decalcomania glass and parcel gilt centre table, decorated with chinoiserie scenes on a green background, glass cracked, restored, early 19thC, 22in (56cm) wide.
$7,500–9,000 *C*

An Anglo-Indian carved ebony and ivory inlaid centre table, the top inlaid with coromandel, sandalwood, satinwood and other various woods in a twist pattern, on a fluted column support, with scroll and foliate carved plinth, on quatrefoil platform base and carved flattened bun feet, c1840, 45in (114.5cm) diam.
$8,500–9,750 *S*

A burr yew and walnut centre table, with shaped top and bronze mounts, with 'Richardson & Son, Bond Street' label, c1870, 51in (129.5cm) wide.
$12,000–13,500 *BUT*

l. A Spanish walnut centre table, on spirally turned legs joined by strapwork carved stretchers and turned wrought iron supports, on bun feet, late 17thC, 50¾in (129cm) wide.
$4,200–4,800 *P*

Console Tables

A satinwood console table, the top veneered in segments radiating from an amboyna wood panel, with burr yew veneered top within a rosewood crossbanding, the blind fluted frieze on square tapering legs with square toes, c1790, 49½in (125.5cm) wide
$5,600–6,300 *S*

A Regency console table, with simulated rosewood graining, the top with rosewood veneer, with brass anthemion mount to the frieze, on giltwood front supports with lion mask and paw feet, on platform base, 51in (129.5cm) wide.
$3,750–4,500 *RBB*

A mahogany console table, in George II style, with a later painted simulated marble banded top, on 6 foliate decorated moulded scroll supports and scroll feet, with stencil mark '18' and letters 'L.D.R.', late 19thC, 63in (160cm) wide.
$1,800–2,250 *CSK*

A Louis XV walnut console table, with shaped grey and pink marble top, the frieze carved and pierced with a central rocaille with trellis and leaves, on curved and carved legs, Liègeois, mid-18thC, 53⅛in (136cm) wide.
$6,000–6,750 *S(Am)*

A giltwood and composition console table, the bowed breakfront white marble top above a fluted frieze centred and ribbon-tied with a wreath on husks, on fluted legs joined by an X-shaped stretcher and urn finial, late 19thC, 45in (114cm) wide.
$4,500–5,250 *P*

A Venetian stained pine, ebonised and parcel-gilt console table, in the manner of Andrea Brustolon, the moulded, shaped demi-lune top covered with simulated fabric, supported by a kneeling figure of Atlas, on an arched plinth with egg-and-dart border and partially covered by simulated fabric with foliage and flowers, restored, 19thC, 32½in (82.5cm) wide.
$14,250–15,750 *C*

Dining Tables

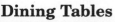

A George II mahogany drop-leaf dining table, on turned and tapered legs with carved hairy paw feet, c1750, 64in (162.5cm) extended.
$3,300–4,000 *S*

A George III mahogany dining table, with 3 pedestals, 2 D-shaped end sections, a central section and 2 extra leaves, restored, the underframe replaced in the 19thC, one leaf reduced, 116in (294.5cm) extended.
$12,000–13,500 *C*

A mahogany dining table, with 2 D-shaped ends and a centre drop-leaf section, on square tapering legs with boxwood stringing, early 19thC, 85¾in (218cm) long.
$2,500–2,700 *P(Sc)*

A mahogany dining table, with 2 pedestals and one extra leaf, early 19thC, 66in (167.5cm) extended.
$1,300–1,450 *CDC*

A mahogany dining table, with 2 pedestals, associated rounded top with tilting ends and reeded border, early 19thC, 110½in (281cm) extended.
$14,250–15,750 *S*

An early Victorian mahogany extending dining table, with 3 extra leaves, on 5 turned and reeded legs with brass casters, 118in (300cm) extended.
$6,750–8,250 *CAG*

A William IV mahogany dining table, stamped 'T. Willson/68 Great Queen Street', 65½in (166.5cm) extended.
$37,500–45,000 *C*

A Regency mahogany dining table, attributed to Gillows of Lancaster, with 7 extra leaves, on turned reeded baluster legs with brass casters, 201in (510cm) extended.
$30,000–33,000 *C*

A Regency mahogany dining table, in the manner of Gillows of Lancaster, comprising 2 D-shaped end sections, a central single flap gateleg section and 3 extra leaves, damaged and restored, 152in (386cm) long.
$6,300–7,200 *C*

A Regency mahogany dining table, with 4 extra leaves, restored, one leaf later, 138in (350cm) extended.
$11,250–12,750 *C*

Gillows

Founded in 1695 in Lancaster by Robert Gillow, a joiner, the firm of Gillows (later Waring & Gillow) grew and prospered in the 18thC, opening a London branch in what is now Oxford Street in 1761. The company's records, which go back as far as 1731, are now preserved in the Victoria & Albert Museum.

An early Victorian mahogany extending dining table, on an octagonal baluster column dividing to reveal a baluster turned leg support, with extra leaf, the rail stamped 'Meyer & Beckenn, St. Mary's Square Birmingham', 78in (198cm) long.
$6,300–7,200 *CSK*

A Victorian mahogany telescopic-action extending dining table, with D-shaped ends and moulded edge, plain frieze, with 6 additional leaves, c1867, 53½in (136cm) extended.
$3,750–4,500 *HAM*

A mid-Victorian mahogany dining table, with 5 extra leaves, 190in (482cm) extended.
$5,250–6,000 *L&E*

A Federal mahogany veneer dining table, in 3 parts, old refinish, Boston, Massachusetts, c1800, 161in (409.5cm) long.
$4,800–5,500 *SK(B)*

An early Victorian mahogany extending dining table, including 2 extra leaves, 70in (178cm) long.
$2,250–2,700 *CSK*

Dressing Tables

A George III mahogany dressing table, the hinged divided top inlaid with stringing, enclosing an adjustable mirror, compartments and lidded boxes, with 3 frieze drawers, on square tapering legs, c1790, 24in (61cm) wide.
$3,000–3,750 *S*

A George III mahogany dressing table, the twin-flap hinged top enclosing a fitted interior with a toilet mirror, on square tapering legs joined by concave undertier, 28in (71cm) wide.
$1,500–1,800 *CSK*

A George III mahogany and inlaid lady's dressing table, the kingwood crossbanded hinged top enclosing an adjustable mirror and 6 lidded compartments, on square tapering legs with brass caps and casters, 24¾in (63cm) wide.
$4,000–4,500 *P*

A George III mahogany enclosed dressing table, the interior with an adjustable mirror and 4 hinged lidded compartments, with a slide below, on square tapering legs with block feet, 27½in (70cm) wide.
$750–900 *DN*

A late George III mahogany enclosed dressing table, with a hinged top enclosing an adjustable mirror, with lidded and other recesses, above 3 false frieze drawers and 2 short drawers, flanking a drawer fitted for a basin, slight damage, 30½in (77.5cm) wide.
$2,000–2,250 *DN*

A late George III inlaid mahogany kneehole dressing table, with boxwood banding and quadrant fan medallions throughout, the top above one long and 2 short drawers, on moulded square tapering legs with spade feet, 40¼in (102cm) wide.
$1,200–1,350 *Bea*

A Victorian burr walnut dressing table, with arched bevelled mirror supported on fretted brackets above 6 small drawers, with central compartment, the bow-shaped table with single drawer and 2 turned front legs, 48in (122cm) wide.
$1,100–1,200 *WIL*

A Regency mahogany knee-hole dressing table, outlined with boxwood stringing, 46¾in (119cm) wide.
$1,100–1,250 *Bea*

An Edwardian mahogany *poudreuse*, in the shape of a harpsichord, with a hinged lid, 47in (119.5cm) wide.
$950–1,100 *WIL*

l. A marquetry dressing table, the lift-up mirrored top inlaid with a vase of flowers, a single small drawer and a writing slide, the square tapered legs with striped veneer, 29in (73.5cm) wide.
$1,100–1,250 *EL*

Drop-Leaf Tables

A George II red walnut drop-leaf table, 37in (94cm) diam.
$3,000–3,750 *P*

A George II mahogany gateleg table, restored, 51½in (131cm) wide.
$670–830 *Bon*

An early George III mahogany drop-leaf dining table, 54in (137cm) extended.
$1,350–1,500 *CSK*

l. A Queen Anne figured walnut drop-leaf dining table, the top with D-shaped hinged leaves above a shaped skirt, on circular tapering legs with pad feet, Newport, Rhode Island, c1750, 57in (145cm) extended.
$3,000–3,750 *S(NY)*

Drop-leaf Tables

In the 18thC the gateleg table was superseded by the more refined drop-leaf dining table. Most of these were constructed in either Virginia walnut or mahogany. They are more comfortable to sit at than gatelegs, as they have fewer legs and no stretchers; also, the overhang of the table is greater.

During the Chippendale period the D-ended dining table was introduced. This consists of 2 D-shaped ends which fit into a rectangular drop-leaf table. They are supported on square chamfered legs, usually 12, which can make the table awkward to sit at. This problem was resolved c1780 with the introduction of the pedestal dining table comprising 2, 3 or 4 pedestals with leaves that clipped in between.

The Victorians introduced dining tables that extended by means of a cranking action and a mechanism of interlocking bearers that did away with the need for excessive numbers of legs. Most have only 4 legs.

Drum Tables

A George III mahogany drum table, restored, 48in (122cm) diam.
$3,750–4,500 *SK*

A George III mahogany drum table, c1800, 41in (104cm) diam.
$17,250–19,500 *S*

A George III mahogany drum table, the gilt-tooled top above 2 frieze drawers and 4 simulated drawers, above a ring turned baluster shaft, on downswept tripod base with brass caps and casters, the base probably associated, 28¾in (73cm) diam.
$10,000–11,250 *C*

A George III mahogany drum rent table, the leather inset top raised above 4 real and 4 dummy drawers, each numbered for rent and with varying keys, raised on a turned and reeded pedestal on 4 reeded legs with brass paw toes and casters, 47in (119.5cm) diam.
$6,750–7,500 *B*

A George IV mahogany drum table, c1820, 40in (101.5cm) diam.
$6,300–7,200 *S*

A George IV stained rosewood drum table, with 4 mahogany lined drawers and 4 hinged compartments, the associated ebony inlaid mahogany base with spreading convex-fronted quadripartite supports, above a concave-fronted square platform, on reed scrolled downswept legs with brass caps and casters, restored, the base early 19thC, 53in (134.5cm) diam.
$5,250–6,300 *C*

Games Tables

A pair of George III bone-inlaid marquetry demi-lune games tables, each top crossbanded and inlaid, opening to a baize-lined playing surface above a frieze inlaid with foliage and a shell, on straight tapering inlaid legs with spade feet, repaired, late 18thC, 36in (91.5cm) wide.
$14,250–15,750 *S(NY)*

A Regency brass-mounted rosewood games table, the removable top with games board on the reverse, early 19thC, 27in (68.5cm) wide.
$2,500–3,000 *S(NY)*

A Regency satinwood, ebonised and parcel-gilt games table, with tripod base, redecorated, c1815, 20in (51cm) square.
$5,250–6,000 *S*

A Regency brass-inlaid and bronze-mounted part ebonised calamander games table, the hinged brass inlaid top above a plain frieze, opening to a baize-lined surface, c1815, 36in (91.5cm) wide.
$25,500–30,000 *S(NY)*

A Victorian rosewood serpentine-shaped games/work table, the folding swivel top inlaid with chequer and backgammon boards and a cribbage scorer, above a drawer and sliding wool bag, on turned legs, 21½in (54.5cm) wide.
$830–1,000 *DN*

A George IV games table, the square tip-up top with a chequerboard and sycamore border decorated with flowers and leaves in penwork, on an ebonised column surmounted by a drawer, painted with beads and leaves, on a triform leaf-carved base, 27½in (70cm) high.
$670–830 *DN*

A French ebonised and thuya wood games table, veneered with a chessboard on one side and a baize-lined surface on the other, with shaped friezes, on cabriole legs with engraved brass sabots, the lockplate engraved 'Alph. Giroux à Paris', c1860, 39in (99cm) wide.
$1,200–1,350 *Hal*

A late Victorian ebony-inlaid satinwood secrétaire games table, the top with sliding central section, inlaid with a chequerboard to the reverse and enclosing a fitted interior with a backgammon board, above a frieze drawer enclosing a writing surface and 6 drawers, on ring turned reeded tapering legs with brass caps and ceramic casters, 29½in (75cm) wide.
$5,600–6,750 *C*

l. An Italian rococo inlaid walnut games table, repairs to top veneer, late 18thC, 30½in (77.5cm) wide.
$4,500–5,250 *S(NY)*

A George IV mahogany games table, the reversible top with a chequerboard, above one drawer and spool borders, on a turned reeded and leaf-carved column on a concave-sided base with turned feet, the column reduced in height, 21in (54cm) wide.
$830–900 *DN*

Hunt Tables

A George III mahogany hunt table, late 18thC,
96in (244cm) long.
$9,300–10,500 *S(NY)*

A mahogany hunt or wake table, late 18thC,
67½in (171.5cm) long.
$5,250–6,000 *S*

l. A mahogany hunt
or wake table, with
a drawer at each end
and 8 square moulded
legs, the centre
4 hinged, late 18thC,
58½in (148.5cm) diam
when open.
$3,000–3,750 *S*

Library Tables

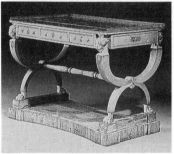

A Regency ormolu-mounted
rosewood and parcel gilt
library table, the top with
three-quarter arcaded gallery,
above beaded frieze drawers
with palmette lockplates and
star-shaped handles, on
X-shaped end supports headed
by leopard masks and joined
by a turned stretcher, on a
stepped plinth with concave
front and back, altered c1830,
46½in (118cm) wide.
$52,500–63,000 *C*

A George III mahogany library
table, the octagonal leather-
inset top above 4 real and
4 false drawers, on a ring
turned stem, with splayed legs,
brass feet and casters, late
18thC, 28in (71cm) high.
$5,250–6,000 *CNY*

A George IV rosewood and brass-
mounted library table, the top
with double brass moulded edge
on a turned column and tricorn
base, with later cast brass
casters, 47¼in (120cm) diam.
$13,000–14,600 *S*

A Regency brass-inlaid
rosewood library table,
attributed to Gillows of
Lancaster, the top with
arabesque band along the
border, above a shallow
frieze with beaded edge,
48in (122cm) diam.
$17,250–19,500 *C*

> **Miller's is a price GUIDE
> not a price LIST**

A William IV rosewood library
table, the top with chamfered
crossbanding, above an ogee
moulded frieze, with 2 pairs of
opposing drawers, the turned
pedestal support with a carved
lotus leaf collar on a shaped
platform base, with foliate scroll
carved feet and casters, c1835,
54in (137cm) wide.
$9,800–10,800 *S*

A William IV mahogany
library table, with leather-
lined top, long shallow frieze
drawer, on double moulded
C-scrolls with scroll feet,
joined by a turned stretcher,
36in (91.5cm) wide.
$1,000–1,100 *WIL*

r. An early Victorian
rosewood library
table, the rounded
top above 2 frieze
drawers, on end
standards with paw
feet, stamped
'T Willson, 68, Great
Queen Street',
57in (145cm) wide.
$3,750–4,500 *CSK*

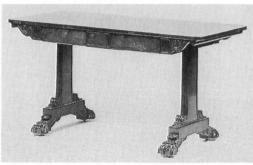

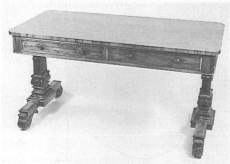

A Regency rosewood library table, the 2 frieze drawers with turned wood handles, on trestle end stretchered supports carved with stiff leaves, on acanthus scroll feet with inset casters, 56¼in (143cm) wide.
$3,750–4,500 *P(G)*

A mahogany double-sided pedestal library table, the moulded top lined in leather, with projecting round corners with lion monopodia, each pedestal with a door in the front and back with arched pierced fret panel, each panelled end carved with a coat-of-arms and hinged to enclose folios, stamped 'Strahan' and with trade label, c1850, 76in (193cm) wide.
$37,500–42,000 *S*

A rosewood library table, the top with canted corners and bead and reel mouldings, a pair of frieze drawers, with flat-shaped end supports, on scroll feet, c1840, 53½in (136cm) wide.
$4,500–5,250 *S*

A Regency brass-mounted rosewood library table, with three-quarter brass gallery, c1815, 41in (106cm) wide.
$33,000–37,500 *S*

A Victorian library table, the top with a deep moulded edge, veneered with random shapes of indiginous and imported cabinet timbers, on a tapering octagonal column, with tricorn platform and scroll feet, c1850, 50in (127cm) diam.
$8,700–9,750 *S*

Nests of Tables

A set of Regency rosewood quartetto tables, on slender ring turned end supports with splayed feet, restored, largest 21in (53.5cm) wide.
$2,250–2,500 *Bea*

A set of George III style satinwood quartetto tables, inlaid with stringing, c1880, largest 20in (51cm) wide.
$5,250–6,000 *S(S)*

Nests of Tables

Nests of tables were an ingenious space-saving late 18thC invention consisting of sets of 3 or 4 tables. Edwardian nest tables are about two thirds the height of Regency ones and considerably less expensive. Early nests of tables are light and elegantly simple in design, becoming more ornate during the 19thC, before returning to the Georgian style in Edwardian times. Rosewood and mahogany are the most common woods used. The largest table top is frequently paler than the small tables, being more often exposed to sunlight.

r. A nest of 3 Edwardian mahogany quartetto tables, largest 21in (53.5cm) wide.
$450–520 *Bon*

l. A nest of 3 Edwardian Sheraton style walnut tables, inlaid with boxwood stringing, on 2 pairs of ring turned columns and splayed feet joined by a stretcher, largest 18in (45.5cm) wide.
$300–380 *Gam*

Occasional Tables

A Victorian figured walnut occasional table, the borders carved with scrolled leafage and oval bead mouldings, on 4 moulded scroll supports with swept-in platform and conforming legs and casters, 48in (122cm) wide.
$2,600–3,000 *CAG*

A Victorian walnut and floral marquetry occasional table, the ebonised turned pillar with a further tier of quadruple ebonised turned supports, on a quatreform base with turned feet, c1860, 28½in (72.5cm) high.
$3,750–4,500 *S*

A pair of George III mahogany tables, c1800, 18in (46cm) wide.
$7,500–8,250 *S*

An Edwardian mahogany and inlaid occasional table, the top with floral inlay decoration, on square section tapering supports tied by a shelf stretcher, 24in (61cm) wide.
$670–750 *Bon*

A mahogany tripod occasional table, the tilt-top on a turned gadrooned column and splayed cabriole legs, with pointed pad feet, 19thC, 54in (137cm) wide.
$900–1,100 *CSK*

r. A Louis XV/XVI transitional parquetry table, the galleried top of Spanish *broccatello* marble, on cabriole legs, joined by a galleried flat stretcher inlaid with a rosette, stamped 'C. Topino Jme', c1775, 12½in (32cm) diam.
$30,000–36,000 *S*

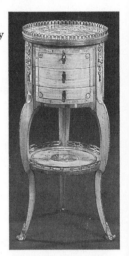

A Louis XVI style ormolu-mounted mahogany occasional table, the veined marble top above a frieze with a single drawer, decorated with playful putti and ribbon-tied floral swags, on fluted turned tapering legs, c1880, 22in (56cm) diam.
$1,800–2,250 *Bon*

A French tulipwood and brass bound occasional table, with a drawer to one end, late 19thC, 16¼in (41cm) wide.
$750–830 *P*

A Louis XV style marquetry inlaid rosewood occasional table, the hinged top inlaid with foliate scrolls with a mirror to the reverse, above a similarly inlaid frieze with a drawer, on square section cabriole legs with foliate gilt metal mounts, c1880, 18½in (47cm) wide.
$2,250–2,700 *Bon*

Pembroke Tables

A George III fiddleback mahogany Pembroke table, crossbanded in tulipwood and inlaid with ebonised and boxwood lines, restored, 38½in (98cm) wide.
$3,000–3,750 *C*

A George III satinwood Pembroke table, the moulded twin-flap top crossbanded in mahogany with ebonised edge and frieze drawer, on turned tapering legs with brass caps and casters, 28¾in (73cm) wide.
$11,250–12,750 *C*

A George III mahogany Pembroke table, the 2 drop leaves with rounded corners and a boxwood and ebony strung border, 39½in (100.5cm) wide.
$600–670 *DN*

A late George III mahogany Pembroke table, the 2 drop leaves with rounded corners, one drawer, on square tapering legs with spade feet, 37in (94cm) wide.
$670–750 *DN*

A George III mahogany Pembroke table, with 2 boxwood strung drop leaves, an ebony edged drawer to each end with brass knob handles, on narrow tapering turned supports with casters, joined by X-shaped stretcher, 36in (91.5cm) wide.
$3,300–3,750 *BWe*

A George IV mahogany Pembroke table, crossbanded in satinwood, fitted with a drawer to each end flanked by carved thistles, 49in (124.5cm) wide.
$900–1,000 *DN*

A satinwood butterfly-shaped flap Pembroke table, the top with central oval mahogany inlay, with crossbanded and line inlaid border, single end drawer, on rosewood-inlaid square tapering legs, late 19thC, 34in (86.5cm) wide.
$3,300–4,000 *HOLL*

An Adam style painted satinwood Pembroke table, with 2 drawers, c1890, 14½in (37cm) wide.
$8,250–9,000 *BUT*

A George III satinwood and marquetry Pembroke table, c1770, 37½in (95.5cm) wide.
$24,000–27,000 *CNY*

l. A satinwood Pembroke table, crossbanded with kingwood, with butterfly-shaped drop leaves and a single drawer, c1890, 34in (86.5cm) wide.
$8,250–9,000 *BUT*

A George III satinwood and marquetry Pembroke table, c1780, 36in (91.5cm) wide.
$135,000–150,000 *CNY*

Pier Tables

A pair of George II carved giltwood pier tables, the marble tops above fluted breakfront friezes, centred by pierced rococo cartouches, the cabriole supports with guilloche and scale-carved decoration, headed by foliate scroll knees and paterae, on scroll feet, with alterations, 34¼in (87cm) wide.
$19,000–21,750 S

A George III marquetry and painted pier table, the semi-circular harewood top with trailing floral border centred by an oval mahogany medallion inlaid with a spray of roses, tulips and dianthus, the base with a swag decorated frieze, on moulded tapering square legs headed by paterae, c1780, 50in (127cm) wide.
$6,000–6,750 S

A George IV rosewood pier table, with carved capitals to the front legs, c1825, 29in (73.5cm) wide.
$3,000–3,750 WLi

Reading Tables

l. A William IV satin birch pedestal reading table, the rounded top with hinged ratcheted surfaces, on adjustable lotus-carved column and quadripartite base, with reeded bun feet, 42in (106.5cm) wide.
$1,100–1,300 CSK

r. A mahogany reading table, with adjustable top, beaded edge, and adjustable melon-lobed column, on 3 swept legs with brass caps and casters, 19thC, 20in (51cm) wide.
$750–820 WL

Serving Tables

A George III mahogany serving table, the quarter-veneered moulded serpentine top above a frieze with a panelled drawer with stylised heart-shaped tracery, on tripartite fluted columnar supports, with a central hatched block and terminating in a fluted block foot, slight damage and minor restoration, 66½in (169cm) wide.
$60,000–67,500 C

A Victorian mahogany three-tier marquetry serving table, with lift-off glass tray, c1890, 33in (84cm) wide.
$4,800–5,700 BUT

A George III mahogany serving table, the eared canted crossbanded top inlaid with a boxwood and ebonised line above a plain frieze centred by a laurel swag, on fluted square tapering legs on collared feet, minor restorations, 53½in (136cm) wide.
$13,000–15,000 C

l. A Regency brass-mounted mahogany serving table, with Etruscan black and palm wrapped border, an ormolu enriched frame and Egyptian bas-relief frieze tablet displaying Ureus, emblematic of the sun god Re, slight damage and some veneer restored, 102¼in (259.5cm) wide.
$30,000–36,000 C

A late George III mahogany serving table, the square tapering legs with pierced fret brackets, 75½in (192cm) wide.
$3,300–3,750 DN

Side Tables

A William and Mary oyster olivewood side table, the top with concentric oval sycamore stringing and banding, the frieze drawer above ash spiral twist turned supports joined by shaped stretchers, on later bun feet, drawer relined, c1690, 31½in (80cm) wide.
$7,500–8,250 *S*

A Regency mahogany side table, the grey fossil marble top above a plain moulded frieze, on quadripartite pillars on a square plinth and rectangular base, some damage and losses to veneer, 72¼in (183.5cm) wide.
$60,000–67,500 *C*

An Irish George III oak side table, with a pierced Gothic arcaded frieze, restored, 78½in (199.5cm) wide.
$14,250–16,500 *C*

A George III mahogany side table, the top above a plain frieze with carved ribbon and paterae beading, the moulded chamfered square legs headed by Gothic blind-fret angle brackets, c1760, 73½in (187cm) wide.
$4,500–5,250 *S*

Side Tables

Side tables, used as serving tables, became fashionable from c1730 and remained popular until the Regency period. Early examples, frequently with marble tops, were of imposing proportions and heavily carved. Some were gilded. Thomas Chippendale developed a lighter style which continued to the end of the 18thC. While the emphasis of the late 18thC was on restrained elegance, a grander style returned during the Regency period, exemplified by the designs of Thomas Hope and George Smith.

A George III satinwood side table, inlaid with stringing and kingwood crossbanding, c1780, 45¼in (115cm) wide.
$10,500–12,000 *S*

A George II walnut side table, the shaped apron with a central shell motif, on cabriole legs with palm leaf carved knees and paw feet, c1735, 35in (89cm) wide.
$9,000–10,500 *S*

A George II mahogany side table, the later breccia marble top above a curved frieze and moulded apron, on cabriole legs headed by acanthus carving and flowerhead terminals, on claw-and-ball feet, 39½in (100.5cm) wide.
$26,250–30,000 *C*

A George II mahogany side table, the associated marble top with stepped moulded edge, above an egg-and-dart cornice and plain frieze, with ribbon-and-rosette edge, the front centred by a later bold pierced acanthus scroll, on cabriole legs on lion paw feet, restorations and shape possibly altered, 51¾in (131.5cm) wide.
$24,750–30,000 *C*

A William IV mahogany side table, with a plain top and apron, cabriole front legs, carved with stylised leaves, anthemion, rosettes, on claw feet, on a concave-fronted platform base with a nulled border, 72¾in (185cm) wide.
$4,800–5,500 *DN*

A German giltwood side table, the marble top above a pierced frieze carved with a central confronting C-scroll and flowerhead-carved cartouche, marble chipped and repaired, split to stretcher, mid-18thC, 47in (119.5cm) wide.
$15,000–18,000 *C*

A George IV mahogany side table, the reeded top above 3 frieze drawers, raised on ring turned tapered legs, altered, c1820, 40in (101.5cm) wide.
$450–530 *Hal*

A William IV Anglo-Indian padouk side table, the 3 frieze drawers with nulled borders, on leaf and tracery carved end supports joined by a shaped platform, 2 scroll brackets missing from base, 54in (137cm) wide.
$1,000–1,100 *DN*

A Dutch walnut and floral marquetry side table, with a drawer in the shaped frieze, on cabriole legs with floral ornament, 18thC, 29in (74cm) wide.
$4,500–5,250 *P*

A pair of Edwardian satinwood demi-lune tables, each top painted with 12 roundels depicting allegorical figures and inlaid with foliage and radiating panels, 60in (152.5cm) wide.
$27,750–30,000 *S(NY)*

An early Louis XV giltwood side table, the later serpentine-fronted liver marble top above a pierced waved frieze centred by a foliate adorned female mask within a C-scroll cartouche flanked by acanthus and foliate trails on a hatched ground, gilding restored, printed label, 62½in (159cm) wide.
$70,000–75,000 *C*

Sofa Tables

A Regency rosewood sofa table, the top with rounded corners, broad border and diamond pattern inlay, with a pair of frieze drawers, on a pair of turned pillars and canted sabre legs, c1815, 58½in (148.5cm) long extended.
$5,250–6,000 *S*

A Regency brass-inlaid and ebonised sofa table, the twin-flap top crossbanded in rosewood, above a pair drawers, flanked by foliate panels, on twin spirally reeded end supports and panelled scrolled downswept legs, with brass caps and casters, restorations, 66¼in (168.5cm) wide.
$7,500–9,000 *C*

A mahogany sofa table, with a moulded edge, 2 drop leaves, 2 centrally locking frieze drawers, on boxwood strung end supports with splayed legs, chased brass terminals and central turned stretcher, early 19thC, 55¼in (140.5cm) wide.
$1,500–1,800 *DN*

A Regency rosewood and brass-inlaid sofa table, the crossbanded top with a pair of hinged leaves, above a frieze containing a single drawer, inlaid with foliage and flowerheads, raised on a baluster profile stem and 4 down-curved legs ending in brass lions' paw feet and casters, c1815, 60in (152.5cm) long extended.
$2,000–2,500 *Hal*

A Regency rosewood sofa table, inlaid with tulipwood bandings, c1815, 60½in (154cm) long extended.
$6,600–7,200 *S*

Sofa Tables

The sofa table was developed from the Pembroke table towards the end of the 18thC. It is longer and usually narrower than the Pembroke, and has flaps at each end. The best examples were made during the last quarter of the 18thC and in the Regency period, although production continued on a smaller scale until the mid-19thC. After this most were copies or interpretations of the styles of an earlier period.

Sofa tables from the Sheraton period are the most sought after, especially those that are not deeper than 24in (61cm). Good quality sofa tables are found in rosewood and mahogany, as well as a variety of exotic woods, with oak or mahogany lined drawers. Rosewood veneer with brass inlay was used from c1800.

The end supports with a high stretcher is more sought after than a low positioned stretcher or a central pedestal. Later tables often have a lower, sometimes rather heavy stretcher to stabilise the table; this can interrupt its elegant lines.

> **Did you know?**
> *MILLER'S* Antiques Price Guide *builds up year-by-year to form the most comprehensive antiques photo-reference library available.*

A brass-inlaid satinwood and ebonised sofa table, the top with broad rosewood crossbanding, 2 true and 2 false similarly banded frieze drawers, restored, early 19thC and later, 65½in (166.5cm) wide.
$7,000–7,800 *Bon*

A Regency mahogany sofa table, with ebony strung borders, 2 drop leaves with rounded corners, 2 frieze drawers, on lyre-shaped end supports with ebonised roundels, turned stretcher and splayed legs with chased brass terminals, top split, 56¼in (143cm) long extended.
$1,800–2,000 *DN*

A Regency mahogany sofa table, the twin-flap top above 2 frieze drawers, on end standards and splayed legs, 56in (142cm) wide.
$5,250–6,000 *CSK*

A Regency mahogany and rosewood crossbanded sofa table, with rounded plum pudding top, 2 cedar lined frieze drawers and 2 dummy drawers flanked by anthemion mounts, on twin column supports with overswept reeded legs and joined by a ring turned stretcher, 64in (162.5cm) long extended.
$3,000–3,750 *CSK*

A Regency rosewood and brass-inlaid sofa table, the top with satinwood inlaid border band, the frieze and 2 frieze drawers with elaborate foliate scroll gilt-metal mounts, anthemion mounts at the corners, the supports and splay legs inlaid with brass string lines, brass paw feet and casters, 40½in (103cm) wide.
$12,000–13,500 *P(S)*

A Regency mahogany and rosewood sofa table, line-inlaid and crossbanded, the twin-flap above 4 frieze drawers, on standard end supports, joined by a later stretcher, on outswept feet, 55in (140cm) long extended.
$4,500–5,250 *CSK*

A William IV mahogany sofa table, the top above 2 frieze drawers with opposing dummy drawers, on twin column end supports joined by a similar stretcher, with hipped reeded downswept legs, top split and faded, 58in (147.5cm) extended.
$2,700–3,300 *CSK*

A William IV mahogany sofa table, with 2 drop leaves and 2 drawers, centred by a leaf-carved tablet, on a turned column with nulled border and leaf-capped splayed legs, with brass casters, 60in (152.5cm) long extended.
$4,500–5,250 *DN*

A rosewood sofa table, the twin-flap top above 2 frieze drawers, on end standards and splayed legs, joined by a ring turned stretcher, 19thC, 51in (129.5cm) wide.
$1,800–2,250 *CSK*

Sutherland Tables

A Victorian walnut Sutherland table, the burr veneered top inlaid with a geometric banding, c1860, 42in (107cm) long extended.
$2,500–2,700 *S*

A late Victorian burr walnut Sutherland table, with moulded top and fluted legs, with gadrooned collars and outswept moulded feet, 42in (106.5cm) extended.
$1,300–1,500 *CSK*

A Victorian walnut Sutherland table, with a twin-flap top of serpentine outline, 40in (101.5cm) long extended.
$600–670 *CSK*

Sutherland Tables

Sutherland tables were introduced in the 19thC and named after the Duchess of Sutherland. They are drop-leaf tables with a distinctive narrow centre section, and end columns which are normally joined by a central stretcher.

l. A mid-Victorian burr walnut Sutherland table, the oval twin-flap top on turned baluster end supports joined by a turned stretcher, on foliate capped downswept legs with scrolling feet, 34in (86.5cm) wide.
$1,000–1,200 *CSK*

A Victorian walnut Sutherland table, the serpentine top with moulded edge, on barley-twist legs, 44in (112cm) long extended.
$1,200–1,350 *AH*

Tea Tables

A mahogany and walnut tea table, the shaped foldover top with projecting corners, the conforming frieze with a drawer, on cabriole legs with shell-carved knees and claw-and-ball feet, restored, c1735, 35½in (89.5cm) wide.
$6,000–6,750 *S*

A George II Irish mahogany tea table, the hinged top with rounded corners, a frieze drawer with shell ornament, on cabriole legs with re-entrant C-scrolls and pad feet, 35in (89cm) wide.
$6,000–6,750 *P*

A George II red walnut tea table, the foldover top with outswept corners, on acanthus carved cabriole legs with spade feet, restored, 33in (84cm) wide.
$1,100–1,300 *Bon*

An inlaid mahogany tea table, outlined with boxwood and ebony stringing, the rounded foldover top above a crossbanded satinwood frieze, on tapering reeded legs, early 19thC, 36in (91.5cm) wide.
$1,300–1,450 *Bea*

A George III mahogany tea table, on channelled square section legs, 36in (91.5cm) wide.
$600–670 *Bon*

A George III mahogany D-shaped tea table, with ebony stringing, on reeded tapering legs, 35½in (90cm) wide.
$1,200–1,500 *Bri*

A Regency mahogany tea table, with four-twist turned supports and reeded splayed legs, c1820, 36in (91.5cm) wide.
$3,000–3,750 *ANT*

A George III mahogany spider leg tea table, with 2 drop leaves supported by swinging gates, on slender turned legs with stretchers and pad feet, 30¾in (78cm) wide.
$1,200–1,500 *DN*

A Regency crossbanded mahogany tea table, with stringing and foldover top, on concave-sided inverted tapering column and scrolled quadruple splay support, brass claw feet and casters, slight damage, 36in (91.5cm) wide.
$830–1,000 *MCA*

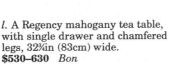

r. A mahogany tea table, the tray top with moulded gallery, on cabriole legs with slipper feet, repaired, Goddard-Townsend School, Newport, Rhode Island, c1750, 20¾in (52.5cm) wide.
$29,250–33,000 *S(NY)*

l. A Regency mahogany tea table, with single drawer and chamfered legs, 32¾in (83cm) wide.
$530–630 *Bon*

Tripod Tables

A George II mahogany tripod table, the top with moulded edge and pierced baluster gallery, inlaid with a brass line, on a fluted columnar shaft and spirally reeded bulb with egg-and-dart socle, the legs headed by carving, on claw-and-ball feet, restoration to gallery, 16in (40.5cm) wide.
$30,000–36,000 C

A mahogany tripod table, the piecrust hinged top on a birdcage support and turned, tapered, fluted and stop-fluted column, the leaf-carved cabriole feet, associated, c1745, 23in (58.5cm) diam.
$6,500–7,500 S

A mahogany tripod table, the octagonal top with pierced fret gallery, baluster stem and leaf-carved cabriole legs, with claw-and-ball feet, c1755, 10½in (26.5cm) diam.
$3,000–3,750 S

A mahogany tripod table, on a turned baluster column and tripod base, with cabriole legs and pad feet, c1755, 12in (30.5cm) diam.
$10,500–12,000 S

A mahogany tripod table, with mottled tilt-top above a birdcage support, the baluster turned stem on cabriole legs with claw-and-ball feet and casters, c1750, 33¾in (85.5cm) diam.
$3,000–3,750 S

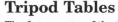

A mahogany tripod table, with moulded tilt-top above a birdcage support, the fluted turned stem with a spiral reeded knop, on cabriole legs with acanthus cabochon carving and claw-and-ball feet, c1755, 30¼in (77cm) diam.
$11,250–13,500 S

Tripod Tables

The forerunners of the tripod table were the small, round-topped tables designed to support a lantern or candlesticks – a type popular in England during the second half of the 17thC. The tripod table was introduced in the 1730s and made in varying sizes. Except in the smallest tripods, the tops are made so that they can tilt to a vertical position and fit neatly into the corner of a room. The heyday of the tripod table was the Chippendale period, when they were most often made in mahogany, with carved decoration. Tripods were largely an English phenomenon and were far less popular on the Continent.

In England in the mid-18thC small tripod tables were made as stands for silver tea kettles and their heaters; but they were undoubtedly used in the drawing room next to armchairs for other purposes, as they still are today.

A brass inlaid padouk tripod table, in the manner of John Channon, the scalloped top with dished centre and outer dished rim inlaid with shell motifs, on cabriole legs headed by brass leaf tips and inlaid pad feet, mid-18thC, 26½in (67.5cm) diam.
$21,000–23,250 CNY

A mahogany tripod table, the moulded top with inverted corners, crossbanded in rosewood, on a turned tapering fluted stem, with swirl-carved baluster sections, on leaf-carved moulded legs with scroll toes and brass casters, c1765, 31in (78.5cm) wide.
$4,800–5,500 S

A George II mahogany tripod table, the tilt-top above a birdcage support, the pillar on cabriole legs with pad feet and brass casters, c1750, 29½in (75cm) diam.
$2,700–3,000 S

A mahogany tripod table, with spindled gallery tilt-top, on a columnar and fluted urn stem, cabriole legs and pointed pad feet, c1770, 28in (71cm) diam.
$4,200–5,000 *CNY*

A George III mahogany tripod table, the tilt-top on a turned column with reeded vase and birdcage, with 3 splayed legs, one leg repaired, 30¼in (77cm) diam.
$900–1,000 *DN*

A George III mahogany tripod table, with tilt-top on a turned and fluted vase column with 3 splayed legs, 32¼in (82cm) diam.
$830–1,000 *DN*

A George III mahogany and padouk tripod table, with dished tilt-top above a birdcage support, adapted, 22in (56cm) diam.
$4,800–5,500 *S(NY)*

A burr elm pedestal tripod table, c1800, 18in (45.5cm) diam.
$2,700–3,000 *DeG*

A Regency mahogany tripod table, the top on a part ebonised ring turned shaft and tripod base, 13in (33cm) diam.
$530–630 *CSK*

A George IV mahogany tripod table, on a turned column with 3 splayed legs, 19⅜in (50cm) wide.
$450–530 *DN*

A burr walnut and parquetry tripod table, the chrysanthemum inlaid top on a turned shaft and acanthus carved downswept legs, with scrolling feet, associated, 19thC, 42in (106.5cm) diam.
$1,800–2,000 *CSK*

A mahogany and brass moulded tripod table, the underside of the top with a brass tablet inscribed 'Vue Sormani et fils, 10 Rue Charlotte, Paris', late 19thC, 21¼in (54cm) wide.
$3,300–3,750 *P*

r. A late George III mahogany tripod table, the tilt-top on a turned column with spiral fluting and 3 splayed legs, restored, 42in (106.5cm) diam.
$1,000–1,200 *DN*

A George III mahogany tripod table, c1820, 23in (58.5cm) diam.
$1,350–1,500 *ANT*

Work Tables

A Regency mahogany drop-leaf work table, outlined with boxwood stringing, with a rosewood crossbanded rounded top, 2 frieze drawers above a sliding work compartment, on a U-shaped support with 3 splayed legs and scroll feet, 27½in (70cm) wide.
$1,200–1,350 *Bea*

A Regency rosewood work table, the rounded drop-leaf top above a frieze drawer and sliding well with U-shaped basket, 19in (48.5cm) wide.
$1,800–2,300 *CSK*

A Regency mahogany sewing table, with 2 satinwood-banded drop leaves, old repair, 30in (76cm) wide extended.
$1,800–2,000 *WL*

Work Tables

Special tables for embroidery and needlework were introduced in the second half of the 18thC. These are usually compact and fitted with a silk bag with compartments for reels, bobbins and so on.

Work tables are characterised by their combined regard for elegance and practicality. They are rarely found with their original bags; replacements, often in pleated silk, are generally acceptable. Not all work tables had bags: some tops lift up to reveal a fitted interior with lidded compartments. Alternatively, some work tables from the mid-19thC of conical shape, usually on a tripod base, have tops that rise to reveal an unfitted interior for holding wools and materials. The most common type of Victorian work table is either made in walnut or papier mâché, with an octagonal lift-up lid and a deep compartment below the top.

A Louis XV style kingwood and marquetry work table, applied with gilt brass edge mouldings, work bag missing, 24¼in (61.5cm) wide.
$1,500–1,800 *Bea*

A George III oak, elm, boxwood, yew and rosewood twin drop-leaf work table, all original, c1820, 28in (71cm) wide extended.
$2,300–2,700 *PHA*

A George IV mahogany work table, c1820, 35in (89cm) wide extended.
$1,350–1,500 *Hal*

An early Victorian mahogany work table, with 2 drop leaves, 2 drawers and a sliding wool box, on a U-shaped support and concave-sided base, with scroll feet, 30in (76cm) wide.
$830–1,000 *DN*

A Federal mahogany work table, with bird's-eye maple and flame birch veneer, mahogany crossbanding, damaged, Portsmouth, New Hampshire, c1710, 17in (43cm) wide.
$3,000–3,750 *SK(B)*

r. A Federal tiger maple work table, slight damage, New England, c1820, 19in (48.5cm) wide.
$1,500–1,800 *SK(B)*

Writing Tables

A George II brass-mounted mahogany writing table, the top with a moulded brass edge and spring-loaded reading support, with 2 mahogany-lined frieze drawers, a fitted spring-loaded mahogany-lined side drawer with 2 glass inkwells and a small Chinese blue and white porcelain well, 24in (61cm) wide.
$37,500–45,000 *C*

r. A George III provincial satinwood writing table, the crossbanded top above a fitted writing drawer, c1790, 41in (104cm) wide.
$6,000–6,750 *S*

A George III mahogany writing table, with rosewood banded top, c1790, 23¼in (59cm) wide.
$7,500–8,300 *S*

Writing Tables

Early writing tables fetch far higher prices than later, chunky ones which are still quite readily available and relatively inexpensive. Late 18thC writing tables are raised either on slender square tapering legs or on slender turned legs of simple outline. Both types terminate in casters. In the early 19thC a heavier leg turned with rings became more popular; it became steadily more robust as the century progressed. An early 19thC development was the writing table with end supports.

Some writing tables have had their legs replaced by slender square tapering legs to give an earlier and more expensive appearance. The original legs have to be cut off and completely replaced. As timber is very difficult to match, there may be discrepancies between the old and new timbers. Casters can be useful dating aids, for example lions' paw feet are probably post c1800. Modern casters are less finely cast, the wheels frequently being solid rather than hollow, as antique casters were.

l. A pair of George III harewood, kingwood and marquetry writing tables, in the manner of Pierre Langlois, c1765, 25¼in (64cm) wide.
$19,500–22,500 *S*

A mahogany partner's writing library table, with leather-lined top and 6 frieze drawers, on ring turned tapering legs, one caster loose, restorations, early 19thC, 60in (152.5cm) wide.
$2,500–3,000 *CSK*

r. A George III double-sided writing table, attributed to J. Taylor, the moulded leather-lined top above 3 frieze drawers, c1800, 52¼in (132.5cm) wide.
$60,000–67,500 *S*

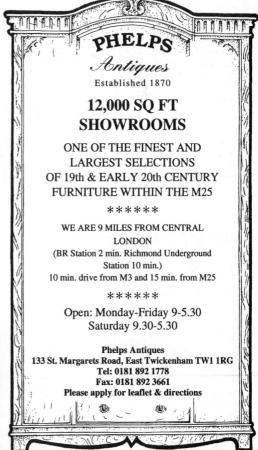

A Regency amboyna and simulated bamboo writing table, mounted overall with black and gilt japanned foliate panels, with pressed metal label 'M97', 38½in (98cm) wide.
$19,500–22,500 *C*

A Regency ormolu-mounted rosewood writing table, the canted top above 2 panelled frieze drawers, with simulated drawers to the reverse, the ends of the frieze inlaid with geometric stringing flanked by reeded panels, on solid end supports joined by a later stretcher, on downswept legs with brass caps and casters, repaired, 35in (89cm) wide.
$11,250–12,750 *C*

A Regency brass-mounted rosewood writing table, with later three-quarter pierced Vitruvian scroll gallery above 2 short drawers, with simulated panelled fronts and lion mask and ring handles, the reverse with simulated drawers, on trestle end supports with panelled sides headed by a scrolling bracket, with arched stretchers and brass scrolling paw feet and casters, restorations, 43in (109cm) wide.
$26,250–30,000 *C*

A George IV mahogany writing table, the top with a brass gallery, c1820, the gallery possibly later, 33in (84cm) wide.
$4,500–5,250 *S*

A George IV mahogany writing table, with 2 frieze drawers flanked by rounded reeded corners, on turned and reeded legs with brass casters, 38in (96.5cm) wide.
$1,500–1,800 *DN*

A William IV mahogany double-sided writing table, with inset leather top, c1835, 48in (122cm) wide.
$4,500–5,250 *ANT*

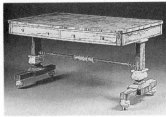

A William IV rosewood and parcel-gilt writing table, the leather-lined top above a panelled frieze with 2 drawers to each side, on trestle end supports joined by a ring turned and reeded baluster stretcher, on spreading shaped bars and foliate gadrooned feet, restored, regilt, 58¼in (148cm) wide.
$6,500–7,500 *C*

An early Victorian mahogany writing table, with 3 opposing freize drawers, on turned and tapering reeded legs and brass wheel casters, c1840, 59¾in (152cm) wide.
$7,800–9,000 *S*

A writing table, veneered in walnut with rosewood crossbanding and boxwood stringing, with gilt-metal mounts, mid-19thC, 41in (104cm) wide.
$1,800–2,300 *Bon*

A Victorian walnut kidney-shaped writing table, stamped 'Wilkinson & Son 7786, 8 Old Bond Street', c1850, 48½in (123cm) wide.
$2,700–3,000 *Bon*

A Victorian mahogany writing table, 47½in (120.5cm) wide.
$530–600 *Hal*

A Victorian kidney-shaped writing table, the top veneered in calamander, with a gilt tooled leather inset and a gallery with baluster turnings, on an ebonised and parcel gilt base, in the manner of C. & R. Light, 48½in (123cm) wide.
$9,000–10,500 *DN*

A late Victorian Georgian style mahogany writing table, with green morocco insert, 60in (152.5cm) wide.
$900–1,000 *CDC*

r. A tulipwood, sycamore and marquetry writing table, in the Louis XV/XVI transitional style, the cartouche brass bound top with a spray of flowers within purplewood strapwork and trellis reserves, the frieze with a moroccan leather inset slide, with drawer below incorporating a toilet mirror, on cabriole legs with gilt bronze sabots, late 19thC, 27½in (70cm) wide.
$3,750–4,500 *P*

A Louis XV ormolu-mounted tulipwood and kingwood parquetry writing table, the top inset with brown leather and surrounded by a moulded ormolu border, fitted at the corners with clasps, signed 'P. Garnier', mid-18thC, 82in (208.5cm) wide.
$45,000–52,500 *S(NY)*

l. A Napoleon III ebonised, ormolu-mounted and brass marquetry writing table, in the Louis XVI style, damaged, 51½in (131cm) wide.
$600–670 *P*

r. A French boulle marquetry writing table, with ebonised detail and gilt ormolu mounts, 19thC, 57¾in (147cm) wide.
$1,800–2,250 *WL*

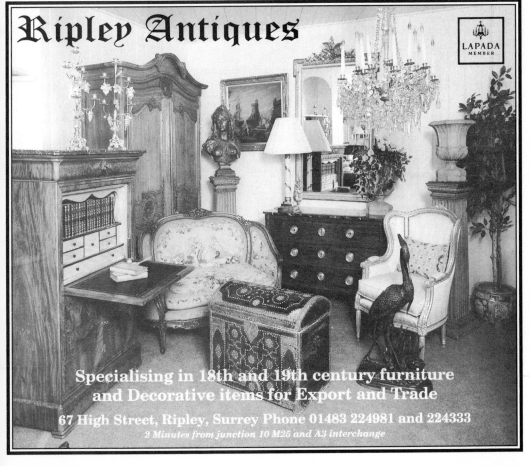

Miscellaneous Tables

A late George III mahogany table, with swivel drawer to each end, on straight legs with a stretcher shelf and leather-covered casters, 24in (61cm) wide.
$600–670 *DN*

An Oriental rosewood altar table, inlaid with mother-of-pearl, 19thC, 38in (96.5cm) wide.
$1,100–1,350 *CDC*

A George III satinwood and kingwood marquetry *vide-poche*, in the French style, 29in (74cm) wide.
$9,750–11,250 *P*

Vide-poches are small tables with a rim around the top. They were intended for use in the bedroom to hold the contents of a man's pockets when he undressed.

Teapoys

A Victorian octagonal teapoy, the hinged lid decorated with a harp motif surrounded by floral sprays, shamrocks and yew banding opening to reveal a fitted interior, Killarney, 30in (76cm) high.
$3,000–3,750 *JAd*

An early Victorian walnut teapoy, the hinged top enclosing 2 lidded compartments, with fluted column and scroll carved tripod base, 17¾in (45cm) diam.
$830–900 *P(C)*

A Victorian walnut teapoy, the hinged lid enclosing 3 lidded canisters and a glass mixing bowl in a gadrooned body, with barley-twist tapering column and triform base, 16in (40.5cm) diam.
$2,000–2,250 *P(Sc)*

A William IV mahogany teapoy, the hinged lid with a moulded handle and rim, enclosing a fitted interior, 15½in (39cm) wide.
$600–670 *CSK*

> **Miller's is a price GUIDE not a price LIST**

A William IV walnut teapoy, with hinged coffered top, containing 4 lidded caddies and spaces for 2 bowls, on spiral turned supports and a concave-sided base with leaf-carved urn-shaped finial and C-scroll and acanthus carved legs, 16½in (42cm) wide.
$1,000–1,200 *DN*

Trays

A George III mahogany tray-on-stand, with chequer inlaid gallery and brass handles, c1780, on a modern stand with square splayed legs, 30¼in (77cm) wide.
$5,500–6,300 *S*

A George III mahogany tray-on-stand, with a shaped fretwork gallery and pierced carrying handles, c1780, on a modern stand with chamfered square legs, headed by pierced angle brackets, 31in (79cm) wide.
$6,000–6,750 *S*

A mahogany tray-on-stand, with pierced semi-elliptical sides and countersunk brass hinges, c1800, on later stand with square tapering legs, 34¾in (88cm) wide.
$4,500–5,250 *S*

A Regency tôle tray, c1810, on a later stand, 24in (61cm) wide.
$2,500–3,000 *MM*

MILLER'S COMPARES . . .

I A George III mahogany tray-on-stand, the tray with brass inlaid waved gallery and a pair of brass loop handles, c1770, on modern stand with splayed legs, 30in (76cm) wide.
$6,750–7,500 *S*

II A mahogany tray-on-stand, the tray inlaid with a compass point medallion, the waved gallery with brass handles, c1780, on modern stand with splayed legs, 31½in (80cm) wide.
$3,000–3,750 *S*

Both trays were manufactured within a decade of each other, are in similar condition, and are both on modern stands. However, two factors made *item I* special: the brass inlay around the gallery, which is very unusual, and a footnote added to the catalogue description stating that a similar tray was supplied by Thomas Chippendale to William, 5th Earl of Dumfries, for Dumfries House. Association with a known maker can sometimes increase the saleroom value of a piece, although experts are reluctant to attribute items without conclusive evidence. *S*

Washstands

A teak campaign washstand, in the form of a Pembroke table, with 2 drop leaves and a hinged centre section enclosing various compartments, 19thC, 34¾in (88cm) wide.
$600–670 *DN*

A Dutch mahogany and floral marquetry washstand, enclosing a metal-lined cistern, early 19thC, 22½in (57cm) wide.
$1,800–2,250 *L*

A George III mahogany and ebony string inlaid washstand, with folding top, the undershelf with drawer with brass knob handle, on baluster turned supports and stretchers with circular stand, 28in (71cm) wide.
$600–670 *AH*

r. A Federal figured maple inlaid cherrywood basin stand, New England, probably Vermont, c1815, 18in (45.5cm) wide.
$3,000–3,600 *S(NY)*

A mahogany washstand, mid-19thC, 41½in (105.5cm) wide.
$450–530 *Bon*

Whatnots

A Regency four-tier whatnot, the moulded hinged top with adjustable ratchet action, above slender turned and square supports, the plinth base with a drawer, on conforming turned legs and brass casters, c1810, 19¼in (49cm) wide.
$5,250–6,000 *S*

A George IV mahogany four-tier whatnot, with ring turned supports and bun-shaped finials, one drawer at the base with turned wood handles, on turned legs with casters, 18in (45.5cm) wide.
$2,250–2,600 *DN*

A mahogany four-tier whatnot, the top with ratchet easel and detachable book rest, turned supports, the central drawer with wood knob handles, on turned feet with casters, early 19thC, 20in (50.5cm) wide.
$2,000–2,500 *WW*

A George IV mahogany four-tier whatnot, the upper tier with spindle turned three-quarter gallery, with turned pillars and a drawer, on turned legs and brass casters, c1820, 17¾in (45cm) wide.
$9,750–11,250 *S*

A William IV mahogany two-tier whatnot, with 2 fitted drawers and inlaid boxwood stringing, 28in (71cm) wide.
$2,250–2,700 *HOLL*

A French marquetry étagère, with ormolu border, c1880, 32in (81cm) high.
$750–900 *APO*

A Victorian butt walnut four-tier corner whatnot, 57in (144.5cm) high.
$830–1,000 *Mit*

A Victorian rosewood six-tier whatnot, the serpentine shelves supported on open barley-twist columns, the upper 3 tiers with mirrored backs, 22in (55cm) wide.
$1,200–1,350 *WL*

r. A Victorian burr walnut whatnot/canterbury, the 2 upper tiers with tulipwood crossbanding, the top tier with brass rail and turned supports, the base with fret panels and a drawer, on turned feet, 44in (112cm) high.
$1,300–1,500 *DN*

l. A mahogany whatnot, c1860, 34in (86cm) high.
$450–530 *APO*

An early Victorian rosewood four-tier corner whatnot, with carved scroll decoration, 30in (76cm) high.
$1,500–1,800 *MR*

Window Seats

A George IV window seat, c1820, 41in (104cm) wide.
$6,000–6,750 *S*

A George III painted and parcel-gilt window seat, with twin scroll ends decorated with stylised foliage, c1780, 50in (127cm) wide.
$3,300–3,750 *S*

A George III mahogany window seat, with paterae and harebell carved decoration, restored, 36in (91.5cm) wide.
$900–1,000 *CDC*

A French walnut window seat, 19thC, 47in (119cm) wide.
$5,500–6,000 *S(NY)*

Wine Coolers

A George III mahogany octagonal cellaret-on-stand, the hinged top revealing a later metal liner, the sides with brass lion mask ring handles, on tapering square legs with brass feet and casters, c1780, 24¾in (63cm) high.
$3,000–3,750 *S*

A George III mahogany cellaret, the hinged top and tapering sides with brass bandings, raised on fluted square tapering legs, damaged, c1780, 20¾in (52.5cm) wide.
$750–900 *Hal*

An early George III mahogany and brass-bound octagonal cellaret, the hinged moulded lid enclosing a later brass liner, carrying handles at the sides, the stand with square chamfered and moulded legs, on casters, 17¾in (45cm) wide.
$3,500–4,000 *P*

A George III mahogany cellaret, the coopered sides with 2 brass bands, lion mask and loop handles, on a stand with straight splayed legs with scroll brackets and casters, 28in (71cm) wide.
$4,500–5,250 *DN*

A George III mahogany cellaret, the satinwood banded top centred by a paterae, the sides with lion mask loop handles, c1785, 21¾in (55cm) wide.
$2,000–2,500 *S*

l. A George III brass-bound mahogany wine cooler-on-stand, with label to the underside 'Norman Adams', 24in (61cm) wide.
$3,000–3,750 *C*

r. A George III mahogany cellaret, the top opening to reveal a fitted interior, 22in (56cm) wide.
$3,750–4,500 *JAd*

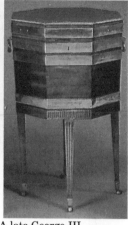

A George III mahogany brass-bound cellaret, the hinged octagonal top with 8 radiating veneers, strung with box, interior fitment missing, 18in (45.5cm) wide.
$2,000–2,700 *P(HSS)*

A George III mahogany cellaret-on-stand, with canted corners and tapering body, the sides with 3 brass bands and lion mask carrying handles, the stand with square tapering legs and brass casters, c1800, 20in (51cm) wide.
$3,750–4,500 *S*

A late George III mahogany brass-bound cellaret, the hinged moulded top with a partially lined divided interior and handles, 18¼in (46cm) wide.
$2,250–2,700 *P*

A late George III mahogany and brass-bound cellaret, with hinged moulded lid and carrying handles, the stand with square moulded tapering legs and casters, 17¾in (45cm) wide.
$2,250–2,700 *P*

A Regency mahogany brass-bound wine cooler, the open top with plain sides and ring handles, on a later plinth base with bun feet and casters, 46in (117cm) wide.
$5,250–6,300 *C*

A pair of Regency mahogany and brass-mounted wine coolers, with liner and tapered panelled sides, banded in rosewood, with lion mask mounts, on paw feet, 26½in (67.5cm) wide.
$1,500–1,800 *CSK*

Miscellaneous

l. A Transitional tulipwood amaranth parquetry and marquetry *coiffeuse*, by Germain Landrin, the hinged top with a cartouche of a basket of flowers enclosing a mirror, restored, damaged, stamped 'G. LANDRIN and JME', late 18thC, 19½in (49.5cm) wide.
$26,250–31,500 *C*

A set of George III harewood shelves, the doors inlaid with urn medallions and tulipwood crossbanding, the shaped sides with trailing flowers, c1780, 28in (71cm) wide.
$7,000–7,800 *S*

r. A George III mahogany kettle stand, on a turned tapering stem with swirl turned and moulded sections, on a plain tripod base, c1780, 10¼in (26cm) diam.
$17,250–20,250 *S*

A Victorian satin birch boot rack, the curved top rail with a pierced handle, on shaped and pierced supports joined by stretchers, on scroll feet, c1860, 33in (84cm) wide.
$300–360 *Hal*

A pair of Chinese export reverse paintings on mirrors, each with an arch of foliage, flowers and standing birds, in pierced giltwood frames, late 18thC, 24½in (62cm) high.
$30,000–35,000 *C*

A pair of Chinese reverse paintings on mirrors, landscape and architectural settings, with figures, in giltwood frames, paint worn in places, late 18thC, 29in (73.5cm) high.
$15,750–18,000 *C*

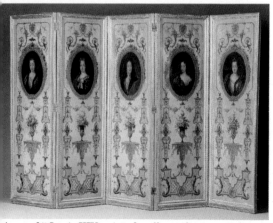

A set of 5 Louis XIV painted wall panels, mounted as a screen, each with an oval portrait surrounded by flowers, trellis and scrolls, each leaf 75¼in (191cm) high.
$52,500–60,000 *C*

A mahogany serpentine sideboard, with 7 drawers, extensively restored, c1790, 72in (183cm) wide.
$3,750–4,500 *Bon*

A Federal satinwood inlaid mahogany sideboard, with a pair of convex doors, a centre concave drawer and 2 doors, c1800, 70in (178.5cm) wide.
$12,750–14,250 *S(NY)*

A carved mahogany pedestal sideboard, with 3 centre drawers, flanked by a pair of projecting drawers and cupboards, c1820, 86in (218.5cm) wide.
$3,500–4,000 *S*

A Federal satinwood inlaid mahogany sideboard, with 4 drawers and a cupboard, Rhode Island, c1800, 48in (121.5cm) wide.
$11,500–13,500 *S(NY)*

An inlaid mahogany sideboard, with a pair of cupboard doors flanked by short drawers, repaired, Rhode Island, c1800, 45in (115cm) wide.
$14,250–15,750 *S(NY)*

A George III mahogany and marquetry sideboard, with demi-lune top and 2 frieze drawers flanked by cabinet doors, 44in (112.5cm) wide.
$9,500–10,000 *CNY*

A George III mahogany, satinwood inlaid and boxwood strung serpentine sideboard, with central frieze drawer, flanked by 2 short drawers and one deep wine drawer, 66in (168cm) wide.
$6,000–8,250 *P(Sc)*

A brass inlaid mahogany sideboard, the backboard with a plate rack on pairs of small pillars, the inverted breakfront with 3 drawers flanked by a pair of doors, c1820, 96in (244cm) wide.
$12,750–13,500 *S*

A George III mahogany sideboard, the veneered front with a frieze drawer, flanked by 2 deep drawers, restored, c1800, 60in (153cm) wide.
$10,000–12,000 *S*

A mahogany breakfront sideboard, with kingwood crossbanding, boxwood stringing, 4 drawers and a tambour shutter, early 19thC, 70in (178cm) wide.
$3,000–3,500 *Bea*

A George III painted beechwood settee, the needlepoint upholstery monogrammed with the initials 'LA', with carved moulded surround, on painted fluted legs with shaped feet, late 18thC, 89in (226cm) long.
$7,500–9,000 *S(NY)*

A George III white and gilt sofa, with padded beaded toprail, the trellis-filled arms with scroll handles, the bowed padded seat on 4 reeded sabre front legs, c1800, 84in (213.5cm) long.
$6,000–6,750 *S*

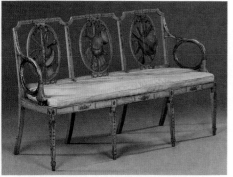

A suite of painted furniture for a music room, comprising 9 armchairs and a pair of triple chairback settees, each back designed as a lyre, with bowed cane seats, c1790, settees 63in (160cm) long.
$67,500–70,000 *S*

A pair of George III mahogany sofas, with outscrolled arms carved with foliage, and serpentine seats, covered in floral cut velvet, restored, 60in (152.5cm) long.
$45,000–52,500 *C*

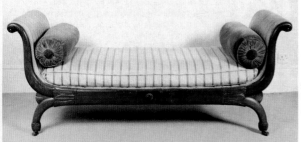

A Regency mahogany window seat, the Egyptian style show-wood frame carved with lotus details, fluting and scroll finials, upholstered in striped damask, on down turned supports with brass casters, 84in (213.5cm) long.
$10,500–12,000 *RBB*

A William IV mahogany settee, with carved shaped back and scroll arms, 84in (213.5cm) long.
$9,750–11,250 *TMA*

A Louis XV beechwood sofa, carved with leaves and flowers, with padded back and loose cushion seat, on cabriole legs, mid-18thC, 82in (208.5cm) long.
$6,000–6,500 *S*

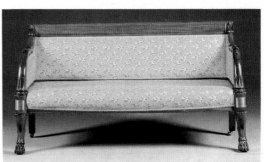

A German brass mounted and inlaid mahogany sofa, with panelled toprail, downswept arms headed by scrolling acanthus leaf, on lion paw legs, restored, early 19thC, 65in (165cm) long.
$6,000–6,500 *C*

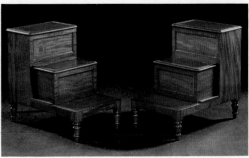

A set of oak Gothic Revival library steps, with 3 moulded red leather lined treads, later brass pole support, c1820.
$4,000–4,750 *S*

A set of George III mahogany library steps, with 4 treads and turned column supports, on a plinth, c1770, 24in (61cm) high.
$6,500–7,000 *S*

A pair of mahogany bed steps, each with 3 leather lined treads, 2 hinged tops and a pull-out centre section, on turned feet, c1820, 25½in (65cm) high.
$7,500–9,000 *S*

A walnut stool, the seat covered in green cut silk velvet, the cabriole legs carved at the knee, on claw-and-ball feet, c1730, 17½in (44.5cm) wide.
$5,250–6,000 *S*

An Italian neo-classical parcel gilt walnut curule stool, with gilt carved rams' heads and hooved paw feet, early 19thC, 23in (58.5cm) high.
$5,250–6,000 *S(NY)*

A set of mahogany library steps, the gallery with 2 turned columnar supports and X-form stretchers, 9 steps, scrolled hand rail, on plinth with casters, c1835, 82in (208.5cm) long.
$18,250–20,250 *S(NY)*

A pair of William and Mary walnut stools, with floral tapestry upholstered padded seats, the inverted baluster turned legs with stretchers, on peg feet, one stool with new rail, c1700, 24in (61cm) wide.
$4,000–4,750 *Bon*

A pair of Queen Anne walnut stools, with original tapestry covered seats, plain cabriole legs with scroll brackets and pad feet, c1710, 21½in (54cm) wide.
$26,250–27,750 *S*

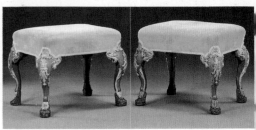

A pair of Charles II ebonised stools, with horsehair seats, block and volute feet, carved arched front and back stretchers, 20½in (52cm) wide.
$6,250–8,250 *C*

A pair of walnut and parcel gilt stools, on cabriole legs with shells and foliate clasps, ruffled ankles and shell form pad feet, mid-18thC, 23½in (59.5cm) wide.
$60,000–65,000 *CNY*

A mahogany architect's table, with hinged top, baize lined slide and compartments, c1760, 33in (84cm) wide.
$4,500–5,250 *S*

A George I burr walnut card table, with concertina action, on carved cabriole legs, with claw-and-ball feet, 32in (81cm) wide.
$19,500–21,000 *DN*

A red walnut card table, with projecting round corners, and a drawer, on cabriole legs, c1730, 34in (86.5cm) wide.
$3,750–4,500 *S*

A walnut card table, with projecting round corners and single drawer, on tapering legs, c1740, 33in (84cm) wide.
$3,750–4,500 *Bon*

An amboyna card table, with lyre shaped end supports and outswept legs with stretcher, c1810, 36in (91.5cm) wide.
$5,250–6,000 *Bon*

A Louis XV carved oak console table, with marble top, scrolled apron, carved cabriole legs and rockwork stretcher, 45in (115cm) wide.
$6,750–8,250 *P*

A mahogany card table, with baize lined interior, a frieze drawer, and carved cabriole legs, c1755, 33in (84cm) wide.
$3,750–4,500 *S*

A Regency brass inlaid rosewood card table, with D-shaped top, tapering stem and hipped splayed legs with brass caps and casters, 36in (91.5cm) wide.
$3,000–3,750 *Bea*

A burr walnut veneered and marquetry card and games table, with a drawer, on cabriole legs, mid-19thC, 32in (81.5cm) wide.
$3,250–3,750 *Bea*

A satinwood inlaid demi-lune card table, with green baize interior, c1880, 36in (91.5cm) wide.
$5,250–6,000 *GAS*

A satinwood and decorated D-shaped card table, with baize lined hinged top, 18thC and later, 36in (91.5cm) wide.
$2,700–3,000 *CSK*

An ormolu mounted console table, with galleried marble top and undertier, and one drawer, c1800, 39in (99cm) wide.
$4,500–5,250 *C*

A mahogany breakfast table, the top with Greek key inlaid border, with 3-sided inlaid concave base, repaired, early 19thC, inlay later, 60in (152.5cm) diam.
$9,750–11,250 *S(NY)*

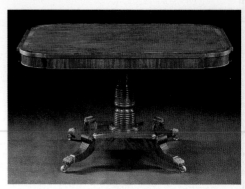

A mahogany breakfast table, with tilt-top, brass stringing and rosewood crossbanding, splayed legs and brass paw casters, c1815, 50in (127cm) wide.
$7,000–7,750 *S*

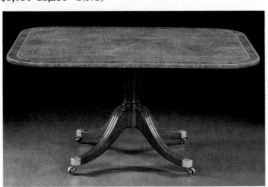

A mahogany breakfast table, the tilt-top with satinwood and rosewood crossbanding, the turned tapering pillar on splayed legs with brass caps and casters, c1810, 60in (152.5cm) wide.
$10,500–11,250 *S*

A rosewood breakfast table, the tilt-top with crossbanded border, a carved giltwood 'water lily' moulding to base, c1820, 49in (124.5cm) diam.
$11,250–12,750 *S*

A mahogany three-pedestal dining table, with moulded top, urn turned standards, brass feet and casters, 3 leaves, restored, late 18thC, 79in (200.5cm) long.
$14,250–15,750 *S(NY)*

A Victorian mahogany extending dining table, on a baluster shaft and reeded scrolled legs with brass caps, 8 leaves, 70in (178cm) diam without leaves.
$100,000–112,500 *C*

A William IV pollarded oak and ebony inlaid breakfast table, by James Mein, Kelso, with maker's label, 56in (142cm) diam.
$26,250–30,000 *P(Sc)*

A mahogany extending dining table, on reeded tapering legs, 2 later leaves, top and base associated, c1830, 42in (106.5cm) wide.
$5,250–6,000 *Bon*

A nest of 4 yew, rosewood and maple quartetto tables, c1820, the smallest 23in (58.5cm) wide.
$7,000–7,750 *CNY*

A rosewood marble-topped low table, with lyre supports, c1820, 17½in (44.5cm) wide.
$2,700–3,200 *S*

A painted table, the top decorated with flowers, c1795, 22½in (57cm) wide.
$18,750–20,250 *S*

A Louis XVI tulipwood, parquetry and marquetry writing table, restored, 17in (43.5cm) wide.
$11,250–12,750 *C*

A William IV rosewood marble-topped pedestal games table, the top inset with a chessboard and surrounding backgammon board, on a tapering column, with carved collar, on raised platform with 3 carved scroll feet, 26½in (67.5cm) diam.
$5,500–6,500 *TMA*

A rosewood inlaid games and work table, with a single drawer and workbox, on casters, c1890, 21½in (55cm) wide.
$2,000–2,500 *GAS*

A George III mahogany tripod silver table, with fretwork gallery, spiral fluted column, and carved legs, possibly associated, 35in (89cm) wide.
$67,500–75,000 *CNY*

A Portuguese rosewood low table, with frieze drawer, 19thC, 23½in (60cm) wide.
$2,000–2,500 *P*

A Federal mahogany veneer serpentine work table, Boston, 1790, 19in (48.5cm) wide.
$6,750–7,500 *SK*

A satinwood work and writing table, with leather-lined top and work bag, c1795, 21½in (55cm) wide.
$6,500–7,000 *S*

A rosewood writing table, with 2 central drawers, one with book rest, on lyre supports and sabre legs, c1805, 28in (71cm) wide.
$6,000–6,750 *S*

An Irish George III mahogany side table, the moulded frieze with central scallop shell, on cabriole legs headed by a scallop shell and stiff-leaf, with paw feet, restored, 60in (152.5cm) wide. **$11,000–11,750** *C*

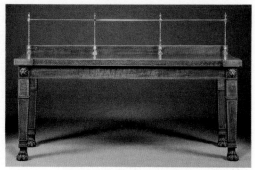

An inlaid mahogany brass-mounted serving table, the top with line inlaid border and brass splash rail, the plain frieze with lions' masks, on tapering legs with paw feet, c1810, 74in (188cm) wide. **$21,000–24,000** *S(NY)*

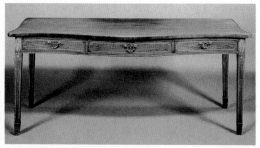

A mahogany serpentine serving table, the 3 frieze drawers with boxwood stringing, on similarly strung square tapering legs with spade feet, headed by inlaid paterae, restored, c1785, 81in (205.5cm) wide. **$4,000–4,750** *Bon*

A part-ebonised mahogany serving table, with projecting centre section, a panelled frieze with 2 drawers, on leaf-carved spiral turned legs with lions' paw feet, early 19thC, 95in (241.5cm) wide. **$8,250–9,000** *S(NY)*

A brass-mounted rosewood sofa table, the top crossbanded in calamanderwood, with canted corners, a pair of drawers, on panelled end supports set with bosses, on winged gilt brass lions' paw feet, c1815, 59in (150cm) wide. **$16,500–18,000** *S*

A George III rosewood sofa table, the top crossbanded in partridgewood with boxwood and ebony lines, with 2 drawers and dummy drawers to reverse, on splayed legs with brass caps and casters, 60in (152.5cm) wide extended. **$7,500–9,000** *P*

A brass-inlaid rosewood sofa table, the top banded in calamander, with 2 drawers, 4 turned supports and hipped sabre legs, damaged, c1810, 59in (150cm) wide. **$6,000–6,750** *S*

A mahogany sofa table, with rosewood-banded top, frieze drawers inlaid with calamander banding, the end supports with scroll brackets, on brass-mounted splayed legs, c1815, 56in (142cm) wide extended. **$6,000–6,750** *S*

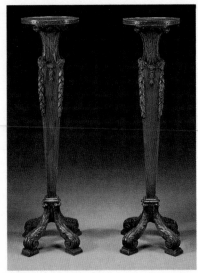

A pair of walnut torchères, the tops with Vitruvian scroll edges, foliate carved necks and square tapering shafts headed by shells and husks, on foliate carved legs, mid-18thC, 49½in (125.5cm) high.
$30,000–33,000 *CNY*

A pair of mahogany torchères, with balustrade galleries, on turned stems, c1760, 39in (99cm) high.
$15,000–18,000 *S*

A Georgian mahogany corner washstand, with arched splashback, single drawer and shaped undertier, 40in (101.5cm) high.
$675–825 *AAV*

An early Victorian polychrome painted and parcel-gilt papier mâché tray, 29in (73.5cm) wide.
$2,250–3,000 *C*

A rosewood table book tray, with a drawer and brass feet, c1820, 16½in (42cm) wide.
$6,000–6,750 *S*

A mahogany cellaret, with carved edge and sides, c1770, 26in (66cm) wide.
$8,000–9,000 *S*

A mahogany wine cooler, with lead-lined interior, restored, early 19thC, 27in (68.5cm) wide.
$7,500–8,250 *CNY*

A mahogany washstand, with cupboard and drawers, c1780, 42½in (108cm) high.
$2,550–3,000 *S*

A rosewood three-tier whatnot, with gallery top, on turned feet and brass casters, c1825, 36½in (92.5cm) high.
$4,500–5,250 *S*

An ebony and palmwood three-tier whatnot, early 19thC, 42in (106.5cm) high.
$6,250–6,750 *C*

A mahogany four-tier whatnot, with a drawer, on tapering legs with casters, c1825, 49½in (125.5cm) high.
$5,250–6,000 *S*

A French carved pine bed head, upholstered in chintz, c1860, 39½in (100.5cm) wide.
$300–375 *SAU*

A pine coffer, with panelled front, on bracket feet, c1850, 48½in (123cm) wide.
$600–675 *HOA*

A German pine trunk, with domed top, brass knob and escutcheon, c1870, 39in (99cm) wide.
$255–300 *COW*

A French pine chest, the 3 long drawers with wooden handles, carved at each front end, on bun feet, c1880, 43in (109cm) wide.
$640–720 *COW*

A Victorian pine chest, the 2 short and 3 long drawers with porcelain handles, 38in (96.5cm) wide.
$390–460 *FOX*

A pine chest, the 3 graduated drawers with wooden handles, c1880, 42in (106cm) wide.
$450–500 *AHO*

A Scandinavian pine chest, with 3 long drawers and brass handles, c1880, 43in (109cm) wide.
$450–525 *SAU*

A French pine chest, the 4 long drawers with original brass handles and escutcheons, c1850, 52in (132cm) wide.
$1,000–1,200 *HOA*

A Dutch pine chest, with 3 long drawers, carved at each front end, shaped front legs, c1870, 43in (109cm) wide.
$375–450 *AHO*

An Irish ash and elm armchair,
the arms with flattened
terminals, c1870.
$450–550 *OD*

A pine and satinwood commode,
with 2 central back supports,
downcurved arms and turned
legs, c1880.
$120–150 *AHO*

A set of 8 elm harlequin
chairs, with bobbin-turned
bar-back and turned legs
with stretchers, c1870.
$750–900 *AHO*

A Victorian pine kitchen
chair, with shaped back splat
and 2 turned spindles, turned
legs and stretchers.
$60–75 *FOX*

A pine chair, with
decorative back and arms,
rush seat, turned legs and
stretchers, c1820.
$185–225 *SAU*

A pine bacon settle, the back made from
5 planks of wood, with 2 cupboard doors
to the reverse and 2 beneath the seat,
restored, 19thC, 73in (185.5cm) wide.
$1,350–1,500 *CSK*

An elm primitive chair,
with single stretcher to the
back, c1860.
$60–70 *AL*

A pine carver chair, with bar-
back, curved arms and turned
legs with stretchers, c1880.
$270–300 *AL*

A Scandinavian pine settle, with shaped
and panelled back, c1860,
48in (122cm) wide.
$375–450 *SAU*

A Continental pine cupboard, the single door with brass knob, c1860, 23½in (60cm) wide.
$200–240 *AHO*

A corner cupboard, with 2 shelves and glazed door, c1890, 32in (81.5cm) wide.
$500–560 *COW*

A pine bowfront corner cupboard, with 3 shaped shelves, c1830, 27in (68.5cm) wide.
$925–1,000 *AL*

A pine hanging corner cupboard, with panelled door, c1860, 31in (78.5cm) wide.
$340–415 *AL*

A pine standing cupboard, with 3 drawers and panelled door, c1850, 40in (101.5cm) wide.
$525–600 *SAU*

A pine corner cupboard, with 2 doors, c1860, 50in (127cm) wide.
$900–1,000 *COW*

A pine cupboard, with panelled door and sides, shelves to the interior, on a plinth base, c1870, 38in (96.5cm) wide.
$300–345 *AL*

A pine cupboard with a single drawer and 2 doors, c1870, 34in (86.5cm) wide.
$375–450 *SAU*

A Scottish pine cupboard, with 2 drawers, 2 doors and decorative pillars, c1870, 47in (119.5cm) wide.
$675–825 *AL*

A Scandinavian pine cupboard, with 2 drawers and 2 doors, c1860, 39½in (100.5cm) wide.
$375–450 *SAU*

A Victorian pine pot cupboard, with galleried top and brass door knob, 15½in (39.5cm) wide.
$185–225 *AHO*

A pine cupboard, with a single drawer and one panelled door, on a plinth base, c1880, 18in (45.5cm) wide.
$270–300 *AL*

r. A Victorian pine cupboard, with 3 drawers and one door, 34in (86cm) wide.
$375–450 *AHO*

A French pine wardrobe, with one drawer, 2 doors and turned pilasters, c1880, 72in (183cm) high.
$975–1,125 *COW*

A Scottish pine linen press, with, 2 short and 2 long drawers, c1850, 84in (213.5cm) high.
$1,500–1,800 *AL*

A Dutch pine pot cupboard, with single drawer and door, c1880, 18in (46cm) wide.
$180–210 *AHO*

ANN LINGARD

ROPE WALK ANTIQUES, RYE, SUSSEX
TEL: 01797 223486 FAX: 01797 224700

10,000 square feet of hand-finished
ENGLISH ANTIQUE PINE FURNITURE
KITCHEN SHOP
and
COMPLEMENTARY ANTIQUES

A Victorian pine pedestal desk, with one central drawer, 3 to the left, and 4 to the right, wooden knob handles, 48in (122cm) wide.
$635–675 *AHO*

A pine pedestal desk, with a mahogany top, the drawers with brass handles, on tunred bun feet, c1880, 60in (152.5cm) wide.
$1,100–1,125 *AL*

A pine desk, the 3 drawers with brass handles, with shaped front, on tapering legs, c1850, 48½in (123cm) wide.
$375–450 *SAU*

A Victorian pine desk, with 2 long and 2 short drawers, on turned legs and casters, 48in (122cm) wide.
$450–525 *AHO*

HERITAGE

RESTORATIONS

ANTIQUE PINE & COUNTRY FURNITURE

CAN'T SEE THE WOOD FOR THE TREES?

FINDING RUN-OF-THE-MILL STRIPPED PINE IS EASY. TRACKING DOWN REALLY WELL RESTORED, INTERESTING FURNITURE IS BECOMING INCREASINGLY DIFFICULT.

WE HAVE THE MOST COMPREHENSIVE STOCK OF GOOD ANTIQUE PINE IN WALES, ALL ORIGINAL & UNUSUAL PIECES RESTORED SYMPATHETICALLY IN OUR OWN WORKSHOPS.

A TREASURE TROVE FOR PEOPLE WHO KNOW THEIR PINE.

- ● ESTABLISHED OVER TWENTY FIVE YEARS.
- ● OPEN 9.00 - 5.30 MONDAY TO SATURDAY.
- ● CLOSED SUNDAYS & BANK HOLIDAYS.
- ● SUPERB RURAL LOCATION - NO PARKING PROBLEMS.
- ● WE CAN DELIVER ANYWHERE.

FOR A COLOUR BROCHURE OR FURTHER INFORMATION PHONE OR FAX JONATHAN GLUCK ON 01938 810384

LLANFAIR CAEREINION, WELSHPOOL, POWYS, WALES SY21 OHD

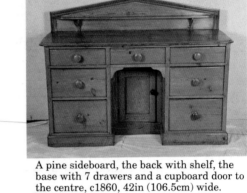

A Victorian pine dresser, the shaped back with 4 small drawers and a shelf, 4 drawers and a central cupboard door below, West Country, 71in (180.5cm) wide.
$2,700–3,000 *AHO*

A pine sideboard, the back with shelf, the base with 7 drawers and a cupboard door to the centre, c1860, 42in (106.5cm) wide.
$675–825 *HOA*

An Irish pine dresser, the top with 3 shelves, 2 panelled cupboard doors below, c1860, 50in (127cm) wide.
$975–1,125 *HOA*

A Welsh pine sideboard, the central mirror flanked by 2 small shelves on barley-twist supports, c1870, 62in (157.5cm) wide.
$1,350–1,500 *AL*

An Irish pine dresser, the top with 3 shelves, 2 drawers and 2 cupboard doors below, in original condition, c1840, 53in (134.5cm) wide.
$1,500–1,800 *COW*

r. A Victorian pine dresser base, with 7 drawers and a pair of panelled doors, on a plinth base, 78in (198cm) wide.
$900–1,000 *Hal*

A French pine dresser, with 3 glazed cupboard doors, above one drawer and 3 panelled cupboard doors below, c1890, 51in (129.5cm) wide.
$1,600–1,800 *COW*

An Irish pine dresser, with 5 shelves above 3 drawers and 2 cupboard doors, c1840, 55in (139.5cm) wide.
$1,500–1,600 *HOA*

An Irish pine breakfront library cabinet, the architectural cornice above 4 cupboards, open book shelves and 4 large cupboards, 19thC, 68in (172.5cm) wide.
$1,900–2,250 *S(S)*

A pine cricket table, with turned legs, c1850, 29in (73.5cm) diam.
$450–525 *AL*

A pine folding table, with square legs and stretchers, early 20thC, 24in (61cm) wide.
$120–150 *FOX*

A pine side table, with 2 drawers, on turned legs, c1870, 36in (91.5cm) wide.
$330–400 *AL*

A pine serving table, with 3 drawers, on turned legs, c1860, 59in (150cm) wide.
$525–600 *HOA*

A pine farmhouse table, with a drawer at one end, on turned legs, c1880, 54½in (138.5cm) wide.
$415–475 *AHO*

A pine folding coaching table, c1890, 26in (66cm) high.
$50–65 *AL*

A Spanish pine table, with a single column and 4 spreading legs, c1860, 38in (96.5cm) square.
$600–675 *SAU*

A pine side table, the 2 turned front columns joined by a stretcher, with a single small drawer, c1870, 38in (96.5cm) wide.
$425–450 *AL*

A pine side table, with turned legs and shaped frieze, c1865, 48in (122cm) wide.
$150–180 *SA*

A Victorian pine farmhouse table, with turned legs, and single drawer, 48in (122cm) wide.
$560–600 *AHO*

A mid-European pine chest of drawers, with original paint decoration, 19thC, 49in (124.5cm) wide.
$560–675 *FOX*

A Swedish pine box, with original paint decoration, initialed 'AMS', and dated '1794', 48in (122cm) wide.
$525–600 *WLD*

A painted pine chest, with an iron escutcheon, and iron handles, c1860, 47in (119.5cm) wide.
$450–525 *SAU*

A Hungarian pine box, with original painted decoration, c1865, 47½in (120.5cm) wide.
$450–525 *WLD*

A Moroccan painted pine wedding chest,
19thC, 24in (61cm) wide.
$1,200–1,350 *LHB*

A pair of north Italian green painted pine corner
cupboards, with later *fleur de pêche* marble tops,
late 18thC and later, 33in (84cm) wide.
$3,000–3,750 *Bon*

A Victorian painted pine table
and mirror, c1880, table 42in
(106.5cm) wide. Table **$415–500**
Mirror **$270–330** *WLD*

A Victorian painted pine washstand, with shaped undertier,
39½in (100.5cm) wide.
$225–270 *OD*

A pine chest of drawers, original
paint and stencil decoration, late
19thC, 42in (106.5cm) wide.
$450–525 *FOX*

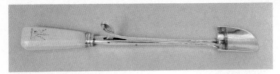

A silver Stilton cheese scoop, with telescopic lever, by Phipps & Robinson, London 1804, 12in (30.5cm) long.
$675–800 *STH*

A stone mineral water jar, for Stevenson's, Tunbridge Wells, Ltd, c1900, 16in (40.5cm) high.
$60–70 *OLM*

A set of wooden spice drawers, each drawer with a label for ingredients, c1900, 10in (25.5cm) high.
$195–225 *WeA*

A Welsh oak two-tier spoon rack, with spoons, c1840, 12½in (32cm) wide.
$330–400 *RP*

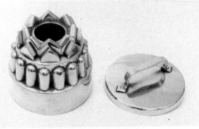

A two-tier copper lined iced pudding mould, with cover, c1860, 6in (15cm) diam.
$450–525 *MB*

An American copper lined iced pudding mould, with hearts and buckle design, c1870, 5½in (14cm) wide.
$180–210 *MB*

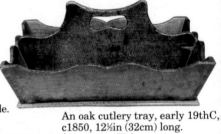

An oak cutlery tray, early 19thC, c1850, 12½in (32cm) long.
$210–270 *Hal*

A brass 'bottle jack' clockwork spit, c1850, 12½in (32cm) long.
$270–300 *WeA*

A pair of sycamore butter scoops and pats, c1800, 10in (25.5cm) long.
$635–710 *PHA*

A Scandinavian salt box, c1920, 8in (20.5cm) wide.
$45–55 *AL*

A set of butter scales, with pottery slab and cast iron weights, c1890, 16in (40.5cm) wide.
$75–90 *AL*

Four sycamore butter prints, c1880, largest 4in (10cm) high.
$50–80 each *AL*

PINE
Benches

A pine side bench, c1880, 60in (152.5cm) long.
$90–120 *AL*

A pine pig bench, c1890, 65in (165cm) long.
$260–290 *AL*

This type of bench was used by butchers when preparing pigs' carcasses.

l. A pine bench, c1890, 54in (137cm) long.
$75–90 *AL*

A pine breakfront bookcase, c1860, 69in (175.5cm) wide.
$3,000–3,750 *SAU*

Bookcases

A pine bookcase, c1860, 60in (152.5cm) long.
$450–520 *SAU*

l. A Yorkshire bookcase, with astragal glazed doors to upper section, c1875, 48in (122cm) wide.
$1,200–1,350 *HOA*

An Irish pine bookcase, with glazed doors to upper section, c1850, 48in (122cm) wide.
$1,100–1,300 *HOA*

l. A pine bookcase, c1880, 79in (200.5cm) wide.
$185–230 *AHO*

Boxes

A pine box, c1890,
12in (30.5cm) long.
$45–55 *AL*

A pine box, c1880, 37in (94cm) long.
$240–170 *COW*

A pine box, c1900,
26½in (67.5cm) long.
$50–65 *AL*

A pine carpenter's box, with fitted
interior and original grained
paint decoration, late 19thC,
33in (84cm) long.
$375–420 *FOX*

A pine filing cabinet, c1920,
19in (48.5cm) wide.
$110–125 *COW*

r. A Scandinavian pine
box, with dummy drawers,
c1900, 27in (68.5cm) long.
$300–375 *BOR*

A collector's miniature pine chest,
c1890, 18in (45.5cm) long.
$90–110 *WLD*

A pine box, with 2 locks and 4 handles, c1880,
49in (124.5cm) long.
$270–330 *AL*

A pine work box, with a tray, c1900,
34in (86.5cm) long.
$150–180 *COW*

There's Original

& there's Quality Original

At Hartwell Antiques you will find a superb selection of *quality* originals, 18th & 19th century antique pine from Britain, Ireland and Europe.

We are one of the largest, specialist antique wholesalers in the UK, offering a wide and varied selection of stripped and polished furniture alongside original hand painted pieces.

The discerning dealer will always find an excellent choice of small and large pieces. We also manufacture superb pine reproductions from 100 year old timber. Visit our warehouse at the side of the A607 and enjoy a cup of coffee while you browse at leisure in an oasis of quality in a desert of mediocrity.

Specialist Wholesalers of 18th & 19th Century Pine Country Furniture

Hartwell Antiques Ltd
Unit 30 Long Furrow
East Goscote
Leicester LE7 3XJ

Hartwell Antiques Ltd

Telephone:
0116 260 3203

Fax: 0116 260 3202

Chairs

A set of 5 rod-back Windsor side chairs,
old black paint, c1810.
$1,800–2,250 *SK(B)*

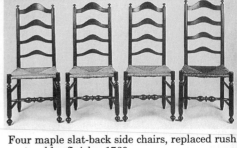

Four maple slat-back side chairs, replaced rush
seats, old refinish, c1760.
$2,250–2,700 *SK(B)*

An Irish ash chair,
with cord seat, c1860.
$150–220 *AF*

r. An elm and yew Windsor
armchair, with shaped cresting
and spindle inset back, saddle
seat and cabriole legs, mid-18thC.
$450–520 *SK*

An Irish famine chair, c1840.
$300–375 *ByI*

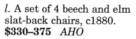

Beware!

When buying stripped pine, check that
the arms and legs are secure, as the
chemical process of stripping the wood
can loosen joints. The softness of pine
can also mean that feet and cornices on
older pieces may have been replaced.
Check that the workmanship is good,
and the colours match.

l. A set of 4 beech and elm
slat-back chairs, c1880.
$330–375 *AHO*

A child's elm chair, c1840.
$110–125 *COW*

l. A Victorian elm and
beech carver chair.
$230–260 *WLD*

Children's Furniture

The children's
furniture illustrated
in this guide no
longer complies with
EC safety
regulations, and
must not be used for
its original purpose.

A child's elm and
beech chair, c1895.
$60–80 *OLM*

A child's ash chair, c1860.
$30–45 *SAU*

Chests of Drawers

A Georgian pine chest of drawers, with original handles and escutcheons, 31¼in (79cm) wide.
$530–600 AHO

A pine chest of drawers, with 2 short and 3 long drawers, c1860, 39½in (100.5cm) wide.
$375–450 SAU

A Scottish pine chest of drawers, c1860, 50in (127cm) wide.
$900–1,000 AL

A Scottish pine chest of drawers, c1860, 55in (139.5cm) wide.
$900–1,000 AL

A stripped pine chest of drawers, with 2 short and 2 long drawers, with original stencil type decoration, c1870, 44in (112cm) wide.
$420–480 AHO

r. A Victorian pine chest of drawers, with glazed cupboard top, 22¾in (58cm) wide.
$530–600 AHO

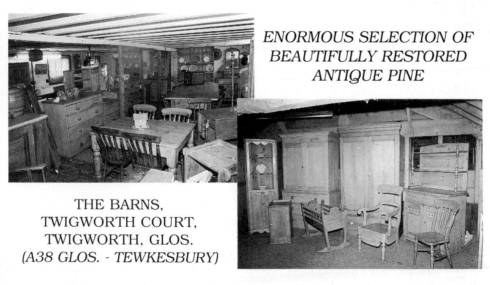

A pine Wellington type chest, c1865, 18in (45.5cm) wide.
$415–480 *HOA*

A pine chest of drawers, c1880, 38in (96.5cm) wide.
$375–415 *AL*

A Victorian pine chest of drawers, with turned feet, 39¼in (100cm) wide.
$450–530 *AHO*

A pine chest of drawers, c1860, 30½in (77.5cm) wide.
$300–375 *SAU*

A Continental pine chest of drawers, c1840, 44in (112cm) wide.
$1,000–1,100 *HOA*

A satinwood dressing chest, with 3 long drawers, c1910, 36in (91.5cm) wide.
$450–530 *COW*

A Dutch pine chest of drawers, with serpentine top, c1890, 44in (112cm) wide.
$675–750 *BOR*

r. A pine chest of drawers, c1890, 36in (91.5cm) wide.
$470–600 *BOR*

Chests

A German pine dome-topped chest, c1880, 41½in (105.5cm) long.
$220–270 *WLD*

A pine plank top chest, with 3 ebonised panels, interspaced by 4 split ebonised spindles, Essex County, Massachusetts, 17thC, 50in (127cm) long.
$7,800–8,700 *B*

Cots

A Continental pine rocking cot, c1880, 36in (91.5cm) long.
$185–225 *ASP*

Cupboards

An Irish pine food cupboard, with fitted interior, c1840, 59in (150cm) wide.
$1,300–1,400 *HOA*

A pine wardrobe, converted from a livery cupboard, c1780, 54¾in (139cm) wide.
$1,000–1,100 *AHO*

A pair of pine pot cupboards, c1880, 32in (81.5cm) high.
$480–530 *AL*

An Irish pine food cupboard, c1840, 55in (139.5cm) wide.
$1,200–1,350 *HOA*

A Welsh pine shelved cupboard, c1860, 64in (162.5cm) high.
$830–1,000 *BOR*

A pine cupboard, c1870, 24in (61cm) wide.
$150–180 *AL*

l. A pine bowfronted corner cupboard, c1830, 28in (71cm) wide.
$900–1,000 *AL*

r. A pine standing corner cupboard, with a pair of astragal glazed doors above a pair of solid panel doors, part possibly early 19thC, 30¼in (77cm) wide.
$1,650–2,000 *S(S)*

A Scottish pine food cupboard, with 2 drawers and brass escutcheons, c1830, 51in (129.5cm) wide.
$1,300–1,400 *HOA*

An Irish pine livery cupboard, c1840, 78in (198cm) wide.
$1,300–1,400 *HOA*

A pine cupboard, with 2 doors, c1880, 36in (91.5cm) wide.
$270–300 *AL*

A pine cupboard, with 2 doors, c1880, 46in (117cm) wide.
$270–300 *AL*

A pine cupboard, with 2 doors, fitted with shelves, c1880, 29½in (75cm) wide.
$210–240 *AHO*

A Scandinavian miniature pine cupboard, c1890, 28in (71cm) wide.
$300–375 *BOR*

A pine pot cupboard, c1880, 33in (84cm) high.
$240–270 *AL*

A pine pot cupboard, c1880, 32in (81.5cm) high.
$220–260 *AL*

l. A Victorian pine cupboard, fitted with shelves, 55¼in (140cm) wide.
$375–450 *AHO*

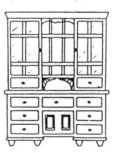

A Victorian pine fitted cupboard, 43in (109cm) wide.
$300–375 *AHO*

A French pine food cupboard, with lead lining, c1860, 48in (122cm) wide.
$530–600 *HOA*

A Danish pine sectional wardrobe, c1900, 72in (183cm) high.
$830–1,000 *BOR*

A French pine wardrobe, c1880, 51in (129.5cm) wide.
$900–1,000 *COW*

A Dutch pine cupboard, with a single drawer, c1880, 35½in (90cm) wide.
$375–450 *AHO*

r. A Victorian pine 2 door cupboard, fitted with shelves, 39in (99cm) wide.
$420–480 *AHO*

A Spanish pine cupboard, decorated with moulded detail, the upper section with a pair of glazed doors, the lower section with a frieze drawer and a pair of panelled doors, on later feet, early 19thC, 39in (99cm) wide.
$2,400–2,700 *CSK*

A French pitch pine buffet cupboard, with 2 glazed and 2 solid doors, c1845, 52in (132cm) wide.
$1,800–2,000 *SAU*

Desks

A mid-Victorian lady's pine writing desk, with slope, c1870, 36in (91.5cm) wide.
$720–820 *HOA*

A Scandinavian pine pedestal desk, c1890, 48in (122cm) wide.
$1,000–1,100 *BOR*

A pine partners' desk, with drawers and cupboards, Cumbria, c1860, 84in (213.5cm) wide.
$1,350–1,500 *HOA*

Dressers

A George III stained pine dresser, 64in (162.5cm) wide.
$3,600–4,200 *KID*

A pine breakfront dresser, with open shelves on each side of glazed breakfront, the lower section with 2 drawers and a potboard, flanked by cupboards, mid-19thC, 147in (373cm) wide.
$6,300–7,500 *WV*

A pine dresser, the upper section with glazed doors, with 3 drawers and a cupboard below, c1870, 65in (165cm) wide.
$600–720 *HOA*

r. A pine dresser, the base with 2 cupboard doors, c1860, 60in (152.5cm) wide.
$1,000–1,100 *HOA*

A pine dresser base, with 3 drawers, c1840, 70in (178cm) wide.
$630–750 *HOA*

A pine dresser base, with 3 drawers and 2 cupboards, c1850, 60in (152.5cm) wide.
$750–900 *HOA*

A pine dresser, with 3 drawers above 2 cupboard doors, c1900, 73in (185.5cm) wide.
$1,500–1,800 *COW*

A pine potboard dresser, c1860, 93in (236cm) high.
$2,200–2,600 *BOR*

A Victorian pine bench dresser, with 4 small doors, on cut-out legs, 63¾in (162cm) wide.
$2,200–2,700 *DOR*

A pine dresser, the lower section with 2 drawers and 2 cupboards, c1860, 72in (183cm) wide.
$1,000–1,200 *HOA*

r. A pine dresser, the base with 2 drawers and 2 cupboard doors, c1860, 60in (152.5cm) wide.
$975–1,125 *HOA*

l. A Victorian pine dresser base, with 2 pairs of doors below 2 drawers, 56in (142cm) wide.
$675–750 *AHO*

r. A Victorian pine dresser, with ornate panelled doors, 40½in (103cm) wide.
$675–750 *AHO*

A pine dresser, the upper section with 2 glazed doors, 2 drawers and 2 cupboard doors below, c1860, 43in (109cm) wide.
$1,200–1,350 *SAU*

A French pine dresser, c1860, 49in (124.5cm) wide.
$1,000–1,200 *SAU*

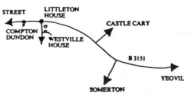

Linen Presses

r. A Scottish pine linen press, c1845, 60in (152.5cm) wide. **$975–1,125** *HOA*

l. A pine linen press, c1840, 48in (122cm) wide. **$1,125–1,300** *HOA*

A Victorian pine linen press, fitted with slides, 2 short and 2 long drawers, 48in (122cm) wide. **$1,500–1,800** *AHO*

Night Commodes

r. A pine commode, with folding back and sides, c1890, 22in (56cm) wide. **$180–220** *AL*

l. A pine commode, c1870, 17in (43cm) wide. **$180–220** *AL*

Pine Manufacturers

Apart from Maples, Heal's, Shoolbreds of London and Gillows of Lancaster, there are few well-known makers of pine furniture in Britain. Some was made in country workshops, giving us engaging primitive pieces, and some for 'the big house' by estate carpenters and joiners, who produced free-standing furniture, one-off pieces, built-in panelling and shutters.

Shelves

A set of pine shelves, c1890, 31½in (80cm) wide. **$90–105** *AHO*

A set of pine shelves, c1890, 44in (112cm) wide. **$450–525** *AL*

A set of pine hanging shelves, c1860, 41in (104cm) wide. **$270–330** *SAU*

Sideboards

A Regency pine sideboard, c1820, 60in (152.5cm) wide. **$675–825** *HOA*

l. A Victorian pine sideboard, with fitted shelves, 38½in (98cm) wide. **$600–640** *AHO*

A Continental pine chiffonier, c1880, 39in (99cm) wide. **$675–825** *HOA*

Steps

A pine step ladder,with platform top, c1900, 27in (68.5cm) high.
$30–45 *AL*

A pine step ladder, c1880, 41¼in (105cm) high.
$75–90 *AHO*

A pine step ladder, c1900, 31in (79cm) high.
$60–75 *AHO*

Stools

A pine stool, c1880, 6in (15cm) high.
$35–50 *AL*

A pine stool, c1880, 14in (35.5cm) wide.
$35–45 *AL*

A pine stool, c1860, 13in (33cm) high.
$35–45 *COW*

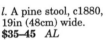

> **Miller's is a price GUIDE not a price LIST**

l. A pine stool, c1880, 19in (48cm) wide.
$35–45 *AL*

A pine stool, c1880, 14in (35.5cm) high.
$30–40 *AL*

A pine shoe shop stool, c1900,
14in (35.5cm) high.
$65–80 *AL*

A pine stool, c1920,
15in (38cm) wide.
$35–45 *AL*

A pine stool, c1890,
19in (48cm) wide.
$45–50 *AL*

A pine three-legged stool,
joined by stretchers, c1880,
19in (48.5cm) high.
$45–60 *OPH*

A pine stool, c1880,
11¾in (30cm) wide.
$35–45 *AHO*

A pine stool, c1900,
22in (56cm) high.
$45–50 *AL*

A Victorian elm stool,
11¾in (30cm) diam.
$50–60 *AHO*

A pine stool, with
wrought iron
stretchers, c1900,
22in (56cm) high.
$35–45 *AL*

A pine stool, c1920,
26in (66cm) high.
$45–50 *AL*

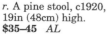

r. A pine stool, c1920,
19in (48cm) high.
$35–45 *AL*

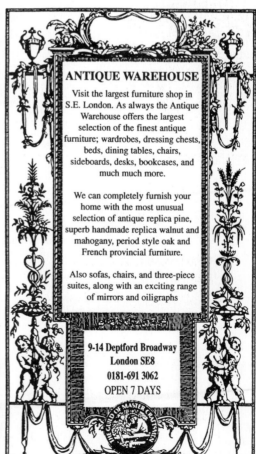

Tables

A Georgian pine side table, c1810, 36in (91.5cm) wide.
$300–340 *WLD*

A pair of X-frame pine trestle tavern tables, each with the original iron banding to the top and central iron stretchers, c1780, 24½in (62cm) wide.
$4,500–5,250 *RYA*

A pine table, c1860, 42in (106.5cm) wide.
$300–375 *SAU*

A pine serving table, with 2 drawers, c1835, 54in (137cm) wide.
$525–675 *HOA*

An Irish pine refectory table, with 2 drawers and double stretchers, c1860, 66½in (169cm) long.
$675–750 *AHO*

A pine cricket table, with turned legs, c1860, 30in (76cm) diam.
$375–450 *AL*

A pine cricket table, c1860, 32in (81.5cm) diam.
$400–450 *AL*

A pine cricket table, c1860, 25½in (63.5cm) diam.
$450–525 *AL*

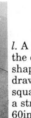

r. A pine side serving table, with 2 drawers, c1870, 45in (114.5cm) wide.
$350–400 *AL*

l. A pine kitchen table, the cleated top above a shaped frieze, single end drawer and raised on square legs, joined by a stretcher, late 19thC, 60in (152.5cm) long.
$375–450 *Hal*

An X-frame pine table, c1870, 89in (226cm) long.
$600–675 *AL*

A pine side table, with 2 drawers, with original patination, c1860, 54in (137cm) wide.
$425–675 *HOA*

A pine tilt-top table, c1870, 28in (71cm) diam.
$375–450 *AL*

A pine side table, with single drawer, c1880, 33in (84cm) wide.
$185–220 *AL*

A pine table, with gallery, single drawer and turned legs, c1880, 34in (86.5cm) wide.
$300–340 *AL*

A pine writing table, with 2 drawers, c1870, 41in (104cm) wide.
$500–550 *AL*

A pine tripod table, c1870, 18in (45.5cm) diam.
$210–240 *AL*

A pine Pembroke table c1870, 33in (84cm) wide.
$300–375 *BOR*

l. A pine Pembroke table, c1880, 35in (89cm) wide.
$240–285 *COW*

r. A pine table, with a single drawer and turned legs, c1880, 48in (122cm) wide.
$450–500 *AL*

l. A pine sofa table, with turned legs, c1880, 48in (122cm) wide.
$225–260 *AL*

A pine table, with straight legs, c1880, 78in (198cm) long.
$300–340 *AL*

A pine drop-leaf table, damaged, c1880, 39in (99cm) diam.
$185–215 *AL*

A pine table, with a shelf, c1890, 35½in (90cm) wide.
$135–175 *AL*

A pine side table, c1880, 37in (94cm) wide.
$225–275 *COW*

A pine side table, c1890, 36in (91.5cm) wide.
$150–180 *AL*

A Victorian pine drop-leaf table, 33in (84cm) wide.
$180–220 *AHO*

A Victorian pine writing table, with a drawer and turned legs, 35in (89cm) wide.
$185–225 *AHO*

A pine table, c1890, 40in (101.5cm) wide.
$225–275 *COW*

A pine cottage table, c1880, 33in (84cm) wide.
$300–375 *BOR*

A Victorian pine kitchen table, with a drawer and turned legs, 38¼in (97cm) wide.
$180–220 *AHO*

A pine table, with straight legs, c1900, 30in (76cm) square.
$150–180 *AL*

A Continental pine table, with a single drawer, late 19thC, 47in (119.5cm) wide.
$400–450 *FOX*

A Spanish pine table, c1855, 41in (104cm) diam.
$600–675 *SAU*

l. A pine drop-leaf table, c1900, 33in (84cm) wide.
$185–215 *AL*

r. An Edwardian pine side table, 71in (180cm) long.
$450–525 *AHO*

Pine Furniture

Pine furniture can largely be divided into regional types. In the south of England one can find conventional chests of drawers, tall closed and open dressers and potboard bases. Wales produced superb dressers and unusual types of chests of drawers. In the north, Scotland is particularly noted for large chests of drawers with twisted panels and various drawer arrangements, wall racks and shelves and low dressers. Typical examples of Irish pine furniture include primitive chairs, substantial food cupboards and one-piece dressers.

Washstands

A pine washstand, c1880, 29in (73.5cm) wide.
$225–275 *AL*

A pine washstand, with faux bamboo legs, c1830, 26½in (67.5cm) wide.
$300–375 *SAU*

Miscellaneous

A German chemist's or apothecary's pine flight of drawers, c1880, 98in (250cm) long.
$1,500–1,800 *HOA*

A pine saddle rack, c1880, 36in (91.5cm) wide.
$210–250 *AL*

A pine meat safe, c1880, 24in (61cm) high.
$90–120 *AHO*

A pine plate rack, c1890, 33in (84cm) wide.
$225–275 *BOR*

l. A pine sack truck, c1900, 41¼in (105cm) high.
$60–75 *AHO*

A butcher's pine block, c1870, 49½in (125.5cm) wide.
$450–525 *AHO*

A pine sledge, c1920, 38in (96.5cm) wide.
$45–55 *AL*

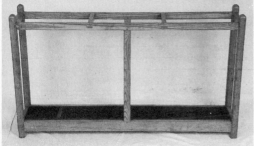

A pine stick stand, c1880, 48in (122cm) wide.
$150–170 *AL*

A pine sledge, inscribed 'Royal Racer', c1930, 40in (101.5cm) wide.
$45–50 *AL*

Painted Pine

An Italian painted pine desk box, the interior decorated with a scene of *The Flight into Egypt,* 17thC, 20in (51cm) wide.
$2,000–2,250 *DBA*

A Continental pine fall-front utility box, painted and decorated in red, green, yellow and brown with houses in landscapes, paint worn, early 19thC, 8¼in (21cm) wide.
$1,200–1,500 *S(NY)*

A painted pine tea caddy, with compartmented interior, mounted with a brass bail handle and escutcheon, on bracket feet, New England, 19thC, 9in (23cm) wide.
$3,400–4,200 *S(NY)*

r. A Czechoslovakian carved and painted pine chest, c1775, 45in (115cm) wide.
$530–600 *WLD*

A Hungarian painted pine box, c1755, 46in (117cm) wide.
$530–600 *WLD*

A grain painted and decorated pine chest, with 3 drawers, some paint missing, Pennsylvania, c1780, 50½in (128.5cm) wide.
$3,000–3,750 *SK*

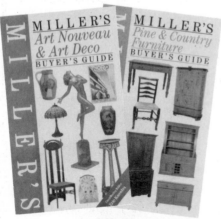

A painted pine blanket chest, signed 'John Selzer', Dauphin County, now Lebanon County, Pennsylvania, dated '1793', 52in (132cm) wide.
$12,750–14,250 *S(NY)*

r. A Hungarian pine box, with original paint, c1858, 50in (127cm) wide.
$450–525 *WLD*

A Czechoslovakian pine box, with original painted decoration, c1870, 39in (99cm) wide.
$300–375 *WLD*

A Romanian painted pine box, c1875, 32in (81.5cm) wide.
$340–420 *WLD*

A Victorian pine box, with original green paint, c1875, 37in (94cm) wide.
$220–300 *WLD*

A painted pine mule chest, decorated with a landscape and figures, on bracket feet, 42in (106.5cm) wide.
$3,000–3,750 *BWe*

A Hungarian pine box, with original painted decoration, c1875, 43½in (110.5cm) wide.
$450–525 *WLD*

l. A pair of George III style green painted cabinets, each with a lead trellis-mullioned glazed door with shelved interior, on bracket feet, 19thC, 35in (89cm) wide.
$10,500–12,000 *S(NY)*

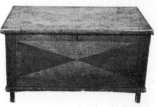

r. A painted pine chest, c1880, 42in (106.5cm) wide.
$230–260 *OD*

A painted pine cupboard, with wire mesh in the door panels, early 20thC, 34in (86.5cm) wide.
$300–375 *FOX*

A red painted pine cupboard, New England, c1740, 35in (89cm) wide.
$13,500–15,000 *S(NY)*

l. A Welsh painted pine food cupboard, with pierced decoration and original hinges, c1720, 24in (61cm) wide.
$970–1,000 *APa*

A bank of chemist's pine drawers, with original paint, worn, c1780, 48in (122cm) wide.
$1,200–1,350 *APa*

An Irish pine dresser, with original paint, c1840, 45in (114.5cm) wide.
$1,100–1,300 *HOA*

A Romanian pine dresser, with original paint, mid-19thC, 46in (117cm) wide.
$900–1,000 *FOX*

r. An Irish green painted pine dresser, c1860, 54in (137cm) wide.
$1,200–1,300 *HOA*

l. An Irish green painted pine dresser, c1860, 48in (122cm) wide.
$825–975 *HOA*

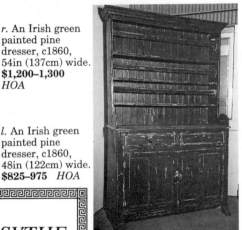

A Polish pine dresser, with original painted decoration, c1875, 37in (94cm) wide.
$850–1,000 *WLD*

l. A Welsh pine settle, with original green paint, c1780, 64in (162.5cm) wide.
$2,250–2,700 *APa*

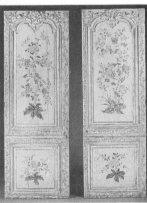

r. A set of 4 Louis XV pine cream and green painted boiserie panels, each with 2 sections painted in the chinoiserie style with birds amidst shrubs, carved on the summit with shells flanked by foliate scrolls, rebacked, widened, now mounted as 4 single doors, distressed, widest 30in (76cm) wide.
$42,000–48,000 *C*

A pine table, with 2 drawers, original paint, reduced in height, 19thC, 54in (137cm) wide.
$300–375 *FOX*

A pine side table, with original painted decoration, mid-19thC, 34in (86.5cm) wide.
$270–330 *FOX*

A mid-European pine wardrobe, with original paint, 19thC, 39in (99cm) wide.
$450–550 *FOX*

A painted pine plate rack, c1820, 18½in (47cm) wide.
$230–260 *WLD*

A set of green painted pine shelves, c1830, 30in (76cm) wide.
$270–300 *APa*

An American pine eagle, carved by Wilhelm Schimmel, painted black, yellow, red and green, c1860, 22¾in (58cm) wide.
$39,000–45,000 *S(NY)*

A mid-European pine and beech spinning wheel, with original red paint, 19thC, 48in (122cm) high.
$200–270 *FOX*

A set of pine spice drawers, with original paint, c1880, 7in (18cm) wide.
$150–180 *WLD*

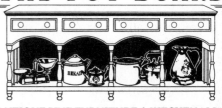

A green painted pine wheelbarrow, c1890, 65in (165cm) long.
$300–375 *AL*

KITCHENWARE

A hand-woven berry
picking basket, c1880,
12½in (32cm) wide.
$80–95 *RYA*

A wicker basket, c1920,
11in (28cm) diam.
$15–20 *AL*

Two American wire baskets,
for eggs or fruit, c1890,
largest 7in (18cm) high.
l. **$45–55**
r. **$110–125** *MB*

A yellow basin, c1900,
10in (25.5cm) diam.
$10–15 *AL*

A brown basin, c1910,
8in (20.5cm) diam.
$10–15 *AL*

A yellow basin, c1920,
8½in (21.5cm) diam.
$15–20 *AL*

A sycamore bowl, with repairs,
19thC, 18in (45.5cm) diam.
$120–150 *FOX*

A pine bread board, c1890,
25in (63.5cm) wide.
$35–45 *ASP*

An enamel bread bin, c1900,
11in (28cm) high.
$20–30 *AL*

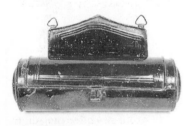

A japanned candle tin, with hinged
lid, c1880, 12in (30.5cm) long.
$150–160 *WeA*

A cardboard shortbread box,
c1920, 9in (23cm) diam.
$15–20 *AL*

A steel cheese iron, used
for testing cheese, c1830,
7½in (19cm) long.
$65–80 *WeA*

A sycamore butter worker,
a pair of butter pats and a
butter curler, c1900,
largest 6in (15cm) long.
$10–15 each *AL*

Two cream pans, c1890, largest
10in (25.5cm) diam. **$20–30 each**
An enamel cream skimmer, c1900,
6½in (16.5cm) diam.
$10–15 *AL*

A 2lb butter crock, inscribed Maypole Dairy Co Ltd, c1910, 5in (12.5cm) high.
$120–150 *WeA*

A silver plated cream can, c1920, 4½in (11.5cm) high.
$20–25 *AL*

A brass display milk churn, engraved with vines and leaves, lid missing, some damage, late 19thC, 11in (28cm) high.
$675–820 *BS*

Coffee Grinders

By the mid-18th century, coffee had become a favourite drink with the middle and upper classes (the only people who could afford to drink it). Although coffee was ground by grocers in large cast iron coffee mills, it also became fashionable to grind beans at home, using small wooden coffee grinders.

In 1815 the iron founder, Archibald Kenrick, patented a new box-type cast iron coffee grinder. The coffee was put into the bowl at the top and when the handle was turned the blades ground the beans so they fell into the drawer at the base. Early grinders had brass or copper bowls. Always check the bowl is in good condition; it is the weakest part of the coffee grinder and prone to cracking or splitting.

The Kenrick coffee grinder design was copied by many other manufacturers and iron founders, such as Clark, Baldwin and Siddons until WWI. They are highly collectable today, particularly the cast iron wall-mounted grinders. Coffee grinders did not change greatly in design during the 19th and 20th centuries and were produced by makers all over Europe and North America.

A cast iron and brass coffee mill, by Kenrick, c1870, 5½in (14cm) high.
$180–220 *WeA*

A cast iron and glass egg timer, c1880, 4in (10cm) high.
$100–120 *WeA*

An all cast iron coffee mill, Cathedral shape, by Kenrick, c1880, 7½in (19cm) high.
$270–300 *WeA*

It is quite rare to find a coffee mill of this type in such excellent condition.

An American food chopper, tin with a wooden handle, 1880s, 8½in (21.5cm) wide.
$110–125 *MB*

An enamel flour shaker, c1900, 4in (10cm) high.
$10–15 *AL*

An ice cream three-way ice cream wafer maker, c1920, 3½in (9cm) long.
$45–55 *AL*

A J. Lyons ice cream cup, c1920, 3½in (9cm) high.
$8–10 *AL*

An ice cream scoop, c1920, 8in (20.5cm) long.
$35–45 *AL*

An ice cream scoop, c1930, 6in (15cm) long.
$10–15 *AL*

A Victorian flat iron stove, 13¾in (35cm) wide.
$200–240 *DOR*

r. An 'egg' iron, by Kenrick, c1870, 8½in (21.5cm) high.
$220–270 *WeA*

After heating on the stove, this iron was held by the shaft, which was often detachable from the base, so that the egg-shaped top could be inserted into the sleeve or skirt of a garment to remove creases from puffs and gathers.

A steel goffering iron, c1800, 9in (23cm) high.
$180–210 *WeA*

A tin fish kettle, c1910, 13in (33cm) long.
$30–40 *AL*

A milk jug, c1930, 5in (12.5cm) high.
$20–25 *AL*

A half gallon measuring jug, c1900, 8½in (21.5cm) high.
$20–25 *AL*

A wooden knife box, c1900, 13in (33cm) wide.
$30–40 *AL*

A wooden butter mould, 19thC, 6in (15cm) diam.
$90–100 *FOX*

An iron 'lazy arm' kettle tilt, c1830, 20in (51cm) long.
$200–220 *WeA*

This piece of apparatus was attached by the ring to the chimney crane, and a kettle was hung on the two hooks below. The long arm was pushed down, which would enable the heavy kettle to pour water without being lifted manually.

l. Two enamel jugs, c1920, largest 12in (30.5cm) high.
$15–20 each *AL*

A tinplate chocolate Easter egg mould,
c1880, 6in (15cm) long.
$20–30 *IW*

A tin chocolate mould, by Letang Fils, Paris, in the shape of a
fish, 1930s, 16½in (42cm) long.
$280–300 *MB*

A tin spiral mould, for
making *gateau de pommes*,
c1880, 8in (20.5cm) diam.
$200–220 *MB*

A pewter ice cream mould,
in 3 pieces, registered 1868,
c1870, 6½in (16.5cm) high.
$160–180 *WeA*

Kitchen Moulds

In the 19th century, moulds were
commonly used in middle and
upper class households, where
cooks would prepare elaborate
meals with either a savoury or a
sweet jelly, blancmange or mousse
as an impressive centrepiece. The
most decorative moulds were made
of copper and Wedgwood creamware,
but they were also produced in white
earthenware. By the turn of the 20th
century, moulds were commercially
made and became available in a
wider variety of materials.

A pewter ice cream mould, hinged top
and bottom, both detachable, c1870,
6in (15cm) wide.
$270–300 *WeA*

A tin and copper
mould, c1880,
6in (15cm) long.
$150–180 *WeA*

A tin iced pudding mould,
shaped as a castle, c1895,
5¾in (14.5cm) high.
$75–90 *MB*

A tin mould, in the shape of a roast
chicken, c1880, 10in (25.5cm) long.
$90–100 *WeA*

A set of 4 tin scallop shell moulds,
c1900, 2½in (6.5cm) wide.
$10–15 *IW*

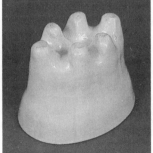

A ceramic jelly mould,
c1880, 6½in (16.5cm) wide.
$15–25 *AL*

l. A pewter hinged marzipan
mould, in the shape of a
bunch of asparagus, c1870,
3in (7.5cm) high.
$60–75 *WeA*

A tin and copper iced pudding
mould, the top with a design
of a rose and thistle, c1890,
6in (15cm) wide.
$150–170 *MB*

A wooden spice box, c1880,
8in (20.5cm) wide.
$60–75 *MofC*

A metal spoon and ladle, c1920,
ladle 16in (40.5cm) long.
$6–10 each *AL*

A Weetabix tin, c1930,
10in (25.5cm) high.
$10–15 *AL*

Two horn spoons:
top. c1820, 8in (20.5cm) long. **$12–18**
bottom. c1890, 7in (18cm) long.
$8–14 *AL*

A tea or coffee tin, with
hinged lid, painted black
with gold decoration, c1880,
5in (12.5cm) wide.
$95–120 *WeA*

A tin urn, the brass tap with
a wooden handle, c1900,
18in (45.5cm) high.
$45–60 *AL*

A pair of steel and brass sugar nips,
on a painted cast iron base, c1870,
12¾in (32.5cm) long.
$240–270 *WeA*

A coffee tin, c1930,
4in (10cm) high.
$8–10 *AL*

Miller's is a price GUIDE
not a price LIST

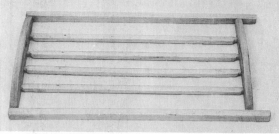

A Victorian pine bath rack, c1900, 28in (71cm) long.
$35–45 *ASP*

A wooden towel rail, c1920, 25in (63.5cm) long.
$30–40 *AL*

A wooden roller towel holder, c1920, 19½in (48.5cm) long.
$25–30 *AL*

A French cast iron miniature waffle iron, with
wooden handle, c1895, 12in (30.5cm) long.
$120–150 *MB*

POTTERY & PORCELAIN

A trend towards specialisation has continued over the past year as more and more dealers have decided to concentrate on one factory, designer or period. Although levels of trading are generally good, dealers cannot sit at home and wait for customers. Many identify fairs most likely to be attended by collectors in their field and take their stock to their customers, or alternatively hold their own specialised exhibitions. The market for items relating to the collector's home town or region is particularly strong, and this interest is further fuelled by collectors' guides and clubs. Success does, of course, require prices to be set at realistic levels.

In some fields this demand for local wares is not a new phenomenon. Liverpool pottery

A Liverpool tin-glazed mug, c1760.
$6,250–6,750 *P*

and porcelain, for example, has always sold well to Liverpool-born collectors. During the year the buoyancy of this market was proved time and time again. For example, a small tin-glazed mug of c1760, just 3¾in (9.5cm) high and decorated with floral sprays in Chinese style, sold for $6,210 at Phillips.

This trend towards regional collecting is also evident in the European market. Maiolica, for example, now sells almost exclusively to trade buyers from Italy.

An Italian maiolica vase, probably Venice, damaged and repaired, mid-16thC, 9in (23cm) high.
$3,750–4,500 *Bon*

What they don't buy may remain unsold; a fact that has brought the light of realism to auction reserves and retail prices.

Over recent years, the main problem for dealers and auctioneers has been finding good quality stock, and though good price levels continue to be achieved, potential vendors have linked the idea of recession with the art market in general and this has affected the number of items being brought in for sale. Turnover may have fallen considerably as a consequence, but this has been in direct proportion to the reduced volume of goods passing through the salerooms, a clear indication that overall price levels have remained stable. Persuading potential vendors of these facts has not proved easy.

The renewed popularity of sumptuously decorated late 19th and early 20th century English porcelain wares has continued. John Sandon of Phillips reports particular enthusiasm for Crown Derby, and cites as examples an inkwell decorated by Albert Gregory (1913) which sold for $8,970 and two pierced plates, decorated and gilded by Desiré Leroy (1902), which made $6,900 and $6,210.

The market has remained steady for several years and, for the most part, relatively predictable. This year the percentage of lots which remained unsold at auction decreased as sellers reacted to the predictability of the market by setting realistic reserves.

A pair of George Jones majolica comports modelled with animal figures representative of Africa and Europe, c1870.
$8,500–9,500 *HDS*

The most bullish and unpredictable field remains that of English majolica. A number of rare and decorative subjects have appeared at auction over the year and almost all have exceeded estimates by a considerable margin. Typifying this trend were a pair of unattributed comports modelled with allegorical subjects representative of the Continents – Europe modelled with a stag and doe, Africa with a lion and lioness. Damage kept the estimate to a modest $750–1,500, but in the end the pair sold for $8,580.

Christopher Spencer

POTTERY
Baskets

A pair of Nove faïence armorial baskets, painted with coloured floursprays, the interiors painted with the arms of Grimani of Venice and Vicenza among trophies of war, some flaking, c1760, 9¾in (24.5cm) wide.
$11,250–12,750 *S*

An English pearlware basket and stand, printed in underglaze blue and white with figures amongst classical columns, floral and diaper borders, lattice piercing and moulded lug handles, printed title 'Ancient Rome' in underglaze blue, c1820, 10¾in (27.5cm) wide.
$450–525 *Hal*

A Minton majolica bowl, pierced with a trellis pattern below a moulded band of flowerheads above oak leaves issuing from branches, supported by 3 doves, enriched in colours, shape No. 874, damaged and repaired, impressed marks, date code for 1867, 12¾in (32.5cm) diam.
$2,250–3,000 *CSK*

Bellarmines

A Continental salt glazed bellarmine, c1670, 8½in (21.5cm) high.
$420–525 *IW*

Bowls & Dishes

An English blue and white delft bowl, c1750, 12in (30.5cm) diam.
$3,750–4,500 *JHo*

r. A delft blue and white shaving bowl, decorated with tools of the trade, inscribed 'JS 1734', crack and damage to rim, 10in (25.5cm) diam.
$4,000–4,500 *KID*

Bottles

A German bellarmine, with moulded mask and central impressed horse-shoes, brown speckled glaze, minor wear, 17thC, 15in (38cm) high.
$450–525 *WIL*

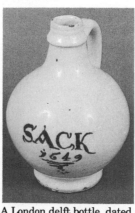

A London delft bottle, dated '1649', 6in (15cm) high.
$6,750–7,500 *JHo*

A Staffordshire salt glazed bottle, c1760, 8¼in (21cm) high.
$3,500–4,000 *JHo*

A Brislington delft fluted dish, painted in blue with a bust portrait of Charles II and inscribed 'CR2' with crown and brooch, both highlighted in yellow, border crack, one chip restored, c1680, 11½in (29.5cm) diam.
$33,000–37,500 *S*

A Bristol delft punchbowl, the exterior painted with a continuous landscape with figures, trees and buildings, the interior painted with a three-masted sailing ship, within a border of diaper panels and stylised flowers, damaged and with restoration, c1750, 18¼in (46.5cm) diam.
$9,750–11,250 *Hal*
Size and quality of decoration on this early English delft bowl made it exceptional and an instance where absolute rarity made the usual concerns over condition almost irrelevant. The damage is quite obvious, and the buyer, who described his purchase as 'one of the most remarkable English delft bowls known to exist', rushed the bowl off to New York for exhibition in the 1995 International Fine Art Fair.
Early English pottery was badly hit by the disclosure a few years ago that both collectors and specialist dealers had been fooled by modern fakes, but the field is still strong for the right pieces.

A creamware bowl, the interior painted with 3 ships, the exterior decorated with transfer printed hunting scenes, impressed 'Wedgwood', c1785, 12½in (32cm) diam.
$2,700–3,000 *JHo*

A pearlware bowl, printed in blue with a central medallion surmounted by a crown, with brown line rim, restored, c1793, 10¼in (26cm) diam.
$450–525 *SAS*

A Derbyshire salt glazed pouring bowl, c1840, 8in (20.5cm) wide.
$60–75 *IW*

A majolica two-handled dish, c1900, 14in (35.5cm) wide.
$225–275 *MofC*

A yellow ground pottery bowl, painted in bright enamel colours, possibly Staffordshire, c1824, 6in (15cm) diam.
$320–420 *HOW*

An Urbino maiolica shallow bowl, painted with an interior scene of an expectant mother seated on a stool, the base painted *en grisaille* with a winged putto on a blue washed ground, outer rim missing and crack, c1570, 6½in (16.5cm) diam.
$5,250–6,000 *P*

Buildings

A Staffordshire model of a castle, c1820, 5in (12.5cm) high.
$300–330 *JO*

A Staffordshire model of a cottage, c1850, 7in (17.5cm) high.
$300–340 *JO*

A Staffordshire cottage group, c1830, 8in (20.5cm) high.
$900–950 *JO*

A Staffordshire model of a cottage, c1870, 10½in (26.5cm) high.
$375–425 *JO*

Busts

A Wedgwood black basalt library bust of Lord Byron, impressed 'Wedgwood' and with title, c1900, 15in (38cm) high.
$1,275–1,425 *Bon*

A Leeds bust of Shakespeare, c1815, 9½in (24cm) high.
$300–375 *SER*

Candlesticks

A pair of Künersberg faïence candlesticks, each modelled in the form of a putto balancing a basket of fruit or flowers, one sconce restuck, c1750, 8¾in (22cm) high.
$26,250–29,250 *S*

Cheese Dishes

A Wiesbaden rococo scroll-moulded candlestick, painted *en camaieu vert* with flowersprays within green line rims, damage to nozzle and restuck, rim chips, c1770, 9in (23cm) high.
$3,500–4,000 *C*

r. A Victorian Jasperware blue and white cheese dish and cover, probably Adams, the cover with a continuous frieze of winged figures and trees, with oak and acorn borders, late 19thC, 10in (25.5cm) high.
$150–180 *Hal*

l. A George Jones majolica cheese bell and stand, moulded in relief with insects and foliage, impressed monogram and registration mark, pattern No. 3432, c1870, 13½in (34cm) high.
$1,500–1,800 *S(S)*

Centrepieces

A Minton majolica four-tiered stand, the bowls formed as oyster shells, with metal mechanism, shape No. 636, damaged and restored, impressed marks and date code for 1872, 10½in (26.5cm) high.
$3,750–4,500 *CSK*

Coffee & Teapots

A Staffordshire red stoneware teapot and cover, by David and John Philip Elers, applied on both sides with flowering branches and acorns, with contemporary silver chain mounts, minor chips some applied decoration missing, c1690, 5in (12.5cm) high.
$11,250–12,750 *S*

A Staffordshire slip cast teapot and lid, c1750, 4¼in (11cm) high.
$2,400–2,800 *JHo*

A Whieldon teapot, in the form of a house, some restoration, c1755, 5½in (14cm) high.
$825–975 *IW*

A Measham ware teapot and cover, applied with sprigs of flowers and a hand protruding from the neck, dark brown glaze, cover restored, late 19thC, 19¼in (49cm) high.
$900–1,000 *S(S)*

A glazed red ware teapot, with sprig decoration, c1750, 3½in (9cm) high.
$300–375 *IW*

A Staffordshire agate ware teapot and cover, minor repairs, c1755, 4¾in (12cm) high.
$4,500–5,000 *JHo*

A Leeds creamware teapot and cover, decorated in iron-red, green and black with roses and leaves, within iron-red bands, c1770, 6in (15cm) high.
$450–525 *DN*

A melon-shaped teapot, with wooden replacement lid, c1765, 4½in (11.5cm) high.
$1,500–1,800 *IW*

A Staffordshire drab ware teapot, c1750, 4in (10cm) high.
$2,500–2,800 *JHo*

A solid agate ware teapot, replacement lid, c1755, 3½in (9cm) high.
$675–825 *IW*

A Staffordshire salt glazed teapot and cover, decorated in coloured enamels with flowers and utensils, cover damaged, c1765, 4¾in (12cm) high.
$600–750 *DN*

A Böttger red stoneware teapot and cover, with part polished body moulded with lambrequin lappets and a mask spout, small chips, c1710, 3¼in (8cm) high.
$30,000–33,000 *Bon*

Small pots with spouts from the early 18thC may be saffron pots rather than teapots.

l. A creamware teapot, probably Yorkshire, with spattered decoration, replacement cover, c1780, 4in (10cm) high.
$300–375 *IW*

Cow Creamers

A pearlware cow creamer, depicting a cow and suckling calf, with coloured sponged decoration, c1780, 4¼in (11cm) high.
$1,200–1,500 *BHa*

A pearlware cow creamer, probably St Anthony's Pottery, minor restoration, c1790, 5in (12.5cm) high.
$1,125–1,425 *BHa*

A Yorkshire cow creamer, with honey-coloured sponged decoration, original lid, c1800, 5¾in (14.5cm) high.
$975–1,275 *BHa*

A Swansea cow creamer, with naturalistic colouring, c1830, 7in (17.5cm) wide.
$525–675 *RP*

Cups

A Derbyshire salt glazed loving cup, c1800, 5¾in (14.5cm) high.
$240–300 *IW*

A Wedgwood encaustic decorated cup and stand, painted in white and terracotta with anthemion and bead borders, cup impressed upper case 'WEDGWOOD', stand impressed lower case 'Wedgwood', c1775.
$675–750 *Bon*

A creamware feeding cup, c1800, 6½in (16.5cm) wide.
$75–100 *IW*

A Gaudy Welsh cup and saucer, c1850, 5½in (14cm) diam.
$50–70 *OD*

l. A pair of Wedgwood *rosso antico* cups and stands, impressed upper case 'WEDGWOOD' and other marks, mid-19thC.
$1,000–1,200 *Bon*

A Victorian cup and saucer, inscribed 'Present from the Isle of Man', saucer 4½in (11.5cm) diam.
$15–25 *OD*

Miller's is a price GUIDE not a price LIST

A lustre ware cup and saucer, chipped, c1830, saucer 5½in (14cm) diam.
$20–30 *OD*

A cup and saucer, with chinoiserie decoration, c1830, saucer 6in (15cm) diam.
$55–65 *OD*

Figures – Animals

A tin glazed figure of a lion, probably Liverpool, decorated in manganese and red, with hollow body and glazed inside, mid-18thC, 8in (20.5cm) high.
$6,750–7,500 *JHo*

A pair of Staffordshire white salt glazed models of hawks, each with incised plumage, brown beaks and blue eyes, some damage, c1755, later Louis XV style ormolu bases, 11in (28cm) high.
$55,000–60,000 *CNY*

A Staffordshire model of a water buffalo, possibly Whieldon, c1760, 7½in (19cm) high.
$1,500–1,800 *JHo*

A Staffordshire creamware model of a recumbent goat, with manganese horns, and naturalistically modelled ground splashed with brown and green glazes, horns restuck, c1790, 7in (18cm) long.
$1,500–2,250 *CNY*

A Pratt ware model of a lion, underglaze decorated with green and blue glazed base, c1800, 12¼in (31cm) long.
$6,750–8,250 *JRe*

An English figure of a squirrel, eating a nut, with translucent green glaze, c1790, 10in (25.5cm) high.
$4,500–5,000 *HOW*

A creamware model of a dog, with enamel decoration over the glaze, c1790, 8in (20cm) long.
$1,425–1,500 *JRe*

A pearlware figure of a lion, enamelled in Pratt colours, c1800, 7¾in (20cm) long.
$1,000–1,350 *Bon*

A Staffordshire bull baiting group, glazed in naturalistic enamels, restoration to ears and horns, one ear missing, chip to base, late 18thC, 7in (18cm) long.
$600–675 *WIL*

A Pratt ware bear group, c1800, 8¼in (21cm) long.
$4,500–5,250 *JHo*

l. A Pratt ware coloured model of a lion, c1810, 7in (17.5cm) long.
$1,800–2,200 *HOW*

Pearlware

- An inexpensive form of pottery developed from Wedgwood's creamware in the late 18thC, using cheaper ingredients and a little cobalt blue.
- Early pearlware was decorated with hand-painted underglaze blue designs in Chinese style.
- Animals decorated in coloured enamels are amongst the most collectable of pearlware shapes.
- Pearlware was made in considerable quantities until about 1875.
- Most later pearlware is decorated with printed patterns in cobalt blue.

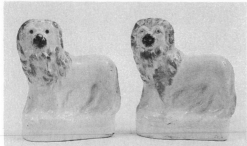

A pair of Staffordshire miniature figures of
lions, maker unknown, c1850, 3½in (9cm) high.
$215–245 each *SER*

A pair of Sherratt type pearlware models
of cows, with flowering bocage,
naturalistically painted in colours, each
base painted with rainbow colours,
restored, c1820, 7½in (19cm) high.
$1,200–1,500 *CSK*

A Staffordshire Enoch Wood
pearlware figure of a greyhound,
overglaze enamel decorated,
c1820, 4in (10cm) high.
$1,000–1,200 *JRe*

A Staffordshire figure of a pug,
enamel painted over a pearl
glaze, c1820, 3½in (9cm) high.
$600–750 *JRe*

A pearlware model of a lion,
enriched in shades of brown,
the globe in pink, the base
painted green above a black
marbled section, some damage,
repaired and overpainting,
c1820, 11¾in (30cm) long.
$1,800–2,800 *CSK*

l. A Staffordshire Enoch Wood
pearlware figure of pointer,
overglaze decorated, c1820,
3¾in (9.5cm) high.
$750–975 *JRe*

A salt glazed stoneware figure of
a lion, c1830, 5in (12.5cm) high.
$750–900 *JRe*

A glazed stoneware figure of a
lion, possibly Yorkshire, c1840,
7½in (19cm) long.
$150–180 *IW*

A Staffordshire group of a
whippet and a spaniel,
'Elegance and Patience',
maker unknown, restored,
c1845, 5½in (14cm) high.
$300–375 *SER*

A pair of Staffordshire groups of red spaniels
with barrels, c1850, 4in (10cm) high.
$100–130 each *SER*

A pair of Staffordshire figures of greyhounds with
hares, c1850, 10½in (26.5cm) high.
$675–825 *RWB*

A pair of Staffordshire figures of spaniels, holding flower baskets in their mouths, c1850, 9in (23cm) high.
$1,500–1,800 *RWB*

A Staffordshire clock face group of a poodle and spaniels, c1850, 9¾in (24.5cm) high.
$675–750 *RWB*

A Staffordshire copper lustre figure of a spaniel, c1860, 9½in (24cm) high.
$90–100 *SER*

A Staffordshire figure of a black and white sponged spaniel, c1860, 10in (25.5cm) high.
$110–140 *SER*

A pair of Staffordshire elephants, each with seated figures and tigers, possibly Kent & Co, c1900, 9in (23cm) high.
$3,000–3,750 *HOW*

A Strasbourg faïence figure of a boar, modelled by J. W. Lanz, the face and ears picked out in pink and the coat in tones of brown and dark green, the body supported by a leafy branch on a grassy base, Paul Hannong period, c1750, 6¾in (17cm) long.
$18,000–22,500 *S*

A model of a seated tortoiseshell cat, stamped 'John Mortlock Pottery Galleries, London', 19thC, 11¾in (30cm) high.
$1,200–1,300 *AG*

A Continental earthenware parakeet, painted in brightly coloured glazes with blue cresting over green and yellow plumage, orange glass inset eyes, black painted monogram to underside, damage, late 19thC, 16in (40.5cm) high.
$180–220 *MJB*

A pair of Staffordshire pearlware figures of recumbent rabbits, each splashed in black and eating a lettuce leaf, cracked, 19thC, 9½in (24cm) long.
$4,500–5,250 *DN*

Collecting Staffordshire Figures

In planning this piece I thought I would be writing about bargains and opportunities, for it struck me how reasonable Staffordshire figures have become. Then, having spent a week sorting and cataloguing an extensive collection of Staffordshire, I came to realise that the state of the market made a great deal of sense.

Many of these figures, I realised, would sell very well, and these were the ones that excited me. I had enjoyed handling and cataloguing a quarter of the collection; the remainder were just naïve fun, decorative and interesting in their own way but just a little bit tedious to catalogue.

I have also become aware that buyers fully share my own likes and dislikes. When it comes to the saleroom view, I know which lots will be asked for most. Absentee bids will be left on the same lots and the run-of-the-mill figures will attract far less interest.

In a sale of Staffordshire animals from the J. H. Bean collection held by Sotheby's in November 1995, two so-called Obadiah Sherratt models, one of a lion, the other a tiger, were each estimated to fetch $1,200–1,800. The lion, with its paw on a ball, was in remarkably good condition but sold for only $1,000. The tiger lacked its tail and had its paw on a rather dead looking lamb – hardly the most appealing of subjects – but even so it sold for a hefty $6,000. The tiger had that exciting combination of rarity and charm that roared 'buy me', while the lion just stood there and purred. Research of recent years has shown that a number of the figures traditionally associated with Obadiah Sherratt were not his work, but the name is still used as a generic term.

With Victorian 'flatback' figures, similar contrasts have been very noticeable. Good portraits, character figures and rarities have been selling as well as ever, but for every Miss Nightingale or Sir Robert Peel, there have been plenty of 'ordinary' figures, mostly untitled equestrian figures, children or Highlanders that have struggled to find buyers. Animals have sold well, and it is clear that collectors discriminate between everyday cuddly comforter dogs and pedigree pooches with character.

A lot of Staffordshire figures seem cheap at the moment, but with the quantity available to be bought all the time, buyers can afford to be selective and many models do not deserve to sell for any more. Good figures and certain rarities, for example some of the named theatrical flatbacks, are probably cheap, however.

Britain has been suffering the effects of the housing slump for ages, it seems, and Staffordshire cottages are by no means exempt. I am astonished at just how inexpensive pastille burner castles and cottages have become – as indeed have cow creamers and Toby jugs.

There has never been a better time to start collecting Staffordshire, and there is no denying how much fun it can be.

John Sandon

A Staffordshire figure of Maria Foot as Arinette in *The Little Jockey*, c1835, 7in (18cm) high. **$750–825** *RWB*

A Staffordshire figure of The Jewish Landlord, from the pantomime *Mother Goose*, c1840, 7½in (19cm) high. **$240–270** *RWB*

Figures – People

A Staffordshire pearl-glazed earthenware group, Tythe Pig, c1815, 6in (15cm) high. **$600–675** *SER*

A pair of Staffordshire Walton fairground musicians, she with a tambourine, he with trumpets, c1820, 6½in (16.5cm) high. **$1,500–1,800** *BHa*

Two Staffordshire pearlware overglaze enamel decorated boxers, Molyneux and Cribb, c1815, 9in (23cm) high. **$6,000–7,500** *JRe*

A Pratt ware figure of
Charity, c1800, 9½in
(24cm) high.
$330–380 *SER*

A Walton figure of a lady
seated reading with a cat,
under an arbour, 1820,
5½in (14cm) high.
$900–1,200 *BHa*

A Staffordshire group of
a pair of lovers, c1820,
8in (20.5cm) high.
$1,200–1,400 *JHo*

A Staffordshire figure
of the Reverend
Charles Spurgeon,
c1856, 11½in (29.5cm)
high, D336.
$300–330 *SER*

Staffordshire Figures

The reference numbers
included in some captions
refer to the cataloguing system
used by P. D. Gordon Pugh in
his book *Staffordshire Portrait
Figures,* published by Antique
Collectors' Club Ltd, 1970.

A pair of Staffordshire figures of a
shepherd and shepherdess, possibly Lloyd
of Shelton, c1835, 7¼in (18.5cm) high.
$450–600 *JO*

r. A pair of Staffordshire
figures, dressed in
Scottish costume, c1840,
5¼in (13.5cm) high.
$450–500 *JO*

An underglaze sponged
figure, probably Newcastle-
upon-Tyne, early 19thC,
6in (15cm) high.
$270–330 *IW*

A Staffordshire figure of
Milton, restored, c1800,
15in (38cm) high.
$500–600 *OD*

Three Staffordshire figures of Napoleon, c1845,
largest 8¾in (22.5cm) high.
$300–450 each *JO*

A pair of Staffordshire figures of the Prince of Wales and Princess Royal, c1846, 7in (18cm) high.
$675–725 *JO*

Two Staffordshire Astleys Circus figures, in a boat, c1850, 10½in (27cm) high.
$225–275 *SER*

A pair of Staffordshire figures of Chelsea Pensioners, c1850, 8½in (21.5cm) high.
$1,200–1,300 *RWB*

A pair of Staffordshire theatrical figures, depicting T. P. Cook as Ben Backstay and companion, c1850, 9¼in (23.5cm) high.
$400–450 *RWB*

A pair of Staffordshire figures of Victoria and Albert, c1850, 11in (28cm) high.
$400–525 *P(E)*

A pair of Staffordshire figures of Harlequin and Columbine, attributed to Thomas Parr, c1855, 6in (15cm) high.
$900–1,000 *HOW*

r. A Staffordshire figure of Eugène, Empress of France, c1854, 11½in (29cm) high, C242, 37, 87.
$160–200 *SER*

A Staffordshire figure of Jim Crow, c1836, 6¼in (16cm) high.
$600–675 *RWB*

A Staffordshire figure of the King of Sardinia, c1854, 13in (33cm) high.
$1,125–1,200 *RWB*

A pair of Staffordshire theatrical figures, some restoration, c1860, 8in (20.5cm) high.
$270–330 OD

A Staffordshire figure of General Roberts, by William Kent, c1900, 14¼in (36cm) high, C313.
$200–260 SER

A Teplitz pottery figural group, modelled as 2 Moroccan males riding camels, restored, Czechoslovakian, late 19thC, 19½in (49.5cm) high.
$600–750 SK

A Naples biscuit group of Marsyas and Olympus, modelled by Filippo Tagliolini, toes missing from right foot of Olympus, c1790, 11in (28cm) high.
$1,300–1,800 C

A pair of Staffordshire figures, William III and Mary II, white and gilt, c1870, 9½in (24cm) high, A175.
$450–500 SER

A Staffordshire figure of William I, King of Prussia, sparsely coloured, with gilt script, by Sampson Smith, c1870, 17in (43cm) high.
$300–340 SER

A Niderviller faïence figure of a huntswoman, painted in *petit feu* enamels, predominantly pink and green, minor chips, Custine period, c1780, 6¼in (16cm) high.
$525–675 S

A ceramic figure of a maiden, her head buried in her arms, wearing a loosely draped dress and leaning on a tree, on a square base, stamped with the number '1031', early 20thC, 46½in (118cm) high.
$1,800–2,200 P

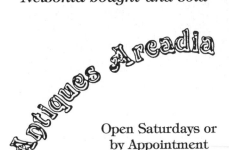

Flasks

A scallop shell-shaped
pearlware flask, c1790,
4½in (11.5cm) wide.
$300–350 *IW*

A London delft blue and white
coaster, c1725, 5½in (14cm) diam.
$1,500–2,000 *JHo*

A Staffordshire creamware
stand, possibly by Thomas
Whieldon, the border with
pierced latticework
alternating with ozier-
moulded panels edged with
embossed fruit and nuts,
sponged decoration in
green and manganese,
and scrolling rim, c1760,
11in (28cm) wide.
$1,700–2,000 *S*

Six Holics plates, painted with horses, the
borders with puce rococo-scroll cartouches
and sprigs of flowers within yellow line rims,
chipped and restored, 'H' marks, c1750,
9¼in (23.5cm) diam.
$9,750–12,000 *C*

Holics is also known as Holitsch.

Flatware

A blue delft polychrome
charger, decorated with Adam
and Eve in the Garden of
Eden, with green foliage, and
a yellow and red serpent,
c1700, 13in (33cm) diam.
$2,500–3,000 *B*

A Bristol delft shallow dish,
painted in underglaze blue,
brown and green enamels,
minor damage, mid-18thC,
13½in (34cm) diam.
$2,500–2,700 *Bea*

r. An English delft blue and
white plate, painted with a
figure by a pagoda, and a
tethered dog barking at a bird
flying overhead, mid-18thC,
8½in (21.5cm) diam.
$230–300 *Hal*

A blue dash charger, probably
Bristol, depicting the Fall of
Man, drawn in primitive style,
decorated in high temperature
faïence pigments of cobalt blue,
manganese and yellow, c1690,
12½in (32cm) diam.
$1,200–1,500 *Mit*

A Staffordshire agate ware
plate, c1755, 6in (15cm) diam.
$3,000–3,750 *JHo*

Holics

- An 18thC Hungarian factory which commenced
  production c1742.
- The factory's patron was Francis of Lorraine.
- Potters from Strasbourg were involved in
  establishing the factory and Holics faïence
  resembles Strasbourg wares, though the quality of
  early Holics decoration is generally inferior.
- In the early 1750s some magnificent table
  ornaments were produced and are amongst the
  finest European examples of baroque and
  rococo style.
- During the 1750s the factory took on workers from
  the Castelli factory and produced wares decorated
  with pastoral subjects in a grey/brown palette.
- Wares of the late 1750s and '60s are easily
  confused with contemporary wares from
  Milan and Pesaro.
- After 1758 a number of workers left the Holics
  factory to take employment at the newly
  established Tata factory.
- From the late 1760s until the factory closed in the
  1790s the quality of Holics faïence, predominantly
  in neo-classical style, declined.

A Swansea creamware plate, decorated in sepia by Thomas Pardoe, c1825, 10in (25.5cm) diam.
$230–300 *RP*

An Italian faïence oval-shaped dish, probably Faenza, Ferniani factory, painted in *famille rose* enamels, minor damage, c1760, 15in (38cm) wide.
$1,450–2,250 *S*

A dish, painted and sponge-decorated with flow blue, c1890, 10in (25.5cm) diam.
$90–120 *IW*

A pottery plate, printed all over in brown with 4 panels, depicting Britannia and Neptune, and Fame mourning at Nelson's tomb, inscribed 'Nelson 21, 1805' against a background of flowers and foliage, orange-lined rim, restored, 8¼in (21cm) diam.
$270–330 *SAS*

A pearlware plate, entitled 'Her Majesty Caroline, Queen of England', with blue-lined rim, chipped, 1821, 6¾in (17.5cm) diam.
$250–300 *SAS*

A Palissy type dish, applied with a coiled serpent, a crayfish, fish, 2 frogs, a toad and snails among flowers and foliage, enriched in colours, minor damages and wear, monogram to one side, 19thC, 15¼in (38.5cm) wide.
$1,800–2,250 *CSK*

A Palissy type dish, applied with a pike among smaller fish, crayfish, a frog, lizard, shells and insects on leaves and a bed of extruded clay, typically coloured, the reverse in brown glazes, chipped and cracked, late 19thC, 17½in (44.5cm) wide.
$900–1,000 *CSK*

l. A Montelupo dish, painted with a figure wearing blue striped breeches, repaired, mid-17thC, 9½in (24cm) diam.
$970–1,100 *Bon*

Flower Bricks

A flower brick, decorated in blue, green and yellow, probably Liverpool, c1760, 6¼in (16cm) long.
$3,000–3,750 *JHo*

A delft blue and white flower brick, decorated with panels of florettes and stylised flowers, 18thC, 6¼in (16cm) long.
$530–670 *HOLL*

Fountains

A Minton majolica fountain, in the form of a crane standing on a grassy mound applied with flowers, its outspread wings supporting a shell, in typical colours, restored, c1870, 34in (86.5cm) high.
$9,750–11,250 *S*

A Lille faïence wall fountain and basin, painted in dark blue with formal borders of lambrequins and stiff leaves, the basin with twin jester mask handles, minor wear, marked 'HV', 'X' and 'M' in blue, c1720, fountain 14½in (37cm) high.
$3,100–3,450 *S*

Jardinières

A pair of Minton majolica jardinières on stands, each with green wreath rim and yellow trelliswork on a blue ground, with climbing flora in relief, the bases fluted blue with wreath to rim and 4 yellow scroll feet, 19thC, 10½in (26.5cm) high.
$11,500–12,500 *DA*

A pair of Minton majolica campana-shaped two-handled jardinières, moulded in relief with vines and picked out in colours, on a deep blue ground, within stiff-leaf and scale moulded bands, minor damage, impressed marks for 1850, 18½in (47cm) high.
$4,000–5,000 *DN*

Jars

l. Two Dutch Delft tobacco jars and domed brass covers, each painted in blue, minor damage, marked 'De Drie Astonnekes', 18thC, 12in (30.5cm) high.
$3,000–3,750 *S(Am)*

r. An Italian maiolica *albarello*, probably Pesaro, painted in *compendiario* style with elaborate grotesques, the central scroll inscribed 'Mostarda Fina', chipped, 17thC, 18½in (47cm) high.
$19,500–22,500 *S*

Dutch Delft

- Tin glazed pottery manufacture was brought to Holland by itinerant potters from Spain and Italy.
- A pottery producing wares with strong Italian influence was established in Antwerp in 1512.
- Subsequently potteries were established in Rotterdam, Haarlem, The Hague and elsewhere.
- By the early 17thC wares were also being made at Delft, which soon became the key centre of production, lending its name to both Dutch and English tin glazed earthenware. However, some authorities argue that the English use of the name derives from 'delved earth'.
- In 1654 a massive explosion destroyed the medieval part of Delft which then became free for development by Delft ware potteries. The names of the former businesses occupying the sites were retained. Many of these were breweries, hence the unusual pottery names, such as The Three Bells, The Metal Pot, The Young Moor's Head and so on. Unlike English delft many Dutch wares bear a mark.
- From the early 17thC Delft pottery emulated Chinese blue and white porcelain – both Wanli wares and the more elaborate Kangxi.
- Later Delft ware was influenced by the various fashions which swept Europe. In particular Meissen shapes were copied and polychrome enamelling techniques adopted.
- Output was reduced greatly in the 18thC because of the success of creamware imported from England.

Jugs

A pearlware jug, decorated in underglaze blue, c1790, 5¾in (14.5cm) high.
$210–240 *IW*

An English delft blue and white puzzle jug, probably London, the reverse decorated with flowersprays, chipped, inscribed, dated '1732', 7½in (19cm) high.
$4,500–5,250 *C*

A Nottingham salt glazed stoneware 'carved' jug, the double-walled body pierced and incised with stylised plants below the horizontally-ribbed cylindrical neck, the whole with ferruginous 'orange peel' dip, minor chips, c1700, 3¾in (9.5cm) high.
$2,700–3,300 *N*

A pearlware jug, printed in black with 2 country seats interspersed with a pink rose and bud spray beneath a bright green neck band and handle, impressed numeral '3', c1810, 6¾in (17cm) high.
$670–820 *Bon*

A transfer printed jug, decorated with the Duke of York, c1800, 5in (12.5cm) high.
$1,200–1,300 *JHo*

r. A pearlware barrel-shaped jug, inscribed 'Richd Cockerman Treburley, Lezant', above a flourish, flanked by flowersprays and leaves in blue, green, yellow and ochre, cracked, c1805, 8½in (21.5cm) high.
$300–375 *DN*

An English earthenware bear jug and cover, probably Staffordshire, applied with shredded clay to simulate its coat, dipped in brown slip, with white clay eyes, paws and teeth, late 18thC, 10¼in (26cm) high.
$10,500–12,000 *S*

A creamware baluster-shaped jug, with loop handle, inscribed in blue 'Lord Weymouth And Success to the Mines', flanked by flowersprays and leaves, beneath a trellis and pendant flower band, c1780, 12in (30.5cm) high.
$1,200–1,500 *DN*

r. An engine-turned black and white jug, early 19thC, 5¾in (14.5cm) high.
$300–360 *IW*

A yellow ground jug, with coloured enamel decoration, probably Staffordshire, c1820, 4½in (11.5cm) high.
$450–550 *HOW*

A Derbyshire salt glazed jug, with mask lip, greyhound handle, decorated with the Oddfellows arms, lip damaged, c1830, 10in (25.5cm) high.
$240–270 *IW*

A red printed earthenware jug, decorated with dogs, c1830, 4¼in (11cm) high.
$180–210 *IW*

A brown stoneware jug, applied in white with portraits centred by superimposed profiles of Victoria and Albert beneath a border of oak leaves and acorns, c1890, 6in (15cm) high.
$180–230 *SAS*

A set of 3 Holdcroft majolica bear-shaped jugs, each carrying a drum on its back, glazed in brown, turquoise and yellow, some chips, c1875, 7½ to 9½in (19 to 24cm) high.
$2,700–3,000 *S*

A Wedgwood majolica jug, moulded with a design of birds on a blossoming branch between fans, raised registration diamond for 1879 and other impressed marks, 6½in (16.5cm) high.
$140–150 *Bon*

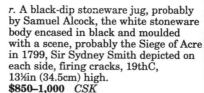

r. A black-dip stoneware jug, probably by Samuel Alcock, the white stoneware body encased in black and moulded with a scene, probably the Siege of Acre in 1799, Sir Sydney Smith depicted on each side, firing cracks, 19thC, 13½in (34.5cm) high.
$850–1,000 *CSK*

A Llanelly Pottery jug, commemorating the death of Prince Albert, c1863, 7¾in (20cm) high.
$450–520 *RP*

A Hanau pewter-mounted baluster-shaped jug, painted in blue, manganese and yellow with an Oriental, damaged, manganese 'OC' mark, the hinged pewter cover with the initials 'F.B.K.M.' and dated '1732', 10¾in (27.5cm) high.
$7,800–9,000 *C*

A metal-mounted stoneware jug, by Engel Kran, applied with a frieze of panels depicting the story of Susanna and the Elders, dated '1584', 13½in (34.5cm) high.
$4,000–5,250 *S*

A Westerwald stoneware pewter-mounted jug, with circular panel decorated in relief, depicting a gentleman seated on horseback, with inscription, hinged pewter lid, early 18thC, 11in (28cm) high.
$4,000–4,800 *S(Am)*

A green transfer printed jug, mid-19thC, 2in (5cm) high.
$50–60 *OD*

Character Jugs

A Portobello Toby jug, depicting a snuff taker, c1830, 7in (18cm) high.
$450–530 *RWB*

A Ralph Wood style Toby jug, depicting a man holding a brown jug of ale, repaired, c1770, 10in (25.5cm) high.
$630–700 *WIL*

A creamware Toby jug, depicting a 'tipsy' man, wearing a frock coat and breeches, repaired, late 18thC, 10¼in (26cm) high.
$11,250–12,750 *S*

A Staffordshire Toby jug, c1780, 10in (25.5cm) high.
$1,500–2,000 *JHo*

Money Boxes

l. An earthenware money box, possibly Sussex, late 19thC, 4in (10cm) high.
$90–120 *IW*

r. A money box, modelled as an owl, possibly Fremington, mid-19thC, 13in (33cm) high.
$1,200–1,500 *BHa*

A Yorkshire money box, modelled as a hen on her nest, c1860, 4¼in (10.5cm) wide.
$100–130 *IW*

Mugs

A Staffordshire salt glazed mug, c1745, 4¼in (10.5cm) high.
$3,000–3,300 *JHo*

A Swansea mug, printed in purple with head and shoulder portraits of Queen Victoria centred by a floral bordered cartouche with crown, 'Victoria Regina' and dates of birth, proclamation and Coronation, the interior rim with scrolling border, damaged, c1838, 3¼in (8.5cm) high.
$530–600 *SAS*

A Staffordshire unglazed red ware mug, with psuedo Chinese mark on base, c1750, 3½in (9cm) high.
$750–900 *JRe*

A pearlware two-handled mug, the brown and blue banded ground decorated in white slip with garlands, inscribed in black 'W. Rogers, Boiler Maker, Moorfields, Bristol', damaged, c1820, 7½in (19cm) high.
$1,350–1,500 *DN*

A silver lustre mug, with lily of the valley decoration, c1815, 3¼in (8.5cm) high.
$120–130 *SER*

A Coronation mug, printed in purple with half length portraits centred by a crown, the interior with union flowers and inscribed ribbons, c1831, 5in (13cm) high.
$260–300 *SAS*

'Holborn Viaduct', No. 202,
4¼in (10.5cm) diam.
$90–100 *SAS*

'The Lovers', No. 119, 1855,
3in (7.5cm) diam.
$160–200 *BHa*

'Sebastopol', No. 208A,
4¼in (10.5cm) diam.
$120–130 *SAS*

'Seven Ages of Man', No. 230,
1860, 4in (10cm) diam.
$150–180 *BHa*

'Osborne House', No. 182,
4¼in (10.5cm) diam.
$100–120 *SAS*

'Volunteers', No. 214, 1860,
3in (7.5cm) diam.
$250–280 *BHa*

'Wimbledon', No. 223, 1860,
4in (10cm) diam.
$150–180 *BHa*

'Wellington', No. 160B,
5¼in (13.5cm) diam.
$120–180 *SAS*

'The Thirsty Soldier', No. 205,
1860, 4in (10cm) diam.
$130–150 *BHa*

Locate the source

The source of each illustration in Miller's Antiques Price Guide *can easily be found by checking the code letters at the end of each caption with the Key to Illustrations located at the front of the book.*

'Deerhound Guarding Cradle',
with marbled border, No. 269,
3in (7.5cm) diam.
$130–140 *SAS*

l. 'The Wolf and the Lamb', by
F. & R. Pratt, No. 361, c1860,
4in (10cm) diam.
$100–110 *SER*

r. 'Church of the Holy Trinity,
Stratford-on-Avon', No. 229,
4¾in (12cm) diam.
$140–150 *SAS*

'Bear Hunting', No. 4,
3in (7.5cm) diam.
$300–330 *SAS*

Quill Holders

A pair of quill holders, modelled as whippets, maker unknown, c1850, 5½in (14cm) wide.
$300–340 *SER*

Services

A Ridgway pearlware dessert service, comprising 18 pieces, painted in green and puce with sprays of flowers and leaves, within orange and pale green bands and vine moulded borders, pattern No. 779 in orange, damaged, c1815.
$825–975 *DN*

A stone china part dessert service, probably Spode, comprising 14 pieces, printed in underglaze blue and enamelled with a central Oriental landscape panel against a whorl ground inside a border scattered with flowers, slight damage, printed mark, c1820.
$900–1,000 *S(S)*

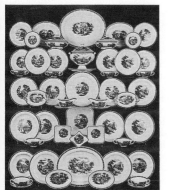

A Wedgwood earthenware dinner service, comprising 85 pieces, decorated in grey, the central circular panel depicting classical architecture within a mountainous landscape, bordered by twisted ribbon, damaged, marked, 19thC.
$1,800–2,200 *S(Am)*

A Pratt ware dessert service, the green ground border with acorn and leaf running garland motif, comprising: 2 oval tazzas, decorated with Highland Music, No. 418, a circular tazza, decorated with the Hop Queens, No. 414, all with projecting handles, together with 9 plates, decorated with The Truant, No. 413, restored, mid-19thC.
$1,200–1,350 *L&E*

An ironstone dessert service, by T. & J. Carey, comprising 15 pieces, decorated in purple and green with flowers and foliage, within a waved border, printed mark 'Saxon china', c1825, plates 8½in (21.5cm) diam.
$330–450 *Hal*

A Giustiniani part dessert service, comprising 7 pieces, decorated in Greek 'black figure' style with warriors and attendants, on a pale terracotta background, the rims with various borders of leaves in black and white, incised script marks, restored, early 19thC.
$2,000–2,500 *P*

A Bayreuth glazed red stoneware armorial part tea service, comprising a teapot and cover, a hot water jug and cover, a tazza on domed circular foot, 5 tea bowls, and 5 saucers, gilt, with the crowned arms flanked by scrolls and foliage within an elaborate gilt scroll and strapwork border, rubbed and restored, c1740.
$9,000–10,500 *C*

A Wedgwood creamware tea set, comprising 8 pieces, each piece decorated with a broad salmon coloured border bearing repeated barley ears, impressed 'WEDGWOOD' and other marks, late 18thC.
$1,125–1,275 *Bon*

Spill Vases

A Staffordshire spill vase, modelled as a deer with a squirrel, early 19thC, 5½in (14cm) high.
$900–1,000 *JHo*

A Staffordshire Pratt ware spill vase, c1800, 8in (20.5cm) high.
$2,250–2,500 *JHo*

A pair of Wood & Caldwell enamelled pearlware spill vases, modelled as a cow and a horse, each base applied with flowerheads, foliage and mosswork naturalistically coloured, impressed upper case mark and 'BURSLEM', restored, c1810, 13½in (34.5cm) wide.
$5,250–6,000 *Bon*

A pair of Staffordshire pearlware spill vases, modelled as a shepherd and shepherdess with a lamb or hound, decorated in coloured enamels, the mound base with applied granitic decoration, damaged, c1825, 7in (18cm) high.
$975–1,000 *DN*

A Staffordshire spill vase, entitled 'Christ Restoring Sight to the Blind', c1850, 10½in (26.5cm) high.
$450–525 *JO*

A spill vase, modelled as a horse with snake, maker unknown, restored, c1850, 9½in (24cm) high.
$450–525 *SER*

This is thought to be a model of Napoleon's horse, 'Marengo', who was killed by a snake bite.

Tankards

A Westerwald tankard, late 17thC, 8½in (21.5cm) high.
$975–1,000 *JHo*

A German salt glazed tankard, damaged, late 17thC, 6¼in (16cm) high.
$210–240 *IW*

An Ansbach faïence pewter-mounted tankard, of a tall ribbed form with a bell foot and rope-twist handle, painted in blue in the manner of Georg Christian Oswald, worn, c1720, 11¾in (30cm) high.
$15,000–16,500 *S*

A Nuremberg tankard, painted in blue with a peacock on a rock in a garden cartouche, against a blue washed reserve of scrolling Renaissance foliage, on a lappet and bird decorated ground, gadrooned pewter mounts with urn thumbpiece, restored, c1740, 8¾in (22cm) high.
$6,750–7,500 *S*

A Westerwald tankard, early 18thC, 6¼in (16cm) high.
$300–400 *JHo*

l. A pearlware tankard, printed in black and decorated in blue, green and yellow with a battlefield scene and the Duke of York on his horse, with a plain handle, entitled 'His Royal Highness Frederick, Duke of York', c1793, 4¾in (12cm) high.
$675–825 *SAS*

Tea Caddies

A Staffordshire pearlware tea caddy and cover, moulded and coloured in yellow and blue with Macaroni figures, the fluted cover enriched in blue and yellow, slight damage, c1790, 6in (15cm) high.
$750–900 *C*

A Leeds tea caddy, c1800, 3½in (9cm) high.
$525–560 *JHo*

A Liverpool delft blue and white tea caddy, c1740, 5in (12.5cm) high.
$2,500–2,700 *JHo*

A Staffordshire agate ware tea caddy, c1755, 4¾in (12cm) high.
$5,250–6,000 *JHo*

Tiles

A panel of 12 delft polychrome tiles, possibly Liverpool, each painted with a bird in blue, yellow, manganese and green, slight damage, c1760, each 5in (12.5cm) square, framed and glazed.
$2,000–2,500 *Bon*

A Liverpool delft tile, decorated in blue and white with a basket of flowers, c1750, 5in (12.5cm) square.
$45–60 *IW*

A Liverpool tile, decorated in manganese with a cow, c1765, 5in (12.5cm) square.
$150–225 *JHo*

An English delft blue and white tile, 1770, 4in (10cm) square.
$90–110 *PHA*

A London tile, decorated in blue and white with Elijah and the Ravens, c1720, 5in (12.5cm) square.
$65–80 *JHo*

An English delft blue and white tile, c1760, 4in (10cm) square.
$75–100 *PHA*

A Dutch Delft blue and white tile, late 18thC, 5in (12.5cm) square.
$50–60 *IW*

A Dutch tile, decorated in blue and white with a swineherd and pigs, c1750, 5in (12.5cm) square.
$45–60 *IW*

Liverpool Delft Tiles

- Delftware is tin-glazed earthenware named after the Dutch town which was the principal production centre.
- Manufacture of delftware in Liverpool commenced in 1710 when a London potter, Richard Holt, established a pottery in Lord Street.
- By 1750 many delft potteries had been established, and Liverpool was the centre of English delft tile making. Vast quantities were produced between 1750–1780, after which time output declined rapidly.
- Liverpool produced the widest variety, including multi-coloured and printed tiles.

Blue & White Transfer Ware

A blue and white bowl, British Views series, decorated with Wanstead House and Water Dog, maker unknown, c1820, 11in (28cm) diam.
$600–700 *GN*

A Spode transfer printed dog bowl, decorated with Tower pattern, c1820, 8in (20.5cm) wide.
$750–1,000 *GN*

A Spode vase-shaped coffee pot, decorated with Woodman design, c1850, 10½in (27cm) wide.
$750–900 *GN*

An Enoch Wood plate, Sporting series, decorated with a pointer, c1820, 8½in (21.5cm) diam.
$300–375 *SCO*

This is a very rare series made for the American market.

A Minton flow blue garden seat, dated '1878', 17in (43cm) high.
$1,000–1,200 *GN*

A Spode soup tureen, decorated in Net pattern, c1820, 11in (28cm) high.
$450–750 *GN*

r. A Turner plate, decorated with The Villagers pattern, c1830, 14½in (37cm) wide.
$450–600 *GN*

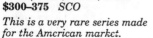

A Ridgway tureen base, decorated with Cowman pattern, c1820, 17½in (44.5cm) wide.
$450–600 *GN*

r. A potted beef dish, advertising 'Snelling's Potted Beef, Rampant Horse St, Norwich', maker unknown, c1835, 3in (7.5cm) wide.
$65–80 *SCO*

A blue and white transfer printed mug, inscribed 'imperial one pint' c1840, 4in (10cm) high.
$75–90 *IW*

A child's Staffordshire dinner service, comprising 42 pieces, decorated with a country house in a landscape setting, early 19thC, largest tureen 4in (10cm) high.
$825–975 *P(G)*

An E. & G. Phillips plate, decorated with British Flowers pattern, c1830, 10in (25.5cm) diam.
$150–180 *Nor*

A Spode tureen stand, Indian Sporting series, decorated with Hunting a Buffalo pattern, impressed and printed marks, c1830, 15½in (39.5cm) wide.
$600–675 *Bon*

An Adams cheese dish and cover, decorated with Cattle Scenery pattern, c1880, 9in (23cm) wide.
$215–255 *Nor*

l. A Wedgwood Botanical series teapot, c1815, 5in (12.5cm) high.
$360–400 *Nor*

A Staffordshire Dr Syntax series sauce tureen stand, c1880, 9in (23cm) wide.
$200–225 *Nor*

A toilet box, decorated with a floral design, maker unknown, c1840, 8in (20.5cm) wide.
$180–225 *Nor*

Mason's Ironstone

A Mason's Ironstone footbath jug, c1820, 13in (33cm) high.
$1,125–1,275 *JP*

A Mason's Ironstone drainer, decorated with Bamboo pattern, c1815, 14½in (37cm) wide.
$480–580 *JP*

A Mason's Ironstone drainer, impressed mark, c1815, 14½in (37cm) wide.
$450–500 *JP*

A Mason's Ironstone flared base mug, crown mark, c1820, 4in (10cm) high.
$300–375 *JP*

l. A Mason's Ironstone drainer, decorated with Blue Pheasants pattern, impressed circle mark, c1813, 15in (38cm) wide.
$330–420 *JP*

A Mason's Ironstone pot pourri vase and domed cover, decorated and gilt in Imari palette with flowering plants issuing from a vase, the rim and base each decorated with a floral garland, damage, impressed mark, c1815, 11in (28cm) high.
$1,000–1,200 *S*

l. A Mason's Ironstone vase and cover, in chinoiserie style, printed and painted with panels of exotic birds perching among flowering branches and figures in landscapes, damage, wear and repair, c1850, 41in (104cm) high.
$4,500–6,000 *CSK*

A Mason's patent Ironstone china part dinner service, comprising 80 pieces, painted and gilt in Imari palette, wear and slight damage, impressed upper case marks, c1815.
$12,750–15,000 *CSK*

A set of 5 Mason's Ironstone octagonal baluster-shaped jugs, with twig-shaped handles, each printed and painted in *famille rose* palette with figures, within scroll cartouches, on an orange diaper ground, some damage, printed marks in black, 19thC, largest 9½in (24cm) high.
$900–1,000 *DN*

Wemyss

A Wemyss bowl, painted with buttercups, 1895, 2½in (6.5cm) wide.
$450–600 *RdeR*

A Wemyss piglet money bank, probably by Karel Nekola, painted with thistles and pink details, chipped, impressed and painted marks, c1920, 6in (15cm) long.
$675–825 *HAR*

A Wemyss pig, c1895, 6¾in (17cm) wide.
$450–600 *RdeR*

A Wemyss bulb bowl, painted with daffodils, c1895, 8½in (21.5cm) wide.
$450–675 *RdeR*

A Wemyss piglet, painted with thistles, impressed 'Wemyss ware RH&S', c1900, 6¼in (16cm) long.
$1,000–1,200 *HAR*

A Wemyss sleeping pig, painted with apples, c1900, 6¼in (16cm) long.
$2,250–3,000 *RdeR*

Wemyss Ware

Wemyss Ware was first produced in the 1880s, when Robert Heron, the owner of the Fife Pottery, brought back to Britain a group of craftsmen he had discovered in Bohemia during his Grand Tour. Their leader, Karel Nekola, became Heron's master painter, and the individual style of painted pottery they produced was an instant success, particularly due to the patronage of Dora Wemyss of Wemyss Castle.

Thomas Goode of Mayfair acquired exclusive selling rights in London and by the turn of the century jam pots, jardinières, candlesticks, inkstands and, of course, the famous pigs and cats, were being produced in a wide range of shapes, sizes and subjects. When Nekola died in 1915 he was succeeded by Edwin Sandland and the Fife Pottery continued its output until 1930, when it fell prey to the economic depression and was forced to close.

The rights and moulds were bought by the Bovey Pottery Company of Bovey Tracey in Devon, who employed Karel's son, Joseph, as painter. He remained with the company, becoming especially renowned for his painted nursery pigs and cats, when the sole agency later passed to a Czechoslovakian, Jan Plichta. Joseph died in 1952 and the pottery ceased production shortly afterwards.

The value of Wemyss Ware is heavily dependent on the quality of the painting and the condition of the piece. It is produced in soft pottery which is fired at a low temperature and is, therefore, very fragile.

A Wemyss quaiche, painted
with raspberries, c1930,
7¾in (20cm) wide.
$300–450 *RdeR*

A Wemyss commemorative
loving cup, painted with
pink ribbon-tied swags
within loop rims, minor
damage, impressed mark,
c1897, 4¾in (12cm) high.
$180–225 *HAR*

A Wemyss plaque, painted by
Karel Nekola, modelled as a
birdcage enclosing a yellow
canary, the base with a
painted view of buildings,
restored, signed in blue 'K. N.',
early 20thC, 11in (28cm) high.
$5,250–6,000 *S(Sc)*

A Wemyss child's mug,
painted with apples, c1895,
3½in (9cm) high.
$150–225 *RdeR*

A Wemyss plaque, decorated
with thistles and inscribed
'I looked for something Scotch
to send you and the thistles
asked if they would do', c1920,
5¾in (14.5cm) long.
$375–450 *RdeR*

A Wemyss comb tray, painted with
roses, c1895, 10in (25.5cm) long.
$300–375 *RdeR*

A Royal Doulton goblet,
made to commemorate
Queen Elizabeth the Queen
Mother's 80th birthday and
the Wemyss centenary,
1985, 7½in (19cm) high.
$375–450 *RdeR*

A Wemyss Gordon plate,
painted with sloes, c1895,
8in (20.5cm) diam.
$300–450 *RdeR*

A Wemyss panelled
vase, designed by
Karel Nekola, painted
in the Chinese style,
with ochre, green
and blue scrolling
foliage, script mark
and 'F. P.' for Fife
Pottery, early 20thC,
22in (56cm) high.
$900–1,000 *S(Sc)*

A Wemyss ware
armorial frog mug,
painted with a coat-
of-arms and motto
'Nulli Inimigus Ero',
on a green ground
shield amongst pink
roses and foliage
within green line
rims, impressed and
painted marks by
James Sharp, c1920,
5¾in (14.5cm) high.
$3,500–3,750 *HAR*

r. A Wemyss pen tray,
painted with cherries,
c1895, 11¼in (28.5cm) long.
$150–225 *RdeR*

A Wemyss heart-shaped tray,
painted with roses, c1895,
11½in (29cm) long.
$225–375 *RdeR*

A Wemyss mug,
decorated in pink,
green and yellow with
a band of growing
tulips, beneath a
green line band,
impressed mark and
printed retailer's
mark for T. Goode
and Co, c1920, 5¾in
(14.5cm) high.
$750–825 *DN*

A Hicks & Meigh mazarine/drainer, decorated with Water Lily pattern, printed Royal Arms mark, c1815, 9in (23cm) wide.
$300–315 *JP*

A Bristol delft charger, decorated in blue, green, yellow and terracotta, c1760, 13in (33cm) diam.
$2,250–2,750 *JHo*

An Hispano-Moresque dish, the centre decorated with monogram 'IHS', restored, Valencia, mid-15thC, 18in (45.5cm) diam.
$90,000–100,000 *C*

A London delft *La Fécondité* dish, probably Southwark, after Bernard Palissy, moulded in relief with Venus, small rim chip, c1675, 18½in (47cm) wide.
$16,500–18,000 *S*

A maiolica istoriato dish, inscribed 'Galatea' on reverse, c1545, 10⅝in (27cm) diam.
$13,500–14,250 *HAM*

A plate, probably by Ralph Wedgwood, decorated with Elephant pattern, c1798, 9in (23cm) diam.
$300–375 *IW*

A plate, the central titled panel depicting Queen Victoria and Prince Albert, c1851, 9in (23cm) diam.
$130–160 *SAS*

An Italian maiolica charger, depicting Sybil, Bacchus and Ceres, signed 'Gro Attansio', of Naples, mid-18thC, 24½in (62cm) wide.
$3,750–5,250 *LHA*

A Liverpool tin glazed plate, decorated with enamels in *famille rose* style, c1755, 8¼in (21cm) diam.
$4,500–5,250 *JHo*

An ironstone part service, possibly Ridgway, printed with chinoiserie designs and hand enamelled, c1830.
$3,000–4,500 *Bon*

A French majolica asparagus cradle, by Gien, c1890, 15½in (39.5cm) wide.
$330–400 *MofC*

A Staffordshire salt glazed teapot, depicting Frederick of Prussia, c1765, 4¼in (11cm) high.
$2,000–2,250 *JHo*

A Yorkshire creamware teapot, some damage, c1750, 4in (10cm) high.
$360–420 *IW*

A Staffordshire spill vase, Red Riding Hood with the wolf, c1850, 10½in (26.5cm) high.
$150–200 *SER*

A Staffordshire spill vase, early 19thC, 4¾in (12cm) high.
$750–825 *JHo*

A Staffordshire model of a castle keep on the coast of Scotland, on a shell base, c1820, 5½in (14cm) high.
$525–600 *JO*

A Staffordshire model of Fantasy Castle, c1860, 11¾in (30cm) high.
$240–280 *SER*

A French faïence basket, by Desvres, c1860, old repairs, 8¾in (22cm) wide.
$180–220 *IW*

A Wedgwood 'Fairyland lustre' vase, designed by Daisy Makeig-Jones, painted with Imps on a Bridge pattern, No. Z5462, c1920, 12in (30.5cm) high.
$5,250–6,000 *S*

A Minton majolica game pie dish and cover, repaired, impressed marks for 1876, 15½in (39.5cm) wide.
$16,500–18,000 *DN*

A hand warmer, made in the form of 2 books, with a hole at one end for hot water, London, c1660, 5¼in (13.5cm) long.
$37,500–45,000 *JHo*

A pair of Le Nove maiolica bottle vases, comet mark in blue, c1900, 19¼in (49cm) high.
$2,700–3,000 *Bon*

A Minton majolica game pie dish and cover, damaged, marked, shape No. 1990, c1880, 18in (45.5cm) wide.
$48,000–52,000 *S*

A pair of Staffordshire models of dalmations, wearing gilt-painted collars, on turquoise floral encrusted bases, c1850, 7in (18cm) long.
$1,500–2,750 *HOW*

A Staffordshire shell and floral piece, repaired, early 19thC, 7¼in (18.5cm) high.
$1,500–1,800 *JHo*

A Staffordshire creamware model of a baby deer with leaf bocage, c1820, 4in (10cm) high.
$300–450 *BHa*

A pearlware model of a performing lion, decorated in underglaze colours, probably Staffordshire, c1800, 7in (18cm) long.
$4,500–5,250 *JHo*

A Staffordshire stirrup cup, c1800, 6in (15cm) long.
$1,850–2,250 *JHo*

A Yorkshire pearlware model of a horse, wearing a saddle cloth and bridle, standing on a green coloured base, restored, c1800, 6in (15cm) long.
$3,000–3,750 *BHa*

A pair of Staffordshire models of black and white dogs, with maroon collars and chains, one restored, c1840, 10in (25.5cm) high.
$300–330 *SER*

A Staffordshire figure of a parrot, c1855, 9in (23cm) high.
$300–375 *RWB*

A Yorkshire Pratt ware group, with a cow, calf and farmer, c1800, 6in (15cm) high.
$1,500–2,000 *RWB*

A Yorkshire pottery cow creamer, sponged and decorated in Pratt ware colours, c1800, 7¼in (18.5cm) wide.
$1,000–1,350 *BHa*

A North Country cow creamer group, with milkmaid, c1810, 5½in (14cm) high.
$825–900 *RWB*

A Scottish pearlware dog and pups, decorated in overglaze enamel colours, c1845, 3¾in (9.5cm) high.
$750–900 *JRe*

A pair of Staffordshire figures of Queen Victoria and Prince Albert, both standing on grey rock bases, 19thC, largest 18½in (47cm) high.
$1,500–2,250 *MSW*

A Staffordshire Obadiah Sherratt tithe pig group, with bocage, c1835, 8½in (21.5cm) high.
$1,500–1,800 *JO*

A Staffordshire Obadiah Sherratt group, depicting Dr Syntax playing cards, c1820, 7½in (19cm) high.
$3,000–3,750 *BHa*

A pair of Staffordshire figures, depicting the Princess Royal and the Prince of Wales, each with a lighthouse and a boat, c1855, 6½in (16.5cm) high.
$1,000–1,200 *HOW*

A Staffordshire figure, entitled 'Princess', c1850, 8in (20cm) high.
$600–675 *RWB*

A Staffordshire pearlware figure of William III, depicted as a Roman emperor, also known as the Duke of Cumberland, c1810, 8¾in (22cm) high.
$5,250–6,250 *JRe*

A pair of Staffordshire figures, The Cobbler and his Wife, by Kent, slight damage, c1880, 12in (30.5cm) high.
$200–285 *SER*

A Staffordshire figure of a skater, depicting 'Winter', c1800, 8in (20cm) high.
$300–375 *SER*

A pair of Staffordshire figures, Betsy Trott and Mr Dick, from *David Copperfield*, c1845, 6¾in (17cm) high.
$750–825 *JO*

A Staffordshire mustard, pepper, and oil or vinegar pot, c1860, largest 6in (15cm) high.
$100–120 each *JO*

A pair of Staffordshire Obadiah Sherratt ale bench groups, c1820, 8in (20cm) high.
$9,000–1,200 *BHa*

A Spode Tiber pattern cream tureen, on fixed base, with original pierced ladle, c1815, 7in (18cm) long.
$600–750 *GN*

A Don Pottery blue and white transfer printed Italian Fountain pattern platter, c1830, 17½in (44.5cm) wide.
$375–525 *IW*

A J. & R. Clewes blue and white transfer ware plate, c1810, 10in (25.5cm) diam.
$100–150 *GN*

A blue and white transfer printed platter, attributed to Ridgway, British Scenery Series, Leamington Baths, c1820, 18½in (47cm) wide.
$750–900 *GN*

A Swansea pottery pearlware plate, transfer decorated from a copper plate engraved by Thomas Rothwell, c1800, 9in (23cm) diam.
$260–340 *RP*

A Minton transfer printed puzzle jug, with serpent handle, c1825, 14in (35.5cm) high.
$1,500–2,250 *GN*

A two-handled tureen, by Jones & Son, printed all over in blue with a Coronation scene, small chip and minor restoration, the base with printed mark of Knowledge and Britannia, c1821, 15in (38cm) wide.
$450–600 *SAS*

A blue and white transfer printed jug, some damage, c1820, 8½in (21.5cm) high.
$150–180 *IW*

A blue and white printed tankard, c1795, 4¾in (12cm) high.
$150–220 *IW*

A blue printed proclamation jug, the base marked 'VR' in a star, c1837, 11in (28cm) high.
$975–1,125 *SAS*

A Robert Hamilton blue and white transfer printed platter, Ruined Castle pattern, c1820, 19in (48.5cm) wide.
$525–675 *IW*

A Ridgway College series platter, showing Trinity College c1820, 10in (25.5cm) wide.
$375–450 *SCO*

A Mason's Ironstone 31-piece dessert service, each piece moulded with cabbage leaf motifs, and hand-coloured in polychrome enamels, c1820.
$2,600–3,000 *Bon*

A Mason's Ironstone drainer, with chinoiserie decoration, c1835, 12½in (32cm) wide.
$450–500 *JP*

A Wemyss plate, painted with violets, c1890, 4¾in (12cm) diam.
$225–375 *RdeR*

A Wemyss mug, painted with daffodils, c1890, 5½in (14cm) high.
$450–600 *RdeR*

A Wemyss two-handled tray, with impressed mark by Karel Nekola, c1900, 17¾in (45cm) wide.
$1,200–1,500 *HAR*

A Mason's Ironstone inkstand, decorated with Bandana pattern, c1835, 8in (20cm) wide.
$1,400–1,800 *JP*

This inkstand is of a rare shape, also found in an even more rare variant on 6 feet.

A Wemyss cat, by J. Plichta, decorated with clover, c1930, 10¼in (26cm) high.
$275–375 *RdeR*

'Our Pets', No. 242, 3½in (9cm) diam.
$270–300 *SAS*

A Wemyss basket, painted with cherries, with fluted sides and twist handle, c1900, 8¾in (22cm) wide.
$600–900 *RdeR*

'Dublin Industrial Exhibition 1853', No. 143, 5in (12.5cm) diam.
$180–200 *BHa*

'Pegwell Bay', stamp for S. Banger, shrimp sauce manufacturer, 4in (10cm) diam.
$900–975 *SAS*

'Golden Horn, Constantinople', No. 204, 4¼in (10.5cm) diam.
$200–270 *SAS*

A pair of Zurich figures, depicting
a maid carrying a tea tray, and a
manservant with a plate of cakes,
1780s, 5¼in (13.5cm) high.
$10,000–11,000 *HAM*

A Chantilly figure of a Chinaman,
seated with a half globe between
his knees, c1730, probably later
inkwell fittings and ormolu stand,
8½in (21.5cm) high.
$16,500–18,000 *WW*

A Meissen elephant group,
restored, crossed swords in
underglaze blue, c1875,
14¾in (37.5cm) high.
$11,250–12,000 *S*

A Buen Retiro Italian
comedy group of spaghetti-
eaters, probably modelled
by Guiseppe Gricci, 4 blue
fleur-de-lys marks, c1760,
7¼in (18.5cm) high.
$60,000–75,000 *C*

An early Derby figure of
Spring, holding a basket
of flowers, one of the
Rustic Four Seasons,
patch marks, c1756,
4¾in (12cm) high.
$1,200–1,500 *TK*

A Meissen group, modelled
by J. J. Kändler, restored,
crossed swords and dot in
underglaze blue, incised 'NG',
c1765, 14½in (37cm) high.
$6,500–6,750 *S*

A Höchst figure of a
vagabond, restored, mark
in underglaze blue, c1775,
10¼in (26cm) high.
$3,750–4,500 *S*

A Meissen group of Pantaloon and
Columbine, modelled by J. J. Kändler,
restored, blue crossed swords mark,
c1738, 6¾in (17cm) high.
$60,000–67,500 *C*

Africa and Europe, from a
set of 4 Samson figures
representing the continents,
c1870, 12in (30.5cm) high.
$8,250–9,750 the set *RA*

A pair of Bloor Derby pierced baskets, encrusted with flowers and gilt, on a yellow ground, c1825, 10in (25cm) wide.
$4,500–5,500 *TK*

A Meissen cream pot, cover and stand, painted with harbour scenes, crossed swords marks, c1735, stand 7in (18cm) diam.
$24,750–27,000 *C*

A Minton floral encrusted vase and cover, date mark for 1846, 12in (30.5cm) high.
$2,250–2,750 *BHa*

A Worcester First Period sweetmeat dish, with 'Blind Earl' moulding, painted in Sunburst pattern, c1758, 6in (15cm) diam.
$3,000–3,600 *CHR*

A Coalport vase, with painted flower panels and floral encrusted decoration, c1840, 12in (30.5cm) high.
$1,800–2,200 *BHa*

A pair of Spode ice pails, covers and liners, painted in pattern No. 2508, restored, c1820, 11½in (29cm) high.
$8,000–8,750 *S*

A Nymphenburg food warmer, cover and stand, painted by G. C. Lindemann, marked, c1765, 9in (23cm) high.
$60,000–67,500 *S*

A Naples two-handled soup tureen and cover, from the Fiordalisi service, restored, marked, c1790, 14¾in (37.5cm) wide.
$15,000–18,000 *C*

A Coalport two-handled vase and cover, marked, c1862, 21in (53.5cm) high.
$3,750–4,500 *CSK*

A pair of Chelsea sweetmeat figures, marked, c1760, 7½in (19cm) high.
$9,000–10,500 *S*

A pair of Meissen tureens and covers, modelled as partridges by J. J. Kändler, slight damage, marked, c1743, 6in (15cm) wide.
$22,500–27,000 *C*

A Meissen *famille verte* plate, the centre painted in underglaze blue with a flowering shrub within a flowerhead and zig-zag pattern, slight rubbing to well, blue crossed swords mark and 2 crossed lines to footrim, c1728, 8¾in (22cm) diam.
$10,500–12,000 *C*

A pair of porcelain dessert plates, painted at the centre with flowers within a border painted with flower festoons, and moulded gilt scrolls, each impressed on the reverse 'Swansea', c1814, 8¾in (22cm) diam.
$525–600 *Hal*

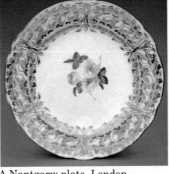

A Nantgarw plate, London decorated in coloured enamels, impressed mark, c1815, 9½in (24cm) diam.
$900–975 *DN*

A Worcester porcelain plate, from the Hope Service made for the Duke of Clarence, decorated by John Pennington, c1792, 9½in (24cm) diam.
$2,700–3,000 *LHA*

A Chelsea Hans Sloane botanical shaped dish, painted with a spray of puce specimen flowers, flowersprays, scattered foliage, butterflies and an insect, with shaped brown line rim, slight rubbing to enamels, red anchor mark, c1755, 12½in (32cm) diam.
$19,500–22,500 *C*

r. A Worcester Sir Joshua Reynolds pattern fluted dish, centrally decorated in Kakiemon style, within a flower panelled gilt diaper band, c1770, 9in (23cm) diam.
$900–1,200 *DN*

A Meissen Imari pattern dish, slight rubbing, blue crossed swords and dot mark, c1730, 14¼in (36cm) diam.
$6,750–8,250 *C*

A Minton bread plate, designed by A. W. Pugin, impressed shape No. '430', mid-19thC, 13¼in (33.5cm) diam.
$550–600 *DN*

A Worcester dish, decorated in enamels with flowers and leaves, blue seal mark, c1770, 7¼in (18.5cm) wide.
$450–500 *DN*

A pair of Derby pastille burners, the pierced rims applied with bearded masks, marked 'S H', late 19thC, 5½in (14cm) high.
$525–750 *Hal*

A Minton floral encrusted inkstand, c1860, 11½in (29cm) wide.
$1,800–2,000 *BHa*

A Derby pot pourri bowl and pierced cover, crowned crossed baton mark in red, c1815, 11½in (29cm) high.
$1,800–2,500 *DN*

A Meissen Hausmaler tankard, inscribed, c1745, 8in (20cm) high.
$15,000–16,500 *S*

A Meissen tankard, painted in the manner of J. G. Höroldt, c1733.
$20,250–22,500 *Bon*

Two Meissen silver gilt mounted pomade pots and covers, marked, *Pressnummer* 23, c1740, 5½in (14cm) high.
$21,000–24,000 *C*

A Derby Crown loving cup, painted by James Rouse Snr, marked and inscribed, date cipher for 1888, 5½in (14cm) high.
$2,500–3,000 *MSW*

A Meissen jar and cover, restored, marked, c1745, 7in (18cm) high.
$18,000–19,500 *C*

A Vienna gilt metal mounted casket, with monogram 'HDL', repaired, blue shield marks, c1785, 6in (15cm) wide.
$4,500–7,500 *C*

A Meissen ewer, emblematic of Air, after a model by J. J. Kändler, slight damage, marked, c1860, 25¾in (65.5cm) high.
$9,000–10,500 *S*

A Meissen ewer and basin, made for the Turkish market, blue crossed swords and star mark, c1790, ewer 13in (33cm) high.
$12,750–14,250 *C*

A Meissen gold-mounted letter box, painted with views of London, inscribed, c1750, 3½in (9cm) long.
$37,500–42,000 *S*

A Doccia gilt-metal-mounted box, in the form of a pug's head, c1770, 2in (5cm) high.
$6,750–8,250 *S*

A Meissen gold-mounted snuff box, the inside cover with 2 pug dogs, c1740, 2in (5cm) high.
$45,000–50,000 *S*

A Meissen gold-mounted snuff box, with a scene of merchants by a quayside, minor damage, c1740, 2in (5cm) high.
$11,250–12,750 *S*

A Meissen silver-gilt-mounted snuff box, painted with battle scenes, minor damage, c1750, 2½in (6.5cm) wide.
$10,500–12,000 *C*

A Belleek shamrock biscuit barrel, 2nd period, 1891–1926, 7½in (19cm) high.
$375–550 *MLa*

A Belleek Neptune cabaret set, 2nd period, 1891–1926, jug 2½in (6.5cm) high.
$1,500–1,850 *MLa*

A Belleek blue and white earthenware tureen, 1st period, 1865–90, 12in (30.5cm) wide.
$375–400 *MLa*

A Belleek earthenware transfer printed and hand painted dish, 1st period, 1865–90, 19½in (49.5cm) wide.
$750–900 *MLa*

A Belleek plate, painted and gilded by Cyril Arnold, 1st green period, 1946–55, 9in (23cm) diam.
$3,000–3,750 *MLa*

A *famille rose* 'Doctors' Visit' vase, after the design by Cornelis Pronk, with a continuous scene of figures, birds and flowering trees, neck restored, c1738, 9in (23cm) high.
$9,750–10,500 *C*

A Chinese vase and cover, decorated in enamels, cracked, mark and period of Kangxi, 17in (43cm) high.
$1,100–1,200 *DN*

A three-piece *famille noire* garniture, comprising a pair of hexagonal baluster vases with covers and a *zun*-shaped vase, restored, Kangxi period, tallest 12½in (32cm) high.
$6,800–7,500 *S(NY)*

A *doucai* jar and cover, underglaze blue four-character seal mark of Qianlong period, 5in (12.5cm) high.
$24,000–27,000 *S(NY)*

A Canton *famille rose* storage jar and cover, restored, Qing Dynasty, 19thC, 26in (66cm) high.
$5,250–6,000 *S*

A *famille verte* rouleau vase, restored, Kangxi period, 18in (45.5cm) high.
$10,500–12,000 *C*

A *doucai* dragon and phoenix meiping, decorated with a scaly dragon and a soaring phoenix amid scrolling vines, multi-coloured blooms and serrated leaves, Yongzheng period, 17¼in (44cm) high.
$36,000–42,000 *S(HK)*

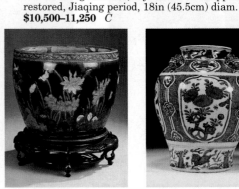

A pair of *famille rose* jardinières, enamelled with butterflies in flight between bands of bat roundels and scrolling hibiscus, *ruyi* heads and lappets, restored, Jiaqing period, 18in (45.5cm) diam.
$10,500–11,250 *C*

A pair of *famille rose* jars and covers, retouched enamels on one cover, 19thC, 16½in (42cm) high.
$13,600–14,200 *C*

A *famille rose* vase and cover, decorated with a lakescape, Yongzheng period, 24¾in (63cm) high.
$10,500–12,000 *C*

A Fahua jardinière, decorated with birds, flowers and insects, cracked, c1600, 11¾in (30cm) high.
$5,250–6,000 *S*

A blue and white jar, with 4 mask handles, restored, Wanli period 12in (30.5cm) high.
$2,700–3,500 *C*

An underglaze blue dish, slight damage and wear, mark and period of Hongzhi, 10¼in (26cm) diam.
$55,000–60,000 *S(HK)*

A pair of Imari dishes, each painted and enamelled with a vase of flowers surrounded by panels of birds, butterflies, prunus and peony on a black ground, the reverse with flowering branches, slight damage, early 18thC, 21¼in (54cm) diam.
$40,000–45,000 *C*

A pair of *rose verte* dishes, each enamelled with a lady and a boy offering a lotus spray to a second lady seated at a table, Yongzheng period, 14in (35.5cm) diam.
$10,500–11,250 *C*

A *famille rose* platter, decorated with Don Quixote, Qianlong period, 18½in (47cm) diam.
$5,500–6,500 *S*

A pair of Chinese export *famille rose* meat dishes, Qianlong period, 17½in (44.5cm) diam.
$9,600–10,000 *DN*

A pair of *famille verte* chargers, the first decorated with 2 lovers being watched by 3 attendants, the second with the lovers being watched by a woman, Kangxi period, 15¼in (39cm) diam.
$42,000–45,000 *S*

A *famille rose* tobacco leaf tureen, cover and stand, Qianlong period, the stand 15in (38cm) wide.
$7,500–9,000 *C*

An enamelled 51-piece part tea service, depicting Le Pêcheur, after an engraving by C. J. Vissher, from a drawing by Abraham Blomaert, Yongzheng/early Qianlong period.
$6,000–6,750 *C*

A Venetian glass footed marriage bowl, by Salviati, painted and gilded, c1870, 7¾in (19.5cm) high.
$3,500–4,000 *MJW*

A Bohemian *Lithyalin* glass bowl, Buquoy Glasshouse, c1835, 7in (18cm) high.
$2,250–3,000 *S*

A Bohemian glass bonbon dish, on a silver base, Vienna, c1844, 5¼in (13.5cm) high.
$1,000–1,125 *MJW*

A Venetian glass footed bowl, gilt with a band of feathering, painted with green, blue and red dots, c1500, 6in (15cm) high.
$75,000–82,500 *S*

An amethyst glass trumpet, with wrythen moulded tube, c1860, 7¾in (19.5cm) long.
$600–630 *Som*

A glass tazza, by Daniel Pearce for Thomas Webb, with cranberry overlay, c1880, 6in (15cm) high.
$1,350–1,400 *MJW*

A Venetian glass pine cone bottle, with a baluster stem on a conical foot, 17thC, 8½in (21.5cm) high.
$6,750–7,500 *S*

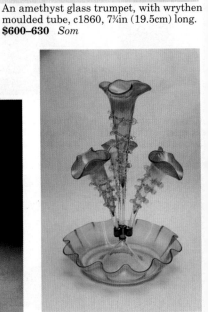

A three-trumpet cranberry glass épergne, c1880, 17¼in (44cm) high.
$1,125–1,200 *MJW*

An amethyst glass bowl, by Stourbridge Glass Co, decorated with dragons and floral designs, c1900, 5in (12.5cm) high.
$1,275–1,300 *MJW*

An opaque pink glass campana-shaped tazza, with ormolu mounts and birds perched on the rim, 19thC, 4½in (11.5cm) high.
$6,000–6,750 *TMA*

A St Louis concentric millefiori carpet-ground paperweight, inscribed '1848', 2¾in (7cm) diam.
$7,750–8,500 *C*

A Paul Ysart concentric paperweight, 1930s, 2¾in (7cm) diam.
$500–650 *SWB*

A Stourbridge concentric millefiori ink bottle and paperweight desk set, in good condition, c1850, bottle 6in (15cm) high.
$1,500–1,800 *SWB*

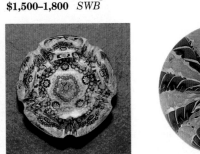

A Clichy patterned millefiori paperweight, with 5 facets and 5 flutes, c1850, 3in (7.5cm) diam.
$3,000–3,250 *SWB*

A St Louis crown paperweight, the twisted ribbon alternating with latticinio thread, mid-18thC, 3in (7.5cm) diam.
$2,250–2,750 *C*

A Baccarat dog rose paperweight, cerise with white petal edges, with 6 side facets, one top facet, stem and 11 leaves, c1850, 3in (7.5cm) diam.
$2,000–2,500 *SWB*

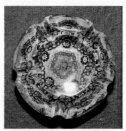

A pair of red overlay wine glasses, c1870, 5in (12.5cm) high.
$225–255 *MJW*

A Bohemian engraved amber glass goblet, c1870, 6¾in (17cm) high.
$475–525 *MJW*

A Lobmeyer goblet, c1890, 7¼in (18.5cm) high.
$650–700 *MJW*

A Stourbridge engraved beaker, late 19thC, 5¼in (13.5cm) high.
$450–525 *Hal*

A goblet, with green overlay, c1870, 5¾in (14.5cm) high.
$370–400 *MJW*

A pair of amethyst wine glasses, with engraved decoration, c1870, 5½in (14cm) high.
$330–370 *MJW*

A set of 6 footed tumblers, with enamel decoration by Fritz Heckert, c1890, 3¾in (9.5cm) high.
$750–800 *MJW*

A Viennese beaker, painted with Tarot cards, one inscribed 'N. Hofman Wien 1806', 4¾in (12cm) high.
$9,000–9,750 *S*

A Viennese beaker, c1825, 4½in (11.5cm) high.
$4,500–5,250 *S*

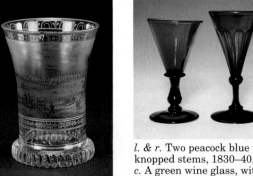

l. & r. Two peacock blue wine glasses, with knopped stems, 1830–40, 5in (12.5cm) high
c. A green wine glass, with part fluted bowl and knopped stem, c1840, 5½in (14cm) high
$100–110 each *Som*

Two cup-shaped wine glasses, c1830, 4¾in (12cm) high:
l. with knopped stem
r. with ribbed bowl and plain drawn stem.
$100–120 each *Som*

A set of 8 green Bristol trumpet-shaped wine glasses, c1840, 5¼in (13.5cm) high.
$760–820 *MJW*

A German enamelled tumbler, painted with a view of the Ochsenkopf mountain, dated '1662', 7in (18cm) high.
$22,500–24,000 *S*

Three scent bottles, c1880, longest 4¾in (12cm) long.
$180–420 each *Som*

A two-compartment scent bottle, with silver gilt mounts, c1880, 3¾in (9.5cm) long.
$1,200–1,500 *Som*

Three scent bottles, c1870, largest 5⅓in (13.5cm) long.
$250–450 each *Som*

A hexagonal cut table scent bottle, with green overlay, and gilt highlights, 19thC, 7in (18cm) high.
$340–400 *AAV*

An opaline scent bottle, probably by Thomas Webb, silver-gilt stopper by Hilliard and Thompson, c1880, 4in (10cm) high.
$1,200–1,350 *BHa*

A cut glass scent bottle, with 18ct gold top marked 'London 1846', 4⅝in (11.5cm) high.
$1,850–2,200 *SHa*

A Clichy scent bottle, with a silver top, mid-19thC, 4in (10cm) long.
$825–975 *BHa*

Two wrythen-moulded cream jugs, and a sugar basin, c1800, jugs 2¾in (7cm) high.
$225–300 each *Som*

A silver-mounted white wine jug, by Stevens & Williams, 1900, 12⅞in (32.5cm) high.
$2,250–2,650 *MJW*

A Nailsea jug, with applied loop handle, c1810, 4¾in (12cm) high.
$525–575 *Som*

A Bohemian jug, engraved with vines and cupids, c1860, 10¾in (27.5cm) high.
$1,850–2,200 *MJW*

A uranium glass jug, c1840, 10in (25.5cm) high.
$1,350–1,400 *MJW*

A pair of French glass opaline vases, with enamel decoration, c1840, 9¼in (23.5cm) high.
$3,000–3,500 *MJW*

A cranberry glass vase, on a mirrored base, decorated with lizards, c1860, 4¼in (11cm) high.
$575–725 *MJW*

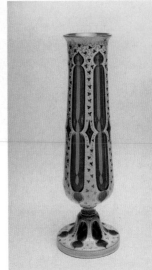

A pair of Bohemian glass vases, c1860, 16in (40.5cm) high.
$3,000–3,500 *MJW*

A St Louis glass millefiori vase, on a gilt metal foot, mid-19thC, 12½in (32cm) high.
$15,000–15,750 *C*

A French opaline glass vase, c1860, 4¼in (11cm) high.
$210–360 *MJW*

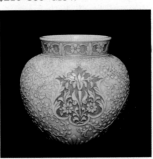

A Webb's ivory cameo glass vase, marked 'Thomas Webb & Sons' on base, c1885, 3¾in (9.5cm) high.
$750–900 *Som*

A Victorian satin glass vase, 7½in (19cm) high.
$70–90 *OD*

A Webb's cameo glass vase, c1885, 5¾in (14.5cm) high.
$1,350–1,450 *MJW*

A purple glass two-handled vase, by Jules Barbe, with gold enamel decoration, c1890, 5in (12.5cm) high.
$300–400 *MJW*

A Bohemian ruby glass vase, engraved with a stag, c1860, 6¼in (16cm) high.
$1,000–1,200 *MJW*

PORCELAIN
Baskets

A Worcester two-handled basket, painted with flowers on a yellow ground, some wear, c1765, 7½in (19cm) wide.
$1,500–2,250 *CNY*

A Worcester First Period pierced basket, printed in underglaze blue with Pinecone pattern, painted border, c1775, 7¾in (19.5cm) diam.
$900–1,000 *CHR*

A Vincennes *bleu celeste* pierced octafoil shallow basket, from the Louis XV service, with painted central bouquet, slight damage, date mark for 1754, painter's mark of Rosset, 9¼in (23.5cm) wide.
$27,750–29,250 *C*

Two Vincennes pierced lobed baskets, painted with scattered bouquets, flowersprays and insects, slight damage, one restored, date letter 'C' for 1755, painter's mark 'B', largest 11¼in (28.5cm) wide.
$14,250–18,000 *C*

A pair of Sèvres pierced trefoil baskets, the centres painted with pilgrim's and vintner's trophies within a flowering garland and gilt flower and scroll cartouche, on a green ground, slight damage, painter's mark of an anchor for Buteux, date letter for 1758, 8½in (21.5cm) wide.
$17,250–18,750 *C*

Beakers

A Meissen flared beaker, one side painted with figures before a palace, the other side with a figure in a landscape, slight damage, c1725, 3¼in (8.5cm) high.
$12,300–13,200 *C*

A Flight Worcester beaker, with tapering sides, decorated in gilt with flowersprays and monogram 'E H', within blue and gilt borders, crescent mark and blue script mark, c1785, 3½in (9cm) high.
$240–270 *DN*

A beaker, possibly by Worcester, with tapering sides, decorated in brown monochrome with figures in a continuous wooded landscape, within gilt bands, c1810, 3¼in (8.5cm) high.
$1,300–1,800 *DN*

Bough Pots

l. A pair of Davenport D-shaped bough pots and covers, painted with floral panels, each on 4 gilt ball feet, slight damage and restoration, impressed marks, c1810, 6¾in (17cm) high.
$6,300–7,500 *S*

r. A Niderviller armorial bough pot and cover, painted by Joseph Deutsch, moulded with elaborate scrollwork, the front decorated with a German coat-of-arms, on 4 scroll feet, restored, signed 'I.D.', purple monogram 'BN', incised 'IH', 6¾in (17cm) high.
$13,800–15,000 *S*

Bowls

A Champion's Bristol porcelain covered bowl, with banded decoration of pink trellis and green leaves enclosed by gilding and interspersed with rose sprays, rose-form finial, c1770, 5in (12.5cm) high.
$700–750 *EL*

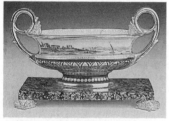

A Sèvres two-handled sucrier, from the *'Service particulier de l'empereur'*, the sides painted with views of *'Vue de Loupssor'*, and *'Vue de Syéné'*, slight damage, stencilled 'M.Imp.le de Sèvres/10' in green, gilder's mark, 1810, 9¾in (24.5cm) wide.
$27,750–29,250 *C*

In October 1807, Napoleon I commissioned a personal service for Fontainebleau, to be decorated with scenes of special significance that brought back happy memories to him.

An Ansbach punchbowl and cover, possibly decorated at The Hague, with a spray of flowers and leaves, the knop formed as a blossom, bud and stem, slight damage, incised letter 'L', stork mark in blue enamel, 1776–80, 11¾in (30cm) high.
$5,250–6,750 *S(NY)*

A Chelsea fluted bowl, in Meissen style, the exterior decorated in coloured enamels with a harbour scene depicting figures and boats, the interior with a spray of flowers and an insect, slight damage, stilt marks, c1752, 5¾in (14.5cm) diam.
$3,250–3,750 *DN*

A Worcester reeded turquoise ground sugar bowl and cover, with bud finial, the gilt borders within shaped bands with scallops and scrolls suspending swags of leaves and flowers, slight damage and wear, 1770–75, 5in (12.5cm) high.
$450–600 *CSK*

A Sèvres écuelle and cover, painted in thick bright enamels with panels depicting figures on the shore, on a blue ground, painted mark in green with date code for 1770, 6¾in (17cm) wide.
$1,000–1,350 *Bea*

r. A pair of Meissen écuelles, covers and stands, each painted with purple vignettes depicting courting couples in architectural landscapes, minor chips, crossed swords in underglaze blue, late 18thC, stands 8in (20cm) diam.
$4,500–5,250 *S(Am)*

A Minton two-handled bowl and cover, decorated by Alboin Birks with a pâte-sur-pâte panel of Diana with a putto, within a gilt cartouche, on a cream ground, signed, printed marks in gilt and pattern number 'DA 1178/5', c1910, 7in (18cm) high.
$2,200–2,700 *DN*

A Meissen sucrier and cover, painted with a continuous chinoiserie scene, minor damage, crossed swords in underglaze blue, impressed Dreher's mark of a star, 1725–30, 3½in (9cm) high.
$12,200–13,500 *S*

A gilt metal and porcelain tazza, the dish decorated with a *fête de campagne* scene, mounted by shell cast decoration with acanthus cast handles, supported by 4 acanthus cast feet linked by garlands, signed 'Pierrin', mid-19thC, 15½in (39cm) diam.
$1,650–2,250 *P*

Boxes

A Royal Worcester reticulated silk box and cover, signed 'G. Owen', the sides with a delicately pierced frieze below a border of acanthus piercing at the shoulder, the lightly stepped cover with a central pierced medallion and cross-hatched panels, printed mark and date code for 1919, 6½in (16.5cm) wide.
$10,500–12,000 *S*

George Owen was the master of reticulated work at Worcester. Piercing is done by hand, at the leather-hard stage of potting, and requires enormous skill and patience.

A Napoleon III porcelain and ormolu mounted ebonised jewellery cabinet, with 4 drawers and a pair of doors, mounted all over with foliate cast bronze and plaques depicting rustic scenes, late 19thC, 12in (30.5cm) wide.
$2,000–2,250 *SK*

A Höchst gilt-metal mounted blue ground tobacco box, cover and weight, painted in sepia with putti, base damaged and restored, c1785, 5in (12.5cm) wide.
$5,000–5,700 *C*

Busts

A Chelsea white head of a boy, damaged, raised anchor period, c1749, 4½in (11.5cm) high.
$5,300–5,700 *S*

A Copeland bust of Milton, on a parian base, c1860, 6in (15.5cm) high.
$60–100 *SER*

Candlesticks

A pair of Chelsea Derby candlestick figures, modelled as scantily clad seated putti, each with one arm round the floral encrusted stick surmounted by tulip sconces, restored, marked with 'D' intersected by anchor mark in iron-red, c1780, 7½in (19cm) high.
$1,650–2,250 *Bon*

A pair of Derby candlesticks, modelled as a boy with fruit and a girl with flowers, the girl with crowned 'D' and baton mark in underglaze blue, late 19thC, 7in (18cm) high.
$390–540 *Hal*

Centrepieces

A Potschappel centrepiece, the bowl raised on a foliate stem with a lady and gentleman dancing around a tree, on a waisted scroll-moulded openwork base, minor repairs, crossed lines and 'T' mark in underglaze blue, late 19thC, 18½in (47cm) high.
$450–525 *S(Am)*

A Dresden centrepiece, the bowl raised on a scrolled stem set with a loving couple seated next to a pedestal, watched by a jealous gentleman, polychrome painted and heightened with gilding, damaged, marked, mid-19thC, 21in (53cm) high.
$930–1,000 *S(Am)*

Clocks

A Meissen blue and white clock, modelled with a cherub writing in a book, the clock surmounted by trophies, restored, crossed swords in underglaze blue, incised 'D 78', c1880, 9½in (24cm) wide.
$2,300–2,400 *N*

A Vienna clock garniture, printed with reserves of Mrs Siddons after Gainsborough, *The Age of Innocence* and the *Infant Samuel* after Reynolds, within a green and claret ground, c1900, 17¾in (45cm) high.
$600–900 *Bon*

A Meissen rococo-scroll clock case, the enamel dial fronting a circular brass movement striking on a bell, with a porcelain stand, both pieces decorated in colours and gilt, damaged and restored, blue crossed swords marks and incised marks, 19thC, 20in (51cm) high.
$4,500–5,250 *CSK*

A Paris porcelain ormolu mounted clock garniture, the enamel dial within a *bleu celeste* case, flanked by ormolu figures of classical women, on a breakfront base mounted with porcelain plaques, painted in colours with a *Watteauesque* scene, the matching tazze painted in the centre with romantic scenes, mid-19thC, 15¾in (40cm) high.
$3,000–3,750 *S(Am)*

A Meissen white clock, in the form of 2 putti supporting a cylindrical clock case, modelled by Professor Paul Scheurich, erased crossed swords in underglaze blue, 14¼in (36cm) high.
$4,200–5,250 *S*

A German porcelain cased mantel clock, the rococo style case with boy and girl figure surmounts and encrusted flower decoration, the striking movement bearing trade stamp of 'Vincento', c1860, 12¾in (32.5cm) high.
$1,800–2,200 *P(Ch)*

Coffee & Teapots

A Chelsea white teapot and cover, modelled as a seated figure of a grinning Putai, holding a parrot, the bird's open beak forming the spout, his fluted conical hat forming the cover with beechnut and foliate finial, slight fire-specking, incised triangle mark, c1745, 6½in (16.5cm) high.
$91,500–97,500 *S*

There are only 4 recorded examples known of this chinaman and parrot teapot, of which this example is one.

A Chelsea hexagonal teapot and cover, painted in *famille rose* palette with birds amongst flowering shrubs and peonies, with a turquoise trellis and flowerhead panelled border, raised anchor period, c1750, 4½in (11.5cm) high.
$9,000–12,000 *S*

A Liverpool, Pennington's Factory, baluster shaped coffee pot and domed cover, in coloured enamels with sprays of flowers and leaves, and scattered flowers, within puce diaper borders, the handle, knop and spout picked out in iron-red, c1775, 9½in (24cm) high.
$1,270–1,430 *DN*

l. A Chelsea hexagonal teapot and cover, painted in Kakiemon palette with The Flaming Tortoise pattern after the Arita original, chip to spout, raised anchor period, c1750, 4½in (11.5cm) high.
$26,250–27,750 *S*

A Worcester teapot and cover, painted in blue with the Mansfield pattern, chip to spout, crescent mark, c1770, 5in (12.5cm) high.
$180–270 *DN*

A Royal Worcester teapot and cover, in Japanese style, with salamander handle and spout, moulded in relief with flowering branches and birds in flight, decorated in brown, green and gilt, chip to rim, moulded mark and registration mark for 1872, 8in (20.5cm) high.
$530–750 *DN*

Comports & Dessert Dishes

A pair of Moore Brothers comports, each modelled as a bowl moulded from lily leaves, supported by 3 cherubs, partly enriched in colours within gilt borders, some damage, impressed marks and registration lozenge, late 19thC, 8in (20.5cm) high.
$1,200–1,300 *CSK*

A pair of Moore Brothers fluted table ornaments, each modelled with flowerheads and leaves, picked out in green and gilt, on twig supports, some damage, printed marks in brown, c1885, 5½in (14cm) high.
$600–680 *DN*

A Lowestoft coffee pot and cover, painted in colours with Oriental figures, on a geometric pattern ground reserved with mono-chrome cartouches of buildings on islands, damaged, firing faults, c1778, 10¼in (26cm) high.
$3,250–3,750 *CSK*

A Royal Worcester white reticulated teapot, by George Owen, double-walled and pierced with tracery, pale blue inner wall and bead highlights, impressed crown over standard round mark, c1862, 4½in (11.5cm) high.
$3,000–3,300 *P(S)*

A Charles Bourne stand and dessert dish, pattern No. 60, c1818, stand 4¾in (12cm) high.
$1,280–1,430 *TVA*

A Worcester teapot and cover, decorated in bright enamels with sprays of summer garden flowers, beneath a stylised red border, c1770, 5¼in (13.5cm) high.
$380–530 *P(E)*

A Vezzi teapot, painted on each side in purple, blue, green, iron-red and yellow with a large flowerspray, spout restored, mark 'V.ª' in iron-red, incised 'A', c1725, 3in (7.5cm) high.
$6,750–7,500 *S*

Registration Marks

These indicate the date when the design was first registered with the Patent Office. Often designs were then produced for a number of years. Further information can be found in *Miller's Pottery & Porcelain Marks*, Miller's Publications Ltd, 1995.

A pair of Continental porcelain comports, with rose encrusted pierced basket tops, the pillars with cherubs and climbing roses on rococo bases, late 19thC, 14½in (37cm) high.
$750–900 *DA*

A pair of Meissen figural comports, decorated in enamel and gilt with male and female figures, repaired, crossed swords marks, late 19thC, 10in (25.5cm) wide.
$1,000–1,200 *SK*

Cups

A Charles Bourne trio, London shape, pattern No. 208, c1820, saucer 5½in (14cm) diam.
$520–600 *TVA*

A Worcester bell-shaped coffee cup and saucer, decorated in coloured enamels with Putai and attendants, within iron-red and gilt spearhead borders, c1760.
$1,500–1,800 *DN*

A Limehouse blue and white cup, with a branch-moulded handle issuing flowering branches, enriched in cobalt, the interior with a band of flowers and foliage, damaged, c1745.
$2,250–2,750 *CSK*

A Chelsea tea bowl and saucer, each piece with scalloped edge, decorated with Tiger and Dragon pattern in the Kakiemon palette, chipped, c1755, saucer 4¾in (12cm) diam.
$1,650–1,800 *Bon*

A Bloor Derby covered chocolate cup and stand, by Leonard Lead, painted with flowers, 1825, 5½in (14cm) high.
$1,000–1,200 *TK*

A Derby coffee can, base inscribed 'On the coast of Sussex', c1810, 2½in (6.5cm) high.
$450–525 *RA*

A Derby coffee can and saucer, the can painted by George Complin, pattern No. 207, with a finch perched on a still life of fruit, within a gilt panel, reserved on a pale pink ground, the saucer with gilt line rim and inner foliate border, puce painted crown, batons and 'D' mark, c1789, 2¼in (6cm) high.
$5,400–6,000 *P(NE)*

A Worcester blue-scale two-handled caudle cup, cover and stand, decorated with reserves of stylised chrysanthemums and insects within mirror-shaped cartouches, the interior with an insect and a flowerspray, interior of cup scratched, blue square seal marks, c1770, stand 5¾in (14.5cm) diam.
$600–750 *CNY*

A Sèvres cup and saucer, painted with scattered pink roses and buds within 2 concentric leaf and berry borders, with a gilt dentil edge, painter's marks for Buteux and Fontaine, interlaced 'Ls' mark, date code for 1778.
$370–450 *P*

A Liverpool transfer printed coffee can, by Philip Christian, Fruit Sprigs pattern, c1770, 2½in (6.5cm) high.
$600–680 *TVA*

Two Sèvres *bleu celeste* coffee cans and saucers, each can later painted with winged putti among clouds, some damage and firing faults, restored, painted blue marks, probably 18thC.
$950–1,200 *CSK*

Cutlery

A Meissen armorial spoon, from the Swan service, modelled by J. J. Kändler and J. F. Eberlein for Count Brühl, the fluted bowl moulded with swans and herons among bulrushes, with decorated borders of *indianische Blumen*, restored, c1740, 7¼in (18.5cm) long.
$14,750–15,450 C

Porcelain spoons are very fragile and, since few survive, they are highly prized.

l. A set of 12 Meissen knife and fork handles, painted with *holzschnitt Blumen* in the manner of Klinger, 5 handles damaged, the re-gilt steel blades and tines with marks for Breslau 1746-58, the handles 3¼in (8.5cm) long.
$9,750–10,500 C

Meissen Porcelain

The Royal Saxon Porcelain factory was founded in 1710 by Augustus the Strong, Elector of Saxony, at Meissen, near Dresden, and the first pieces produced were in the famous red stoneware developed by the factory's administrator, Johann Böttger. In 1713 the factory exhibited Europe's first hard-paste porcelain, the formula for which had been discovered by Böttger and Count Ehrenfried von Tschirnhausen five years previously. The second great phase in the history of the factory began in 1720 with the appointment of the brilliant painter Johann Höroldt, and under his direction Meissen wares acquired the exquisite decorations and palette that were to make them famous.

Production of figures of animals and people was largely unsuccessful until the sculptor Johann Kändler joined the factory in 1731. However, such was his talent that Meissen figures soon became the most admired and sought-after of the factory's products, the most popular subjects being lovers, the commedia dell'arte, satirical characters and street vendors.

The market for Meissen porcelain continues to be very strong, particularly in Germany and Japan. It therefore commands high prices, although 19thC pieces are a little more affordable.

Figures – Animals

A Bow white figure of a lioness, with open jaws revealing 2 rows of pointed teeth, on an irregular shaped rocky base, c1752, 9in (23cm) long.
$3,750–4,500 Bon

A Bow white figure of a lion, with his right forepaw resting on a tree stump, on an irregular shaped rocky base, with applied mosswork, c1752, 8¾in (22cm) long.
$3,750–5,250 Bon

A Copeland and Garrett figure of a recumbent greyhound, naturalistically decorated, on green ground base with gilt borders, chipped and repaired, printed and impressed marks, c1838, 11¼in (28.5cm) long.
$1,500–2,250 DN

The recumbent greyhound is among the most popular animal figures, being made by possibly hundreds of factories, large and small. Copeland and Garrett produced one of the largest, most naturalistic and costly models. These figures were originally sold in pairs and often used as part of a desk set.

l. A pair of Derby bocage figures, 'The Vain Jackdaw' and 'The Cock and Jewell', both with a group of birds and chicks, on rococo scrolling bases and originally fitted with candle sconces, carrying handles to the rear, c1770, 8½in (21.5cm) high.
$1,130–1,280 J&L

l. A Royal Worcester group of young foxes, by Doris Lindner, shape No. 3131, introduced 1936, 2¾in (7cm) wide.
$300–380 TVA

r. A Staffordshire figure of a pointer, with splashed decoration, minor damage, c1850, 5in (12.5cm) high.
$180–260 SER

A group of 3 Derby biscuit figures, modelled as Spring, Autumn and Winter, each on integral plinth, minor damage, incised 'No. 5, G, S,' and other marks, c1790, 8in (20cm) high.
$600–900 *Bon*

A Derby figure of a girl, wearing a white bonnet and carrying a basket, the gilt scroll base surmounted by bocage, restored, incised numeral, c1770, 5in (12.5cm) high.
$130–180 *Hal*

A pair of Minton dancing figures, each brightly coloured, on scroll-moulded bases picked out in gilding, restored, c1840, 7¾in 19.5cm) high.
$420–520 *Bon*

Parian ware

Parian ware is a fine white biscuit porcelain, which is mostly unglazed but sometimes lightly or smear-glazed. Developed in the mid-19th century by William Copeland, the name 'parian' was derived from its similarity to ancient Greek marble from the island of Paros. From 1844 onwards the Copeland (later Copeland and Garrett) factory produced a wide range of extremely popular parian figures and busts, sometimes known as 'statuary' ware.

A Minton parian figure, Solitude, modelled as a semi-draped female seated on a rockwork plinth, with a stork or heron beneath, incised 'J. Lawlor, Sculp. – Art Union of London 1852,' impressed marks under base rim, 20in (51cm) high.
$390–450 *P(E)*

A pair of Robinson and Leadbeater parian figures, depicting north Italian country musicians, decorated in green, red and sand coloured enamels, impressed 'R&L' mark and script marks to base, c1885, 16in (40.5cm) high.
$520–570 *P(E)*

A pair of Royal Worcester figures of Moorish musicians, modelled by James Hadley, both dressed in long flowing robes standing beside obelisks, tinted ivory ground and gilt, signed, date ciphers for 1897, mould Nos. 1084, 13in (33cm) high.
$2,700–3,000 *J&L*

A parian ware figure of the muse of Art, slight chip, unmarked, c1854, 14¼in (36cm) high.
$220–330 *SER*

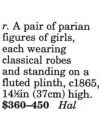

l. A parian ware female figure with a harp, slight chip, unmarked, c1860, 24½in (62cm) high.
$450–530 *SER*

r. A pair of parian figures of girls, each wearing classical robes and standing on a fluted plinth, c1865, 14½in (37cm) high.
$360–450 *Hal*

A Doccia figure group, depicting a man standing on a rocky mound leaning on a tree, wearing a blue jacket and breeches decorated with flowers and a yellow and iron-red hat, a lady seated at his feet, chipped and restored, c1770, 9in (23cm) high.
$4,500–4,800 *S*

A Ludwigsburg figure of a fisherman, emblematic of Water, modelled by Johann Christian Wilhelm Beyer, the naked man striding forward and hauling a blue-scaled dolphin in a net, minor damage, blue crowned interlaced 'C' mark to edge of base, c1765, 8¼in (21cm) high.
$4,450–6,000 *C*

Two Meissen figures of fisherfolk, modelled by J. J. Kändler, he wearing a grey hat, iron-red lined blue jacket, white shirt and yellow rolled breeches, with fish tucked into his shirt, she in black bonnet, white bodice, buff skirt and blue apron, ex Jörg Nelte collection, restored, c1740, female figure with blue crossed swords mark, 7 and 7½in (18 and 19cm) high.
$12,000–12,750 *C*

The Jörg Nelte collection of Meissen porcelain comprised pieces from the great services made for royalty and nobility in the 18th century, as well as pieces from other great collections which were milestones in the history of Meissen manufacture. The sale of the first portion of this collection included the finest and most celebrated wares and figures produced from the earliest years of the Meissen factory, from 1709 until the end of its 'golden age' in 1755.

A Fürstenberg equestrian figure of Marcus Curtius, modelled by Desoches, the Roman centurion wearing a plumed helmet, gilt-edged armour over a yellow tunic, yellow boots and a purple cloak, with short sword to his left side, the base with clouds and leaping flames, the pedestal moulded on each side with military and musical trophies, restored, one end with crowned 'FR' monogram within a laurel wreath, 'F' in underglaze blue, c1773, 19¼in (49cm) high.
$6,000–7,500 *S*

A Meissen figure of a waiter, wearing white cap, apron and stockings, pale-yellow jacket and purple breeches, holding a tray with a beaker and 3 pastries and standing before a tree stump, ex Jörg Nelte collection, blue crossed swords mark at back, c1765, 5½in (14cm) high.
$8,000–10,500 *C*

A Meissen figure of a button seller, wearing white scarf, yellow coat, puce apron and blue and white striped skirt with gilt hem, holding a pierced basket of buttons, ex Jörg Nelte collection, chipped and restored, blue crossed swords mark and impressed '16', c1755, 5¼in (13.5cm) high.
$5,500–7,500 *C*

l. A Frankenthal hunting group, modelled by Joh. Fr. Lück, with a hunter seated on a grassy mound with a hunting horn and a huntress loading a rifle, mounted on a marble plinth, cracked and restored, rampant lion and 'AB' monogram in underglaze blue, c1760, 10½in (26.5cm) high.
$6,000–7,500 *S*

A Meissen group of 2 Freemasons, modelled by J. J. Kändler, one wearing black tricorn hat, turquoise gilt-edged jacket with purple cuffs, white shirt, gilt-flowered iron-red waistcoat, black breeches, blue-edged buff apron and black shoes, the other in black tricorn hat, white jacket with gilt and black flowered grey cuffs, grey waistcoat, buff apron edged in blue, black stockings and shoes, seated and standing to either side of a terrestial globe, ex Jörg Nelte collection, inscribed in Latin, chipped and restored, c1745, 9in (23cm) high.
$109,500–120,000 *C*

A Meissen Marcolini group of Three Graces, probably after a model by J. F. Eberlein, in white, scantily draped, with flowers in their hair, on a shaped base and pedestal with stepped foot, chipped and repaired, crossed swords and '∗' in blue, incised 'No. 536', impressed numeral '50', c1780, 12¼in (31cm) high.
$2,200–2,700 *S*

A Meissen figure of a young lady, holding a gold orb, her other hand behind her back, with flowing blond hair, wearing loose robes enriched in pale green, on a moulded base with entwined meandering bands, enriched in colours and gilt, blue crossed swords mark, *Pressnummer* '105', incised 'Q180', early 20thC, 11½in (29cm) high.
$2,250–2,500 *CSK*

A Meissen musical group, depicting children, each playing an instrument and standing on rocks, pedestals and scrollwork, supported on a waisted circular base, the whole picked out in pastel colours and gilt, damaged, crossed swords in underglaze blue and impressed and incised numerals, c1860, 10¼in (26cm) high.
$1,650–1,800 *N*

A Meissen group of 2 cherubs, allegorical of Summer and Autumn, the base modelled with scrolls and coloured green, pink and blue, minor damage, crossed swords in underglaze blue, incised '1230', impressed '111', c1860, 10¾in (27cm) high.
$2,250–2,650 *S(Am)*

r. A Meissen figure of a Columbine, modelled by J. J. Kändler, wearing a blue bodice, yellow shirt bordered by vines and *indianische Blumen*, and black shoes, playing a hurdy-gurdy, seated on a tree stump, restored, mid-18thC, 4¾in (12cm) high.
$1,800–2,300 *S(Am)*

> **Did you know?**
> *MILLER'S* Antiques Price Guide *builds up year-by-year to form the most comprehensive antiques photo-reference library available.*

A pair of Meissen polychrome porcelain figures of Juno and Minerva, wearing classical costumes and carrying attributes, 19thC, 26in (66cm) high.
$2,250–2,650 *SLN*

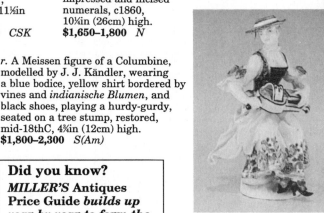

A Meissen group of Venus and Cupid, modelled in sections both drawn in a chariot pulled by swans and doves through clouds, painted in coloured enamel and gilt, crossed swords mark in blue, late 19thC, 18in (45.5cm) wide.
$6,750–9,000 *WW*

A Meissen group of Phoebus in the Chariot of the Sun, after a model by J. J. Kändler, originally executed for the Russian Empress Catherine II, the youthful scantily draped god seated in a rococo chariot drawn through sunrays and clouds by 4 white horses, attended by putti, the shaped base with laurel border, chipped and restored, late 19thC, 19¼in (49cm) wide.
$9,750–10,500 *S*

A Meissen group depicting Cupid's chariot of love, glazed in pastel colours and gilding, the figures seated on a deep crimson cushion, damaged, blue underglaze crossed swords mark, late 19thC, 9in (23cm) wide.
$2,300–2,700 *MJB*

A Paris gilt-metal mounted biscuit figure of Cupid, poised on one knee aiming a gilt metal bow and arrow, on a gilt-edged plinth, bordered in dark green heightened in gilding, minor damage, stencilled mark in iron-red, c1810, 11½in (29cm) high.
$3,300–3,750 *S*

A Sèvres group, modelled as a seated lady resisting the amorous advances of a courtly gentleman, minor damage, incised mark of Bachelier, mid-18thC, 8in (20cm) high.
$2,700–3,000 *Bon*

A pair of Sèvres figures, l'Eté garlanded with wheat and carrying a large sheaf, l'Hiver pulling a cloak around himself, each on a slab base, damaged, incised mark of Bachelier, late 18thC, 6¼in (16cm) high.
$680–900 *Bon*

r. A Wallendorf allegorical figure of Summer, modelled as a young woman holding a sheaf of wheat in her apron, wearing a yellow apron over a puce dress and a green hat lined in iron-red, the scroll-edged grassy base heightened in gilding, damaged and restored, c1775, 5¼in (13cm) high.
$750–1,000 *S*

l. A Sèvres figure group, La Curiosité, modelled as a young boy opening a magic lantern to a girl holding a basket of fruit, a smaller boy at her side, firing cracks, late 18thC, 6¼in (16cm) high.
$3,200–3,800 *Bon*

Flatware

A Chelsea leaf dish, the stem handle with leaf and flower terminal, painted with flowersprays and a moth, with brown line rims, red anchor mark, 18thC, 10¾in (27cm) wide.
$270–330 *P(Ch)*

A Chelsea fluted two-handled dish, decorated in coloured enamels with a spray of flowers, leaves and scattered flowers, within a brown line rim, red anchor mark, c1753, 8¼in (21cm) wide.
$1,000–1,200 *DN*

A Derby Crown Porcelain Co plate, painted by Rouse, the centre with a loose spray of garden flowers within a pink ground, enamelled and gilt border, slight wear, inscribed to the reverse 'J. Rouse Senr Derby', printed and impressed marks, c1880, 8½in (21.5cm) diam.
$670–750 *CSK*

l. A Chelsea Hans Sloane plate, painted in colours with a large botanical specimen on the right, possibly borage, with a sliced fig to the left, surrounded by scattered butterflies and a mushroom, the border moulded with diaper panels alternating with scrolling cartouches, brown line rim, red anchor mark, c1755, 11in (28cm) diam.
$16,500–18,000 *S*

A set of 5 Derby plates, each boldly decorated in coloured enamel with 3 sprays of flowers and leaves, within a gilt dentil border, stained, crowned crossed batons mark in red, c1820, 9¾in (25cm) diam.
$630–750 *DN*

A pair of Longton Hall strawberry-leaf moulded deep plates, the centres painted with loose bouquets and flowersprays, the borders moulded with fruiting strawberries, the leaves edged in green with puce veins, chipped, c1755, 8¾in (22cm) diam.
$2,200–2,400 *C*

A Stevenson & Hancock Derby plate, painted by W. Mosley, with tulips, pink roses and other summer flowers within two-tone burnished gilt scrolling foliate border, signed, crowned crossed batons 'S H' and 'D' marks in red, c1900, 8¾in (22cm) diam.
$630–750 *N*

An English plate, centrally decorated in coloured enamels with flowers in a basket on a ledge, the rim decorated in gilt with bird masks and leaf scrolls, c1820, 8½in (21.5cm) diam.
$2,200–2,700 *DN*

Pâte-sur-Pâte

Pâte-sur-pâte is a technique used to produce low relief decoration by applying successive layers of white clay to a tinted body, each coat or layer being carved to build up the three-dimensional design. The technique was perfected at Minton by Frenchman, Marc Louis Solon, and wares were exhibited for the first time in France in 1865. Alboin Birks was one of a number of apprentices who applied the technique to a wide range of wares after 1904.

Eight Minton plates, each painted in shades of puce, with vignettes of Cupid at various pursuits including attending a cage, riding a goat, holding a bow and arrow and sitting by a basket of fruit, the borders gilt with a band of stylised leaves within gilt bands, slight wear, impressed marks, indistinct date codes, c1865, 9¼in (23.5cm) diam.
$1,200–1,300 *CSK*

A pair of Berlin plates, with gilt band rims, the centre of one decorated with convolvulus, the other with bluebells, blue sceptre and printed double-headed eagle, 'KPM' marks, 1823–32, 9in (23cm) diam.
$450–750 *CSK*

r. A Frankenthal lozenge-shaped dish, decorated in puce *camaieu* with a gentleman and companion in a wooded landscape, the rim with scattered flowers, painted mark in blue and incised repairer's marks, dated inside footrim, c1774, 11¼in (28.5cm) wide.
$930–1,000 *DN*

A Minton pâte-sur-pâte plate, the centre with carved decoration depicting a winged cherub holding balance scales, signed 'Birks', flanked by classically gilt detail, with pierced Greek key stylised border, c1900, 9¾in (25cm) diam.
$1,200–1,400 *RA*

Two Berlin Schumann porcelain plates, with dark blue ground, both painted with views of Venice, each titled to the reverse 'Basilique de s. Marc. a Venise' and 'Pont de Rialto a Venise', underglaze blue and impressed marks, slight wear, c1860, 9¼in (23.5cm) diam.
$2,700–3,000 *CSK*

A set of 4 Berlin cabinet plates, each painted with *Watteauesque* scenes, depicting lovers couples picked out in colours with gilt lined borders and shaped rim, sceptre mark in underglaze blue, orb and 'KPM' in underglaze red, c1900, 9½in (24.5cm) diam.
$1,500–2,250 *S(Am)*

A set of 4 Dresden cabinet plates, painted and parcel gilt, each depicting a different royal lady, slight wear, signed 'Wagner', factory marks, late 19thC, 9¼in (23.5cm) diam.
$2,700–3,000 *SK(B)*

A Vienna plate, the painted reserve depicting figures at an easel, on gilded and jewelled deep blue ground, signed, late 19thC, 9½in (24cm) diam.
$600–750 *AH*

An Austrian cabinet portrait plate, the centre painted with Peter the Great and Catherine the Great, the borders with portrait roundels, late 19thC, 14in (35.5cm) diam.
$1,950–2,250 *SK*

A German portrait plate, depicting the Countess of Harrington, signed 'Wagner', titled on reverse, raised gilt border with simulated jade medallions, c1900, 9½in (24cm) diam.
$520–750 *SK*

A pair of Tournai dishes, decorated in The Hague, painted in colours with vignette, one depicting a seated fisherman in a riverside landscape, the other with 2 exotic birds perched in a garden, within a blue and gilt decorated border and flowering garlands beneath a moulded rim, stork mark in underglaze blue, one with slight damage, late 18thC, 12¼in (31cm) diam.
$1,800–2,300 *S(Am)*

An early Doccia plate, with ozier-moulded border, brightly painted with an adaptation of a Japanese design of banded hedges, flowering peonies and a ho-ho bird in thick enamels and gold, 18thC, 9in (23cm) diam.
$750–900 *P*

A Meissen armorial dish, from the Swan service, by J. J. Kändler and J. F. Eberlein for Count Brühl, moulded with swans in rough water among fish and shells between bulrushes, a heron wading with a fish in its beak, another in flight above, on a spiral shell-moulded ground, the border with *indianische Blumen* and coat-of-arms, within a gilt dentil rim, retouching to gilt rim, blue crossed swords mark, 1737–41, 16½in (42cm) diam.
$50,000–52,500 *C*

The famous Swan Service, made at Meissen from 1737–41, was commissioned by the Elector of Saxony, Augustus III, for presentation to Count von Brühl, the director of the Meissen factory, on his marriage to Anna von Kolowrat-Krakowski. Modelled by J. J. Kändler and J. F. Eberlein, the design has a predominating theme of water, with swans, dolphins, nereids and putti in relief. Each piece bears the arms of the Count (and sometimes those of his wife) and the entire service comprised over 1,400 pieces. The Swan Service was Meissen's first important production in the rococo style, which influenced and inspired the development of this style in other porcelain factories.

l. A Bavarian cabinet plate in Vienna style, the pale puce border decorated with gilding and enamelling, the centre painted with a half-length portrait by Wagner, inscribed on reverse 'Sommer', mark over-painted in gilt, c1900, 9½in (24cm) diam.
$450–520 *P(HSS)*

A Sèvres square fruit dish, the central reserve painted with lovers in a park in a green wreath and floral festoon surround on a deep blue jewelled and gilded ground with painted panels, 19thC, 8½in (21.5cm) wide, and a pair of matching plates.
$950–1,000 *AH*

A pair of Russian gilt ground plates, with blue painted rims framing borders of blue and green flowers among stylised foliage, Imperial cipher of Nicholas II, early 20thC, 9in (22.5cm) diam.
$930–1,200 *CSK*

Ice Pails

A Derby ice pail, cover and liner, from the Earl of Shrewsbury service, painted by John Brewer in puce *camaieu* on both sides, the base with a crown, crossed batons and 'D' marks in red, the liner with mark in red, 1805–10, 13¾in (35cm) high.
$4,550–5,250 *S*

This is one of the 4 ice pails from the service made for the Earl of Shrewsbury.

A pair of Coalport orange ground ice pails, covers and liners, each with gilt wishbone finial and scroll handles, gilt with large paterae on a band of orange enriched with yellow scrolling foliage between wide gilt diamond borders and gilt lines, one cover cracked, c1810, 10¾in (27.5cm) high.
$9,750–10,500 *CNY*

Jars

A pair of Chamberlain's Worcester two-handled jars and covers, of baluster form, applied and painted with flowers and foliage, damaged, early 19thC, 12½in (32cm) high.
$670–750 *Bea*

Inkstands

A Chamberlain's Worcester inkstand and cover, modelled after King John's tomb in Worcester Cathedral, with 3 internal covers and liners, restored, printed mark and historical account in puce, c1850, 8¼in (21cm) wide.
$450–750 *Bon*

A Derby inkstand, painted with panels of flowers on cobalt blue ground, 1815, 11½in (29cm) wide.
$1,275–1,425 *TK*

Miller's is a price GUIDE not a price LIST

A Meissen jar and cover, in the form of a seated bear, with blue and gold collar, holding a wide ribbon with a French inscription proclaiming the merits of wine, one foot restored, incised '1001', c1870, 10½in (26.5cm) high.
$750–900 *Bea*

A Staffordshire shell-shaped inkwell, with swan-neck handle, fitted with a well and 2 quill holders, decorated in coloured enamels with sprays of flowers and leaves, within gilt borders, rim chip restored, c1820, 5½in (14cm) wide.
$330–450 *DN*

A ceramic and ormolu-mounted encrier, the central drum-shaped receiver flanked by 2 turned circular receivers with shell-shaped pen tray, c1825, 12in (30cm) wide.
$2,750–3,000 *P*

Jardinières

A Sèvres bisque and gilt jardinière, 19thC, 18½in (47cm) high.
$8,200–9,000 *S(NY)*

A Royal Worcester jardinière, printed and painted with flowers, printed marks, indistinct shape code, shape number 1459, c1900, 6in (15cm) high.
$670–900 *Bon*

Jugs & Ewers

A Worcester blue and white mask jug, with cabbage leaf moulded body, printed with floral sprays and butterflies, slight damage, c1780, 12in (30.5cm) high.
$450–530 *RBB*

A pair of ewers, each with continuous panels depicting allegorical figures, with snake formed handles, restored, sceptre mark in unglazed blue, 'KPM' red mark, late 19thC, 23½in (59.5cm) high.
$4,800–5,400 *S(NY)*

A Staffordshire porcellaneous Toby jug, the seated figure wearing a red coat, with a black tricorn hat, the scroll handle moulded with a figure and acanthus leaves, mid-19thC, 9¼in (23.5cm) high.
$120–180 *Hal*

A Böttger silver gilt-mounted hot milk jug and cover, with S-scroll handle and pinched gilt lip, decorated with an Oriental and an attendant beneath the spout, the domed cover with gilt button finial, slight damage,mounts with maker's mark of Elias Adam of Augsburg, blue enamel crossed swords mark to base and cover, c1725, 6¼in (16cm) high.
$13,800–15,000 *C*

A Worcester baluster-shaped jug, with loop handle, printed in black by Robert Hancock with 'The Tea Party' and 'The Maid and Page', black line rim, c1770, 3¼in (8cm) high.
$420–520 *DN*

A New Hall boat-shaped jug, painted with grapes and foliage on a mazarine blue ground, pattern No. 779, c1805, 4in (10cm) high.
$270–330 *CHR*

A Flight Worcester cream jug, with pinched lip, in Sèvres style, decorated in coloured enamels with scattered cornflowers and gilt leaves, within gilt borders, script mark in puce, 1785–90, 2¾in (7cm) high.
$210–270 *DN*

A Meissen ewer, emblematic of Earth, after a model by J. J. Kändler, with figures of Diana and Pan, moulded with animals of the chase, the wheatsheaf moulded scroll handle topped with a putto, restored, crossed swords in underglaze blue, incised '309', 1860–70, 26½in (67.5cm) high.
$10,500–11,250 *S*

A Derby baluster-shaped jug, with scroll handle, decorated in coloured enamels with exotic birds, the reverse with a bold spray of flowers and leaves, within a brown line rim, restored, c1760, 8¼in (21cm) high.
$525–600 *DN*

A Sèvres style ewer and stand, painted with portraits of Louis XIV and members of the French court within tooled gilt borders reserved on a dark blue ground, the panels linked by gilt scrolls enriched with turquoise, white and red 'jewels', all within gilt dentil rims, slight damage and wear, script marks and titles to the base, 19thC, 6¾in (17cm) high.
$3,300–3,800 *CSK*

Scent Bottles

Services

A scent bottle, with silver top, commemorating the Royal Naval Exhibition in 1891, 2½in (6.5cm) diam.
$750–900 *BHa*

A Coalport blue ground part dessert service, comprising 35 pieces, with still lifes of fruit and flowers within a gilt scallop surround intersected with a gilt zigzag, the rim gilt with foliate scrolls on the blue ground, some damage and wear, c1805.
$4,800–6,000 *CNY*

A Coalport dessert service, painted by S. Lawrence, comprising 25 pieces, each with a flowerspray in the centre, the border with floral bouquets within elaborate gilt cartouches on a deep blue ground, within yellow and gilt scroll moulded rims, gilt fractional pattern No. 4/412, slight damage, c1840.
$6,300–6,800 *S*

A Royal Worcester 'Victoria R' commemorative perfume flask, with a gilt-metal crown cover, printed mark in gilt 'Rd No. 56943', c1887, with presentation box.
$1,200–1,800 *Bon*

A Charles Bourne part dessert service, comprising 15 pieces, painted and gilt in the Imari palette with spray of peony branches, within shaped gilt line rims, some damage and wear, iron red marks, pattern No. 62, c1820.
$1,000–1,200 *CSK*

A Davenport botanical service, comprising 24 pieces, painted in colours with named botanical specimens, turquoise pearl border and gilt pierced rim, some damage, underglaze blue printed mark, c1845, plate 9in (23cm) diam.
$3,300–4,200 *S*

A Royal Crown Derby part dessert service, comprising 17 pieces, decorated in the Japan pattern, highlighted in gilding, some wear and repair, printed and impressed factory marks, 1878–90.
$900–1,000 *S(S)*

A Derby ornithological part dessert service, Robert Bloor & Co, comprising 9 pieces, the centres painted in the manner of Richard Dodson, some damage, the dishes with crown, crossed batons and 'D' marks in gold, the plates with crown, crossed batons and 'D' marks in iron-red, c1815.
$2,700–3,300 *C*

A Davenport botanical dessert service, comprising 28 pieces, finely painted with botanical specimens, within apple green borders with gilt enrichments, some damage, blue printed marks, c1860, plate 9in (23cm) diam.
$4,900–5,700 *S*

A Royal Crown Derby Imari pattern part dinner service, comprising 53 pieces, painted in iron-red, blue and gilt with a peony and prunus pattern, No. 563, with impressed and printed red marks, 1902, plate 10in (25.5cm) diam.
$970–1,120 *P(E)*

A Ridgway part tea and coffee service, with Imari floral pattern in iron-red, blue and green with gilt embellishments, comprising: 8 tea cups, 4 coffee cups, 5 saucers, 2 saucer dishes, cream jug and sucrier, early 19thC.
$870–930 *AH*

A Ridgway part dessert service, comprising 26 pieces, with loose sprays of flowers within similar scrolling gilt panels divided by beige shaped panels gilt with bouquets on a deep blue ground, with pale blue shaped gilt line rims, moulded with fruiting vines, some damage and wear, iron-red pattern No. 735, 1815–20.
$6,000–6,750 *CSK*

A Spode tea service, comprising 37 pieces, decorated in pink and gilt with roses, slight damage, painted mark in red, pattern No. 3886, early 19thC.
$450–530 *CAG*

A Rockingham part dessert service, comprising 5 pieces, painted with exotic birds within buff ground and gilt scroll borders, some damage, one with puce printed mark, c1830.
$1,200–1,800 *CSK*

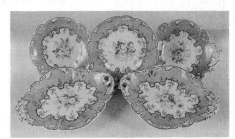

A Staffordshire apple green and gilt bordered dessert service, comprising 22 pieces, the centres painted in colours with floral sprays within shaped gilt reserves, pierced rims with gilt leaf scroll pattern borders, pattern No. 8095, some damage, 19thC.
$450–530 *CAG*

A Spode tea and coffee service, comprising 45 pieces, each decorated in Japan colours with wisteria and stylised flowers, slight damage, red capital Spode mark and pattern No. 2214, mid-19thC.
$3,750–4,500 *P(S)*

A group of Worcester tea and coffee wares, comprising 12 pieces, with gilt framed panels of exotic birds and insects against a blue scale ground, and a Worcester blue scale fluted plate, painted with panels of flowers, extensive damage and repair, fretted square marks in underglaze blue, c1770.
$670–900 *S(S)*

A Chamberlain's Worcester assembled part dessert service, comprising 104 pieces, painted in iron-red, green and underglazed blue enriched in gilt in the Thumb and Finger pattern, wear to gilding, script mark to one plate, pattern No. 276, c1807, plate 8½in (21.5cm) diam.
$6,750–8,250 *CNY*

A Grainger's Worcester tea service, comprising 22 pieces, decorated in the 18thC Worcester manner with birds and butterflies within gold foliate reserves on a blue scale ground, printed mark and date for 1892.
$900–1,000 *Bea*

A Clignancourt cabaret service, comprising 8 pieces, with vignettes of putti bordered by flowerheads *en grisaille*, cobalt and gilt border, Vitruvian scrolls and husk chains, red stencilled monogram of 'protector' Louis-Stanislas-Xavier beneath crown, late 18thC, tray 8½in (21.5cm) wide.
$6,750–7,500 *Bon*

A Worcester fluted part tea and coffee service, comprising 23 pieces, finely gilt with husk swags suspended from rings and paterae in husk ovals and a band of Vitruvian scrolls around the base and inside the cups, the shaped pieces with floral finials, some damage, c1785, saucer 7¼in (18.5cm) diam.
$3,000–3,750 *CNY*

A Meissen ornithological part dinner service, comprising 17 pieces, the centres painted with exotic birds, *en camaieu bleu* borders with loose bouquets within gilt scroll-moulded cartouches on a *Dulong* pattern ground, waved gilt rims, blue crossed swords and dot marks, *Pressnummer* 10, c1775, plate 9¾in (25cm) diam.
$7,500–9,000 *C*

l. A Meissen Marcolini part tea service, with flower bouquets and fruit within ribbon and flower borders and gilt dentil rims, comprising: 11 tea cups and 10 saucers, slight damage, blue crossed swords and star marks, c1780.
$3,400–4,200 *CSK*

A Berlin dinner service, comprising 107 pieces, each with a central spray of flowers surrounded by 3 insects in colours, ozier moulded borders painted with 3 flower sprigs, minor damage, sceptre mark in blue and orb, 'KPM' in red, late 19thC.
$9,000–10,500 *P*

A Meissen tête-à-tête, comprising 13 pieces, with a scene of rustic and resting farm animals within elaborate gilt borders, damaged and restored, crossed swords in underglaze blue and *Pressnummern*, c1830, tray 17¼in (44cm) wide.
$6,750–7,500 *S*

A Meissen cabaret set, in the manner of the Swan service, comprising 10 pieces, with two pairs of swans and herons on a swollen river before reeds and buildings within a gilt line border, some damage, crossed swords in underglaze blue, c1870, tray 16¾in (42.5cm) wide.
$7,500–9,000 *S*

A Meissen breakfast set, in the Purple Indian pattern, comprising: a cup and saucer, creamer, sugar bowl, coffee pot and shaped tray, factory marks, c1880.
$1,500–2,250 *SK*

A Sèvres aquamarine ground part dessert service, comprising 114 pieces, each centre painted with a bouquet of pink roses and green leaves tied with a blue, rose, purple or yellow bow knot, the aquamarine ground body or rim with a gilt berry vine border, some damage, variously marked with Sèvres or 'R F' Sèvres in script, painters' marks in blue or grey enamel, gilders' marks in gold, and many with incised marks, c1800, fruit cooler 10¼in (26cm) high.
$7,000–8,400 *S(NY)*

l. A Paris porcelain part dinner service, comprising 78 pieces, with sprays of multi-coloured flowers, wear lines, mid-19thC.
$1,200–1,500 *SK(B)*

A Sèvres *bleu agate* ground tea service, comprising 17 pieces, gilt with anthemion, scrolls, foliate and flowerhead ornament, gilt cup interiors, blue printed circular masks enclosing monogram 'L P' below a crown flanked by 'Sèvres 1834' and one with '1837', incised marks and gilders' dates and marks, 1834–37.
$3,000–3,750 *C*

A Sèvres *blue celeste* ground tête-à-tête, comprising 10 pieces, decorated with couples in landscapes within a jewelled surround in underglaze blue, mid-19thC, tray 13in (33cm) wide.
$6,000–6,750 *SK*

Miller's is a price GUIDE not a price LIST

A Paris porcelain part tea and coffee service, comprising 9 pieces, decorated in the Empire style, with lions' mask moulded spouts and terminals, painted with garlands of blossom reserved on yellow ground borders within gilt rims, damaged and restored, incised marks, early 19thC.
$1,200–1,500 *CSK*

A Sèvres tête-à-tête, comprising 9 pieces, with figural panels on a cobalt ground, interlacing 'L' mark and a circular crown mark, 'Porcelaines D'Art A. Golse', c1900, with silk lined carrying case.
$3,300–4,000 *S(NY)*

A Vienna cabaret set, comprising 16 pieces, with gilding and bands of scrolling, leaves and stylised flowers in a dark blue ground, restored, shield mark in underglaze blue, impressed date, codes and potters' numbers, 1796–98, tray 15¼in (38.5cm) wide.
$18,750–22,500 *S*

A Vienna cream ground tête-à-tête, comprising 10 pieces, with gilt bands of meandering vine, flanking a band of stylised scrolls, paterae and green foliage, the borders with gilt half flowerheads and zigzag ornament, blue shield marks, various *Pressnummern*, date codes for 1798–1800.
$6,300–7,200 *C*

Snuff Boxes

A Meissen gold-mounted portrait snuff box, the exterior painted with gallants and companions in puce *camaieu* after Watteau, the interior richly gilt and the cover with a half-length portrait of a lady, minor damage, repaired, c1750, 3¼in (8cm) wide.
$6,750–8,250 *C*

A Meissen gold-mounted chinoiserie snuff box, painted with Orientals in the manner of J. G. Höroldt, within gilt line quatrefoil cartouches with Böttger lustre panels and iron-red, purple and gilt scrolls, the underside painted in purple *camaieu* with figures, the interior of the cover with a man holding a bow and a quiver of arrows, slight rubbing, blue 'KPM' above crossed swords mark to the interior of the base, c1725, 2¼in (5.5cm) wide.
$14,250–15,750 *C*

A Meissen gold-mounted snuff box and cover, the exterior of the cover painted with a bust of Athena, the interior with a warrior wearing a plumed helmet within an ogival cartouche on a gilt ground, the exterior with chinoiserie figures on a terrace, the underside with green mosaic within a Böttger lustre band, the interior richly gilt, contemporary gold mount, slight rubbing, blue 'KPM' above crossed swords mark visible through gilding, c1730, 2½in (6.5cm) wide.
$9,000–10,500 *C*

Tankards

A Lowestoft tankard, in the manner of 'Tulip painter', painted with a loose bouquet of flowers, a lesser spray to the reverse, among scattered sprigs, the interior rim painted in pink with a geometric pattern, applied with a strap handle, slight damage, c1775, 5½in (14cm) high.
$3,750–4,500 *CSK*

A documentary Meissen silver-mounted tankard, painted and signed by Carl Wilhelm Böhme in crimson monochrome with a scene of the Rape of Europa after Boucher, with the initials 'C.W.B.', handle embellished with scrollwork, the silver mount with London hallmarks of 1828, traces of crossed swords in blue, handle partially replaced, handle dated '1742', 6½in (16.5cm) high.
$11,250–12,750 *S*

l. A Capo di Monte covered tankard, with relief figural design and finial, gilt bronze eagle-form thumb latch, late 19thC, 12in (30.5cm) high.
$820–900 *EL*

r. A Worcester blue and white tankard, with transfer decoration, open crescent-form mark, c1776, 5in (12.5cm) high.
$260–340 *EL*

A Worcester bell-shaped tankard, with grooved strap handle, printed in black with a bust of George II, a ship in full sail and crowned martial trophies with a scroll inscribed 'Liberty', signed 'R.H. Worcester' with anchor rebus, c1760, 5½in (14cm) high.
$1,500–1,800 *S*

Tea Caddies

A Meissen chinoiserie hexagonal tea caddy and cover, painted with Orientals in the manner of Johann Gregorius Höroldt, the angles and shoulder richly gilt, the cover enriched with gilding, ex Jörg Nelte collection, slight rubbing, blue enamel crossed swords mark, gilder's '87' on both pieces, c1725, 4½in (10.5cm) high.
$8,250–10,500 C

A Meissen armorial tea caddy and cover, from the Mauro d'Averso service, painted in the manner of B. G. Häuer with estuary scenes and equestrian figures, the shoulder with green and iron-red diaper pattern, the angles enriched with gilding, the cover painted with an estuary scene and a gilt band, ex Jörg Nelte collection, slight flaking to gilding, faint blue crossed swords mark, c1740, 4¼in (11cm) high.
$15,750–18,000 C

Thimbles

A German thimble, painted with a bouquet of roses and forget-me-nots within gilt bands, slight wear, 19thC, ¾in (19mm) high.
$330–450 CSK

An English thimble, painted with roses and pansies in a continuous garland within gilt rims, worn, 19thC, 1in (25mm) high.
$210–240 CSK

A Derby thimble, by Stevenson and Hancock, painted around the base with roses and stylised cornflowers above a gilt footrim, slight wear, lilac crown and crossed batons mark, 19thC, 1in (25mm) high.
$380–450 CSK

An English thimble, painted with a geometric design of a band of yellow ovals reserved on an iron-red ground band above diagonal gilt bordered panels enclosing graduated yellow dots within gilt bands, worn, 19thC, 1in (25mm) high.
$190–220 CSK

Trays

A Darte, Paris, tray, painted with a classical scene of a warrior carrying the body of a girl, with a monk and a hound, in a rocky landscape within a gilt border, slight wear, printed marks, early 19thC, 17¼in (44cm) wide, framed.
$1,300–1,800 CSK

A Vienna gold ground tray, painted by Jakob Schufrid with a view of Vienna, inscribed in French on the reverse, signed, impressed 'P', incised 'W', date code for 1816, 16½in (42cm) wide.
$15,000–18,000 C

Jakob Schufrid worked in Vienna as a landscape painter from 1798 to 1857.

Tureens

A Derby yellow ground tureen cover and stand, painted by Cuthbert Lawton, in sepia with birds, 1805, 6½in (16.5cm) wide.
$1,100–1,200 TK

A Höchst two-handled quatrefoil tureen and cover, with green and yellow scroll and foliage handles and feet, painted with bouquets and flowersprays, the cover with artichoke and foliage finial, damaged, manganese wheel mark, 'PB' for Philipp Magnus Bechel, c1755, 13½in (34.5cm) wide.
$1,500–1,800 C

A Meissen two-handled tureen, cover and stand, with *Brühlsche Allerlei* moulding, painted in puce and green *camaieu* with bouquets and flowersprays within gilt-edged moulded cartouches, slight damage, blue crossed swords marks to tureen and stand, c1750, stand 14in (35.5cm) diam.
$5,250–7,500 C

Urns

A Worcester two-handled urn and cover, decorated with flowers on a gilt trellis, the cover tightly encrusted with blossoms, early 19thC, 15in (38cm) high.
$6,000–7,500 *CNY*

A pair of Sèvres style urns, painted by H. Desprez, with continuous scenes depicting Napoleon, within blue ground gilt borders with swans, crowned eagles, oak leaves with acorns, laurel garlands, gilt-metal mounts, damaged and repaired, signed, crowned 'N' marks and anthemion motifs, 19thC, 23½in (59.5cm) high.
$8,250–9,750 *CSK*

A pair of Derby vases, moulded with scrolls and painted with birds, the borders highlighted in gilt and containing bouquets of white flowers and green leaves, some damage and restoration, c1765, 9in (23cm) high.
$520–750 *MSW*

Vases

A pair of Chelsea eel-trap vases, with pierced, galleried shoulders and necks, aquatic weeds and bulrushes forming each handle, restored, gold anchor marks, c1760, 10¾in (27.5cm) high.
$3,400–4,200 *S*

A Derby campana vase, decorated with a view of a Continental city, on an orange ground, c1810, 6¾in (17cm) high.
$1,200–1,800 *TK*

A pair of Dresden vases and covers, with pink ground, gilt conical finials and each painted with 2 scenes of figures wearing 18thC style dress, chipped and repaired, blue 'AR' monograms above stars, c1880, 13¾in (35cm) high.
$900–1,200 *C*

A Swansea vase, with caryatid handles, painted with roses on a black ground, c1815, 9¼in (23.5cm) high.
$1,500–1,800 *TK*

A pair of Swansea vases, by James Goodsby, the border decorated with biscuit flowers, c1815, 11in (28cm) high.
$4,200–5,300 *TK*

A pair of Meissen beaker vases, made for Schloss Hubertusberg, the hunting lodge of Augustus III, the yellow ground reserved and painted with hunting scenes, one with equestrian figures following hounds, gilt line rims, ex Jörg Nelte collection, slight damage, blue crossed swords marks and Dreher's mark to both, c1740, 16in (40.5cm) high.
$172,000–180,000 *C*

A Chamberlain's Worcester pierced flower vase and cover, decorated with a topographical view of Worcester, c1810, 8in (20cm) high.
$1,130–1,430 *TK*

A pair of Meissen pâte-sur-pâte vases and covers, each with 2 reserves of classical figures and Bacchanalian putti, within a scrolled surround, with animal-form handles, restored, late 19thC, 16in (40.5cm) high.
$21,000–24,000 *SK*

A Meissen vase and cover, after a model by J. J. Kändler, the reverse with a cartouche inscribed 'Dieu et mon Droit', the cover with a figure of Jupiter, flanked by fire and an eagle, chipped and restored, crossed swords in underglaze blue, c1860, 24¼in (61.5cm) high.
$4,500–6,000 *S*

A Flight, Barr & Barr Worcester triple vase, painted with canted reserves of flowers, the pale apricot ground with Regency gilding, on 4 lions' paw feet, damaged, unmarked, c1815, 6¼in (16cm) high.
$5,400–6,000 *MSW*

A Chamberlain's Worcester vase, painted on one side with flowers, gilt foliate and lyre decoration on reverse, on a blue ground, mounted with yellow and gilt dolphin handles, marked in red 'Chamberlain & Co, Worcester, 155 New Bond Street, London,' c1820, 17¼in (44cm) high.
$330–450 *Hal*

l. An Italian vase and cover, drawn in manganese and iron-red, painted in strong colours with panels of parrots perched on flowering shrubs in pagoda gardens, within formal borders of strapwork, lattice panels, acanthus and bells, chipped and restored, underglaze blue 'S' mark, c1740, 11½in (29cm) high.
$11,250–12,750 *S*

A pair of Meissen fluted vases, with domed covers, the turquoise flutes divided by pink lines above a moulded horizontal wreath of laurel enriched in gilding, the grounds gilt with *caillouté* pattern, the covers moulded with acanthus and ribbon-tied interlaced double wreath finials, on stepped bases moulded with foliage scrolls, the lower bodies pierced for conversion to table lamps, chipped, blue crossed swords marks, c1900, 12⅝in (32cm) high.
$3,000–3,750 *C*

A cornucopia vase, possibly by Jacob Petit, painted with flowers within gilt cartouches, on a blue ground, with eagle's head terminal, shaped rectangular base, gilt borders and highlights, mid-19thC, 9in (23cm) high.
$180–270 *Hal*

An Austrian vase and cover, with gilt finial and loop handles, the reserves depicting a reclining maiden with cherubs, on gilded scrolling foliate blue ground, matching stand with bracket feet, 19thC, 18½in (47cm) high.
$1,200–1,300 *AH*

Wall Vases

A pair of Worcester wall vases, spirally moulded and painted with Cornucopia Prunus pattern in underglaze blue, traces of crossed swords and other marks, c1758, 8½in (21.5cm) high.
$1,800–2,300 *MSW*

Wine Coolers

A Meissen wine bottle stand, to hold a moon-shaped glass bottle, pierced with strongly moulded white trellis, the undulating top edged with gilt rope-twist and shell motifs, cracked and restored, crossed swords mark and impressed '26', c1740, 8¾in (22.5cm) wide.
$530–750 *P*

A pair of Worcester cornucopia wall vases, the rims moulded with flowerheads and leaves above spiral fluted stems, painted in enamel colours with European flowers, slight damage, c1760, 9¾in (24.5cm) high.
$3,000–3,750 *P(B)*

Multi-coloured vases are rarer than underglaze blue and white examples.

A pair of Coalport wine coolers, with a painted floral frieze including passion flowers, gilt acanthus mouldings and handles, detachable rims, on scroll feet, slight damage, 9½in (24cm) high.
$1,350–1,500 *RBB*

A pair of German porcelain wall vases, each painted with foliage and trelliswork, moulded with a putto and flowerheads, damaged, late 19thC, 13¼in (34cm) high.
$980–1,130 *SK*

A pair of Meissen flared bottle coolers, each moulded in relief with swans and cranes, painted with a swan within a scroll cartouche, within pierced trellis and flowerhead borders, picked out in puce and gilt, on oval bases, marks in blue and impressed and incised numerals, 19thC, 9in (23cm) wide.
$6,750–7,500 *DN*

Miscellaneous

A Royal Crown Derby milk churn-shaped miniature cream jug, decorated in Old Derby Witches pattern, c1904, 2in (5cm) high.
$300–380 *TVA*

A Royal Copenhagen Flora Danica dessert dish and cover, with dentate edge, the bell-shaped cover with pierced basketwork sides applied with gilded leaves and florets and painted with named botanical specimens, the pierced domed top modelled as a canopy of leaves, with bud knop, printed marks, 20thC, 11½in (29cm) high.
$4,500–5,250 *P*

l. A Minton lobed two-handled foot bath, printed and painted with sprays of flowers and leaves, within green line borders, cracked, pattern No. 2615 in red and impressed mark for 1842, 19in (48.5cm) wide.
$1,000–1,200 *DN*

A Minton Dresden match pot, design No. 28, c1830, 5in (12.5cm) high.
$300–380 *TVA*

A Royal Crown Derby miniature kettle, decorated in Old Derby Witches pattern, c1911, 3in (7.5cm) high.
$450–530 *TVA*

Belleek

A Belleek triple bird's nest basket, with glazed two-strand lattice bodies, with non-glazed flower decoration, c1880, 7in (18cm) wide.
$3,000–4,500 *MLa*

A Belleek basket, the lattice body formed from cross strands rising to a looped rim applied with a trail of roses and thistle heads, 2 grog applied twig-shaped handles, with a creamy lustrous glaze, minor chips, applied label with impressed mark, late 19thC, 8½in (21.5cm) diam.
$900–1,000 *WIL*

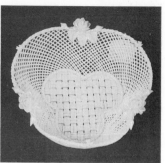

A Belleek shamrock four-strand basket, c1930, 5½in (14cm) wide.
$520–560 *MLa*

On four-strand items, there is no period mark.

A Belleek brooch, encrusted with flowers, First Period, 1¼in (3cm) diam.
$410–450 *MLa*

A Belleek neptune cup and saucer, First Green Period, saucer 5¼in (13.5cm) diam.
$300–380 *MLa*

A pair of Belleek candlesticks, Second Period, 9½in (24cm) high.
$750–1,000 *MLa*

l. A Belleek piano candlestick, Second Period, 9in (23cm) high.
$1,200–1,350 *MLa*

Two Belleek baskets and covers, in open trellis work applied with swags of roses, shamrocks and thistles, crabstock handles:
l. with the word 'Ireland' added, post-1891, 12½in (32cm) wide.
$2,600–3,300
r. impressed 'Belleek Co Fermanagh', pre-1891, 11½in (29cm) wide.
$3,700–4,500 *J&L*

A Belleek Celtic coffee cup and saucer, hand decorated, Third Period, saucer 5in (12.5cm) diam.
$280–330 *MLa*

A Belleek McBirney dish, First Green Period, 5¼in (13cm) wide.
$300–380 *MLa*

Belleek Ware

The Belleek Works were established in 1857 in Co Fermanagh, Northern Ireland by Caldwell Bloomfield, Robert Williams Armstrong and David McBirney. The distinctive, ultra-thin porcelain was first exhibited at the Dublin Exhibition in 1865 and the factory soon became famous for parian ware ornamental items. They were often modelled in the form of shells and other marine objects, which were finished with the characteristic iridescent glaze resembling mother-of-pearl. Services and wares of all types were also produced, including openwork baskets and vases with extremely fine flower encrustation (made possible by the strength of the parian body), as well as ordinary white china and white graniteware.

American Belleek refers to decorative 'eggshell type' porcelain. This was mostly made in the Trenton, New Jersey area of the United States in the last quarter of the 19th century.

A Belleek cardium, with shell feet, Second Period, 4in (10cm) wide.
$150–230 *MLa*

A Belleek urn jug, Second Period, 7in (18cm) high.
$1,100–1,200 *MLa*

A Belleek tazza, First Period, 9in (23cm) high.
$2,700–3,000 *MLa*

A Belleek pot, encrusted with flowers, early Second Period, 4in (10cm) high.
$340–380 *MLa*

A Belleek shamrock Irish harp, Third Period, 8¾in (22.5cm) high.
$300–380 *MLa*

A Belleek figure of Affection, First Period, 14½in (37cm) high.
$2,250–3,000 *MLa*

A Belleek spill vase, in the form of a corn on the cob, First Period, 6¼in (16cm) high.
$380–450 *MLa*

A Belleek moulded shell and coral tea set and tray comprising: a teapot, sugar basin, milk jug, six cups and saucers, Second Period.
$1,000–1,200 *TMA*

A Belleek dragon teapot, First Period, 6in (15cm) high.
$2,700–3,000 *MLa*

The lid has a recipe for tea making inscribed inside the lid.

A Belleek thorn dressing table tray, First Period, 9¼in (23.5cm) wide.
$750–900 *MLa*

A Belleek moulded lace tray, First Period, 14in (35.5cm) diam.
$3,750–4,500 *MLa*

A Belleek hexagonal teapot, Second Period, 5½in (14cm) high.
$450–530 *MLa*

A Belleek princess vase, encrusted with flowers, Third Period, 9in (23cm) high.
$1,000–1,200 *MLa*

Crested

A Belleek vase and cover, modelled in bold relief with putti, the cover with a putto and 3 seahorses, supported by 3 mermaids, on lobed round base, finial damaged, printed marks in black, c1900, 18in (46cm) high.
$970–1,300 *DN*

Belleek Marks & Dates

The first pieces produced at the factory bear impressed or relief name-marks 'BELLEEK, CO FERMANAGH', or 'FERMANAGH POTTERY', or impressed or printed crowned harp mark.

First Period 1863–90

Mark, usually black, showing seated Irish wolfhound, its head turned to face a round tower, an Irish harp to right, all above a banner inscribed 'Belleek' with sprigs of shamrock either side.

Second Period 1891–1926
Mark as above, with a furled banner inscribed 'Co Fermanagh' added below.

Third Period 1926–46
Mark as above, with circular stamp inscribed 'Deanta in Eirinn' (made in Ireland) and registration trademark number 0857 added below.

First Green Period 1946–55
Same mark as above but in green.

Second Green Period 1955–65
Letter 'R' within circle added above the banner inscribed 'Co Fermanagh', to show that the Belleek mark was registered in the USA.

Third Green Period 1965–81
Mark reduced in size and words, 'Co Fermanagh' deleted.

First Gold Period 1981–
Same mark as above but in gold.

A Belleek crested china vase, Second Period, 2¼in (6cm) high.
$150–230 *MLa*

A Belleek two-handled crested china vase, Second Period, 2in (5cm) high.
$150–230 *MLa*

A Belleek crested china jug, Second Period, 3¼in (8.5cm) high.
$150–230 *MLa*

Goss & Crested

A Goss Bagware teapot, with Trinity crest, c1900, 6in (15cm) high.
$130–160 *MLa*

Bagware refers to the blue cording around neck and handle of the teapot.

Four models of lifeboats, 2 Arcadian, an Aldwych and a Podmore, largest 3in (7.5cm) long.
$60–270 each *CCC*

A Savoy British tank, from the Battle of Ancre, dated '1916', 6¾in (17cm) long.
$60–80 *SAS*

A Goss Shakespeare's jug, 1890–1900, 3¼in (8.5cm) high
$40–60 *G&CC*

l. A Goss Capel Madoc stoup, 1915–30, 3¼in (8cm) wide.
$70–110 *G&CC*

A selection of 5 Goss flower girls, 1920–1930, 5–5½in (13–14cm) high.
$120–180 each *G&CC*

Three Arcadian busts, depicting Lord Roberts, King of the Belgiums and Sir John French, a Savoy of Admiral Beatty and a Shelley of Sir John French, tallest 8in (20.5cm) high.
$90–120 each *CCC*

A collection of Goss crested china, depicting a cenotaph, Gloucester jug, Welsh hat, Whitstable Seal ashtray and Worcester jug, largest 2½in (6.5cm) high.
$40–140 each *CCC*

A Willow Art WWI aeroplane, 6in (15cm) long
$90–110 *SAS*

l. Two Arcadian Collie dogs, a Savoy King Charles Spaniel, a German puppy and a Willow Scottie, largest 2½in (6.5cm) high.
$30–50 each *CCC*

A Swan WWI dispatch rider, 3½in (9cm) long.
$90–110 *SAS*

A Victoria boy on a scooter, 1910–30, 4in (10cm) high.
$30–40 *G&CC*

A Grafton WWI grenade thrower, 5½in (14cm) high.
$190–210 *SAS*

A Goss Lloyd George's early home, 1913–30, 4¼in (10.5cm) long.
$180–210 *G&CC*

An Arcadian charabanc, 1920–30, 5½in (13.5cm) long.
$40–60 *G&CC*

A Carlton spinning wheel, inscribed 'Irish Spinning Wheel', 1910–30, 4in (10cm) high.
$60–100 *G&CC*

A crested WWI infantryman, 4¼in (12cm) high.
$220–240 *SAS*

An Arcadian nurse, inscribed 'Soldier's Friend', 1914–18, 5¼in (13.5cm) long.
$90–120 *G&CC*

l. A Goss Bettws-y-Coed ancient kettle, 1910–30, 4¼in (11cm) high.
$60–80
r. A Goss Portland lighthouse, 1914–30, 4¾in (12.5cm) high.
$90–110 *G&CC*

Chinese Dynasties and Marks

Early Dynasties

新石器時代	Neolithic	10th – early 1st millennium BC	唐	Tang Dynasty	AD 618 – 907
商	Shang Dynasty	16th Century – circa 1050 BC	五代	Five Dynasties	AD 907 – 960
周	Zhou Dynasty	circa 1050 – 221 BC	遼	Liao Dynasty	AD 907 – 1125
秦	Qin Dynasty	221 – 206 BC	宋	Song Dynasty	AD 960 – 1279
漢	Han Dynasty	206 BC – AD 220	北宋	*Northern Song*	AD 960 – 1127
三國	Three Kingdoms	AD 220 – 265	南宋	*Southern Song*	AD 1127 – 1279
晉	Jin Dynasty	AD 265 – 420	西夏	Xixia Dynasty	AD 1038 – 1227
南北朝	Southern & Northern Dynasties	AD 420 – 589	金	Jin Dynasty	AD 1115 – 1234
隋	Sui Dynasty	AD 581 – 618	元	Yuan Dynasty	AD 1279 – 1368

Ming Dynasty Marks

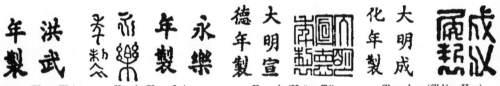

Hongwu (Hung Wu) 1368–1398

Yongle (Yung Lo) 1403–1424

Xuande (Hsüan Té) 1426–1435

Chenghua (Ch'éng Hua) 1465–1487

Hongzhi (Hung Chih) 1488–1505

Zhengde (Chéng Té) 1506–1521

Jiajing (Chia Ching) 1522–1566

Longqing (Lung Ching) 1567–1572

Wanli (Wan Li) 1573–1620

Tianqi (Tien Chi) 1621–1627

Chongzhen (Ch'ung Chêng) 1628–1644

Qing (Ch'ing) Dynasty Marks

Shunzhi (Shun Chih) 1644–1661

Kangxi (K'ang Hsi) 1662–1722

Yongzheng (Yung Chêng) 1723–1735

Qianlong (Ch'ien Lung) 1736–1795

Jiaqing (Chia Ch'ing) 1796–1820

Daoguang (Tao Kuang) 1821–1850

Xianfeng (Hsien Féng) 1851–1861

Tongzhi (T'ung Chih) 1862–1874

Guangxu (Kuang Hsu) 1875–1908

Xuantong (Hsuan T'ung) 1909–1911

Hongxian (Hung Hsien) 1916

CHINESE CERAMICS
Basins

A Ding Yao basin, the exterior carved with 3 rows of overlapping upright leaves below a plain band at the rim, applied overall with an even ivory coloured glaze, the rim of the bowl and the foot rim left unglazed, some damage, Northern Song/Jin Dynasty, 13in (33cm) diam.
$300,000–337,500 *S(HK)*

A Chinese export basin, decorated in underglaze blue with pagodas and buildings in a river landscape, the rim with cell diaper border, the exterior with prunus, peony, lotus and chrysanthemum sprays, cracked, Jiaqing period, 24½in (62cm) diam, on a wood stand.
$1,500–1,800 *DN*

Bottles

A bottle, the tall ringed neck with a stylised phoenix head, covered overall in a buff-coloured glaze, Northern Song Dynasty, 13¾in (35cm) high.
$10,500–12,000 *S(NY)*

This bottle was made in the Guangzhou province for the Indonesian export market.

Beakers

A pair of beakers, painted on the exterior in iron-red and gold with carp, later mounted in silver, with pewter covers to fit, with a silver spoon, fitted into a covered wooden box as tea-caddies, together with a key, Kangxi period, mounted cups 4¾in (12cm) high.
$9,000–9,750 *S(HK)*

A deep U-shaped beaker, gold decorated on a coffee ground with an archaistic dragon scroll band between upright leaves and hanging florets, the interior with red fish amidst green weed, seal mark and period of Daoguang, 2¾in (7cm) high.
$3,000–3,750 *S(HK)*

A Lianzi blue and white bowl, boldly painted in deep underglaze blue tones with 'heaping and piling' on the interior, the exterior decorated with a frieze of narrow petal flutes radiating from the foot beneath a key fret band encircling the rim, minor damage, Xuande period, 8in (20.5cm) diam.
$33,000–36,000 *S(HK)*

A *yuhuchun*, decorated in copper-red tones with speckles of apple-green, showing 2 scaly dragons, amid a dense frieze of undulating slender stems in bright underglaze blue tones, firing crack in foot rim, mark and period of Yongzheng, 13¾in (35cm) high.
$550,000–600,000 *S(HK)*

Bowls

A moulded celadon bowl, the interior with a florette in the centre below chrysanthemums, the exterior carved with ribs, all resting on a short foot, covered overall in an olive-green glaze, Northern Song Dynasty, 7in (18cm) diam.
$6,000–6,750 *S(NY)*

l. A pair of *kraak porselein* dishes, with grasshopper designs, Wanli period, 6in (15cm) diam.
$1,200–1,500 *ORI*

Kraak porselein is named after the Dutch trading vessels of the same name.

A pair of blue and white bowls, painted around the exterior with monkeys, one bowl chipped, marks and period of Yongzheng, 3¾in (9.5cm) diam.
$24,000–25,500 *S(NY)*

An underglaze blue decorated bowl, painted with 4 iron-red five-clawed dragons, amongst scrolling clouds, some speckling to glaze, mark and period of Yongzheng, 8½in (21.5cm) diam.
$12,000–13,500 *S(NY)*

A *doucai* bowl, painted in yellow, purple, green and iron-red enamels, with 5 clusters of flowers forming medallions, in underglaze blue around the rim of the plain interior, damaged, six-character Yongzheng mark within a double square on the base, 4½in (11.5cm) diam.
$16,500–18,000 *S(NY)*

A Canton *famille rose* punchbowl, depicting courtly interiors with patriarchs, ladies and servants, 19thC, 20in (51cm) diam.
$3,750–4,500 *SLN*

Canton famille rose *wares are termed 'rose medallion' wares in the United States of America.*

A Canton *famille rose* punchbowl, decorated with mandarins, c1830, 16in (40.5cm) diam.
$825–975 *EL*

Boxes

A blue and white five-lobed box, painted with a plunging dragon encircling a 'flaming pearl', some damage, mark and period of Wanli, 5½in (14cm) diam, with wood stand and cover.
$15,000–18,000 *S(HK)*

A *famille rose* and cobalt blue fish bowl, painted with small vignettes of landscapes and flowers, moulded gilt lion mask handles, the interior painted with carp amidst seaweed and other underwater creatures, mid-Qianlong period, 24in (61cm) diam.
$15,000–16,500 *S(NY)*

A glazed bowl, covered overall with a thick glaze of bright turquoise and copper imitating peacock feathers, restored, the slightly countersunk base inscribed with four-character Yongzheng period seal mark, 8in (20.5cm) diam.
$1,500–1,800 *S(NY)*

Brush Pots

A pierced blue and white box and cover, the cover painted and pierced with a scene of 16 boys, mark and period of Wanli, 12½in (31.5cm) wide.
$75,000–82,500 *S(HK)*

A blue and white brush pot, painted with a continuous landscape, the base with 3 short bracket feet, Kangxi period, 8¾in (22cm) diam.
$3,500–3,750 *C*

A blue and white brush pot, painted with a continuous scene of 3 wispy bearded scholars, with 2 boys playing in the foreground, six-character mark inscribed in a countersunk well in the centre of the base and period of Yongzheng, 5¼in (13.5cm) diam.
$67,500–75,000 *S(HK)*

Candleholders

A pair of *famille rose* elephant candlesticks, each supporting a hexagaonal candleholder above jewelled and painted trappings, Qing Dynasty, 7in (18cm) high. $2,250–2,600 *S(S)*

Cisterns

A *famille verte* cistern and cover, with a flat back, the rim applied with 2 dragon carp flanking a shell, the base with a pierced mask spout, restored, Kangxi period, 16½in (50cm) high. $5,250–6,000 *C*

An Imari cistern and cover, with a design after Cornelis Pronk, finely enamelled, painted and gilt on each side with a lady washing her hands, restored, c1737, 28¾in (73cm) high. $42,000–50,000 *C*

MILLER'S COMPARES . . .

I A pair of *famille rose* candleholders, each modelled as a lady wearing pink and green robes decorated with dragon motifs, restored, late Qianlong period, 10½in (26.5cm) high. $2,600–3,000 *C*

II A pair of *famille rose* candleholders, each modelled as a lady wearing long pleated robes, restored, Qianlong period, 16in (40.5cm) high. $22,500–24,000 *C*

Chinese export porcelain is largely bought by Western collectors for its decorative qualities and, therefore, condition and size are both crucial in establishing the price.

Item I is a much smaller pair of figures than Item II, is in poorer condition, more common as a model, less striking as a design, and has been restored to a greater extent. Most collectors consider the detailed design of the robes and faces on Item II to be significantly more striking and interesting than Item I. The large price difference between Item I and Item II demonstrates that in a specialist market such as this collectors are prepared to pay much more for objects of significantly larger size, in better condition, and greater rarity. *C*

Censers

A celadon glazed tripod censer, incised to the exterior with clouds in trellis pattern, c1500, 14in (35.5cm) diam. $1,125–1,275 *CSK*

Miller's is a price GUIDE not a price LIST

A *blanc de chine* censer, of bombé form, applied with a rich ivory glaze missing part of the interior, late Ming Dynasty, 8in (20.5cm) diam. $2,400–2,700 *S(HK)*

Cups

A *famille verte* wine cup, painted in underglaze blue and enamels with a blossoming peach tree, the reverse with couplet, mark and period of Yongzheng, 2½in (6.5cm) diam. $10,000–10,500 *S(HK)*

A wine cup, with loop handles in the form of archaistic dragons, applied on the outside with a translucent yellow glaze, the interior glazed white, Kangxi mark and period, 1¾in (45mm) high. $3,000–4,500 *S(NY)*

Ewers

A pair of ormolu-mounted *famille verte* ewers and covers, modelled as seated deer, the covers moulded in the shape of ears and a pair of tall antlers, restored, the porcelain Kangxi period, the ormolu later, 10⅞in (27.5cm) high.
$39,000–45,000 *C*

A monk's cap ewer, engraved with an undulating lotus stem, above double line borders and a band of lappets, applied overall with a white glaze extending over the base, mark and period of Yongle, 7¾in (19.5cm) high.
$255,000–300,000 *S(HK)*

A *famille verte* ewer and cover, enamelled on one side with a pair of phoenix on rockwork, on the other with a pair of pheasants in oval panels reserved on a scrolling lotus ground, damaged, Kangxi period, 14in (35.5cm) high.
$3,500–4,500 *C*

Figures – Animals

A grey pottery figure of a horse, with legs slightly turned out, on a plinth, the head held downwards, the neck decorated with applied floret trappings, with layers of flaring blankets over a wide saddle, restored, Northern Wei Dynasty, 10¼in (26cm) high.
$20,250–21,750 *S(NY)*

A red pottery figure of a horse, with angular neck, the sculpted head held forward with jaw open to reveal clenched teeth, large flared nostrils beneath the protruding eye sockets and spiky ears, restored, Han Dynasty, 19in (48.5cm) high.
$2,600–4,500 *S(NY)*

A painted grey pottery figure of a mythical beast, with bulging eyes, flaring nostrils and pricked ears, a pair of wings sprouting from its shoulders, remains of a white slip with black overpainting and painted details on the wings, Six Dynasties, 16in (40.5cm) long.
$8,250–9,750 *S(NY)*

A Compagnies des Indes figure of a pug dog, the simulated fur brushed in sepia and with a bell hung on an iron-red collar, Qianlong period, 9½in (24.5cm) high.
$8,000–8,800 *S*

A pair of ormolu-mounted green glazed figures of parrots, each standing astride a pierced brown glazed rockwork base, the bodies covered with a deep green glaze, the beaks and feet unglazed, on gilt-bronze bases, the porcelain Kangxi period, the ormolu 19thC, 9⅜in (25cm) high.
$7,500–8,250 *C*

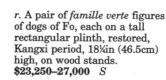

r. A pair of *famille verte* figures of dogs of Fo, each on a tall rectangular plinth, restored, Kangxi period, 18¼in (46.5cm) high, on wood stands.
$23,250–27,000 *S*

Figures – People

A pair of painted grey pottery figures of attendants, naturalistically painted, the facial features picked out in black on a pink ground, Han Dynasty, 18½in (47cm) high.
$8,800–9,500 *S(NY)*

A pair of green and ochre glazed pottery fiugres of attendants, each wearing flowing robes and tall hats, on hexagonal bases, late Ming Dynasty, 19½in (49.5cm) high.
$1,350–1,500 *CSK*

Two *famille rose* figures, one modelled as *Li Tieguai* leaning on his staff, wearing black ground floral robes, 12½in (32cm) high, the other as Budai, his bag of happiness in his left hand and a rosary in his right hand, damaged, early 19thC, 12in (30.5cm) high.
$2,000–2,700 *C*

A *famille verte* biscuit figure of a warrior, wearing an aubergine glazed phoenix robe with clouds above leg armour, restored, Kangxi period, 8in (20.5cm) high.
$3,400–4,400 *C*

A biscuit group of 2 laughing boys, dressed in brightly coloured jackets, Kangxi period, 8¼in (21cm) high.
$31,500–34,500 *S*

A pair of nodding-head figures, depicting an official and his wife, he wearing a black hat, a chestnut-brown blue collared jacket over robes, she wearing a blue floral robe, seated on rockwork on square chequer pattern bases, restored, 18thC, 24½in (62cm) high.
$34,500–45,000 *C*

Locate the source

The source of each illustration in Miller's Antiques Price Guide *can easily be found by checking the code letters at the end of each caption with the Key to Illustrations located at the front of the book.*

l. A red pottery figure of a fat man, dressed in a low waisted robe with the draped folds falling straight at the feet, the clay covered with a white slip, restored, Tang Dynasty, 18¼in (46.5cm) high.
$17,250–18,750 *S(NY)*

A pair of *wucai* figures of boys, each wearing a short robe, decorated with a *shou* character panel reserved on a cell pattern ground below a *ruyi*-shaped collar, standing on rectangular bases, each with a smaller boy clinging on to his robe, restored, 17thC, 13in (33cm) high.
$5,800–6,800 *C*

Flasks

A blue and white quatrefoil moon flask, painted in the Ming style with 2 birds perched on a fruiting quince branch, neck restored, Yongzheng seal mark, 19¾in (50cm) high.
$31,500–37,500 *C*

A celadon glazed flask, the body surmounted by a ring-moulded neck of capstan form rising to an onion-shaped bulb with incurving mouth, applied overall with a rich sea-green glaze thinning to pale green along the rim of the mouth and edges of the handles, mark and period of Yongzheng, 9in (23cm) high.
$187,500–195,000 *S(HK)*

A Longquan celadon barbed dish, carved with numerous flutes radiating from and encircling the centre, early Ming Dynasty, 24½in (62cm) diam.
$65,000–67,500 *S(HK)*

Flatware

A moulded blue and white dish, painted with a scene from a Yuan play, the unglazed flat base burnt orange in the firing, slight damage, Yuan Dynasty, 6in (15cm) diam.
$22,500–27,000 *S(HK)*

It is unusual to find a Yuan blue and white dish with a figure design, or a dish of this form with parts of the design raised in relief.

A blue and white saucer, the centre painted with a single lotus spray, encircled by a continuous band of scrolling lotus blooms, cracked, mark and period of Xuande, 4¾in (12cm) diam.
$30,000–37,500 *S(NY)*

A *wucai* five-lobed saucer, mark and period of Longqing, 4⅜in (11cm) wide.
$15,000–22,500 *S(HK)*

r. A blue and white *kraak porselein* deep plate, Ming Dynasty, 13in (33cm) diam.
$1,350–1,500 *ORI*

A blue and white saucer dish, the interior painted with 3 *lingzhi* and cloud scrolls, slight damage, drilled six-point collector's mark on base, mark and period of Wanli, 7in (18cm) diam.
$6,250–6,750 *S(HK)*

A blue ground dish, decorated in the centre with a dense frieze of 5 cranes soaring amid 4 leafy fruiting peach sprigs, firing crack, mark and period of Jiajing, 13in (33cm) diam.
$112,500–120,000 *S(HK)*

A pair of Chinese export monogrammed *famille verte* plates, painted and gilt with central entwined foliage below coronets within borders of spearhead and floral sprays, rims repaired, early 18thC, 12½in (32cm) diam.
$1,200–1,500 *CSK*

A pair of *wucai* saucers, the centres decorated with 2 scaly dragons, one picked out in translucent green enamel, one in underglaze blue, amid iron-red and green enamelled flame scrolls, marks and period of Kangxi, 5¾in (14.5cm) diam.
$22,500–27,000 *S(HK)*

A blue and white saucer, painted in Ming style with a lotus bouquet surrounded by a composite floral scroll and a classic band at the rim, seal mark and period of Qianlong, 4¾in (12cm) diam.
$7,500–9,000 *S(HK)*

A blue and white porcelain plate, six-character Yongzheng mark on base, Qing Dynasty, 10½in (26.5cm) diam.
$150–225 *EL*

An armorial plate, painted in *famille rose* with the arms of Pigot below a wolf's head crest, decorative bands in gilding, small chip to rim, Qianlong period, 9in (23cm) diam.
$1,500–1,800 *S*

A pair of octagonal plates, each decorated in *famille rose* and underglaze blue with a river landscape within spearhead and decorative borders, cracks, Qianlong period, 12¼in (31cm) diam.
$450–525 *DN*

A pair of blue and white octagonal plates, painted with fishermen before pagodas in a mountainous river landscape, minor restoration and rim frits, Qianlong period, 13¼in (33.5cm) diam.
$450–525 *CSK*

An armorial plate, painted in *famille rose* with the arms of Michel of Kingston Russell, Dorset, above the motto 'Nil Conscire Sibi', Qianlong period, 9in (23cm) diam.
$2,400–2,700 *S*

A *grisaille* and gilt armorial plate, inscribed with the gilded initials 'Obando', Qianlong period, 9in (23cm) diam.
$1,800–2,250 *S*

A *famille rose* dish, enamelled with iron-red, lime green, pink and dark brown feathery leaves and hibiscus blooms, small rim chip, Qianlong period, 15in (38cm) wide.
$2,250–2,700 *C*

Sauce Boats

r. A *famille rose* silver-shaped sauce boat, painted and gilt with chrysanthemums and peonies issuing from rockwork in a fenced garden, chip to rim, Qianlong period, 9½in (24cm) long.
$340–420 *CSK*

A blue and white gravy boat, painted with birds among peonies and prunus issuing from rockwork, Qianlong period, 9in (23cm) long.
$525–600 *CSK*

Services

A *famille rose* part dinner service, comprising 71 pieces, made for the Swedish market, decorated with detached sprays of flowers below an iron-red and gold stylised florette and C-curl border, Qianlong period.
$24,750–26,250 *S*

A Chinese export porcelain armorial part dinner service, comprising 82 pieces, each piece painted in iron-red, blue, black, yellow and gold with the arms of Percy Clinton Sydney Smith, Viscount Strangford, inscribed 'Virtus Incendit Vires', within a gilt band and gilt edged rim, wear to gilding, Qing Dynasty.
$10,500–13,500 *S(NY)*

Snuff Bottles

A snuff bottle, decorated in *famille rose* enamels, rim slightly worn, seal mark and period of Qianlong, 2¼in (60mm) high.
$900–1,000 *S*

An enamelled snuff bottle, moulded as an olive green squirrel on a fruiting vine, the flat base carved with leaves of varying shades of green with finely etched details, slight damage, Qing Dynasty, 3in (75mm) high.
$2,250–3,000 *S(NY)*

A snuff bottle, of shield form, moulded and reticulated around the sides with lions and brocade balls between *ruyi* head borders, covered in blue, the rim and foot rim gilded, slight fritting, late Qianlong/early Jiaqing period, 2½in (65mm) high.
$750–1,200 *S*

r. A snuff bottle, decorated in *famille rose* enamels with figures and a horse in a fenced garden scene, the reverse with a dedication by Huang Runquan to Bo Long, dated to the year *wuxu* (1838), Daoguang period, 2¼in (60mm) high.
$525–600 *S*

A snuff bottle, incised on each side with a dragon in flight, covered in a crackled white glaze, slight wear, the base incised with 3 characters 'cun de tang', Jiaqing/Daoguang period, 2¼in (60mm) high.
$2,600–2,800 *S*

A snuff bottle, moulded in the form of a monkey, the eyes highlighted in black, slight damage, Jiaqing period, 3in (76mm) high. $525–675 S

A snuff bottle, decorated in copper-red with a dragon on a blue and white ground of peonies, the base with a double circle encircling a 'flaming pearl' in copper-red, some damage, Jiaqing period, 3¼in (83mm) high. $750–900 S

A porcelain snuff bottle, decorated in famille rose enamels with warriors fighting outside a city wall, some wear, Tongzhi/Guangxu period, 3in (75mm) high. $600–750 S

A porcelain pear-shaped snuff bottle, painted in iron-red with demons, all between ruyi head borders, supported by an oval foot, worn, Daoguang/Xianfeng period, 2¾in (70mm) high. $675–825 S

An enamelled snuff bottle, moulded in the form of an artemisia leaf, the base with a four-character mark, Qing Dynasty, 2⅞in (72mm) high. $450–600 S(NY)

r. A famille rose snuff bottle, enamelled overall on a yellow ground with stylised lotus, lip worn, four-character mark in iron-red on the base, Qing Dynasty, 2¼in (60mm) high. $525–675 S(NY)

l. A famille rose porcelain snuff bottle, painted on both sides with a grasshopper in various shades of green, iron-red and purple, slight wear, Qing Dynasty, 3in (75mm) high. $450–600 S(NY)

Trays

A pair of blue and white quatrefoil trays, the centre decorated with a poetic inscription, 12 spur marks, marks and period of Jiaqing, 6¼in (16cm) wide. $7,500–9,000 S(HK)

Spice & Supper Boxes

A famille rose 'tobacco leaf' supper set, comprising a central octagonal box and cover and 8 fan-shaped boxes and covers, all in an octafoil dish, damaged, Qianlong period, 15½in (39.5cm) diam. $9,750–11,250 C

An armorial triple spice box and cover, from a French Royal service, painted in underglaze blue, enamelled and gilt, on 3 coral-glazed paw feet, the top joined to the bottom by a metal fitting to hold the 2 sections together while rotating, repaired, small frits, c1720, 5¾in (14.5cm) wide. $21,000–24,000 C

A pair of yellow ground famille rose trays, set at the centre with boys with a three-legged toad on their backs, slight damage and restoration, iron-red marks, seal marks and period of Daoguang, 5¾in (14.5cm) wide. $12,000–13,500 S(HK)

Tureens

A Chinese export armorial soup tureen, decorated with the arms of Garfoote, minor chips, c1765, Qing Dynasty, 13in (33cm) wide.
$5,250–6,000 *SK(B)*

A *famille rose* tureen and cover, the double rabbit head handles in iron-red, Qianlong period, 13in (33cm) wide.
$6,500–6,750 *S*

A *famille verte* tureen and cover, modelled as a cockerel, moulded and enamelled with green, blue, iron-red and *grisaille* feathers, the head with serrated comb in iron-red, protruding yellow eyes and sharp beak, rim chip restored, 2 rim cracks to cover, probably Kangxi period, 9¾in (25cm) high.
$50,000–52,500 *C*

Vases

A pottery vase, covered overall with an iridescent green glaze, Han Dynasty, 17½in (44.5cm) high.
$6,750–7,500 *S(NY)*

A pair of blue and white vases, with 6 panels decorated with flower designs, Kangxi period, 8in (20.5cm) high.
$1,000–1,125 *ORI*

A celadon glazed lobed *zhadou* vase, covered overall with a soft bluish-green glaze, the underside with six-character Yongzheng seal mark, 5¼in (13.5cm) high.
$60,000–75,000 *S(NY)*

r. A baluster blue and white vase, decorated in shallow relief with a magnolia tree, slight damage, Kangxi period, 17¼in (44cm) high.
$3,750–5,250 *S(HK)*

A vase, decorated to simulate *cloisonné* enamel with lotus scrolls in bright enamels and gold on a turquoise ground, the waisted neck set with 2 handles shaped as stylised dragons, with gilt seal mark on the base, Qianlong seal mark and period, 4¾in (12cm) high.
$7,500–9,000 *S(NY)*

A *famille verte* rouleau vase, painted in bright enamels, Kangxi period, 17½in (44.5cm) high.
$7,500–9,000 *S(NY)*

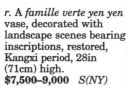

r. A *famille verte* yen yen vase, decorated with landscape scenes bearing inscriptions, restored, Kangxi period, 28in (71cm) high.
$7,500–9,000 *S(NY)*

A Transitional rouleau vase, decorated in underglaze blue with a continuous river landscape, the neck with flowering prunus, cracked, late Ming Dynasty, 19¼in (49cm) high.
$1,900–2,300 *DN*

A Transitional baluster blue and white vase, c1650, early Qing Dynasty, 15in (38cm) high.
$1,500–1,800 *ORI*

A pair of baluster vases, decorated in underglaze blue with temple landscapes, within shagreen borders, gilt twin scrolling pierced handles to neck, Qianlong period, 14in (35.5cm) high.
$2,250–2,600 *J&L*

A pair of baluster vases, the domed covers with dog of Fo finials, painted with water birds amongst lakeside flowering plants and willow branches in coloured enamels and gilt, flanges chipped, 19thC, 28in (71cm) high.
$3,000–3,750 *RBB*

l. A blue and white vase, painted with plantain and bamboo growing in a garden beside rocks and a balustrade, mark and period of Guangxu, 9½in (24cm) high.
$4,500–6,000 *S(HK)*

r. A Chinese export *famille rose* baluster vase, painted in bright enamels in shaped recessed panels with figural scenes alternating with birds amongst flowering branches, the interior fitted with a brass liner, restored, 18thC, 22¼in (56.5cm) high.
$12,000–13,500 *S(NY)*

Miscellaneous

A Canton bidet, damaged, 19thC, Qing Dynasty, 24in (61cm) long.
$600–750 *SK(B)*

A *famille rose* wine cooler, painted with sprays of chrysanthemums, roses and other flowers, between a pair of upright handles, Qianlong period, 8in (20.5cm) high.
$2,750–3,500 *S(S)*

A Ding Yao pillow, sculpted in the round as a plump boy sleeping beneath a lotus leaf, covered overall with a clear glaze of greenish tint in the carved detail, slight damage, Song Dynasty, 8in (20.5cm) wide.
$135,000–150,000 *S(NY)*

A celadon glazed water pot, with 6 boys surrounding a tank, 2 moulded fish to the interior, damaged, Ming Dynasty, 4in (10cm) high.
$375–450 *CSK*

A pair of hexagonal tea canisters, painted with blue celestial dragons amongst clouds on a white ground, on a raised base, c1900, 11¼in (28.5cm) high.
$1,500–1,800 *Gam*

A blue and white brush rest, moulded in high relief with scaly dragons, firing cracks around base, six-character mark inscribed in a line within a double rectangle, Wanli period, 6¾in (17cm) wide.
$12,750–15,000 *S(HK)*

JAPANESE CERAMICS
Bowls

A Satsuma bowl, decorated with cartouches of butterflies, mon and good luck symbols, the base with overglaze blue Satsuma mon, marked in iron-red 'Dai Nihon Satsuma Yaki Koseki Ga', Meiji period, 3¼in (8.5cm) high.
$600–750 *WW*

A Satsuma bowl, the interior decorated with chrysanthemums, the exterior with 2 panels, one depicting a cockerel and quail in a flowering landscape, the other with adults and children by a riverside, signed 'Dai Nihon, Kyoto, Tojiki Goshigaisha, Ryozan Sho', above a Shimazu mon, Meiji period, 16in (40.5cm) diam.
$17,250–20,250 *SK*

An Arita *wucai* style bowl, painted and gilt to the exterior with Immortals and attendants in a garden, the interior with a coiled dragon, underglaze blue Jiajing six-character mark and of the period, 4¼in (11cm) diam.
$180–225 *CSK*

Japanese copies of Chinese ceramics, such as this piece, often include reign marks.

Figures

Japanese Imari
Japanese Imari dishes of the 19thC and 20thC are amongst the most commonly seen Japanese ceramics. Quality, and thus value, varies enormously. An early 20thC dish, with underglaze blue decoration applied by stencil, could be worth less than £50, but a large 19thC charger with well-detailed decoration could be worth £500–800.

Two Satsuma figures, both decorated in red enamel, Meiji period, 19thC, 4½ and 7in (11.5 and 18cm) high.
$2,500–3,000 *JH*

Two Imari figures of bijins, late 19thC, 10 and 10½in (25.5 and 26.5cm) high.
$330–375 *JH*

Flatware

An Imari dish, the lobed rim with carefully drawn decoration, late 19thC, 8½in (21.5cm) diam.
$150–180 *ORI*

A Satsuma earthenware charger, decorated with panels of figures and lakeland landscapes, Satsuma mon and mark in gilt, late 19thC, 10¼in (26cm) diam.
$525–600 *P(HSS)*

A set of 8 Imari dishes, each with a roundel pierced border picked out in green within 2 underglaze blue bands, centrally decorated with a courtesan smoking a pipe and reading a scroll before a screen, some damage, late 17thC, 10½in (26.5cm) diam.
$14,250–15,750 *DN*

Japanese Chronology Chart

Jomon period (Neolithic)	circa 10,000 – circa 200 BC	Muromachi (Ashikaga) period	1333 – 1573
Yayoi period	circa 200 BC – circa 200 AD	Momoyama period	1573 – 1614
Tumulus (Kofun) period	200 – 552	Edo (Tokugawa) period	1614 – 1868
Asuka period	552 – 645	Meiji period	1868 – 1911
Nara period	645 – 794	Taisho period	1912 – 1926
Heian period	794 – 1185	Showa period	1926 –
Kamakura period	1185 – 1333		

Koros

A Satsuma earthenware koro, with a metal cover, damaged and repaired, Meiji period, 6in (15cm) high.
$1,900–2,250 *S(S)*

A Satsuma earthenware koro and cover, the sides painted with a border of flowers, the shoulder with 4 panels of figures, the cover with waterfowl at a pond side, slight damage, signed 'Dai Nihon, Tojiki Goshigaisha, Ryozan', below the Yasuda company trade mark, Meiji period, 5½in (14cm) wide.
$6,000–7,500 *S(S)*

Koro

A koro is an incense burner. The typical shape of 4 curved sides narrowing from a shouldered square top to a smaller base is taken from archaic bronze vessels of the same form and use.

A decorated and enamelled lozenge-shaped koro, with pierced cover, signed 'Etsuseki', c1890, 5in (12.5cm) high.
$2,700–3,000 *MER*

Vases

An Imari beaker vase, painted and gilt with peonies and oxen before a retreat, restored, c1700, 26in (66cm) high.
$800–1,000 *CSK*

An Imari vase, painted with a phoenix in flight above flowering plants, small hair crack, 18thC, 15¾in (40cm) high.
$675–750 *L*

r. A pair of Kinkozan Satsuma vases, in double gourd form, decorated with cherry blossoms on dark green grounds, c1900, 12in (30.5cm) high.
$450–600 *EL*

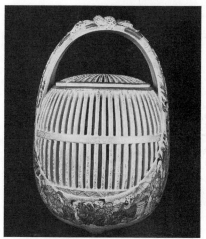

A Satsuma baluster vase, decorated with 2 panels, late 19thC, 17½in (44.5cm) high.
$975–1,125 *JH*

An Oribe type vase, with *lingzhi* shape handles, green glaze extending from rim, patterned design on a grey ground below, mark on base, Meiji period, 16in (40.5cm) high.
$525–675 *SK*

A pair of Satsuma earthenware vases, the pale yellow shaded ground decorated with partridges, foliage, flowers and butterflies in coloured enamels, painted and impressed marks, c1900, 22in (56cm) high.
$420–500 *P(HSS)*

A Satsuma earthenware trumpet vase, painted with panels of figures and mountain temples, reserved on a midnight-blue ground densely covered in wistaria and cherry blossom, signed and with impressed seal 'Kinkozan', each panel signed, one 'Senzan', the other 'Seizan', Meiji period, 6in (15cm) high.
$8,000–8,750 *S*

A Satsuma lozenge-shaped box and cover, decorated on one side with a panel containing numerous birds amidst blossoming foliage and the reverse with a panel of figures, probably Kinkozan, Meiji period, 3¼in (8.5cm) wide.
$2,600–3,000 *HDS*

Miscellaneous

A Satsuma teapot, decorated with panels of figures, signed 'Kichizan', c1890, 7in (18cm) high.
$1,500–1,800 *MER*

A Satsuma kettle, decorated with a design of figures and flowers, small floral borders above and below, the lid with floral design, raised on 3 feet, late 19thC, 6in (15cm) diam.
$1,800–2,200 *SK*

A Louis XVI style gilt bronze mounted Imari potpourri vase, the domed lid above a pierced gilt bronze rim, the body flanked by rams' head handles, late 19thC, 19in (48.5cm) high.
$5,750–7,250 *S(NY)*

A Satsuma cricket cage, c1880, 12in (30.5cm) high.
$3,750–2,850 *MER*

An Imari garden seat, painted with panels of birds among peony and prunus, *ho-o* medallion, on a foliate ground, enamel worn, Meiji period, 20½in (52.5cm) high.
$900–1,200 *S(S)*

A Satsuma pottery urn, with foliate neck over a gilt and peony decorated body, Meiji period, 19in (48.5cm) high.
$12,000–13,500 *LHA*

An Imari teapot and cover, painted in underglaze blue, iron-red, green and yellow with 2 figures on a boat, the reverse painted with figures and an ox and 2 figures seated before a flask marked 'F.W.', the cover with recumbent *shishi* knop, slight damage, Edo period, c1700, 4¾in (12cm) high.
$3,800–4,500 *S(S)*

KOREAN CERAMICS
Bottles

A celadon mallet form bottle, the glazed underside with 5 spur marks, Koryo Dynasty, 11thC, 9½in (24cm) high.
$97,500–105,000 *S(NY)*

A blue and white bottle, painted with butterflies and tufts of grass growing beside rockwork, the reverse with a flowering chrysanthemum bloom, restored, Choson Dynasty, 19thC, 14½in (37cm) high.
$12,750–13,500 *S(NY)*

Bowls

A celadon deep bowl, the sides inlaid in white slip with a central chrysanthemum spray roundel bordered by *yo'i*-heads, the exterior inlaid in *sanggam* with a band of peony scrolls, the glazed foot with 3 spur marks, Koryo Dynasty, 12thC, 8in (20.5cm) diam.
$36,500–39,000 *S(NY)*

A celadon bowl, the centre moulded with a floral spray, the foot with 3 spur marks, Koryo Dynasty, 12thC, 7¼in (18.5cm) diam.
$3,500–4,000 *S(NY)*

Cups & Cupstands

A celadon foliate cupstand, each panel of the ten-petalled everted tray inlaid in *sanggam* with a chrysanthemum spray, the lobed countersunk well incised with fish, the domed support carved and incised with lotus petals, all below the raised ring encircling a *sanggam* floret, on a foliate foot with matching decoration, Koryo Dynasty, 12thC, 6in (15cm) diam.
$6,750–8,250 *S(NY)*

A celadon foliate cupstand, the everted tray of eight-petalled outline decorated with double floral spray clusters, the lobed countersunk well incised with fish and waves, Koryo Dynasty, 12thC, 5½in (14cm) diam.
$9,750–10,500 *S(NY)*

A white glazed cup with saucer, the saucer sides moulded as a pair of cranes with spread wings, Choson Dynasty, 19thC, saucer 5¾in (14.5cm) wide.
$14,250–15,750 *S(NY)*

Dishes

A blue and white dish, the centre decorated with a stylised *su* character roundel, encircled by a band of chrysanthemums on leafy stalks, the exterior decorated with bamboo stalks, on a glazed foot, Choson Dynasty, 19thC, 12½in (32cm) diam.
$18,000–19,500 *S(NY)*

A blue and white dish, painted with a catfish, 2 carp, waves and rockwork, on a high foot, Choson Dynasty, 19thC, 6in (15cm) diam.
$85,000–95,000 *S(NY)*

A blue and white dish, painted with a cluster of grapes and scrolling vines, on a foot ring, Choson Dynasty, 19thC, 6in (15cm) diam.
$12,000–13,500 *S(NY)*

l. A blue and white dish, painted with a waterside landscape of rockwork and mountains beneath a half visible sun, the underside decorated with ribboned florettes between line borders, Choson Dynasty, 19thC, 6in (15cm) diam.
$12,750–13,500 *S(NY)*

Vases

A celadon *maeby'ong* vase, painted in iron-brown with curled three-petalled leaves, Koryo Dynasty, 12thC, 10¾in (27.5cm) high.
$15,750–17,250 *S(NY)*

A baluster vase, covered overall with a deep brown glaze, Yi Dynasty, 12in (30.5cm) high.
$4,500–6,000 *SK*

A celadon *maeby'ong* vase, painted in iron-brown with a stylised leafy spray between collars of abstracted leaf design at the neck and base, Koryo Dynasty, 12thC, 10¾in (27.5cm) high.
$5,250–7,500 *S(NY)*

Miscellaneous

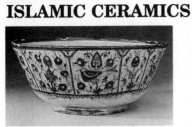

A bamboo brush pot, the sides decorated overall with engraved vertical lines, the underside naturally counter-sunk, Choson Dynasty, 19thC, 6in (15cm) high.
$3,750–5,250 *S(NY)*

A *punch'ong* flask, carved in sgraffito with a leafy arabesque, covered overall with a celadon glaze, on a glazed foot, Choson Dynasty, 15th/16thC, 8¾in (22cm) high.
$65,000–67,500 *S(NY)*

A pale bluish glazed koro and pierced domed cover, with knop finial and upright handles, cover damaged, Koryo Dynasty, 6in (15cm) high.
$900–1,200 *CSK*

ISLAMIC CERAMICS

A Persian plate, painted in olive green and cream with a calligraphic roundel and a border of foliate roundels, glaze discoloured, dated '1285H' (1780), 9in (23cm) diam.
$225–375 *CSK*

A Safavid blue and white bowl, the interior painted with a central spray of stylised flowers and leaves, the exterior with shaped panels of birds alternating with scrolling lotus flowers, damaged, 17thC, 13¼in (33.5cm) diam.
$725–900 *CSK*

A Qajar moulded blue, black and cream baluster jar, decorated with floral sprays, buildings and birds, slight discolouration, 19thC, 11in (28cm) high.
$575–625 *CSK*

r. A Persian blue and white *kendi*, in the form of a frog, damaged, probably 18thC, 6in (15.5cm) wide.
$7,000–7,500 *S(S)*

l. A Safavid blue and white bowl, the interior painted with a bird perched on rockwork in a fenced garden, the exterior with deer and birds among pine and flowers issuing from rockwork, small chip, 17thC, 8½in (21.5cm) diam.
$750–900 *CSK*

GLASS
Bottles, Decanters & Flasks

An amethyst spirit bottle, with flute cut body, cut pouring spout and cork/metal stopper, c1840, 13in (33cm) high.
$375–450 *Som*

A glass decanter, with trailing decoration to the neck, c1840, 11in (28cm) high.
$225–300 *MJW*

A glass decanter, engraved 'White Wine' within engraved cartouche and fruiting vines, c1790, 11½in (29.5cm) high.
$750–900 *CB*

A mallet-shaped wine bottle, with string neck fastening, c1780, 5¾in (14.5cm) high.
$90–120 *OD*

r. A set of 4 green glass spirit bottles, with canted edges and gilt labels for 'Rum', 'Brandy', 'Hollands' and 'Shrub', with gilt ball stoppers, in a fitted mahogany box, c1800, bottles 7in (18cm) high.
$1,800–2,200 *Som*

A bell-shaped glass decanter, cut with strawberry diamonds, with mushroom stopper, c1830, 13in (33cm) high.
$1,275–1,475 *FD*

A Bristol blue glass decanter, with silver neck, c1838, 16½in (42cm) high.
$600–725 *MJW*

l. & r. A pair of green glass flagons, with metal mounts and cork/metal stoppers, c1830, 7¾in (19.5cm) high.
$300–420
c. An amber glass flagon, with loop handle, c1830, 7½in (19cm) high.
$225–300 *Som*

A pair of glass liqueur decanters, decorated in gilt, c1880, 10in (25.5cm) high.
$525–600 *MJW*

A glass decanter, c1890, 14in (35.5cm) high.
$300–375 *MJW*

A central European opaque white glass spirit flask, painted in bright colours with a half-length portrait of a lady holding a bloom within a roundel issuing foliage, minor damage, 18thC, 5in (12.5cm) high.
$340–420 *CSK*

l. A pair of late Victorian amber glass decanters, the necks applied with prunts and ribbon moulding, the beaded silver collars and stoppers with Chinese ivory finials carved with a reclining sage holding a spray of flowers and a child grinding rice, the mounts by John Aldwinckle and Thomas Slater, London 1885, 8in (20.5cm) high.
$550–600 *DN*

Decanters

The original use for a decanter is to contain liquid that has been poured from a storing vessel into a more decorative item. This ensures that the sediment is left behind and that the wine served at the table is clear.

The first glass bottles appeared in Britain around 1650. They were dark green, squat, and stamped with glass seals, which identified the owner of the bottle, and sometimes the date of manufacture.

Decanters made in shapes that are familiar today first appeared at the beginning of the 18th century. Early decanters tended to be plain, but the rising popularity of wheel cutting and engraving in the 18th century meant that decorated decanters became more common, so that by the late 18th century they had become heavily ornamented with elaborate cut decoration. Examples produced in the 19th century used many of the innovative techniques developed by British glasshouses, and were displayed at the international exhibitions held during this period.

Bowls

A glass salad bowl, with turnover rim cut with diamond pattern, a similar band below, on knopped stem and domed circular foot with notched edge, c1790, 10in (25.5cm) high.
$2,000–2,500 *Som*

l. An Irish cut glass bowl and detachable stand, minor chips, probably Waterford, c1825, 9½in (24cm) high.
$2,250–2,750 *S*

A glass fruit bowl, the double ogee body with a band of vesica cut decoration and notch cutting round the rim, a band of hollow facet chequer pattern below, on a knopped stem and square domed lemon squeezer foot, c1810, 9in (23cm) high.
$1,275–1,500 *Som*

Two canoe-shaped pedestal bowls, English or Irish, slight chips to both, c1800, 12½in (32cm) wide.
$3,750–4,500 *CSK*

r. A ribbed glass sweetmeat, with double ogee bowl, on teared knop, pedestal and domed foot, c1745, 6¼in (16cm) high.
$900–1,000 *FD*

A Stourbridge rock crystal yellow and green intaglio and cameo overlay bowl, by Stevens & Williams, late 19thC, 9½in (24cm) diam.
$3,000–3,500 *HAM*

A pair of glass bowls and covers, facet cut above square-shaped feet, the domed covers surmounted by shaped finials, 19thC, 15¼in (39cm) high.
$3,000–3,750 *S(Am)*

A glass bonbonnière, with blue thread decoration, c1890, 7¼in (18.5cm) high.
$375–400 *MJW*

r. A Liège 'Traforato' fruit bowl and stand, 18thC, 10in (25.5cm) diam.
$300–375 *FD*

Candlesticks

A pair of brass and cut glass table lights, each of the candleholders with lustre drop-hung drip pans supported by leaf cast arms and centred by a cone finial, the cut glass tapered stem with a gilt-brass moulding and lions' paw feet, c1825, 13¾in (35cm) high.
$4,500–5,250 *S*

> **Miller's is a price GUIDE not a price LIST**

A pair of crystal glass candlesticks, 1870, 8¾in (22cm) high.
$1,275–1,425 *MJW*

A pair of Edwardian cut glass candlesticks, the trumpet-shaped stems and bases cut with hobnail ornament, supporting thistle-shaped nozzles, 15in (38cm) high.
$1,500–1,800 *CSK*

Centrepieces

A Thomas Webb & Sons Queen's Burmese ware centrepiece, the central trumpet vase with crimped end tapering to a tripod brass fitting, each brass tripod arm holding a crimped bowl to enclose the Clarke's Patent Fairy Light fittings and support the enamelled shades, some wear to enamels, c1886, 11in (28cm) high.
$2,700–3,000 *CSK*

A cranberry tinted glass épergne, with applied clear glass borders, fitted with a central trumpet-shaped vase and 3 smaller vases, flanked by scroll supports suspending 3 baskets, on dished round base, late 19thC, 15½in (39.5cm) high.
$775–825 *DN*

A Bohemian amethyst flash and cut glass three-tiered stand, chipped, c1860, 22¾in (58cm) high.
$1,800–2,200 *C*

Drinking Glasses
Beakers & Tumblers

A Bohemian engraved heavy-walled glass beaker, with 3 cartouches within scrollwork, engraved with monograms 'IL', 'EL', 'CL', and 'TL' within polished circlets, the base with a stylised flower, c1690, 4½in (11.5cm) high.
$2,500–3,000 *S*

A German diamond-point engraved glass humpen, probably Bohemian, with green tint, inscribed, applied foot ring and kick-in base, cracked, dated '1617', 10½in (27cm) high.
$10,500–11,250 *S*

A Venetian 'calcedonio' *trembleuse* cup and saucer, the marbled brown and green glass with aventurine inclusions, late 17thC, 3½in (9cm) high.
$6,800–7,500 *S*

> **Miller's is a price GUIDE not a price LIST**

A German engraved glass beaker, the thick flared sides cut with facets and polished circlets round the base, engraved on one side in polished *tiefschnitt* with Eve offering the apple to Adam, after Dürer, the reverse inscribed, the base with pontil polished out and engraved with a hand holding a goblet issuing from clouds, early 18thC, 5¼in (13.5cm) high.
$2,000–2,500 *S*

A Bohemian flared glass tumbler, enamelled in transparent colours, inscribed in gilt, on an amber flash cartouche, on a cut base, slight wear, c1845, 4½in (11.5cm) high.
$1,500–1,800 *C*

A Vienna enamelled glass beaker, painted in sepia with classical figures, the foot rim with a dentil cut above a star cut base, worn, 19thC, 4in (10cm) high.
$375–450 *CSK*

A Baccarat cut glass tumbler, enamelled in colours on gilt foil with the crowned Badge of the Légion d'Honneur, the centre with a portrait of Henri IV, slight damage, mid-19thC, 3¾in (9.5cm) high.
$525–600 *C*

A Lobmeyr glass tumbler, engraved and gilt filled, 1880, 4in (10cm) high.
$180–220 *MJW*

A Baccarat cut glass tumbler, enamelled in colours on gilt foil with a loose bouquet of flowers, mid-19thC, 3¾in (9.5cm) high.
$1,300–1,500 *C*

A Baccarat cut glass tumbler, enamelled in colours on gilt foil with a pansy on a raised oval panel and cut with diamonds on a wide band, minor chips, mid-19thC, 3½in (9cm) high.
$975–1,000 *C*

A Baccarat cut glass tumbler, enamelled in colours on gilt foil, with flowerspray on an oval red-ground medallion within a shield-shaped cartouche, chips to rim, mid-19thC, 3½in (9cm) high.
$825–900 *C*

Wine Glasses & Goblets

A wine glass with cylinder knop, on folded foot, c1720, 7in (18cm) high.
$3,750–4,500 *CB*

A Jacobite wine glass, with balustroid stem, bell-shaped bowl engraved with a rose and one bud, the stem with a cushion, air-beaded cushion, inverted baluster and base cushion knops, on domed folded foot, c1740, 6¾in (17cm) high.
$2,250–3,000 *Som*

l. A Dutch engraved Royal armorial light baluster goblet, engraved in the manner of Jacob Sang, with the crowned Royal arms of England above scroll ornament, the stem with an angular knop above a beaded inverted baluster section and basal knop, on a conical foot, c1750, 7in (18cm) high.
$3,800–4,500 *C*

A pair of Jacobite light baluster wine glasses, the flared funnel-shaped bowls engraved with a rose and bud, supported on a cushion knop above a beaded knop, the swelling stems terminating on a basal knop, on domed and folded feet, one bowl stained, c1750, 7in (18cm) high.
$1,120–1,420 *C*

A mercury twist wine glass, with 2 spirals outside single cable, hammered round funnel bowl, c1760, 6in (15cm) high.
$450–500 *FD*

A balustroid wine glass, the bell-shaped bowl on a stem with central cushion knop, on plain domed foot, c1720, 6½in (16.5cm) high.
$480–580 *Som*

A green glass goblet, the ovoid bowl and drawn plain stem, on plain conical foot, c1760, 6½in (16.5cm) high.
$600–630 *Som*

A pair of wine glasses, with bell-shaped bowls, on stems with multiple spiral air-twists and swelling shoulder knops, on folded conical feet, c1745, 6½in (16.5cm) high.
$1,000–1,350 *Som*

A wine glass, with bell-shaped bowl and drop knop, on folded foot, c1740, 6in ((15cm) high.
$2,200–2,700 *CB*

A Beilby wine glass, the funnel-shaped bowl enamelled in white with fruiting vine motif, the stem with a double series opaque twist, on plain conical foot, c1765, 6in (15.5cm) high.
$2,250–3,000 *Som*

A wine glass, with bell-shaped bowl, multi-spiral air-twist stem, with shoulder knop and conical foot, c1760, 6¼in (16cm) high.
$375–425 *FD*

A colour-twist wine glass, the stem with an opaque laminated twisted core entwined by 2 opaque ribbons and 2 translucent blue threads, on a conical foot, c1765, 6½in (16.5cm) high.
$3,000–3,750 *C*

An engraved colour-twist ale flute, engraved with 2 ears of barley and a hop spray, c1765, 6½in (16.5cm) high.
$2,700–3,000 *C*

A Jacobite wine glass, with bell-shaped bowl, on opaque, green and blue twist stem, c1770, 6½in (16.5cm) high.
$2,700–4,300 *CB*

A wine glass, with engraved bowl, on double series opaque twist stem, c1770, 5½in (14cm) high.
$300–375 *FD*

An Oliver Goldsmith commemorative goblet, engraved with a profile bust portrait, inscribed 'Oliver Goldsmith' below, the reverse inscribed 'A Man he was, to all the Country Dear, Obitt. April 1774', set on a double series opaque-twist stem and conical foot, 2 restored foot rim chips, c1774, 7½in (19cm) high.
$2,700–3,000 *S*

A wine glass, engraved with a continuous horse racing scene, the stem cut with diamond facets, on a conical foot, c1780, 6in (15cm) high.
$1,200–1,500 *C*

An Irish rummer, with ovoid bowl cut with alternate panels of small diamonds and sunbursts, bands of prisms and slanting blazes, cushion-knopped stem, on plain conical foot with star cut beneath, c1810, 5in (12.5cm) high.
$135–175 *Som*

An opaque-twist cordial glass, with faint fluted bowl, on a multi-strand stem and conical foot, mid-18thC, 5¾in (14.5cm) high.
$180–230 *Hal*

r. Two blue glass naval rummers, the bowls inscribed in gilt, below a gilt rim line, gilt worn, early 19thC, 5in (12.5cm) high.
$1,200–1,350 *CSK*

A set of 4 Georgian wine glasses, with rounded funnel-shaped bowls, opaque-twist stems and plain feet, 6in (15cm) high.
$570–630 *Sim*

Three green wine glasses, with conical bowls, plain stems with shoulder collars, c1830, 5¼in (13cm) high.
$60–90 each *Som*

A set of 19 port glasses, the shallow cup-shaped bowls with fine flute cutting, on knopped stems, c1830, 3in (7.5cm) high.
$1,000–1,125 *Som*

A set of 4 green wine glasses, with cup-shaped bowls, plain stems, on plain conical feet, c1830, 4¾in (12cm) high.
$300–360 *Som*

A Venetian enamelled goblet, with everted rim, painted in pale blue and white with a band of dots and with faint traces of red enamel and gilding, late 16thC, 4½in (11.5cm) high.
$5.250–6,000 *S*

A Venetian wine glass, with wide cup-shaped bowl set on a hollow slender tapering stem between collars, on a wide conical foot with folded rim, late-16thC, 4¾in (12cm) high.
$2,000–2,700 *S*

A Stourbridge glass ewer and 2 goblets, probably Richardson's, each piece engraved with stars and the triple-feather crest, the motto of the Prince of Wales on one side and that of the City of London on the other, c1860, ewer 10¾in (27.5cm) high.
$2,700–3,000 *S*

A set of 12 hock glasses, with facet cut amethyst rims, c1900, 7¼in (18.5cm) high.
$1,500–2,000 *MJW*

A Venetian winged glass goblet, the stem applied with opposing turquoise scrolls edged with clear pincered ornament, on a conical foot, late 17thC, 5¼in (13.5cm) high.
$1,350–1,450 *C*

l. A façon de Venise glass drinking vessel, with everted rim supported on a short hollow stem with shoulder and basal knops, late 16thC, 4in (10cm) high.
$1,800–2,250 *C*

A Venetian wine glass, with yellow tint, the conical bowl with ribbed lower section and trailed band above, set on an incised twisted openwork stem with blue-tinted C-scroll wings, flanked by collars, above a wide conical foot with folded rim, late 16thC, 6¾in (17cm) high.
$18,000–22,500 *S*

A Bohemian armorial marriage goblet, the bowl engraved with a coat-of-arms to either side and inscribed below 'Heinrich von Brombsem' and 'Magdalena von Kirchering', very small blown bubble to inside of the rim, early 18thC, 11¼in (28.5cm) high.
$2,000–2,700 *C*

A Dutch-engraved composite-stemmed light baluster goblet, the funnel-shaped bowl engraved with Noah's Ark on a continuous band of water, c1760, 7in (18cm) high.
$1,200–1,500 *C*

A Saxon Royal portrait goblet and cover, the bowl with Dutch engraving of Princess Anne of Hanover beneath tasselled drapery, damaged and restored, c1755, 15in (38cm) high.
$3,750–4,500 *C*

An armorial light baluster goblet, the funnel-shaped bowl Dutch engraved and polished, in the manner of Jacob Sang, with the arms of Willem V of Orange and Nassau within the mottoed Garter, c1760, 8¾in (22cm) high.
$3,750–4,500 *C*

An armorial goblet, possibly Saxon, engraved with a coat-of-arms above tied laurel branches, on a folded conical foot, 18thC, 9in (23cm) high.
$1,275–1,425 *CSK*

A Russian glass goblet, engraved with the crowned monogram 'EAII', for Catherine II, flanked by martial trophies, late 18thC, 8½in (21.5cm) high.
$1,300–1,500 *C*

A German goblet and cover, engraved with a female figure below the title 'Unico', matched cover, 18thC, 11¼in (28.5cm) high.
$600–750 *CSK*

A Bohemian ruby flash goblet and cover, engraved with a stag in a continuous sparsely wooded landscape, c1875, 10¾in (27.5cm) high.
$1,000–1,200 *C*

A Bohemian goblet, with red flashing, one side engraved with 3 deer in a woodland scene, the other side with a circle of 6 lenses surrounded by baroque scrolling, on cogwheel foot, c1860, 5½in (14cm) high.
$450–600 *Som*

r. A Bohemian glass goblet, with white and gilt overlay, c1850, 11in (28cm) high.
$1,200–1,350 *MJW*

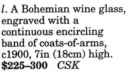

l. A Bohemian wine glass, engraved with a continuous encircling band of coats-of-arms, c1900, 7in (18cm) high.
$225–300 *CSK*

A Lobmeyr enamelled decorative glass, c1890, 7½in (19cm) high.
$600–675 *MJW*

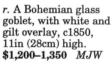

Jugs

A pair of silver and crystal glass claret jugs, c1889, 11¾in (30cm) high.
$12,000–12,750 *MJW*

A Victorian glass wine jug, with stopper, c1860, 14in (35.5cm) high
$375–450 *MJW*

A Rockingham ware claret jug, by Stevens & Williams, with brown, green and clear glass overlay, silver top, c1893, 9¼in (23.5cm) high.
$5,750–4,250 *MJW*

A pair of French glass jugs, with torsaded filigree decoration, c1870, 12¾in (32.5cm) high.
$4,500–5,000 *MJW*

r. An American amber blown pattern-moulded glass pitcher, with threaded neck, ribbed sides and strap handle, small crack, c1840, 6in (15cm) high.
$2,250–3,000 *S(NY)*

Two late Victorian silver-mounted green glass overlay jugs, in the form of griffins, by J. T. Heath and J. H. Middleton, slight damage, Birmingham 1894 and 1899, 7½in (19cm) high.
$1,100–1,200 *DN*

Lustres

A matched garniture of cut glass table lustres, comprising: a three-light gilt-metal mounted candelabrum, and a pair of lustres, damaged and repaired, 19thC, tallest 15¾in (40cm) high.
$825–900 *S(S)*

l. A pair of ruby glass two-tier lustres, decorated with polychrome floral enamelling, embellished with gilt-turned ebonised bases and glass domes, late 19thC, 14½in (37cm) high.
$600–750 *WIL*

Panels

A stained glass heraldic panel, 19thC, 16 x 12½in (40.5 x 32cm).
$225–300 *P(Sc)*

A pair of stained glass panels, each depicting a man and woman, 19thC, 18 x 14½in (45.5 x 37cm).
$675–750 *P(Sc)*

Paperweights

A Baccarat scattered millefiori paperweight, with large brightly coloured canes including silhouettes of a monkey, elephant, cockerel, horse, goat, dog and butterflies, with a cane inscribed 'B 1847', very slight surface wear, 3¼in (8.5cm) diam.
$2,500–2,700 *C*

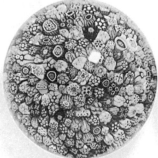

A Baccarat close-pack millefiori paperweight, with 9 silhouettes, dated '1847' in cane, 3in (7.5cm) diam.
$2,000–2,500 *SWB*

A Baccarat millefiori paperweight, with double trefoil garland of white, green, red and blue canes, on a colourless base, c1850, 3in (7.5cm) diam.
$2,250–2,500 *MLa*

l. A Baccarat close millefiori paperweight, with brightly coloured canes in shades of blue, lime green, pink and white, with a cane inscribed 'B 1847', 3¼in (8.5cm) diam.
$2,700–3,000 *C*

Miller's is a price GUIDE not a price LIST

A St Louis paperweight, with 3 red/yellow pears and 5 green leaves, the stems pulled near a base of deeply cupped, double white latticinio basket, c1850, 2¾in (7cm) diam.
$2,600–2,800 *MLa*

A Baccarat paperweight, the dark red clematis with furrowed pointed petals, honeycomb centre cane and green leaves and stem, c1850, 3in (7.5cm) diam.
$2,500–2,700 *MLa*

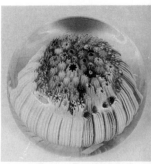

A George Bacchus & Sons concentric millefiori paperweight, with shallow colourless dome, c1850, 2¾in (7cm) diam.
$525–600 *MLa*

A New England Glass Co
paperweight, with a lampwork
cluster of 5 yellow/red pears,
with dark green leaves, and
white latticinio basket, c1860,
2¼in (5.5cm) diam.
$525–575 *MLa*

A Baccarat close pack
mushroom paperweight,
with blue torsade, c1850,
2¾in (7cm) diam.
$1,600–1,700 *SWB*

A Clichy paperweight, with
central pink rose, green sepals
and various pastry mould canes,
c1850, 2¾in (7cm) diam.
$1,600–1,700 *SWB*

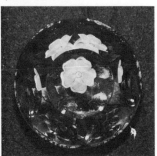

A Baccarat paperweight, with a
cerise dog rose with white petal
edges, 6 side facets and one top
facet, stem and eleven leaves,
c1850, 3in (7.5cm) diam.
$2,000–2,500 *SWB*

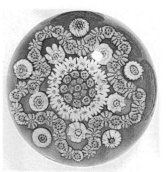

A Clichy blue ground patterned
millefiori paperweight, the
3 circles of canes in shades of
pink, turquoise and white,
surrounded by 5 large white
and blue canes, slight damage,
mid-19thC, 3in (7.5cm) diam.
$975–1,125 *C*

A St Louis crown paperweight, the
red and green twisted ribbon
alternating with white entwined
latticinio thread, radiating from a
central white, green and blue set-
up, mid-19thC, 2½in (6.5cm) diam.
$1,300–1,500 *C*

A Clichy red ground patterned
millefiori paperweight, mid-
19thC, 2¾in (7cm) diam.
$1,600–1,900 *C*

A Clichy patterned millefiori
paperweight, the large central
pink pastry mould within 2
circles in shades of green, pink
and blue, with an outer circle
of pink roses and 6 horseshoe-
shaped garlands, in shades of
pink, blue, green, purple and
white, on a star-cut base,
slight chips to foot rim, mid-
19thC, 3in (7.5cm) diam.
$1,600–1,900 *C*

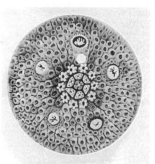

A St Louis green carpet-
ground millefiori paperweight,
with a central set-up in shades
of red and white, surrounded
by 6 silhouette canes, thread
of cullet to one side, mid-
19thC, 2¾in (7cm) diam.
$2,800–3,000 *C*

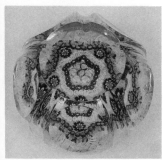

A Clichy patterned millefiori
paperweight, with 5 facets,
5 flutes and one top facet,
on a muslin base, c1850,
3in (7.5cm) diam.
$3,000–3,500 *SWB*

r. A St Louis concentric millefiori
mushroom paperweight, the tuft
with 5 circles of canes in shades of
blue, pink, white, and green,
around a white centre, bruise to
side, mid-19thC, 3in (7.5cm) diam.
$1,200–1,300 *C*

Scent Bottles

A matched pair of Victorian cut glass scent bottles, the glass bodies decorated with birds, flowers and foliage, the hinged silver tops by William Comyns, London, c1888–1900, 5¼in (13.5cm) high. **$1,200–1,300** *Bea*

l. A blue opaline flat disc scent bottle, with silver gilt mount, c1870, 2⅜in (6cm) diam. *c.* An opaque white flat disc scent bottle, with embossed silver mount and chain, c1870, 1¾in (4.5cm) diam. *r.* A green opaline flat disc scent bottle, with silver gilt mount and chain, c1870, 2½in (6.5cm) diam. **$300–350 each** *Som*

An amethyst cut scent bottle, with gold screw cover, the flattened sides cut with diamond facets, one side enamelled in colours with doves perched on a tree trunk, minor damage, c1760, 2¾in (7cm) high. **$3,000–3,750** *C*

Scent Bottles

The first British made scent bottles appeared at the beginning of the 18th century. Early examples followed European designs and were flat in shape, but had characteristic British features such as heavy, lead crystal bodies with cut decoration. British style scent bottles began to be made in the mid-18th century in a variety of colours of glass, including blue, white, pale green and occasionally amethyst. Bottles were often made in pairs to go inside a travelling case – one for perfume and one for smelling salts.

l. A pair of late Victorian silver-mounted cut glass cologne bottles, in a plush and quilted satin-lined tooled leather case, Drew & Sons, London 1892, 6in (15cm) high. **$1,800–2,200** *CSK*

Services

A Venetian ruby coloured glass set, comprising 78 pieces, early 20thC, tallest 6in (15cm) high. **$2,200–3,000** *S(S)*

An Edwardian cased glass strawberry set, the opaque white glass overlaid in pink translucent glass, enamelled and gilt with sprays of flowers and foliage, wear and minor chips. **$2,500–3,000** *CSK*

Tazzas

An enamelled gilt metal mounted glass tazza, by J. & L. Lobmeyr, engraved with fruit and foliage, c1880, 7¾in (20cm) diam. **$1,800–2,200** *C*

A pair of mercury glass tazzas, by Henry Walker, USA, c1869, 6½in (16.5cm) high. **$975–1,000** *MJW*

A Venetian diamond point engraved glass tazza, with panels of stylised foliate scroll within a leaf border, c1600, 4½in (11.5cm) diam. **$10,500–11,250** *S*

Vases

A pair of French turquoise overlay opaque glass vases, possibly St Louis, the turquoise grounds gilt with anthemion and stylised foliate ornament, the circular feet and rims enriched with gilding, slight wear to gilding, c1860, 15¾in (40cm) high.
$3,500–4,500 C

A façon de Venise crisselled two-handled vase, applied with large strawberry prunts, the reeded scroll handles applied with pincered ornament, slight damage, possibly Venice, early 18thC, 11¾in (30cm) high.
$5,250–6,000 C

A pair of Bristol blue glass vases, c1840, 7in (18cm) high.
$600–675 MJW

A Bohemian glass overlay trumpet vase, in an English plated and gilt stand, marked 'Published by Elkington Mason & Co, April 1851', 18½in (47cm) high.
$825–900 P

An opaline glass vase, painted with flowers, c1860, 20in (51cm) high.
$1,200–1,400 CB

A bronze glass two-handled vase, by Webb, made as an experimental piece, c1818–80, 9¼in (23.5cm) high.
$600–675 MJW

A cameo glass vase, overlaid in white with stylised leaves and ribbons, with stiff leaf and geometric bands, on a brown ground, 19thC, 4½in (11.5cm) high.
$525–600 DN

Miscellaneous

An Irish cut glass potato ring, c1820, 7in (18cm) diam.
$100–150 FD

A bowl of potatoes would have been served on a potato ring at the dining table.

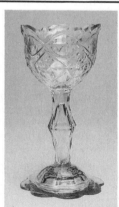

A facet-cut sweetmeat glass, on a domed scalloped foot, c1770, 7in (18cm) high.
$300–400 CB

Three jelly glasses, with trumpet bowls and plain conical feet, c1780–1800, tallest 4¼in (11cm) high.
$70–80 each Som

A French glass ruler or paperweight, c1850, 6½in (16.5cm) long.
$375–450 MJW

CLOCKS

Variations in type, style, design and size, as well as the materials used in the manufacture of antique clocks, ensure that this is a diverse collecting area and a fascinating subject for study. Even the most experienced dealers and collectors are constantly coming across clocks, the like of which they have never seen before.

Traditional areas of collection are constantly widening, from carriage, longcase, bracket and wall clocks – those most frequently seen in a domestic setting – to mystery, novelty and fantasy clocks, even into such precise areas as clocks in WWII aircraft.

Some specialisations may be guided by price, but there remain areas in which substantial sums may be involved. These include 16th and 17th century German clocks, early English clocks by eminent makers and fine French technical clocks.

From around 1760 France supplanted England as the source of the very finest clocks. Their complex movements were made to a much higher standard and were often contained in outstanding cases, which perhaps incorporated Sèvres or Meissen panels or were decorated with fine bronze mounts.

Fig.1
An ebony veneered bracket clock, by Thomas Tompion, with pull quarter repeat on one bell operated by cords to either side of the case and with fast/slow and strike/silent regulation, c1695. $128,000–160,000. *DRA*

Good quality and well proportioned clocks of most types are always popular and even though demand eased during the recession, prices held up remarkably well. Over the last 12–18 months prices have been rising quite strongly.

It was only at the top of the price range that clocks by such celebrated makers as Tompion, Graham or Knibb fell back, when the market was to some extent stretched as the need of some owners to recover property or

investment losses saw rather too many top of the range clocks coming onto the market at one time. However, there has been quite a strong recovery in this area and the best 17th century English clocks (*fig.*1) have probably increased in value by 15–25% over the last 18 months. This rise is likely to continue.

An example of how strong that part of the market is becoming is provided by two Tompion bracket clocks sold at Sotheby's in December 1995. A good, early and interesting example was sold at $365,250, against an admittedly somewhat conservative estimate of $100,000–135,000, while a very rare *grande sonnerie* clock made a rather more predictable $431,250, against an estimate of $270–330,000.

There has undoubtedly been a marked change in emphasis regarding the desirability of various types of clock over the last five or more years; the age of the item becoming far less important than quality and, above all, artistic merit or appeal. Increasingly, even clocks of considerable technical merit and those demonstrating the highest standards of craftsmanship are only sought after if they are pleasing to the eye. However, when a beautiful design is combined with superb quality and good technical features, then the price will soar.

Fig.4
Most French porcelain panelled carriage clocks were produced between 1860 and 1900. Their value is affected by the number and quality of the panels, the size and style of the case, whether or not it is engraved, and the complexity of the movement. Most will fall in the $4,500–10,500 price range but the very finest examples can command much more. *DRA*

This tendency has been seen most strongly in the field of carriage clocks, the best of which have probably increased in value more in recent times than any other type of clock. For instance, a fine and complex carriage clock by J. F. Cole, dating from 1823 and possibly the first made in this country, still managed to fetch $255,750 at the height of the recession. English carriage clocks, long undervalued, have increased in price strongly during the last few years, largely due to their superb quality and comparative scarcity. Only a relatively small number were produced and these were nearly always made by the finest clockmakers (*fig.*3).

As far as French carriage clocks are concerned, it is again the most beautiful examples that are now most eagerly pursued. Those with porcelain panels (*fig.*4), for instance, or with finely engraved or decorated cases, are likely to be at a premium.

Fig.3
A giant striking and repeating carriage clock, by Dent of London, 10½in (26.5cm) high including the handle. Made around 1900, it is thought to have belonged to the Buckney family, who were partners in the firm of Dent. $30,000–37,500. *DRA*

There are also the collectors' pieces, of course, carriage clocks that might feature moon phase dials, calendar work (particularly if it is perpetual), complex escapements, additional dials for world time, sundials, etc.

If one were to try and pick the likely winners during the next few years the list would probably include:

• The best of the Georgian mahogany longcase clocks, by which I mean those of reasonable size and good proportion. Longcases that fit easily into most homes have risen in value rapidly and are likely to continue to do so. Relatively large and poorly proportioned North Country clocks of later date, as well as those with plain cases, tend to be out of favour.

• Good mahogany, rosewood or walnut bracket clocks from c1750-1850, especially of small size.

Fig.5
A mahogany longcase clock, by Ambrose Vowell, London, c1765, standing 86in (218.5cm) high without the finial. A fine, fully restored London mahogany longcase clock now costs around $15,000, with a lesser example selling for maybe $12,000 and good country clocks in the $7,500–12,750 range. *DRA*

• Beautiful and fine carriage clocks, be they English or French.

• Fine 17th century longcase and bracket or spring clocks (to give them their original name) by well-known makers, particularly if the provenance is known.

• French clocks of great artistic merit, such as the beautiful Sèvres porcelain lyre clocks (*fig.* 2) and some of the best designs emanating from the great French bronzers, enamellers and porcelain manufacturers.

It is an indisputable fact that fine antique clocks are still seriously under-valued when related to some other areas of collecting, particularly in relation to their intrinsic value or cost of production. Until that gap is closed, prices will undoubtedly go on rising.

Derek Roberts

Fig.2
A Sèvres 'Beau Bleu' porcelain lyre clock, the superb jewel enamelled dial by Coteau decorated with zodiacal signs. Sèvres porcelain lyre clocks will vary in value from $60,000–$150,000, depending on complexity, condition and age, c1788. *DRA*

Bracket Clocks

A George II ebonised bracket clock, the dial signed 'Wm Audouin LONDON' on a silvered disc in the arch, silvered chapter ring with matted centre and mock pendulum aperture, gilt-metal foliate spandrels, pierced blue steel hands, the 5 pillar single wire fusee movement with knife edge verge escapement, passing strike on bell, pendulum holdfast to the foliate engraved backplate, 10in (25.5cm) high.
$3,500–4,000 *CSK*

An ebonised bracket timepiece, with pull quarter repeating, the 7¼in (18.5cm) dial with a wide silver and Arabic chapter ring, matted centre with mock pendulum and calendar apertures, dummy winding hole, signed within the arch 'Thomas Blundell, Dublin', the single fusee movement with a verge escapement and bob pendulum similarly signed on the backplate and striking on 2 bells from above, c1770, 17in (43cm) high.
$4,500–5,250 *Bon*

A mahogany verge escapement bracket clock, the silvered dial with hour repeat strike/silent, engraved backplate, signed 'John Clarke LONDON', c1800, 17in (43cm) high.
$5,500–6,500 *ALS*

Timepieces

A timepiece is a clock which tells the time only, with no striking mechanism. A pull repeat piece, which incorporates a chord to pull to make it strike, would strictly be termed a timepiece.

An ebonised bracket clock,
inscribed 'Holmes London',
c1795, 13in (33cm) high.
$7,500–8,250 *TUR*

*John Holmes is considered
one of the most eminent
clockmakers of the late 18thC.*

A Regency mahogany bracket
clock, signed 'Jos. Phillips,
London', the 8-day double fusee
movement with anchor escapement, striking/repeating the hours
on a bell, raised on brass ball feet,
together with brass inlaid bracket,
c1830, 16in (40.5cm) high.
$5,250–6,000 *PAO*

A mahogany verge bracket
clock, with gilt mounts,
inscribed 'Wm. Pybus London',
c1790, 19¾in (50cm) high.
$8,250–9,000 *DSP*

Ebonised Bracket Clocks

Ebonised cases for bracket clocks
were common from c1705. Early
examples have a square dial, with
arched dials more common on later
ones. They were made in London,
generally using pale fruitwood veneer,
such as apple or pear wood, stained
black. Veneers were applied to the
back and sides as well as to the front.
If worn, the pale coloured fruitwood
shows through. Typical features of
ebonised brackets include a brass
carrying handle, brass side frets,
case mounts and a brass dial with
applied chapter ring and spandrels.

An ebonised bracket timepiece,
with pull quarter repeating,
the dial with silvered Roman
and Arabic chapter ring, matted
centre with mock pendulum
and calendar aperture, signed
in the arch on a silvered plaque
'Martin Hall, Yarmouth', the
5 pillar single fusee movement
with verge escapement and bob
pendulum, engraved foliage backplate and repeating on 3 bells,
c1750, 17½in (44.5cm) high.
$3,750–4,500 *Bon*

A George III mahogany and
brass-mounted bracket clock,
the dial with strike/silent,
signed 'John Green, London', the
movement with fully engraved
backplate and verge escapement,
c1780, 24in (61cm) high.
$8,000–9,000 *CLC*

A bracket clock, with double
fusee movement, inscribed 'Wᵐ
COSENS & SON LONDON',
1820s, 11in (28cm) high.
$8,300–9,300 *TUR*

An ebonised bracket clock,
with pull quarter repeat on
6 bells, inscribed 'Nicholas
Lambert LONDON', c1750,
15¾in (40cm) high.
$6,000–6,750 *DSP*

A brass inlaid bracket clock,
with painted dial and double
fusee movement, inscribed
'ROWELL OXFORD', c1840,
21¾in (55cm) high.
$2,700–3,000 *DSP*

A Victorian ebonised bracket clock, with gilt-brass Corinthian columns at the corners, the arched brass dial engraved with scrolling foliage and flowers, the silvered chapter ring inscribed 'Smith & Sons, Clerkenwell', 3 subsidiary dials in the arch for regulation, chime/silent, full chime/Westminster chime, the 3 train fusee movement chiming on 8 bells and a wire gong, standing on gilt-brass ogee bracket feet, 18¾in (47.5cm) high.
$1,200–1,500 *P(S)*

A mahogany bracket clock, with double fusee movement, inscribed 'Webster Queen Victoria St London', c1872, 14¾in (37.5cm) high.
$3,000–3,500 *ROD*

r. A Regency rosewood bracket timepiece, with flat top, arched silvered Roman dial, signed 'Turner, Colchester', and fusee movement, c1830, 7¾in (20cm) high.
$2,400–2,700 *WL*

l. A mahogany bracket clock, by Benjamin Ward, London, with brass dial, 8-day movement with verge escapement, striking the hours on a bell and repeating, c1770, 20in (51cm) high.
$8,250–9,000 *PAO*

A mahogany bracket clock, the dial and movement signed by 'Rivers & Sons London', with fusee movement striking and repeating on a bell, c1810, 13½in (34cm) high.
$4,000–5,000 *CLC*

An ebonised and fruitwood bracket clock, by John Richardson, London, with strike/silent feature to the arch, the 8-day 5 pillar movement striking the hours on a bell and repeating, c1765, 15in (38cm) high.
$9,750–11,250 *PAO*

An ebonised timepiece, the 6¾in (17cm) dial with a silvered Roman and Arabic chapter ring, signed in the matted centre on a silvered plaque 'John Pyke London', with concentric alarm setting mask, a calendar subsidiary in the arch, the single fusee movement with verge escapement and bob pendulum, fully engraved backplate and pull quarter repeating on 6 bells, standing on brass bun feet, c1730, 20in (51cm) high.
$3,000–3,750 *Bon*

A mahogany bracket/mantel clock, with a lancet top, chiming on 8 bells or 4 gongs, c1895, 12in (30.5cm) high.
$2,600–3,000 *TUR*

A Victorian gilt-bronze musical bracket clock, the dial with 7½in (19cm) chapter ring with Roman and Arabic numerals, the 3 subsidiary dials for chimes, speed regulator and chimes indicator, 3 train fusee movement with anchor escapement, striking 7 bells on the quarter-hour, 17in (43cm) high.
$4,000–4,500 *S(NY)*

An ebonised bracket clock, with 8in (20.5cm) dial, subsidiary dials in the arch for regulation and chime selection, the 3 train fusee and chain movement with anchor escapement, gong striking and chiming on 8 bells, the case with brass basket top, decorated with gilt mounts, with a similar wall bracket, c1875, clock 24in (61cm) high.
$2,600–3,000 *S*

l. A Regency mahogany bracket clock, by S. & C. Joyce, London, 21in (53.5cm) high.
$1,500–1,800 *DN*

r. A mahogany bracket clock, with triple fusee movement and 8 bell chimes, c1850, 19in (48cm) high, with bracket.
$5,250–6,000 *ROD*

A Victorian ebonised bracket clock, with 6½in (16.5cm) dial and subsidiary dials in the arch for chime/silent, regulation and chime selection, 3 train fusee and chain movement with deadbeat escapement, maintaining power, rise and fall regulation, chiming on 8 bells or 4 gongs with a further hour gong, the case with gilt-brass mounts and a similarly decorated wall bracket, c1885, clock 26½in (67cm) high.
$2,250–2,750 *S*

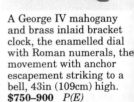

A George IV mahogany and brass inlaid bracket clock, the enamelled dial with Roman numerals, the movement with anchor escapement striking to a bell, 43in (109cm) high.
$750–900 *P(E)*

l. A German black lacquer and chinoiserie decorated chiming bracket clock, the silvered dial with black painted Arabic chapters, the triple barrel movement with pin barrel chimes on 5 gongs, stamped on the backplate for 'W & H', early 20thC, 16¾in (42.5cm) high.
$900–1,000 *CSK*

A German ebonised bracket clock, with quarter striking ting tang, by Winterhalder and Hofmeier, c1880, 12in (30.5cm) high.
$1,800–2,000 *ROD*

Ting tang is the onomatopoeic name for the quarter chime on 19thC Black Forest clocks.

r. A Louis XV gilt-bronze and boulle bracket clock, veneered in brass with polychrome flowers in horn and mother-of-pearl, with 8-day movement, rack repeating mechanism striking the hours and quarters, the movement signed 'P. Jaquet-Droz à La-Chaux de Fond', the whole mounted with scrollwork, on similarly decorated bracket, the case stamped 'A. N. T. Foullet, JME', the case and base with the inventory number '976/89', restored, with bracket, mid-18thC, 55in (140cm) high.
$55,000–65,000 *S*

A German mahogany chiming bracket clock, the dial with silvered chapter ring and matted centre, subsidiary slow/fast and chime/silent rings, the twin barrel movement with anchor escapement, with hour strike on gong and chimes on further gong, stamped 'W & H' on the backplate, with foliate carving to a frieze below the dial, lacking cresting, early 20thC, 14½in (37cm) high.
$500–600 *CSK*

A French cut brass and polychrome tortoiseshell inlaid bracket clock, the 9in (23cm) cast and chased gilt-brass dial with enamel numeral cartouches, engraved outer minute ring and bearing a dependent plate signed 'M. Boucher', the twin train movement with countwheel strike on a bell and later anchor escapement, 18thC, 32½in (83cm) high, together with matching bracket.
$4,000–5,000 *P*

A French red boulle bracket clock, with 9in (23cm) 12-piece enamel cartouche dial, bell striking Japy Frères movement No. 775 with Brocot escapement, the case veneered with red shell-inlaid with brass and outlined with gilt-brass mounts, the similarly decorated wall bracket with plumed mask corner mounts, c1860, clock 34in (86.5cm) high.
$4,500–5,250 *S*

Carriage Clocks

A Corinthian cased carriage clock, with satin gilded and silvered strike repeat, signed by 'T. Martin, London', c1880, 6⅓in (16cm) high.
$1,800–2,000 *ROD*

A carriage clock, with a cast case and bell striker, c1835, 5½in (14cm) high.
$1,500–1,800 *ROD*

A carriage clock, with engraved and gilded one-piece case, the strike/repeat alarm on a bell, c1835, 5½in (14cm) high.
$2,000–2,500 *ROD*

An Edwardian brass carriage clock, by Richards, with scroll engraved dial, cream chapter ring, lever escapement with hour repeater and striking movement, 7½in (19cm) high.
$800–900 *RBB*

A carriage clock, with a gilded case, masked dial and strike repeat alarm, c1880, 5½in (14cm) high.
$18,000–20,250 *ROD*

Escapements

The escape wheel, or escapement, controls the speed at which a clock runs, thereby regulating its timekeeping. It releases, at equal intervals, the energy from hanging weights or a coiled spring, and transmits it from the movement to the hands. The escapement is usually an arm with 2 *pallets*, which engage with the teeth of the escape wheel.

Types of escapement include:

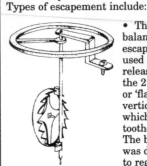

• The oscillating balance wheel escapement, *left,* used until c1670, releases in turn the 2 pallets, or 'flags', on the vertical bar, which engage the toothed wheel. The balance was difficult to regulate.

• The verge escapement, *right,* also uses pallets, but the short pendulum enabled the clock to be more accurately regulated. The verge was used on lantern clocks, as well as on most bracket clocks.

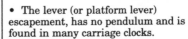

• The anchor escapement, *left,* was used – first in longcases – from c1670, and became standard for longcases, brackets, and many wall clocks. The anchor engages at intervals with the teeth of the escape wheel.

• The lever (or platform lever) escapement, has no pendulum and is found in many carriage clocks.

• The cylinder escapement, found in inexpensive late 19thC French carriage clocks.

l. A satin gilt carriage clock/timepiece, with filigree masked dial and sides, in satin gilt case, c1880, 5in (12.5cm) high.
$975–1,125 *ROD*

r. A satin gilt timepiece, with filigree masked dial, c1880, 5in (12.5cm) high.
$975–1,125 *ROD*

A carriage clock, with gilded case, by Achille Brocot, and strike repeat, c1870, 6in (15cm) high.
$1,500–1,800 *ROD*

A gorge cased carriage clock, by Drocourt, with strike repeat, c1870, 5½in (14cm) high.
$1,900–2,250 *ROD*

A silver and tortoiseshell 8-day carriage clock, the white enamel dial with Roman numerals, blue steel hands, movement with gilt lever platform, uncut balance with spiral hairspring, the panels of tortoiseshell each inlaid with a decorative foliate pattern in engraved silver, hallmarked Birmingham 1912, 3in (7.5cm) high.
$1,500–1,600 *PT*

l. A Regency style satin gilded carriage clock, by Couaillet, c1895, 5½in (14cm) high.
$750–900 *ROD*

A French gorge cased *grande sonnerie* carriage clock, with alarm, the enamel dial signed 'Drocourt, 28 Rue Debelleyme, Paris', the movement No. 22692 with the stamp of 'Drocourt', striking on 2 gongs and with ratchet tooth lever escapement, the similarly numbered gorge case dated '*Février* 1887', with strike control lever in the base and engraved on the top glass with a monogram, 5⅜in (14.5cm) high, with a travelling case.
$5,000–5,750 *S*

A satin gilded cased carriage clock, by Lamaille, with strike repeat and blue enamel panels, c1890, 4¾in (12cm) high.
$2,250–2,750 *ROD*

A corniche cased carriage clock, by Henri Jacot, with strike repeat, c1890, 5¼in (13cm) high.
$1,500–1,800 *ROD*

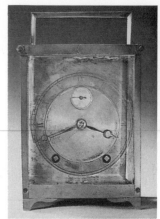

A French porcelain mounted *grande sonnerie* carriage clock, with alarm, the movement No. 2435 with club tooth lever escapement and striking on 2 gongs, the six-sided moulded case inset on the sides with 4 colourful panels painted with maidens representing the seasons, signed 'Le Comte', the back with an armorial panel and a strike control lever in the base, 6¼in (16cm) high.
$15,500–17,000 *S*

A French *grande sonnerie* carriage clock, with alarm, the 2in (5cm) enamel dial signed by 'Payne & Co, New Bond Street' and set in an engine-turned silvered surround, similarly signed movement 'No. 6067', with ratchet tooth lever escapement and striking on 2 gongs, gilt-brass gorge case with strike control lever in the base, c1870, 5¾in (14.5cm) high, with travelling case.
$3,500–3,750 *S*

A French quarter striking carriage clock, the 4in (10cm) silvered dial with subsidiary seconds, the 2 train movement No. 52 striking on 2 bells and with ratchet tooth lever escapement, the case with sliding glasses at the front and rear retained by folding arms, c1835, 6in (15cm) high.
$850–1,000 *S*

r. A French gilt-metal striking carriage clock, with alarm and white chrome dial, the case with foliate engraving and bevelled glasses, c1880, 6½in (16.5cm) high.
$1,500–1,800 *RAF*

A French carriage clock, the white enamel dial inscribed 'R. & W. Sorley, Paris', with lever escapement, and bevelled glass panels, late 19thC, 7in (18cm) high, in red morocco travelling case.
$600–675 *RBB*

A miniature alarm carriage clock, c1890, 3½in (9cm) high.
$900–1,000 *ROD*

A French gilt metal carriage clock, c1880, 7in (18cm) high.
$3,000–3,750 *RAF*

r. A French calendar carriage timepiece, the enamel dial with gilt filigree centre, central date hand and subsidiary dials below for day of the week and month, the 8-day movement with ratchet tooth lever escapement, the sides with applied mounts, c1900, 4¾in (12cm) high.
$525–600 *S*

A French brass cased carriage clock, with enamelled dials, striking movement, alarm and repeater, 19thC, 5in (13cm) high, in original leather case.
$900–975 *RBB*

A French *grande sonnerie* and alarm carriage clock, with 2 enamel dials set into gilt and engraved mask, with the movement striking on 2 gongs, ratchet tooth lever platform escapement, c1900, 7in (18cm) high.
$2,700–3,500 *S*

l. A French 8-day carriage clock, with English silver case, c1915, 3in (7.5cm) high.
$900–1,000 *ROD*

Longcase Dials

Square dials, *top left* and *top centre,* were used until c1715. From c1715, the arched dial became standard. The arch may be signed by the maker, *top right;* show the phases of the moon, *bottom left;* or have a strike/silent dial, *bottom centre.* Square dials were used in the provinces until the 1840s, *bottom right.*

A mahogany longcase clock, by John Christian of Aylsham, with arched brass dial, c1780, 84in (213.5cm) high.
$8,500–10,000 *TUR*

A late George III oak longcase clock, the painted arched dial with fans and flowers, subsidiary seconds and date aperture, signed 'Ed. Camm, Brigg', 85in (216cm) high.
$1,000–1,300 *DN*

An oak longcase clock, by James Common, Coldstream, the painted dial with flowers to each corner and bird scene in the arch, the 8-day movement striking the hours on a bell, c1805, 86in (218.5cm) high.
$4,000–5,000 *PAO*

An oak longcase clock, the 11½in (29cm) brass dial with Roman numerals and subsidiary seconds and date aperture, engraved and the centre with scrolling foliage and birds, urn and eagle spandrels, signed 'George Cresswell,' the 2 train 8-day movement with anchor escapement striking on a bell, late 18thC, on a later plinth base, 74in (188cm) high.
$2,500–3,000 *Hal*

An oak longcase clock, by William Cockey, Yeovil, the 12in (30.5cm) square brass dial, with engraved centre, showing seconds and date, with 8-day movement striking the hours on a bell, c1770, 79in (200.5cm) high.
$5,750–6,750 *PAO*

An inlaid oak and mahogany longcase clock, with arched brass dial, signed 'John Carter, London', with 8-day movement, c1775, 69½in (176.5cm) high.
$7,800–9,000 *AH*

An early Victorian flame mahogany longcase clock, the painted arched Roman dial with subsidiary seconds and date, signed 'Cremonini Bilston', 8-day movement, 82¾in (210cm) high.
$1,150–1,350 *WL*

A mahogany longcase clock, by William Crighton, Headington, with white painted arched dial showing seconds and date, the corners with painted flowers, the arch with masonic symbol and owner's name, the 8-day movement striking the hours on a bell, c1790, 91in (231cm) high.
$7,000–8,250 PAO

A London style mahogany longcase clock, the hood with reeded and brass inlaid pillars, the sides retaining the original sound frets, by Thomas Dicker, Reading, the engraved silvered brass dial showing seconds and date, the arch with bird automata and the inscription 'Time Flieth', the 8-day 5 pillar movement striking the hours on a bell, c1780, 88in (223.5cm) high.
$9,000–10,200 PAO

l. An oak longcase clock, by Valentine Downs, Louth, the brass dial with silvered chapter ring and recessed second dial, the 8-day 5 pillar movement incorporates a visual date, has a repeat mechanism and strikes the hours on a bell, c1780, 87in (221cm) high.
$6,000–6,750 PAO

An oak longcase clock, by John Draper, Maldon, the brass dial with silvered chapter ring, showing seconds and date, the 8-day 5 pillar movement striking the hours on a bell, c1765, 81in (205.5cm) high.
$5,400–6,400 PAO

An oak and mahogany banded longcase clock, by Thomas Crofts, Leeds, the brass dial with seconds and calendar aperture, with 8-day striking movement, mid-18thC, 86in (218.5cm) high.
$2,700–3,300 M

A mahogany longcase clock, by John Ellicott, London, the brass dial with silvered brass chapter ring, showing seconds, date and strike/silent feature to the arch, the 8-day 5 pillar movement with deadbeat escapement, striking the hours on a bell, c1765, 92in (233.5cm) high.
$14,250–15,750 PAO

John Ellicott, London, was clockmaker to King George III.

A mahogany longcase clock, the 12in (30.5cm) dial with centre penny moon and lunar date apertures, below further apertures, the arch with day of the week and date dials flanking a calendar dial, signed 'John Davis, Windsor', with 2 train rack and bell striking movement, driving work for subsidiary dials and apertures removed, movement c1730, straight grained mahogany stained case c1800, 82½in (209.5cm) high.
$5,250–6,000 S

An oak and mahogany longcase clock, with boxwood stringing, by George Greenway, Broadsummerford, the dial with moon phases, with 8-day movement, early 19thC, 83in (211cm) high.
$4,500–5,250 *ALS*

A mahogany longcase clock, by Thomas Hall of Romsey, the 12in (30.5cm) arched brass dial with wide chapter ring, subsidiary seconds and date aperture, with 8-day 5 pillar striking movement, late 18thC, 91in (231cm) high.
$2,000–2,250 *CAG*

A George III mahogany longcase clock, the 13in (33cm) brass and silvered arched dial engraved in the centre and with scalloped subsidiary seconds and date aperture, signed in the arch 'John Hamilton, Glasgow', with 8-day 4 pillar movement with rack strike, 89in (226cm) high.
$2,000–2,400 *DN*

A walnut crossbanded longcase clock, by Charles Gretton, London, the 10in (25.5cm) dial with seconds, calendar aperture and cherub spandrels, the 5 pillar latched bell striking movement with outside countwheel and bolt and shutter maintaining power, c1695, 75¾in (192.5cm) high.
$15,750–18,750 *S*

Charles Gretton, a famous maker who had premises in Fleet Street, London, was apprenticed c1662 and Free of the Clockmakers' Company from 1672. He served as Master in 1700. Records indicate that he worked until c1733 when it is presumed he died at the age of 84.

l. A George II gilt-decorated black japanned longcase clock, the door, base and sides with chinoiseries in tones of red and gold, the 10in (25.5cm) square brass dial with silvered chapter ring, Roman and Arabic numerals, matt centre with calendar aperture and subsidiary dial, the chapter ring inscribed 'F. Ford de Bucks', the 2 train 4 pillar movement with anchor escapement striking the hours on a bell, restored, mid-18thC, 83in (211cm) high
$4,000–4,800 *S(NY)*

r. A George III mahogany longcase clock, by William Holliwell, Liverpool, the brass and silvered dial with painted moon phase in the arch, inscribed 'Time Shews The Way of Lifes Decay', subsidiary seconds dial below, the movement striking on a bell, restored, 98½in (250cm) high.
$2,400–3,000 *Bea*

A George III oak longcase clock, the 11in (28cm) square brass and silvered dial with Roman and Arabic numerals and fleur-de-lys half-hour markers, engraved matt centre with date aperture, signed 'Jams. Head, Evesham', the 30-hour 4 pillar movement with outside countwheel strike, slight damage, 78½in (199.5cm) high.
$1,800–2,300 *DN*

An oak longcase clock, with mahogany crossbanding to the sides, by A. Jacobs, Torquay, the painted dial with seconds and date, with 8-day movement striking the hours on a bell, c1820, 88in (223.5cm) high.
$4,500–5,250 *PAO*

An oak and mahogany longcase clock, by Hancock, Yeovil, with painted dial and 8-day movement, c1790, 79in (200.5cm) high.
$3,500–4,000 *ALS*

An oak and mahogany longcase clock, by Chas. Hulbert, Marshfield, the dial with a stag hunting scene in the arch, with 8-day movement, c1825, 81½in (207cm) high.
$3,000–3,750 *ALS*

A lacquered longcase clock decorated with Oriental chinoiserie to trunk door and base, by William Hayler, Chatham, with brass dial showing seconds and date, the 8-day 5 pillar movement striking the hours on a bell, c1765, 87in (221cm) high.
$8,250–9,500 *PAO*

A mahogany veneered longcase clock, by John Holmes, London, the brass dial with silvered chapter, seconds and strike/silent, gilt spandrels and maker's name on a cartouche, the 8-day 6 pillar striking movement with deadbeat escapement, bolt and shutter maintaining power and Holmes crutch and double bob pendulum with beat scale, restored, c1765, 88in (223.5cm) high.
$28,500–31,500 *PAO*

l. A Charles II olivewood parquetry and boxwood, ebony and green stained bone marquetry longcase clock, by Joseph Knibb of Oxford, the 10in (25.5cm) square dial with silvered chapter ring, blued steel hands, matt centre with calendar aperture and winged cherub spandrels, the 5 ringed pillar movement with outside countwheel strike on a bell, anchor escapement with spring suspended butterfly nut rated pendulum, on inlaid plinth with later bun feet, restored, 70in (178cm) high.
$55,500–63,000 *CNY*

r. A walnut and crossbanded longcase clock, by Tho. Kefford, Royston, the 12in (30.5cm) square brass dial with engraved bird and foliage to the centre, silvered chapter ring, applied gilt metal urn and foliate scroll spandrels, seconds and date aperture, the twin train movement with anchor escapement and bell strike, early 18thC, 88¾in (225.5cm) high.
$4,000–4,500 *P(E)*

A stellar inlaid oak longcase clock, by Samuel Quarman, Temple Cloud, with 8-day movement, c1760, 79in (200.5cm) high.
$5,250–6,250 *ALS*

A burr walnut longcase clock, by W. James, London, with 8-day movement striking on a gong, c1881, 67½in (171.5cm) high.
$4,800–5,600 *ROD*

A mahogany longcase clock, with rosewood crossbanding, by Peters, Arbroath, the painted dial showing *The Lady of the Lake* after Sir Walter Scott, the corners showing poets of the time, with 8-day movement striking the hours on a bell, c1850, 82in (208.5cm) high.
$5,000–5,750 *PAO*

r. A mahogany longcase clock, by James Paterson of Banff, the 12in (30.5cm) silvered arched dial with subsidiary seconds and date, decorated with scrolled leafage and floral ornament, with 8-day striking movement, late 18thC, 85in (216cm) high.
$2,700–3,300 *CAG*

An oak longcase clock, by William Robb of Montrose, with painted dial and 8-day movement, c1815, 84in (213.5cm) high. **$3,000–3,500** *PNF*

An early Victorian mahogany longcase clock, the 11¾in (30cm) painted dial with Roman figures, subsidiary seconds and date, signed 'G. Stromier, Glasgow', with 8-day movement striking on a bell, 78¾in (200cm) high. **$1,500–1,800** *WL*

A mahogany longcase clock, with boxwood stringing, by Richard Roynon, Compton Martin, the dial with moon phases, with 8-day movement, early 19thC, 82in (208.5cm) high. **$6,750–7,500** *ALS*

A mahogany longcase clock, by Joseph Testi, Somerton, the dial with moon phases in the arch, with 8-day movement, c1840, 86in (218.5cm) high. **$5,250–6,500** *ALS*

A mahogany longcase clock, by Wm. Taylor, King St, Whitehaven, the brass dial with moon phase and concentric calendar, with 8-day movement, c1780, 89in (226cm) high.
$9,750–11,000 *ALS*

l. An oak longcase clock, by William Tompson, Wolverhampton, the 11in (28cm) square matt brass dial with pierced cherub spandrels, Roman numerals, date indicator and name cartouche, with 30-hour movement, mid-18thC, 81in (205.5cm) high.
$1,500–1,800 *GH*

r. An oak longcase clock, with giltwood finials, by John Wenham, East Dereham, the brass dial with silvered chapter rings, engraved in the arch, inscribed 'Tempus Fugit', late 18thC, 82in (208.5cm) high.
$6,000–6,500 *CLC*

A mahogany longcase clock, by Thompson, Acle, Norfolk, the painted dial with moon phases, c1810, 91¾in (233cm) high.
$9,000–10,500 *DSP*

l. An oak longcase clock, crossbanded in mahogany, by Joseph Thristle, Stogursey, the dial with seconds and date, painted with fruit and foliage to each corner, 8-day movement striking the hours on a bell, c1830, 78in (198cm) high.
$3,250–4,000 *PAO*

A mahogany longcase clock, with boxwood stringing, by D. Whitelaw, Edinburgh, the round white dial showing seconds and date, the 8-day movement striking the hours on a bell, c1820, 79in (200.5cm) high.
$5,500–6,500 *PAO*

l. A mahogany longcase clock, by William Webster, London, with 3 train movement quarter striking on 8 bells, c1760, 103¼in (263cm) high.
$15,000–18,000 *GUN*

A George III mahogany longcase clock, by John Whitfield of Clifton, the brass and silvered arched dial with matt centre, subsidiary seconds and date, a moon phase with landscape and marine scenes in the arch, with 8-day 4 pillar movement with rack strike, case early 19thC, 88¾in (225.5cm) high.
$1,150–1,350 *DN*

An oak longcase clock, crossbanded in mahogany, by Wright, Northwich, the brass dial showing seconds and date, with moon phase in the arch, the corners with brass spandrels denoting the 4 seasons, with 8-day movement striking the hours on a bell, c1770, 84in (213.5cm) high.
$6,900–7,500 *PAO*

An oak and mahogany longcase clock, by Wright of Swineshead, with 8-day movement, c1815, 82in (208.5cm) high.
$3,300–3,900 *PNF*

A mahogany and oak inlaid and crossbanded longcase clock, the painted arched dial with floral decoration, Roman numerals, seconds and date indicator, with 8-day movement striking on a bell, mid-19thC, 90in (228.5cm) high.
$1,250–1,450 *GH*

A mahogany veneered longcase clock, inlaid with satinwood banding, by William Young, Dundee, the 13in (33cm) painted dial showing seconds and date, with 8-day movement striking the hours on a bell, c1830, 81in (205.5cm) high.
$5,300–6,300 *PAO*

l. An Edwardian mahogany longcase clock, the 12in (30.5cm) arched brass dial with silvered chapter ring, gilt Arabic numerals and seconds dial, chime/silent, Whittington and Westminster chime dials in the arch, with 8-day 3 train movement striking on tubular gong and chiming on 8 tubular gongs, 100in (254cm) high.
$5,500–6,300 *CAG*

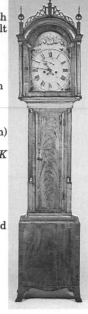

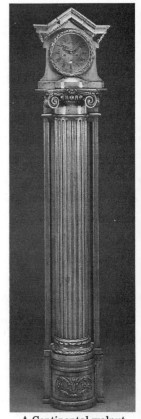

A Federal mahogany longcase clock, by A. Kennedy Miller, Elizabethtown, New Jersey, feet replaced, some repairs, c1800, 98in (249cm) high. $5,700–6,300 **S(NY)**

A mahogany longcase clock, the 10½in (26.5cm) brass dial with silvered chapter ring, Roman numerals, subsidiary seconds and 3 winding apertures, the 3 train repeating movement with deadbeat escapement, striking on 6 gongs, c1920, 88in (223.5cm) high. $2,700–3,300 **Hal**

r. A Federal mahogany and mahogany veneer longcase clock, with polychrome and gilt floral dial, with seconds and calendar aperture, with 8-day weight driven brass movement, minor damage, Massachusetts, c1800, 87in (221cm) high. $12,750–14,250 **SK**

l. A French tulipwood and gilt-bronze mounted longcase clock, the white enamel dial with Roman and Arabic numerals, the angles applied with rocaille mounts, 19thC, 98in (249cm) high. $6,000–6,750 **CSK**

A tiger maple longcase clock, the dial inscribed 'William Stillman in Hopkinton 1786', the wood and paper dial with pen and ink compass and numerals, with wooden movement, the case incomplete, 83in (211cm) high. $7,500–8,250 **SK(B)**

A Continental walnut columnar form longcase clock, the dial with an engraved steel chapter ring, the 2 train movement with anchor escapement striking the hours on a bell, movement associated, case repaired, early 19thC, 97in (246.5cm) high. $16,200–18,000 **S(NY)**

Mantel Clocks

A Victorian four-glass mantel clock, the double fusee movement with silvered and engraved dial signed 'Kleyser & Co, 66 High Street, Southwark', c1845, 10¼in (26cm) high.
$3,300–3,700 *RAF*

A mahogany balloon-shaped mantel clock, with boxwood string inlay and oval marquetry flower, by Barraud & Lund, London, the 4in (10cm) enamel dial and backplate signed, the 8-day double fusee movement striking the hours on a bell, c1850, 10½in (26.5cm) high.
$4,500–5,500 *PAO*

English fusee mantel clocks of this size and style are very rare.

r. A Victorian mahogany mantel clock, the painted dial with Roman numerals and inscribed 'Brock, 64 George Street, Portman Sqe.', 25½in (65cm) high.
$2,300–2,700 *S(NY)*

An Edwardian mahogany inlaid balloon clock, by W. Bruford & Son, Eastbourne and Exeter, 8in (20.5cm) high.
$450–550 *ROD*

l. A red boulle mantel clock, the dial marked 'Goldsmiths & Silversmiths Co', the 8-day French movement striking on a gong, late 19thC, 17in (43cm) high.
$2,250–2,500 *CLC*

A Regency rosewood mantel timepiece, the 8-day movement by Vulliamy London, No. 501, with gilt-metal mounts and handle, 9in (23cm) high.
$9,500–10,500 *RBB*

A gilt-bronze and blue porcelain self-levelling mantel clock, c1850, 18in (45.5cm) high.
$3,000–3,600 *ROD*

A late Victorian mahogany mantel clock, with floral inlay, the 8-day movement striking on a gong, 11½in (29cm) high.
$1,500–1,800 *CLC*

An oak mantel clock, with oak leaf inlay, the 8-day movement striking on a coil gong, c1895, 11½in (29cm) high.
$1,200–1,400 *CLC*

A satinwood mantel timepiece, with 8-day movement, c1910, 6in (15cm) high.
$900–1,200 *ROD*

l. A Viennese or German gilt-brass and porcelain mantel timepiece, the 8-day movement with enamel dial and cylinder escapement in a drum case enclosed by 4 dark blue porcelain columns, highlighted with gilt and surmounted by a porcelain dome painted with colourful mythical figures, the porcelain base with similar vignettes, dome cracked, c1900, 11½in (29cm) high.
$1,750–2,000 *S*

An Austrian giltwood mantel timepiece, with 2¼in (5.5cm) enamel dial, standing barrel silk suspension movement, raised on a simulated marble base, c1800, 12in (30.5cm) high.
$2,500–3,000 *S*

A French bronze-mounted marble mantel clock, the 4¼in (11.5cm) enamel dial signed 'Hemon A Paris', bell striking silk suspension movement, the case with arched bronze cresting, the corners with bearded masks above sphinxes, c1815, 20½in (52cm) high.
$2,300–2,700 *S*

A white marble and gilt-metal mantel clock, the white enamel dial signed 'Bigot, Bourges' and painted with swags of roses, on a portico base, late 19thC, 19in (48cm) high.
$1,750–2,000 *S*

An Edwardian mahogany and boxwood strung mantel clock, with brass columns and finials, floral dial, striking on a gong, 9¼in (23.5cm) high.
$1,350–1,450 *CLC*

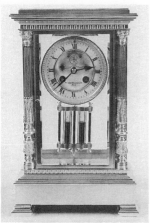

A silvered and gilt Corinthian-cased mantel clock, signed 'Sir John Bennett Ltd, Paris', with visible self-levelling mercury compensating Brocot escapement, c1878, 12½in (32cm) high.
$2,000–2,400 *ROD*

A Napoleon III gilt-bronze mantel clock, the dial signed 'Deluaux', within a shaped case surmounted by an urn flanked by scrolls, late 19thC, 29½in (75cm) high.
$4,000–4,500 *S(NY)*

A French Louis VI style ormolu striking mantel clock, by Henry Marc, Paris, c1850, 11¾in (30cm) high.
$1,350–1,500 *ROD*

A *pendule d'officier*, signed 'Le Roy, Paris', c1890, 11in (28cm) high.
$1,800–2,000 *ROD*

A French bronzed and gilt-spelter mantel clock, with 4¾in (12cm) gilt dial, bell striking Samuel Marti movement, on a shaped red marble plinth raised on gilt paw feet, c1890, 37¾in (96cm) high.
$2,400–2,800 *S*

l. A French giltwood and composition mantel clock, the white enamel Roman dial with steel moon hands, signed 'H.ry Marc à Paris', the twin barrel movement with countwheel strike on bell, damaged, 19thC, 19¾in (50cm) high.
$300–375 *CSK*

An Empire bronze and gilt striking mantel clock, signed 'Hy Marc A Paris', with silk suspension, c1815, 15½in (39.5cm) high.
$1,650–1,950 *ROD*

A French ormolu mantel clock, by Marti, Paris, with painted porcelain panels, c1845, 11¼in (28.5cm) high.
$2,600–3,000 *ROD*

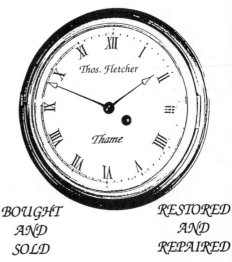

A French gilt mantel clock, by Miroy Frères, Paris, with 8-day striking movement, and porcelain panels with cherubs, flowers and foliage, 19thC, 26in (66cm) wide.
$4,700–5,700 *E*

A French red boulle and ormolu mounted mantel clock, by Miroy, Paris, with 8-day bell striking movement, c1870, 12in (30.5cm) high.
$1,800–2,000 *ROD*

A Louis XVI ormolu mantel clock, attributed to Robert Osmond, with two-tone gilding, the enamelled dial signed 'Julien le Roy', the movement signed 'Julien Le Roy A Paris', stamped on the back 'Osmond', 25¼in (64cm) high.
$82,500–93,000 *C*

l. A French Second Empire ormolu-cased mantel timepiece, by Le Roy, Paris, c1850, 7in (18cm) high.
$900–1,000 *PNF*

A French ormolu rococo style mantel timepiece, with 8-day movement by Silvani of Paris, c1860, 10in (25.5cm) high.
$1,500–1,800 *PNF*

A French bronze and gilt mantel clock, by Marti & Co, with a bronze cupid on a column, 1860, 13¼in (33.5cm) high.
$1,500–1,800 *ROD*

A French ormolu and bronzed salon clock, with a 3½in (9cm) turned silvered Roman dial, the silk suspension on 8-day bell striking movement, signed 'En Quillet', c1830, 23½in (60cm) high.
$1,125–1,275 *WL*

A French porcelain mantel clock, signed 'Pons, Paris', with 8-day bell striking movement, and silk suspension, c1860, 11½in (29cm) high.
$1,600–2,000 *ROD*

A Napoleon III gilt-bronze and marble figural mantel clock, late 19thC, 11½in (29cm) high.
$4,000–4,500   S(NY)

A Louis XV style gilt-bronze mantel clock, the dial signed 'Voisenetz, Paris', late 19thC, 25in (63.5cm) high.
$2,800–3,300   S(NY)

An Empire ormolu and malachite-veneered mantel clock, the glazed dial enclosed by a serpent devouring its tail, inscribed with Roman numerals and signed 'Thomire à Paris' and 'Moinet aine Hger.', within a spreading pylon case, movement and plinth also signed, minor repairs, 21¼in (54cm) high.
$22,500–27,000   C

A French hand-painted porcelain mantel clock, c1860, 9in (23cm) high.
$750–900   BWC

A Napoleon III bronze and Siena marble mantel clock, the silvered dial with Roman chapter ring and steel spade hands, the twin barrel movement with countwheel strike on bell, bell missing, 24in (61cm) high.
$1,300–1,500   CSK

A French Empire mantel timepiece, with 8-day movement and silk suspension, c1810, 13in (33cm) high.
$1,200–1,350   ROD

A French ormolu striking mantel clock, with floral porcelain panels, 1880, 11in (28cm) high.
$2,400–2,700   TUR

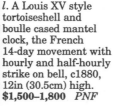

l. A Louis XV style tortoiseshell and boulle cased mantel clock, the French 14-day movement with hourly and half-hourly strike on bell, c1880, 12in (30.5cm) high.
$1,500–1,800   PNF

A French 4 glass mantel clock, with Corinthian columns, the striking movement with mercury compensated pendulum, c1880, 14in (35.5cm) high.
$2,000–2,500 *TUR*

A French 4 glass regulator mantel clock, the enamel dial with green border and Arabic numerals, the 8-day duration movement striking the hours and half hours on a gong, the brass case with doors to both front and rear, c1890, 12in (30.5cm) high.
$1,500–1,800 *PAO*

A Continental porcelain mantel clock, with 8-day striking movement, the case with flowers and foliage in relief and painted with panels of flowers, on scroll feet, 19thC, 15in (38cm) high.
$825–975 *E*

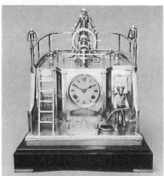

l. A nautical mantel clock, the brass and silvered case in the form of a ship's poop deck, the French 8-day movement striking on a gong, the pendulum in the form of a sailor holding the ship's wheel, another sailor below coiling rope, on a black marble base, late 19thC, 11in (28cm) high.
$3,500–4,000 *Bea*

r. A German mantel clock, by Winterhalder & Hofmeier, c1910, 8¾in (22cm) high.
$1,450–1,650 *CLC*

A German 4¼in (11cm) symphonion disc musical mantel clock, the centre drive disc playing on a single comb, the clock with 2in (5cm) annular dial with Arabic numerals, c1900, 11in (28cm) high, with approximately 15 discs.
$975–1,200 *Hal*

A Swiss gilt-bronze and black marble mantel timepiece, the 3½in (9cm) white enamel dial signed 'Chevron 8 Jours' with outer dark brown ring and gilt numerals, 8-day lever movement, c1920, 9½in (24cm) high.
$1,400–1,500 *S*

Table Clocks

A George III mahogany table clock, by Barwise, London, inlaid with brass and ebony, the enamel convex dial with Roman hours and Arabic minutes, the 8-day movement striking and repeating the hours on a bell, the backplate with engraved borders and maker's name, strike/silent facility, c1795, 21in (53cm) high.
$3,750–4,250 *PAO*

A burr walnut table timepiece, the 7in (18cm) arched gilt dial signed 'Thos. Cole' in an elaborate cartouche, the fusee and chain movement with offset winding, maintaining power and deadbeat escapement with jewelled pallets, the pendulum with roller suspension and spherical bob, plaque on underside of case inscribed 'GWR 2929', c1860, 14½in (37cm) high.
$8,500–9,500 *S*

Makers

Not all clocks are marked; some carry the name of the retailer. Those makers who did sign their clocks usually used their full name, or, in the case of later French clocks, an abbreviation of it, or a stamp.

A George III painted musical table clock, by Henry Brown, made for the Turkish market, the arched dial with a 6in (15cm) silvered chapter ring with Turkish numerals, the matt centre with calendar and false pendulum apertures, blued-steel scroll-cut hands, the arch with a strike/silent dial, signature plate and silvered arch with tune indicators above a spray of painted flowers with bells, the 3 train 7 pillar fusee musical movement with verge escapement and cylinder playing 6 tunes on 9 bells, repaired, gilt-bronze finials later, late 18thC, 23in (58.5cm) high.
$12,750–14,250 *S(NY)*

l. A mahogany bracket/table clock, by James Howe, London, the brass dial with separate chapter ring and spandrels showing the date and strike/silent feature to the arch, the 8-day 5 pillar movement with verge escapement and striking the hours on a bell, backplate profusely engraved with scrolls and the maker's name, c1765, 18in (45.7cm) high.
$13,500–15,000 *PAO*

r. A George III brass-mounted ebonised musical table clock, the 9¾in (25cm) dial with calendar aperture, signed 'Eardley Norton, London', strike/not strike and chime/not chime dials, tune selection dial, similarly signed 8 pillar 3 train fusee and chain bell striking movement with deadbeat hammers, 9¼in (23.5cm) pinned barrel, restored, hands replaced, c1775, 35¾in (91cm) high.
$16,500–19,500 *S*

Wall Clocks

A miniature silvered dial twin fusee dial clock, with verge escapement and pull hour repeat, signed 'Chas. Absolon, London', c1805, dial 6in (15cm) diam.
$6,750–7,500 *ALS*

A hooded wall clock, by Birtles of Market Harborough, with a white dial and original painted pine case, 1830, 23½in (60cm) high.
$1,800–2,400 *DSP*

A rosewood wall timepiece, probably by Atkins Whiting & Co, Bristol, Connecticut, with 30-day wagon spring movement, mid-19thC, 25½in (65cm) high.
$675–825 *SK(B)*

Miscellaneous

A skeleton clock, by Barry of Cardiff, with engraved silvered dial and fusee movement, c1850, 10in (25.5cm) high.
$1,500–2,000 *ROD*

A miniature tortoiseshell clock, with silver gilt mounts, Swiss lever 8-day movement, hallmarked 'London 1904', 2½in (6.5cm) high.
$1,000–1,200 *ROD*

A mahogany triple-decker mirror clock, by C. & L. C. Ives, Bristol, Connecticut, with 8-day brass wagon spring driven movement, slight damage, c1831, 36½in (92.5cm) high.
$3,750–4,500 *SK(B)*

A corner case astronomical master timepiece, by Tiffany & Co, the movement with 18in (45.5cm) chapter ring with visible escapement, dials and indicators for world time, strike/silent, high/low tide and 5 slave dials for alarms, the lower section with subsidiary calendar dial, with an 8in (20.5cm) mercury pendulum, c1880, 86in (208cm) high.
$55,500–63,000 *SK*

Skeleton Clocks

The earliest examples of skeleton clocks were probably French, although their origins may lie with Austrian clocks. It was in England, where they were produced between c1820–1870, that they underwent the greatest development. The earliest examples are simple, but later they became very complex, often incorporating architectural motifs and elaborate striking mechanisms.

r. A French bronzed spelter swinging mystery timepiece, by Guilmet, with 3¼in (8.5cm) enamel dial, movement stamped and with 'No. 6914', contained in a drum case forming the upper part of a grid-iron pendulum held by a figure of a young girl standing on a leaf-moulded plinth, c1880, 30in (76cm) high.
$2,600–3,000 *S*

l. A French First Empire ormolu library clock, with silk suspension movement striking on a bell, c1800, 14in (35.5cm) high.
$2,250–2,550 *CLC*

A mahogany bracket clock, by J. W. Benson, with striking carriage-type movement, c1890, 9½in (24cm) high. **$975–1,200** *ROD*

A Victorian walnut bracket clock, by Jackman, 10½in (26.5cm) high. **$1,000–1,200** *AAV*

A bracket clock, by Joseph Knibb, 17thC, 12½in (32cm) high. **$16,500–18,500** *DN*

A Transitional ormolu cartel clock, surmounted by a beaded laurel-cast part-fluted urn with reeded scrolled handles, signed 'Martinot à Paris', c1770, 32¾in (83cm) high. **$8,000–8,500** *C*

l. An ebonised musical bracket clock, signed 'Moore, Ipswich', playing 7 tunes on 12 bells every 3 hours, c1780, 24½in (62cm) high. **$6,750–8,250** *Bon*

A rosewood and brass inlaid bracket clock, by Adams, London, with 8-day, 5 pillar fusee movement, c1840, 16in (40.5cm) high.
$4,000–4,500 *PAO*

A Cuban mahogany bracket clock, by Geo. Blackie, Musselburgh, c1810, 17in (43cm) high.
$5,500–6,500 *ALS*

An ebonised bracket clock, engraved on dial 'Wm Hughes, High Holborn, London', c1780, 13½in (34.5cm) high.
$9,000–9,750 *ALS*

A tortoiseshell and cut brass inlaid bracket clock, 18thC, 54in (137cm) high overall.
$5,500–6,200 *P(B)*

A William IV pollard oak bracket clock, by Walker of Clerkenwell, 22½in (57cm) high.
$2,800–3,200 *CAG*

A George III giltwood cartel clock, signed 'Peter Amyot, Norwich', with brass chapter dial, restored, 42in (106.5cm) high.
$13,750–15,250 *C*

A Regency painted bracket clock, with enamel dial, bracket later, 23¼in (59cm) high.
$7,800–8,500 *C*

A French ormolu and bronze mantel clock, signed 'Baltazar, Paris', on the back of a bronze bull, on a base, early 19thC, 23½in (59.5cm) high.
$3,500–4,000 *CAG*

A mahogany bracket clock, inscribed 'John Prichard, London', c1785, 18½in (46.5cm) high.
$9,000–9,750 *Gam*

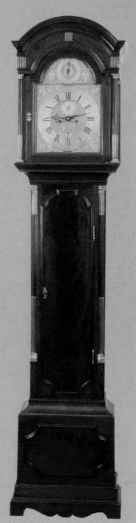

A French brass carriage clock, by Henri Jacot, the enamel dial with Roman chapters and steel hands, with 8-day movement, c1870, 7in (18cm) high.
$1,900–2,300 *PAO*

A French champlevé enamel repeating carriage clock with alarm, c1890, 6½in (16.5cm) high.
$4,000–4,500 *S*

A French carriage clock, with 8-day movement, striking on 2 gongs, signed 'Z. Barraclough & Sons Paris', c1875, 5⅝in (14.5cm) high.
$2,400–2,700 *S*

A miniature carriage clock, with Corinthian columns and 8-day movement, c1890, 3¼in (8.5cm) high.
$1,200–1,500 *ROD*

A clock garniture, decorated with gilding, silver and bronze, with porcelain panels and enamelled birds and butterflies, c1870, the clock 20¾in (52.5cm) high.
$2,700–3,500 *ROD*

A silvered and gilt-bronze Rheims cathedral clock, with 2½in (6.5cm) enamel 'rose window' dial, c1860, 19in (48.5cm) high.
$4,500–5,250 *S*

A 'jewelled' porcelain mounted gilt-bronze composed clock garniture, with 4in (10cm) painted dial, Japy Frères movement No. 7400, c1890, clock 19¼in (49cm) high.
$5,500–6,500 *S*

A gilt and white marble garniture, c1880, clock 16½in (42cm) high.
$2,000–2,500 *ROD*

A miniature gilt-bronze and champlevé decorated clock garniture, the clock with 2in (5cm) dial, with 8-day lever escapement movement, including two-light candelabra supported by cherubs, c1880, clock 9in (23cm) high.
$2,400–2,700 *ROD*

A French gilt-bronze white marble wall clock, with 8-day movement, c1900, 8½in (21.5cm) high.
$1,500–1,800 *S*

A French gilt-bronze and bisque clock garniture, with drum-shaped movement, the base mounted with 2 bisque groups of Cupid and Psyche, c1900, clock 16in (40.5cm) high.
$3,000–3,500 *SK*

A Swiss silver-gilt and enamel miniature clock, with 8-day movement, c1810, 1½in (4cm) high, contained in original case.
$1,125–1,350 *ROD*

A mahogany longcase clock, by Ashton Bredbury, c1765, 81in (206cm) high. $6,000–7,000 ALS

A walnut longcase clock, by James Bush, London, c1740, 85in (216cm) high. $16,500–18,750 PAO

A mahogany longcase clock, by John Baxter, c1825, 84in (214cm) high. $5,250–5,750 PAO

A walnut musical longcase clock, by Stephen Asselin, c1720, 95in (242cm) high. $13,800–16,500 Bon

A mahogany longcase clock, by John Baxter, c1825, 84in (214cm) high. $5,250–5,750 PAO

An oak and mahogany longcase clock, by Bothamley, Boston, c1830, 83in (211cm) high. $3,000–3,500 ALS

A mahogany longcase clock, by Bryson, Edinburgh, c1830, 79in (201cm) high. $4,500–5,500 PAO

An oak longcase clock, by John Barnish, Rochdale, c1780, 82in (208cm) high. $3,200–3,500 ALS

An oak longcase clock, by Archibald Buchan, Perth, c1800, 82in (208cm) high. $3,800–4,700 PAO

An oak longcase 8-day clock, by George Way, Wincanton, c1790, 86in (218.5cm) high.
$3,500–4,000 *PAO*

A mahogany longcase clock, by Thomas Williams, Haverfordwest, c1775, 83in (210.5cm) high
$9,750–10,750 *PAO*

A mahogany 8-day longcase clock, by Edouard Renouf, Jersey, c1780, 84in (214cm) high.
$10,750–12,000 *PAO*

A mahogany 8-day moon-phase longcase clock, by Robert Smith, Nottingham, c1795, 89in (226cm) high.
$7,500–9,000 *PNF*

A 30-hour long-case clock, by John Younge Darby, c1700, 80in (203cm) high.
$3,000–3,500 *Bon*

A walnut marquetry longcase clock, by J. Windmills, c1700, 71in (180cm) high.
$24,000–27,000 *S*

A longcase clock, by Edward Walters, c1840, 90in (228cm) high.
$6,500–7,500 *PAO*

An 8-day longcase clock, by James Warren, c1800.
$3,750–4,500 *CAG*

An oak 8-day longcase clock, by Samuel Whitmore, Daventry, with engraved and silvered brass dial, c1780, 84in (214cm) high.
$3,500–4,000 *ALS*

A mahogany long-case clock, by E. G. Williams, c1840, 91in (231cm) high.
$6,000–7,000 *PAO*

A longcase clock, by Wm Wright, c1715, 87in (221cm) high.
$15,000–17,250 *PAO*

A mahogany 8-day long-case clock, by John Warry, Bristol, early 19thC, 83in (210cm) high.
$6,000–7,000 *ALS*

A green lacquer 8-day
striking longcase clock,
by Thomas Harris, London,
c1775, 97in (246.5cm) high.
$7,500–8,500 *PAO*

A Queen Anne
scarlet lacquer
longcase clock,
by Jno Martin,
London, 123in
(312cm) high.
$24,750–27,000 *C*

A mahogany crossbanded oak 8-day
longcase clock, with painted dial
and pull hour repeat, by Holmes,
Cheadle, c1790, 74in (188cm) high.
$4,000–5,000 *ALS*

A mahogany year-
going longcase
timepiece, by
John Holmes,
The Strand, c1790,
91in (231cm) high.
$3,600–4,200

A mahogany 8-day
longcase clock, by
Charles Lunan,
Aberdeen, c1790,
84in (213cm) high.
$8,500–9,200 *PAO*

A mahogany 8-day striking
longcase clock, by Thomas
Lock, Bath, c1810,
89in (226cm) high.
$6,000–6,500 *PAO*

A mahogany
longcase clock, by
William Parr,
London, c1780,
87in (221cm) high.
$5,250–6,250 *S*

A mahogany longcase 8-day
clock, by William Pringle,
Edinburgh, with silvered
brass dial, c1830, 82in
(208cm) high.
$4,500–5,500 *PAO*

An oak 8-day longcase clock,
by R. Mason, Kelso, with
white dial and painted with
flowers to the arch, c1790,
84in (213cm) high.
$4,000–4,500 *PAO*

An oak longcase 8-day clock, by
Henry Messer, Southampton,
striking the hours on a bell,
with strike/silent, c1760,
84in (213cm) high.
$4,750–5,750 *PAO*

A mahogany 8-day longcase
clock, by J. Snelling, Alton,
the white dial with subsidiary
seconds dial, early 19thC,
78in (198cm) high.
$3,500–4,000 *ALS*

RAFFETY

FINE ANTIQUE CLOCKS

34 KENSINGTON CHURCH STREET, LONDON W8 4HA   TELEPHONE / FAX 0171-938 1100
and by appointment at 39 LEDBURY ROAD, LONDON W11 2AA

*W*e have the largest selected stock in Central London of genuine antique clocks and barometers dating from 1650 - 1880.

- All our clocks are chosen for their exceptional quality, originality and decorative appeal.

- Whether you are looking for a longcase or bracket clock by a leading London maker or a more modest country made example, we may well have what you are seeking in our wide ranging selection.

- Each of our clocks are sympathetically restored and fully guaranteed.

- We are always keen to purchase items of a similar type.

- Please call and see us in London or contact us with a specific interest you may have.

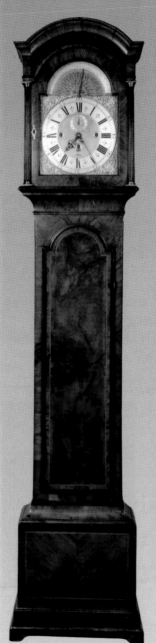

Left:

JONATHAN MARSH, LONDON

A rare London walnut musical longcase clock playing eight tunes.

Circa 1740
Height:
7' 11" (242 cms)

Top right:

JOHN GRAHAM, LIVERPOOL

A good two day marine chronometer in its original numbered case (no.181).

Circa 1850

Lower right:

JOHN DWERRIHOUSE, BERKLEY SQAURE, LONDON

A fine quality mahogany belltop bracket clock with 8 day brass dial movement and strike/silent.

Circa 1780
Height:
20" (51 cms)

A minute repeating chronograph, with silver gilt and enamel full hunter case, signed 'Henry Sandoz, Le Locle', hallmarked London 1895, 55mm diam.
$3,750–4,500 *PT*

An /English verge watch, with gilt champlevé dial, in a shagreen-covered gilt-metal consular case, signed 'Henry Mafsey', c1705, 57mm diam.
$1,900–2,250 *PT*

An English verge watch, with painted enamel dial in silver pair cases, signed 'Thos Norris Wittlesea 545', hallmarked London 1808, 58mm diam.
$750–850 *PT*

A Swiss verge watch with calendar, in an 18ct gold consular case, the bezel bordered with a band of marcasites, late 18thC, 47mm diam.
$4,500–5,000 *PT*

A Continental verge watch, in three-colour gold consular case, signed 'Sauvaistre à Jonzac', c1770, 39mm diam.
$1,000–1,250 *PT*

A gold open-faced keyless perpetual calendar minute repeating chronograph pocket watch, signed, 'Patek Philippe c1880, 56mm diam.
$52,500–60,000 *C*

A gold and enamel verge watch, with royal cipher of King George III, and fob, by Thomas Grey, c1790, watch 48mm diam.
$5,000–6,000 *S*

r. A German silver pair cased verge watch, signed 'Heinrich Pepfenleuser', c1700, 59mm diam.
$3,750–4,500 *C*

r. An English verge watch, with poly-chrome dial, in silver pair cases, signed 'Jno Smith, York', hallmarked London 1753, 50mm diam.
$900–1,000 *PT*

A Continental gold, enamel and split pearl cylinder watch, some restoration, c1810, 54mm diam.
$5,000–5,750 *S*

A Continental gold and enamel verge watch, unsigned, restored, c1790, 47mm diam.
$1,350–1,500 *S*

An 18ct gold half-hunter pocket watch, signed 'Dent, 61 Strand & Royal Exchange, London', c1898, 50mm diam.
$3,750–4,500 *BWC*

A Longines 18ct gold single button chronograph wristwatch, with register, tachometer and telemeter, c1929, 35mm diam.
$5,250–6,000 *S(G)*

A Jaeger LeCoultre stainless steel and gold reverso wristwatch, signed, c1945, 38mm long.
$4,000–5,000 *S(G)*

A Cartier 18ct gold and diamond bracelet wristwatch, with date aperture, quartz movement, water-resistant type case, bezel set with single cut diamonds, signed, c1985, 36mm wide.
$9,000–10,500 *S(G)*

A lady's Cartier 18ct gold and diamond bracelet wristwatch, quartz movement, 4 jewels silvered dial, diamond set winder, signed, c1985, 31mm long, leather Cartier pouch.
$6,800–7,800 *S*

A gentleman's Omega 15ct gold Seamaster automatic wristwatch, with date aperture, link bracelet strap, c1969.
$1,125–1,275 *BWC*

A Patek Philippe 18ct gold wristwatch, nickel level movement, signed, No. 910804, c1940, 32mm diam.
$3,500–4,000 *S(G)*

A Breguet 18ct gold wristwatch, with circular gilt lever movement, signed, No. 2157, c1930, 35mm long.
$3,500–4,000 *S(G)*

A Gerald Genta 18ct gold, diamond, ruby and mother-of-pearl bracelet watch, quartz movement, c1985, 32mm diam.
$5,500–6,500 *S(G)*

A Hamilton 'Bomb Timer' silvered metal duo-dial military wristwatch, with refinished black dial, 17 jewels, signed, winder replaced, c1944, 31mm long.
$1,000–1,200 *S*

A Cartier 18ct gold self-winding 'Tank' wristwatch, circular nickel level movement, glucydur balance, 17 jewels, signed, c1980, 34mm long.
$5,000–5,500 *S(G)*

A Movado 18ct gold self-winding wristwatch, with date and dual time zone, nickel level movement, signed, c1990, 36mm diam.
$1,500–1,800 *S(G)*

A Patek Philippe 18ct pink gold two-piece case wristwatch, signed, c1940, 24mm wide.
$5,000–5,500 *S(G)*

An oak cased barograph, with bevelled glass and 2 bellows, c1910, 15in (38cm) wide.
$750–825 *RTW*

A mahogany cased display barograph, with chart roll, 1960s, 15½in (40cm) wide.
$825–975 *RTW*

An Edwardian oak-cased pluviograph, by Pastorelli & Rapkin, 11in (30cm) wide.
$750–900 *RTW*

An oak-cased thermograph, with bevelled glass and chart drawer, by M. W. Dunscombe Ltd, Bristol, c1908, 14in (35.5cm) wide.
$1,350–1,500 *RTW*

A Victorian brass-cased barometer and altimeter, by Lancaster, 3½in (9cm) diam.
$185–200 *RTW*

A French barometer, with enamelled scale, c1910, 4in (10cm) diam.
$65–80 *RTW*

An oak-cased display barograph, with ivory scale thermometer, complete with drawer in base, by Aitchison, London, 1930s, 14in (35.5cm) wide.
$750–900 *RTW*

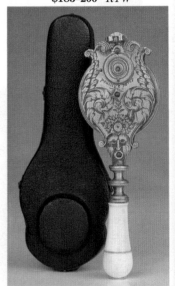

A French microscope, with turned ivory handle, parts lacking, signed 'Pouilly à Paris', late 17thC, 5¼in (13cm) long.
$12,200–13,700 *Bon*

A brass-cased aneroid barometer, by Short & Mason, 1960s, 5¼in (13cm) diam.
$90–105 *RTW*

A pair of polished and lacquered brass and leather field glasses, fully restored, signed Dollond, c1870, 3½in (9cm) long.
$120–150 *Tem*

A Victorian hand-held brass and leather telescope, fitted with sun shade, c1880, 15in (38cm) long.
$180–225 *Tem*

A pair of telescopic field glasses, fitted with sun shades, by Negretti & Zambra, c1870, 13½in (34.5cm) long.
$225–270 *Tem*

A brass ship's engine room repeater telegraph, by Chadburn & Co, c1936, 18in (45.5cm) high. **$675–750** *Tem*

An 8-day marine chronometer, by Army & Navy, c1880, 8in (20.5cm) square. **$7,500–9,000** *TMe*

A 2-day marine chronometer, by Victor Kullberg, c1865, 7in (18cm) square. **$6,500–7,500** *TMe*

A brass lifeboat binnacle, fitted with original oil lamp and compass, c1950, 9in (23cm) high. **$225–255** *Tem*

A brass naval sextant, signed 'J.W. Norie & Co', late 19thC, 8in (20.5cm) index arm. **$900–975** *DN*

An 8-day mantel chronometer, by Thomas Mercer, c1925, 11½in (29cm) high. **$5,250–6,000** *TMe*

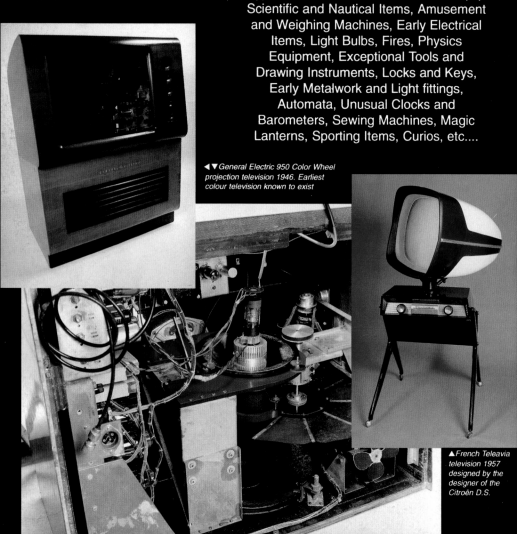

▲A selection of metalwork
17th - 19th Century.

▶Double goffering iron
early 19th Century.

▲EMGs and an Expert gramaphone.

▲Parts of Leoll. The worlds first commercial main
frame computer as supplied to Stewart & Lloyds
in 1957 with associated ephemera.

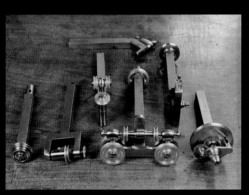

▲A selection of spindles and toolholders by Holtzapffel.

▲Silver plate Naperian coffee maker c.1860.

TV and TV related material bought and sold.

Books available: "Historic Televisions & Video Recorders" ISBN 0-9521057-0-5. World's first book illustrating television design 1936-1982. 64pp 297 x 210mm: 121 col ill. £15 (GB) £18 (elsewhere). "Tv is KING" ISBN 0-9521057-1-3. Specially produced to go with an exhibition at Sotheby's illustrating televisions from 1930-1982. 66pp 297 x 210mm, 120 col ill. £17 (GB) £20 (elsewhere). Credit cards accepted, prices include post and packing. Orders from any bookshop or direct from "Early Technology"

EARLY TECHNOLOGY

Tel: 0131 226 1132 Fax: 0131 665 2839 Mobile: 0831 106768
World Wide Web: www.presence.co.uk/earlytech
E-mail address: earlytech@presence.co.uk

A pair of 15in (38cm) library globes, by John Senex and Benjamin Martin, London, on mahogany stand, restored, the celestial with maker's label of 1740 and updates to 1757, 42in (106.5cm) high.
$45,000–52,000 *CSK*

A 21in (53cm) globe, by Cary, on mahogany stand, early 19thC.
$5,500–6,200 *CSK*

A 15in (38cm) table globe, by Newton & Son, some damage, dated '1849', 28in (71cm) high.
$7,500–8,250 *CSK*

A pair of 12in (30.5cm) celestial and terrestrial globes, by Cary, restored, 1816 and 1812, 35in (89cm) high.
$22,500–27,000 *S(NY)*

A pair of 17in (43cm) mahogany table globes, by Cary, 1800, altered and lacking compasses.
$17,250–20,250 *C*

An 18in (45.5cm) terrestrial globe, by Newton & Son, London, with mahogany stand with horizon circle, some damage, dated '1 January 1850', 44in (111.5cm) high.
$6,500–7,000 *CSK*

A 28in (70cm) terrestrial globe, by Cruchley, late Cary's, restored, c1800.
$9,500–10,500 *S*

A pair of 12in (30.5cm) table terrestrial and celestial globes, by Cary, on mahogany stands, restored, 25in (64cm) high.
$7,000–8,000 *CSK*

An 18in (45.5cm) merchant shipper's globe, by George Philip, 20thC, 48in (122cm) high.
$2,000–2,700 *CSK*

A pair of 12in (30.5cm) table globes, by Cary, the terrestrial showing the routes of Cook, Gore, Pickersgill and others, on mahogany stands, some restorations, 17½in (44.5cm) high.
$6,500–7,000 *CSK*

Regulators

A Viennese regulator, the spring-wound timepiece with pendulum, c1880, 13in (33cm) diam.
$1,600–1,800 *CLC*

A mahogany regulator, made in London, c1820, 73in (185.5cm) high.
$9,750–11,250 *DSP*

A Viennese mahogany striking *grande sonnerie* 8-day regulator, the case with fan top and maple stringing, the enamel dial with engine-turned bezel, c1840, 48in (122cm) high.
$10,500–12,000 *GeC*

A Viennese rosewood veneered striking *grande sonnerie* regulator, in a serpentine case with maple decoration and applied carving, 8-day movement, c1850, 48in (122cm) high.
$9,750–11,250 *GeC*

l. A French 4 glass regulator, the silvered brass dial set into a mask backplate with an aneroid barometer and a temperature gauge, the 8-day movement striking the hour and half-hour on a gong, stamped 'M.S.', c1890, 15in (38cm) high.
$2,250–2,750 *PAO*

A French brass 4 glass regulator, the case inlaid with champlevé enamel, with elaborate inlaid dial, the 8-day movement striking the hours on a gong, the mercury compensated pendulum also inlaid, c1870, 12in (30.5cm) high.
$2,700–3,300 *PAO*

A Vienna walnut miniature wall regulator, the glazed case with arched top and turned finials, the spring-driven single train movement with deadbeat escapement and gridiron pendulum with beat adjustment and indicator, 19thC, 18in (45.5cm) high.
$825–975 *DN*

Watches

A hunter pocket watch, by Waltham, with enamel dial, 15 jewels, separate jewelled bearings and micrometer, c1920, 50mm diam.
$160–200 *PSA*

A silver cased open-face pocket watch, by J. W. Benson, London, c1898, 50mm diam.
$130–150 *PSA*

A verge watch, signed 'Thos. Holmes, Cheadle, 786', the gilt-metal dial with Roman numerals and blued steel hands, the edge inscribed 'Keep me clean and use me well and I to you the truth will tell', maker's mark 'VR', hallmarked Birmingham 1826, 55mm diam.
$600–700 *PT*

A gilt-metal repoussé pair cased verge watch, decorated with a classical scene, signed 'Thos Gardner, London, 1506', the full plate fire gilt movement with square baluster pillars, fusee and chain with worm and wheel barrel setup between the plates, the white enamel dial with Roman and Arabic numerals, later blued steel beetle and poker hands, c1760, 47mm diam.
$750–825 *PT*

An 18ct gold and enamel lady's half hunter lever watch, signed 'Le Roy & Fils, To the Queen, 211 Regent Street, London, 13 & 15 Palais Royal, Paris, 47654', the white enamel dial with black Roman and red Arabic numerals and blued steel hands, the back cover decorated with a monogram in dark blue enamel, signed gold cuvette, c1880, 35mm diam.
$600–660 *PT*

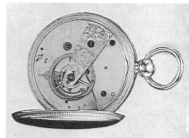

An 18ct gold open-face duplex watch, signed 'Vulliamy London, axxa', with gilt full plate movement, polished steel three-arm balance, the cock engraved with grotesque mask, gold cuvette, silvered matt dial, Roman numerals, eccentric subsidiary seconds, Vulliamy heart-form hands, bezels and reeded band, monogrammed engine-turned case, hallmarked, London 1819, 48mm diam.
$1,800–2,100 *S(NY)*

A gilt-metal pair cased verge watch, the outer covered in horn underpainted with a polychrome village scene, signed 'John Wontner, London, 1325', the full plate fire gilt movement with round pillars, white enamel dial with Arabic numerals and gilt hands, slight damage, c1790, 50mm diam.
$900–1,000 *PT*

A gilt-metal enamel and pearl open-face jump seconds watch, for the Oriental market, with gilt lever movement, bridges engraved overall with foliate scrolls, polished steel balance with halberd style weights, glazed cuvette, white enamel dial, Roman numerals, the case polychrome enamelled, c1850, 61mm diam.
$3,750–4,500 *S(NY)*

A 18ct gold hunter cased dual-time watch, with gilt lever movement, 25 jewels, white enamel dial, 2 eccentric meantime dials, subsidiary seconds dial, engine-turned case with stop slide in the reeded band for independent seconds, some damage, c1830, 52mm diam.
$2,000–2,500 *S(NY)*

A silver cased half hunter pocket watch, with Swiss 17 jewelled movement by Syren, separate jewel bearings, micrometer adjuster to regulator, Birmingham 1923, 50mm diam.
$300–350 *PSA*

A silver open-face keyless lever goliath watch, the white enamel dial with Roman and Arabic numerals, subsidiary dials for day, date and constant seconds with moon phase, c1900, 78mm diam, with a leather-covered desk stand inscribed 'Giraudon, Rue de la Paix, Paris'.
$950–1,000 *CSK*

An 18ct gold quarter repeating watch, with gilt cylinder movement, gold three-arm balance, rack regulator, single hammer repeating on gong, gilt metal cuvette engraved 'Rep.par Breguet', silvered matt chapter ring, Roman numerals, engine-turned centre, subsidiary dials for date, constant seconds and wind indicator arc, engine-turned case, the case stamped with Paris goldmarks for 1798-1809, 55mm diam.
$5,250–6,000 *S(NY)*

A 14ct gold hunter cased quarter repeating automaton watch, signed 'Audemars Frères', with gilt lever movement, bimetallic compensation balance, gold cuvette, central white enamel dial flanked by applied vari-coloured gilt figures of dancing gypsies striking instruments, subsidiary seconds, in an engine-turned case, push repeat, cuvette and case signed, c1900, 56mm diam.
$5,000–5,500 *S(NY)*

A gold keyless open-face split second chronograph pocket watch, dial and movement signed 'Agassiz', No. 254784, the nickel-plated movement jewelled to the centre with bimetallic balance and micrometer regulation, the white enamel dial with Arabic numerals, blued steel spade hands, and subsidiary dials, c1890, 47mm diam.
$1,500–1,800 *C*

> **Miller's is a price GUIDE not a price LIST**

r. A gold and enamel hunter cased pocket watch, signed 'Jacot Brothers, Locle', No. 28625, the gilt bar movement with straight line lever escapement, the white enamel dial with Roman numerals and subsidiary seconds, in engine-turned case with raised decoration highlighted with black enamel, c1890, 43mm diam, with gold and enamel chain, seal and key.
$1,000–1,150 *CSK*

A gold hunter cased quarter repeating independent seconds watch, signed 'Le Roy & Fils, Parish, Palais-Royal 13 and 15', with nickel 2 train lever movement, wound separately by key, bimetallic compensation balance, gold cuvette, white enamel dial, Roman numerals, polished case, lock on band for seconds, cuvette signed, c1870, 52mm diam.
$3,500–4,000 *S(NY)*

A German verge watch, by Herman Neuburg, in repoussé gold pair case, with full plate fire gilt movement with square baluster pillar, push pendant quarter repeating on a bell, the signed gilt champlevé dial with Roman and Arabic numerals, later blued steel hands, c1750, 48mm diam.
$6,750–7,500 *PT*

German watches of this period are now scarce.

Wristwatches

A gold wristwatch, signed 'International Watch Co', with jewelled lever movement No. 1206249, the matt gilt dial with raised alternating Arabic and dagger numerals, sweep centre seconds, the snap-on back with maker's mark No. 1237019, with associated woven gold bracelet and clasp, c1950, 36mm diam.
$975–1,125 *C*

r. A gold chronograph wristwatch, signed 'Eterna', the nickel-plated movement jewelled to the centre with gold alloy balance, the black dial with outer tachymetric and telemetric scales, Arabic numerals, subsidiary dials for running seconds and elapsed minutes, sweep centre seconds, snap-on back numbered '3058285', case and dial signed, c1950, 36mm diam.
$1,125–1,275 *C*

l. A lady's platinum and diamond set wristwatch, signed 'European Watch Co Inc', case No. 4866. 31482, the nickel-plated duo-plan movement with bimetallic balance, 17 jewels, adjusted to temperature and to 2 positions, the matt white dial with Arabic numerals, with flexible platinum and diamond set 2 stranded bracelet and pink gold clasp, movement signed, case numbered, 1920s, 25mm long.
$8,500–9,750 *C*

r. A gentleman's steel wristwatch, signed 'Longines', No. 1956 43, the nickel-plated movement jewelled to the third with bimetallic balance and micrometer regulation, the matt white dial with raised gilt baton numerals, subsidiary seconds, c1930, 43mm long.
$600–750 *C*

A WWII airman's steel chronograph wristwatch, signed 'Glasshutte', the gilt and nickel finished movement No. 200307, mono-metallic compensation balance, the matt black dial with Arabic numerals, subsidiary dials for constant seconds, 30 minute recorder, case No. 207766, c1940, 39mm diam.
$2,000–2,700 *C*

A gentleman's pink gold wristwatch, signed 'Jaeger-LeCoultre', No. 360817, the gilt movement jewelled to the third with gold alloy balance, the white dial with raised pink dagger numerals and subsidiary seconds, pink hands, snap-on back with maker's stamp, c1950, 28mm diam.
$900–1,000 *C*

A white gold asymmetric wristwatch, signed 'LeCoultre', No. 4048, the nickel-plated movement jewelled to the centre with gold alloy balance, the matt white dial with raised dot and dagger indexes, subsidiary seconds, c1950, 38mm long.
$1,275–1,500 *C*

A WWII airman's steel wristwatch, signed 'A. Lange & Sohne, Glasshutte I SA.', No. 211259, the matt gilt movement jewelled to the centre with bimetallic balance and micrometer regulation, the black dial with luminous Arabic numerals and minute ring, luminous hands and sweep centre seconds, with original leather strap, 1940s, 55mm diam.
$2,000–2,500 *C*

r. A lady's 18ct white gold wristwatch, by Hamilton, with diamond surround, c1980, 20mm long.
$975–1,125 *BWC*

r. A lady's 18ct white gold and diamond bracelet watch, signed 'Patek Philippe & Co, Genève', No. 1247513, circular nickel lever movement, gyromax balance, free sprung, 20 jewels, adjusted to heat, cold, isochronism and 5 positions, silvered matt dial, with applied baton numerals, the bezel set with round-cut diamonds and sapphire crystal, case, dial and movement signed, with integrated 18ct white gold Patek Philippe bracelet, c1975, 19mm wide, with fitted leather box.
$5,250–5,750 *S(G)*

A gentleman's pink gold automatic water resistant wristwatch, signed 'Omega, Constellation', the pink gilt movement with 24 jewels, gold alloy balance and micrometer regulation, brushed silvered dial with raised baton numerals, date aperture and sweep centre seconds, case, dial and movement signed, c1950, 34mm diam.
$1,125–1,275 *C*

An airman's steel flyback stopwatch, signed 'Longines Patent', the nickel-plated movement jewelled to the centre with gold balance, the silvered dial with Arabic numerals and subsidiary seconds, 1940s, 33mm diam.
$5,000–5,500 *C*

r. A pink gold triple case water resistant wristwatch, signed 'Patek Philippe', No. 851921, the nickel-plated movement jewelled to the centre with gold alloy balance, the pink dial with raised square quarter hour marks, dot 5 minute indexes and pink gold hands, snap-on back No. 508257, with maker's black leather strap and gold buckle, c1940, 31mm long, presentation box and outer packaging.
$8,000–8,750 *C*

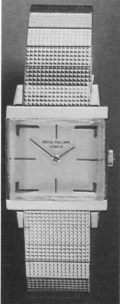

An airman's stainless steel wristwatch, signed 'Longines', the nickel-plated movement jewelled to the centre with gold alloy balance, the matt white dial with Arabic numerals, luminous hands, and sweep centre seconds, snap-on back No. '22384,217', c1940, 33mm diam.
$180–220 *C*

An 18ct pink gold wristwatch and bracelet, signed 'Patek Philippe, Genève', No. 784816, circular nickel lever movement, 18 jewels adjusted to 5 positions, heat, cold and isochronism, free sprung gyromax balance, silvered dial with quarter hour baton numerals, 18ct pink gold Patek bracelet of rectangular engine-turned links, Ref. 3406, case, dial, movement and bracelet signed, c1956, 27mm wide.
$4,000–5,000 *S*

An 18ct gold step-sided wristwatch, signed 'Patek Philippe & Co', No. 832367, octagonal nickel lever movement, 18 jewels adjusted to 5 positions, heat, cold and isochronism, re-finished dial, with Arabic and baton numerals, subsidiary seconds, c1935, 40mm long, with 18ct gold Patek buckle.
$9,750–10,500 *S*

A gentleman's pink gold wristwatch, signed 'Patek Philippe & Co', No. 173132, the frosted gilt bar movement jewelled to the third with bimetallic balance and lever escapement, the white enamel dial with Breguet numerals and blued steel hands, case No. 281503, with maker's leather strap and gold buckle, 1920s, 32mm diam.
$6,500–7,000 *C*

This is an early model of the Patek Philippe Officer's watch using an ebauche by LeCoultre developed in 1922.

An 18ct gold wristwatch, signed 'Patek Philippe & Co', No. 804923, the circular gilt lever movement, with bimetallic compensation balance, the silvered matt dial, with Arabic numerals, with 18ct Patek Philippe buckle, c1925, 37mm long.
$7,000–8,250   *S(G)*

An 18ct pink gold chronograph wristwatch, signed 'Patek Philippe, Genève', No. 868776, with nickel lever movement, precision regulator, mono-metallic compensation balance, 23 jewels, 8 adjustments, silvered matt dial, applied baton and Arabic numerals, 2 subsidiary dials indicating constant seconds and register for 30 minutes, outer ring calibrated for tachometer, Ref. 530, case, dial and movement signed, with 18ct Patek Philippe buckle, c1955, 36mm diam..
$46,000–52,000   *S(G)*

A lady's 18ct white gold and diamond wristwatch, signed 'Patek Philippe & Co', No. 1240342, circular damascened nickel lever movement 20 jewels adjusted to 5 positions, heat, cold and isochronism, grey dial, white baton and Roman numerals, diamond-set bezel, 18ct white gold Patek bracelet, case, dial, movement and bracelet signed, London import mark for 1969, 23mm wide.
$2,700–3,000   *S*

A lady's gold bracelet watch, signed 'Patek Philippe', No. 840739, the nickel-plated movement jewelled to the centre with gold alloy balance, the pink gilt dial with baton numerals, snap-on back No. 628629, with heavy gold bracelet and clasp, c1930, 25mm long, with presentation box.
$5,250–6,000   *C*

A platinum wristwatch, signed 'Patek Philippe & Co, Genève', No. 830223, with silvered dial, blue enamel baton 5 minute divisions to the bezel, c1935, 35mm long.
$13,000–15,000   *C*

A stainless steel water resistant wristwatch, signed 'Rolex', No. 6244, the nickel-plated movement with alloy balance jewelled to the third, the white textured dial with alternating Rolex crown emblem and baton numerals, gold hands and sweep centre seconds, c1930, 32mm diam.
$2,700–3,000   *C*

A 9ct two-colour gold wristwatch, signed 'Rolex, Prince', the nickel-plated extra prima observatory quality movement jewelled to the third and timed to 6 positions, with alloy balance, No. 72878, the two-tone silvered dial with Arabic numerals and subsidiary seconds, hinged back No. 73587, Ref. 971, import mark 'Glasgow 1930', 43mm long.
$6,750–7,500   *C*

A gentleman's gold wristwatch, signed 'Rolex Chronometer', the nickel-plated movement with gold alloy balance, timed to 6 positions, No. E29203, the matt gilt dial with raised gilt baton numerals and sweep centre seconds, Ref. 4364, 1945, 36mm diam.
$2,500–3,000   *C*

r. A lady's 9ct gold wristwatch, signed 'Rolex Precision', with tonneau nickel lever movement, patented superbalance, 17 jewels, silvered matt dial, baton and applied dot numerals, case, dial and movement signed, c1930, 29mm long.
$525–600   *S(G)*

An 18ct gold self-winding sweep seconds wristwatch, signed 'Rolex Oyster Perpetual', with nickel lever movement, white matt dial, applied gold triangular numerals, luminescent hands and aperture for date, water resistant case, Ref. 6105, c1955, 35mm diam.
$2,300–2,700 *S(G)*

A pink gold automatic water resistant wristwatch, signed 'Rolex Oyster Perpetual Date Chronometer', Model No. 1601, the nickel-plated movement with 26 jewels, adjusted to 5 positions and to temperatures, with gold alloy balance No. D59553 the black dial with raised pink baton numerals, date aperture under magnifying glass and sweep centre seconds, 1950s, 36mm diam.
$3,500–3,750 *C*

r. A lady's pink gold and diamond set wristwatch, signed 'Rolex', No. 4489, the nickel-plated movement jewelled to the third, the matt silvered dial with raised pink alternating dagger and Arabic numerals, in pink gold rectangular case with scalloped sides, diamond set lugs, with fluted pink gold and diamond set hinged bracelet and clasp, c1950, 21mm long.
$2,700–3,000 *C*

l. A 9ct pink gold wristwatch, signed 'Rolex', with tonneau nickel lever movement, 17 jewels, patented superbalance, black matt dial, applied Arabic and baton numerals and subsidiary seconds, Ref. 4010, c1935, 38mm long.
$2,500–3,000 *S(G)*

A gold water resistant chronograph wristwatch, signed 'Universal Compur', No. 12482, the gilt movement jewelled to the centre with gold alloy balance No. 210706, the matt silvered dial with Arabic numerals, outer tachymetric scale, subsidiary dials for running seconds and elapsed minutes, sweep centre seconds, late 1950s, 38mm diam.
$2,250–2,750 *C*

A 9ct gold wristwatch, signed 'Rolex', with nickel finished jewelled lever movement, mono-metallic balance, silvered dial with applied Arabic numerals and subsidiary seconds, the case No. 20789 2467, together with a rolled gold associated bracelet and clasp, import mark 'Glasgow 1935', 30mm diam.
$1,800–2,200 *C*

r. A 14ct gold wristwatch, signed 'Rolex Precision', the circular nickel lever movement with 17 jewels, re-finished dial, with Arabic numerals and centre seconds, case, dial and movement signed, c1945, 34mm diam.
$3,000–3,750 *S*

A gold and stainless steel hooded wristwatch, signed 'Rolex Oyster Royal', with nickel lever movement, 17 jewels, timed 6 positions, silvered matt dial, luminescent Arabic numerals and sweep seconds, tonneau water resistant case, the case, dial and movement signed, c1935, 21mm diam.
$5,000–5,500 *S(G)*

A gentleman's gold water resistant wristwatch, signed 'Vacheron & Constantin', the nickel-plated movement with 17 jewels adjusted to temperature, No. 458557, the silvered dial with alternating raised dot and Arabic numerals, inner minute ring and sweep centre seconds, No. 293361, c1950, 32mm diam.
$2,000–2,250 *C*

BAROMETERS

The latest economic recession has brought no lull in demand for antique mercury barometers, particularly the better quality examples.

Barometers simply measure changes in atmospheric pressure – the weight of the atmosphere. High pressure, associated with fine, settled weather, is able to support a longer column of mercury (over 30 inches) than low pressure (around 29 inches or less), typified by unsettled conditions.

Instruments fall into one of two style categories, stick and wheel. Stick barometers display at least part of the mercury column, enabling the current height to be read directly against a register plate. Until the mid-19th century these plates were usually made of brass decorated with a scale that was hand-engraved, filled with black wax and then silvered and lacquered. From around 1840, ivory and then bone became increasingly popular for register plates. Wheel barometers use a simple pulley mechanism that allows a reading to be made on a dial that is usually circular and made of silvered brass.

Significant numbers of barometers were made as scientific instruments, and were used to determine altitude as well as give accurate air pressure readings. However, the vast majority have traditionally served as domestic wall furniture.

Stick barometers were made in England from the latter part of the 17th century, but although wheel barometers, popularised by Italian immigrant workers, did not appear until around 1780, they were then sold in large and growing numbers throughout the 19th century. They enjoyed enormous popularity until supplanted by the cheaper, smaller and more portable aneroid barometer, introduced at the Great Exhibition in 1851.

Stylistically, mercury barometers were as subject to the whims of fashion as more conventional pieces of furniture, principally in the matter of case styles. The choice of wood, embellished by carving or inlay, as well as the overall shape, saw continual fashion-driven changes, both subtle and fundamental.

Walker & Walker

Mercury

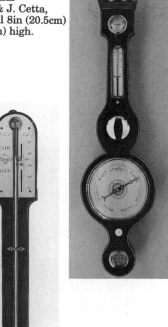

r. A mahogany 5 dial barometer, by J. & J. Cetta, Stroud, c1845, dial 8in (20.5cm) diam, 38½in (98cm) high.
$830–1,000 *ALS*

A George III mahogany stick barometer, the silvered plate and vernier signed 'C. Aiano, fecit', with thermometer to the side and behind a glazed door, the chevron veneered trunk bordered with chequered stringing, c1810, 39in (99cm) high.
$1,800–2,000 *S*

A rosewood wheel barometer, by R. Blakeborough, Ripon, c1830, dial 6in (15cm) diam, 36½in 92.5cm) high.
$1,800–2,000 *W&W*

l. A mahogany stick barometer, with hemispherical cistern cover, by Dollond, London, c1840, 37in (94cm) high.
$2,700–3,000 *W&W*

A figured mahogany bowfronted stick barometer, by Casartelli, Liverpool, with ivory plates, c1850, 39½in (100.5cm) high.
$4,500–5,250 *W&W*

A carved walnut stick barometer, by Boxell, Brighton, with ivory scales, c1850, 42in (106.5cm) high. **$1,800–2,000** *W&W*

A tortoiseshell veneered stick barometer, by T. Blunt, London, c1800, 38in (96.5cm) high. **$7,000–8,000** *W&W*

MILLER'S COMPARES . . .

I A figured mahogany bow-fronted stick barometer, signed 'Callaghan, London', with staged pediment above engraved ivory dials and vernier, insert with fahrenheit mercury thermometer with ivory scale, terminating in mahogany urn-shaped cistern cover, c1850, 39in (99cm) high. **$3,700–4,500** *W&W*

II A flame mahogany bow-fronted stick barometer, signed 'Dollond, London', with staged pediment above engraved silvered-brass register plate and vernier, ebony strung and inset with silvered brass fahrenheit mercury thermometer, terminating in an ebonised cistern cover, c1850, 39in (99cm) high. **$5,250–6,000** *W&W*

These two stick barometers are apparently similar, however, *item II* has several significant features which make it generally a more desirable barometer. The cistern cover is ebonised rather than plain mahogany. The case is also wider and more imposing and the register plate is silvered-brass, a feature which is particularly popular with collectors. *Item I* has ivory scales and plates with typically less fine and defined engraving. In general terms, these appeared after 1840 and, therefore, denote a later piece. *Item II* has an overall appearance of a much more impressive domestic instrument, and as such in some cases will command as much as **$1,500 difference in price.** *W&W*

A George II mahogany stick barometer, signed 'George Doncaster, Halifax fecit', the concealed tube with broken arch brass plates and vernier bordered with wheat ear engraving, c1735, 36¾in (93.5cm) high. **$5,000–6,000** *S*

A mahogany clock barometer, signed 'Della Torre Londra' on the level, the silvered dial with blued steel hand, brass register hand, timepiece with 4in (10.5cm) white enamel dial, Roman chapter, brass hands and verge movement signed 'Willm Terry 430 London', c1815, 48in (122cm) high. **$1,100–1,300** *Bon*

Pediment Styles

The most common styles encountered on mercury barometers include:

Wheel Barometers		Stick Barometers
Usually 1780-1810	Round or Arched Top	Usually 1760-1820 (Silvered brass scales) 1850-1880 (ivory or bone scales)
Commonly 1830-1850 (occasionally 1790-1810)	Swan-neck	Usually 1780-1820
Usually 1790-1830	Break-arch or Architectural	Usually 1770-1840 (1820-40 especially Italian makers)
Usually 1860-1880	Onion Top	
Usually 1850-1870	Scroll-Top	
	Staged	Usually 1850-1880 (also found on bowfronted stick barometers from c1790)

A mahogany barometer, with tulipwood cross-banding and bowed thermometer box, by McAll, Tower Hill, London, c1820, 39in (99cm) high.
$3,000–3,750 *RAY*

An inlaid mahogany wheel barometer, the shaped case with broken moulded cresting, urn finial, inlaid with shells in contrasting woods and outlined with ebony and box stringing, the 8in (20.5cm) silvered dial signed 'A. Mantegani, Wisbech', with thermometer above, c1810, 38¾in (98.5cm) high.
$750–900 *S*

A mahogany wheel barometer, by John Newman, London, with silvered brass scales, c1840, dial 8in (20.5cm) diam, 38in (96.5cm) high.
$1,500–1,800 *PAO*

John Newman exhibited at the Great Exhibition of 1851 and was regarded as the leading scientific barometer maker of his day.

A mahogany and boxwood strung wheel barometer, the case with replaced swan neck pediment above a hygrometer, thermometer and convex mirror, the 8in (20.5cm) silvered dial and level signed 'L. Realini', 19thC, 38½in (98cm) high.
$900–1,000 *P*

A mahogany Sheraton shell barometer, by Mazzuchi & Co., Gloucester, c1820, dial 8in (20.5cm) diam, 39in (99cm) high.
$1,000–1,200 *ALS*

A rosewood brass and mother-of-pearl wheel barometer, signed 'Negretti & Zambra, Instrument Makers to Her Majesty London', c1855, 42½in (108cm) high.
$1,000–1,100 *Bon*

r. A mahogany stick barometer, signed 'J. Testi & Co, Chester', with exposed tube and thermometer, the turned cistern cover outlined with ebony and box spiral stringing, c1810, 38in (96.5cm) high.
$1,500–1,800 *S*

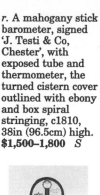

A mahogany stick barometer, signed 'J. Ronchetti, Manchester', with silvered engraved scales, c1810, 36in (91.5cm) high.
$2,250–2,700 *RAY*

A flame mahogany wheel barometer, by Silvani, Brighton, c1830, dial 4½in (11.5cm) diam, 35½in (90cm) high.
$3,000–3,750 *W&W*

l. An Irish stick barometer, by Spears, Dublin, with ivory register plates, c1840, 37in (94cm) high.
$2,700–3,000 *W&W*

A mahogany wheel barometer, with ebony and boxwood stringing, by A. Tacchi, Bedford, c1835, 38in (96.5cm) high.
$900–1,000 *CLC*

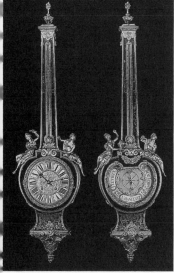

A Régence ormolu-mounted and brass inlaid brown tortoiseshell cartel clock and matching barometer, each spreading shaft enclosing a glass thermometer, the clock numbered according to the *échelle de florence*, with a gilt-bronze decorated dial, movement signed 'Pierre Margotin A Paris' and with altered chiming bells, restored, the barometer numbered according to the Réaumur scale, the Louis XVI dial with enamel cabochon-set outer border, the steel inner dial signed 'Carcani' and inscribed, later door to reverse and some later mounts, c1715, both 45in (114.5cm) high.
$165,000–187,500 *C*

A mahogany clock barometer, the 11¾in (30cm) silvered dial signed 'Mattw Woller, Birmingham', the trunk set with a timepiece, level, thermometer and hygrometer, c1810, 45¾in (116cm) high.
$1,650–2,000 *Bon*

A walnut pillar barometer, the silvered plates inscribed in French within a foliate engraved brass hood with finials to adjust the scales, c1710, 38¼in (97cm) high.
$12,750–14,250 *S*

A mahogany stick barometer, signed 'W. Youle, 79 Leadenhall St, London', the case with swan neck cresting and urn finial, the veneered trunk with a moulded edge, circular cistern cover, c1810, 39in (99cm) high.
$2,700–3,000 *S*

l. A Louis XVI mahogany, gilt bronze, and enamelled barometer and clock, attributed to Weisweiler, both dials signed 'Coteau', one also signed 'Furet à Paris' and with phases of the moon, surmounted by doves, garlands of flowers and vines, the lower section flanked by caryatids, the whole with scrolling mounts, c1785, 23¾in (60cm) high.
$27,750–33,000 *S*

r. A Louis XVI giltwood barometer, with hand painted dial, original thermometer on the dial, c1790, 38in (96.5cm) high.
$5,250–5,700 *RAY*

Aneroid

r. A late Victorian carved oak combination aneroid barometer and clock, the white enamel Roman timepiece dial with steel moon hands, the main register below signed 'Geo. Birley & Co, Worcester', with brass presentation plaque to the terminal, 42in (106.5cm) high.
$1,100–1,300 *CSK*

l. An oak cased aneroid barometer, with concave porcelain dial and exposed movement, c1880, 27in (68.5cm) high.
$530–600 *W&W*

A lacquered-brass cased aneroid barometer, signed 'J. Goldschmid, Zurich', the silvered dial with various altitude scales, with glass cursor, thermometer and sighting tubes, late 19thC, 6in (15cm) long, in a plush-lined case.
$670–830 *CSK*

Barographs

A half size barograph, in an oak case, by Negretti & Zambra, London, c1900, 9in (23cm) wide.
$2,000–2,250 *W&W*

A micro-barograph, by Casella, in a black japanned metal case with bevelled glass, 1950s, 13in (33cm) wide.
$630–750 *RTw*

A brass dial barograph, with a 4½in (11.5cm) silvered chapter and 8 tier vacuum, in an oak and bevelled glass case with drawer below, on bracket feet, 19thC, 14in (35.5cm) wide.
$1,000–1,100 *P*

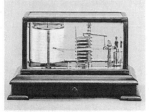

A mahogany barograph, the 8 day movement with lever escapement, the pen controlled by a stack of 8 vacuum discs, signed 'John Davis & Son Ltd, Derby', the base containing a chart drawer, in a glazed cover, c1940, 8½in (21.5cm) wide.
$780–900 *S*

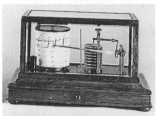

An oak barograph, with 8 aneroid bellows, lacquered brass mechanism and clockwork recording drum, in a bevelled glass case with chart drawer in the base, c1900, 14½in (36.5cm) wide.
$670–750 *Bon*

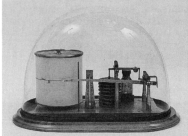

A glass domed barograph, by Richard Frères of Paris, with thermometer, c1912, 13in (33cm) wide.
$830–1,000 *RTw*

SCIENTIFIC INSTRUMENTS

Collecting scientific instruments encompasses a wide scope of interests as the area includes apparatus used in the more popular collecting areas of navigation, surveying, astronomy, microscopy and medicine. Although 18th and early 19th century examples can fetch thousands of pounds, there are still items made in the late 19th and early 20th century that can be purchased for much less. Unlike some collecting areas, prices of scientific instruments have remained steady over the last five years.

The important factors in determining whether a piece is worth buying are the maker (George Adams, Troughton & Simms, the Dollond family and Negretti & Zambra are particularly well-known), condition, and whether it is still in working order. Many instruments come in mahogany cases – look out for vacant compartments within the case as this implies that some of the accessories are missing and will consequently lower the price.

Jon Baddeley

Dials

A silvered brass equinoctial compass sundial, signed, 'J. Long London', with engraved hour circle, lacquered brass spring-loaded gnomon, printed paper compass card and blued needle, the underside of the compass frame inscribed in ink 'Royal Military College, 1852', in mahogany case, lid missing, 5½in (14cm) square.
$850–950 *CSK*

A silver octagonal dial, signed 'Butterfield, Paris', engraved beneath with the latitudes of 30 Continental cities and towns, set with a compass dial and spring-loaded bird gnomon with a degree scale for latitudes, the upper surface engraved with hour scales for latitudes 43°, 46°, 49° and 52°, 18thC, 3¼in (8.5cm) long.
$1,000–1,200 *DN*

A brass universal equinoctial ring dial, with engraved latitude and hour scales, bridge with sliding cursor moving over calendar scale, mid-18thC, 5in (12.5cm) diam.
$1,700–2,000 *S*

l. A French brass universal equinoctial dial, by Auguste Patte, the octagonal dial with silvered compass rose, 2 spirit levels, hinged latitude and hour scale, signed, early 19thC, 5½in (14cm) wide.
$1,125–1,275 *S*

r. An Italian brass mechanical equinoctial dial, signed 'Philipo et Xavier Fratteli De Bianchy 1764 Noᵐ3', the shaped brass base plate with engraved scrolling decoration, levelling screws and sights missing, 10in (25.5cm) long.
$8,500–10,000 *S*

A brass universal equinoctial dial, signed 'Andr. Vogle' on the base, the octagonal dial with engraved decoration, inset glazed compass well, silvered compass, blued needle, folding latitude arc, hour ring with gnomon, and folding plumb bob, the base engraved with the latitude of Augsburg, Paris, Cracaau, Prag, Leipzig and Cölln, late 18thC, 2¾in (7cm) diam.
$900–1,200 *Bon*

A silver octagonal Butterfield type compass dial, signed on the underside 'Martinot à Paris', the horizontal plate with scales for latitudes 40°, 45°, 50° and 55°, the underside engraved with the latitudes of 32 Continental cities and towns, with leather display base, 18thC, 4in (10cm) long.
$2,300–2,700 *CSK*

A brass heliochronometer, by Negretti & Zambra, with hour and calendar scales and sights, on a cast brass stand, c1900, 9in (23cm) high.
$800–900 *S*

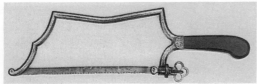

An amputation saw, the shaped frame with blade and trefoil adjusting screw, with ebony handle, 18thC, 18in (45.5cm) long.
$750–850 *CSK*

A surgeon's bone saw, with steel blade in engraved silver plated mount and decorative chased handle, early 19thC, 13in (33cm) long.
$500–600 *S*

A silver apothecary funnel, engraved with monogram, in fitted sycamore case, the screw lid with monogrammed plaque, late 18thC, 4¾in (12cm) long.
$650–750 *CSK*

A brass-cased fleam, stamped with the maker's mark 'I.D.', with floral decoration, in chamois leather-lined domed case, possibly German, late 18thC, 2¾in (70mm) wide.
$320–420 *CSK*

A fleam is a lancet used for letting blood.

A fruitwood monaural stethoscope, incised on the base 'Plowrig', 19thC, 6¾in (17cm) long.
$600–650 *CSK*

A leather-covered brass ear trumpet, with gilded interior and brass ear piece, early 19thC, 8¾in (22cm) long.
$900–1,000 *CSK*

A surgeon's part amputation and field service set, with saws, scalpels, trocars, forceps, catheters, trepanning instruments, swabs, elevators and other items, in brass-bound military pattern mahogany case, possibly by Savigny & Co, 19thC, 18in (45.5cm) wide.
$1,500–1,800 *CSK*

A case of trepanning instruments, the forceps stamped 'Gotzand', the trephine handle with brass attachment and spring catch, 2 trephines, elevator knife and other items, in plush-lined mahogany case, the arrowhead perforator and reamer later replacements, early 19thC, 8in (20.5cm) wide.
$900–1,000 *CSK*

A pair of honed steel razors, by Palmer, the blades stamped with the Royal cipher of crown over 'G.R.', with tortoiseshell guards, in leather-covered card case, inscribed 'Baker Esq', 6½in (16.5cm) long.
$2,500–3,000 *CSK*

With these razors is a label which reads 'These razors were taken from George III when he was deranged, by his physician Sir George Baker, and they were given to me by his grandson, Arthur Baker Esq of ? Blackheath'. This is accompanied by a letter of provenance.

A set of Capron surgeon's instruments, the leather-covered case with brass carrying handle and baize-lined interior, fitted with large tourniquet, Liston knives, bullet extractors, bone brush, large bone saw with chequered ebony handle, elevators, trephine with 2 crown saws, scalpels and other instruments, late 18thC, the case 22½in (57cm) wide.
$4,500–5,500 *S*

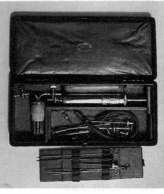

l. A set of surgical drains, in leather-lined case, c1940, 9in (23cm) wide.
$40–60 *ET*

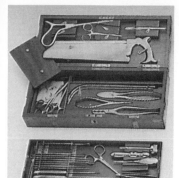

A set of surgeon's instruments, stamped 'Mayer and Meltzer, London', the brass-bound mahogany case fitted with lift-out tray containing Liston knives, trephine, bone saw, catheters and various forceps, late 19thC, 16½in (42cm) long.
$750–850 *S*

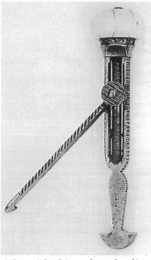

A burnished iron dental pelican, stamped on the lower body 'Leron', with screw adjustment, ivory handle, decorated body and claw shank, 18thC, 5¼in (13cm) long when closed.
$4,000–4,800 *CSK*

A surgeon's part set of trepanning, dental and other instruments, by Stodart, 401 Strand, including bone saw with spine and rosewood handle, 2 trephines with chequer grip ebony handle, finger saw, 4 Liston knives, various trocar and cannulae, bullet forceps, catheters, 2 tourniquet and other items, in red plush-lined fitted brass-bound mahogany case, late 19thC, 14½in (37cm) wide.
$5,200–6,000 *CSK*

A dental extracting key, with turned rosewood handle, single detachable claw and hatched steel bolster, c1840, 5¼in (13cm) long.
$120–150 *CS*

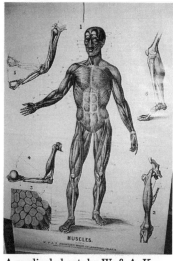

A medical chart, by W. & A. K. Johnston, showing the muscles of the human body, 20thC, 36 x 27in (91.5 x 68.5cm).
$60–80 *ET*

An Edison pattern electric dental drill, c1880, 12½in (32cm) high.
$700–900 *ET*

A Ritter dental X-ray machine, c1910, 86in (218.5cm) high.
$500–600 *ET*

An iron tooth extracting key, with single claw, baluster-turned shank, the crossbar of the handle fashioned for use as chisel and elevator, 18thC, 4¾in (12cm) long.
$750–900 *CSK*

A French phrenology patch box, 'Cranologie du Docteur Gall', the case carved in relief with 3 aspects of the human skull, also with numbers corresponding to the table of human characteristics on the base, mid-19thC, 3in (7.5cm) diam.
$900–1,000 *S*

Meteorological

A zinc plated dial rain gauge, by Callachan & Co, London, early 19thC, 13in (33cm) high.
$550–650 *RTw*

A mahogany cased weather station, by Negretti & Zambra, London, comprising: timepiece, with silvered chapter ring and subsidiary seconds dial to the 8-day fusee movement, aneroid barometer with silvered dial and with attached recording barograph, and maximum and minimum thermometers, all within the mahogany case, the front formerly glazed, 19thC, 26in (66cm) wide.
$2,400–2,700 *CAG*

A swinging plate anemometer, with various scales, by A. W. Gamage, c1925, 8in (20.5cm) high.
$500–600 *RTw*

An American Signal Corps. anemometer, by J. P. Friez & Sons Baltimore, c1942, 20in (51cm) high.
$600–675 *RTw*

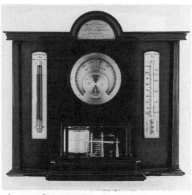

A recording station, by Negretti & Zambra, in mahogany overmantel, c1920, 36in (91.5cm) wide.
$3,800–4,500 *W&W*

A French table thermometer, by Salon Reaumar, c1830, 11½in (29cm) high.
$900–1,000 *MM*

A pocket sympiesometer, by Peovery, London, with ivory plate, vernier and mercury tube, c1850, 7in (18cm) high.
$1,800–2,200 *W&W*

A green and purple gysler lamp, c1870, 12½in (32cm) high.
$230–270 *ET*

A tortoiseshell and ivory thermometer, c1850, 10in (25.5cm) high.
$350–450 *W&W*

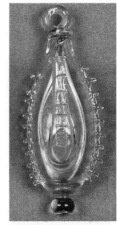

A Dutch glass weather recorder, or 'donderglas', c1820, 7½in (19cm) long.
$350–450 *W&W*

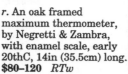

r. An oak framed maximum thermometer, by Negretti & Zambra, with enamel scale, early 20thC, 14in (35.5cm) long.
$80–120 *RTw*

Microscopes

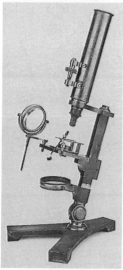

A brass compound monocular microscope, signed 'Abraham, Liverpool', the rectangular section pillar with compass joint at base, rack-and-pinion stage adjustment, fine adjustment to focusing on the body tube, with bull's-eye condenser, 2 objectives, specimen forceps and other items, in a mahogany case, early 19thC, 10½in (26.5cm) wide.
$675–825 *CSK*

A brass compound monocular microscope, by Abraham & Co, focusing by rack-and-pinion and lever and screw, 14½in (37cm) high, in mahogany case with 2 lieberkuhns, 2 oculars and 3 objectives, together with a mahogany case fitted with ten drawers containing a collection of specimen slides, mid-19thC, the case 16in (40.5cm) high.
$900–1,000 *S*

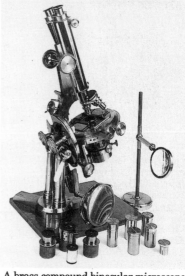

A brass compound binocular microscope, with rack-and-pinion focusing and triple nosepiece, stand signed 'R. & J. Beck, London, No. 11477', in a fitted mahogany box with a quantity of accessories including lenses by J. Swift & Son, Ross, and others, early 20thC, 20in (51cm) high.
$5,000–6,000 *P(S)*

A compound monocular microscope, the stand signed 'R. & J. Beck Ltd, London, 26107', the calibrated body tube with rack-and-pinion coarse and micrometer screw fine focusing, 4 objective attachment, above a stage with specimen finder and scale above a mechanical sub-stage with condenser and micrometer fine focus control, in a mahogany case with a Carl Zeiss binocular attachment and various objectives and oculars, c1880, 14½in (37cm) high.
$2,000–2,400 *S*

A brass and mahogany lucernal microscope, signed 'W. & S. Jones, No 135, Holborn, London', the back with condensing lens and ground glass screen and simple lens on brass support, together with a drawer of accessories including 7 objectives, and a collection of slides, c1795, the case 27½in (70cm) long.
$7,000–8,000 *S*

A brass stage focusing cuff microscope, signed 'Adams, London', with folding tripod foot, square pillar with sliding collar for the plano-concave mirror, rackwork to the wing stage, Bonanni stage, an arm with transverse and rotating movement supporting the body tube, late 18thC, 16¼in (41cm) high, with accessories, in a mahogany box with pasted label 'Earl of Stradbroke'.
$3,000–3,800 *Bon*

r. An ebony, tooled-leather and brass compound microscope, signed 'I. Marshall', the optical tube in 2 pasteboard sections, covered with red leather on the outer and green vellum on the inner, the nosepiece with a 3mm biconvex objective lens in a screw-on cell, the top of the inner with a 30mm biconvex field lens, the eyepiece with a 26mm biconvex eye lens, dust cap missing, c1710 12in (30.5cm) high.
$31,500–37,500 *CSK*

John Marshall (1663–1725), a Freeman of the Turners' Company in the City of London, was the best-known optical instrument maker of his day, producing by 1693 his famous large compound microscope with an inclining joint in the form of a ball-and-socket. He also sold large multi-draw terrestrial telescopes.

A lacquered-brass compound monocular microscope, signed 'Powell & Lealand, London', with rack-and-pinion focusing, double nosepiece sub-stage condenser, specimen forceps and various accessories, plano-concave mirror, with accessory case, in a mahogany carrying case, 19thC, 17in (43cm) high.
$750–850 *CSK*

A lacquered-brass compound monocular microscope, signed 'M. Pillischer, London, No. 371', with rack-and-pinion focusing, mechanical stage, sub-stage condenser and plano-concave mirror, with 3 eyepieces, 3 objectives, live box, specimen forceps and other items, in a mahogany case, 19thC, 17in (43cm) high.
$750–850 *CSK*

A universal rotating and inclining compound binocular microscope, signed 'Ross London 5437', with rack-and-pinion coarse focusing, long screw and shank fine focusing, calibrated swinging stage and mechanical sub-stage, condenser above a plano/concave mirror, with accessories including 2 pairs of oculars, 8 numbered objectives, and 4 piece objective holder, c1880, 20½in (52cm) high.
$30,000–33,000 *S*

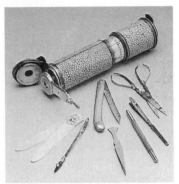

A combined microscope and étui, signed 'Ribright Optician Fecit London', and 'By Ye Kings Royal Patent', the pink ray skin covered pocket case with silver mounts opening to a set of implements, the hinged section at the end with lens, lieberkuhn and stage, late 18thC, 4½in (11.5cm) long.
$6,500–7,500 *S*

A French lacquered-brass compound monocular microscope, signed 'F. Villette Opticien du Prince à Liège', the eyepiece with primary lens, the extension tube with lens, mounted on a pillar support with fine screw focusing adjustment, the pillar fixed to a pair of scroll and quadrant limbs with cross stretcher incorporating a mirror, on a plinth base with accessory drawer containing 5 numbered objectives, 8 point specimen carrier and other items, some damage to lenses, in a stained wood carrying case, 18thC, 17in (43cm) high.
$18,750–21,000 *CSK*

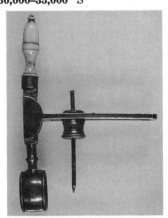

A botanist's brass and ivory folding pocket microscope, c1775, 2in (50mm) long.
$150–180 *CS*

An Italian compound microscope, in tiger wood, pasteboard covered in green vellum, black leather and gilded brass, signed and dated 'François Baillou à Milan L'Année 1738', in a leather covered case, microscope 4¾in (12cm) high.
$13,500–15,000 *CSK*

This microscope is one of only eight known instruments with Baillou's signature, and apart from one compound microscope similar to the large Marshall microscopes, all the other six are telescopes or opera glasses.

r. A Culpeper type compound monocular microscope, the turned lignum vitae body tube having a threaded eyepiece and velum draw tube with leather covering and sleeve of grey-dyed ray skin, on a base with a drawer containing accessories, mid-18thC, 16¼in (41.5cm) high, in an oak case.
$8,500–9,500 *S*

Surveying & Drawing

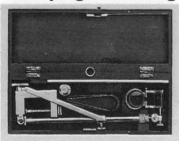

A lacquered-brass camera lucida, signed on the clamp 'Dollond, London', with telescopic arm, steadying bars, prism and 2 lenses, in a fitted mahogany case arranged with a brass tie bar to fold open and flat for use as a sketching surface, 19thC, the case 9½in (24cm) wide.
$375–450 *CSK*

The camera lucida was attached to a microscope or other instrument so that the image and drawing surface could be viewed simultaneously, thereby facilitating the sketching of the image.

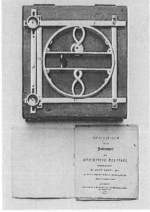

A brass ellipsograph, signed 'Farey Invt, London', with instruction booklet dated '1812', in a plush lined and fitted mahogany case, compass missing, 6in (15cm) wide.
$1,500–1,700 *CSK*

r. A pair of brass drawing proportional dividers, signed 'W. & S. Jones, London', with fine screw adjustment, engraved scales, in a plush-lined fishskin covered case, early 19thC, 7¼in (18.5cm) long.
$375–450 *CSK*

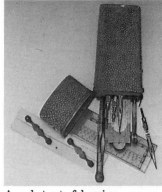

A pocket set of drawing instruments, by George Adams, signed, the shagreen-covered case fitted with a hinged parallel rule, brass and ivory sector, compass, dividers and accessories, late 18thC, 6¾in (17cm) high.
$1,000–1,200 *S*

A lacquered-brass drum sextant, signed 'Cary, London', with silvered scale, vernier and magnifier, telescope with variable eyepiece, draw tube focusing and 2 shades, the screw-on cover forming the base engraved 'J. R. Young, 1st Prize for Military Surveying Royal Military College, December 1871', 19thC, 3in (7.5cm) diam, in an ebony strung fitted mahogany case, 4¾in (12cm) wide.
$900–1,000 *CSK*

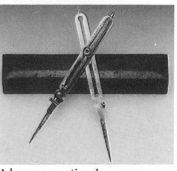

A brass proportional compass, signed 'Thomas Jones & Sons, 62 Charing Cross London', with engraved scale and milled screw adjustment, in a mahogany case, late 18thC, 8¾in (22cm) long.
$450–525 *S*

A boxwood moon phase slide rule, signed 'Nat Smith Fecit', the 6 double-sided sliders with stamped phase scales, the base with calendar scale for a 4 year period, with 3 brass mounts, 18thC, 9¼in (23.5cm) long.
$2,700–3,100 *CSK*

A pair of German gilt brass compasses, signed and dated 'C.S.S.: 1587', with iron points, one unscrewing for a pen, a square-sectioned column engraved with the four seasons, four elements, four humours, four properties and the zodiac, topped by the globe, engraved with the equator, marked every 10° to 360°, tropic of Cancer, arctic circle and ecliptic circle, the legs opening to reveal 2 sets of scales, late 16thC, 7½in (19cm) radius.
$127,500–142,500 *CSK*

Christoph Schißler Senior was a renowned precision instrument maker of Augsburg. His workshop had an immense level of production, specialising in sundials, astronomical compendia, gunners' compendia and armillary spheres.

l. A patent omnimeter, signed 'Elliot Bros, London' and 'Eckholds Patent Omnimeter 206', with telescope, rack focus, level, silvered vertical circle, twin silvered verniers and magnifiers, periscope, cross bubble all on A-frame, with level, micrometer, enclosed horizontal silvered circle, on 3-screw tripod base, late 19thC, 17¾in (45cm) high, with accessories in a mahogany case.
$1,300–1,500 *Bon*

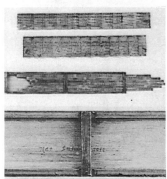

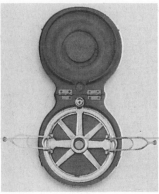

A brass swinging arm protractor, signed on the adjustment arm 'Troughton & Simms, London' with 'East India Company' trademark, the folding arms with pins, with rack-and-pinion adjustment, silvered circle scale and 2 verniers, the centre glass etched with a centre point cross, in a shaped mahogany case, 19thC, 7¼in (18.5cm) long.
$675–750 *CSK*

A quill cutter, signed 'G. Adams, No. 60 Fleet Street London' on the face, with steel key, c1770, 2¼in (58mm) high, in a green shagreen case with red velvet lining.
$3,600–4,200 *Bon*

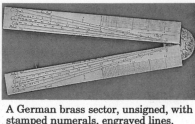

A German brass sector, unsigned, with stamped numerals, engraved lines, scale divisions, symbols and labels, comparisons for 'Rheinland, London, Rome, Paris' inches, the hinge decorated with acorn and foliate design, 17thC, 19⅝in (50cm) long unfolded.
$3,750–4,500 *CSK*

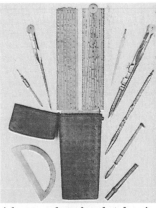

A brass and steel pocket drawing set, by Watkins & Hill, Charing Cross, with boxwood sector and scale rule, and brass protractor, in a fishskin covered case, 19thC, 6⅜in (17cm) long.
$530–600 *CSK*

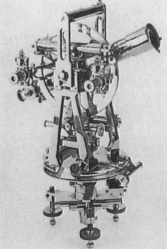

A polished brass transit theodolite, by Cary, London, the telescope with rack-and-pinion focusing, micrometer eyepiece with fine adjustment, lens hood and dust slide, the trunnion counter weight and 7in (18cm) vertical circle with graduated bubble level and twin micrometer magnifiers with axis on the twin A-frame supports over the horizontal plate with level, the chamfered silvered scale with twin verniers and magnifiers on 3-screw tripod mounting incorporating a trough compass, 19thC, 17¼in (44cm) high.
$1,500–1,800 *CSK*

An oxidised brass transit theodolite, signed 'Keuffel & Esser Co, New York' on the silvered compass dial, the telescope with rack-and-pinion adjustment, graduated bubble level, engraved 4in (10cm) vertical circle with silvered scale and vernier, supported on 2 A-frames from the horizontal plate with enclosed circle, level and cross bubble, with fine vernier adjustment, on 4-screw tripod attachment, in a fitted case with maker's metal label stamped '24058', late 19thC, 13¾in (35cm) high.
$900–1,000 *CSK*

A German brass theodolite, signed 'Neuhofer & Sohn Kohlmarkt 8', the telescope with rack-and-pinion focusing and a quarter circle of degrees with silvered scale, vernier and magnifier, scale divided 50-0-50, above a horizontal circle with twin verniers and magnifiers, late 19thC, 13in (33cm) high.
$1,000–1,100 *S*

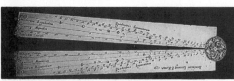

A brass sector, signed 'Dominicus Lusuerg F. Romae 1730', both sides finely engraved with scales, 16⅝in (42.5cm) long opened.
$3,400–4,200 *Bon*

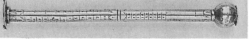

A silver penner, unsigned, divided into 6 sections for use as a compass, with hinged cover, a pen-nib guard, a writing pen, a pocket knife and pencil, a pencil guard and an ink cistern forming the base, engraved with a coat-of-arms, the whole engraved with foliate decoration and linear scales with stamped numerals, 17thC, 5¾in (14.5cm) long.
$3,000–3,750 *CSK*

Telescopes

A brass 1⅝in (45mm) 3-draw refracting telescope, signed 'Abraham Optician, 7 Bartlett St, Bath', the mahogany body tube with draw tube focusing, raised on a pillar folding tripod stand with screw clamp, in a fitted mahogany case with trade label, 19thC, 10½in (26.5cm) wide.
$530–600 *CSK*

A 2¾in (70mm) refracting telescope, signed on the backplate 'Adams, London', with tapering mahogany body tube, rack-and-pinion focusing and lens cap, raised on a tapering pillar support and tripod stand, the cabriole legs terminating in pad feet, 19thC, tube 43in (109cm) long.
$830–900 *CSK*

A brass monocular microscope, No. 9, by Arnold & Sons, London, with rack-and-pinion focusing, in a fitted mahogany case with additional oculars, objectives and other accessories, 19thC, 14¼in (36cm) high.
$375–450 *Bea*

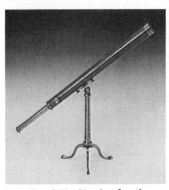

A Newtonian 8in (20.5cm) reflecting telescope-on-stand, the cast iron and brass-mounted tube mounted with sighting telescope, on a heavy cast iron columnar support with maker's plaque engraved 'John Browning, London', together with a case of 6 eyepieces, signed, and other accessories, late 19thC, tube 72in (183cm) long.
$850–1,000 *S*

A Dollond 2in (5cm) refracting telescope, the mahogany body tube with rack-and-pinion focusing, 2 eyepieces and extension tube, on a cabriole leg tripod stand, in a fitted case, c1800, telescope 29in (74cm) extended.
$1,650–2,000 *S*

A brass 3¼in (8.5cm) refracting astronomical telescope-on-stand, signed 'Negretti and Zambra', with a leather-bound body, 3-draw tubes, rack-and-pinion focusing, star finder and tripod with fitted clamp to the body tube, in a fitted mahogany carrying case with 2 eyepieces, early 20thC, telescope 20in (51cm) long.
$1,000–1,200 *S*

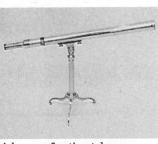

A brass refracting telescope on stand, with rack-and-pinion focusing, on a folding tripod base, in a fitted mahogany case with sunken handles and accessories, early 19thC, tube 32¼in (82cm) long.
$750–900 *Bea*

A lacquered-brass 4in (10cm) telescope, with 57in (145cm) body tube in 2 stages, rack-and-pinion and draw tube focusing, lens cap, 4 eyepieces and a sighting telescope, in a pine box with a wood tripod, 19thC.
$1,500–1,800 *DN*

A lacquered-brass 2½in (6.5cm) reflecting telescope, by James Short, London, numbered '1741 114/306=9.5', the 14in (35.5cm) tube with speculum mirrors and screw rod focusing, on tapered pillar with knuckle joint attached by a plate to an oak carrying case, mid-18thC, 17¼in (44cm) long.
$1,650–2,000 *P*

Weighing & Measuring Equipment

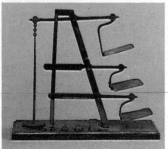

A set of 10 brass imperial measures, made for the County of Surrey, measuring from a bushel to a half gill, the larger measures with shaped handles, dated '1825', bushel 19½in (49.5cm) diam.
$7,000–7,800 *S*

A ladder scale, the brass frame stamped 'De Grave Short & Co, London', with stepped 5 settings and 5 numbered weights fitted into the wooden base, mid-19thC, 13½in (34.5cm) high.
$1,650–2,000 *S*

r. A Japanese gold beam balance, the bronze pans supported on a wooden beam between 2 collapsible uprights and mounted on a wooden cabinet with drawers, wrought iron handles and 7 bronze weights, c1790, 29in (73.5cm) wide.
$1,300–1,500 *S*

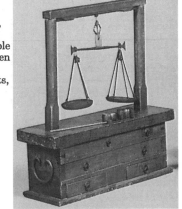

A set of 7 bronze standard bell-shaped weights, by De Grave, Short & Fanner, London, set No. 1264 for the County of Ayr, dated '1859', stamped with numerous proof marks for 56lbs, 28lbs, 14lbs, 7lbs, 4lbs, 2lbs and 1lb, 19thC.
$2,000–2,250 *CSK*

r. A Japanese gold beam balance, with brass pans supported on a wrought iron folding bracket and mounted on a brass-bound hardwood case with drawers and 15 brass weights, c1850, 23¼in (59cm) wide.
$900–1,000 *S*

A set of 6 imperial standard bronze measures, by Bate, London, made for the County of Middlesex, with hardwood side handles, inscribed 'Middlesex' and 'London County Council', and Victorian and later Excise marks, mid-19thC.
$3,400–4,200 *B*

A set of 7 bronze standard cylindrical measures, each engraved 'London County Council, Kent, No. 19', for gallon, half gallon, quart, pint, half pint, gill and half gill, each stamped '1405', 19thC.
$1,300–1,400 *CSK*

Miscellaneous

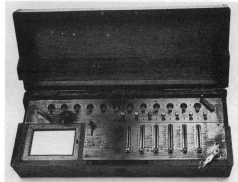

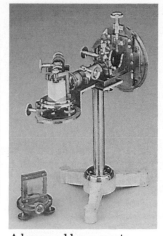

An arithmometre, No 1462, the oak case with brass mechanism inscribed 'Thomas de Colman, Inventeur, 44 Rue d'Chateaudun, Paris' and 'Prudential Assurance Co Ltd,' c1877, 18½in (47cm) wide.
$1,500–1,800 *HDS*

The arithmometre was invented in 1810, and was the first multiplication instrument to be made commercially. At the time it was a breakthrough for technology, but as the costs of production were so high only around 100 were manufactured each year. However, the design proved to be a successful one and the machines were produced well into the 20th century.

A lacquered brass spectro-analysis instrument, by A. Hilger, London, with 2 telescopes, rack-and-pinion adjustment mechanical circuit adjustment, prism and some accessories, with brass and iron pillar and tripod stand, in a plush lined fitted pine case, late 19thC, 14in (35.5cm) wide.
$1,350–1,500 *CSK*

A triple-globe vacuum demonstration apparatus, unsigned, with lacquered-brass fittings, and spreading foot, 19thC, 13¾in (35cm) high.
$250–300 *CSK*

l. A brass goniometer, signed 'Cary London' with engraved scale and vernier read-out, with twin adjusting wheels, raised on an inverted V-frame, on mahogany plinth base (cut at edge), with plush-covered ebonised base and glass dome, early 19thC, 7¼in (18.5cm) high.
$5,000–5,700 *CSK*

This machine was used for measuring the angles between the faces of a crystal.

A brass calendar for the year 1688, signed 'E. C. fecit', probably for Edward Culpeper, engraved on both faces with scales for calendar, zodiac signs, saints days, and lettered 'Easter 1688, Key=Day South Epact', dated '1688', 2½in (6.5cm) diam.
$3,000–3,300 *S*

A Swedish Hagelin encryption machine, No 4048, Type 0489A, with a winding handle, 6 rotors, numbered cylinder with various settings against a numbered scale divided 1-0-6, 3 digit counter, double tape printer and inking roller, in a lidded fitted case with 2 paper tapes, tweezers, screwdriver, and 2 cylinders containing spare inking rollers, c1950, 8in (20.5cm) wide.
$560–675 *S*

A Dollond 'Dr Brewster's Patent' kaleidoscope, signed, the red morocco-bound tube with adjustment to the mirrors by rack-and-pinion, with accessories and 5 glass and brass discs containing various shapes and coloured glass, one missing, c1850, 7½in (19cm) wide.
$5,000–6,000 *S*

An ornamental turning lathe, signed 'J. Evans & Son, maker No. 957, 104 Wardour Street, Soho, London', with double mahogany frame, 4 tool drawers, iron bed, treadle gear and fitted with an electric motor, various boring tools and cutters, in a fitted box, early 19thC, 42in (106.5cm) wide.
$6,000–6,750 *Bon*

MARINE
Charts & Pictures

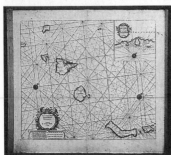

A double page engraved chart,
'Canaria, Tenerifa, Forteventura',
by Hendrick Doncker,
Amsterdam, with outline colours,
laid down on linen, c1680,
16½ x 19½in (42 x 49.5cm).
$530–600 *S*

A double page engraved chart,
'Oost Indien', by Hendrick
Doncker, Amsterdam, showing
the outline of Australia, c1680,
16½ x 19½in (42 x 49.5cm).
$2,000–2,300 *S*

A woolwork picture, portraying
HM *Victoria & Albert*, with
3 paddle steamers in the
foreground, mid-19thC,
24 x 31in (61 x 78.5cm).
$4,000–4,500 *S*

Chronometers

A two-day marine chronometer
by Wempe, c1945, case
7¼in (18.5cm) square.
$750–900 *TMe*

A two-day marine chronometer,
by Joseph Sewill of Liverpool, with
2 prize medal award cartouche
panels for 1862 and 1867, all in a
mahogany three-piece case, with
a key, 7½in (19cm) wide.
$2,700–3,000 *P(HSS)*

A two-day marine chronometer
by Barraud, c1820,
5¼in (13.5cm) square.
$6,750–8,250 *TMe*

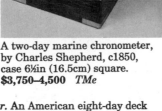

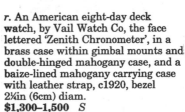

A two-day marine chronometer,
by Fletcher, c1845,
6½in (16.5cm) square.
$3,750–4,500 *TMe*

A chronometer, by James
Murray, Royal Exchange,
London, the engraved silvered
dial with seconds and up/down
subsidiary dials, numbered '547',
mounted in gimbals and housed
in a square two-stage mahogany
case with carrying handles,
19thC, 7½in (19cm) wide.
$3,750–4,500 *P(C)*

A two-day marine chronometer,
by Charles Shepherd, c1850,
case 6½in (16.5cm) square.
$3,750–4,500 *TMe*

r. An American eight-day deck
watch, by Vail Watch Co, the face
lettered 'Zenith Chronometer', in a
brass case within gimbal mounts and
double-hinged mahogany case, and a
baize-lined mahogany carrying case
with leather strap, c1920, bezel
2¼in (6cm) diam.
$1,300–1,500 *S*

Figureheads & Carvings

l. A carved and polychromed oak hancing piece, depicting Ajax, late 18thC, 83in (211cm) high.
$45,000–52,500 *S*

A hancing piece was a form of ship's decorative carving used to enhance the step from one level to another. This could be from the poop to upper deck or in this case probably used to decorate the starboard stern quarters as the base has been made to slightly tilt the figure forward and to the right.

r. A carved wood ship's figurehead, with rope decoration, 19thC, 28in (71cm) high.
$2,500–3,000 *S*

A carved and painted sailor's trade figure, depicting Billy Budd, probably American, late 19thC, 82in (208.5cm) high.
$50,000–57,000 *S(NY)*

A carved and painted wooden figurehead, depicting a woman wearing a feathered bonnet and sash, late 19thC, 40in (101.5cm) high.
$5,000–6,000 *S*

Foghorns

A ship's foghorn, the olive-green painted cylindrical metal case with hand plunger and horn mounted at the side, mid-19thC, 27in (68.5cm) high.
$660–700 *S*

A ship's brass foghorn, with hand plunger, cylindrical case with shaped trumpet at the side, c1900, 29in (73.5cm) high.
$850–1,000 *S*

Lamps

A brass Bialaddin storm lamp, model No. 300X, c1940, 13in (33cm) high.
$60–70 *HEM*

A chrome anchor oil lamp, c1940, 13in (33cm) high.
$80–90 *HEM*

r. A brass tilley lamp, with enamel top, c1940, 13½in (34.5cm) high.
$60–70 *HEM*

l. A brass bulkhead electric lamp, c1960, 11in (28cm) diam.
$90–100 *Tem*

A copper signal lamp, with original oil burner, c1880, 14in (35.5cm) high.
$230–270 *Tem*

A brass and glass ship's companion-way lamp, c1960, 7in (18cm) high.
$90–100 *Tem*

A copper glass and brass gas trawling lamp, c1960, 14in (35.5cm) high.
$130–160 *Tem*

A Trinity House copper and brass mooring buoy gas lamp, c1950, 21in (53.5cm) high.
$300–375 *Tem*

Marine Barometers

r. A mahogany marine barometer, the concealed tube with angled bone plates and vernier, signed 'Cox, Devonport', enclosed by a door applied with a thermometer, the case with cushion cresting and brass cylindrical cistern cover, damaged, mid-19thC, 37in (94cm) high.
$2,000–2,500 *S*

l. A marine barometer, signed 'Mangave à Bordeaux', with silvered plates and adjustable vernier, mahogany case with cylindrical cistern, brass bracket and gimbals, mid-19thC, 39in (99cm) high.
$3,000–3,600 *S*

Model Ships

A half block model of a merchant ship, with laminated pine hull, mounted on a mahogany backboard, late 19thC, 38in (96.5cm) long.
$550–600 *S*

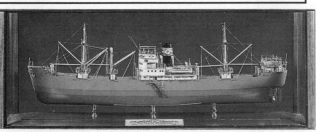

A model of the cargo vessel SS *Oslo*, with gilt brass fittings, in a mahogany case with maker's plaque detailing specifications of builders Short Brothers Ltd of Sunderland, mid-20thC, 40in (101.5cm) long.
$8,600–9,750 *S*

A display model of a fishing smack, c1910, 45in (114.5cm) long.
$450–530 *Tem*

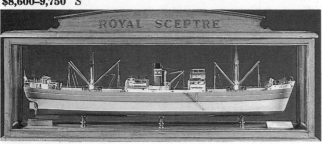

A model of the steel screw steamer *Royal Sceptre*, built for Hall Brothers Steam Ship Company Ltd, Newcastle Upon Tyne, the wooden hull painted grey and pink with brass screw and deck details, in a glazed mahogany case, the double arched pediment with name repeated in brass, c1937, case 60in (152.5cm) long.
$5,250–6,000 *S*

A French prisoner of war bone model of a 42-gun ship of the line, the pinned and planked hull with horn strakes, on an ebonised wood stand, early 19thC, 13in (33cm) long, in a later glazed display case.
$3,750–4,500 *S*

Navigational Instruments

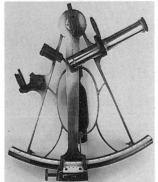

A ship's bearing compass, with pivoted compass card, in a brass drum case, with circular silver scale, 2 verniers, sights and filters, in gimbal mounts and mahogany carrying case, late 19thC, 9in (23cm) diam.
$1,300–1,500 *S*

A German brass lattice frame octant, signed 'R. Jmme Berlin 619', pinhole and telescope sight, bone vernier, tangent screw and clamp, 2 mirrors, 2 sets of shades and mahogany grip, mid-19thC, 9½in (24cm) radius.
$1,000–1,200 *Bon*

A ship's brass direction finder, by Alex Dobbie & Son, in a brass case with carrying handles and dome above, damaged, late 19thC, 15in (38cm) high.
$750–830 *S*

r. A Somalvico ebony octant, with ivory scale vernier and maker's plaque, peephole sight and one set of coloured filters, in a shaped mahogany case, early 19thC, 10in (25.5cm) radius.
$830–1,000 *S*

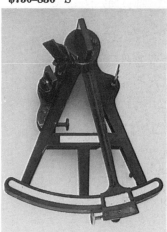

l. A Chadburns brass and glass propeller revolution indicator, c1940, 5in (12.5cm) diam.
$90–100 *Tem*

l. A brass and glass compass, marked 'Veb GRW Teltow', c1940, 5¼in (13cm) diam.
$90–100 *Tem*

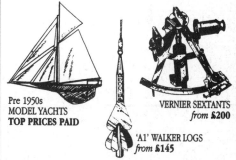

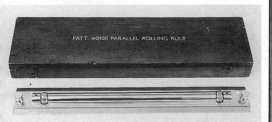

A brass parallel rolling rule, pattern No. 160100, c1960, 19in (48.5cm) long.
$110–120 *Tem*

A set of nickel-plated proportional dividers, in a fitted box, c1950, 10in (25.5cm) long.
$50–60 *Tem*

A Spencer Browning rust ebony quadrant, with 2-0-129 degree scale, mirrors and maker's plaque missing, in an oak case, early 19thC, 15in (38cm) radius.
$2,500–3,000 *S*

A John Stancliffe brass sextant, signed, with angled and silvered scale and vernier, tangential screw adjustment to the index arm, magnifier, 2 sets of coloured filters, detachable telescope mount and 2 telescopes, faceted mahogany handle, in a shaped mahogany case with accessories, early 19thC, 5in (12.5cm) radius.
$5,500–6,300 *S*

A mahogany Hadley's quadrant, with boxwood scale and vernier, peephole sight, horizon glass and reflector, c1770, 15½in (39.5cm) radius.
$1,300–1,500 *S*

A marine micrometer sextant, standard naval pattern, in a fitted box, c1960, 11in (28cm) wide.
$675–750 *Tem*

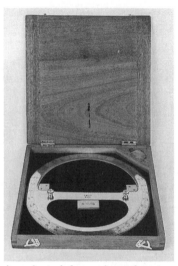

A navigator's brass circumferentor, with carrying case, c1950, 13in (33cm) diam.
$100–120 *Tem*

A Kelvin Hughes star globe, 1975, case 10½in (26.5cm) square.
$900–1,000 *Tem*

Miscellaneous

l. A ship's brass bell, engraved 'Manx Maid', late 19thC, mouth 16in (40.5cm) diam.
$600–675 *S*

r. A scrimshaw whale's tooth, entitled 'Nelson Ship Victory', engraved, chips to base, mid-19thC, 6¾in (17cm) high.
$2,500–3,000 *S*

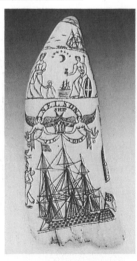

An engraved scrimshaw sperm whale tooth, signed 'R. Sherman, Wilmington', dated '1850', the obverse engraved with a stylised figure of a lady with an American flag entitled 'Carolina', 6in (15cm) high.
$2,250–2,700 *S(NY)*

r. A scrimshaw cow horn, decorated with a portrait of a merchant ship and lettered 'From Heareas Shepperd 80 Reg To W. A. Brown Carpenter Ship China', mid-19thC, 19in (48.5cm) long.
$480–560 *S*

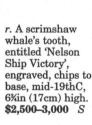

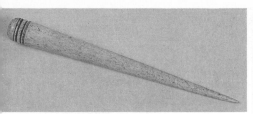

A whalebone fid, used for rope splicing at sea, early 19thC, 18in (45.5cm) long.
$1,300–1,450   *AEF*

A line throwing gun, made by Schermully, c1900, 23in (58.5cm) long.
$225–250   *Tem*

Miller's is a price GUIDE not a price LIST

A pair of double telescope binoculars, by Negretti & Zambra, c1890, 7in (17.5cm) long.
$225–270   *ET*

A painted papier mâché snuffbox, decorated on the lid with a portrait of a brig, lettered on the front 'Caledonia, built at Dumbarton 1850', mid-19thC, 2½in (6.5cm) long.
$1,100–1,200   *S*

An oak and ebony display barometer, c1890, 16in (40.5cm) wide.
$375–450   *Tem*

A brass naval gunsight, c1920, 20in (51cm) long.
$225–270   *Tem*

A chrome naval Officer of the Watch telescope, sun shade missing, c1950, 13in (33cm) long.
$90–100   *Tem*

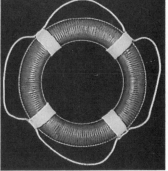

A teak and brass ship's wheel, by John Hastie, c1900, 36in (91.5cm) diam.
$550–600   *Tem*

A Sankey Biston patent copper life buoy, the ribbed copper life belt with rope hand holds, mid-19thC, 28in (71cm) diam.
$260–300   *S*

A brass ship's bulkhead clock, by E. & E. Emanuel, marked 'The Hard, Portsea, 1868', 5in (12.5cm) diam.
$450–530   *Tem*

A brass speaking trumpet, the single draw telescopic tapering tube with shaped mouthpiece and circular mouth, early 19thC, 39¼in (99.5cm) long.
$850–1,000   *S*

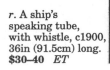

r. A ship's speaking tube, with whistle, c1900, 36in (91.5cm) long.
$30–40   *ET*

CAMERAS

A kingwood photograph viewer, with enlarging mirror, 1880, 14in (35.5cm) wide.
$250–300 *ET*

Camera Condition

Some of the cameras in this section have a condition code which relates to the table below. The first digit refers to cosmetic condition and the second to mechanical condition. A good/average camera will score 5F. The condition class given is only a guide to the AVERAGE condition of a piece. Specific defects may be noted.

Cosmetic

0 – New, never used, sold with warranties.

1 – As new. No warranty but with box or original packaging.

2 – No signs of wear. No packaging.

3 – Very minimal signs of wear.

4 – Signs of light use, but not misuse. No other cosmetic damage.

5 – Complete, but showing signs of normal use or age.

6 – Complete, but showing signs of heavy use. Well used.

7 – Restorable. Some refinishing necessary. Minor parts may be broken or missing.

8 – Restorable. Refinishing required. May be missing some parts.

9 – For parts only or major restoration.

Mechanical

A – As new, functioning perfectly, with factory and/or dealer warranty.

B – As new, functioning perfectly, but not warranted.

C – Everything functioning, recently cleaned or overhauled, and guaranteed.

D – Everything functioning, major functions professionally tested.

E – Everything functioning, major functions professionally tested.

F – Not recently cleaned, lubricated or overhauled. Accuracy of shutter or meter not guaranteed.

G – Fully functioning. Shutter speeds and/or meter probably not accurate. Needs adjusting or cleaning only.

H – Usable, but not fully. Shutter may stick on slow speeds. Meter may not work.

J – Not usable without repair or cleaning. Shutter meter, film advance may be stuck, jammed or broken.

K – Probably not repairable.

A mahogany and brass biunial magic lantern, with black metal chimney, rack and thumbscrew focusing and screw carrier mounts, converted to electric illumination, on base with ebonised edging, some damage, 19thC, 27½in (70cm) high, with painted pine carrying case.
$900–1,000 *Bea*

A quarter plate wooden body Royal Mail camera, by W. Butcher & Son, with 15 lenses, c1910, condition 5F.
$1,850–2,250 *CSK*

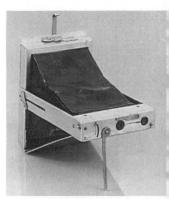

A 65 x 90mm alloy body Pocket Cyco No. 1 camera, by J. J. Griffin, London, c1902, condition 5F.
$600–680 *CSK*

A Rolleiflex 120 rollfilm E2 TLR camera, No. 2352793 with meter, by Franke and Heidecke, a Heidosmat f/2.8 80mm viewing lens No. 800792 and a Carl Zeiss Planar f/2.8 80mm taking lens No. 2384231, in a Synchro-Compur shutter, with instruction booklet, in maker's ever ready box, c1959, condition 2F.
$1,350–1,550 *CSK*

r. An Agfa Speedex O export version camera, for 127 film, c1935.
$80–90 *VCL*

A Neuca camera No. 1013, by Franz Robert Neubert, with Carl Zeiss, Jena Sonnar T f/1.5 50mm lens No. 2793392, c1946, condition 5F.
$1,275–1,425 CSK

It is likely that fewer than 30 examples of the Jena-made Neuca camera were produced c1946–7.

A Kodak Girl Guide camera, the blue enamelled body with Guide emblem, black bellows and blue ever ready case, together with another camera, 1930s.
$210–240 *P(Ba)*

l. A Rolleiflex Old Standard twin lens reflex camera, by Franke and Heidecke, with Zeiss Tesar 3.5 75mm lens, Compur shutter 1 sec–1/300, levers for setting shutter speed and aperture, lever film wind and calibrated distance scale, a spirit level within the viewfinder, with leather case, c1935.
$60–80 *DN*

A 35mm wooden body hand-cranked 1909 patent cinematographic camera No. 170, by Moy & Bastie, with hand-crank, 2 wood film magazines, one with metal plate 'W. K. Co. Ltd' and a Dallmeyer Pentac f/2.9 50mm lens No. 123505, together with a cinematographic tripod.
$1,000–1,300 *CSK*

A black Leica III camera No. 118047, with a Leitz Summar 50mm f/2 lens No. 248223, in maker's ever ready case, Leitz Elmar 35mm f/3.5 lens No. 400563, Leitz Elmar 90mm f/4 lens No. 453872, VIOOH finder and a BAZOO set, in box, 1933, condition 5F.
$1,000–1,200 *CSK*

An 18 x 24mm red body Korelle K camera, by F. Kochmann, with Carl Zeiss, Jena Tessar f/3.5 35mm lens No. 2757824 in a rimset Compur shutter, 1933, condition 4F.
$560–620 *CSK*

A 120 rollfilm Exakta 66 SLR camera No. 600771, by Ihagee Dresden, with a Carl Zeiss, Jena Tessar f/2.8 80mm lens No. 4849077, 1954, condition 4F.
$1,800–2,000 *CSK*

A chrome Leica M3 camera No. 1046554, with Leitz Summicron f/2 50mm lens No. 1887259 and a Leica-Meter MC, in maker's ever ready case, 1962, condition 4F.
$1,850–2,250 *CSK*

A chrome Leica IIIf camera No. 529567, with black dial and Leitz Summitar 50mm f/2 lens No. 760521, in maker's ever ready case, 1950, condition 5F.
$530–600 *CSK*

A Leica IIIc Monté en Sarre camera No. 359421, with Leitz/Taylor-Hobson Xenon 50mm f/1.5 lens No. 490823, 1948, condition 5F.
$3,550–3,750 *CSK*

A black Leica III camera No. 126801*, with a Leitz Summar 50mm f/2 lens No. 280354, in an ever ready case, 1934, condition 5F.
$860–980 *CSK*

The asterisk suffix usually indicates a factory duplicated serial number.

A postcard rollfilm Tropical Challenge camera, by J. Lizars, with polished teak body, Aldis Anastigmat lens, in a leather case, c1910.
$680–720 *S*

A Marion & Co Ltd, Tropical Reflex camera, with Tessar 150mm f/4.5 lens, teak body with brass mounts, red leather bellows and viewing hood, revolving back, in leather carrying case, and Teleros 13in f/5.5 lens, 1920s.
$2,700–3,000 *S*

A Prominent camera No. B.55650, by Voigtländer, Germany, with Voigtländer Nokton f/1.5 50mm lens No. 3918765, Voigtländer Dynaron f/4.5 100mm lens No. 3971555 and a Voigtländer Turnit 3 finder, 1954, condition 4F.
$670–750 *CSK*

Cameras

Camera collectors should be aware that there are many types of films and bulbs which are no longer manufactured because they do not fit into modern cameras. They can still be found at auctions and in private collections. Many dealers in classic cameras also carry stocks of these items.

A Nikon F camera No. 6909969, with photomic head, Nippon Kogaku Nikkor-H auto f/3.5 28mm lens No. 648535, Nippon Kogaku Nikkor-Q Auto f/3.5 135mm lens No. 749444 and a Nippon Kogaku Nikkor-Q Auto f/4 200mm lens No. 183700, c1960, condition 6F.
$330–380 *CSK*

A Nicca Camera Co, Japan, Tower Type-3 camera No. 31486, with Leitz Summitar 50mm f/2 lens No. 561780, 1949, condition 6F.
$330–380 *CSK*

A 2¼in (64mm) Zeiss Ikon Baby-Box Tengor camera, c1934.
$40–60 *VCL*

A Voigtländer Bessamatic 35mm SLR camera, f/2.8 Color-Skopar, c1963.
$120–150 *VCL*

r. A Zeiss Ikon 90 x 120cm tropical Adoro 230/5 camera No. O.54578, with polished wood body, nickelled fittings, tan leather viewing hood and bellows, a Carl Zeiss, Jena Tessar f/4.5 135mm lens No. 1004078 in a dial-set Compur shutter, with 6 single metal slides, in a fitted leather case, c1930.
$680–750 *CSK*

A PDQ camera, with Wollensak Velostigmat Series VII 3in f/3.5 lens No. 255543, internal processing tank and accessories, c1935, condition 4F.
$960–1,000 *CSK*

A Voigtländer Vito B, 35mm camera, 1954.
$40–60 *VCL*

A Russian Zorki-3 'Leica copy' camera, with f/2 rigid lens, c1953.
$120–150 *VCL*

A Thornton-Pickard 120 rollfilm Mk. IIIH camera gun No. 4048 with lens, in maker's fitted wooden box, c1915, condition 5F.
$1,800–2,000 *CSK*

SILVER
Baskets

A George III silver openwork shaped oval cake basket, the swing handle cast with a rococo cartouche and foliate scrolls, the base engraved with a rococo cartouche, by John Henry Vere and William Lutwyche, London 1762, 14in (35.5cm) wide, 24oz.
$1,800–2,000 *P(S)*

A George III silver swing handled bonbon dish, with ropework borders, the wirework sides applied with fruiting vines, by William Plummer, 1764, 6in (15cm) wide, 4.5oz.
$830–900 *P*

A George II silver cake basket, the centre engraved with a band of diaper work and scrolls, the swing handle engraved with the King crest, pierced and engraved on the outside with scrolling foliage and centred on either side with roundels enclosing the King crest and baron's coronet, by John White, London 1734, 12¾in (32.5cm) wide, 80.75oz.
$99,000–108,000 *S*

The crest is that of John, 2nd Lord King and Baron of Ockham (1706–40), the eldest son and heir of Lord Chancellor King.

r. A George III silver panelled octagonal cake basket, with reeded edge, swing handle, the centre with a pierced band and border of bright cut foliate swags, engraved with a crest of a horse's head, on a reeded pedestal foot, London 1788, 15¾in (40cm) wide, 26oz.
$1,400–1,600 *P(HSS)*

Changes in Style of English Silver

English silver design seems to change every 30 or 40 years largely due to European influences. Before 1660, English silver design and quality was mediocre because of the Civil War, but with the restoration of Charles II to the throne styles became more exuberant owing to the influence of the Dutch. With the influx of the Huguenots from France after 1685, designs were simple and heavy, steadily becoming more elaborate and culminating in rococo styles in the mid-18thC. However, the influence of Adam and neo-classicism made for elegant, more flimsy designs, but by 1800 silver had become heavier and more substantial, still with classical influences. By Queen Victoria's reign, designs became extremely elaborate.

A Victorian silver sweetmeat basket, by Nathan & Hayes, Chester 1898, 5¼in (13.5cm) wide.
$300–330 *TVA*

A George III silver sweetmeat basket, by Tudor & Leader, Sheffield 1776, 3in (7.5cm) high.
$630–700 *TGa*

A pair of Edwardian silver baskets, Birmingham 1903, 4¾in (12cm) wide.
$330–360 *TGa*

Bowls

A Charles II silver bowl and cover, the bowl engraved with armorials between crossed plumes, maker's mark 'GC' in monogram reversed, 'WS' on bowl, London 1681, 5½in (14cm) diam, 19.25oz.
$26,250–30,000 *S*

A James II silver porringer, engraved with initials 'M.C.' over 'A.W.', with a band of stiff leaves, 2 scroll handles, maker's mark 'E G' between mullets, 3¾in (9.5cm) diam, 5oz.
$1,600–2,000 *DN*

A Swedish silver bowl, the plain spherical body with moulded rim, on 3 feet in the shape of dolphins with swept tails, maker's mark of C. G. Hallberg, Stockholm 1911, 12¼in (31cm) diam, 73.3oz.
$2,700–3,000 *C(G)*

A Dutch silver brandy bowl, the body chased with lobes and dots, the centre engraved with a scene of a meeting, the pierced handles cast with flowers, the reverse stamped with initials 'RY/GC', 8¾in (22.5cm) wide, 6.5oz.
$4,000–4,500 *S(Am)*

Did you know?

MILLER'S **Antiques Price Guide** *builds up year-by-year to form the most comprehensive antiques photo-reference library available.*

A Victorian silver miniature bowl, import marks for Sheffield 1894, 2in (5cm) diam.
$65–75 *TVA*

A French silver *coupe de mariage*, the plain bowl with a griffin's head and scroll handles, engraved under the lip, on a waisted foot chased with foliage and ovolo and with spreading border, by Morlaix, c1740, 5½in (14cm) wide, 4.2oz.
$4,200–4,800 *C(G)*

A George III silver sugar bowl, the sides pierced with flowers, leaves and scrolls, a ropework rim and swing handles, on a trumpet foot, with blue glass liner, by William Vincent, 1770, 3¼in (8cm) diam, 2.75oz.
$500–600 *P*

A French silver-gilt *coupe de mariage*, with cover, stand and liner, the bowl on a spreading base with cornucopia handles each terminating in a ram's mask, applied twice with classical scenes, the cover with detachable finial formed as Hebe, the stand on 4 winged lion's mask and paw feet and with anthemion borders, the plain liner with 2 hinged handles, mark of Jean Baptiste Claude Odiot, Paris, c1820, 9½in (24cm) high, 69oz.
$16,500–19,500 *C*

A 16thC style silver quaiche, the lobed bowl with a central rose head boss, flat scroll pierced handles, inscribed 'IF', by J. Parkes & Co, London 1933, 7½in (19cm) wide.
$190–230 *DN*

A silver bowl, the scroll handles with lion mask finials, with egg-and-dart borders, on a spreading foot, by B.P. & S. Ltd., c1935, 12¼in (31cm) diam, together with a matching pair, 44oz.
$500–680 *P(C)*

Boxes

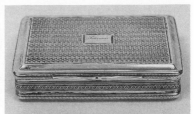

A George I silver soap box, the plain spherical body on a spreading circular foot, the domed cover engraved with initials 'GW' beneath an earl's coronet, maker's mark of Isaac Liger, London 1717, Britannia standard, 3¾in (9.5cm) high, 11oz.
$22,500–27,000 *C*

The initials are those of George, 2nd Earl of Warrington.

A George II silver box and cover, the plain body and detachable domed cover engraved with a coat-of-arms beneath an earl's coronet, on a moulded rim foot, maker's mark of James Shruder, London 1745, 5in (12.5cm) diam, 20oz.
$22,500–27,000 *C*

James Shruder was an exponent of some of the most individual English rococo designs. Little is known of Shruder's life and work but, because of his patronym, he is thought to have been of German origin. He is recorded working in the parish of St Martin-in-the-Fields, London, and was declared bankrupt in 1749.

A George III silver snuff box, Birmingham 1795, 2½in (6.5cm) wide.
$330–380 *TGa*

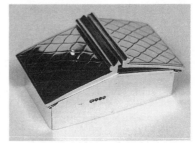

A silver-gilt snuff box, by John Keith, London 1852, 1½in (3.5cm) wide.
$680–720 *AMH*

Caddies

A George II silver caddy set, comprising a circular bowl and cover and 2 oblong caddies, each applied on either side with rococo cartouches enclosing the crest and armorials of King, also applied with shells, bulrushes, scrolls and flowers, by James Shruder, London 1748, caddies 5¾in (14.5cm) high, 64oz.
$102,000–112,500 *S*

The arms of King are for Thomas King (1712–79), 4th son of Lord Chancellor King who succeeded his 3 elder brothers as 5th Lord King and Baron of Ockham in 1767.

A George III silver lobed tea caddy, with engraved cartouches, panels of shells and foliage, fixed overhead handle, 2 lidded compartments, 2 keys, by Henry Chawner and John Emes, London 1796, 6¼in (16cm) wide, 14.25oz.
$1,600–1,800 *P(S)*

Caddy Spoons

A silver caddy spoon, by Thomas Evans, London 1789, 3½in (9cm) long.
$380–400 *AMH*

A silver caddy spoon, with a daisy bowl, by Joseph Taylor, Birmingham 1797, 2½in (6.5cm) long.
$200–240 *STH*

A George III silver caddy spoon, with fiddle handle, by Powell & Coates, London 1822, 3in (7.5cm) long.
$180–200 *STH*

A silver caddy spoon, by F. Higgins, London 1859, 4in (10cm) long.
$330–380 *AMH*

A George III silver caddy spoon, by George Nangle, 1800, 3½in (9cm) long.
$90–100 *TGa*

A silver caddy spoon, by Wardell & Kempson, Birmingham 1818, 3½in (9cm) long.
$600–680 *AMH*

Candlesticks & Candelabra

A pair of George II cast silver tapersticks, the baluster stems with fluted shoulders, spool-shaped holders on welled moulded shaped square bases, by John Cafe, London 1749, 4½in (11.5cm) high.
$2,400–2,700 *WW*

A pair of George II cast silver table candlesticks, with knopped fluted stems and square-shaped bases, by Bennett Bradshaw and Robert Tyrill, London 1740, 6½in (16.5cm) high, 27.75oz.
$3,000–3,300 *P(Sc)*

A pair of George III silver candlesticks, by Ebenezer Coker, London 1768, 10in (25.5cm) high.
$3,800–4,200 *TGa*

A George IV silver candelabrum, the triform base on 4 shell feet, each side with a cartouche enclosing armorials or a crest, 6 anthemion decorated scroll branches supporting drip pans and sconces with detachable nozzles, by Paul Storr for Storr & Mortimer, London 1825, 28½in (72.5cm) high, 246oz.
$43,500–51,000 *S*

A pair of George III silver table candlesticks, engraved with a coat-of-arms, the plain oval bases and detachable nozzles with scalloped edges, maker's mark indistinct, London 1795, 9in (23cm) high.
$3,300–3,800 *Bea*

r. Four Georgian silver Corinthian column table candlesticks, each with a papyrus sconce, fluted column and bead edging, on a stepped spreading square base, maker's mark 'I.C.' possibly for J. Collins, London 1759 and 1767, 13in (33cm) high.
$5,250–6,000 *Bea*

A pair of late Victorian silver three-light candelabra, the fluted stems decorated with creeping ivy motifs, the detachable nozzles and borders with beaded decoration, by Charles Boyton, 1892, 20in (51cm) high.
$3,450–3,750 *P(B)*

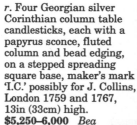

Four George III silver table candlesticks, the bases cast and chased with flutes and paterae and engraved with armorials, detachable nozzles engraved with a crest and the same armorials, by Peter Desvignes, London 1775, 11in (28cm) high, 90oz.
$19,200–21,800 *S*

A set of 4 Victorian silver table candlesticks, the stems entwined with a serpent with gem-set eyes, leaf decorated sconces with plain detachable nozzles, each on 3 lion's leg supports conjoined by classical foliage and cartouches, engraved with crest, initials 'RJM' and inscription, by Thomas Smiley, London 1842, 11½in (29cm) high, 86oz.
$10,500–12,000 *S(NY)*

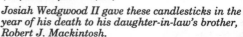

Josiah Wedgwood II gave these candlesticks in the year of his death to his daughter-in-law's brother, Robert J. Mackintosh.

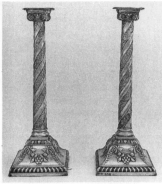

A pair of late Victorian silver candlesticks, with Ionic capitals, with spiral fluted columns engraved with flowers, the bases embossed with swags of flowers, shell and leaf scroll corners, gadrooned borders, by J. N. Mappin, Britannia standard marks for London 1896, 14½in (37cm) high.
$2,300–2,700 *DN*

Two Dutch silver candlesticks, with shaped bases, octagonal baluster stems and slightly differing vase-shaped sockets, maker's mark of Hendrick van Beest, Rotterdam 1715 and 1723, 6¾in (17cm) high, 20.5oz.
$6,000–6,750 *C(G)*

A set of 6 Italian silver candlesticks, each on a circular base with moulded border, baluster stem, spool-shaped socket and circular drip pan, engraved with initial 'F' with crown above, maker's mark probably of Contardo Buccellatti, c1765, 5in (12.5cm) high, 42oz.
$27,750–33,000 *C*

The initial on these candlesticks is that of Franz I of Austria (1745–65).

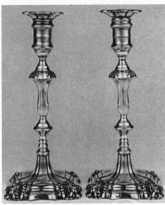

A pair of George II style silver table candlesticks, with detachable nozzles, spool-shaped sconces, knopped baluster stems, shell-capped spreading square bases, Sheffield 1904, 10in (25.5cm) high.
$750–900 *N*

A pair of silver candlesticks, with tapering Corinthian columns bound with spiral swags of acorns, on square spreading bases with urns, leaf scroll corners, gadrooned borders, by Goldsmiths & Silversmiths Co Ltd, London 1903, 10in (25.5cm) high.
$1,500–1,800 *DN*

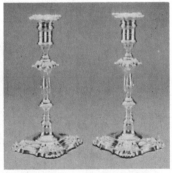

A pair of George V silver table candlesticks, the square bases, knopped stems and detachable nozzles with anthemion shell corners, by Hawksworth Eyre and Co Ltd, Sheffield 1911, 9¾in (25cm) high.
$825–975 *Bea*

r. A Spanish silver library lamp, for 2 lights, cast, chased and applied with leaves and foliage, the silk-fitted sliding screen surmounted by a dove, laurel leaf finial, by Domingo Estrada, Zaragosa, marked on base and sconces, c1780, 26in (66cm) high, 50.7oz.
$2,600–3,000 *S(G)*

r. A pair of Edwardian silver Corinthian column candlesticks, decorated with swags and beaded edging, by Harrison Bros & Howson, Sheffield 1905, 8½in (21.5cm) high.
$825–975 *MAT*

A silver chamberstick, Sheffield 1923, 4in (10cm) wide.
$300–340 *TGa*

A set of 4 American silver table candlesticks, each on a pierced shaped base of flowers and foliage, the knopped stems rising to 3 ancient Egyptian busts, the bell-shaped sconces with everted pierced floral borders and detachable nozzles, by Samuel Kirk & Son, Baltimore, Maryland, c1845, stamped, 9¾in (25cm) high, 71oz.
$6,800–7,500 *S(NY)*

Cruets

A set of 4 late George III silver crested oval salts, with flared rims, gadrooned and leaf scroll and acanthus chased borders, on scroll bracket and angled paw feet, by Philip Rundell, London 1819, 4½in (11.5cm) diam, 28oz.
$2,700–3,000 *DN*

A pair of Edwardian silver novelty pepperettes, in the form of milk churns, Birmingham 1903, 1¾in (4.5cm) high.
$200–230 *TVA*

A George III mustard pot, London 1789, 2¼in (5.5cm) high.
$380–420 *TGa*

A French silver condiment set, comprising an oval sugar bowl and stand, a pair of oval salt cellars and a circular mustard pot, the stand engraved with monogram 'FD' beneath a count's coronet, maker's mark of Antoine Boullier, c1783, bowl 7¾in (19.5cm) wide, 43.7oz.
$4,500–5,250 *C(G)*

l. A Belgian silver cruet stand, moulded with matted rococo ornaments, pierced central handle, maker's mark of a crowned shell (Stuyck 1612), Brussels 1773, 11in (28cm) wide, 15.9oz excluding 2 associated glass bottles and stoppers.
$2,500–3,000 *S(G)*

A George II Scottish silver Warwick cruet stand and fittings, the stand on 4 leaf-capped shell feet, applied with rococo cartouche, fitted with 3 casters each with pierced domed cover and baluster finial, and 2 silver mounted cut glass oil and vinegar bottles, the cartouche engraved with a coat-of-arms, the casters with later monogram within motto, maker's mark of Douglas Ged, Edinburgh 1755, stand 10¼in (26cm) high, 52oz.
$5,250–6,000 *C*

Cups & Goblets

A George II silver two-handled bell-shaped cup and cover, applied with classical profiles and cartouches enclosing arms and a crest, gilt interior, by Paul de Lamerie, London 1728, Britannia standard, 12in (30.5cm) high, 95oz.
$183,000–202,500 *S(NY)*

A George II silver two-handled cup and cover, applied with infant Bacchic busts, the finial formed as a bunch of grapes topped by a bee, engraved with arms in a rococo cartouche, by Paul de Lamerie, London 1750, 12½in (32cm) high, 75oz.
$90,000–105,000 *S(NY)*

A George II silver-gilt cup and cover, with applied armorials of King on either side, floral swags above with sea monsters and figures below, the shaped square foot cast with shells and rocaille, foliate double scroll handles, the unmarked domed cover cast with the crest of King, by John White, London 1737, 14in (35.5cm) high, 110oz.
$81,000–90,000 *S*

Influence of the Huguenots

The revocation in 1685 of the Edict of Nantes, in France, denying freedom of worship to Protestants, resulted in a flood of hard-working French craftsmen emigrating, many of them to England. The French silversmiths were highly successful and revitalised the trade in England, their styles eclipsing the ornate Dutch-inspired silver which had become so popular with the Restoration of Charles II in 1660. Platel, Pantin, Courtauld (silversmiths originally), Le Sage and, arguably the greatest of them all, Paul de Lamerie, were all prolific makers until the middle of the 18th century.

A George III silver porringer or christening cup, of Guernsey type, the S-scroll handles with beaded rat-tails, inscribed 'I.S.C., P.L.R., 1769', maker's mark 'IH' attributed to John Hardie, Guernsey, c1769, 2¾in (7cm) high, 4oz.
$1,300–1,500 *P*

A George III silver cup, and domed part fluted cover with fluted finial, with reeded scroll handles and a cartouche crest engraved with the arms of Hall of London and Warnham, Sussex, on a round gadrooned column and square pierced base with ball feet, by Andrew Fogelberg, London 1773, 15½in (39.5cm) high, 50oz.
$1,600–2,000 *DN*

A George III silver two-handled cup, the body with a moulded girdle, later initials 'JAM' within a wreath, on a moulded spreading base, by Hester Bateman, London 1782, 6½in (16.5cm) high, 12.5oz.
$750–830 *DN*

A George III silver-gilt presentation Kiddush cup, the campana-shaped body applied with a collar of grapevine and chased with a band of lobes outlined by matting, engraved with inscription, pedestal foot with egg-and-dart border, by John W. Storey, London 1808, 8¾in (22cm) high, 32oz.
$30,000–36,000 *S(NY)*

An American silver spout cup and cover, the wide baluster body with slender swan-neck spout swelling at the base, scroll handle, moulded rim and raised collet foot, stepped domed cover with baluster finial, by Samuel Vernon, Newport, RI, c1730, base engraved with initials 'M*B' and 'A' above 'C*B', 6¼in (16cm) high, 14.5oz.
$78,000–90,000 *S(NY)*

A Baltic parcel-gilt silver beaker, the tapering sides with a gilt and moulded rim, on a gadrooned foot with a zig-zag band, inscribed, marks probably for Riga, maker's mark 'ID' beneath a crown, probably for I. D. Revald, c1730, 7in (18cm) high, with an associated cover, 15½oz.
$2,700–3,000 *DN*

A William IV silver-gilt cup and stand, the bell-shaped cup applied with flowers and thistles, on a moulded base, the stand of shallow dish form with a border of trailing vine leaves, maker's mark of John Bridge, London 1830, stand with maker's mark of William Bateman for Rundell Bridge & Co, London 1836, 15½in (39.5cm) high, 106oz.
$5,400–6,300 *Bon*

A pair of George III silver thistle-shaped goblets, with basal fluting and reeded conical feet, gilt interiors, by Joseph Craddock and William Reed, London 1817, 6½in (16.5cm) high, 18.75oz.
$1,000–1,200 *P(S)*

Cutlery

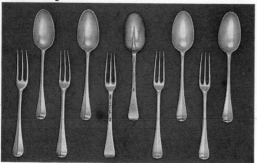

A set of 18 George I silver-gilt Hanoverian pattern dessert spoons and dessert forks, the spoons with rat-tail bowls, the forks three-pronged, maker's mark of Philip Robinson, London 1714, some marks indistinct, spoons 6½in (16.5cm) long, 48oz.
$45,000–52,500 *C*

A Queen Anne silver two-pronged fork, 8in (20.5cm) long.
$450–550 *TGa*

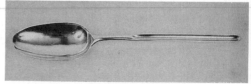

A George II silver spoon by John Wirgman, London 1747, 8½in (21.5cm) long.
$270–300 *TVA*

A George III silver fish slice, London 1804, 11½in (29cm) long.
$230–270 *TGa*

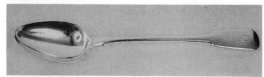

A George III silver stuffing spoon, by William Eley and William Fearn, London 1816, 12in (30.5cm) long.
$200–240 *TVA*

A Victorian silver flatware fiddle thread, and shell pattern table service, comprising 48 pieces, by George W. Adams, London, c1842, 97oz.
$1,200–1,400 *HCH*

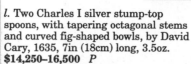

r. A Victorian silver Old English thread pattern matched part-canteen, comprising 44 pieces, by Mary Chawner, John and Henry Lias and Elizabeth Eaton, c1850, retailed by Carrington & Co, crested, 107oz, in fitted oak box.
$1,200–1,400 *P(B)*

l. Two Charles I silver stump-top spoons, with tapering octagonal stems and curved fig-shaped bowls, by David Cary, 1635, 7in (18cm) long, 3.5oz.
$14,250–16,500 *P*

A Victorian silver christening set, by George Unite, Birmingham, c1857, cutlery 6½in (16.5cm) long.
$150–180 *TVA*

An Irish silver pudding slice, with ebonised turned wood handle and shell and scroll mount, the rounded triangular blade pierced with quatrefoils, foliage and a shell, the reverse engraved with a crest, by James Graham, Dublin, apparently with no date letter, probably c1760, 13in (33cm) long.
$2,300–2,700 *CSK*

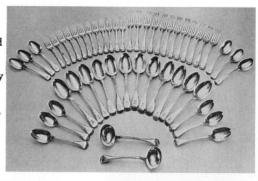

A set of 6 Victorian silver dessert knives and forks, with mother-of-pearl handles, by George Unite, Birmingham 1873, in carved walnut case, 12½in (32cm) wide.
$600–675 *TVA*

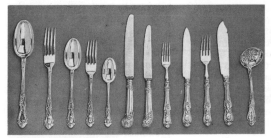

A Victorian silver muffin fork, mark erased, c1890, 11in (28cm) long.
$60–80 *OD*

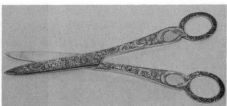

A pair of Victorian silver-gilt grape scissors, London 1889, 6⅞in (17.5cm) long.
$450–500 *TGa*

An Edwardian silver rococo scroll pattern canteen, comprising 201 pieces, maker's mark of Elkington & Co, monogrammed, Birmingham 1903 and 1904, together with 3 pairs of electroplated nut crackers, 12 table knives, 12 dessert knives and a three-piece carving set with foliate pistol handles, London 1965 and 1972, 330oz, in a fitted six-drawer mahogany case.
$5,700–6,700 *Bon*

r. A French silver dessert/table service, by G. Fouquet-Lapar, Paris, engraved with armorials, c1880, 244.25oz, contained in 3 lined and fitted maroon leather travelling cases.
$10,200–11,250 *P*

Six silver ice cream spoons, by Aldwinkle & Slater, London 1880/81, 5in (13cm) long.
$230–270 *AMH*

A Victorian child's silver cutlery set, London 1894-98, in a fitted box, 8in (20.5cm) long.
$150–170 *TGa*

A set of late Victorian silver fiddle pattern cutlery, comprising 62 pieces, by George Maudsley Jackson, London 1893, 109oz.
$1,800–2,250 *WW*

A French silver-gilt christening set, comprising 12 pieces, marked with retailer's name 'A. Aucoc, R. de la Paix', with a hand inscribed paper ticket 'Mgr. Le Duc d'Orléans à sa Filleule', in a plush and satin-lined tooled leather case, 19thC, pan 9¼in (23.5cm) overall.
$1,600–2,000 *CSK*

A Belgian set of table silver for 12 persons, by Wolfers Frères, some pieces with maker's marks Philippe Wolfers, Brussels, the majority c1929, 202oz excluding table and cheese knives with steel blades.
$7,200–8,250 *S(G)*

A French silver parcel-gilt fiddle pattern table service, comprising 126 pieces, the stems chased with vine foliage, pearls and ribbons enclosing a cartouche engraved with armorials, the reverse chased with a hunting trophy, the knives with silver-gilt mounts, mother-of-pearl handles and steel blades, maker's mark 'PQ and Odiot', Paris, c1880, 277oz.
$12,000–14,250 *C(G)*

A set of 12 silver coffee spoons and a pair of sugar tongs, by Walker & Hall, Sheffield 1910, in a fitted case, 11in (28cm) wide.
$330–380 *TVA*

Jugs

A George III silver cream jug,
London 1760, 3½in (9cm) high.
$380–430 *TGa*

A George III silver beer jug, by
William Cripps, London 1762,
8in (20.5cm) high, 28oz.
$4,200–4,800 *JSH*

A George II silver baluster-
shaped jug, the applied girdle
above engraved armorials and
crest, with scroll handle and
thumbpiece, the stepped
hinged cover with knop finial,
on a spreading foot, by
Gabriel Sleath, 1731,
10in (25.5cm) high, 33oz.
$19,500–22,500 *P(B)*

A George III silver cream jug,
London 1779, 4in (10cm) high.
$350–380 *TGa*

An American silver water pitcher,
of Liverpool pottery type, plain
barrel-shaped body, short spout
rising from 3 diminishing beads,
partly faceted slender hollow
scroll handle with strut support,
marked on base 'Pittman',
Providence, Rhode Island, c1800,
9in (23cm) high, 22oz.
$7,500–8,250 *S(NY)*

A George III silver hot water
jug, fluted at the angles,
engraved initial 'B' below a
baron's crest with drapery
cartouche below foliate band, the
pedestal base with a single band
of foliage, hinged cover, ball
button, and carved ivory handle,
by Henry Chawner, London
1795, 12½in (32cm) high, 28oz.
$2,000–2,250 *S*

A George III silver cream jug,
London 1805, 3½in (9cm) high.
$200–230 *TVA*

A George III silver cream jug,
with reeded rim, loop handle
and base, London 1799,
10in (25.5cm) high, 3oz.
$180–230 *AH*

r. A George IV silver-gilt water pitcher,
the body partly chased with water
leaves and flowerheads, with leaf and
bellflower-clad tubular scroll handle,
the rim with an everted band of stiff
leaves, engraved with a crest, helm and
coat-of-arms within undulating foliate
mantling, maker's mark of Paul Storr,
London 1827, 11½in (29cm) high, 55oz.
$9,750–11,250 *C(SP)*

A German silver parcel-gilt
baluster-shaped ewer, applied
with a bearded mask, embossed
and chased with acanthus and
gadroons and with entwined
handle, marked on body and
foot, by Johann Mittnacht I,
Augsburg 1690–95, 12in
(30.5cm) high, 40oz.
$9,750–11,250 *S(G)*

Mirrors

r. An Edwardian silver-mounted dressing table mirror, with strut, decorated with floral rococo scrolls, cartouche and covered in blue velvet, London 1907, 16in (40.5cm) high.
$530–600 *MAT*

l. An Irish silver dressing table mirror, the ogee-moulded frame with a gadrooned border applied with stylised leaves at the corners, the centre engraved with a coat-of-arms, helm, crest and motto within engraved foliate scroll mantling and flanked by chased crossed fronds, with wood backing, maker's mark John Humphreys, Dublin 1696–98, 28in (71cm) high.
$21,000–24,000 *C*

The arms are those of Thompson impaling those of Wilmot.

Mugs & Tankards

A George III silver tankard, with applied rib band on rim foot and scroll handle, maker Langlands & Robertson, Newcastle mark 1784, 6in (15cm) high, 17oz.
$900–1,000 *AG*

A William III silver 3 pint tankard, the flat moulded top with corkscrew thumbpiece, the body engraved with armorials, on moulded foot, by John Sutton, London 1686, 7in (18cm) high, 29oz.
$13,500–15,000 *P(G)*

An Irish silver tankard, the tapering shape with twisted scroll thumbpiece, the handle with beaded rat-tail, the front engraved with a contemporary armorial, the cover engraved on top with a later crest, by David King, Dublin 1702, 6¾in (17.5cm) high, 23.75oz.
$6,300–7,500 *P*

l. A William IV silver-gilt tankard, the body applied with an oval plaque depicting a horse race within leaf and berry surround, the part-fluted detachable cover cast with matted acanthus and detachable finial formed of acorns, by William Eaton, London 1832, 12⅛in (31.5cm) high, 122oz.
$9,800–10,800 *S*

A George IV silver tankard, with reeded bands, inscribed 'Arundel Christmas Market 1828 ... 10 Fat South Down Ewes', and initials, and engraved with a bird of prey, by William Bateman, London 1828, 5in (13cm) high, 15oz.
$750–830 *DN*

Plates

Two matching George III silver dinner plates, with shaped gadrooned borders and crests, by James Young, London 1776 and by John Wakelin and Robert Garrard I, 1793, 9½in (24cm) diam, 32oz.
$750–900 *DN*

r. Four silver dinner plates, with gadrooned border and anthemion clusters, each engraved with a coat-of-arms and a crest and motto in 18thC style, by Sydney Bellamy Harman, London 1901/02, 11⅛in (29cm) diam, 135oz.
$1,800–2,000 *S*

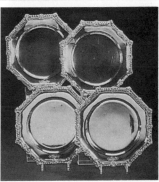

Pots

A James II silver chocolate pot, of baluster form derived from Chinese porcelain, with swan neck spout at right angles to the wood C-scroll handle, the cover attached by a chain and with sliding urn finial, the lower handle terminal engraved with contemporary initials 'ED' surrounded by mullets, engraved with later inscription above moulded base band, monogram mark '(?)PB', London 1686, 7½in (19cm) high, 21.25oz.
$52,500–60,000 *S(NY)*

A Victorian silver teapot, with spirally reeded body, finial and spout, with wood scroll handle on a plain foot rim, by Edward Hutton, London 1886, 6¾in (17cm), 128.8oz.
$500–600 *Bea*

An Italian silver pear-shaped coffee pot, with S-shaped spout terminating in a bird's head, wood harp-shaped handle, the hinged cover fluted with scroll thumbpiece rising to a flower-shaped finial, with plain spreading reeded foot, marked on base and cover, Genoa 1757, 10½in (26.5cm) high, 33oz.
$27,000–30,000 *C(G)*

A George II silver baluster-shaped coffee pot, richly chased and embossed with flowerheads and foliage, with partly fluted curved spout, reverse scroll handle with acanthus thumbpiece, hinged cover with further foliage decoration and pine cone finial, on spreading base, by Daniel Piers, 1748, the base with later presentation inscription, 12¼in (31cm) high, 56oz.
$3,500–4,000 *C(S)*

A Victorian silver pear-shaped coffee pot, half-gadrooned with armorial crest, hinged lid, ebonised handle and finial, Sheffield 1881, 10in (25.5cm) high, 14oz gross.
$350–380 *WIL*

A George IV silver pear-shaped teapot, with hinged cover, leaf-capped spout, scrolling wood handle with knop, on cast scroll feet, London 1822, 8in (20.5cm) high, 25.25oz.
$450–530 *L&E*

An early George II silver teapot, with a band of fine diaper and scroll engraving at the shoulder and lid rim, straight tapered spout, moulded foot, by Edward Bennett, London 1728, 4¼in (11cm) high, 14oz.
$5,500–6,000 *P(G)*

A George III silver baluster-shaped coffee pot, the cover with spiral reeded finial, leaf chased spout, wood handle and round moulded foot, by Francis Crump, London 1764, 10¾in (27.5cm) high, 30.50oz.
$2,000–2,700 *DN*

A Belgian silver baluster-shaped teapot, the ribbed body, hinged cover and bird's head spout engraved with *Régence* strapwork, husks and foliate latticework on matting, wood handle and rim foot, by Petrus van Eesbeeck, Brussels, c1730, date letter illegible, 6¾in (17.5cm) high, 20oz gross.
$70,500–75,000 *S(G)*

A George IV silver teapot, by William Traies, London 1822, 10in (25.5cm) wide.
$830–900 *TVA*

Salvers & Trays

A George I silver salver, the centre later engraved with a coat-of-arms within a rococo cartouche, the reverse engraved with a presentation inscription, on 8 shaped bracket feet, maker's mark of Benjamin Pyne, London 1718, Britannia standard, 15½in (39.5cm) diam, 56oz.
$45,000–52,500 *C*

A George I silver-gilt salver, engraved with a band of rosettes and diaperwork, the centre with a lozenge-of-arms within a cartouche, the reverse with later presentation inscription, on 4 bracket feet, maker's mark of Abraham Buteau, London 1723, 12¼in (31cm) square, 45oz.
$18,750–22,500 *C*

A George II silver salver, by Joseph Sanders, London 1743, 6in (15cm) diam.
$680–750 *TGa*

A George III silver two-handled tea tray, engraved with armorials within scrolls, flowers, foliage and fruit on matted ground, the border with thread edging, by William and John Fisher, London 1797, 25in (63.5cm) wide, 86oz.
$2,000–2,400 *Bea*

A George II silver salver, engraved with armorials within a foliate and rocaille cartouche below a flat chased band of floral festoons and scrollwork designs, a waved and ribbed border with shell and scale motifs, on 4 vine leaf panel supports, by Paul de Lamerie, London 1744, 10in (25.5cm) diam, 22.5oz.
$25,800–30,000 *S*

A late George II silver salver, engraved with an armorial within a flower wreath and ribbon tied cartouche, within a shell and C-scroll border, on hoof feet, by Ebenezer Coker, London 1756, 10¾in (27.5cm) diam, 18oz.
$1,200–1,400 *DN*

Miller's is a price GUIDE not a price LIST

A George III tea tray, engraved with a coat-of-arms, the handles chased with flowers and acanthus leaves, shell, acorn and gadrooned border, by John Watson, Sheffield 1817, 19¼in (49cm) wide, 81.6oz.
$3,150–3,750 *P(Sc)*

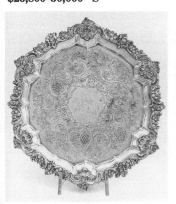

A William IV Scottish silver salver, with shell and vine chased border, flat chased with flowers, foliate and shell scrolls and central monogram, on shell scroll bracket feet, possibly by William Cunningham, Edinburgh 1835, 10½in (26.5cm) diam, 24.5oz.
$500–570 *DN*

A Victorian silver salver, the centre engraved with a crest within a band of scrolling foliage, the raised moulded border with a rococo scroll edge, on panel feet, by Charles Rawlings and George Summers, London 1846, 14½in (37cm) diam, 41oz.
$975–1,125 *WW*

A Victorian silver salver, with a raised piecrust, shell and scroll decorated border with engraved scrolling flower and leaf inner decoration and coat-of-arms, on 4 scroll leaf feet, by John Hunt and Robert Roskell, stamped 'Hunt and Roskell late Storr and Mortimer 5018', London 1868, 25¼in (64cm) diam, 196oz.
$3,500–4,200 *P(Ch)*

Sauce Boats

A pair of George III sauce boats, by Wm Skeen, London 1769, 5¼in (13.5cm) wide.
$1,350–1,500 *AMH*

Services

A Victorian composite silver four-piece tea and coffee set, the bodies embossed with flowers, scrolls and diaper or scale ornament above scroll panel supports, the pots with flower finials, coffee pot by R. Harper, London 1859, remainder by E. Barnard & Sons, London 1871, coffee pot 10in (25.5cm) high, 72oz gross.
$1,800–2,300 *S(S)*

r. A four-piece silver tea and coffee service, with monogram 'J.B.', teapot by Richard Cooke, London, c1800, coffee pot, creamer and sugar, London, c1884, 64oz.
$1,275–1,425 *SK*

A pair of George II silver sauce boats, the handles capped by monsters' heads, the sides centred by shells in chased cartouches below the gadroon rims, the fronts engraved with arms, by Paul de Lamerie, London 1744, 8½in (21.5cm) wide, 42oz.
$157,500–172,000 *S(NY)*

A silver tea and coffee set, London, c1895, milk jug London 1809, teapot 7in (18cm) high.
$2,000–2,450 *TGa*

A pair of silver double-lipped sauce boats, of early Georgian design, the moulded oval bodies with shaped rims and flared lips, spreading bases, each with 2 cast scroll handles, by William Comyns & Sons Ltd, London 1925, 7¾in (19.5cm) wide, 29oz.
$1,400–1,500 *S*

A George IV composite silver three-piece tea set, the melon fluted bodies chased with panels of matted foliage, the teapot with leafy collar and flower embossed circular foot, the others with leaf capped scroll handles, on leaf chased shaped circular bases, teapot by William Hunter, London 1823, the others Thomas Ballam, London 1821, teapot 7½in (19cm) high, 52oz gross.
$1,400–1,600 *S(S)*

A Victorian silver four-piece tea and coffee set, the circular bodies with fluted divisions and engraved scroll leaf and trailing flower decoration, all with leaf capped scroll handles and scroll feet, by Robert Hennell, London 1847, 68.5oz gross.
$1,500–1,800 *P(Ch)*

A George IV silver four-piece tea and coffee service, of panelled and globular form, embossed with foliage and flowers, on leaf and shell cast feet, by Rebecca Emes and Edward Barnard, London 1826, 82.3oz.
$3,300–3,800 *P(HSS)*

l. An early Victorian silver four-piece tea and coffee service, of circular baluster form, with engraved decoration, on scroll feet, Birmingham 1860, 90oz.
$1,600–2,000 *JAd*

A Victorian three-piece silver-gilt bachelor tea service, decorated with foliage in the Indian manner, by George Fox, London 1874 and 1875, spoons and tongs by George Adams, London 1874 and 1875, teapot 3¼in (8.5cm) high, 17oz, in a brass-bound rosewood box with plate engraved with retailer's name, 'R. & S. Garrard & Co'. $1,500–1,800 CSK

An Irish silver four-piece tea service, the plain ground repoussé with bands of Celtic motifs, by Weir and Sons, Dublin 1918, 80oz gross. $1,400–1,500 P(HSS)

A Victorian silver seven-piece tea and coffee service, each lobed and embossed with cartouches within flowers, scrolling foliage and shells, with an engraved crest, on paw feet, ivory handles and finials, by Mappin Bros, Sheffield 1898, 237.75oz. $7,500–8,250 P(S)

An Edward VII silver six-piece tea and coffee service, in late Georgian style, edged with beadwork, with reeded handles, the lower sections engraved with a crest and motto, by Goldsmiths & Silversmiths Company, coffee pot London 1900, tea kettle London 1902, teapot, sugar basin and milk jug London 1903, hot water jug by Martin Hall & Co, Sheffield 1901, 118.2oz gross. $2,400–2,700 P(HSS)

A four-piece silver tea and coffee set, the swirl-fluted bodies on gadrooned bases, the flared collars pierced with arabesques, tea and coffee pots with carved horn angular handles, by Gibson & Langman for the Goldsmiths and Silversmiths Co., London 1894, coffee pot 9¼in (23.5cm) high, 79oz gross. $3,000–3,300 S

A Victorian silver four-piece tea and coffee service, the oval bodies engraved with sprays of ferns, with bead edges, the milk jug and sugar basin with gilt interiors, by Henry Stratford, Sheffield 1882, 66oz gross. $1,800–2,300 WW

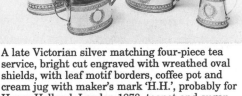

A late Victorian silver matching four-piece tea service, bright cut engraved with wreathed oval shields, with leaf motif borders, coffee pot and cream jug with maker's mark 'H.H.', probably for Henry Holland, London 1878, teapot and sugar bowl with maker's mark 'J.A.J.S., London 1881, 63.25oz gross, in a lined oak case. $2,700–3,000 MCA

A silver four-piece oblong-shaped tea service, the teapot and hot water jug with compressed handles and knobs, Sheffield 1932, 56oz gross. $1,000–1,125 DN

Serving Dishes

l. A George III silver meat dish and cover, the gadrooned rim with anthemion, shell and acanthus, the border engraved with crests, engraved with a baron's armorials, maker's mark of Paul Storr, London 1808, 17in (43cm) long, 120oz. $12,750–14,250 C(SP)

A matched pair of George III silver entrée dishes and covers, with gadrooned edging, engraved with a coat-of-arms and decorated with fruit, flowers, and scrolling foliage, detachable handles, by T. & J. Guest and Joseph Craddock, London 1810, one cover by another maker, marks worn, London 1813, 98.6oz. $1,800–2,000 Bea

Sugar Casters

r. A pair of George III silver vase-shaped casters, with urn finials, beaded borders, engraved covers, crests and round bases, by Jabez Daniell and James Mince, London 1770, 6¾in (17cm) high, 14oz.
$1,275–1,425 *DN*

l. A pair of Victorian silver sugar casters, decorated with spiral fluting and foliage and with C- and S-scroll and floral cartouches engraved with crests and mottos, each on a rocaille decorated rising foot, by Joseph Bradbury & John Henderson, London 1886, 8½in (21.5cm) high, 18.25oz, in a lined case.
$1,350–1,500 *CSK*

Toast Racks

l. A silver toast rack, by Aldwinkle & Slater, Birmingham 1861, 8¼in (21cm) wide.
$480–530 *AMH*

A Victorian silver toast rack, by William Spooner, Birmingham 1849, 6½in (16.5cm) wide.
$390–450 *TGa*

Tureens

A Victorian silver soup tureen with later cover and stand, the tureen by D. & C. Houle, London 1843, finial by Robert Garrard, London, c1835, stand and cover by Sydney Bellamy Harman, London, c1916, stand 26in (66cm) wide, 318oz.
$16,500–19,500 *S*

A pair of George III silver soup tureens, covers and liners, with leaf-capped reeded lion's mask scroll handles, later engraved with coats-of-arms, crests and coronets, maker's mark of Paul Storr, London 1812, 15in (38cm) wide, 372oz.
$78,000–90,000 *C*

A Georgian silver crested Adam style oval tureen, the domed lid with urn finial, reeded loop handles, oval base and beaded edging, by Henry Greenway, London 1779, 9in (23cm) wide, 18.35oz.
$900–1,000 *AH*

A George III silver two-handled oval half-fluted soup tureen, on an oval foot with gadrooned borders, finial repaired, maker's mark 'J.S.' for John Schofield, London 1789, 9in (23cm) high, 66oz.
$4,000–4,500 *MCA*

r. A pair of early George III silver soup tureens, with gadrooned borders and domed covers, pomegranate finials, on rococo scroll feet, engraved with crests and armorials, by George Methuen, 1760, 17in (43cm) wide, 194.5oz.
$15,000–18,000 *P*

Paul Storr

Paul Storr was the most prolific of the early 19th century silversmiths. He had a long working life, registering his first mark in 1794 and his last in 1834, retiring shortly afterwards.

Until about 1800 his pieces were of average quality but subsequently he became a master of the heavy neo-classical styles which became very fashionable, and with Philip Rundell, an astute and avaricious businessman, and John Bridge, with whom he was associated from 1813 to 1820, his workshop produced enormous quantities of silver and silver-gilt. George III and the Prince of Wales became patrons and virtually every fashionable household in the country followed suit. It is calculated that at their height his workshops would have employed over 100 craftsmen. His designs were so heavy and robust that many pieces have survived in excellent condition, and are widely sought-after by collectors today.

Urns

A George III silver tea urn, with engraved shield, 2 handles and on a plain base, maker's mark of Paul Storr, London 1793, 18in (45.5cm) high, 96oz.
$9,750–11,250 *EL*

A Dutch silver vase-shaped urn, with spool shaped cover and finial, 2 loop handles, silver-mounted wood tap, on trumpet shaped stem with bayonet mount and base with bun feet, maker BN, Amsterdam 1785, 17in (43cm) high, 89oz.
$3,900–4,500 *DN*

Vases

A pair of American silver vases, chased with bands of foliage, the handles topped by bearded masks, initialled and dated '1863', marks not visible, 13in (33cm) high, 42oz.
$1,275–1,425 *S(NY)*

A Victorian silver baluster-shaped vase, with gadrooned rim, engraved with hatched motifs and bands including, anthemions, forks, scrolls, vitruvian scroll and key pattern bands, maker Robert Hennell, London 1869, 18½in (47cm) high, 50oz.
$2,300–2,700 *P(S)*

Miscellaneous

A set of 6 silver buttons, with motif of a cherub kissing a lady, Birmingham 1905, 1in (25mm) diam, in original box.
$380–420 *AMH*

A pair of miniature Royal Worcester plaques, with contemporary pierced silver surrounds, each signed 'Raymond Rushton', date code for 1912, 4in (10cm) diam.
$1,350–1,500 *TVA*

A silver and glass butter dish and knife, maker John Thomas Heath and John Hartshorne Middleton, London, c1889, 4¾in (12cm) wide, in a lined case.
$520–600 *AMH*

A novelty silver vesta, in the form of a coffee pot, Birmingham 1905, 3¼in (8cm) high.
$340–400 *AMH*

An American silver presentation fireman's trumpet, embossed and chased with floral sprays, engraved with presentation inscription and 2 suspension rims, by Conrad Bard & Son, Philadelphia, c1845, 22in (56cm) long, 20oz.
$10,500–12,000 *S(NY)*

r. A set of 6 silver buttons, with motif of a lady, Birmingham 1902, 1in (25mm) diam, in original box.
$380–400 *AMH*

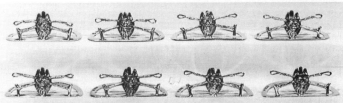

A set of 8 Edwardian menu holders, each with fox hunting trophy, Birmingham 1906, 2½in (6.5cm) wide, 3oz.
$500–600 *AH*

SILVER PLATE

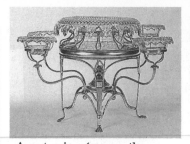

A Victorian folding double shell-shaped biscuit box, with pierced liner, cast rustic branch stand and handle, late 19thC,
8in (20.5cm) wide.
$450–525 *N*

A centrepiece épergne, the circular frame with ropework borders, the cut glass bowl with wirework support, a framework supporting a dome with stiff leaf decoration surmounted by a leafy knop finial, flanked by 4 branches each supporting a cut glass bowl, raised on reeded claw feet, c1800, 14in (35.5cm) high.
$1,800–2,300 *P*

A pair of electrotype silvered chargers, the outer rim depicting astrological panels, the interior with titled months of the year and frolicking putti, late 19thC, 21in (53.5cm) diam.
$1,800–2,300 *S(NY)*

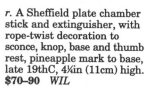

A Victorian silver plated tray, chased and engraved with C- and shell-scrolls, crest, 2 leaf and shell-scroll handle, on rococo feet, 28½in (72.5cm) wide.
$520–630 *DN*

The crest and motto of Brownrigg of White Waltham, Berks.

A pair of Regency Sheffield plate sauce tureens, with gadroon borders and reeded shell scroll corners, the covers with lamb and pennant crest, leaf scroll ring handles, on leaf applique paw feet, 7½in (19cm) wide.
$850–930 *WW*

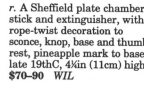

r. A Sheffield plate chamber stick and extinguisher, with rope-twist decoration to sconce, knop, base and thumb rest, pineapple mark to base, late 19thC, 4¼in (11cm) high.
$70–90 *WIL*

l. A Sheffield plate standish, with foliate scroll borders, glass wells with hinged covers, chamber stick, detachable sconce, on lion paw feet, 19thC, 13½in (34.5cm) wide.
$660–720 *N*

Sheffield Plate

The increasing prosperity of the merchant and trading classes led to a search for a silver substitute, which resulted in 1740 in the invention of Sheffield plate. Sheffield plate is a specialist collecting area in its own right. It is always less expensive than silver but can command high prices when in good condition.

Sheffield plate was made by binding a sheet of sterling silver to an ingot of copper and fusing them together in a furnace. The resultant metal was rolled or hammered into sheet and made up into objects.

The so-called 'double-sandwich' dates from c1770. Used for pieces that had a visible interior (mugs, bowls and so on), it consisted of a sheet of silver each side of a piece of copper; early makers applied a film of solder over the bare edge of copper; such pieces are very rare. Late in the 18th century, borders were applied with a U-shaped section of silver wire to conceal the copper (this can be felt as a lip on the underside). The silver border has often worn through to the dull lead beneath – a useful identification point.

From the end of the 18th century the borders of Sheffield plate pieces became increasingly florid, more so than on sterling silver wares, probably because they could be produced far less expensively than solid silver borders. Borders should be carefully examined for wear. A little copper showing is generally considered attractive, but more than that is not.

A Sheffield plate table, chased with rococo ornament, with oak backing, knopped column stem, on 3 paw feet, c1835, 24in (61cm) diam.
$7,500–8,250 *S(NY)*

WINE ANTIQUES

A William III silver monteith, the detachable rim with wavy foliate scroll edge applied with putto masks, the sides matted to simulate shagreen and embossed with gadrooned scrolls framing plain panels, one engraved with armorial, lion mask drop ring handles, by Timothy Ley, 1696, 13¼in (33.5cm) diam, 89oz.
$30,000–33,000 *P*

A Victorian silver punchbowl, in monteith style, with notched rim and scroll edging with masks above reeded girdle, lion mask drop ring handles, by Robert Garrard, London 1881, 12½in (32cm) diam, 66oz.
$3,000–3,750 *Bea*

A Victorian silver monteith type punchbowl, with lobing to the lower body, shaped scroll rim inscribed 'Won by Robert Usher's "Reiver" by Rostrevor', by Martin Hall & Co, 1883, retailed by Brook & Son of Edinburgh, 12¾in (32.5cm) diam, 64oz.
$2,300–2,700 *C(S)*

A Victorian silver punchbowl, with moulded waved border, embossed flowers, foliate scrolls and leaf band, on stem foot, London mark for 1889, 10½in (26.5cm) diam, 35oz.
$1,800–2,250 *AG*

A late Victorian silver punchbowl, with embossed gadrooned, bead, scroll and floral decoration, by W. G., J. L., retailed by Goldsmiths Co, 9¾in (25cm) diam, 25oz.
$680–750 *Gam*

A silver plated tantalus, with 3 cut glass decanters, c1880, 11¾in (30cm) wide.
$1,500–1,800 *MM*

A Danish silver punch ladle, with wood and ivory handle, 19thC, 17in (43cm) long.
$850–900 *AEF*

A George III silver punch ladle, London 1775, 11½in (29cm) long.
$225–260 *TGa*

An Edwardian oak mirror-back tantalus, fitted with 3 square section decanters and compartments, with hinged lid above a secret drawer decorated with carved panels, one decanter damaged, 12½in (32cm) high.
$300–330 *WIL*

A silver stand, with 4 spirit bottles, by William Bateman II, c1828, 10in (25.5cm) high.
$2,250–2,600 *Har*

A silver plated tantalus, with 3 cut glass decanters, c1890, 12in (30.5cm) wide.
$1,350–1,500 *GAS*

A pair of George III silver wine coasters, with pierced and beaded galleries, on turned walnut bases, by Robert Hennell I, London 1776, 5in (12.5cm) diam.
$1,350–1,500 *DN*

Three George III silver wine coasters, crested at the centre, the rims and bases with gadroon edging, by William Burwash & Richard Sibley, London 1809, 5⅝in (14.5cm) diam.
$3,750–4,500 *Bea*

A set of 3 George III silver wine coasters, by William Stevenson, London 1780, 4¾in (12cm) diam.
$3,000–3,600 *TGa*

A George III Sheffield plate wine cooler, with 3 reeded bands and loop handles, engraved with an armorial, 8¼in (21cm) high excluding handles.
$2,000–2,250 *DN*

A creamware wine coaster, marked 'Wedgwood', c1790, 6in (15cm) diam.
$420–450 *Har*

A George IV Irish silver two-handled wine cooler, engraved with a coat-of-arms and presentation inscription, the upper section of the body embossed with 2 foliate scroll cartouches, each surmounted by an eagle, the lower section embossed with flowering acanthus leaves and flowers against a matted background, with detachable liner, maker's mark of Edward Power and Edward Twycross, Dublin 1826, 11¼in (29cm) high, 104oz.
$6,000–6,750 *Bon*

A George III Sheffield plate urn-shaped wine cooler, with gadrooned borders, part fluting and 2 reeded handles with satyr mask terminals, on a round base, engraved with crests and armorials, 9¼in (23.5cm) high.
$900–1,000 *DN*

r. A mahogany hexagonal urn-shaped wine cooler, with boxwood and ebony Tunbridge ware type parquetry borders, the detachable cover with a finial, lead lined interior with drain hole, stamped beneath 'New Custom House', 19thC, 28¼in (72cm) high.
$900–1,000 *DN*

A pair of Regency Sheffield plate wine coolers, engraved with contemporary armorials, 2 wrythen grip handles with scallop shell appliqués, gadroon borders, with detachable liners, 8in (20.5cm) high.
$2,400–2,700 *WW*

Two silver gilt wine coolers and liners, applied with cast trailing vines, vine tendril handles, plain collars and liners, engraved twice with coats-of-arms, the liners and collars with a crest of the Guelphic Order, with maker's mark of William Eley II, London for 1828 and 1830, 11¾in (30cm) high, 325oz.
$27,000–30,000 *C*

A steel double-folding pocket corkscrew, with decorative spine and helical worm, c1790, 4½in (11.5cm) long.
$150–180 *CS*

A brass frame corkscrew, with turned wooden handle and brush, c1860, 7½in (19cm) long.
$120–140 *CS*

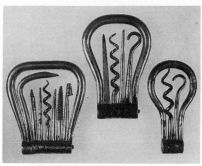

Three all-steel folding bow corkscrews, c1860:
l. A 7-tool combination, 2¾in (7cm) long. $80–90
centre A 4-tool combination, 3in (7.5cm) long. $60–70
r. A 2-tool combination, corkscrew and buttonhook, 2¾in (7cm) long. $18–25 *CS*

Two steel picnic corkscrews, with plain tapering sheaths and baluster shanks, c1790, 4½in (11.5cm) long.
$75–90 each *CS*

l. A wide rack King's Screw corkscrew, with turned wood handle, turned bone side handle and outer bronze barrel with Royal coat-of-arms and maker's name 'Dowler', c1820, 7½in (19cm) long.
$225–250 *CS*

r. A Thomason type double-action corkscrew, with turned bone handle and brass barrel, applied coat-of-arms with maker's name 'J. Heeley & Sons', c1840, 7in (18cm) long.
$150–180 *CS*

A metal Thomason type bell corkscrew, by T. Dowler, c1800, 5½in (14cm) long.
$225–250 *PSA*

A Dowler wide rack King's Screw corkscrew, c1840, 7½in (19cm) long.
$450–530 *Bar*

r. A simple corkscrew, with bone handle, c1860, 5in (12.5cm) long.
$45–60 *Bar*

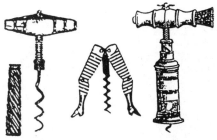

The Evolution of the Corkscrew

Originally wine bottles were onion or mallet-shaped and sealed with wooden plugs wrapped in waxed linen. Corks, imported in great numbers from the Iberian peninsula, made their first appearance in the latter half of the 18thC, when it was discovered that wine improved by being laid down and that the bottles, therefore, needed to be properly sealed. This is also when the shape of the bottle changed to the one we recognise today.

With the advent of corks came the invention of innumerable ingenious corkscrews, designed not only to extract the cork, but also to perform other functions such as cutting through the sealing wax and lead cap and brushing away dust and loose particles off the seal or cork. Such is the appeal of the corkscrew to inventors that between 1795 and 1908 almost 350 British patents were taken out on them.

A double-action barrel type brass corkscrew, with rosewood handle and plaque inscribed 'Dowler, Patent, Ne Plus Ultra', 19thC, 7½in (19cm) long.
$525–600 *Bea*

A late Victorian corkscrew, with mahogany handle, rusty and with brush missing, 5½in (14cm) long.
$35–45 *WIL*

An Italian all-steel lever corkscrew, with maker's name 'Vogliotti', c1910, 5in (12.5cm) long.
$60–70 *CS*

A German all-steel folding pocket corkscrew, by Hollweg, c1895, 2¾in (7cm) long.
$35–45 *CS*

Two Scandinavian corkscrews, c1920, 4in (10cm) long.
$60–75 *Bar*

A Baby Polly waiter's friend corkscrew, c1900, 4in (10cm) long.
$18–25 *Bar*

A French Debouchtout concertina corkscrew, 20thC, 4in (10cm) long.
$45–60 *Bar*

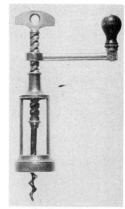

An Italian grinder corkscrew, late 19thC, 5½in (14cm) long.
$525–625 *Bar*

A French rack corkscrew, early 20thC, 7in (18cm) long.
$65–75 *Bar*

A Guild of Sommeliers concertina corkscrew, c1960, 4¾in (12cm) long.
$45–55 *Bar*

A selection of American simple corkscrews, c1900, 4¼in (11cm) long.
$25–30 each *Bar*

A silver plated decanting cradle, decorated with grapes and vine leaves, on goats' feet, c1850, 12in (30.5cm) high.
$780–880 *Har*

A Victorian claret jug, c1881, 9¾in (25cm) high.
$825–900 *TGa*

r. A pair of Geoge III wine cups, by Edward Farrel, London 1785, 7in (18cm) high.
$1,800–2,000 *TGa*

A set of 4 hollow dog shaped wine decanters, with loop tails as handles, 19thC, 7in (18cm) high.
$600–675 *AG*

A Victorian silver-mounted claret jug, the glass body etched with ivy leaves, with applied flower chased silver collar, caryatid scroll handle, mask, spout and domed cover, with lion rampant and shield finial, maker's mark 'C.F.', Sheffield 1883', 11½in (29cm) high.
$3,450–4,200 *S*

A George III wine funnel, London 1799, 6in (15cm) long.
$630–700 *TGa*

A silver plated twin coaster decanter wagon, the coasters with gadrooned rim and fluted sides, on 4 wheels, the swivelling pull with loop handle in the form of a trailing vine, 19thC, 20½in (52cm) long.
$675–750 *AH*

A Victorian silver wine funnel, by Robert Garrard, London 1840, 5½in (14cm) long, 7⅜oz.
$420–480 *HCH*

A Victorian silver Armada pattern ewer, embossed with scrolls and masks, with applied beasts heads and figures flanking vacant cartouches, the cover with articulated handle lever, by Job Frank Hall, London 1894, 12in (30.5cm) high, 28oz.
$1,800–2,000 *S*

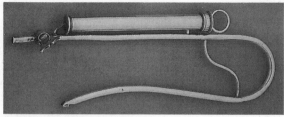

A George III silver wine syphon, with a syringe form plunger, inscribed, flattened bell-shaped tap, by Phipps & Robinson, London 1803, 15in (38cm) long, 11oz.
$4,500–5,250 *S(NY)*

A selection of hallmarked silver decanter labels, including unusual names 'QUINCE', 'WHITE', 'MONTILLA', and 'CALCAVELLA', c1770–1840, 2in (5cm) wide.
$60–90 each *CS*

l. A ceramic wine bin label, marked 'Farrow & Jackson', c1870, 3¼in (8.5cm) diam.
$25–30 *Har*

A ceramic wine bin label, 'PORT', c1870, 5in (12.5cm) wide.
$75–80 *Har*

Three William IV wine labels, by Unite & Hillard, 1¾in (4.5cm) wide.
$300–330 *TGa*

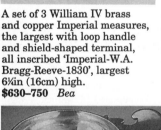

A set of 3 William IV brass and copper Imperial measures, the largest with loop handle and shield-shaped terminal, all inscribed 'Imperial-W.A. Bragg-Reeve-1830', largest 6¼in (16cm) high.
$630–750 *Bea*

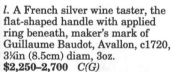

A ceramic wine bin label, 'HOLLANDS', c1870, 5in (12.5cm) wide.
$80–90 *Har*

l. A French silver wine taster, the flat-shaped handle with applied ring beneath, maker's mark of Guillaume Baudot, Avallon, c1720, 3¼in (8.5cm) diam, 3oz.
$2,250–2,700 *C(G)*

A pair of Scottish provincial wine labels, engraved with stiff leaf borders and foliate motifs in each corner, backs engraved with a script initial 'S', incised 'MADEIRA' and 'SHERRY', maker's mark 'MH', for Mark Hinchsliffe, Dumfries, c1820.
$600–750 *P*

A George IV mahogany bottle carrier, the partitions radiating from a central post with brass ring-turned handle, c1825, 15in (38cm) wide.
$900–1,100 *P*

A French wicker-covered flat ovoid bottle, c1840, 15in (38cm) high.
$270–300 *Har*

A George III mahogany decanter carrier, with canted corners and 2 brass bands, with a green japanned metal divided interior and a central brass loop handle, 12in (30.5cm) wide.
$2,500–3,000 *DN*

A George II silver basket, in the form of a scallop shell, on 3 cast dolphin feet, the handle later engraved with a crest and motto, maker's mark of Phillips Garden, London 1754, 13½in (34.5cm) wide, 58oz.
$50,000–54,000 *C*

A George II silver basket, by Peter Archambo I, with pierced sides, the cartouches engraved with a coat-of-arms and motto, engraved crested handle, London 1734, 12in (30.5cm) wide, 69oz.
$52,000–57,000 *S*

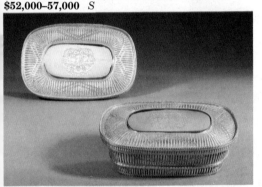

A pair of silver boxes and covers, in the form of baskets, maker's mark of Gabriel Sleath, London 1713, 7in (18cm) wide, 37oz.
$42,000–48,000 *C*

A Victorian punch bowl, on spreading foot, the sides embossed and chased with floral and fish motifs, gilt interior, by John Mortimer and John Samuel Hunt, 1843, 15¼in (38.5cm) wide, 66oz.
$3,750–4,500 *P(B)*

A George V tortoiseshell and silver jewellery box, by Levi & Salaman, Birmingham 1917, 6in (15cm) wide.
$650–750 *TGa*

An Edwardian sweetmeat dish, with pierced sides, by Charles Stuart Harris, London 1903, 6in (15cm) wide.
$300–380 *TGa*

A Victorian parcel-gilt punch bowl, maker's mark of Charles Frederick Hancock, London 1858, 21½in (54.5cm) diam, 329oz.
$45,000–50,000 *C*

A pair of George III silver-gilt spice boxes, covers and stands, engraved with crests and an earl's coronet, maker's mark of John Wakelin and Robert Garrard, London 1800, stands 8¾in (22cm) wide, 37oz.
$50,000–57,000 *C*

A Victorian silver casket, chased with rococo ornament, dragons and demi-lions, hinged cover with lion's head finial, by Charles Reily and George Storer, London 1844, 16½in (42cm) wide, 275oz.
$19,000–22,000 *S(NY)*

A set of 4 silver candlesticks, by François de la Pierre, c1717, 8⅜in (22cm), high, 89.25oz.
$80,000–87,000 *S(G)*

A set of 4 German silver candelabra, bases by Johann Philipp Heckenauer, c1767, 13¼in (33.5cm) high, 149oz.
$48,000–52,000 *S(G)*

A pair of parcel-gilt table candlesticks, by L. R. Ruchmann, Paris, c1825, 8¼in (21cm) high, 83oz.
$18,000–22,000 *S(NY)*

A French silver-gilt *confiturier*, maker's mark 'LJMH', Paris, 1789, 10½in (26.5cm) high, 27oz.
$2,500–3,000 *C(G)*

A chamberstick, by William Grundy, London 1758, 6in (15cm) diam.
$1,000–1,100 *TGa*

A Victorian silver plated table centre épergne, 33in (84cm) high.
$3,700–4,200 *J&L*

A pair of Regency silver four-light candelabra, by William Pitts, London 1809, 8in (20.5cm), 415oz.
$33,000–37,000 *S(NY)*

A Victorian silver centrepiece, The Goodwood Cup, by R. & S. Garrard, London 1840, 21in (53.5cm) overall height.
$30,000–37,000 *S*

A pair of George III salt cellars, London 1786, 2in (5cm) high.
$370–450 *TGa*

A silver Warwick cruet, with original bottles, by James Ker, Edinburgh, c1735, 9⅞in (25cm) high, 40oz.
$4,500–5,300 *JSH*

A silver and glass centrepiece, by Bolin, Moscow, c1896, 15¼in (38.5cm) high.
$50,000–52,000 *S(G)*

An early Victorian mustard and salt set, by Barnard & Co, London 1838, 2in (5cm) high.
$630–700 *TGa*

A silver coffee pot, by Jacob Kuchler, Philadelphia, with monogram 'EGL', c1805, 15in (38cm) high, 48oz gross. **$16,500–19,000** *S(NY)*

A Maltese silver coffee pot, maker's mark 'MC', c1770, 10½in (26.5cm) high, 28oz. **$3,800–4,500** *C(G)*

A Belgian parcel-gilt coffee pot, attributed to Guillaume Dengis, Liège 1768, 13¾in (35cm) high, 57oz. **$60,000–67,000** *S(G)*

An Imperial Austrian silver travelling breakfast service, by E. & T. Schiffer, Vienna 1864, case 20¼in (51.5cm) wide, 150oz gross. **$10,500–12,000** *S(G)*

A Dutch silver-gilt cup and cover, restored, Zwolle 1682, 20in (50.5cm) high, 62oz. **$27,000–30,000** *Bon*

A German silver-gilt 'coin' beaker, maker's mark of Gottlieb Menzel, Augsburg, c1709, 8in (20cm) high, 17oz. **$10,500–12,000** *C(G)*

A German silver tea and coffee service, by Wollenweber of Munich, c1880, lacquered wood tray 34in (86.5cm) wide, 204.75oz, contained in an oak case. **$10,000–11,000** *S*

A French silver-gilt tray, on lion's paw feet, the underside with wood panelling, attributed to Jean-Charles Cahier, Paris 1819–38, 33in (84cm) wide. **$30,000–36,000** *C(G)*

A Belgian silver hot water kettle and burner, maker's mark of Jean-Melchior Dartois, Liège 1772, kettle 7½in (19cm) diam, 86.5oz. **$110,000–120,000** *C(G)*

A silver beer jug, by Thomas
Mason, London 1739,
8½in (21.5cm) high, 38.5oz.
$14,000–15,500 *S*

A parcel-gilt tankard,
maker's mark 'O' in a shield,
possibly Austrian, c1640,
8in (20cm) high, 22.4oz.
$11,000–13,500 *S(G)*

A Victorian matched pair of Cellini
pattern ewers, in Renaissance style,
by Stephen Smith, 1869–71,
11½in (29cm) high, 51oz.
$3,000–3,300 *P(B)*

A pair of silver-gilt
flagons, attributed to
Roger Stevens, London
1638, 13½in (34.5cm) high.
$85,000–97,000 *S*

A silver two-handled vase and cover,
by Benjamin Smith, for Rundell,
Bridge & Rundell, London 1807,
15¼in (39cm) high, 115oz.
$28,000–33,000 *S*

A parcel-gilt tankard, with domed cover,
by George Angell, probably chased by
Frederick Courthope, London 1866,
12¾in (32.5cm) high, 71.5oz.
$11,000–13,500 *S(NY)*

A pair of silver second course dishes, each with
coat-of-arms and gadrooned border, maker's
mark of George Methuen, London 1757,
16in (40.5cm) diam, 108oz.
$30,000–36,000 *C*

A pair of silver sauce boats, each with
engraved coat-of-arms, maker's mark of Paul
de Lamerie, London 1730, Britannia
Standard, 7¾in (19.5cm) long, 30oz.
$67,000–75,000 *C*

A pair of silver meat dishes and covers, the dishes
with maker's mark of Thomas Heming, c1774, the
covers William Brown and William Somersall,
London 1838, 16in (40.5cm) wide, 171.75oz.
$7,800–8,500 *S*

A pair of silver sauce tureens, covers and
liners, engraved with monogram and
coronet, after a design attributed to
E. Hodges Baily, by Paul Storr, London 1817,
9¾in (24.5cm) wide, 135oz.
$48,000–54,000 *S(NY)*

A Victorian silver wine ewer, with stopper, by Walker & Hall, Sheffield 1896, 14½in (37cm) high.
$2,200–2,500 *AMH*

A pair of French silver wine coolers, maker's mark of Pierre-François Turquet, Paris 1838–55, 10in (25.5cm) high, 186.5oz.
$5,200–6,000 *S(G)*

A mahogany spirit barrel, with brass bands, c1790, 13¾in (35cm) high.
$2,500–3,000 *S*

A Dutch walnut and marquetry decanter box, with 6 gilded decanters, early 19thC, 9in (23cm) high.
$1,100–1,200 *FD*

A gilt-bronze wine cooler, attributed to Matthew Boulton, c1775, 9in (23cm) high.
$19,000–22,000 *S*

An oak three-bottle tantalus, with secret drawer containing playing cards, c1890, 14in (35.5cm) wide.
$640–700 *Har*

A Pontypool ware bottle carrier, marked 'Farrow & Jackson, London & Paris', c1860, 9in (23cm) long.
$240–280 *Har*

A silver plated claret bottle holder, c1864, 12in (30.5cm) high.
$120–150 *Har*

A French silver wine cooler and metal liner, maker's mark of Maison Odiot, Paris, c1920, 13¼in (33.5cm) high, 107.7oz.
$6,700–7,500 *S(G)*

A set of 3 Edwardian copper measures, 2 gallon, one gallon and half gallon, with licence stamps.
$330–380 *TMA*

A pair of silver campana-form ice pails, each chased to the front and back with a coat-of-arms, with reeded and shell-capped scroll handles, maker's mark of Paul Storr, London 1818, 10in (25.5cm) high, 235oz.
$57,000–63,000 *Bon*

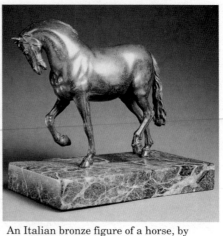

An Italian bronze figure of a horse, by Francesco Fanelli, early 17thC, 9in (23cm) high, on green mottled marble base. **$26,000–31,500** *S*

A bronze figure of a boy, by S. Bizard, signed, 19thC, 11½in (29cm) high. **$300–360** *HEI*

A French bronze group of La Sirène, after the model by Denys Puech, c1890, 42in (106.5cm) high. **$13,000–14,000** *S*

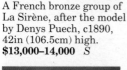

An Austrian cold painted bronze fruit basket, signed 'Geschutzt', early 20thC, 11¾in (30cm) high. **$1,400–1,700** *Hal*

A Restauration bronze and gilt-bronze rhinoceros inkwell, 2 pen holes in place of ears, the back opening to reveal a gilt-bronze fitting, c1825, 5in (12.5cm) high. **$6,000–6,800** *S*

A pair of French bronze figures of Eros and Psyche, after Eugène Laurent, c1890, 19¾in (50cm) high. **$10,500–12,000** *S*

A bronze model of Ariadne, after Michel Anguier, late 17thC, 18½in (47cm) high. **$21,000–23,000** *C*

A pair of French bronze putti, with dark patina with lighter brown highlights, each on a modern square wooden base, 18thC, 11½in (29cm) high. **$11,000–12,800** *C*

A moulded and gilded-copper grasshopper weathervane, by L. W. Cushing & Son, Waltham, Massachusetts, c1883, 18in (46cm) high. **$13,000–13,800** *SNY*

A bronze crocodile, green patina with touches of reddish-brown, by Antoine-Louis Barye, stamped underneath, early 19thC, 7¾in (19.5cm) long. **$6,000–6,800** *S*

A Viennese enamel
scent bottle, with silver
mounts, decorated with
classical figures, c1875,
2¼in (57mm) high.
$1,100–1,300 *BHa*

A pair of Bohemian enamelled
humpen and covers, Haida,
c1870, 26¼in (66.5cm) high.
$5,500–6,300 *S*

A Regency ormolu-mounted tortoiseshell and
black marble inkstand, with 2 cornucopiae,
2 candlesticks and a drawer, 12in (30.5cm) wide.
$12,000–13,000 *C*

A champlevé enamel and copper-gilt
reliquary chasse, with the Martyrdom
of St Saturninus, Limoges, late 12thC,
6½in (16.5cm) high.
$225,000–270,000 *S*

A pair of ormolu and polychrome painted chenets, each chinoiserie
figure wearing pointed hats and robes, 19thC, 13¾in (35cm) high.
$12,000–13,500 *C*

A Victorian cloisonné
vase, by Elkington & Co,
signed and dated '1876',
5in (12.5cm) high.
$750–900 *DN*

A polychrome and gilt roundel,
by Leonard Limousin, 1554,
10in (25.5cm) wide, framed.
$12,000–13,500 *S*

A Regency ormolu-mounted burr yew,
bronze and brass inkstand, with a
cedar and mahogany lined drawer,
10½in (26.5cm) wide.
$5,000–6,000 *C*

A pair of ormolu campana urns,
decorated with vines and figures,
on a fluted waisted foot and square
plinth, 19thC, 10½in (26.5cm) high.
$3,300–3,750 *C*

An ormolu stand, inscribed
and engraved in Russian
with masonic emblems,
18thC, 8in (20.5cm) high.
$2,400–2,700 *C*

A pair of ormolu-mounted porphyry
urns, each body with a satyr's mask,
fruiting vines and swags, 19thC,
10¾in (27.5cm) high.
$9,000–10,500 *C*

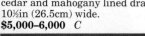

A marble bust, by Pietro Calvi, signed and dated '1874', on a turned socle, 26½in (67.5cm) high.
$5,500–6,300 *Bon*

An alabaster figure, emblematic of history, on a naturalistic base, signed 'A. Giuliani', restored, late 19thC, 36in (91.5cm) high.
$6,300–7,300 *C(SP)*

A white marble figure of Venus, standing by a flower-adorned urn, signed 'Gaetano Mercanti', on a rocky base, late 19thC, 37in (94cm) high.
$28,500–33,000 *C(SP)*

An Italian white marble figure, depicting Venus crouching, 19thC, 33½in (85cm) high.
$4,800–5,200 *CSK*

A French terracotta figure of a lady, c1910, 33½in (85cm) high.
$830–1,000 *HIS*

A white marble bust of a girl, after the antique, wearing a ribbon in her hair, late 18thC, 19in (48.5cm) high.
$7,500–8,200 *P(H)*

A French *bleu tureau* marble study of a horse, on a naturalistic base inscribed 'H. Merlini Editeur, Boulogne', and '5/5', on a *griotte* marble plinth, late 19thC, 21in (53.5cm) high.
$6,700–7,500 *C(SP)*

An Italian carved marble group of 2 cherubs playing with a billy goat, on a naturalistic base, and a group of 2 cherubs stroking a spaniel, late 19thC, 36½in (93cm) high.
$12,000–13,500 *P*

A white marble figure, entitled 'Mignon', signed 'F. Galli Galeria Prof. P. Bazzanti Florence', late 19thC, 43½in (110.5cm), on a marble column.
$13,000–14,200 *S*

An American white marble bust, inscribed 'Venezia', signed 'L. G. Mead', late 19thC, with a green marble socle, 27in (68.5cm) high.
$10,000–10,800 *S*

A Welsh beech love spoon, pierced with rosettes, with 2 quiver finials, early 19thC, 19½in (49.5cm) long.
$5,000–5,700 *CSK*

A pair of George II giltwood brackets, with Zephyr masks and scallop shell backplates, regilt, 14¾in (37.5cm) wide.
$7,800–8,800 *C*

A George III giltwood jardinière, with leaf handles, paw feet and a copper liner, repaired, late 18thC, 29in (73.5cm) wide. **$9,000–10,500** *S(NY)*

A pair of polychrome painted rams, each on a gadrooned plinth, damaged, late 19thC, 19in (48.5cm) wide. **$13,500–15,000** *S(NY)*

A French boxwood lever-action type nutcracker, dated '1750', 6in (15cm) high.
$1,500–1,800 *CSK*

A Norwegian burr birchwood *kasa*, with a horse's head on each side, c1780, 14in (35.5cm) wide.
$1,500–1,800 *RYA*

A polychrome and parcel giltwood panel, of the Virgin and Child, possibly Spanish, late 17thC, 22in (56cm) high.
$1,800–2,000 *CSK*

A Flemish carved oak panel, depicting putti, 17thC, 18½in (47cm) wide.
$900–1,000 *DBA*

A Continental carved oak panel, c1620, 18in (45.5cm) high.
$1,500–1,800 *PHA*

A pair of Régence giltwood sphinxes, each with long braids and a headdress, a cloth with husk-trails over its back, the reverse with a plaque with a flowerhead and foliage, on a moulded shaped base and later simulated marble plinth, re-gilt, 15½in (39.5cm) wide.
$5,200–5,700 *C*

A grand pianoforte, by John Broadwood & Son, No. 2200, dated '1801', 42in (106.5cm) wide.
$10,500–12,000 *S*

A mahogany two-manual harpsichord, by Andreas Ruckers, Antwerp, the later baton inscribed and dated '1623', 37in (94cm) wide.
$135,000–150,000 *S*

A mahogany-cased chamber organ by James Grange Hancock, London, inscribed on a plaque, c1900, 46½in (118cm) wide.
$16,500–19,500 *S*

A walnut spinet, No. 1243, by Thomas Hitchcock the Younger, London, inscribed and signed, early 18thC, 73½in (186.5cm) long.
$16,500–19,500 *S*

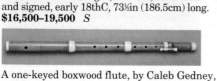

A one-keyed boxwood flute, by Caleb Gedney, mid-18thC, sounding length 21¼in (54cm).
$5,200–6,000 *S*

A one-keyed rosewood flute, by Thomas Stanesby Jr, mid-18thC, 21½in (54.5cm), long.
$14,000–16,500 *S*

A concert guitar, No. 257, by Ignacio Fleta, dated '1962', length of back 19½in (49.5cm), cased.
$26,000–30,000 *S*

A Bechstein decorated rosewood grand piano, No. 42684, c1900, 80in (203cm) long.
$13,500–15,000 *CSK*

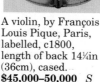

An Italian violoncello, by Giovanni Battista Guadagnini, labelled, 1757, length of back 28in (71cm).
$250,000–270,000 *C*

A violin, by François Louis Pique, Paris, labelled, c1800, length of back 14¼in (36cm), cased.
$45,000–50,000 *S*

A violin, by Antonio Stradivari, Cremona, labelled, 1728, the head later, length of back 14in (35.5cm).
$210,000–240,000 *S*

An Italian violin, by Sanctus Seraphin, labelled, c1700, length of back 14in (35.5cm), cased.
$52,000–57,000 *C*

A pair of Japanese bronze elephants, with dragon
medallions, Meiji period, 34in (86.5cm) wide.
$39,000–42,000 *S*

A mottled green jade boulder, carved with
2 horses on a path, late Qing Dynasty,
14½in (37cm) wide.
$7,800–8,800 *C*

A finely cast gilt-bronze
figure of Buddha, Ming
Dynasty, 14½in (37cm) wide.
$17,500–20,000 *S*

A carved wood figure of
the Priest Honen, 18thC,
27¼in (69cm) high.
$3,000–3,750 *S(NY)*

A carved jade figure of a horse, with
bulbous eyes and flaring nostrils,
Ming Dynasty, 10¼in (26cm) wide.
$55,000–60,000 *S(NY)*

A gilt-bronze figure of a
Bodhisattva, 17th/18thC,
16in (40.5cm) high.
$8,300–9,000 *S(NY)*

A lacquer gilt-bronze figure
of a Bodhisattva, on a carved
wood stand, Ming Dynasty,
24½in (62cm) high.
$19,500–22,000 *S(NY)*

A pair of iron figures of Yan Wang,
the backs inscribed, on shaped stands
dated for 1517, 36½in (92.5cm) high.
$26,000–30,000 *C*

A Korean gilt-bronze
figure of Buddha,
Unified Silla period,
5in (12.5cm) high.
$68,000–78,000 *S(NY)*

A pair of gilt-bronze
cloisonné and champlevé
enamel elephants,
Qianlong period,
11¾in (30cm) high.
$16,500–19,500 *C*

Three Japanese papier mâché and woo
dolls, each dressed as a warrior in
lacquered armour and brocade robes,
damaged, 19thC, 7in (18cm) high.
$900–1,000 *S(NY)*

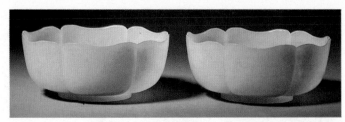

A pair of white jade flower-shaped bowls, with lobed sides and undulating rims, incised Qianlong four-character marks and of the period, 6in (15cm) diam.
$55,000–60,000 *C*

A Canton enamel dish, restored, Qianlong mark, 8in (20.5cm) diam.
$570–670 *S(NY)*

A cloisonné enamel meiping, Ming Dynasty, damaged, 16th/17thC, 12in (30.5cm) high.
$4,500–5,300 *S*

A cloisonné enamel beaker vase, the sides set with 4 vertical flanges, some damage, Ming Dynasty, 16in (40.5cm) high.
$4,800–5,500 *S*

A Ginbari cloisonné enamel vase, with silver rims, Meiji period, 12in (30.5cm) high.
$1,000–1,200 *S(NY)*

A jadeite two-handled vase and cover, late Qing Dynasty, 10¼in (26cm) high, on wooden stand.
$12,000–13,500 *C*

An imitation gilt-bronze censer, the mark carved in relief within a countersunk square, Qianlong period, 4¼in (11cm) diam.
$18,000–20,000 *S(HK)*

A pair of Canton enamel dishes, decorated with European scenes, the rim with 5-shaped panels, Qing Dynasty, 13½in (34cm) diam.
$13,500–15,000 *S*

A cloisonné enamel vase, signed 'Tamura', Meiji period, 12¼in (31cm) high.
$1,350–1,500 *S(NY)*

A pair of Japanese bronze vases, with *ho-o* handles, decorated in relief with bands of raised panels of kirin and dragons, above borders of angular lappets, raised seal marks to the base, c1900, 14in (35.5cm) high.
$1,500–2,300 *CSK*

A Japanese compressed circular silver bowl, with everted rim, on a carved hardwood stand, the bowl signed, late 19thC, 10½in (26.5cm) diam.
$4,000–4,500 *DN*

A pair of black lacquer horseshoe-back armchairs, each upper panel with a beaded cloud medallion, 17th/18thC.
$4,500–5,200 *S(NY)*

A pair of Chinese elmwood horseshoe-back chairs, with cane seats, c1860.
$2,700–3,000 *ORI*

A child's rattan chair, designed for the Brighton Pavilion, c1820.
$750–820 *ORI*

A Chinese carved walnut floor standing cabinet, c1870, 42in (106.5cm) wide.
$3,000–3,300 *ORI*

A pair of Chinese carved elmwood square backed chairs, with hardwood seats, c1870.
$2,700–3,000 *ORI*

A Chinese coffer, the top with everted ends, the frieze with 3 drawers, above 2 doors flanked by removable panels, 18thC, 71½in (181.5cm) wide.
$9,300–10,000 *S(NY)*

A tall stand, with carved apron, restored, 18thC, 48in (122cm) high.
$11,300–12,300 *S(NY)*

A Japanese gilt-decorated lacquered rosewood table, 19thC, 14in (35.5cm) wide.
$4,500–5,200 *S(NY)*

A Chinese black lacquer and gilt eleven-fold screen, decorated with figures, pagodas and foliage, dated '1782', 104in (264cm) high.
$45,000–52,000 *CSK*

A Chinese export lacquer eight-leaf screen, decorated with a scene of palace life and a foliate border with birds and insects perched in trees, 19thC, 85in (216cm) high.
$12,000–13,500 *C*

A lacquered wood *norimono*, with sliding door on each side, hinged flap in roof, interior with padded back support and armrests, lined with gold paper, 18th/19thC, 33in (84cm) wide.
$82,000–90,000 *S*

A glass snuff bottle, carved in high relief, Qianlong period, 3in (75mm) high.
$420–500 *S*

A glass snuff bottle, of flattened spherical form with a waisted neck, decorated with swirls, 1740–1800, 2¾in (70mm) high.
$1,275–1,425 *S(HK)*

A glass snuff bottle, by Chen Zhongsan, with figures searching for prunus, the other side with a grasshopper, 1918, 2⅜in (60mm) high.
$2,250–2,750 *S*

A single overlay snuff bottle, 19thC, 2¾in (70mm) high.
$550–630 *S*

A decorated *laque burgauté* snuff bottle, 1900–39, 3in (75mm) high.
$1,400–1,500 *S(NY)*

A double overlay glass snuff bottle, Daoguang period, 2in (50mm) high.
$3,750–4,500 *S*

A gold lacquer three-case inro and netsuke, by Masayuki, with *shibayama* decoration, 19thC, inro 4¼in (110mm) high.
$9,750–11,250 *S*

A *mito-kinko* carved tsuba, with gilt edging, 19thC, 2¾in (70mm) high.
$2,800–3,500 *C*

A *laque burgauté* snuff bottle, with mother-of-pearl inlay, c1800, 3¼in (85mm) high.
$4,500–5,250 *S*

An inlaid *sentoku* tsuba, depicting Daikoku, signed 'Inabanosuke Terusugu', Meiji period, 4in (100mm) wide.
$2,250–2,750 *S(NY)*

A four-case gold ground inro, decorated in gold and silver, minor chips, signed 'Toyo Saku', 19thC, 3¼in (85mm) high.
$5,250–6,000 *C*

A gold and *gyobu* ground jar-shaped five-case inro, signed 'Toshihide', late 19thC, 3¼in (85mm) high.
$8,000–9,750 *C*

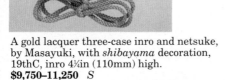

A Chinese Imperial dragon
robe, with 8 dragons in gilt
threads, and 12 symbols, over
a sea-wave, probably re-lined,
altered, 19thC.
$9,400–9,800 *CSK*

A Chinese summer dragon
robe, with 4 Imperial symbols,
and 9 dragons, 19thC.
$11,250–12,750 *CSK*

A fine gauze dragon robe, with
couched gold dragons and *shou*
medallions, late 19thC.
$3,000–3,750 *S(NY)*

A Chinese informal coat,
the peonies worked in
Peking knots, 19thC.
$600–675 *CSK*

A pair of Chinese reverse mirror paintings
depicting female deities riding Buddhist
lions, in giltwood frames, one mirror
cracked, 18thC, 22 x 16in (56 x 41cm).
$6,000–6,750 *P*

An embroidered court official
rank apron, the top with original
gilt rings, Choson Dynasty, 19thC,
23½ x 10½in (59.5 x 26.5cm).
$4,500–5,250 *S(NY)*

A scroll, attributed to
Lang Shining, 1784,
73 x 35½in (185 x 90.5cm).
$5,000–5,800 *C*

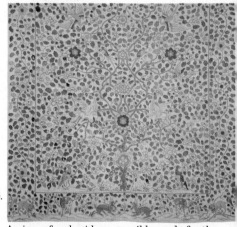

A piece of embroidery, possibly made for the
Portuguese market, depicting blossoms, birds,
mythical beasts and deer, within a floral border,
now backed, c1700, 62½ x 63in (159 x 160cm).
$2,250–2,700 *S(NY)*

A New Year's robe, with narcissus
roundels, black borders, and flowering
prunus, late 19thC, 55½in (141cm) long.
$4,500–5,250 *S(NY)*

A Chinese mirror painting, painted with figures, a horse
and deer, probably depicting the estuary of the Pearl
River, mid-18thC, in a gilt frame, 29 x 49in (74 x 124cm).
$13,000–14,250 *S*

A pair of George III giltwood two-light girandôles, re-gilt and later mirrors, 41in (104cm) high. **$14,000–15,000** *C*

A pair of bronze candelabra, c1795, 24in (61cm) high. **$12,000–13,500** *S*

A pair of French ormolu lanterns, 20thC, 58in (147cm) high. **$26,250–28,500** *C*

A pair of George III giltwood two-light girandôles, restored, 33½in (85cm) high. **$21,000–24,000** *C*

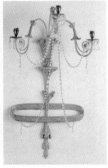

A pair of giltwood and plaster wall lights, c1860, 33in (84cm) high. **$3,500–4,000** *S*

A pair of George III giltwood girondôles, 36in (91.5cm) high. **$27,000–30,000** *S(NY)*

A pair of French bronze candelabra, 25¼in (64cm) high. **$8,000–9,200** *S*

A pair of Louis XVI ormolu, bronze and marble twin-light candelabra, drilled for electricity, on later wooden plinths, 21¼in (54cm) high overall. **$16,500–18,000** *C*

A pair of Louis XV ormolu and Meissen porcelain two-light candelabra, after the model by J. J. Kändler and P. Reinicke, restored, c1745, 10½in (26.5cm) high. **$16,500–18,000** *C*

A set of 3 American Baccarat glass and brass oil lamps, each with octagonal cut-glass urn and lid and 3 shell-cut glass feet, minor damage, mid-19thC, 24¾in (63cm) high. **$8,400–9,200** *S*

A pair of Louis XVI ormolu and white marble three-light candelabra, with urn-shaped bodies and panelled bardiglio marble collar, ribbon-twist handles, on square plinths, 24¾in (62cm) high. **$10,500–12,000** *C*

A bronze and gilt-bronze light, the bowl applied with anthemion, divided by male masks, c1815, 48in (122cm) high.
$33,000–37,500 *S*

A Baltic neo-classical gilt-metal and glass chandelier, early 19thC, 25in (63.5cm) diam.
$17,250–20,250 *S(NY)*

A Victorian brass hall lantern, late 19thC, 18in (45.5cm) high
$4,000–5,250 *S(NY)*

An Edwardian brass and stained glass hall lantern, 29in (73.5cm) high.
$1,200–1,350 *CSK*

A Victorian brass Gothic style hall lantern, 46½in (118cm) high.
$6,500–7,500 *C*

A brass hanging lantern, with four-branch candelabrum, ball finials and feet, late 19thC, 46½in (118cm) high.
$5,500–6,200 *S*

An Italian neo-classical painted alabaster light, decorated with signs of the zodiac, c1830, 21in (53.5cm) high.
$17,250–18,750 *S*

A pair of mid-Victorian papier mâché ebonised and parcel-gilt six-light torchères, inlaid with mother-of-pearl foliage, on later plinths, some damage, 75in (190.5cm) high.
$7,700–8,000 *C*

A cut glass and gilt-brass chandelier, attributed to Perry & Co, the 12 scrolled arms with drop-hung drip-pans joined by double swags of cut glass drops and pendants, mid-19thC, 55in (140cm) high.
$30,000–33,000 *S*

A white marble and gilt-metal standard lamp, the shade applied with glass beads, early 20thC, 67½in (171.5cm) high.
$1,500–1,800 *CSK*

A Coalbrookdale fern and blackberry pattern cast iron seat, with metal slats, stamped 'C. B. Dale, No. 113617', c1870, 75in (190.5cm) wide.
$1,400–1,800 S(S)

A lead urn, with a frieze of putti beneath foliage, on an associated Portland stone base, adapted, mid-18thC, 25in (63.5cm) high.
$5,200–6,000 S(S)

A bronze figure of Diana the Huntress, with a hound, signed 'A. J. Oakley 1931', 48in (122cm) high.
$10,500–12,000 S(S)

A cast iron garden seat, with wooden planked seat and back, the end supports in the form of hissing serpents, late 19thC, 66in (167.5cm) wide.
$900–1,200 S(S)

Two lead figures of Autumn, by the Bromsgrove Guild of Applied Arts, both cherubs wearing oversized helmets, early 20thC, 18in (45.5cm) high.
$6,000–6,750 each S(S)

An Italian white marble figure of Raphael, in Renaissance dress, titled and signed 'Zoachi Emilio Fece 1869 Firenze', on a square panelled pedestal, 19thC, 78in (198cm) high.
$13,500–15,000 S(S)

A pair of Pulham stoneware lidded urns, with rope twist decoration, on a square base, c1900, 39in (99cm) high.
$5,000–5,500 S(S)

A pair of terracotta garden urns, with flared necks, decorated with fruit and leaves, riven snake handles, late 19thC, 30½in (77cm) high.
$3,400–4,200 S

A set of four Italian carved marble figures, depicting the four seasons, c1700, largest 91in (231cm) high.
$360,000–420,000 CSK

A pair of limestone square pedestals, carved in relief with military trophies, flanked by buttresses, late 17thC, 42½in (108cm) high.
$7,000–7,800 CSK

A Chippendale paint-decorated door surround, in 13 pieces, with swan-necked pediment, 4 columns each with Corinthian capitals, New England, c1775, 192in (488cm) high.
$18,000–21,000 *S(NY)*

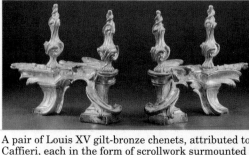

A pair of Louis XV gilt-bronze chenets, attributed to Caffieri, each in the form of scrollwork surmounted by 2 scrolled finials, c1740, 14in (36cm) high.
$9,750–11,200 *S*

A George III pine and composition fire surround, with moulded shelf above a panel depicting a shepherd, the jambs with flowers and foliage, c1780, 55⅛in (141cm) high.
$2,700–3,300 *S*

A set of 3 brass and steel fire irons, each with turned stems and pineapple finials, c1830.
$4,000–4,500 *S*

A set of 3 brass fire irons, with turned stems and scroll and mask cast finials, c1830
$2,700–3,300 *S*

l. A pair of brass fire tongs, late 17thC, 31in (79cm) long.
$450–530 *KEY*

A Victorian brass fire screen, with leaded glass, c1880, 33in (84cm) high.
$150–180 *ASH*

A George III carved pine chimney piece, 54in (137cm) high.
$2,700–3,300 *SWO*

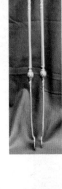

A late Georgian cast iron fuel trough, with ring pull handles and rolled copper edging, 15in (38cm) wide.
$375–450 *TMA*

A Victorian cast iron fireplace, with tiled surround, 38¼in (97cm) high.
$600–675 *DOR*

A pair of Louis XVI gilt-bronze chenets, with ribboned swags of flowers, 14½in (37cm) high.
$7,800–8,800 *S*

A brass and iron fire grate and fireback, carved with a battle scene, and a set of 3 fire irons, c1835, grate 43¼in (110cm) wide.
$7,800–8,800 *S*

ARCHITECTURAL ANTIQUES
Bronze & Iron

A set of 4 Italian bronze urns, derived from the Borghese and Medici vases, after the antique, c1820, 19in (48.5cm) high.
$46,500–52,500 *HDS*

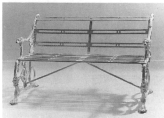

A white painted cast iron garden bench, with a slatted wood seat, 19thC, 48in (122cm) wide.
$1,400–1,500 *CAG*

A Victorian Coalbrookdale cast iron garden bench, in serpent and grape pattern, the arms with dogs' head terminals, registration mark for 1844, 50in (127cm) wide.
$750–900 *Bri*

A bronze group of the infant Bacchus seated on the shoulders of Pan, after the antique, on a base cast with a tree trunk draped with a ram's pelt and hung with pan pipes, weathered green patination, late 19thC, 72in (183cm) high, on a stone plinth.
$17,250–19,500 *S(S)*

A wrought iron tree seat, early 19thC, 72in (183cm) diam.
$3,000–3,750 *GHA*

A French cast iron bridge, the sides cast in the form of rustic branches, with wooden planked base, c1880, 245in (622cm) long.
$15,750–18,000 *S(S)*

A cast iron plant stand, of semi-circular form, arranged in 3 tiers pierced with octagons, 37½in 95.5cm) high.
$1,800–2,000 *S(S)*

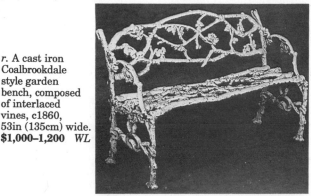

r. A cast iron Coalbrookdale style garden bench, composed of interlaced vines, c1860, 53in (135cm) wide.
$1,000–1,200 *WL*

l. A pair of cast iron urns, the sides cast with cartouches flanked by flowers beneath a frieze of 10 signs of the zodiac, the sides with satyr masks below winged Egyptian beasts, on rising circular feet and square bases, 29½in 75cm) high.
$3,000–3,750 *S(S)*

A wrought iron garden bench, 19thC, 74½in (189cm) wide.
$750–900 *Hal*

Iron

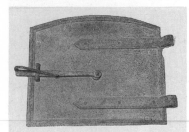

A cast iron bread oven door, c1860, 17¾in (45cm) wide.
$100–125 *DOR*

An Ideal Standard cast iron radiator, with 10 sections, 1930s, 23¼in (59cm) wide.
$100–120 *DOR*

A pair of cast iron garden urns, the campana-shaped bodies decorated with scrolling arabesques, on square bases and plinths, 19thC, 48in (122cm) high.
$1,500–1,800 *WW*

A pair of Victorian cast iron garden urns, probably Coalbrookdale, the fluted and reeded campana-shaped bodies with egg-and-dart rims, each on a fluted trumpet-shaped foot and stepped square base, late 19thC, 20in (51cm) high.
$750–900 *Hal*

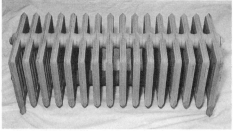

A Crane cast iron radiator, c1930, 37in (94cm) wide.
$130–150 *DOR*

Lead

A lead cistern, with panelled front and sides, the front with initials 'RSM' inside an oval, and the date '1785' between foliate decoration, 64½in (164cm) wide.
$7,000–7,800 *S(S)*

A Victorian cast iron water pump, 76in (193cm) high.
$450–530 *DOR*

A lead garden ornament, depicting a curly-headed child looking at her right hand, on a circular base, 19thC, 28in (71cm) high.
$750–900 *DA*

Marble

A pair of Italian marble lions, early 16thC, 14in (35.5cm) high.
$3,700–4,500 *DBA*

A white marble bust of a girl, wearing a low-cut dress with a brooch, signed 'S. S. Bricoli, Roma', c1900, 29in (73.5cm) high.
$2,700–3,000 *S(S)*

A carved marble bust of Hercules, 18thC, 21in (53.5cm) high.
$3,750–4,500 *TMA*

A pair of white marble urns, each of semi-lobed campana form with everted rim, on a rising circular foot and square base, late 19thC, 27in (68.5cm) high.
$3,300–3,700 *S(S)*

Stone

A white marble figure of a boy, holding a conch shell to his ear, signed 'C. Steinhausen Fec, Rome 1860', 37¾in (96cm) high.
$5,500–6,300 *S(S)*

A Victorian Gothic variegated marble column, the triform top on an octagonal plinth, the cluster column with a quatrefoil centred with an 'S' and headed by flanking angels, on a grey octagonal plinth, 54in (137cm) high.
$1,600–2,000 *P(Sc)*

An Italian white marble group of 2 children, dressed in classical robes, c1870, 40in (101.5cm) high.
$4,000–4,800 *S(S)*

A limestone trough, 18thC, 36¼in (92cm) wide.
$750–900 *DOR*

A quantity of York flagstones, 19thC.
$50–60 per sq yd *DOR*

A pair of limestone finials, each of semi-lobed baluster form, carved with cherubs' masks below a flame finial, c1760, 55in (139.5cm) high.
$2,250–2,500 *S(S)*

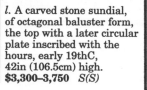

A stoneware pedestal, of baluster form moulded in relief with wisteria on a trellis, on an acanthus cast foot, stamped 'Doulton Lambeth', c1900, 42in (106.5cm) high.
$2,000–2,300 *S(S)*

l. A carved stone sundial, of octagonal baluster form, the top with a later circular plate inscribed with the hours, early 19thC, 42in (106.5cm) high.
$3,300–3,750 *S(S)*

A carved sandstone figure of a lion, unfinished, on a rounded base, 19thC, 36in (91.5cm) high.
$1,800–2,000 *S(S)*

A Coade stone figure of Ceres, on a rectangular base, late 18thC, 60in (152.5cm) high, on a Portland stone base.
$9,000–10,500 *S(S)*

A carved stone figure of a soldier of the 88th Foot Connaught Rangers, early 19thC, 80in (203cm) high.
$6,300–7,500 *S(S)*

r. A stoneware figure of Diana de Gabies, possibly by Blashfield, on a square base, late 19thC, 64in (162.5cm) high.
$2,300–3,000 *S(S)*

l. A limestone figure of Autumn, depicting a girl in classical dress with vines entwined in her hair, one arm held aloft, on a bowfronted base, 18thC, 61in (155cm) high.
$6,300–7,500 *S(S)*

A sandstone urn, carved in high relief with fruiting vines, on a baluster column carved in the form of 3 birds, on a shaped square foot and paw supports, birds' heads missing, c1870, 62in (157.5cm) high.
$3,000–3,300 *S(S)*

A Coade stone keystone, modelled in relief with the mask of a laughing satyr, the base stamped 'Coade, Lambeth, 1797', 10½in (26.5cm) high.
$3,400–4,000 *S(S)*

A sandstone birdbath, the bowl carved with stylised waves on 3 overscrolled supports, on a cruciform base, 19thC, 30in (76cm) diam.
$2,300–2,700 *S(S)*

A carved sandstone figure of a lady, 19thC, 57in (145cm) high.
$2,000–2,700 *Mit*

A York stone seat, with arched back, 4 panels carved in relief with flowers, a scrolled central section, on 5 scrolled fluted supports, 19thC, 144in (366cm) wide.
$6,000–6,700 *S(S)*

Terracotta

r. A terracotta figure of Bacchus, draped in a lion skin, next to a tree stump entwined with vines, on a square base, 20thC, 56in (142cm) high, on a pedestal.
$4,500–5,250 *S(S)*

l. A pair of terracotta urns, late 19thC, 21in (53.5cm) high, on square panelled pedestals moulded with laurel leaves.
$3,000–3,300 *S(S)*

A quantity of terracotta half-divided stable paviours, late 19thC, 9in (23cm) long.
$1–2 each *DOR*

Bathroom Fittings

A cast iron roll-top enamelled bath, with enamelled soap dish, no overflow, on ball-and-claw feet, 19thC, 72in (183cm) long.
$1,200–1,300 *DOR*

A zinc bath, with original marbling decoration and central waste, on casters, late 19thC, 69¾in (177cm) long.
$1,200–1,300 *DOR*

l. A cast iron roll-top enamelled bath, with kneed feet, late 19thC, 70in (178cm) long.
$530–670 *DOR*

A Victorian multi-coloured floral basin, 27in (68.5cm) wide.
$1,700–2,250 *WRe*

l. An Edwardian cloakroom basin, 23in (58.5cm) wide.
$370–530 *WRe*

A spongeware kidney-shaped sink, with leadless glaze, marked 'The Pearl', with original solid nickel taps, c1890, 40¼in (102cm) wide.
$500–560 *DOR*

A ceramic wash basin, by Twyfords, with pedestal, c1930, 25in (63.5cm) wide.
$260–300 *BAS*

An Edwardian corner basin, by Royal Doulton, together with pedestal, 30in (76cm) wide.
$750–900 *WRe*

A Victorian blue and white floral basin, marked 'Meda', together with nickel-plated mixer taps, 27in (68.5cm) wide.
$1,800–2,000 *WRe*

A German marble washstand, c1930, 46in (117cm) wide.
$1,500–1,800 *WRe*

A copper and brass shower mixer, c1920, 20in (51cm) high.
$80–100 *HEM*

A fire clay barber's basin, by Ogee, c1920, 37in (94cm) wide.
$600–750 *WRe*

A bidet, with brass fittings, c1930, 27in (68.5cm) wide.
$570–670 *WRe*

A high level cistern, by J. Duckett & Son Ltd, c1900, 20in (51cm) wide.
$450–530 *WRe*

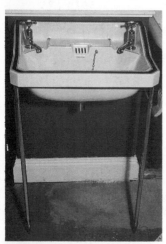

A black and white basin, by Whieldon, on a chrome stand, c1930, 22in (56cm) wide.
$600–700 *WRe*

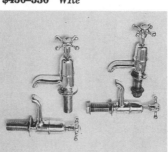

A pair of nickel plated bath taps, 1930s, 9in (23cm) high.
$180–230 *WRe*

l. Two pairs of matching brass sink and bath taps, with pottery heads, c1920, bath 9¼in (23.5cm) high.
$150–170 *HEM*

A pair of chrome taps, c1930,
9in (23cm) high.
$110–125 *BAS*

A pair of Edwardian quarter-turn
basin taps, with china handles,
5in (12.5cm) high.
$150–180 *WRe*

A black toilet pan, c1930,
16in (40.5cm) high.
$450–530 *WRe*

A Victorian blue and white
floral pattern toilet pan, by
Shanks, with octagonal
pedestal, 17in (43cm) high.
$1,300–1,500 *WRe*

The Velox wash-down closet,
with blue and white transfer
print, c1860, 17in (43cm) high.
$600–670 *BAS*

The Vaal toilet pan, c1900,
16½in (42cm) high.
$240–300 *DOR*

l. The Unitas
wash-out closet,
with Florentine
design, late 19thC,
17¼in (44cm) high.
$450–530 *DOR*

*This model was
the first all-ceramic
pedestal wash-out
closet, invented by
Thomas Twyford
in 1883.*

A Bostel's Excelsior rim-flush toilet, late 19thC,
17¼in (44cm) high.
$630–750 *DOR*

Doors & Door Furniture

An oak planked door, c1650, 71¾in (182.5cm) high.
$530–560 *DOR*

Four Victorian pine-panelled double beaded doors, 78in (198cm) high.
$75–90 each *DOR*

A Victorian pine planked front door, with iron studs, 71in (180cm) high.
$240–270 *DOR*

An Arts and Crafts oak door, c1910, 67in (170cm) high.
$150–230 *DOR*

r. A brass bell push, c1880, 3½in (9cm) high.
$60–70 *HEM*

l. A Georgian brass door lock, c1790, 7in (18cm) wide.
$100–120

A brass bell push, inscribed 'Tradesmen', c1890, 4in (10cm) diam.
$60–75 *HEM*

A brass door handle, inscribed 'Pull', c1930, 12in (30.5cm) high.
$15–20 *HEM*

A cast brass door knocker, in the form of a face, c1880, 7in (18cm) high.
$90–100 *HEM*

A pair of brass 'beehive' door knobs, c1860, 2½in (6.5cm) long.
$90–100 *HEM*

Fireplaces

A cast iron fender, dated '1840', 47¼in (120cm) long.
$500–550 *DOR*

A Victorian cast iron fender, with brass decorations, 57in (145cm) long.
$530–600 *WRe*

A cast iron fireback, c1663, 24in (61cm) high.
$450–530 *KEY*

A cast iron fireback, c1660, 26in (66cm) high.
$600–670 *KEY*

A pair of Italian wrought iron firedogs, with brass finials, 17thC, 28in (71cm) high.
$1,500–1,800 *KEY*

l. An Edwardian fire basket, 25in (63.5cm) high.
$530–600 *WRe*

r. A pair of wrought iron and brass firedogs, c1680, 18in (45.5cm) high.
$1,200–1,300 *KEY*

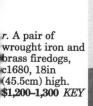

An hourglass-shaped hob grate, 18thC, 39in (99cm) wide.
$1,100–1,300 *WRe*

A Regency cast iron register hob,
36in (91.5cm) high.
$630–750 *WRe*

A hob grate, late 18thC,
28in (71cm) wide.
$560–670 *WRe*

An early Victorian hob grate,
c1840, 38in (96.5cm) wide.
$530–600 *VF*

A cast iron register grate, with
boilers, 1830s, 36in (91.5cm) high.
$600–670 *WRe*

A Georgian cast iron register
grate, with cast relief decoration,
c1810, 39in (99cm) high.
$1,500–1,800 *WRe*

A Victorian cast iron hob grate,
c1840, 62in (157.5cm) wide.
$530–600 *VF*

r. A Victorian fireplace with twelve-
tile insert, c1885, 48in (122cm) wide.
$530–600 *VF*

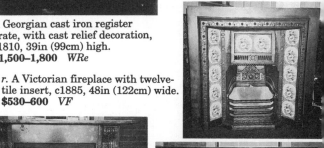

A Victorian combination grate,
c1890, 48in (122cm) wide.
$450–530 *VF*

A Belgian red fossil marble fireplace
surround, with scrolled corbled
decoration, 64in (162.5cm) wide.
$1,000–1,100
A Victorian insert with brass
hood, c1890.
$600–670 *VF*

A Victorian mahogany fire surround,
c1890, 68in (172.5cm) wide.
$900–1,000
A Victorian tiled insert, c1900.
$530–600 *VF*

A cast iron bedroom fireplace,
c1860, 36in (91.5cm) high.
$230–260 *BAS*

A cast iron fireplace and grate,
with tiled decoration, c1900,
52in (132cm) wide.
$670–820 *BAS*

An Art Nouveau fireplace,
with green tiled insert, c1905,
44in (112cm) wide.
$530–600 *VF*

A mid-Victorian arched marble fireplace surround, with matching register grate, 69in (175.5cm) wide. **$2,000–2,500** *WRe*

An Edwardian oak fire surround, with Delft tiles, 52in (132cm) high. **$1,650–1,800** *WRe*

An Art Nouveau cast iron fire surround, with reproduction tiles, c1900, 47in (119.5cm) high. **$600–670** *BAS*

A set of 3 polished steel fire irons, the cylindrical shafts with inverted trumpet-shaped grips with knop finials, the waisted shovel pierced with a foliate motif, mid-19thC, 24in (61cm) long. **$710–780** *CSK*

r. A steel footman, the D-shaped top with fretwork decorated frieze, on 3 slender legs with pad feet, 18thC, 12½in (32cm) high. **$670–750** *WIL*

An Edwardian mahogany fireplace, 50in (127cm) high. **$750–1,200** *WRe*

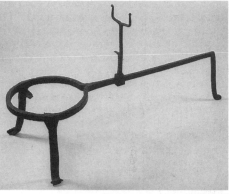

A wrought iron trivet, early 18thC, 24in (61cm) long. **$120–150** *TMA*

A set of 3 brass and steel fire irons, the brass handles with leaf and fleur de lys castings, the shovel with a pierced bell-shaped pan, c1830, 24in (61cm) long. **$4,000–4,200** *S*

A late Victorian patinated cast iron fireside companion set, modelled as a suit of armour, stamped 'NESTOR', 26in (66cm) high. **$390–450** *CSK*

METALWARE

A lot of people who now collect antique metalware started off buying furniture and, when they had acquired all that their home would reasonably take, moved on to collecting things to put on those pieces of furniture – brass candlesticks for the side tables, or pewter plates for the kitchen dresser, for example. If this course appeals, then I would advise trying to keep the period of the items, the candlesticks, plates, tankards or whatever, as close as possible to the date of the piece of furniture.

From the early years of the 18th century until around 1780, brass candlesticks were made by casting the stem in two halves and if you look carefully you will see a vertical join. The underside of the base of such a candlestick would have been cleaned off by turning and scraping. Reproductions of this type are usually heavier than the real thing and still have the sand casting marks under the base.

One of the few items that have not been copied and reproduced in any number are keys. A group of old keys displayed against a plain wall can make an interesting decorative feature and they can cost as little as a few cents for a 19th century example, or as much as $1,500 for a fine French masterpiece key of the 17th century.

Hundreds of different designs have been utilised in the manufacture of keys and it remains an area where bargains can still be found. Keys have a long history, but while splendid specimens from the Medieval and Renaissance periods are occasionally to be found, the majority of those that the collector will come across will date from the Georgian and Victorian eras, and are usually available for under $30.

Where there were keys there were once locks – but never as many. Locks of great decorative beauty and technical ingenuity can be found and do provide another collecting field, but they are much less frequently found and the costs are likely to be much greater.

Another collecting area worth considering is that of wrought iron work. More and more people are going back to open fires and it is better to have a pair of genuine fire dogs than the modern mild steel equivalent, which in some cases may actually be more expensive. Other objects made in wrought iron include chimney cranes, adjustable pot hooks, cooking forks and rushlight holders, but the list does not end there and prices are still very reasonable, starting from a few dollars and rising into the hundreds.

Whether you buy from a car-boot sale or from an auction room, always remember that the item you are thinking of buying was made to be used. Look for signs of wear and tear, such as cut marks on pewter plates or smooth, rubbed areas on the bases of objects such as candlesticks.

One final word of advice – always buy the best you can afford.

Danny Robinson

Brass

A German decorative brass alms dish, 17thC, 21in (53.5cm) diam.
$900–975 *KEY*

A pair of Irish gilded-brass candlesticks, c1890, 14in (35.5cm) high.
$155–185 *SAU*

A pair of gilt-brass candlesticks, in the manner of Matthew Boulton, each candleholder cast with rams' heads, replacements, c1775, 12in (30.5cm) high.
$4,500–5,250 *S*

l. A pair of brass doorstops, shaped as dolphins, on moulded plinths, c1850, 15¾in (40cm) high.
$4,000–4,500 *S*

A pair of brass candlesticks, the drip pans surmounted by fleur-de-lys and applied with flowerheads, made by Hardman Powell & Co, for the Palace of Westminster, c1860, 43in (109cm) high.
$4,000–4,500 *Bon*

FURTHER READING
Rupert Gentle & Rachael Field,
English Domestic Brass 1680–1810,
Elek Books, 1975
Peter Hornsby, *Collecting Antique
Copper & Brass,* Morland
Publications, 1989
Peter and Nancy Schiffer, *Antique
Iron,* Schiffer Publications, 1979

A French brass cockerel,
c1840, 29½in (75cm) high.
$1,125–1,275 *HIS*

A brass jardinière, with a
circular repoussé panel
depicting a character in 17thC
costume raising a glass to a
woman in his arms, the sides
with lion mask ring handles,
19thC, 21½in (54.5cm) diam.
$2,800–3,600 *S*

A brass two-piece lock plate and lock,
pierced with scrolls and engraved with
flowerheads, 18thC, 12½in (32cm) wide.
$100–120 *DN*

A German raised and cast
brass schnabelstitze, c1830,
12in (30.5cm) high.
£680–750 *WLi*

*This brass schnabelstitze is
rare as they are usually
produced in pewter.*

A brass rocking beam letter
balance, the pillar modelled
with stylised lotus leaf
decoration, the letter holder
with one arm missing, 19thC,
5¾in (14.5cm) wide.
$540–620 *CSK*

A brass fish
slice, c1800,
16in (40.5cm) long.
$200–225 *KEY*

A brass skimmer,
c1700, 19in
(48.5cm) long.
$210–240 *KEY*

r. An engraved brass plate
depicting a woman,
possibly representing
summer, signed and dated
'Daniel Keisereisen, fecit
1742', 4½in (11.5cm) high.
$900–1,000 *C*

A bright-cut decorated brass and wrought iron
bed warmer, the bowl with hinged domed lid
decorated at the top with stamped and chased
scrolls and rosettes, with a projecting tapered
handle ending in a hooked terminal, early
18thC, 38¾in (98.5cm) long.
$1,800–2,000 *S(NY)*

l. A Victorian brass desk stand, modelled on
Landseer's painting of Queen Victoria's favourite
pets, with a parrot on a perch above a King
Charles spaniel and a begging terrier, candle
nozzles detached, 12in (30.5cm) high.
$1,200–1,400 *DN*

A brass candle snuffer
and stand, early
18thC, 6in (15cm) high.
$525–600 *KEY*

Bronze

A bronze mortar, dated '1664',
4½in (11.5cm) high.
$375–450 *KEY*

A set of 4 Victorian bronze
and parcel-gilt candlesticks,
each with a cluster column
surmounted by a foliate finial
and waisted spreading
platform with pierced Gothic
arches and a foliate baluster
nozzle, on a spreading base
with twisted quatrefoil within
a roundel and foliate finials to
the angles, 20in (51cm) high.
$2,500–3,000 *C*

A gilt-bronze and boulle
inkstand, inlaid with foliate
cut brass, with raised central
inkwell, long pen tray with
engraved monogram, on scroll
feet, 19thC, 13in (33cm) long.
$550–620 *Bea*

A pair of bronze and gilt-
bronze ewers, with a handle
in the form of a cherub, on a
plinth, early 19thC,
16½in (42cm) high.
$7,500–8,250 *S(Am)*

A gilt-bronze figural inkstand,
the 2 wells flanked by figures of
grizzly bears, on a naturalistic
oval base and scroll feet, 19thC,
17¾in (45cm) long.
$525–600 *P*

A bronze figure of a pointer,
signed 'E. Samson' and stamped
with a Paris foundry mark,
19thC, 14in (35.5cm) high.
$1,500–1,800 *Bon*

An Austrian cold painted
bronze figure of a hare, with
one paw raised, early 20thC,
2in (5cm) high.
$325–375 *Hal*

A bronze head of a bear,
with dark brown patina and
white painted marks inside,
by Antoine-Louis Barye,
early 19thC, signed,
3⅓in (8.5cm) high.
$3,000–3,750 *S*

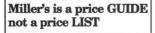

Miller's is a price GUIDE
not a price LIST

r. A bronze group of a gladiator
fighting a lion, the nude male
figure holding a spear to the
chest of the lion, dark brown
patination, on a stepped and
moulded marble and slate base,
after Edme-Nicolas Faillot,
early 19thC, 18in (45.5cm) high.
$2,300–2,700 *Hal*

A bronze seated schnauzer, by
Maximilien Fiot, late 19thC,
signed, 5½in (14cm) long.
$2,600–2,400 *S*

A bronze figure of Amphitrite, cast after a model by Michael Anguier, 18thC, 14½in (37cm) high.
$6,800–7,800 *C*

A bronze of a child sitting on a recumbent goat, by Antoine-Louis Barye, early 19thC, signed, 3¾in (9.5cm) high.
$3,250–3,750 *S*

A portrait bronze of a champion racehorse and its jockey, after Isidore Bonheur, brother of Rosa Bonheur, cast by Hippolyte Peyrol, c1870, 24in (61cm) high.
$3,600–4,400 *HAM*

A bronze, 'Peace', on green and black-veined marble plinth, signed and dated 'E. Onslow Ford, London, 1889', figure 21¾in (55.5cm) high.
$3,600–4,400 *S*

A French bronze figure of a standing female nude holding a drape, on marble plinth, signed 'Prof. J. Buese', late 19thC, 14in (35.5cm) high.
$1,800–2,000 *GH*

A French bronze figure of a woman wearing flowing robes, stamped 'F. Barbedienne Fondeur', on marble base, 19thC, 15½in (39.5cm) high.
$900–975 *E*

A two-coloured bronze figure of a minstrel, with a viola tucked under his arm, standing on a stool, signed 'E. Picault', 19thC, 20½in (52cm) high.
$1,000–1,200 *P*

A French bronze model of a soldier, with armour breast-plate, sword at his hip and rifle to shoulder, standing on a simulated cobble ground base, stamped 'Ligueur' and dated '1847', 22in (56cm) high.
$1,000–1,200 *CSK*

A French bronze group of a nymph and satyr on a see-saw, the nymph being aided by 4 putti, inscribed 'Clodion', on a cream-veined marble base, early 19thC, 19½in (49.5cm) high.
$1,800–2,200 *WW*

A pair of French bronze figures of an Arab warrior and a female water carrier, both wearing tribal dress, the woman carrying a water jar, the man a flintlock musket, by Jean Jules Salmson (1823–1902), 19¾ and 17in (50 and 43cm) high.
$10,500–12,000 *S*

An art bronze bust of Mercury, with the seal 'Bronze Garanti au Titre, Paris', and signed by the foundry 'Sudre', the veined marble plinth with brass plaque 'Prix de Concours Ecole de Beaux, Paris', 19thC, 12in (30.5cm) high.
$1,600–1,900 *TMA*

A German bronze group of a classical muse seated on a low stool, instructing a putto in pipe blowing, by Alexandre Schoenewerk, signed, late 19thC, 11in (28cm) high.
$1,000–1,350 *RBB*

A seated cast bronze figure of a nude Orpheus, playing a flute, holding a snake beguiled in his other hand, on base, signed 'A. Thabard', 19thC, 18in (45.5cm) high.
$1,000–1,200 *L&E*

An Italian/French bronze bust, 'Grande Dame Patricienne', silvered, gilt, patinated and set with a semi-precious stone, on a green marble base with gilt-bronze mount, signed 'Grange Colombo', late 19thC, 15¾in (40cm) high.
$9,000–10,500 *S*

A Florentine bronze figure of Andromeda, resting against a tree trunk, a manacle attached to her left foot, right index finger missing, attributed to the workshop of Pietro da Barga, 16thC, 11in (28cm) high, on plinth.
$11,250–12,750 *S*

A pair of French bronze putti, the male depicting a harvester of corn, the female of grapes, 19thC, 8in (20.5cm) high, on marble bases, one cracked.
$900–1,000 *L&E*

A bronze of a boy, inscribed 'Les Boules sur la Neige', c1890, 14in (35.5cm) high.
$1,350–1,500 *GAS*

A pair of French bronze figures, after Falconet and Allegrin, each semi-naked figure shown standing and drying themselves, on square bases, 19thC, 17¼in (44cm) high.
$3,750–4,500 *CSK*

A pair of Italian bronze urns and covers, cast with female masks and foliate swags, with twin loop scroll side handles and domed pierced covers, on foliate bases, 19thC, 13in (33cm) high.
$1,600–1,900 *S*

A bronze figure of a metal worker smelting, on a marble base, inscribed 'Richard W. Lange, 1924', 8¾in (22.5cm) high.
$450–525 *P(Sc)*

Ormolu

A Charles X Palais Royale mother-of-pearl and ormolu *nécessaire à broder*, in the form of a basket, banded overall with flowerheads, the oval hinged lid with central lozenge suspended by 2 winged lions, with a fitted red velvet and pale silk interior, work tools missing, 4½in (11.5cm) high without handle.
$2,200–2,700 C

A pair of Regency ormolu and bronze candlesticks, after a design by Thomas Hope and possibly by Alexis Decaix, each with 3 Egyptian figures, supporting a concave-sided triangular capital with hieroglyphics to the sides, above an urn-shaped nozzle with a frieze showing a ceremonial procession, on white marble bases, 11½in (29cm) high.
$34,500–42,000 C

A set of 4 ormolu pillar candlesticks, decorated in the classical manner, the sconces with lion masks and paw supports, the columns in the form of female caryatids, early 19thC, 12½in (32cm) high.
$8,250–9,000 CAG

A pair of Régence ormolu *presse-papiers*, decorated with acanthus scrolls, the handles decorated with stiff leaves, 16 x 21½in (40.5 x 54.5cm).
$13,500–15,000 C

A pair of French ormolu candlesticks, the tapering columns with profile masks and octagonal capitals, early 18thC, 9¾in (25cm) high.
$1,400–1,600 DN

Ormolu

Ormolu derives from the French *or moulu*, ground gold, meaning the gold leaf used for gilding metals. Strictly speaking the term applies to cast bronze items which were subsequently finely chiselled and fire-gilt, but the word has come to be applied to all gilt-bronze objects including those which were dipped in acid and finely lacquered, and to a gold-coloured alloy of copper, zinc and tin. The high point of ormolu craftsmanship was in the latter half of the 18th century when exquisite pieces were produced, the most common items being candlesticks, mounts for porcelain and furniture, firedogs, clock cases, wall sconces and chandeliers.

A pair of Empire ormolu urns, each with tapering circular body cast in relief with a Bacchanalian procession of rams and panther-drawn putto playing cymbals and eating grapes, the plinth applied with overflowing baskets of fruit, drilled for electricity, re-threaded and with wooden blocks to the base, 20½in (52cm) high.
$21,000–24,000 C

A pair of George III ormolu cassolettes, by Matthew Boulton, each with domed lapetted lid with foliate finial, with socle surmounted by a beaded band and stiff-leaf brace, both restored, the interior with printed label, 9½in (24cm) high.
$16,500–19,500 C

A pair of Louis XVI ormolu vases, the sides centred by lion masks and hung with drapery and fruiting laurel swags, the bases with ribbed and panelled sides, on later red griotte marble plinths, re-threaded, probably originally furniture mounts, possibly North European, 12in (30.5cm) high.
$18,000–21,000 C

Copper

A gilt-copper and enamel plaquette, in a later velvet-covered surround and moulded wooden frame, with a label on the reverse inscribed '188', restored, Limoges, 13thC, 3½in (9cm) high.
$9,750–11,250 *C*

A copper firemark, from the Salop Fire Office, c1830, 7¾in (19.5cm) high.
$150–180 *KEY*

A gilt-copper and enamel corpus figure, the eyes inset with glass, minor damage, Limoges, 13thC, 6½in (16.5cm) high.
$8,000–9,000 *C*

Enamel

An enamel plaque of the Pietà, in a copper frame, now mounted on a textile ground, under glass, in a giltwood frame, Limoges, restored, 15/16thC, 3in (7.5cm) high.
$800–900 *C*

A set of 6 enamelled plates, in the manner of Jean de Court, enamelled *en grisaille* with the months July to December, incorporating the signs of the Zodiac, Limoges, c1570, 7½in (19cm) diam.
$50,000–60,000 *HDS*

A south German hexagonal enamel dish, embellished with elaborate gilt decoration and painted with 3 interior scenes of a barber's shop, an armourer's shop and a mint, the underside of the foot painted with polychrome floral decoration, minor damage and restoration, c1700, 9in (23cm) wide.
$2,000–2,400 *C*

A polychrome enamel and silver-gilt mirror, depicting the freeing of Andromeda, Perseus astride Pegasus attacking the sea monster at her side, from the workshop of Jean de Court, Limoges, late 16thC, 4 x 2½in (10 x 6.5cm), in contemporary silver-gilt frame.
$12,750–14,250 *S*

Gold

A Swiss gold bonbonnière, the top and base engine-turned, with diminishing circular motif, within trailing foliate border, maker's mark 'R' within 2 pellets, 19thC, 2in (5cm) diam.
$1,500–1,800 *Bon*

A gold thimble, enamelled in black and white with beaded swags on a pale blue background, together with tooled leather case with trade label for Giuliano, c1880.
$4,600–5,200 *HAM*

Iron

A south German iron pricket candlestick, with deep drip pan, a straight stem and domed foot with rope twist border etched with scrolling acanthus leaf scrollwork, initialled 'WG', dated '1591', probably Nüremburg, 12½in (32cm) high.
$8,500–9,750 *S*

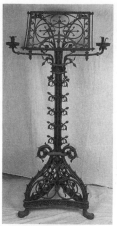

A wrought iron lectern, c1880, 57in (145cm) high.
$1,900–2,300 *COW*

A cast iron and brass tobacco box of Mr Punch, with original decoration, c1870, 6in (15cm) high.
$1,000–1,200 *LEN*

A silhouette sheet cut iron cockerel, with traces of original decoration, c1720, 18in (45.5cm) high.
$975–1,125 *RYA*

A Nüremburg wrought iron strong box, 17thC, 20in (51cm) long.
$1,275–1,425 *KEY*

A selection of English and Continental iron keys, 18thC, largest 5in (12.5cm) long.
$100–120 *KEY*

An iron flintlock tinder pistol, 18thC, 5½in (14cm) long.
$575–675 *KEY*

Miscellaneous

A pewter chalice, c1770, 10in (25.5cm) high.
$225–275 *KEY*

A lead figure of a putto, on an integrally cast circular base, minor damage, 19thC, 40½in (103cm) high.
$3,250–3,750 *C*

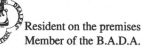

ALABASTER

An Italian alabaster figure of a mother and child, late 19thC, 20½in (52cm) high.
$2,400–3,000 *S*

Two alabaster allegorical figures, depicting spring and summer, both with a putto, Naples 18thC, 25¾in (65.5cm) high.
$7,500–9,000 *S*

Alabaster

Alabaster, a granular form of gypsum, has been popular in Europe since the Middle Ages for small sculpture. It is a smooth, pale-coloured stone, which sometimes has a yellow or pink hue, or is veined due to impurities. It can be painted without an underlying ground of gesso, which made it particularly popular from the 14th century for tomb effigies and religious carvings. In modern times its popularity has been limited because the smooth, polished surface makes it easy to carve but does not allow for the subtleties of texture with which many of today's sculptors concern themselves.

An Italian alabaster vase, after the antique, of fluted campana form, carved in relief with classical figures, late 19thC, 20in (51cm) high.
$1,800–2,200 *S*

An alabaster group of Cupid and Psyche, after Canova, 19thC, 28¾in (73cm) wide.
$800–900 *P*

l. An Italian alabaster Egyptian urn, with a baluster body, scroll handles, early 19thC, 26½in (67.5cm) high.
$9,000–10,500 *S*

An Italian alabaster figure of a female water carrier, on an Algerian onyx stand, turned column and square plinth, 19thC, 79½in (202cm) high.
$2,400–2,700 *AH*

An Oriental alabaster vase and cover, after the Roman antique, the lid with a later gilt bronze pine cone finial, 17th/18thC, 20½in (52cm) high.
$16,500–19,500 *S*

An alabaster relief of the Lamentation, in a later velvet-covered mount, traces of gilding and polychromy, cracks and losses, Nottingham, 15thC, 16¼in (41.5cm) high.
$16,500–18,750 *CSK*

An alabaster bust of a girl, signed 'Kochendorfer', incised with numerals and bearing a Munich Art Medal seal, late 19thC, 8½in (21.5cm) high.
$360–420 *Hal*

r. A pair of Italian alabaster fiorito tazze, on a turned socle with grey marble base, the marble probably reused from an antique column, variations in carving, c1800, 7½in (19cm) high.
$16,500–19,500 *C*

MARBLE

A marble bust of a maiden, after the antique, her hair in a plaited top-knot, late 18thC, 21in (53cm) high.
$5,400–6,000 *P(H)*

A white marble bust of Princess Charlotte Augusta, by Joseph Nollekens, on a marble socle, minor chips to socle, signed and dated on reverse '1812', 19in (48.5cm) high.
$13,500–15,000 *C*

A carved white marble bust of a young maiden wearing a garland of flowers in her hair, on a turned and waisted socle, 19thC, 24¾in (63cm) high.
$1,350–1,650 *P*

A white marble figure, entitled 'A Mother's Kiss', signed 'H. Weekes RA', on a white-veined marble column with gilt metal Corinthian capital and laurel-bound base mount, mid-19thC, group 38½in (98cm) high.
$15,000–16,500 *S*

A French white marble seated figure of Diana bathing, by Louis Gossin, on a shaped naturalistic base, signed, on a cream coloured marble plinth, late 19thC, 23in (58.5cm) high.
$14,250–15,750 *C(SP)*

A white marble group of a spaniel playing with a kitten, signed by Joseph Gott, the dog crouching over an overturned basket of fruit, damaged and repaired, mid-19thC, 27in (68.5cm) wide.
$7,500–9,000 *S*

r. A white marble figure of a girl, by Mathurin Moreau, leaning on a water stoup, holding a sickle and corn sheaves, perhaps allegorical of summer, signed, late 19thC, 34¾in (88.5cm) high.
$10,500–12,000 *S*

A marble group of the Virgin and Child, probably French, crown missing, chipped and restored, c1400, 16in (40.5cm) high.
$9,000–9,750 *CSK*

A white marble bust, 'La Génie de la Danse', by Jean-Baptiste Carpeaux, signed, mid-19thC, 26in (66cm) high.
$24,000–27,000 *S*

This bust is taken from the central figure of Carpeaux' notorious group made as one of the four monumental reliefs on the façade of the Paris Opèra.

A marble bust of a nobleman,
circle of Artus Quellinus the
Elder, late 17thC,
31½in (80cm) high.
$45,000–52,500 *S*

A white marble bust of
Napoleon, by R. Trentenove,
after Canova, signed and
inscribed on the frieze, dated
'1825', 22in (56cm) high.
$7,500–8,250 *P(H)*

An Italian white marble bust of a
lady in the Renaissance manner,
possibly Isabella von Aragon, the
dress engraved with embroidery
and infilled with pigment, mid-
19thC, 24½in (62cm) high.
$4,000–4,500 *S*

An Italian white marble figure of
a naked child, resting on a
cushion with a dove in his arms,
c1880, 14in (35.5cm) high.
$4,000–4,500 *S*

A marble figure of a flute
player, by Emanuele Caroni,
on a wrought iron stand,
mid-19thC, 59in (150cm)
high overall.
$13,500–15,000 *S(NY)*

An Italian Siena marble
ewer, carved with an eagle
handle and ram spout, on a
fluted trumpet stem and
verde antico base, c1880,
18in (45.5cm) high.
$3,750–4,500 *S*

A pair of Italian marble busts
of gypsy girls, on waisted socles
with green marble bases,
19thC, 24½in (62cm) high.
$3,500–4,000 *P*

PORPHYRY

A pair of Italian brèche violette marble urns,
late 18thC, 15in (38cm) high.
$27,000–30,000 *C*

An Empire ormolu-mounted
Swedish porphyry urn, the
moulded everted rim above a
waisted body, on a ring turned
spreading socle and square
plinth, on an ormolu pedestal,
22½in (57cm) high.
$55,000–65,000 *C*

A Louis XV ormolu-
mounted porphyry
vase and cover, the
reeded domed top with
a foliate pomegranate
finial, originally with
handles and further
foliage, restored,
27½in (70cm) high.
$40,000–45,000 *C*

TERRACOTTA

A terracotta figure, by Aimé-Jules Dalou, entitled 'Paysanne Française Allaitant Son Enfant', signed, c1875, 20in (51cm) high, on an ebony base.
$21,000–24,000 *S*

A terracotta group, depicting a benefactor and child in 17thC dress, early 19thC, 21¾in (55.5cm) high.
$4,500–5,250 *S*

A terracotta bust, by Albert-Ernest Carrier-Belleuse, entitled 'Le Sommeil', on a painted wooden socle mounted on a square plinth, signed, mid-19thC, 23¼in (59cm) high.
$22,500–27,000 *S*

A terracotta bust, 'signed 'Emmeline Halse', late 19thC, 14¾in (37.5cm) high, on a waisted wooden socle.
$3,300–3,750 *S*

This bust is probably Mabel, daughter of W. Clark Lawrence, which Emmeline Halse is recorded as exhibiting at the Royal Academy in 1888.

l. A glazed terracotta portrait relief of a woman, from the Della Robbia workshops, Florence, early 16thC, 16¼in (41.5cm) diam, in a carved giltwood frame.
$18,000–21,000 *S*

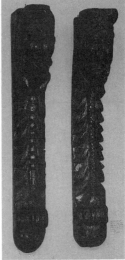

r. A French terracotta group of a lion and a royal infant, the reverse unfinished, infant's foot missing, minor chips, c1800, 6¾in (17cm) high.
$1,350–1,500 *C*

WOOD

A Georgian mahogany cheese coaster, the turned ends with ivory roundels, with moulded base and leather casters, 17¼in (44cm) wide.
$375–450 *AH*

A carved giltwood crest, in the form of 2 ovals with motifs, surrounded by carved scrolling foliage centred by a helmet, 19thC, 36in (91.5cm) wide.
$3,000–3,300 *P(S)*

l. An Italian carved giltwood book stand, the coat-of-arms with initials 'AL' and dated '1777', 19in (48cm) wide.
$10,000–10,800 *S*

A pair of oak carvings, possibly part of a hammer-beam roof, the extended corbel ends depicting a male and a female head, some original gilding, c1680, 37in (94cm) high.
$6,000–6,750 *SEL*

A Tyrolean parcel-gilt and polychrome carved wooden figure of a saint, damaged and repaired, c1500, 40in (101.5cm) high.
$7,500–9,000 *C*

A Flemish boxwood group, depicting Charity, 17thC, 9in (23cm) high.
$7,500–8,250 *AEF*

A collection of 5 carved oak terminals, in the form of figures in 16thC costume, on mask-applied bases, 17thC, 19¾in (50cm) high.
$3,800–4,800 *P(Sc)*

A pair of American decoy mallard ducks, c1900, 14in (35.5cm) long.
$250–280 *HIS*

An oak carving from a bed canopy, depicting 2 cherubs holding a garland of flowers, 17thC, 25in (63.5cm) wide.
$4,500–5,000 *AEF*

Two French gilded cherubs, 18thC, 18in (45.5cm) high.
$3,750–4,500 *DBA*

A Flemish carved oak group, depicting the Virgin and St Anne, c1620, 13½in (34.5cm) high.
$5,250–6,000 *AEF*

A Burgundian carved oak figure of St John, with hand raised and holding a book, c1500, 35in (89cm) high.
$4,000–4,500 *L&E*

A Spanish carved wooden figure of St Sebastian, with polychrome decoration, 16thC, 33in (84cm) high.
$3,000–3,300 *KEY*

A carved gilded eagle, late 18thC, wingspan 30in 76cm) wide.
$1,300–1,400 *DBA*

r. A pair of south German polychrome carved wooden putti, damaged, late 17thC, largest 28½in (72.5cm) high.
$15,750–18,000 *CSK*

A north Netherlandish polychrome and giltwood relief of 2 magi on horseback, and a terrier eating a bone, c1500, 17in (43cm) high.
$45,000–52,500 *S*

An oak panel of the Madonna, within a sunburst, 16thC, 14in (35.5cm) high.
$1,350–1,500 *AEF*

A carved fruitwood panel, by Putman, Paris, signed and dated '1790', 21¾in (55.5cm), in a later glazed frame.
$15,250–17,250 *S*

A pair of carved oak panels, with Romayne heads, 16thC, 14in (35.5cm) high.
$2,400–2,700 *AEF*

A pair of oak panels, c1480, 15in (38cm) high.
$830–900 *AEF*

An Italian carved walnut panel of Saturn seated on an armillary sphere, 16thC, 31½in (80cm) high.
$1,000–1,100 *DBA*

l. A Regency mahogany framed double-sided mirror, c1810, 5½in (14cm) diam.
$230–280 *JC*

A pair of carved oak panels, with Romayne heads, 16thC, 14in (35.5cm) high.
$2,000–2,500 *AEF*

A German carved walnut panel, depicting Shadrach, Meshach and Abednego, c1580, 23in (58.5cm) wide.
$2,250–2,500 *DBA*

According to the book of Daniel, in the Old Testament, Shadrach, Meshach and Abednego survived the burning furnace, having refused to worship a golden image of King Nebuchadnezzer.

A pair of carved oak panels, depicting Death and a Gallant, 16thC, 14in (35.5cm) high.
$2,400–2,700 *AEF*

TREEN

An oak water barrel,
painted green, c1875,
10in (25.5cm) wide.
$80–95 *WLD*

A Scottish christening cup,
with the arms and motto of
the McPherson clan, c1840,
5in (12.5cm) diam.
$1,800–2,000 *AEF*

A sycamore bowl, with traces
of original paint, c1860,
19½in (49.5cm) diam.
$65–80 *WLD*

A braid loom, late 18thC,
12in (30.5cm) long.
$300–340 *COT*

A cedar wood
miniature urn,
late 18thC,
5½in (14cm) high.
$180–210 *COT*

A lignum vitae
tobacco jar, c1790,
10½in (26.5cm) high.
$900–1,000 *AEF*

A spoon rack, the
top carved with
birds, 18thC,
29in (73.5cm) high.
$1,800–2,000 *AEF*

A rosewood watch stand,
inlaid with mother-of-pearl,
c1860, 2½in (6.5cm) high.
$200–220 *COT*

A mahogany pincushion, inlaid
with satinwood, in the form of
a sarcophagus, c1820, 5½in
(14cm) wide.
$180–200 *COT*

A snuff box, in the form of a
horse's head, with pattern and
inscription 'Forget Me Not' in
brass pins, 19thC, 4in (10cm) wide.
$1,300–1,500 *AEF*

A wooden container, with an
iron handle and wooden lid,
c1880, 11in (28cm) wide.
$110–115 *MofC*

A pair of carved wooden shoes,
c1880, 3½in (9cm) long.
$50–60 *PSA*

A boxwood snuff box, in the shape of a boat,
c1850, 5in (12.5cm) long.
$270–300 *Tem*

LEATHER

A Georgian leather and brass-bound trunk, c1749, 42in (106.5cm) wide.
$600–675 *WLD*

A Rhenish gilt-copper mounted leather-covered casket, the wood carcass overlaid with leather panels, with hinged hasp over iron lockplate, c1400, 9¼in (23.5cm) wide.
$30,000–33,000 *S*

A leather costrel, late 17thC, 9in (23cm) long.
$220–300 *KEY*

A costrel is a leather, wooden or earthenware bottle.

A leather-covered wooden casket with iron mounts, French or Spanish, with hasp and lockplate, steel key and rope-twist handles, early 16thC, 8¾in (22cm) wide.
$33,000–37,500 *S*

A Dutch parcel-gilt leather casket, the domed lid opening to reveal a silk-lined interior with a removable tray, one end of the casket with concealed drawer, some damage, lining and key later, early 17thC, 7¾in (19.5cm) high.
$4,000–4,800 *C*

PAPIER MACHE

A maroon papier mâché inkstand, inlaid with mother-of-pearl, painted with a landscape scene, the pair of glass ink pots with cast brass lids, central lidded stamp compartment, c1860, 9¾in (24.5cm) wide.
$1,100–1,300 *JC*

A pair of cream ground papier mâché coasters, early 19thC, 5in (12.5cm) diam.
$1,500–1,700 *LEN*

A papier mâché letter holder, mid-19thC, 6¾in (17cm) wide.
$90–100 *PSA*

l. A Victorian papier mâché and brass tray-on-stand, decorated in red and gold, the tray with maker's stamp 'Henry Loveridge & Co', with registration mark of 1882, the stand stamped 'Howard & Sons', 28½in (72.5cm) wide.
$9,750–11,250 *S*

A papier mâché tray-on-stand, the tray painted with birds, flowers and foliage on a black ground, on a gold and black painted turned stand, joined by an X-shaped stretcher, the tray c1850, stand modern, 31in (79cm) wide.
$1,400–1,500 *S*

BOXES

A Louis XIV ormolu-mounted
boulle copper, brass and mother-
of-pearl inlaid tortoiseshell box,
re-mounted and re-carcassed,
14¾in (37.5cm) wide.
$5,250–6,000 *C*

A beadwork casket, c1860,
8in (20.5cm) wide.
$1,000–1,200 *LEN*

A Venetian rock crystal,
lacquer and silver-gilt casket,
later giltwood feet, restored,
c1600, 18in (45.5cm) wide.
$69,000–75,000 *S*

A walnut brass-mounted *coffre
fort,* the fall-front revealing a
writing section and concealed
drawers, screw attachment to
sides, cast carrying handles,
c1690, later restorations,
19¾in (50cm) wide.
$1,650–2,000 *WL*

*A coffre fort is a safe, and the
screw attachment to the sides is
to render the piece immobile.*

An oak box, with brass
lock and handle, c1895,
13½in (34.5cm) wide.
$80–95 *OLM*

An ebony and ormolu casket,
in Renaissance style, the case
inset with rock crystal panels
to the cover and sides, the
reverse carved in relief with
grotesques, distressed, 19thC,
9¼in (23.5cm) wide.
$3,000–3,300 *CSK*

A French brass-mounted
rosewood and oyster-walnut
coffre fort, the hinged cover and
front with applied strapwork,
enclosing an interior with a
well, 2 drawers and secret
compartments, the sides with
carrying handles, late 17thC,
15in (38cm) wide.
$2,000–2,400 *AG*

A wallpaper-covered hat box,
New England, minor damage,
c1830, 21½in (54.5cm) wide.
$7,500–8,250 *S(NY)*

A cast iron casket, with brass
decoration, including an armorial
shield, probably German, c1650,
13in (33cm) wide.
$4,500–5,250 *DBA*

A silver-gilt presentation
cigarette case, the sunburst
reeded case set with the
Imperial eagle with sapphire
centre cabochon, the raised
thumbpiece set with a
cabochon garnet, maker's
mark 'A.F.', possibly of
A. Fuld, St Petersburg,
c1910, 4in (10cm) wide.
$2,000–2,300 *S(G)*

A Charles X mother-of-pearl
and ormolu casket, printed
label inscribed 'Lares et
Penates', and inscribed in
black ink, 5in (12.5cm) wide.
$1,200–1,350 *C*

A green japanned tôle coal box,
with gilt decoration, 19thC,
19in (49cm) wide.
$900–1,000 *TMA*

A pair of George III satinwood and rosewood crossbanded knife boxes, later painted with cherubs, portrait medallions, trophies and flowers, with interior compartments for cutlery, lined in velvet and paper, 14in (35.5cm) high.
$8,250–9,750 *CSK*

A Staffordshire enamel patch box, inscribed 'Affection', c1770, 1½in (4cm) long.
$530–600 *BHa*

A south Staffordshire enamel patch box, inscribed 'Peace, Love, United', c1770, 2½in (6.5cm) long.
$630–750 *BHa*

A tortoiseshell sewing box, with ivory stringing, original silk-lined interior, brass lion mask handles and claw-and-ball feet, c1810, 9½in (24cm) wide.
$3,300–4,000 *BHa*

An Irish satinwood inlaid sewing box, with fitted interior and various sewing implements, early 19thC, 12in (30.5cm) wide.
$1,800–2,000 *P*

A silver and silver-gilt snuff box, the case engraved with the initials 'HH', by Yapp & Woodward, Birmingham 1846, 3in (7.5cm) long, in original fitted case.
$1,350–1,500 *C*

It is likely that this box was a gift from the composer Cipriani Potter (1792–1871) to the viola player Henry Hill (1808–56), son of the violin maker Henry Lockey Hill (1744–1835).

A French mother-of-pearl and gilt-bronze *nécessaire*, early 19thC, 6¼in (16cm) wide.
$3,000–3,300 *Bea*

A George IV 18ct gold snuff box, the cover set with a late 18thC enamelled portrait miniature of a gentleman, the box engine-turned and edged with raised borders of oak leaves and acorns, by A. J. Strachan, 1824, 3¼in (8cm) diam.
$12,750–15,000 *P*

A George III gold and banded agate snuff box, stamped only with date letter for London 1809, 3¼in (8cm) wide.
$2,250–2,700 *Bon*

A papier mâché box, shaped as a dog's head, c1870, 2in (5cm) long.
$375–450 *EUR*

l. A gold presentation snuff box, the cover with inscription, by Jacques-Felix Viennot, Paris, c1800, 3¾in (9cm) long.
$2,000–2,300 *C*

A Dutch gold and tortoiseshell snuff box, probably by Johan Doede or Johannes van Deventer, The Hague, 1736, 3¼in (8cm) long.
$12,750–15,000 *P*

MILLER'S COMPARES . . .

I A late George III satinwood tea caddy, with 2 lidded compartments, painted overall with drapery, ribbons, baskets of flowers and foliage, within flowerhead and foliate bands, 8in (20.5cm) wide.
$1,500–1,700 *Bea*

II A George III inlaid partridgewood tea caddy, with 2 lidded compartments, inlaid with shells and foliage, 7¼in (18.5cm) wide.
$560–680 *Bea*

These two tea caddies are of a similar size, shape and date, but *item I* fetched a higher price at auction because the painted design is particularly attractive and unusual, whereas the shell motif on *item II* is far more common. In contrast to the rather plain interior of *item II*, the interior of *item I* is painted throughout, the colours remaining fresh and vibrant. Moreover, the painted decoration is contemporary with the caddy, rather than painted later as is more usual, and this increased its value, as did the fact that it was made of satinwood, which has always been an expensive cabinet wood. *Bea*

An Edwardian oak till, with brass fittings, 19in (48cm) long.
$70–80 *OLM*

A Scandinavian trunk, with iron strapwork, a handle to the hinged cover, painted with initials, dated '1793', 21in (53cm) wide.
$750–900 *WW*

An early Victorian brass-mounted coromandel tea caddy, containing 2 lidded compartments, 10in (25.5cm) long.
$560–640 *Bea*

A Victorian walnut toilet box, with 4 bottles, 2 with silver plated lids, c1830, 10in (25.5cm) wide.
$220–270 *PSA*

A Victorian coromandel vanity box, the hinged top enclosing morocco and velvet fitted interior including 7 glass bottles and boxes with electroplated covers, by J. Bradshaw & Sons, Liverpool, 12½in (32cm) wide.
$675–750 *CDC*

A Victorian papier mâché tea caddy, with floral motifs and scalloped edge, 13in (33cm) wide.
$450–530 *PSA*

A pair of Regency mahogany miniature tea caddies, with brass stringing, c1815, 4in (10cm) long.
$1,500–1,800 *WLi*

TARTAN WARE

A tartan ware pen nib cleaner, c1860, 3½in (9cm) long.
$450–500 *EUR*

A tartan ware snuff box, with gilding, c1845, 3in (7.5cm) wide.
$270–300 *EUR*

A pair of tartan ware spill vases, with pink interiors, c1845, 6in (15cm) high.
$2,000–2,400 *EUR*

A tartan ware sewing casket, c1838, 2½in (6.5cm) wide.
$300–330 *EUR*

A tartan ware vesta box, in the shape of a bell, in Stuart and Colquhoun tartans, c1850, 5in (12.5cm) high.
$520–600 *EUR*

> **Miller's is a price GUIDE not a price LIST**

A Tunbridge ware stationery box, bearing label of William Upton, Brighton, c1860, 8in (20.5cm) wide.
$750–830 *AMH*

TUNBRIDGE WARE

A Tunbridge ware matchbox cover with Masonic emblem, c1880, 2½in (6.5cm) high.
$230–250 *AMH*

A Tunbridge ware box, in original condition, c1860, 6in (15cm) square.
$330–400 *PSA*

A Tunbridge ware pleating box, labelled, c1860, 4in (10cm) long.
$750–830 *PSA*

l. A Tunbridge ware box, the top decorated with small cube-work, c1850, 4in (10cm) long.
$150–170 *AMH*

A Tunbridge ware inkstand, late 19thC, 4in (10cm) diam.
$450–480 *PSA*

r. A Tunbridge ware letter rack, early 19thC, 8in (20.5cm) wide.
$530–600 *PSA*

CARD CASES

Twenty-five years ago, a collector purchased a locally made silver card case for just a few dollars at a Birmingham market. Just how far the market in card cases has progressed since then was shown at a Bonhams auction recently, when that same early Victorian 'castle-top' case, depicting a view of St Margaret's Chapel, Edinburgh Castle, was sold for $6,200!

That same Bonhams sale of two major collections of 19th century card cases saw price levels for some of the rarer and more exquisite examples amaze even the most avid collectors and dealers. Whilst card cases have appealed to collectors for many years, it is only recently that the market has produced some really outstanding results.

Originally used by the nobility and upper classes of the Regency and Victorian periods, card cases were an essential part of everyday social etiquette.

Silver card cases were the earliest and most popular, particularly 'castle-top' cases, and these are among the most collectable today. They were so-called because they were embossed or engraved with a view of a tourist attraction such as the castles of Windsor, Kenilworth or Warwick. Prices for these types range from $375–1,200, but rarer views of St Paul's Cathedral, the Palace of Westminster, and Chatsworth House, to name but a few, are more desirable and can be worth anything from $2,250–3,750.

It is essential before buying to be aware of quality and condition, as repairs and splits in the silver may be difficult to detect with the naked eye. Other points to consider are the maker and the town where the silver case was made.

A Victorian silver 'castle-top' card case, with a view of Malvern Abbey Church, 4in (10cm) long.
$4,500–5,250 Bon

Birmingham was the great centre of production for silver 'toys' and it was here that Nathaniel Mills established his firm which became the most prolific manufacturer of silver card cases. Other recognised makers are Taylor & Perry, Joseph Wilmore, Yapp & Woodward, Hilliard & Thomason, Frederick Mason and George Unite, who took over Nathaniel Mills' firm in 1864. London and Scottish examples are more unusual and likely to be more expensive.

Less expensive but still exquisitely designed card cases are those made of papier mâché, mother-of-pearl and abalone shell – or indeed any combination of these materials. In the latter part of the 19th century, Jennens & Bettridge of Birmingham introduced the inlay of abalone and mother-of-pearl into their popular papier mâché card cases, but as early as the 1830s one of their designers, Edward Haselar, was making papier mâché cases painted with flower and fruit themes within ornate gold-coloured, rococo style borders, a style that remained popular for 30 years.

The value of these will vary according to a number of factors – condition and decoration, for example – but the collector should still be able to find examples ranging from $60–375. Those with a 'castle'-top' view will again command the higher prices.

Between 1830 and 1880 the Cantonese were producing intricately carved ivory and tortoiseshell examples, which often feature crustacea or figures in a town or riverbank setting. They generally range in value from $300–600.

Japanese ivory card cases were also made in the shibayama style, an inlay technique using a variety of materials ranging from malachite, coral and horn to mother-of-pearl, tortoiseshell and abalone. The finest examples can be very elaborate and often depict exotic birds and flowers. High- and low-relief-carved lacquer work, depicting similar subjects, is also seen and often the different techniques were combined, transforming a plain piece of ivory into a work of art. Japanese card cases made during the Meiji period (1868–1912) are particularly desirable, not only amongst card case collectors but also with Oriental art enthusiasts, making the market very strong and competitive. Prices as high as $4,500 are known, but it should be possible to find examples from $375.

One way of making a start on a collection might be to look out for one of the mixed lots that go through auction from time to time. These can provide a variety of different styles, materials and dates at a reasonable price and will help in gaining a feel for the subject. The more experienced collector will find the rarer examples harder to find and that only a determined and constant search of shop, fair, market or saleroom will reveal the prize.

Card cases provide a varied and rewarding field for collectors and though the present market may be strong, it is still possible to acquire unusual and interesting examples at both ends of the market.

Isobel Ward

A Victorian silver 'castle-top' card case, with a view of Windsor Castle in low relief on one side and Warwick Castle on the other, both scenes flanked by floral engraving, by Nathaniel Mills, Birmingham 1840, 4in (10cm) long, 2oz.
$1,000–1,100 *P*

A Victorian silver embossed 'castle-top' card case, with a view of Gloucester Abbey in relief on one side flanked by chased floral scrolls, the reverse with a lobed oval cartouche engraved with a vase of flowers, flanked by chased floral scrolls, by Taylor & Perry, Birmingham 1844, 4in (10cm) long, 2.5oz.
$3,000–3,750 *P*

An early Victorian silver 'castle-top' card case, with a view of St Paul's Cathedral within foliate scroll decoration, the reverse with vacant scroll cartouche within foliate scrolls, maker's mark of Cronin & Wheeler, Birmingham 1847, 4in (10cm) long.
$1,300–1,400 *Bon*

An early Victorian silver 'castle-top' card case, with a view of St Anne's Chapel, Edinburgh Castle, within foliate scroll decoration, the reverse with vacant cartouche within foliate scrolls, maker's mark of Fredk Mason, Birmingham 1856, 4in (10cm) long.
$5,500–6,000 *Bon*

A Japanese ivory card case, decorated in gold, silver and red *hiramakie, takamakie* and *okibirame* and *shibayama* style inlay, with an argus pheasant among peonies, the reverse with a pair of courting doves on a branch of flowering plum, late 19thC, 4¼in (11cm) long.
$2,000–2,500 *Bon*

An early Victorian silver 'castle-top' card case, with a view of Westminster Abbey within foliate scroll decoration, the reverse with crested and monogrammed scroll cartouche within foliate scrolls, with maker's mark of Nathaniel Mills, Birmingham 1845, with French import marks, 4in (10cm) long.
$2,000–2,300 *Bon*

A mid-Victorian silver engraved 'castle-top' card case, with a view, possibly Burghley House, within scroll decoration, the reverse with monogrammed central cartouche, within scroll decoration, maker's mark of Foxall & Co, Birmingham 1850, 4in (10cm) long.
$530–600 *Bon*

r. A Victorian silver engraved 'castle-top' card case, with a view of the Houses of Parliament, the river Thames and paddle steamers in the foreground, bordered by foliate scrolls on a hatched ground, the reverse engraved with a vacant shield cartouche flanked by similar foliate scrolls, by Foxall & Co, Birmingham 1850, 4in (10cm) long, 2.5oz.
$1,500–1,800 *P*

ORIENTAL
Cloisonné

A Chinese cloisonné box and cover, made for the Tibetan market, decorated with a central double *vajra* design within shaped cartouches of precious objects and bands of scrolling flowers, the underside with bats and geometric designs, on a short foot, pitted and restored, 17thC, 6¾in (17cm) diam.
$1,200–1,350 *CSK*

Cloisonné

Cloisonné is formed by applying a network of fine metal strips to the surface of an object and pouring enamel into the 'cloisons', or compartments. The strips remain exposed and separate the different coloured enamels from one another. The process may have originated in Ancient Mesopotamia, but first appears as a major art form in the Byzantine Empire from as early as the 6th century AD. It was also used very successfully by Celtic craftsmen. By the end of the 14th century the technique had travelled from Byzantium to China and from there throughout the Oriental world.

An Imperial cloisonné enamel censer and cover, decorated with a pair of phoenix within dense grounds of feathery lotus scrolls on turquoise grounds, repeated on the cover dividing a middle register with reticulated flower scrolls and pendant tassels, surmounted by a Buddhistic lion finial, on 4 gilt lion mask feet with a pair of phoenix handles, minor damage, Qianlong period, 31in (78.5cm) wide.
$15,000–18,000 *C*

A Chinese cloisonné enamel ewer, with turquoise ground, decorated with scrolling lotus divided by a band of *ruyi* heads at shoulder and below the rim, with a dragon forming the serpentine handle, minor damage, Jiaqing period, 11¾in (30cm) high.
$2,200–2,700 *C*

A Chinese cloisonné box and cover, decorated with bands of stylised lotus surrounding a central character, 18thC, 2in (5cm) diam.
$350–420 *CSK*

A Japanese cloisonné enamel tray, with a greyish-white dove shown in profile, the beak, eye and talons worked in gold wire, against a grey ground shading to a pale orange, with *shakudo* rim, the reverse with cherry blossoms on a dark brown ground, cracked, with the signature and seal of the artist Settei, Namikawa Sosuke mark, Meiji period, 11½in (29cm) square.
$1,800–2,000 *S(NY)*

A Chinese cloisonné enamel and gilt-metal clock, the domed top with lion finial, the edges applied with prunus branch mounts, the sides with cloisonné enamel panels with flowers, the tiered base with pierced apron, with key, 19thC, Qing Dynasty, 19¼in (49cm) high.
$2,700–3,300 *S*

A pair of Japanese cloisonné vases, decorated with birds flying among flowers, on a midnight-blue ground, Meiji period, 7in (18cm) high, on wood stands.
$1,800–2,200 *Bea*

A Japanese cloisonné enamel vase and cover, worked in brass and silver wire with oval panels of various colours, overlaid with floral medallions, the cover with gilt *kiku* knop, cracked, by Namikawa Yasuyuki, late 19thC, 4¼in (11cm) high.
$8,000–9,000 *S*

Enamel

A Canton enamel saucer, painted with insects among fruit and foliage, within a cell pattern border interspersed with flowersprays, the ruby-coloured reverse with further floral designs, 18thC, 6in (15cm) diam.
$675–750 *CSK*

A pair of Chinese champlevé enamel and gilt *gu* vases, decorated overall with scrolling lotus and foliage between bands of lappets and stylised leaves, within key fret borders, 18thC, 10⅞in (27.5cm) high.
$1,200–1,350 *CSK*

r. A Chinese repoussé painted enamel panel, moulded in repoussé technique to enhance the design of European figures on a sward of grass, in front of 18thC style houses, with ships in the distance, mounted in giltwood frame, chipped and restored, mid-18thC, Qing Dynasty, 27¾ x 47½in (70.5 x 120.5cm).
$52,500–60,000 *S*

A Canton enamel table screen, painted with a bird and butterflies among flowering chrysanthemums on a mauve ground, within a scrolling border, the reverse with vases, censers and precious objects, chipped, 18thC, 7¼in (18.5cm) high.
$1,800–2,000 *CSK*

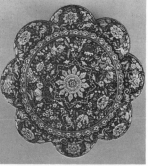

A Canton enamel octafoil lobed box and domed cover, painted with a central flowerhead within *ruyi* heads, a panel of butterflies and bats among flowers, within a wider band of similar decoration and lappet borders, on a blue ground, the turquoise interior fitted with a tray, damaged, c1800, 14½in (37cm) wide.
$3,250–3,750 *CSK*

Glass

A Peking yellow glass *zhadou*, with widely flaring neck, bulbous centre section, on cylindrical foot, with four-character mark on base, Qianlong period, 4in (10cm) high.
$10,500–12,000 *S(NY)*

A Chinese green glass bowl, with steeply rounded sides rising from a flat countersunk base, the translucent yellow metal with a greenish hue, suffused with minute air bubbles and fine crizzling, minute chips to rim, four-character mark on the base, Qianlong period, 6½in (16.5cm) diam.
$2,200–2,700 *S(NY)*

A Chinese yellow ground glass bottle, with red overlay, a *chilong* amidst cloud swirls around the neck, and carved flowers sprouting from ornamental rocks encircling the base, 18thC, 6¾in (17cm) high.
$7,500–9,000 *S(NY)*

A Chinese turquoise ground with yellow overlay glass vase, with long neck, carved in deep relief with pheasants amid flowering branches, a frieze of rocks surrounding the base, 18thC, 8½in (21.5cm) high.
$7,500–9,000 *S(NY)*

r. A set of 4 Chinese glass cups, coloured red, blue, purple and turquoise, the steeply rounded sides flaring towards the rim, carved around the sides in deep relief with flowering branches, on short countersunk bases, 19thC, 3¼in (8.5cm) diam.
$3,750–4,500 *S(NY)*

Jade

A Chinese two-tone jade Three Friends of Winter double vase, carved and undercut using the black and grey colours of the stone, in the shape of 2 slender naturalistic pine and prunus tree trunks with a tall bamboo stalk, encircled overall by blooming prunus and pine branches, a long-beaked egret perched on a branch and *lingzhi* growing at the base, Qianlong period, 6in (15cm) high.
$5,300–6,000 *S(NY)*

A Chinese celadon jade dragon pendant, both sides with a low relief pattern of intertwined swirls, pierced with one hole drilled from both sides, the semi-translucent stone suffused with fine dark and russet flecks, now with areas of opaque white mottling from burial, tail restuck, possibly slightly reduced, Eastern Zhou Dynasty, 4in (10cm) wide.
$5,250–6,250 *C*

A Chinese yellow jade figure, carved as a recumbent unicorn curled to one side and scratching his right brow with his hoof, the eyes, brows, pricked-back ears, horn, paws and spine well defined, Song Dynasty, 3½in (9cm) long.
$3,750–4,500 *C*

A mottled grey jade brush washer, carved as an upturned lotus leaf, with incurved edges forming the bowl, the interior carved with a lotus pod and the exterior carved in relief with branches of lotus flowers and leaves, 17thC, 5in (12.5cm) wide.
$3,750–4,500 *C*

A Chinese celadon jade vase, carved in shallow relief with a band of *taotie* below 2 *shou* characters divided by fixed-ring bat handles at the sides, a band of lappets at the rim, the stone with russet and darker inclusions, Ming Dynasty, 6¼in (16cm) high.
$4,500–5,250 *C*

A pair of Chinese celadon jade bowls, each decorated in gilding with dragons among scrolling flowers and foliage, the exteriors with lappet bands to the footrims, chipped, Qianlong period, 4¾in (12cm) diam.
$4,000–4,500 *Bea*

A Chinese jade box and cover, the sides carved with The Twelve Ornaments in roundels, the top with a large roundel containing the *qian* Trigram within stylised dragons, surrounded by an ornamental disc from which project 4 dragons' heads alternating with stylised leaves, on an incised swirling ground, with wood stand, Guangxu period, dated '1887', 4¾in (12cm) wide.
$16,500–18,500 *S*

l. A Chinese grey and black jade flattened vase and cover, with coiled mythical dragon handles, above rams among rockwork and clouds below a flaming pearl, 17th/18thC, 7in (18cm) high.
$1,500–1,700 *CSK*

A Chinese spinach jade lobed dish, carved in the centre with scrolling peonies and tendrils forming a roundel, Qing Dynasty, 5¾in (14.5cm) diam.
$1,200–1,350 *S*

r. A Chinese celadon jade *ruyi* sceptre, the top carved with an openwork dragon amid clouds, the handle with a knotted prunus bough and a bat at the end, Jiaqing period, 17¼in (44cm) long.
$9,000–10,500 *S*

Lacquer

A red lacquer bowl, the exterior carved with 2 striding dragons chasing a flaming pearl amid cloud swirls, the interior of dark brown negoro lacquer, damaged, incised six-character Qianlong mark on the base, the footring added later, 11¼in (28.5cm) diam.
$6,000–7,500 *S(NY)*

A Chinese export gilt decorated black lacquer needlework box, the interior fitted with lidded compartments and containing various ivory accoutrements, with drawer to the base, early 19thC, 14in (35.5cm) wide.
$1,200–1,400 *P(S)*

A Chinese red lacquer box and cover, carved with 2 parakeets in flight among peonies and chrysanthemums, chipped and cracked, Ming Dynasty, 6¼in (16cm) diam.
$1,800–2,000 *CSK*

A Japanese black lacquered table cabinet, on conforming stand with 2 drawers, 19thC, 19¾in (50cm) wide.
$1,800–2,000 *DN*

A Japanese lacquered workbox, the interior with lift-out tray containing sewing accessories, a single drawer, on gilded paw feet, 19thC, 14½in (36cm) wide.
$450–525 *WL*

A Japanese lacquered table box, c1760, Edo period, 12in (30.5cm) long.
$975–1,125 *WLi*

r. A lacquer tea cabinet, the drop-front door opening to 2 deep drawers beneath a pair of sliding grid-framed panels, Meiji period, 16½in (42cm) wide, together with a black lacquered storage box.
$7,000–8,000 *S(NY)*

A *shibayama* rounded rectangular box and cover, with silver rims, signed, Meiji period, 3¼in (8cm) wide.
$2,200–2,700 *P*

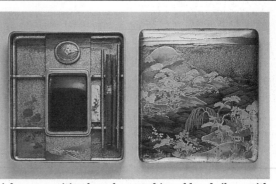

A set of 3 Chinese export crimson ground lacquered trays, c1870, largest 22in (56cm) long.
$1,800–2,000 *LEN*

A lacquer writing box, decorated in gold and silver, with the original wood box bearing the seal of the Marquis of Maeda, 19thC, 9½in (24cm) wide.
$36,000–42,000 *S(NY)*

Metalware

A Chinese silver bowl, possibly
Sing Fat and Chao-Ch'ang, early
20thC, 9in (23cm) diam, 24oz.
$975–1,125 *SK(B)*

A gilt-bronze figure of Guanyin,
Ming Dynasty, 29in (73.5cm) high.
$36,000–42,000 *S*

A cast iron figure of an
official, damaged, Ming
period, 16in (40.5cm) high.
$4,500–5,250 *C*

A Japanese bronze incense
burner and cover, modelled
as a Buddhistic lion, with
green patination, Edo period,
14¼in (36cm) high.
$975–1,125 *MSW*

A pair of gilt-bronze figures of crouching
Bodhisattvas, some encrustation, Tang
Dynasty, 2in (55mm) high.
$7,000–8,000 *S*

An inlaid bronze
vase, by Genryusai
Seiya, applied in
high relief with
vessels, a model of
an elephant and
a hawk, signed,
Meiji period,
18in (45.5cm) high.
$6,500–7,500 *S*

A Japanese bronze incense
burner, in the form of a
seated *shishi*, 19thC,
18in (45.5cm) high.
$2,200–2,700 *P(S)*

l. A Chinese
Yixing pewter
encased teapot
and cover, with
jade handle,
spout and finial,
signed 'Zhu Jian'
and dated, early
19thC, 4¾in
(12cm) high.
$675–825 *CSK*

A Japanese metal charger, by
Komai, signed, Meiji period,
22½in (57cm) diam.
$30,000–36,000 *S*

A Japanese inlaid iron dish,
by Komai, Meiji period,
13½in (34cm) diam.
$6,750–7,500 *Bea*

An inlaid bronze warrior,
signed 'Miyao zo', Meiji period,
7¼in (18.5cm) high.
$4,500–5,250 *S(NY)*

Marble

A Chinese marble sculpture of a standing Bodhisattva, standing on a lotus plinth on an inscribed stand, holding attributes, the head surmounted by a mandorla, damaged, Northern Wei Dynasty, 8in (20.5cm) high.
$1,850–2,250 *S*

A Chinese white marble head of a Dvarapala, carved with an *urna* between large eyebrows, protruding eyes, curved nose, pendulous earlobes and smiling open mouth revealing the teeth and tongue, with buff patina, chipped, Liao/Song Dynasty, 11in (28cm) high, on metal stand.
$9,000–10,500 *C*

r. A Chinese marble sculpture of a seated Bodhisattva, in the posture of contemplation, the stand inscribed with the possible date 'zheng guang yuan nian', damaged and restored, possibly 520, Northern Wei Dynasty, 10½in (26.5cm) high.
$6,500–7,500 *S*

Stone

A Chinese soapstone group, seated with a basket of peaches beside a female Immortal holding a *lingzhi* spray, 18th/19thC, 2½in (6.5cm) wide.
$120–140 *CSK*

A pair of Chinese carved soapstone pagodas, each multi-tiered, on octagonal bases, damaged, c1900, 21in (53.5cm) high.
$4,750–5,250 *S(NY)*

l. A Burmese stone head of Buddha, with stepped headdress and serene expression, metal base, 14th/15thC, 9in (23cm) high.
$540–600 *CSK*

Wood

A Chinese wood model of a seated official, wearing long robes, on a scrolling base, the head painted and gilt, damaged, 16th/17thC, Ming Dynasty, 27in (68.5cm) high.
$1,000–1,200 *CSK*

A carved wood figure of a seated official, wearing a loosely draped gown and official hat, pigment on gesso, traces of gilt, damage, Ming Dynasty, 33in (84cm) high.
$900–1,000 *SK*

An inscribed hardwood brush pot, carved in high relief with a topical, long prose inscription, the wood with a dark lacquered surface simulating *zitan,* and a small illegibly inscribed seal, 18th/19thC, 9¼in (23.5cm) high.
$2,200–2,700 *S(NY)*

A Japanese wood model of a seated Buddha, wearing long flowing robes, on a throne above a rockwork base, damaged, 18thC, 13in (33cm) high.
$725–825 *CSK*

Furniture

A Chinese elmwood storage
cabinet, c1860,
76in (193cm) high.
$3,000–3,500 *ORI*

A Chinese coromandel cabinet,
with carved ivory and shell
inlaid decoration, late 19thC,
60in (152cm) wide.
$7,500–8,250 *RBB*

Miller's is a price GUIDE
not a price LIST

A Chinese hardwood table, carved and
painted with central bird issuing from
foliate decoration, on carved block
legs, 18thC, 79in (200cm) long.
$3,500–4,000 *SLN*

A Chinese elm horseshoe-back
open armchair, with plain splat
and cane seat, c1870.
$1,150–1,350 *ORI*

A pair of Chinese walnut tea
tables, with railed shelf,
c1880, 33in (84cm) high.
$1,200–1,350 *ORI*

r. A bamboo table, with pierced
lattice work frieze and recessed
legs, 18thC, 64in (162.5cm) long.
$5,000–6,000 *S(NY)*

A Chinese elm 'official's hat'
armchair, with plain back
splat and cane seat, c1870.
$1,500–1,700 *ORI*

A pair of Chinese rosewood
vase stands, c1870,
33in (84cm) high.
$1,600–1,900 *ORI*

A pair of bamboo tables, each
with black lacquer top above a
lattice work frieze, on slender
legs joined by shaped brackets,
18thC, 33in (84cm) wide.
$10,000–12,750 *S(NY)*

A pair of Chinese elm
side chairs, each with
cane seat, c1860.
$2,000–2,500 *ORI*

Inros & Netsuke

A lacquered sheath inro, decorated in gold, silver and colours, the inlaid iron *ojime* signed 'Komin', the lacquered wood netsuke of a red fish with double inlaid eyes, signed, 19thC, 3½in (8.5cm) high.
$6,750–7,500 *S(NY)*

A gold lacquer 3 case inro, with *shibayama* decoration, one side decorated with poultry and chrysanthemums, the other with mice dressed in leaves and human attire enacting a parody of a drama, unsigned, the netsuke with inlaid copper birds, slight damage, signed 'Koku', 19thC, 4½in (11.5cm) high.
$8,000–9,000 *S*

Inros & Netsuke

Craftsmanship of miniature works of art such as inro, netsuke and tsuba flourished in Japan in the Edo period (1603–1868). The inro was a small sectional medicine case which was hung from the sash by means of a netsuke, or toggle. The tsuba was a sword-guard, often elaborately decorated. After the defeat of the Shogunate in 1868, Japan embarked upon a fervid period of westernisation, and items such as these, which reminded the Japanese only too well of their feudal past, were exported to the west where they found an enthusiastic collecting market.

A four-case gold and silver inro, decorated in red lacquer and ivory inlay, depicting Daikoku on one side and Ebisu on the other, with a reticulated ivory *ojime*, signed 'Shokasai', 19thC, 3½in (8.5cm) high.
$3,000–3,500 *S(NY)*

An ivory four-case inro, decorated in gold lacquer inlaid in coral, mother-of-pearl and tortoiseshell, Meiji period, 4in (10cm) high.
$3,000–3,750 *S(NY)*

An inlaid lacquered two-case inro, decorated in gold and inlaid with ivory, tortoiseshell and mother-of-pearl, 19thC, 5in (12.5cm) high.
$4,500–5,250 *S(NY)*

A lacquered five-case inro, decorated with gold turtles, the wooden netsuke in the form of a retracted turtle, signed 'Yutokusai Hogyoku', 19thC, 3¾in (9.5cm) high.
$4,000–4,500 *S(NY)*

A lacquered five-case inro, decorated in gold with 3 mounted warriors in combat, signed 'Kajikawa saku' with seal, 19thC, with an ivory netsuke of an elephant and groom, early 19thC, 3½in (8.5cm) high.
$5,000–5,250 *S(NY)*

A lacquered wood netsuke, in the form of a filleted fish, decorated with brown lacquer, the flesh in red, Meiji/Taisho period, 4¼in (11cm) long.
$675–750 *P*

An ivory inro, in the form of a large jar, inlaid in mother-of-pearl, tortoiseshell and stained ivory, repaired, signed 'Meishun', Meiji period, 4¾in (12cm) high.
$3,750–4,500 *S(NY)*

SNUFF BOTTLES

One of the most resilient areas of collecting for several years has been that of Chinese snuff bottles, and prices have been rising steadily. The market has been kept buoyant by the ever growing numbers of collectors from around the world, but over the past four or five years, an added impetus has come from Chinese collectors in Hong Kong, Taiwan and Singapore. During the same period much serious research in this field has been published, and collectors now have a solid core of reference works to guide them.

A laquered wood snuff bottle, in the form of a purse, 1780–1850, 2in (5cm) high. **$3,750–4,250** *RHa*

Beautiful, tactile and so varied in style and material as to be endlessly fascinating, snuff bottles embody the same superb skill in their manufacture as the best of China's art, only reduced in scale to minuscule proportions.

Snuff bottles were made in every material known to the Chinese: glass, porcelain, jade and other hardstones, ivory, coral, lacquer, amber, wood, etc, and though the high point in the manufacture of most types of bottles was the 18th century, many high quality bottles continued to be made during the 19th century. The early bottles are generally in greatest demand, but fine workmanship must always be the dominant criterion.

At the top end of the market, prices for unusual and wonderful bottles can be startling; witness the $25,500 paid at Sotheby's recently for a rare 19th century hornbill bottle, or the $130,000 paid at the same sale for a superbly carved nephrite bottle from the Suzhou school!

Beginners should take heart, however, as fine old bottles can still be obtained at affordable sums. The field is almost entirely dominated by collectors, and consequently there is very little speculation. The vast majority of snuff bottles are in private hands and therefore are, or will become, available.

A Suzhou School nephrite snuff bottle, 1750–1820, 2¾in (7cm) high **$18,500–22,500** *RHa*

Although increasing demand for the highest quality porcelain has had a corresponding effect on their cost, new collectors would nonetheless do well to start with either porcelain or plain glass examples. A very good bottle in either category may be purchased from $750–1,000.

Collectors should be on the alert for serious damage or visible restorations; either reduce the monetary value unless the example is so rare that the chances of finding one in perfect condition are practically non-existent. On the other hand, it should be remembered that these objects were made for daily use for a period of well over a hundred years, and buyers should not be put off by some slight restoration to an otherwise delightful bottle.

Finally, discriminating collectors should shun modern reproductions, which are now in plentiful supply. 'Copying antiquity' is a fine old Chinese tradition, and some new bottles are of amazingly high quality, but they do not have a place in a meaningful collection.

Robert Hall

A rock crystal snuff bottle, in the form of a mallow flower, carved in the centre of each side with radiating flower petals, the stone of smoky grey tone, slight damage, Qianlong period, 2¼in (6cm) high. **$3,250–3,750** *S*

A limestone snuff bottle, of flattened pear form, the dark matrix suffused with light grey fossils, slight damage, Qianlong period, 2⅛in (6.5cm) high. **$900–1,000** *S*

A silver snuff bottle, chased with Manchurian script on one side, and Mongolian on the other, matching stopper encrusted with coral and turquoise, Qianlong period, 2¾in (7cm) high. **$725–825** *S*

An amber snuff bottle, carved in the form of a pig, 1780–1850, 2¼in (5.5cm) long.
$5,250–6,750 *RHa*

A rock crystal snuff bottle, flattened pear shape with a smoky hue, on a dimpled base, with a pink glass stopper, 1780–1850, 2¼in (5.5cm) high.
$1,000–1,200 *RHa*

A celadon jade snuff bottle, shaped as a vase with 2 boys either side, 1780–1850, 2in (5cm) high.
$2,500–3,000 *S(NY)*

r. A cameo agate snuff bottle, decorated with a white crane, deer and *jui* design on a grey ground, with an agate stopper, early 19thC, 2in (5cm) high.
$1,000–1,200 *EL*

A cloisonné enamel snuff bottle, decorated in coloured enamels with butterflies and plants against a dark blue ground, 1820–50, 2½in (6.5cm) high.
$1,500–1,800 *S(HK)*

A glass snuff bottle, with carved red overlay fish amidst bubbles, 18thC, 2½in (6.5cm) high.
$4,000–4,500 *RHa*

r. A figure-shaped porcelain snuff bottle, in the form of the immortal Li Tieguai, with a yellow double gourd tied to his back, 19thC, 3in (7.5cm) high.
$1,500–1,800 *S(HK)*

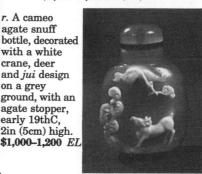

A rock crystal snuff bottle, carved with a magpie on a prunus branch, Daoguang period, 2½in (6.5cm) high.
$600–675 *S*

A cinnabar and green lacquer snuff bottle, 19thC, 2¼in (5.5cm) high.
$3,000–3,600 *RHa*

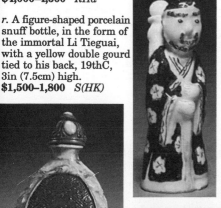

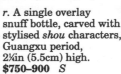

A porcelain snuff bottle, moulded in the form of a leaf-covered in iron-red and gilding, reserved on each side with a large panel of diaper pattern in blue, Daoguang/Xianfeng period, 2½in (6.5cm) high.
$1,000–1,800 *S*

l. A cloisonné enamel snuff bottle, decorated with scholarly objects, plants and fruits in various colours, on a powder blue ground, Qianlong mark on base, matching stopper, 19thC, 2½in (6.5cm) high.
$975–1,125 *S(HK)*

r. A single overlay snuff bottle, carved with stylised *shou* characters, Guangxu period, 2¼in (5.5cm) high.
$750–900 *S*

Robes

A blue Imperial 12 symbol robe, worked with couched metallic gold dragons, satin-stitched bats, clouds, rolling waves and a typical wavy *lishui* stripe, the symbols arranged in 3 groups of 4, the *fu* symbol and other decoration in fine satin-stitch, Qianlong period, 56in (142cm) long.
$30,000–33,000 *S(NY)*

A silk robe, finely embroidered in bright colours and gold thread with numerous Buddhist emblems on a floral and *wan* diaper blue ground, the applied hems with a similar design on a darker blue ground, 18thC, Qing Dynasty, 55in (140cm) long.
$5,000–5,750 *S*

A Chinese red silk dragon robe, woven in *kossu* with 10 dragons in coloured silks and gilt thread, lined in pale blue silk, late 19thC, 58in (147.5cm) long.
$850–1,000 *CSK*

A Chinese short robe, the purple silk damask woven with cicada and trimmed with black satin, embroidered with flowers, lined with pink cotton, c1900, 18in (45.5cm) long.
$420–500 *CSK*

A Chinese theatrical costume, comprising robe and leggings of purple satin embroidered in ivory silks with cranes and plum blossom, with gilt thread outlines, and another brown satin damask robe, c1900.
$500–600 *CSK*

A robe with matching skirt, the ground of red satin with couched gilt threads with shades of mainly pink and blue silks, lined in pink silk, the skirt panels similarly worked, early 20thC.
$580–620 *CSK*

Textiles

An embroidered coral silk satin hanging, with a central roundel of 2 dragons, a lion in each corner, the upper section with a phoenix and lotus, 17thC, 108 x 78in (274.5 x 198cm).
$1,200–1,350 *CSK*

A child's silver pheasant rank badge, the blue-black silk satin-stitched with the bird on a rock amid trailing clouds, all with couched gold detailing, Qianlong period, 5¾ x 6in (14.5 x 15cm).
$1,800–2,200 *S(NY)*

A Chinese Imperial cover of yellow gauze, finely embroidered in coloured silks, the central cartouche depicting a water landscape, lined in yellow silks, c1800, 50 x 36in (127 x 91.5cm).
$4,500–5,250 *CSK*

r. A pair of Chinese embroideries on white silk, showing figures in gardens, couch work, watercolour and bullion work, framed and glazed, 19thC, 15¾ x 30⅜in (40 x 78cm).
$600–675 *WL*

Arms & Armour

A white laced *tosei gusoku*, the leather 6 plate hip guards light purple laced and bear fur trimmed, the white laced shoulder guards with *kiri mon* decoration, the armoured sleeves with pierced design of blossoms, associated iron chainmail thigh guard and shinguards, 18thC, mid-Edo period, helmet 19thC.
$13,500–15,000 C

A composite suit of armour, black and russet lacquered, laced in dark blue, with a wooden armour box listing the contents, c1900.
$9,000–10,500 S

Japanese Armour

From the 5th–8th century AD, Japanese armour was very similar to that of China and Korea, being made from strips of small metal plates laced together. However, the lace holes weakened the metal and could be penetrated by weapon points, and the laces were found to be impractical because they became sodden and filthy in the damp climate. By the 15th century the armour had been adapted for the particular needs of the Samurai, so it was shaped to ensure comfort during the long campaigns, and was made of fewer, larger metal strips which were lacquered to prevent rusting. After guns made their appearance in the 16th century strong rivets were used for breastpieces in order to withstand the impact of musket balls.

An *eboshi* style *kawari kabuto*, the 2 plates black lacquered with 5 stage blue laced *shikoro*, some old damage, 18thC, Edo period.
$7,500–9,000 C

A Chinese style *kawari kabuto*, of 6 plates, each with an additional decorated plate, with silver *nunome* characters riveted, the top with *kiku* form *tehan* of iron attached with decorative rivets, c1700, early Edo period.
$18,000–21,000 C

A Japanese russet iron *mempo*, with detachable nose, horsehair moustache, the interior lacquered in red, 2 plate *yodarakake*, Edo period, 9½in (24cm) high.
$1,200–1,500 BWe

r. A *wakizashi* blade, ascribed to Umetada Yoshinobu, 17thC, 13⅜in (35cm) long.
$2,000–2,500 S

A *hoshi-bachi*, by Miochin Munenaga, with 24 plate russet iron bowl, signed and dated '1812'.
$5,000–6,000 S

A pair of inlaid iron *kaga abumi*, decorated with numerous birds and netting, the underside with rafts and flowers on water, in silver *nunome* and *honzogan*, the interior lacquered red, slight damage, signed, 18thC.
$7,500–9,000 S

l. A *tanto*, signed 'Soshu ju Masahiro', 16thC, 7½in (19cm) long.
$1,800–2,000 C

A *wakizashi* and mount, the blade carved with a dragon, signed 'Echigo no kami Fujiwara Kunitomo', early 17thC, 15⅝in (40cm) long.
$12,750–14,250 *C*

The swordsmith Echigo no Kami Fujiwara Kunitomo, from Yamashiro province, was a distinguished student of Horikawa Kunihiro and his blades were famed for their exceedingly sharp cutting edges.

An *efu tachi koshirae*, signed 'Osafune Norimitsu saku', dated for 1470, the scabbard of deep gold decorated with 14 *izutsu-mon*, late Edo period, 25½in (65cm) long.
$45,000–52,500 *C*

A *ken*, with a *Masamune* signature and dated '1329–30', late 19thC, 8in (20.5cm) long, in a natural wood mounting carved and inlaid with dragons in ivory, mother-of-pearl and ebony, late 19thC.
$2,500–3,000 *C*

Pseudo archaic blades were not uncommon in the Meiji period, made by smiths such as Miyamoto Kanenori and Hayama Enshin among others.

A *tachi*, signed, 19thC, 25in (63.5cm) long, in a black lacquered *saya* with gilt and embossed cherry blossom, 19thC.
$4,000–5,000 *C*

A *katana zutsu*, decorated with *mon* showing wistaria within a circle in rubbed gold *takamakie* on a ground of crushed *raden*, the interior of *roiro*, some chips, 17thC, 43¼in (110cm) long.
$4,500–5,250 *S*

An *aikuchi*, the blade ascribed to Tadayoshi, mounts by Harunaga, 19thC, blade 9½in (24cm) long.
$5,250–6,000 *S*

A *tachi* with mounts, 19thC, 27¾in (70.5cm) long, in an *aogai saya* with mounts of blackened brass with foliage, 19thC.
$3,750–4,500 *C*

Tsuba

A *sentoku tsuba*, in the form of a badger teapot, a blind man touching its tail, with 2 loose rings suspended from each side, signed 'Yasuchika', Meiji period, 3¼in (8.5cm) wide.
$6,000–6,750 *S(NY)*

A copper *tsuba*, decorated in *iro-e takazogan* with a fish swimming among reeds and lotus, signed 'Iwamoto Chokan', Meiji period, 3½in (9cm) wide.
$3,000–3,500 *S(NY)*

A *shakudo nanako tsuba*, the plate depicting warriors of the Mongolian war in silver, in Goto style, 18thC, 3in (7.5cm) diam, with a box.
$3,500–3,750 *C*

CROSS REFERENCE
Inros and Netsuke
page 545

l. An iron *tsuba*, carved and inlaid with soft metals with a frightened man observing a badger dancing under a silver moon, signed 'Naoshige' with *kakihan*, Meiji period, 3¼in (8.5cm) wide.
$6,750–7,500 *S(NY)*

A *shibuichi tsuba*, depicting Omori Hikohichi carrying the demon on his back, the detail traversing from front to back, the reverse with a large tree, signed 'Yoshitoshi', and a gold seal, 19thC, 2¾in (7cm) wide.
$7,500–8,250 *C*

MUSIC
Musical Boxes

A ratchet-operated cylinder musical box, playing 6 airs, with change/repeat and play/stop levers, in an inlaid rosewood and stained wood case, late 19thC, 14in (35.5cm) wide, cylinder 6in (15cm) wide.
$1,125–1,275 *P(F)*

A Swiss overture musical box, by Nicole Frères, No. 23158, the 11¾in (30cm) cylinder playing 4 overtures by Rossini, Weber and Mozart as listed on tune sheet, the key-wound movement contained in a rosewood veneered case with marquetry inlaid lid, lacking glazed panel and part of tune sheet, mid-19thC, 19¾in (50cm) wide.
$6,300–7,500 *S*

A Swiss Paillard Vaucher Fils overture cylinder musical box, the 12½in (32cm) comb playing 4 overtures by Verdi and Rossini as listed on tune sheet, contained in a veneered rosewood case inlaid with marquetry, c1880, 21½in (54.5cm) wide.
$6,000–6,750 *S*

A lever-wind musical box, No. 26038, playing 12 airs, with 13in (33cm) cylinder, contained in a rosewood, ebonised and inlaid case, the hinged lid decorated with a basket of flowering plants and garden implements, mounted on bracket feet, late 19thC, 25½in (65cm) wide.
$1,000–1,200 *P(E)*

A Swiss *'harpe harmonique oiseau'* musical box automaton, by Langdorff, the 13in (33cm) cylinder playing 6 airs on 2 combs as listed on tune sheet, contained in a walnut veneered case, with automated feathered bird mounted behind a glass window, cast brass carrying handles at the sides, c1870, 23in (58.5cm) wide.
$7,500–9,000 *S*

A Swiss automata and bells-in-sight musical box, the 19¼in (49cm) cylinder playing 8 popular airs, accompanied by 8 saucer bells, struck by 2 painted plaster mandarin figures, a seated monkey and 2 butterflies, contained in a rosewood veneered case, c1880, 26⅜in (67cm) wide.
$9,750–11,250 *S*

A Swiss rigid notation musical box, probably by François Nicole, the 10in (25.5cm) cylinder playing 6 operatic airs on the comb made in 4 sections, contained in fruitwood case with 3 exposed control levers at the sides together with 2 turned brass carrying handles, the bedplate and lid applied with plaques engraved with the retailer's details, c1820, 17¾in (45cm) wide.
$15,000–18,000 *S*

A Swiss mandolin expressive musical box, by Nicole Frères, No. 46485, the 12¾in (32.5cm) cylinder playing 8 airs as listed on tune sheet, contained in a rosewood veneered inlaid case with marquetry inlaid lid, c1880, 22½in (57cm) wide.
$4,500–5,250 *S*

A Swiss 12 air musical box, by Nicole Frères, No. 37423, the 13in (33cm) cylinder with two-piece steel comb, contained in rosewood and floral marquetry case, mid-19thC, 21in (53.5cm) long.
$3,750–4,500 *CAG*

A Swiss lever-wind musical box, by Nicole Frères, No. 42950, with 11in (28cm) cylinder playing 8 tunes, in an ebonised, rosewood and marquetry case, late 19thC, 20½in (52cm) wide.
$1,000–1,200 *DN*

A Swiss bells-in-sight musical box, No. 7144, playing 12 airs with 12⅛in (32cm) cylinder, accompanied by 6 saucer-shaped bells, zither and song sheet, contained in a crossbanded, inlaid and transfer-decorated case, c1890, 24¾in (63cm) wide.
$1,800–2,000 *Bon*

A Swiss musical box, with 13in (33cm) cylinder and zither attachment playing 12 tunes as listed on the tune sheet, in a rosewood crossbanded walnut case, late 19thC, 26¾in (68cm) wide.
$1,200–1,350 *Bea*

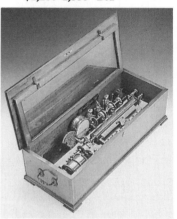

A Swiss Ducommun-Girod pianoforte musical box, the 12½in (32cm) cylinder playing 6 airs on 2 combs as listed on tune sheet, contained in a veneered mahogany case with domed lid and brass inlaid coat-of-arms, c1880, 21½in (54.5cm) wide.
$3,750–4,500 *S*

A Swiss musical box, the interior with 3 painted metal Chinamen playing 8 tunes accompanied by 6 bells, 19thC, 22in (56cm) wide.
$2,250–2,700 *EL*

A Swiss bells-drum-and-castanets-in-sight interchangeable musical box, by Nicole Frères, the single 15¼in (39cm) cylinder playing 8 popular airs as indicated by pointer, accompanied by snare drum, 6 saucer bells struck by 3 seated gilt-metal mandarins and castanets, the comb covered by a zither and movement with double-spring barrel, contained in mahogany veneered case with trade transfer applied to the interior, late 19thC, 35½in (90cm) wide.
$11,250–14,250 *S*

l. A Swiss Paillard 'Amobean' interchangeable musical box, No. 72311, with seven 7½in (19cm) cylinders, each playing 6 airs, in an inlaid, crossbanded and strung case, c1900, 22½in (57cm) wide, with 2 boxes each containing 3 cylinders.
$2,250–2,700 *Bon*

Gramophones

r. A French autophone two-selection oak cased juke box, with hearing tubes, c1906, 71in (180cm) high.
$4,500–5,250 *ET*

l. An HMV Model No. 194 gramophone, No. 1940000090, with re-entrant tone chamber enclosed by doors and fret, 5a soundbox, enclosed motor with lubricator and mahogany case with panelled doors, carved spandrels and gilt internal fittings, restored, c1930, 44¼in (112.5cm) high.
$2,700–3,000 *CSK*

An HMV Model No. 156 gramophone, in an oak cased cabinet, with 2 doors and compartmented interior, the base with turned supports tied by stretchers, 1928, 19in (48cm) wide.
$17,250–19,500 *EB*

Polyphons

A 24½in Polyphon disc musical box, with twin-comb movement, coin mechanism, drawer and instruction label, in an upright walnut case, lacking gallery, c1900, 45½in (115.5cm) high, with 9 discs.
$9,750–11,250 *CSK*

A 14⅛in Polyphon Style 48 table model, the periphery driven movement playing on 2 combs accompanied by 12 saucer bells, contained in a walnut veneered case, the lid interior with inset print, the exterior with marquetry inlaid floral motif, German, c1910, 30¼in (77cm) wide, together with 12 discs.
$4,200–4,800 *S*

A 19⅝in Polyphon disc musical box, the periphery drive movement playing on 2 combs, with coin-operated mechanism and glazed motor cover contained in an upright walnut veneered case, German, c1910, 50in (127cm) high, together with 53 discs.
$7,000–8,000 *S*

Symphonions

A Victorian Symphonion, contained in a walnut case, c1880, 20in (51cm) wide, together with 18 discs.
$5,250–6,750 *BUT*

l. A 11¾in Symphonion 'Rococo' disc musical box, No. 284775, with twin-comb arrangement contained in an oak case, German, c1900, 20in (51cm) wide, with 12 metal discs.
$6,000–7,200 *CAG*

Mechanical Music

A hurdy-gurdy, the body in guitar form, the table edged with ebony and ivory segments, the keybox with stamped decoration, the keybox cover, wheel cover and tailpiece overlaid with stained walnut ivory stringing, the keys of ebony and ivory, the pegbox also with stamped decoration surmounted by the carved head of a bearded man, S-shaped iron handle with ivory knob, labelled internally 'Massety à Paris 1768', 24¼in (61.5cm) long without handle.
$4,500–5,250 *S*

A Bontems coin-operated automaton, with gilt-brass cage enclosing 4 feathered birds with moving heads, tails and beaks to the sound of birdsong, the gilt gesso-shaped base with moulded decoration and coin drawer, with key at the side, French, c1910, 24in (61cm) high.
$5,250–6,300 *S*

A Bruder barrel organ automaton, the 23 note instrument with 3 stops, 50cm pinned wooden cylinder playing 10 airs as listed on sheet, contained in mahogany case with winding handle at the back and sides with 3 stop controls, the front with marquetry inlay panel and bands together with set of pressed brass organ pipes, the upper section hinged to open to a scene with 12 automated carved and painted wooden figures who move, dance and play musical instruments to the accompaniment of the organ music, German, restored, late 19thC, 23½in (60cm) wide.
$45,000–54,000 *S*

The Bruder family were among the foremost makers of barrel organs in Germany throughout the 19thC. It is rare to find an example with a set of automated figures.

Musical Instruments

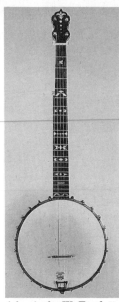

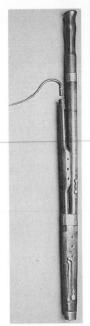

An American five string banjo, 13in (33cm) hoop orchestra Model No. 2, labelled 'S. S. Stewart, Phil'a P.A.', restored, the vellum replacement by 'C. Essex, Compton Str., London', stamped on the back, c1890, with fitted leather case.
$450–525 *Bon*

A banjo, by W. Temlett, the 10½in (26.5cm) engraved hoop with 24 gold plated shoes and tensioners, the ebony fingerboard and peghead inlaid with mother-of-pearl, the triple spliced neck also with mother-of-pearl side position dots, c1905, with fitted case.
$560–660 *Bon*

A bell-shaped cittern, the two-piece back of irregular curl, the ribs similar, the pierced parchment rose edged with ebony and ivory stringing, the head with a mother-of-pearl plaque, ebony fingerboard, 10 strings in 5 capo tasto positions, unlabelled, late 18thC, 28¼in (72cm) long, with fitted leather-covered wooden case.
$3,300–4,000 *Bon*

A nine-keyed fruitwood bassoon, by Jacob Georg Larshoff, with brass mounts, stamped 'I. Larshof' on the boot joint, Copenhagen, c1800, 49½in (125cm) long.
$1,800–2,000 *S*

An eight-keyed rosewood flute, by Charles Joseph Sax, with silver mounts, silver keys on pillar mounts with crescent base plates, with domed circular covers, tuning slide and graduated stopper, stamped 'Sax, Fac^r du Roi à Bruxelles', c1830, sounding length 23¼in (59cm).
$1,500–1,800 *S*

A blackwood conical Boehm flute, by Clair Godfroy Aîné, with silver mounts and keywork, stamped with the device of a lion and the monogram 'CG', c1860, sounding length 23in (58.5cm).
$5,250–6,300 *S*

An eight-keyed boxwood flute, by August T. A. Knochenhauer, with ivory mounts, brass keys with circular covers, graduated stopper, stamped with the device of an eagle, c1830, sounding length 22½in (57cm).
$2,700–3,000 *S*

A four-keyed rosewood flute d'amore, by Tebaldo Monzani, with ivory mounts, silver keys with square covers, stamped with crowns and 'Monzani, No. 3, Old Bond St, London, 509', c1805, sounding length 26½in (67cm).
$1,800–2,000 *S*

A six-keyed boxwood and ivory clarinet, the brass keys with square covers, with a period mouthpiece and cover, stamped 'J. Green, London', c1820, 26¼in (66.5cm) long.
$560–660 *SK*

A one-keyed ivory flute, probably French, the single key of silver with bevelled octagonal cover, later end cap, late 18thC, sounding length, 22¼in (56.5cm) in mahogany case.
$7,500–9,000 *S*

A four-keyed boxwood flute, by Carl Augustin Grenser I, with ivory mounts, silver keys with bevelled square covers, graduated stopper and foot register, stamped with crossed sword device on all joints, except the foot joint, the latter stamped 'A. Grenser Dresden, all stamped, c1790, sounding length 20½in (52cm).
$2,250–2,700 *S*

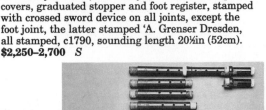

A one-keyed rosewood flute, by Carl Augustin Grenser I, some parts missing, stamped, late 18thC, in mahogany case.
$9,750–11,250 *S*

l. A French rosewood and rosewood veneer guitar, probably by Lacote, the table of medium grain spruce, the edges decorated with bands of ebony and ivory, the soundhole similarly decorated, the brass machines stamped 'Jerome', the ivory tuners, silver frets with upper registers set into the table, labelled 'Rue Louyois No. 10, Lacote & Cie Luthiers, Paris, Médaille Al, Exposition 1839, Brevetés d'Invention', length of back, 17¼in (44cm).
$720–780 *Bon*

A harp, by James Hanley, manufacturer of Sebastian Erard's Patent, 28 Grafton Street, Fitzroy Square, London, the neck painted to simulate rosewood with gilt lines, the soundboard similarly painted outside and with a design of leaf scrolls on a cream ground, lacking strings, 19thC, 66½in (169cm) high.
$1,800–2,000 *DN*

A concert guitar, by Daniel Friederich, stamped internally on the heelblock 'D. Friederich' and labelled, Paris 1981, length of back, 19¼in (48.5cm), in case.
$12,300–14,500 *S*

A concert guitar, by Manuel Ramirez, labelled, 1899, length of back 19¾in (50cm), in case.
$4,200–4,800 *S*

The table is a replacement by José Ramirez IV.

A Neapolitan mandolin, by G. and A. Vinaccia, the body of rosewood strips and decorated with mother-of-pearl and tortoiseshell, labelled and import labelled, c1803, 23½in (60cm) long.
$4,200–4,800 *Bon*

A two-keyed boxwood oboe, by Thomas Cahusac, the Elder, with onion and cotton reel finial, the keys of silver with circular covers, the C key with fish-tailed touchpiece, twinned G holes, stamped, late 18thC, 22½in (57cm) long.
$3,750–4,500 *S*

A two-keyed boxwood oboe, by Carl Augustin Grenser I, with onion and cotton reel finial, horn top ring, brass keys with octagonal covers, the C key with fishtailed touchpiece, twinned G holes, later bell joint by Steinke & Hoeprich, stamped 'A. Grenser, Dresden' with the device of crossed swords, c1800, 22⅛in (57cm) long.
$4,800–5,800 *S*

An American mandolin, by Gibson Inc, the two-piece back of irregular curl, the top of medium to wide grain, with mahogany neck, the fingerboard rosewood bound with pearl eyes, labelled 'Gibson Mandolin No. A-8772 is hereby guaranteed against faulty workmanship and materials, Gibson, Inc. Kalamazoo, Mich. USA', c1951, length of back 12¾in (32.5cm), with original case.
$2,700–3,000 *SK*

A set of Northumbrian small pipes, by Robert Reid and others, the blackwood chanter with 7 brass keys with circular covers, the 4 blackwood drones with brass and ivory mounts, with tuning beads on all drones, but undrilled on the G drone, leather bag with green velvet cover, the bellows by Tom Clough, the chanter and drone stock stamped 'Reid', c1820, length of chanter 10¾in (27.5cm), in case.
$3,300–4,000 *S*

Henry Clough (1854–1936) and his son Tom (1881–1964) were members of a family that produced 5 generations of pipers. Tom was to become the most acclaimed performer of the 20thC on the Northumbrian small pipes, and earned the title 'Prince of the Pipers'.

Pianos

A Bremar mahogany
piano/bureau, c1930,
60in (152.5cm) wide.
$3,750–4,500 *PEx*

A Victorian walnut cottage
grand pianoforte, No. 212,
by John Broadwood, c1880,
54in (137cm) wide.
$1,800–2,000 *GH*

An Erard straight-strung grand
piano, with rosewood case, c1890,
65in (165cm) wide.
$1,500–1,800 *PEx*

A Steinway Model O grand piano,
with ivory keyboard and rosewood
case, c1900, 60in (152.5cm) wide.
$7,500–9,000 *PEx*

A Neumeyer baby grand piano,
in an ebonised case, retailed
by Harrods, late 1920's,
63in (160cm) wide.
$1,500–1,800 *SEM*

A Blüthner satin mahogany
grand piano, reconditioned,
c1938, 59in (150cm) wide.
$10,500–12,000 *PEx*

r. A Napoleon III gilt-
bronze mounted boulle
marquetry ebonised
upright piano, works by
Erard, No. 16177, with
hinged panel revealing
keys, putti figures,
busts, foliate and
beaded trim, 19thC,
56in (142cm) high.
$12,750–15,000 *S(NY)*

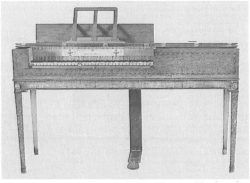

A mahogany square piano, by Thomas Haxby of
York, the hinged top with half-hinged fascia panel
opening to reveal the keyboard backed by a
satinwood and cream painted panel, flanked by
pair of neo-classical urns, opening to reveal the
movement, the stand with a folding pedal board,
on square tapering supports, headed by oval gilt
metal foliate rosettes and terminating in spade
feet, the whole inlaid with chequered stringing,
inscribed with maker's name dated '1788',
61in (155cm) wide.
$1,200–1,425 *P(HSS)*

A George III mahogany, satinwood and rosewood crossbanded square piano, the hinged lid enclosing straight strung frame above a keyboard of 5 octaves, on base with square tapering legs, inscribed 'Christopher Garner, London, fecit 1785, No. 17 Broad Street, Golden Square', 61½in (156cm) wide.
$2,000–2,500 *P(Sc)*

Violas

l. A Steinway upright piano, No. 111559, overstrung and under-damped, in a rosewood and ebonised case with turned and fluted uprights, 1904.
$2,700–3,000 *CSK*

An Italian viola, by Marengo Rinaldi, Turin, the two-piece back of broad curl, the ribs and scroll similar, the top of fine to medium grain, with orange varnish, labelled, 1899, length of back 16¼in (41.5cm).
$18,000–21,000 *SK*

A south German viola, the one-piece back of broad irregular curl, the ribs of strong broad curl, the scroll of narrow curl, the top medium to wide grain, red-gold varnish, labelled 'Antonio Testore, Milano Anno 1732', length of back 16in (40.5cm).
$9,000–10,500 *SK*

Violins

A violin, by John Barrett, the two-piece back of medium curl, the ribs and scroll faint curl, the top of fine to medium grain, with orange varnish, labelled, c1734, length of back 14in (35.5cm), with case.
$3,000–3,300 *SK*

A violin, by John Lott after Antonio Stradivarius, London, labelled, the two-piece back of broad curl, the ribs and scroll similar, the table of medium grain, with rich golden-red varnish, c1840, length of back 14in (35.5cm).
$27,750–30,000 *Bon*

A Markneukirchen violin, made for John A. Gould & Sons, the one-piece back of medium curl, the ribs and scroll similar, the top of medium grain, with red varnish, labelled, c1928, length of back 14in (35.5cm), with case.
$4,500–5,250 *SK*

A violin, by Georges Chanot, the two-piece back of faint medium curl, the scroll similar, the ribs broader, the table of medium grain, with orange-gold varnish, labelled, and inscribed 'Imitation HRH The Duke of Edinburgh Violin/G. Chanot 1877', length of back 14¼in (36cm).
$10,500–12,000 *C*

A French violin, ascribed to Pierre Pacherel, the one-piece back of small curl, the ribs and scroll similar, the table of narrow grain, with golden varnish, labelled, c1846, length of back 14in (35.5cm).
$15,750–18,000 *C*

r. An Italian violin, by Eugenio Degani, the two-piece back of medium curl, the ribs and scroll similar, the table of medium grain, with golden-brown varnish, labelled, c1896, length of back 14in (35.5cm).
$27,750–30,000 *Bon*

l. An Italian violin, by Giuseppe Rocca, the one-piece back of irregular curl ascending slightly from left to right, the ribs of similar curl, the head of medium curl, the table of medium grain, with orange-brown varnish, labelled, 1861, length of back 14in (35.5cm).
$65,000–72,000 *S*

Violins

From the late 18th century the design of the violin changed to incorporate a longer fingerboard, a longer, more acutely angled neck and a larger bass bar. These technical innovations allowed violinists to play at the increased volume needed in the large concert halls which were being built at that time. They also facilitated the playing of the new style of music being produced by composers, which required the 7th and higher fingering positions to be used.

An Italian violin, by Carlo Antonio Testore, labelled, the two-piece back of narrow curl ascending slightly from the joint, the ribs and head of similar curl, the table of fine grain, with golden-brown varnish, incised simulated purfling on the back, mid-18thC, length of back 14in (35.5cm), in case.
$45,000–52,500 *S*

Violoncellos

An Italian violoncello, by Giovanni Battista Gabrielli, the two-piece back of narrow curl descending slightly from the joint in the lower bout, the ribs and head of similar curl, the table of medium grain in the centre opening out towards the flanks, with golden-brown varnish, c1750, length of back 30in (76cm), in case with cover.
$111,000–120,000 *S*

A violoncello, by Bernhard Simon Fendt, London, after Andreas Amati, the two-piece back of irregular medium horizontal curl, decorated with the arms of Charles IX of France flanked by the figures of Justice and Piety and columns with putti above, the ribs of medium curl, decorated with gilt borders and inscribed in gilt, the scroll of narrow curl with further gilt decoration, the table of fine to medium grain widening towards the flanks, with golden red-brown varnish, unlabelled, c1830, length of back 29¾in (75.5cm), fitted wooden case.
$27,000–30,000 *Bon*

A French violoncello, by Charles Jean Baptiste Colin-Mezin, Paris, signed, the two-piece back of medium broad curl, the ribs and scroll similar, the table of medium even grain, with golden-orange varnish, labelled, 1889, length of back 29¾in (75.5cm).
$23,250–27,000 *Bon*

A French Mirecourt School three-quarter size violoncello, with two-piece back and orange-brown varnish on a golden ground, c1900, length of back 27¾in (70.5cm), with a bow and canvas cover.
$750–900 *Hal*

Miscellaneous

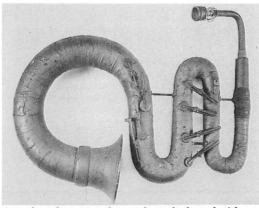

A Charles X adjustable fruitwood music stand, with 2 candle holders, the facetted stem above a triform base, on giltwood paw feet, c1825, 69¼in (176cm) high.
$4,500–5,250 *S*

A ten-keyed serpent, the wooden tube bound with fabric painted a dull gold colour, flared bell, brass keys with circular covers, brass crook with boxwood mouthpiece, c1840, 106in (269cm) long.
$1,350–1,500 *S*

This serpent has no finger holes, and all the tone holes are controlled by keys.

A French beechwood duet music stand, the adjustable music rest with telescopic candle holders, above a hexagonal shaft, on 3 down-swept legs, late 18thC, 54in (137cm).
$375–450 *CSK*

l. A pair of Regency music stands, the pierced fret music rests painted in gilt, with oak leaves and acorns around a central panel with brass rods, on adjustable brass columns and triform bases, 50in (127cm) high.
$3,000–3,600 *DN*

r. A French child's wooden music stand, painted with Mickey Mouse, c1930, 33½in (85cm) high.
$675–825 *C(NY)*

LAMPS & LIGHTING

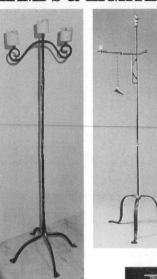

A wrought iron three-branch pricket candle-stand, c1600, 42in (106.5cm) high.
$2,000–2,250 DeG

A cruciform-based wrought iron rushlight with candleholder, in original condition, c1740, 7in (18cm) high.
$680–750 RYA

r. A pair of Venetian gilt-metal and painted torchères, the lanterns surmounted by hinged flags each with a winged lion, the lobed bases mounted with 3 winged cherubs, on knopped stems and faceted tapered bases, late 19thC, 86½in (219.5cm) high.
$380–450 Hal

l. A brass and wrought iron candlestand, the standard with brass finial, rectangular cage and single adjustable arm with brass drip pan and snuffer, on arch supports with disc feet, repaired, probably New England, c1800, 59½in (151cm) high.
$1,500–1,800 S(NY)

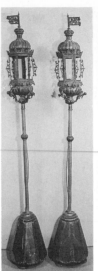

A Scottish wrought iron cruse lamp, 18thC, 16in (40.5cm) high including hook.
$120–150 KEY

A mahogany and brass storm lamp, the tulip-shaped glass shade with moulded brass support, on an anthemion carved stem and turned base, c1790, 23in (58.5cm) high.
$3,000–3,600 S

A pair of Wedgwood gilt-brass and glass storm lights, the engraved shades on bead-moulded and leaf-cast pierced supports, the drum bases depicting classical scenes, on bead moulded feet, re-gilded, c1775, 19¼in (49cm) high.
$5,250–6,000 S

A pair of Victorian Gothic bronze lamps, each with a square shaft with simulated brickwork inset with 3 tiers of Gothic arched and columned windows, surmounted by the gas burner, with glass shaft and an associated outer glass etched with vines, on a stepped base and plinth, with ebonised wooden socle, fitted for electricity, with old label inscribed 'Eaton Hall/ .../2.is', 30¼in (77cm) high.
$9,750–11,250 C

Probably supplied to Robert, 2nd Earl Grosvenor, for Eaton Hall, Cheshire.

A pair of bronze and gilt-bronze candlesticks, each with leafy nozzle above a band of leaves hung with icicle pendants, the reeded stem on square base, c1815, 12in (30.5cm) high.
$2,300–2,700 S

A wood and iron rushlight, with candleholder, c1780, 10in (25.5cm) high.
$300–350 WeA

l. A late Victorian oil lamp, with glass reservoir, on a reeded tapering column, round base with nulled and beaded border, etched globe, by Collis and Co, 20in (51cm) high.
$675–825 DN

A wrought iron rushlight nip, with original spring mechanism, c1800, 8in (20.5cm) high.
$350–420 *RYA*

An American three-socket electric table lamp, the patinated brass lamp of floral design, the sockets stamped 'Edison patented', with 3 original light bulbs labelled 'Gilmore Electric', c1893, 14½in (37cm) high.
$750–900 *S*

A ten-branch cut glass chandelier, each scroll arm with drop hung drip pans, united by swags of drops and with swags rising to 10 drop hung scrolled arms with spires, beneath a cascade of drops and a scroll and drop hung corona, restored, late 19thC, 63in (160cm) high.
$15,750–17,250 *S*

A pair of embossed gilt-brass colza wall lights, with tapered octagonal panelled bodies with shaped finial lids, single scrolled arm with light fitting, c1850, 14½in (37cm) high.
$2,300–2,700 *S*

A pair of glass hanging lights, the tulip-shaped bodies with cut trellis pattern, supported on chains from a brass rim, with birds' head hooks and a glass smoke shade, early 19thC, chains later, 24in (61cm) high.
$5,250–6,000 *S*

A set of 6 silvered-brass wall sconces, in 17thC style, the twin scrolling branches with cartouche-shaped backplates, cast with vacant escutcheons surmounted by flambeau urns, flanked by cherubs, early 20thC, 10½in (26.5cm) high.
$2,300–2,700 *CSK*

A Continental brass six-branch chandelier, c1760, 19in (48.5cm) wide.
$1,600–1,800 *KEY*

A brass hanging lantern, with the original glass, c1860, 32in (81.5cm) high.
$5,700–6,700 *LEN*

An Edwardian brass ceiling light, the domed shade with fluted glazing bars, a pierced circlet hung with beaded chains, surmounted by outspreading acanthus leaves, with open scrolling corona above a stiff-leaf wrapped terminal, 21in (53.5cm) high.
$1,200–1,400 *CSK*

A Genoese cast and embossed brass twelve-light chandelier, of inverted trumpet shape, the circlet with bands of Greek key pattern and stiff leaf ornament, hung with chains of graduated and faceted glass beads and silvered glass spheres, 19thC, 50in (127cm) high.
$975–1,125 *CSK*

ICONS

A Provincial Byzantine icon of Archangel Michael, shown half-length, in a red vestment over a blue shift, holding a lance in his left hand, the neck and face heightened with white, 13thC, on new panel, 18 x 14½in (45.5 x 37cm).
$150,000–165,000 *C*

A Cretan icon of the Dormition of the Virgin, the Apostles gathered round the Virgin's bier and the figure of Christ encompassed by a mandorla painted with angels, holding the soul of his mother represented as a new born infant, by a follower of Andreas Ritsos, late 15thC, 24 x 18½in (61 x 47cm).
$120,000–135,000 *S*

A Cretan icon of the Nativity of Christ, against an elaborate mountain setting, depicting the Virgin and infant, Joseph, the 3 Magi, a shepherd, his flock and angels, the blue arc of the sky bears traces of a gilt Latin inscription, early 15thC, 25¾in x 24¾in (65.5 x 63cm).
$398,250 + *C*

A Byzantine icon of Saint Kyriake, wearing Imperial purple and crown, holding an orb in her left hand with an inscribed image of the Christ child, her stole decorated with 5 roundels of female saints, one section missing, early 15thC, 14½ x 8¾in (37 x 22cm).
$38,250–45,000 *C*

A Greek icon of the Synaxis of the Archangels Michael and Gabriel, shown supporting a cosmic disc with the image of Christ Emmanuel, each holding a lance, late 17thC, 14 x 10½in (35.5 x 26.5cm).
$10,500–12,000 *C*

A Cretan icon of Christ King of Kings and Great Hierarch, seated upon an elaborate gilt throne, vested as Great Hierarch, the Imperial mitre with pendant jewels and pearls, stole and episcopal omophorion, his feet resting upon a winged seraphim, the panel reduced on either side, late 17thC, 52 x 34in (132 x 86.5cm).
$52,500–63,000 *C*

l. A Greek icon of Saint John the Baptist before a chalice containing his severed head, in a rocky landscape, the lower part of the panel with traces of a black inscription, 16th/17thC, 12¼ x 10¼in (31 x 26cm).
$5,000–6,300 *C*

r. A Cretan icon of Saint George Slaying the Dragon, with Saint George mounted on a grey charger, transfixing the dragon with his lance while the Princess escapes, the King and his soldiers on the ramparts of a tower, School of Emmanuel Tzanes, late 17thC, 10 x 8in (25.5 x 20.5cm).
$24,750–27,000 *C*

A Greek icon of the Bishop Saint, Dionysis, on a gold ground, 19thC, 5½ x 4in (14 x 10cm). $450–530 P

A Russian icon of the Hodigitria, with gold haloes, ochre background and stars on the Virgin's robe, Christ in orange-red garments, holding a scroll in his left hand, 15thC, 25¼ x 18in (64 x 46cm). $42,000–48,000 S

A Russian icon of the Dormition of the Mother of God, painted against a celadon green ground, the figure of Christ with green mandorla behind it, late 15thC, 19½ x 14½in, (49.5 x 37cm). $120,000–127,500 S

An icon of Saint Theodore of Tiron and Theodore Stratilates, probably Syria/Lebanon, the 2 warrior saints depicted as bearded young men, on an olive green ground, Theodore Tiron with a yellow halo, riding a grey horse, Theodore Stratilates with a red halo, riding a chestnut, an inscription in Greek between the horses hooves, possibly 13thC, 32¼in x 17¾in (82 x 45cm). $142,500–165,000 C

A Russian icon of the prophet Elijah in the wilderness, seated in contemplation at the mouth of the desert cave where he lived, the mountainous desert appears as a series of stepped cubic rock, 16thC, 9¼ x 7in (23.5 x 18cm). $5,250–6,000 S

A Russian icon of the Mother of God of the Sign, the Virgin depicted with her hands raised in a gesture of prayer, displayed on her chest is a roundel containing a bust portrait of the Emmanuel, Mary is surrounded by a two-tone blue mandorla which spreads at the side onto the raised border, the remainder of the border and the background are covered in strips of fine repoussé silver basma, 16thC, 18 x 14¼in (46 x 36cm). $69,000–78,000 S

A Russian icon of the Birth of the Virgin, 17thC, 15¾in x 14¼in (40 x 36cm). $4,000–4,800 C

A Russian icon of the Anastasis, flanked by the birth of the Virgin and the Annunciation, with the Mother of God below, surrounded by 4 groups of Saints, 18thC, 32¼ x 28¼in (82 x 72cm). $5,000–6,000 P

A Russian icon of the Doubting of Thomas, 17thC, 16½ x 14½in (42 x 37cm). $7,500–9,000 C

PORTRAIT MINIATURES

The market for portrait miniatures has remained buoyant over the past year. This is probably due to the growing number of collectors in Britain, Continental Europe and the United States.

Miniatures of outstanding quality continue to hold their value and in some cases that value can be seen to have risen considerably. For example, a 1792 portrait by the celebrated English miniaturist John Smart of his sister-in-law, Mrs Charles Smart, that had been sold at auction for $10,500 in 1992 was sold for $30,000 when it reappeared in a London saleroom barely two years later. Children and officers in their regimental finery continue to be the most popular subjects, but as a general rule portraits of distinguished or at least identified sitters will command higher prices than unknown subjects.

As the miniatures of the 16th and 17th century become harder to find, those that do emerge tend to bring ever higher prices. World records have been set at auction for miniatures by such established names as Samuel Cooper and Nicholas Hilliard.

Miniatures by American artists have performed well at auction in London recently, reflecting a strong demand from both US collectors and dealers. A signed miniature dating from 1790 by James Peale, younger brother of naturalist and painter Charles Willson Peale, whose full-size portrait of George Washington is an American icon, was sold for $3,300 against an estimate of just $750–1,200. A portrait of Captain Strawbridge by Robert Field, *see above,*

an English born and trained miniaturist who went to work in America in 1794, also achieved that same sum. A characteristic of his work is the use of tiny white hatch marks as highlighting technique, just visible on the collar of his subject.

However, miniatures painted in England from the middle of the 19th century onwards still remain relatively inexpensive and many examples may still be found priced at under $450. Few artists of this period signed their work, which makes it hard to make attributions with any degree of certainty, and this has traditionally made them less popular. The quality evident in miniatures of the period is nevertheless usually high and new collectors could benefit by taking a closer look at such works.

When looking at miniatures it is advisable to examine them carefully with a magnifying glass to ensure that the ivory, the most commonly found painting surface for miniatures from the early 18th century onwards, is not cracked. Check also for any signs of mould. Cracked miniatures can rarely be repaired successfully and once cracked, they tend to loose their value. Mould can be professionally removed but it is not always easy to open up the frames without damaging the glass or frame.

Finally, the serious collector should avoid miniatures housed in rectangular ivory frames, usually backed with old newspaper. These were mass-produced on the Continent at the end of the 19th century and are decorative pastiches made for the tourist market.

Claudia Hill

A portrait miniature on ivory, of an aristocratic lady, by Richard Corsway, in the form of a gold locket with a lock of hair in the back, c1800, 2½in (65mm) high.
$4,500–5,000 *BHa*

A portrait miniature of a gentleman, by Peter Paillou, signed on obverse, dated '1805', gold frame, 2¾in (70mm) high.
$830–930 *Bon*

A portrait miniature on ivory of a gentleman, by Horace Hone, ARA, in gold frame, the reverse with central hair reserve and seed pearl monogram 'W.C.', c1800, 2¾in (70mm) high.
$900–1,000 *N*

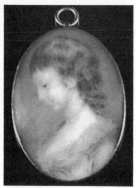

A profile miniature of a young girl, in a white dress trimmed with a turquoise ribbon, wearing a pearl choker, by John Smart, signed with initials, in gold frame, c1780, 2in (50mm) high.
$6,000–6,750 *Bon*

Profile miniatures by Smart are usually of family members or close friends and are, therefore, not always dated. This example bears a close resemblance to Sophia Dighton, 1770–93, Smart's 3rd daughter by his first wife.

A portrait miniature of a lady with pearls in her hair, by Augustin Ritt, c1795, 2½in (65mm) diam, in a gilt-metal bezel.
$7,200–8,200 *S*

A portrait miniature of a lady, by Mrs Anne Mee, c1815, 2½in (65mm) high, in giltwood frame.
$550–630 *CSK*

r. A portrait miniature of Miss Eleanor Elizabeth Normansele in white dress, by Henry Birch, signed on reverse, dated '1802', stamped gilt-mounted papier-mâché frame, 3in (75mm) high.
$1,125–1,275 *Bon*

A portrait miniature, attributed to Samuel John Stump, c1820, 4¼in (110mm) high.
$750–830 *TVA*

l. A portrait miniature on ivory of a gentleman, by Sir William Charles Ross, RA, signed, c1810, 3½in (90mm) high.
$2,000–2,400 *BHa*

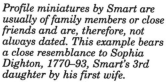

r. A portrait of Marie Justine Duvenesy, by Mlle Henriette Juegel, c1760, 3½in (90mm) high.
$1,800–2,000 *BHa*

Marie Justine Duvenesy was a famous French actress of the Comic Opera.

l. A portrait miniature on ivory of a junior officer of the 5th Regiment of Foot, Royal Northumberland Fusiliers, English School, c1820, 4¾in (120mm) high.
$1,200–1,400 *BHa*

FABERGÉ

The House of Fabergé was created by Gustav Fabergé, who was of Huguenot descent. His ancestors fled from France in 1685 and settled in St Petersburg. For a time Gustav was an apprentice to the jewellers Spiegel & Co, but in 1842 he left and founded the House of Fabergé in a small basement flat in Bolshaya Morskaya Street. It was his son Peter Carl Fabergé, born in 1846, who was to transform the family business to become famous throughout the world.

Carl Fabergé worked in Germany, London and Paris where he was greatly influenced by the designs and craftsmanship of each city. When he took over the family business in 1870, he introduced new creative ideas which brought him success at the Russian Fair in 1886 with his animal carvings and *objets d'art*. His success with Easter eggs led to him being granted a Royal Warrant by Tzar Alexander III in 1884 after the delivery of the First Imperial Egg to the Tzar and Tzarina. This theme was to become his namesake.

Carl was a man of great inspiration and restless imagination. It was his continual driving force, attention to quality and detail that raised him above all other craftsmen at that time. He employed the finest craftsmen working in Imperial Russia such as François Birbaum, Fabergé's head designer, and Michael Perchin, the most important of all the workmasters of the House of Fabergé. They created the most wonderful pieces using the most diverse range of techniques that were available, such as objects hand carved from nephrite jade and agates from the great mine of Ekaterinburg to the finest guilloche enamels that were fired countless times to produce the many different shades of colour.

Other important workmasters were August Holmström, August Hollming, Fedor Affanassiev and Johan Victor Aarne. There were in total, at the height of Fabergé's career, some 30 workmasters producing for his shops in St Petersburg, Moscow, Odessa, Kiev and London.

Each workmaster had their own workshop and mark, normally the initials of the workmaster – ie for Michael Perchin the mark was МП. The marks of the most famous workmasters were normally preceded by the Fabergé mark in full or the initials of КФ and the gold or silver standard mark and town mark. In certain cases only the workmasters mark is found without the Fabergé mark. This is due to the fact that a great many items were produced from many different sources, thus accounting for a variety of different marks.

Fabergé items have always performed well on the market in popularity and price over the last 40 years. The 'opening up' of Russia has helped provoke renewed interest of Fabergé there and in other former Soviet countries. Prices have actually risen recently and should continue to rise steadily in the future as more collectors fall for the undiminished beauty of these wonderful items. Items have remained recession-proof due to the fact that they are prized pieces and sought-after by many people.

Fabergé covers a huge diversity of items ranging from several hundreds of pounds for small silver items to many thousands of pounds for the more exotic pieces and is indeed a worthy challenge for the avid collector.

Sheldon Shapiro

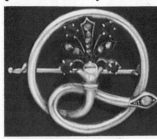

A Fabergé 14ct gold and jewelled pin, in the form of a spray of flowers set with sapphires and diamonds, encircled by a serpent with a diamond-set head, workmaster Erik Kollin, St Petersburg, marked with workmaster's initials and 56 standard, c1890, 1¼in (32mm) diam.
$2,250–2,700 *S(NY)*

A Fabergé 14ct gold and diamond brooch, the round openwork decorated with a swirling pattern, set with diamonds, workmaster August Hollming, St Petersburg, marked with initials and 56 standard, c1900, 1in (25mm) diam.
$5,250–6,000 *S(NY)*

A Fabergé gold, ruby and rose quartz miniature Easter egg, workmaster E. Schram, St Petersburg, c1890, 1in (25mm) long.
$4,700–5,700 *SHa*

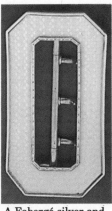

A Fabergé silver and gold buckle, with translucent oyster enamel over a guilloche ground, with gold borders, workmaster Michael Perchin, St Petersburg, marked with Cyrillic initials of workmaster, Fabergé in Cyrillic and 88 standard, c1890, 3in (76mm) long.
$2,600–3,000 *S(NY)*

l. A pair of Fabergé gold enamel and 'cat's-eye' cufflinks, workmaster Johan Victor Aarne, St Petersburg, c1896, 1in (25mm) long.
$6,300–7,000 *SHa*

Fabergé Marks

К.ф.   Fabergé mark (abbreviated version)
фАБЕРЖЕ   Full Fabergé strike

Important Workmasters' Marks

МП	Michael Perchin	(1860–1903)
H.W.	Henrik Wigström	(1862–1930)
A*H.	August Hollming	(1854–1915)
A.H.	August Hollström	(1829–1903)
O.A.	Fedor Affanassiev	(unrecorded)
B.A.	Johan Victor Aarne	(1863–1934)
E.K.	Erik Kollin	(1836–1901)
I.P.	Julius Rappoport	(1864–1916)
A.N.	Anders Nevelainen	(1858–1933)

The above marks are normally preceded by the Imperial Russian gold or silver standard and the town marks.

r. A Fabergé cut glass scent bottle, the body decorated with thistles and dandelions, with a rose gold collar, the cover in salmon pink guilloche enamel, the neck overlaid with rose-cut diamond set two-colour gold sprays, with a cabochon chalcedony finial within a rose-cut diamond border, decorated with ribbon-tied garlands, the knots set with rose-cut diamonds, maker's mark, scratched inventory number '24224', St Petersburg, c1890, 4¾in (12cm) high.
$19,500–21,750 *CNY*

A Fabergé Louis XV style silver jardinière, the lower part of the body cast and chased with lobes, the everted sides chased with shaped panels, with rocaille border and foliate side handles, on rocaille feet, maker's mark with Imperial warrant, Moscow, 1880–93, with metal liner, 21½in (54.5cm) wide.
$25,500–28,500 *CNY*

A Fabergé silver-mounted tazza, the red jasper column supporting a caryatid, with a wide agate dish on her head, workmaster Julius Rappoport, St Petersburg, maker's mark, before 1899, 6¾in (17cm) high.
$7,000–7,800 *CNY*

A Fabergé canteen of cutlery for 12, comprising 158 pieces, the handles decorated with scroll and rocaille bordered cartouches engraved with monogram, 2 spoons missing, maker's mark below the Imperial warrant, 84 zolotnik mark, Moscow, 1908–17.
$18,000–21,000 *S*

A Fabergé gem-set silver-gilt-mounted hardstone cane handle, the top mounted with a carved recumbent tigress in reddish-brown agate, workmaster August Hollming, St Petersburg, maker's mark, 1908–17, 4in (10cm) high.
$17,250–19,500 *CNY*

A Fabergé Bowenite carving of a baby cormorant, the eyes set with rubies, restored, c1890, 2½in (65mm) high.
$9,300–10,500 *CNY*

l. A Fabergé carved nephrite jade hippopotamus, set with demantoid garnet eyes, c1930, 2in (50mm) long.
$13,500–15,000 *SHa*

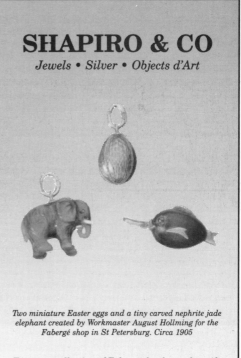

DECORATIVE ARTS
Arts & Crafts Furniture

A carved oak 'Eagle' chair, designed by E. W. Godwin for the library at Dromore Castle, Limerick, in 1869, manufactured by William Watt, with a cane seat and drop-in cushion, re-upholstered in brown leather cloth, c1869.
$27,750–30,750 *C*

An Arts and Crafts oak fireside chair, the wing panels and front apron carved with oak leaves and acorns within a roundel, the right-angled arms supported on 2 open uprights, labelled 'Baker & Co, Broad Street, Oxford', c1905.
$750–900 *C*

An Arts and Crafts oak umbrella stand, with cut-out decoration to front and sides, 30in (76cm) wide.
$560–660 *APO*

An Arts and Crafts oak armchair, in the manner of Bernard Maybeck, of pegged construction, with high slab back, curved flat arms, shaped board seat and canted rear legs, in original medium finish.
$1,800–2,000 *SK*

An Arts and Crafts fruitwood open armchair, with waved slats to the back and a rush seat.
$420–500 *APO*

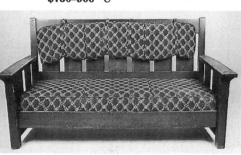

An Arts and Crafts 'Lifetime' oak settle, No. 719¾, with wide crest rail above 7 wide slats, flat drop arms and spring cushion seat, original medium finish, Hastings, Michigan, c1910, 75½in (192cm) long.
$2,000–2,250 *SK*

An Aesthetic Movement pine wardrobe, with painted cornice above 3 doors, the centre one with mirror, the flanking doors panelled and painted in maroon, grey and black, enclosing hanging space and drawers, 76½in (194cm) wide.
$1,500–1,800 *P*

An Arts & Crafts chair, by Carlo Bugatti, with vellum covered back, legs and seat, applied with beaten copper and wood roundels, the wood inlaid with yellow and blue metal, c1900.
$9,000–10,500 *S*

An Arts and Crafts oak settle, designed by Charles Annesley Voysey, for J. S. Henry, the upper section with a mirror flanked by 2 cupboard doors with brass handles and hinges, the backrest with 9 splats inlaid with pewter panels, with projecting coat rail and chest seat, 72in (183cm) wide.
$31,500–36,000 *S*

An Arts & Crafts
mahogany inlaid chair,
with soft seat.
$420–500 APO

An Arts and Crafts mahogany
occasional table, the plank sides
cut with ovals and shelves,
21½in (55cm) high.
$600–700 P

An Arts and Crafts oak chair,
by Gustav Stickley, No. 369,
the slant arms above spindles,
front and rear seat apron with
through tenons, original
medium finish, c1907.
$9,300–10,000 SK

Arts & Crafts and Art Nouveau Furniture

Furniture bearing a designer's
monogram, or other evidence that
allows attribution to a known designer,
always increases the desirability of a
particular piece to a collector.

An Arts and Crafts oak
cabinet, the
superstructure with a
pair of glazed doors
flanking a pierced grille
panel, above a shelf,
with frieze drawer, a
pair of panelled
cupboard doors and an
open recess, on shaped
feet, 27in (69cm) wide.
$750–900 CSK

An Aesthetic Movement oak
kneehole desk, with rounded
apron, stamped 'Gillow & Co,
Lancaster', 53½in (136cm) wide.
$3,750–4,500 P

An Aesthetic Movement
triangular ebonised wall
cabinet, the door stencilled
with a fruiting apple tree in
a small pot, the interior
with a single shelf, c1870,
19½in (49.5cm) wide.
$1,000–1,100 C

An Arts & Crafts oak canted
breakfront sideboard, the low
panel back pierced with heart
motifs, a central drawer and
carved panel door beneath,
original anodised metal handles,
on bracket feet,
54in (137cm) wide.
$670–830 WIL

An Arts & Crafts walnut
dressing table, probably
by Norman & Stacey,
labelled 'Liberty & Co
Ltd, London', early 20thC,
41in (104cm) wide.
$550–650 TMA

An Arts and Crafts mahogany
side table, possibly designed
by Phillip Webb, manufactured
by Morris & Co., the top
supported on 4 turned legs,
with lower shelf, c1900,
28in (71cm) high.
$750–900 C

Arts & Crafts Carpets & Textiles

Three William Morris 'Bird' design curtains, woven in blue, green, yellow and red, c1900, largest 150 x 64in (381 x 162.5cm).
$3,750–4,500 *Bon*

A Donegal carpet, the design attributed to Gavin Morton and G. K. Robertson, the deep blue field with central lozenge, intersecting motifs and formalised floral and foliate design, buff border with stylised palmettes, c1900, 106¾ x 89¾in (271 x 228cm).
$5,500–6,300 *C*

A hand-knotted 'Hammersmith' rug, designed by William Morris, the central blue field with scrolling flowers and leaves in beige, pink and green, outer border with floral running design on duck-egg blue ground, plain toffee outer border, with woven hammer and 'M' cipher, double knotted fringe, c1880, 80¼ x 54in (204 x 137cm).
$13,000–15,000 *C*

l. A Donegal wool carpet, 'The Donnemara', designed by C. F. A. Voysey, the field woven in alternate scrolling cartouches of poppies and tulips, supported by sinuous foliage against a reserve of leaves, within tulips and band striped borders, in shades of reds, greens and dusty pinks, c1902, 140¼ x 134¼in (357 x 342cm).
$15,000–18,000 *C*

Art Nouveau Furniture

l. A pair of side chairs, by Louis Majorelle, the shaped tapering back rests inlaid in fruitwoods with fern leaves and bronze mounts, the outward curving legs with bronze fern sabots, re-upholstered, c1900.
$7,000–7,800 *S*

A pair of black-painted armchairs, designed by Fritz Nagel, with scalloped-shape tops above curved panelled backs pierced with ovals, re-upholstered green leather seats, c1905.
$1,650–2,000 *C*

A rocking chair, designed by Josef Hoffmann, carved with stylised foliate, floral and geometric motifs, re-upholstered, c1912.
$3,600–4,000 *S*

An Austrian brass-mounted table, the top inset with 16 individual yellow iridescent glass tiles attributed to Loetz, in swirled peacock and red, with brass border, on square tapering legs with brass sabots, c1905, 27in (69cm) high.
$3,750–4,500 *C*

A suite of white painted garden furniture, designed by Josef Hoffmann, comprising 2 benches, a pair of armchairs and a pair of tables with open lattice stretchers, c1902, benches 101½in (258cm) long
$8,000–9,000 *C*

A fruitwood marquetry, mother-of-pearl, abalone and ash cabinet, by Louis Majorelle, in 2 parts, the framework carved with woodbine leaves and berries, c1900, 75½in (192cm) high. $21,000–24,000 S(NY)

A fruitwood display case, by Louis Majorelle, with central glazed section flanked by open shelves, carved with clematis flowers and leaves, c1900, 74½in (189cm) high. $9,000–10,500 S

An Austrian wicker conservatory plant stand, possibly manufactured by Prag-Rudniker, c1905, 56½in (144cm) high. $3,000–3,750 C

A music cabinet, by Louis Majorelle, inlaid with various fruitwoods, with top glazed drop-front cabinet, above silk back panel, small drawer, cupboard and music shelves, with marquetry butterflies, clematis flowers and stylised tulips, c1900, 57in (145cm) high. $5,500–6,300 S

An Art Nouveau brass double bed, attributed to Liberty & Co, with brass struts and turned uprights, bud motifs inset with blue and turquoise ceramic plaques, 72in (183cm) long. $1,500–2,000 P

A French Art Nouveau gesso wall mirror, the carved foliate surround with large floral blooms, buds and tendrils, surmounted by a foliate crest, 42in (107cm) high. $1,425–1,650 P

A dark stained brass-mounted table, the design attributed to Otto Wagner, the base and outer supports applied with flat brass banding, c1900, 51in (129cm) wide. $4,500–5,250 C

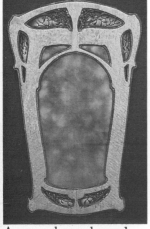

A cameo glass and carved bird's-eye maple mirror, by Jacques Gruber, the shaped frame carved with mistletoe blossoms and leafage, backed by glass panels cut and enamelled in purple and ivory, c1900, 68½in (174cm) high. $9,300–10,500 S(NY)

A carved giltwood overmantel mirror, the plate flanked by clumps of tall irises and framed by massed flowerheads above and 3 lily pads below, the panelled lower edge carved with a frieze of salamanders and mushrooms, c1900, 53in (135cm) wide. $14,250–16,500 C

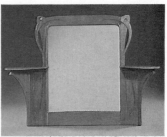

A carved pearwood mirror, by Hector Guimard, the glass flanked by shaped shelves, with carved organic motifs, c1900, 62½in (159cm) wide. $2,250–2,700 S

Arts & Crafts and Art Nouveau Metalware

An Art Nouveau WMF sardine dish, cover and stand, with a fish knop, 8½in (21.5cm) long.
$330–400 *DN*

An Art Nouveau WMF dressing table mirror, cast with flowers and diaphonously clad girl looking into the glass, 14in (35.5cm) high.
$1,200–1,350 *N*

An Art Nouveau WMF decanter, c1900, 10in (25cm) high.
$375–450 *CSA*

A silver glass holder, by Omar Ramsden, hallmarked London 1927, with later glass, 5in (12.5cm) high.
$1,500–2,000 *SHa*

A finger bowl in the Japanese style, silver coloured metal, gilt silver coloured metal interior, everted petalled rim, 4 scroll feet, cast and chased with a frieze of stylised blossom, gold coloured metal inlaid detail, stamped 'Tiffany & Co 4759 M 8886....797', c1885, 4in (10cm) diam.
$1,800–2,000 *S*

An Art Nouveau WMF mirror, 20in (51cm) high.
$1,800–2,700 *ASA*

A Liberty Tudric hammered pewter clock, with 3½in (9cm) Roman dial and copper chapter ring around peacock blue centre, the case with presentation inscription dated '1924', 11¾in (30cm) wide.
$375–450 *WL*

Miller's is a price GUIDE not a price LIST

A WMF shaped dish, with a female figure, c1900, 8in (20.5cm) high.
$900–1,350 *ASA*

An Art Nouveau WMF kettle and stand, c1900, 11in (28cm) high.
$750–825 *SHa*

A WMF brass-mounted 11-piece hammered copper punch set, decorated with random hammered pattern and impressed design, with stylised brass finial, supports and mounts, impressed marks, glass cup liners missing, c1905, 18in (45.5cm) high overall.
$900–1,000 *SK*

A pewter and enamel clock, designed by Archibald Knox for Liberty & Co, the dial of green and blue enamel, stamped registration No. '0629', with key, c1905, 6¾in (17cm) high.
$3,000–3,600 C

Liberty Pewter

Tudric is the trade name used by Liberty for their decorative Art Nouveau pewter. Although no obvious indication is given on individual pieces, those items known to have been designed by Archibald Knox are most eagerly sought-after.

An Art Nouveau polychromed bronze dish, with lotus flowers and leaves and sleeping figure of a girl, 9½in (24cm) wide.
$675–825 JL

A silver plated toast rack, designed by Christopher Dresser, manufactured by Hukin & Heath, c1881, 4¾in (12cm) wide.
$950–1,100 SHa

A silver plate and glass claret jug, designed by Christopher Dresser, of baluster form, with vertical ivory rod handle and flat-hinged cover, maker's mark of Hukin & Heath, c1881, 8½in (21.5cm) high.
$2,500–2,700 S(NY)

A pair of Art Nouveau gilt-bronze vases, by François-Raoul Larche, inscribed and numbered 'N963' and 'N964', 16¼in (41.5cm) high.
$30,000–36,000 S(NY)

A pewter basket with handle, designed by Archibald Knox for Liberty & Co, c1905, 9¼in (23.5cm) long.
$110–120 GOO

A silver and enamel photograph frame, by Hutton & Sons, embossed with entwined plant forms heightened with blue/green enamels, stamped maker's marks, London hallmarks for 1903, 4in (10cm) high.
$900–1,000 P

A silver coloured metal tankard, attributed to Dominic & Haff, decorated with a dragonfly hovering above a lily pond, underside stamped 'Wm Wilson & Son' and numbered '114', 4in (10cm) high.
$975–1,100 S

A silver picture frame, embossed in bold relief with chrysanthemums and poppies, with J. W. Benson Ltd retailer's stamp, maker's marks for Chester 1904, 13½in (34cm) high.
$1,000–1,200 P

An electroplated sugar basin, designed by Christopher Dresser and stamped 'Elkington & Co,' c1880, 3¼in (8cm) high.
$14,250–15,750 C

Arts & Crafts and Art Nouveau Jewellery

l. An Art Nouveau gold brooch, set with pearls, c1900.
r. An Art Nouveau gold locket, c1900.
$1,200–1,425 each *JES*

A silver plated châtelaine, probably French, c1880.
$300–330 *TVA*

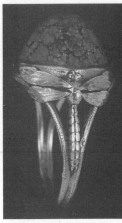

A French gold and turquoise ring, decorated with a dragonfly, c1900.
$1,500–1,800 *JES*

An oxidised silver brooch, set with olivine, by C. R. Ashbee, c1900.
$1,500–1,800 *JES*

A gold dragonfly brooch, attributed to Boucheron, the 4 sprung wings in pale green shading to pale blue enamel, each set with a blue cabochon and bordered on one side with diamond rosettes, the body studded with rose diamonds, the head green enamel and set with a diamond, c1900, 4¾in (12cm) wide.
$36,000–39,000 *S(G)*

A gold pendant/brooch, by Maison Vever, modelled as 2 peacocks holding a diamond between their beaks and a large pearl between their feet, enamelled in blue and green, their wings set with diamonds mounted in silver, the tails with cabochon sapphires and rose diamonds, c1900, pendant 2½in (65mm) long, in original lined maroon leather case.
$32,000–36,000 *S(G)*

An Art Nouveau pocket watch, with clear white enamelled dial and black numerals, the back with the profile head and shoulders of a Mucha style maiden, framed by lilies, the outer edge with holly, signed on case 'Huguenin dep', 2in (5mm) diam.
$600–675 *P*

A German Art Nouveau gold and enamel pendant/brooch, with pearl drop, c1900, 1½in (40mm) high.
$4,200–4,500 *JES*

An Austrian carved amethyst brooch, with diamond set stem, c1900, 2½in (65mm) high.
$2,250–2,700 *JES*

A hair comb, by René Lalique, of carved and patinated horn, in the form of 2 stalks of corn, each applied with a carved and patinated bee, the wings heightened with metallic paint, stamped 'Lalique', c1900, 8in (20.5cm) long, in modern case.
$57,000–63,000 *S(G)*

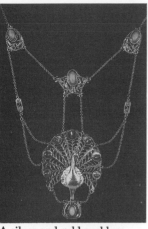

A silver and gold necklace, set with abalone, by C. R. Ashbee, c1900. $4,200–4,800 *JES*

A symbolist hair comb, by Charles Boutet de Monvel, tortoiseshell and openwork silver, centred by a female head with green, yellow and mauve enamel flowers, surmounted by an owl with gem-set eyes, c1901, 5½in (14cm) long, in modern case. $3,750–4,200 *S(G)*

Miller's is a price GUIDE not a price LIST

An Art Nouveau silver buckle, c1905, 2½in (65mm) high. $150–180 *GOO*

A gold pendant, by René Lalique, modelled as 2 scaly enamelled talons clutching a large eagle with a cabochon ruby eye, c1898, 3in (7.5cm) long, on a later gold chain, in modern case. $28,500–33,000 *S(G)*

A jade pendant necklace, by René Lalique, the central jade pendant carved in *entrelac* design, suspended from an openwork frame of dark green enamel, each corner with a stylised pearl flower, with 2 further jade pendants, the green enamelled chain interspersed with pearls, c1904, 13in (33cm) long, in a modern wallet. $36,000–42,000 *S(G)*

r. An 'Anemone' dog collar plaque, by René Lalique, the gold frame with entwined leaves and stems of rose and brilliant-cut diamonds, carved opals and enamel, with detachable pin and later collar of 14 parallel strings of small pearls, c1897, 3in (7.5cm) wide, in modern case. $66,000–72,000 *S(G)*

An apple blossom tiara, by Paul Liénard, with gold branch, the leaves and blossoms carved from transluscent horn, the flowers centred by rose diamonds, the buds small pearls, with 2 pendant twigs, c1900, 6¼in (16cm) long, in lined paper-covered case with gilt mark. $15,000–18,000 *S(G)*

A gold, diamond, enamel and pearl brooch, in a fan-shaped design of seaweed fronds, incised mark 'G. Fouquet', c1905, 4½in (11.5cm) wide. $105,000–112,500 *S(G)*

A French gold and amethyst ring, by Antoine Bricteux, c1900. $2,000–2,250 *JES*

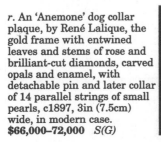

Art Nouveau Glass

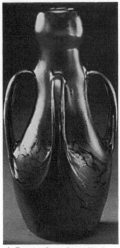

A Queen's Burmese ware glass vase, with rolled-over rim, decorated with green garlands of ivy, signed 'Thos. Webb & Sons', c1890, 7in (18cm) high.
$600–675 *JL*

An Art Nouveau Bohemian glass and copper bowl-on-stand, the green bowl with wavy rim, enhanced with iridescent blue webbing, on 4 pierced foliate columns, 13¾in (35cm) high.
$780–930 *P*

A Daum martelé *veilleuse*, c1900, 7in (18cm) high.
$3,000–3,750 *JES*

Cameo Glass

Cameo is produced from 2 or more layers of different coloured glass cut away from the base vessel leaving the subject standing out in relief. Smaller sized examples with several layers of glass and pieces decorated with landscapes are particularly popular.

A Loetz four-handled glass vase, the pale green washed with purple, with blue and green-gold iridescence, engraved mark 'Loetz Austria', c1910, 9¾in (25cm) high.
$6,600–7,800 *S*

A Tiffany Favrile glass vase, amber over white, decorated with rows of iridescent green peacock feathers, with 'pea-eyes' in iridescent blue, brown and grey-green, inscribed 'Louis C. Tiffany-Favrile/1997 C.', c1908, 10in (25.5cm) high.
$4,200–4,800 *S(NY)*

A Loetz yellow iridescent glass vase, inscribed 'Loetz/Austria', c1900, 9¾in (25cm) high.
$18,750–21,750 *S(NY)*

A Gallé grey glass vase, internally decorated with pink, overlaid with lilac and olive-green and etched with flowering sprays, cameo mark 'Gallé', c1900, 10in (25.5cm) high.
$1,300–1,500 *S*

l. A *pâte-de-verre* glass vase, decorated with mauve and purple and moulded with a frieze of green fish swimming through stylised waves, with intaglio moulded mark 'G. Argy-Rousseau', c1925, 6¼in (15.5cm) high.
$18,000–21,000 *S*

l. A Gallé grey-green carved and applied glass pitcher, carved mark on the handle 'Gallé', c1905, 9in (23cm) high.
$78,000–90,000 *C*

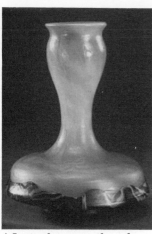

l. A Gallé yellow glass aquatic vase, cameo mark 'Gallé', c1900, 9⅞in (25cm) high.
$3,600–4,200 *S*

A Loetz glass vase, the pale yellow washed with bands of peach and purple iridescence at the foot and neck, the central section with lustrous ripples of pale green-gold iridescence, the underside with engraved mark 'Loetz Austria', c1900, 7½in (19cm) high.
$8,700–10,000 *S*

r. A Tiffany Favrile glass vase, in brick red, the foot and rim wrapped with black, decorated about the neck and shoulder with silvery-grey stringing, inscribed 'L. C. Tiffany-Inc. Favrile 5020 N.', c1918, 9¼in (23.5cm) high.
$5,700–6,300 *S(NY)*

A Loetz clear glass vase, the dimpled body washed with golden-pale blue iridescence and with 5 trailing lily pad applications in red and iridescent stripes, engraved mark 'Loetz Austria', c1900, 8¼in (21cm) high.
$4,200–4,800 *S*

A Daum glass vase, internally mottled with yellow, orange and green, etched and enamelled with a distant riverbank and flowering alliums, mark 'Daum Nancy' with a cross of Lorraine, c1910, 10⅝in (27cm) high.
$6,750–7,500 *S*

Art Nouveau & Studio Ceramics

A Martin Brothers double-faced stoneware jug, with a loop handle, chipped, incised 'R. W. Martin & Bros, London & Southall', c1900, 6½in (16.5cm) high.
$2,000–2,500 *S*

A pair of Théodore Deck polychrome earthenware vases, decorated with clusters of enamelled flowers, and with a bird and butterflies, against an eau de nil ground, damaged and restored, mark 'T. H. Deck' and factory mark, c1880, 23¾in (60.5cm) high.
$6,300–7,500 *S*

A charger, by C. H. Brannam, designed by Frederick Baron, c1904, 14in (35.5cm) diam.
$270–330 *GOO*

A ceramic iridescent jardinière, by Clement Massier, with bronze mount, dated '1892', 11¾in (30cm) diam.
$1,350–1,500 *SUC*

A Moorcroft pottery table lamp, with Clematis pattern, on deep blue ground, with wooden stand, 13½in (34.5cm) high.
$675–780 *AH*

A pair of Moorcroft pottery spill vases, with Pomegranate design on deep blue ground, 12½in (32cm) high.
$950–1,100 *AH*

A Moorcroft baluster-shaped vase, decorated with orchid type flowers on a blue ground, 11¾in (29.5cm) high.
$375–450 *P(C)*

A Moorcroft two-handled vase, with Pomegranate design, green signature, repaired, 14in (35.5cm) high.
$1,500–1,800 *RBB*

A Moorcroft Florian ware vase, c1900, 8½in (21.5cm) high.
$750–900 *HEA*

A ceramic iridescent vase, by Clement Massier, decorated with butterflies, c1892, 8¾in (22cm) high.
$1,200–1,425 *SUC*

A pair of Moorcroft MacIntyre miniature ovoid vases, decorated with flowers and leaves, on a blue and orange ground, printed marks in brown and No. '4', c1900, 3in (7.5cm) high.
$1,200–1,425 *DN*

A William De Morgan Persian vase, the double-gourd form with 2 loop handles, painted in the Damascus manner with a symmetrical design of peacocks amidst scrolling foliage, chipped, c1880, 15¼in (38.5cm) high.
$7,200–8,500 *S*

A William Moorcroft compressed bottle-shaped vase, of Claremont pattern, impressed mark and painted signature, 'Rd. No. 420081', 7in (18cm) high.
$975–1,100 *MSW*

A ceramic plaque, by Webb & Co, c1910, 14¼in (36cm) diam.
$300–360 *DAF*

A hand-painted wall plaque, probably on a Wedgwood blank, depicting a girl with golden hair, enclosed by a border of red, orange and yellow flora with butterflies, signed and dated 'Louis J. Rhead 1880', 16¼in (41cm) diam.
$8,250–9,750 *P*

A Pilkington bottle vase, designed by Walter Crane and decorated by Richard Joyce, c1907, 10in (25.5cm) high.
$2,700–3,000 *SUC*

A Villeroy & Boch coffee jug, c1900, 9in (23cm) high.
$225–270 *SUC*

A Dutch Rozenburg eggshell porcelain jar with lid, designed by Sam Schellink, c1904, 6½in (16.5cm) high.
$3,000–3,600 *OO*

A Poole Pottery (Carter & Co) moulded vase, designed by Owen Carter, the white stoneware covered with a red/gold lustre glaze, incised in script 'Carters Poole 1905', 12½in (32cm) high.
$600–720 *PP*

Lighting

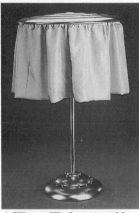

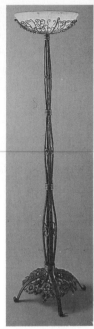

A Wiener Werkstätte table lamp, designed by Josef Hoffmann, the stem supporting a shallow domed ribbed shade hung with silk, stamped with designer's monogram and 'WW' registration mark, c1905, 22in (56cm) high.
$10,500–12,000 *C*

A Daum and Majorelle tea rose lamp, the shade with mark 'Daum Nancy' with a cross of Lorraine, the base marked 'L. Majorelle, Nancy', c1905, 19in (48.5cm) high.
$21,000–24,750 *S*

A pair of Arts & Crafts embossed copper and glass wall lanterns, the side panels cut and embossed with various scenes of New York city, enclosing striated opalescent glass panels in shades of green, red and white, both suspended from a scrolling bracket with small chains, unsigned, c1915, 9½in (24cm) high.
$1,800–2,000 *S(NY)*

A French Art Deco parcel-gilt, wrought iron and alabaster floor lamp, c1925, 70in (178cm) high.
$8,700–10,000 *S(NY)*

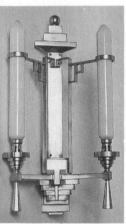

A bronze and alabaster table lamp, designed by Albert Cheuret, modelled as 3 tulips, c1925, 14¾in (37.5cm) high.
$10,500–12,000 *C*

A Rosenthal white glazed porcelain figural lamp base, probably designed by Gerhard Schliepstein, the seated nude female holding a conical torchère, on a triangular base, c1925, 24in (61cm) high.
$1,800–2,000 *S(NY)*

A set of 4 Art Deco bronze wall lights, c1920, 13¾in (35cm) high.
$1,500–1,800 *ASA*

An Emile-Jacques Ruhlmann silvered-bronze three-arm table lamp, some damage, c1925, 25½in (65cm) high.
$20,250–22,500 *S(NY)*

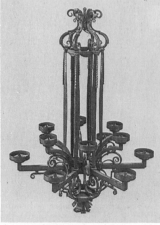

A wrought iron chandelier, with 12 arms, c1925, 41in (104cm) diam.
$2,700–3,000 *C*

An Edgar Brandt and Daum chandelier, the shade with mark 'Daum Nancy' with a cross of Lorraine, ceiling rose stamped 'E. Brandt', c1925, 26in (66cm) diam.
$3,300–4,000 *S*

A French Art Deco light fitting, enclosing multiple light sockets, contained within silver-plated mounts, c1920, 20in (51cm) diam.
$1,500–1,800 *ASA*

A Keith Murray pottery lamp base, of stepped cylindrical form, the grey body banded with silver colour, marked 'Wedgwood' and 'Keith Murray', c1920, 8in (20.5cm) high.
$600–700 *P*

A John B. Salterini wrought iron lamp, the standard cast with stylised perching bird, c1930, 36in (91.5cm) high, fitted with a modern parchment shade.
$2,700–3,000 *S(NY)*

l. An American Art Deco parcel-gilt wrought iron floor lamp, the finial cast as a stylised bird above 3 candle-cup lamps, raised on twisted standard wrought with berries and leafage, c1930, 71in (180.5cm) high, fitted with a modern parchment shade.
$5,700–6,700 *S(NY)*

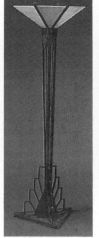

An Art Deco metal and glass ceiling light, designed by Ray Hille, 1935, 22½in (57cm) high, and 4 wall lights made by Galliers, London.
$530–630 *P*

A Degué Art Deco wrought iron and glass standard lamp, signed on the shade 'Degué', c1920, 70⅞in (179.5cm) high.
$3,750–4,500 *P*

A wrought iron floor lamp, the flared shade with 4 flat alabaster panels, c1930, 66½in (169cm) high.
$1,300–1,500 *CSK*

A Margo Kempe bronze figural lamp, the standard cast with a stylised bird, c1930, 26½in (67.5cm) high, fitted with a modern parchment shade.
$3,300–4,000 *S(NY)*

r. A pair of Venetian five-branch wall lights, each branch internally bubbled, tapering into fluted supports, c1930, 11in (28cm) high.
$4,000–4,800 *C*

An Art Deco set of 3 silver-plated bronze ceiling lights, with frosted glass, c1930, 12in (30.5cm) diam.
$1,200–1,350 *DAF*

A pair of Art Deco wall lights, the opalescent disc-shape shades moulded with seashells and aquatic tendrils, partly enclosed by a gilt-metal wall bracket with frosted glass side panels, moulded 'Verlys France', 12½in (32cm) long.
$1,200–1,350 *P*

An Art Deco uplighter, with central column of glass rods and original sand-blasted Perspex shade, 56in (142cm) high.
$375–450 *DAF*

Tiffany Lighting

A Tiffany Favrile glass and bronze Laburnham table lamp, impressed mark 'Tiffany Studios New York, No. 368', c1910, 27in (68.5cm) high.
$87,000–100,000 *DN*

A Tiffany Favrile glass and bronze Dragonfly lamp, shade impressed 'Tiffany Studios/New York/1495', base impressed 'Tiffany Studios/New York/533', c1900, 24in (61cm) high.
$45,000–52,500 *S(NY)*

A Tiffany Favrile glass and bronze Daffodil lamp, impressed 'Tiffany Studios/New York', c1900, 24in (61cm) high.
$46,500–54,000 *S(NY)*

A Tiffany Favrile glass and gilt-bronze Parasol lamp, shade impressed 'Tiffany Studios/New York', base impressed 'Tiffany Studios/New York/1651', c1900, 28in (71cm) high.
$11,250–12,750 *S(NY)*

A Tiffany Favrile glass and bronze Wisteria lamp, shade impressed '30025/02', base impressed '30250', c1900, 25½in (65cm) high.
$142,500–165,000 *S(NY)*

A Tiffany Favrile glass and bronze Butterfly lamp, shade unsigned, base impressed 'Tiffany Studios/25918', c1900, 23¾in (60.5cm) high.
$90,000–100,000 *S(NY)*

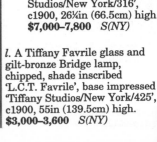

A Tiffany Favrile glass and gilt-bronze Linenfold lamp, shade impressed 'Tiffany Studios/New York/1950/PAT. Applied For', base impressed 'Tiffany Studios/444', c1900, 24½in (62cm) high.
$4,800–5,800 *S(NY)*

A Tiffany Favrile wheel-carved paperweight glass and bronze lantern, shade inscribed 'L. C. Tiffany/Favrile/114 G.', c1912, 13in (33cm) high.
$27,000–30,000 *S(NY)*

A Tiffany Favrile glass and bronze two-arm lamp, each shade inscribed 'L.C.T.' base, impressed 'Tiffany Studios/New York/316', c1900, 26¼in (66.5cm) high.
$7,000–7,800 *S(NY)*

l. A Tiffany Favrile glass and gilt-bronze Bridge lamp, chipped, shade inscribed 'L.C.T. Favrile', base impressed 'Tiffany Studios/New York/425', c1900, 55in (139.5cm) high.
$3,000–3,600 *S(NY)*

Art Deco Furniture

A bentwood rocking chair, designed by Antonio Volpe, the continuous oval legs widening to form the arms, supporting a wicker seat, with adjustable back, c1922, 45in (114.5cm) high.
$9,500–10,500 *C*

A pair of French bergères, the frames in stained mahogany with swollen reeded stiles heightened with silver gilt, upholstered in beige striped fabric, c1925.
$6,300–7,000 *S(NY)*

A pair of Oscar Bach hammered wrought iron and bronze chairs, of curule form, the sides set with geometric bronze panels, upholstered in leopard patterned hide, c1925.
$4,500–5,250 *S(NY)*

A curule chair is an upholstered folding seat with curved legs, used by the highest civil officials of ancient Rome.

A Thonet Model No. MR10 chair, by Ludwig Mies van der Rohe, with bent nickel-plated tubular steel frame and brown leather seat and back, 1927.
$1,200–1,350 *Bon*

An adzed oak armchair, by Robert Thompson of Kilburn, with straight crest, leather back and seat, panelled sides and square supports and stretchers, inscribed 'R.A. 1935'.
$1,000–1,200 *AH*

A satin birch settee, designed by Ray Hille, with curving padded button-down back above similar squab cushion, on plinth base, 68in (172.5cm) wide, and a pair of corresponding shelves, each with curved shaft supporting 2 tiers, on eliptical plinth base, each 15in (38cm) wide, 1929.
$3,300–3,750 *CSK*

A pair of Art Deco Dryad cane armchairs, each seat and back woven as a continuous form, between bent and combined cane arms and supports.
$530–600 *P*

r. An Art Deco chaise longue, the seat raised at one end, covered in a black and white zebra pattern fabric, the shallow back upholstered in black velvet, on a black painted wood frame, on casters, 82in (208.5cm) wide.
$720–820 *P*

A satin birch and part ebonised three-piece suite, upholstered in cream leather, sofa 69in (175.5cm) wide.
$4,800–5,500 *CSK*

A Barcelona chair and ottoman, by Ludwig Mies van der Rohe, the sprung steel X-frame with loose seat and back cushion in cream leather, with a matching ottoman, 1929.
$2,000–2,500 *Bon*

A Jules Leleu mahogany and gilt-bronze dining table, the inlaid top enclosing radiating marquetry, above U-form supports raised on tapering legs, with gilt-bronze mounts, leaves missing, c1930, 73½in (187cm) long.
$7,000–8,300 *S(NY)*

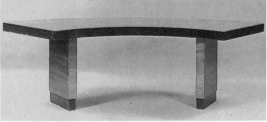

A pair of Art Deco walnut and black painted curved writing tables, each with a curved top edged in black and raised on solid, angled plank supports, 29in (74cm) high.
$2,000–2,500 *P*

An Art Deco coffee table, the octagonal top with geometric veneer, 21½in (55cm) diam.
$270–300 *DAF*

A mahogany writing table and chair, by Süe et Mare, the frieze with 3 drawers and carved with a fabric drape effect, on tapering legs, with key, the upholstered armchair with low back, the mahogany frame running into the armrests and terminating in a tight scroll, c1925, table 30in (76cm) long.
$36,750–42,750 *S*

An Art Deco bird's-eye maple and walnut serving table, with 3 drawers and open shelves beneath, with U-shaped sides and solid base, 34in (87cm) wide.
$1,000–1,200 *P*

A Continental Art Deco figured walnut occasional table, the circular top with geometric design, 31½in (80.5cm) diam.
$750–900 *DAF*

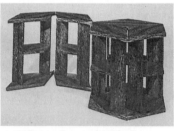

A folding palmwood table, by Eugene Printz, in 5 parts, each lozenge-shaped section with a lower open shelf, 23½in (60cm) high.
$21,750–24,000 *S*

An Art Deco three-tiered walnut veneered coffee table, repolished, 24in (61cm) diam.
$530–600 *DAF*

An Art Deco hardwood dining room suite, comprising an extending table with gilt-metal surround, and a set of 8 dining chairs, each with a leopard print padded seat, table 104in (264cm) long extended.
$1,350–1,500 *CSK*

A French Art Deco mahogany low table, by L. Marx, the top inset with an etched glass panel depicting Diana the Huntress amidst exotic flora and fauna, in shades of ivory and brown, signed, c1930, 36½in (92.5cm) diam.
$7,000–7,500 *S(NY)*

An Art Deco Epstein burr walnut dining room suite, comprising: a table with 2 leaves, on square uprights, a set of 4 matching dining chairs, each with shaped padded back and seat, on square tapering legs, and a matching sideboard, table 70in (178cm) long extended.
$4,000–4,800 *CSK*

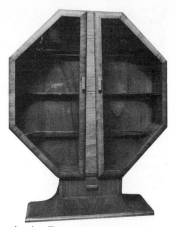

An oak dressing table, by Heals, with 2 short and one long drawer, ring handles, c1920, 36in (91.5cm) wide.
$830–980 *APO*

An Art Deco walnut veneered 'rocket' cabinet, the twin centrally hinged glazed doors enclosing 3 glass shelves, 41in (104cm) wide.
$670–800 *BWe*

An Art Deco octagonal display cabinet, with a single drawer in the pedestal, 40in (102cm) wide.
$750–900 *DAF*

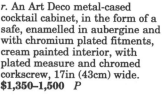

r. An Art Deco metal-cased cocktail cabinet, in the form of a safe, enamelled in aubergine and with chromium plated fitments, cream painted interior, with plated measure and chromed corkscrew, 17in (43cm) wide.
$1,350–1,500 *P*

l. A French Art Deco burr maple and thuya wardrobe, with 4 cupboard doors enclosing hanging space and a bank of drawers, on plinth base, 93in (236cm) wide.
$2,250–2,500 *CSK*

A headboard and footboard, by Marcel Breuer, of bent plywood, light brown grained maple, from Gane House, Bristol, 1935, 42in (107cm) wide.
$1,500–1,800 *Bon*

A French Art Deco mahogany, marble and gilt-bronze sideboard, the shaped pink marble top above a gilt-bronze foliate cast trim, 2 short drawers above 2 glazed doors mounted with elaborate gilt-bronze framing, flanked by 2 doors mounted with gilt-bronze panels of naked maidens opening to a shelved interior, on large ball feet, c1925, 92in (234cm) wide.
$4,500–5,250 *S(NY)*

Art Deco Carpets & Textiles

A Wilton wool carpet, 'Omega Vases' pattern, designed by Duncan Grant, in shades of lemon, light blue, beige, cream and pink, one end cut, 1932, 126 x 138½in (320 x 352cm).
$21,750–24,000 *S*

A French hooked rug, woven with large stylised flowerheads in vivid shades of pink, blue, dusty rose, orange and yellow reserved against a beige ground, within a brown border, c1930, 118 x 81in (300 x 206cm).
$3,750–4,500 *S(NY)*

An Art Deco hand woven carpet, with a radiating semi-circular pattern and dramatic linear zig-zag pattern, in red, brown and blue, against a two-toned beige field, 127½ x 107in (324 x 272cm).
$1,000–1,200 *P*

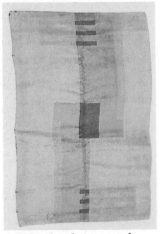

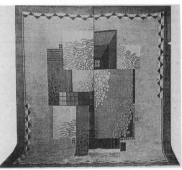

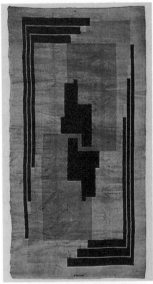

A Wilton hand woven wool carpet, 'Wessex' pattern, designed by Edward McKnight Kauffer, beige ground with geometric design in scarlet, dusty pink, shades of brown and lime green, monogrammed in the weave 'EMcKK', c1928, 84 x 55in (213.5 x 139cm).
$7,000–8,250 *S*

An Art Deco machine-made carpet, woven with overlapping geometric panels, bubbles, linear and curvilinear patterns, in blue, green and shades of brown against a beige field with triangular motif border, 127½ x 107in (324 x 272cm).
$1,000–1,200 *P*

A wool carpet, by da Silva Bruhns, woven with a geometric design in black against a salmon pink ground, signed and monogrammed, c1930, 252 x 132in (640 x 335cm).
$67,500–75,000 *S*

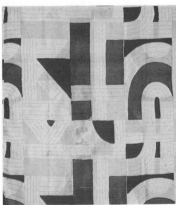

An Art Deco silk sample, by the Wiener Werkstätte, 16in (40.5cm) square.
$1,100–1,200 *JES*

A Wilton wool carpet, 'Omega' pattern, by Vanessa Bell, polychrome decoration incorporating stylised flowers and foliage, c1932, 144 x 98in (365.5 x 249cm).
$20,250–22,500 *S*

A printed damask panel, 'Number', by Ben Nicholson, woven with daisy-like flowers and printed with a blue horizontal strip, with a dark sea-green design of scattered numbers and letters, early 1940s, after a lino block first made in 1933, 17 x 20½in (43 x 52cm), framed and glazed.
$1,300–1,400 *CSK*

Art Deco Metalware

An Art Deco figural bronze and ivory clock, the circular face flanked by 2 metal columns, fronted by the reclining figure of a borzoi dog, signed 'Lemo', 26½in (67cm) long.
$780–930 *P*

An Art Deco enamelled cigarette case, decorated with 2 overlapping triangles, one blue, one simulating eggshell, against a coral-coloured ground, within a simulated eggshell border, indistinct maker's mark and '925', 3¼in (8.5cm) wide.
$300–360 *P*

A Wiener Werkstätte hammered brass vase, designed by Josef Hoffman, of waisted form, ribbed and fluted, stamped with designer's monogram, c1920, 6¾in (17cm) high.
$5,250–6,000 *C*

An Art Deco silver plated and bronze clock, with a figure of a Chinese pheasant on top, standing on a wooden base, 12½in (32cm) high.
$600–675 *DAF*

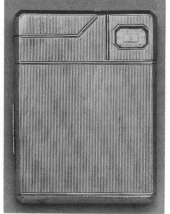

A gold combined cigarette case, lighter and timepiece, with fine linear engine-turned decoration, the timepiece case and door marked '9ct', and London hallmarks for 1930, 4in (10.5cm) high.
$2,300–2,500 *P*

An American silver Scandinavian style compote, by Gorham Manufacturing Company, designed by Eric Magnussen, the bowl fluted into 6 panels and raised on 3 heron supports, each standing on a ball above a carnelian disc screwed to a flat ring base, c1930, 6¼in (16cm) diam, 15oz.
$1,800–2,000 *S(NY)*

An Art Deco figural bronze and marble clock garniture, the marble body of pentagonal outline, having twin supports formed as semi-naked girls with green patination, 17in (43cm) high.
$1,500–1,800 *P*

r. Two Wiener Werkstätte hammered brass bowls, designed by Josef Hoffman, each above a knopped inverted trumpet form base, impressed marks, c1925, 13in (33cm) diam.
$37,500–45,000 *S(NY)*

A silver-coloured metal four-piece tea and coffee service, by Jean E. Puiforcat, each piece with a central double band of silver gilt, the wooden lids centred by gilt-metal roundels, with wooden handles, each piece stamped, c1930, coffee pot 5½in (14cm) high.
$9,000–10,500 *S*

A silver-coloured metal four-piece tea and coffee service, by Jean E. Puiforcat, with square section rosewood handles, the covers inset with rosewood, each with an inlaid geometric design, each piece stamped, c1930, teapot 4in (10cm) high.
$3,000–3,750 *S*

A five-piece 'Cosmos' tea and coffee service, by Georg Jensen, designed by Johan Rohde, the 4 vessels with hammered fluting at the base, coffee pot and cream jug with ribbed carved ebony handles terminating in scrolling tendrils with berries, the tray with beaded border and ebony handles in fluted mounts, all pieces stamped and with designer's monogram, Jensen marks for 1933–44.
$12,000–14,250 *C*

An Art Deco four-piece silver tea service, by Alexander Clark Co. Ltd, the panelled bodies with scroll spouts, teapot and hot water jug with ivory finials to the hinged covers and ivory scroll handles, milk jug and sugar basin with moulded scroll handles, on panel feet, Sheffield 1937, 53oz.
$2,000–2,500 *WW*

An Art Deco silver plated coffee or chocolate set, 1930s, tray 14in (35.5cm) wide.
$750–900 *BEV*

A set of 6 silver-coloured metal 'Cannes' oyster spoons, by Jean E. Puiforcat, each with maker's monogram, c1930, each 5in (13cm) long.
$1,200–1,400 *S*

An Acanthus pattern 94-piece flatware service, by Georg Jensen, marked, and with dates from pre- and post-war production.
$4,800–5,800 *C*

A Danish silver Blossom pattern five-piece coffee set, with matching tray, by Georg Jensen Silversmithy, Copenhagen, numbered '2/2B/2D/2E', marked on bases, after 1945, tray 22¾in (58cm) wide, 222oz.
$17,250–20,250 *S(NY)*

An Art Deco enamelled cigarette case, with engine-turned decoration, the front with a radiating design in lemon and black enamels, marked 'BBS Ltd', Birmingham 1931, 3¼in (8.5cm) wide.
$230–270 *P*

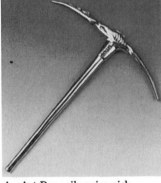

An Art Deco silver ice pick, the blades modelled as a streamlined racing greyhound, marked 'R P C Co', Sheffield 1942, 8¾in (22cm) high.
$750–900 *CSK*

A silver-coloured metal bowl, by Georg Jensen, with 4 pendant openwork handles modelled as bunches of grapes, the lobed base with an openwork frieze of fruiting vines with leaves, numbered '296 A', designed 1919, manufactured post-1945, 14½in (36.5cm) wide.
$7,500–9,000 *S*

A silver-coloured metal jug, by Kay Fisker for A. Michelsen, Copenhagen, of fluid baluster form, the line of the lip sweeping back to form the semi-circle of the handle, on a low flared base, designer's and maker's marks, numbered 'E9 C', c1935, 9½in (24cm) high.
$2,600–2,800 *S*

Art Deco Jewellery

A pair of Art Deco diamond earclips, of openwork scroll design with diamond collet detail, French assay and unknown maker's marks, c1930.
$3,450–4,000   C

An Art Deco diamond brooch, the pierced ribbon bow of stylised palmette design set with circular and cushion-cut diamonds, c1925, 3in (7.5cm) wide.
$3,750–4,500   C

A diamond and platinum fan-shaped double clip brooch, with pavé-set diamond draped folded scrolls and rays of tapering baguette diamonds, c1930, 2in (50mm) wide.
$4,800–5,500   DN

An Art Deco rock crystal and diamond brooch, by Mauboussin, of geometric design, the carved buckle with cushion and baguette-cut diamond terminals to the central diamond panel of openwork form, with baguette and cushion-cut diamond detail, signed, maker's marks, c1925, 2¼in (55mm) wide.
$8,700–10,000   C

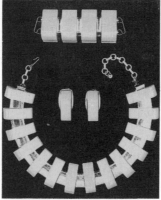

An Art Deco gilt-metal and plastic necklace, bracelet and earrings, c1930.
$230–350   JES

An Art Deco diamond brooch, the central brilliant-cut diamond collet on a pierced panel with crescent terminals, c1925, 2in (50mm) wide.
$5,000–5,500   C

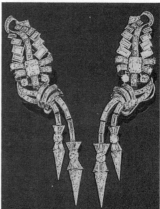

A pair of Art Deco diamond pendant earrings, each set with a diamond to a surround of stylised collet and scroll design with baguette-cut diamond detail, suspending 2 tassels with arrowhead terminals of baguette-cut scroll and collet detail, c1925.
$8,500–10,000   C

A pair of Art Deco diamond chandelier earrings, of geometric design, each suspending a baguette and circular-cut diamond collet flexible fringe to a graduated crescent and openwork palmette surmount, c1925.
$10,500–12,000   C

A pair of Art Deco jadeite, diamond and onyx earrings, each with diamond cupola mount suspended from a rose-cut diamond, onyx and black enamel surmount, c1925.
$3,750–4,500   C

A French Art Deco minaudière, the case with polychrome enamel and engraved decoration depicting naturalistic forms, the interior with lipstick, twin compartments and mirror, the outer case with calibré sapphire and cabochon sapphire thumb pieces to an enamelled bar hoop and chain suspension.
$6,000–6,750   CSK

An Art Deco ruby and diamond fob watch, the pavé-set diamond cylindrical pendant watch with carved ruby and onyx applied foliate detail, the concealed watch on a sliding mechanism, with pearl crown, the flexible panel suspended from an openwork diamond panel top with carved ruby detail, c1925, 4in (10cm) high.
$38,250–42,000   C

An Art Deco diamond bracelet, the central openwork diamond panel with vari-cut diamond vase of flowers with navette and baguette-cut diamond detail, the two-row bracelet of openwork diamond links with baguette-cut diamond detail, c1925, 6¼in (16cm) long.
$8,800–9,800   C

An Art Deco black opal and diamond bracelet, set with 5 opals joined by oval links accented by round diamonds, set in platinum, some abrasions.
$2,000–2,500 *SK*

A pair of Art Deco diamond clip brooches, each in the form of an openwork scroll with baguette and brilliant-cut diamond collet detail to a graduated pavé-set fan-shaped demi-surround, with French control marks, c1930, each 2in (50mm) wide.
$7,000–7,500 *C*

An Art Deco ruby and diamond bracelet, the ruby 3 stone centre with a baguette-cut diamond surround with ruby border to pavé-set diamond crescent shoulders, the bracelet with baguette and diamond collet geometric detail to ruby collet clusters, c1930, 6¼in (16cm) long.
$10,500–12,000 *C*

r. A pair of Art Deco dress clips, each set with a cabochon ruby within a geometric-shaped diamond mount, ruby 9.6mm wide.
$17,250–19,500 *SK*

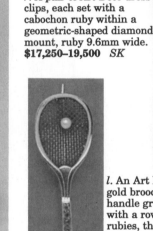

l. An Art Deco gold brooch, the handle grip set with a row of 10 rubies, the mesh strings set with a pearl tennis ball, stamped on reverse '15ct', 2in (50mm) long.
$1,000–1,100 *P*

A tortoiseshell and gold piqué brooch and earrings, c1930, brooch 2in (50mm) wide.
$670–830 *JES*

A chrome and Bakelite pendant necklace, c1930, 24in (61cm) long.
$60–75 *GOO*

An Art Deco Movado enamelled pocket watch, edged with blue, green and red champlevé enamelled borders, the top surmounted by a Mexican head incorporating the winder, with a hinged loop attached, the white dial with black Arabic numerals, mechanism marked '15 Jewels, 4 Adjust', the case stamped with Swiss *poinçon* and '18K', numbered '0634442', 1¾in (45mm) wide.
$1,350–1,500 *P*

A pair of Art Deco diamond cuff links, of graduated baton design, each larger link with a central line of baguette-cut diamonds to stepped terminals, c1925.
$6,750–7,500 *C*

A silver gilt, pearl and sapphire brooch and pair of ear clips, by Sibyl Dunlop, c1935.
$3,000–3,750 *JES*

A chrome and Bakelite chain link necklace, c1930, 10in (25.5cm) long.
$60–75 *GOO*

A sapphire and diamond bracelet, with 7 square cut sapphire links bordered by brilliant-cut diamonds alternating with diamond square buckle links, set in platinum, c1930, 7in (18cm) long.
$6,000–6,750 *DN*

Art Deco Glass

An Art Deco cameo rainbow glass biscuit barrel, decorated with enamelled pink waterlilies and green leaves, acid etched ground, floral pewter lid with Cupid, 6in (15cm) high.
$600–720 *JL*

A German glass and metal overlay decanter set, of faceted octagonal form, decorated with foliate overlay against a lime-green ground, comprising a decanter and stopper, 8in (20cm) high, and 6 matching liqueur goblets.
$975–1,125 *P*

A clear glass and black enamel decanter and 8 glasses, the decanter with a silver rim, 1920s, glasses 4in (10cm) high.
$270–300 *GOO*

A pair of Jobling frosted glass panels, designed by Alan Howes, each modelled in relief with an Art Deco cherub playing a musical instrument, with metal mounts, impressed 'AH' monogram, chips to edge, 9in (23cm) high.
$680–750 *CSK*

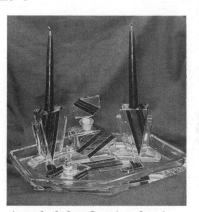

An etched glass five-piece dressing table set, of bold geometric form, c1930, tray 12in (30.5cm) wide.
$300–380 *WTA*

A cameo glass vase, the grey glass internally mottled and streaked with orange, red and yellow, overlaid with maroon and cut with stylised flowers and leafage, signed in cameo 'Charder', signed in intaglio 'Le Verre Français', c1925, 28in (71cm) high.
$3,750–4,500 *S(NY)*

A glass jug, by Le Verre Français, decorated with orange butterflies on a pale ground graduating to turquoise, with a black handle, c1925, 12¼in (32cm) high.
$1,200–1,500 *SUC*

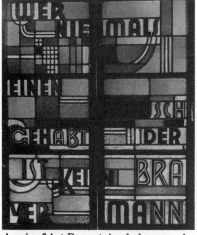

A pair of Art Deco stained glass panels, possibly by Hoffman, the mauve, red and blue patterned panels worded in black with verse, in a pair of triple panelled wood frames, each 46½ x 19½in (118 x 49.5cm).
$1,800–2,000 *CAG*

These panels were removed from a café bar in Munich during the early 1950s, and the closest translation of the verse is 'A man who has not had a hangover is not a real man'.

A Continental Art Deco blue and clear cut glass decanter set, tray 28in (71cm) diam.
$300–380 *DAF*

A dark amber and frosted glass Serpent vase, intaglio moulded mark 'R. Lalique', after 1924, 10in (25.5cm) high.
$9,000–10,500 *Bon*

A smoked glass vase, 'Bacchantes', by René Lalique, the exterior moulded in relief with a continuous frieze of bacchanalian figures, wheelcut mark, c1927, 9¾in (24.5cm) high.
$17,250–19,500 *CSK*

A Graystan blue vase, signed, c1920, 7¼in (18.5cm) high.
$1,200–1,400 *MJW*

An opalescent glass vase, 'Farandole', by René Lalique, moulded in low and medium relief with a band of cherubs and leafage around the base, acid stamped, c1930, 7in (18cm) high.
$11,500–13,500 *S(NY)*

An Orrefors glass vase, designed by Simon Gate, of ribbed tapering cylindrical form, on a short splayed foot, cut and etched with a mermaid in bubbled water, engraved factory mark 'Orrefors Gate 1133.14.R', c1930, 8¼in (21cm) high.
$750–830 *CSK*

A clear and opalescent glass vase, 'Prunes', by René Lalique, moulded with plums and leaves, heightened with blue staining, small repair, stencilled mark on underside, after 1930, 7in (18cm) high.
$4,500–5,250 *S*

Lalique Glass

It is always wise to examine pieces of Lalique glass carefully. It is not unusual to find that pieces have been ground down where damage has occurred. Naturally, this constitutes a flaw and will affect the value.

r. A moulded glass vase, 'Bacchantes', by René Lalique, the rich golden opalescent glass moulded in high relief with a frieze of nude maidens, inscribed, minor chips to base, c1927, 9½in (24cm) high.
$15,750–18,000 *S(NY)*

A frosted glass vase, 'Palestre', by René Lalique, with satin finish moulded with a frieze of male nudes, c1930, 15¾in (40cm) high.
$24,000–27,750 *S*

An Orrefors glass vase, 'The Javanese Dancer', engraved by Simon Gate, engraved on base 'Orrefors S. Gate 1387 EA', c1930, 10¼in (26cm) high.
$1,900–2,000 *SK*

A vase of tapering stepped form, 'Chevreuse', No. 1081, by René Lalique, consisting of 5 graduated concentric rings, 6in (15cm) high.
$750–900 *AAV*

Art Deco Ceramics

A Beswick wall plaque, 1930s,
6in (15cm) high.
$380–450 *DAF*

A pair of Art Deco Carlton Ware vases,
painted with abstract floral blooms and
berry clusters in red, yellow, green,
mauve and black against a blue ground,
marked, 8in (20cm) high.
$300–360 *P*

A ceramic vase, by Boch
Frères, Kéramis
potteries, Belgium,
decorated with orange
on a black and grey
ground, c1920, 10½in
(26.5cm) high.
$150–180 *GOO*

A Gouda pottery charger,
decorated by H. Breedvelt, c1925,
16¾in (42.5cm) diam.
$600–750 *OO*

An Aynsley ware
lustre vase, c1932,
7in (18cm) high.
$90–100 *WTA*

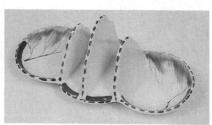

An Art Deco Burleigh ware toast rack,
7in (18cm) high.
$18–24 *OD*

A Shelley composite tea set, comprising
Yellow Sunray Vogue teapot, Yellow
Block Mode cups, saucers and side
plates, minor damage, painted mark
'11791', c1930, teapot, 4½in (11cm) high.
$1,000–1,200 *CSK*

An Art Deco Crown Devon coffee service,
decorated in gilt with zigzag bands on a powder
blue ground, printed marks in black and
pattern No. '2614', c1930.
$870–970 *DN*

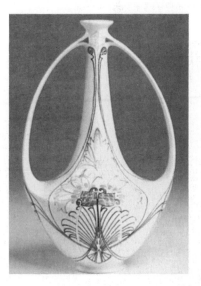

A set of 6 Art Deco plates, each painted with a geometric design in dark blue against a light blue ground, signed 'Susie Cooper 545', 9in (23cm) diam.
$1,000–1,200 *P*

A New Hall lustre dish, by Lucien Boullemier, 1935, 12½in (32cm) wide.
$70–90 *CSA*

A Maling ware embossed Peony pattern chocolate cup, c1935, 4½in (11.5cm) high.
$60–80 *CSA*

A Poole Pottery (Carter Stabler & Adams Ltd) white earthenware book end, designed by John Adams, the glaze sprayed in light and dark brown colours, shape No. 831, impressed marks, c1935, 8in (20.5cm) high.
$380–450 *PP*

A Poole Pottery (Carter Stabler & Adams Ltd) red earthenware vase, designed by Truda Carter, painted in greens, blue and grey by Ann Hatchard, incised shape No. 337, pattern PU, c1931, 9¾in (25cm) high.
$750–830 *PP*

A Maling ware green Primrose Border wall plate, c1936, 11½in (29cm) diam.
$150–180 *CSA*

r. A Poole Pottery (Carter Stabler & Adams Ltd) red earthenware vase, designed by Truda Adams, painted in blue, green, yellow, orange, purple, crimson and blue by Winifred Collett, incised shape No. 979, pattern HE, c1930, 8½in (22cm) high.
$380–450 *PP*

A Poole Pottery (Carter Stabler & Adams Ltd) vase, c1930, 9in (23cm) high.
$120–150 *GOO*

A Maling ware blue Rosine pattern vase, c1940, 8in (20cm) high.
$100–120 *CSA*

A ceramic wall mask, by Goldscheider, with Myott, c1939, 5in (13cm) high.
$300–340 *WTA*

r. A selection of Noritake china, from a design by Frank Lloyd Wright, decorated with circular and geometric forms in orange, yellow, green and grey, in production 1922–68, pre-date machine coding.
$600–720 *P*

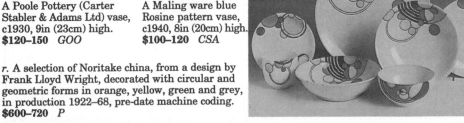

Charlotte Rhead

A Burleigh Ware Beverley bowl, designed by Charlotte Rhead, decorated with Vine pattern, No. 4113/A, c1928, 11in (28cm) diam.
$380–450 PC

A Crown Ducal bevelled-edge bowl, designed by Charlotte Rhead, pattern No. 5623, c1938, 10in (25.5cm) diam.
$210–250 PC

A Shorter Bramble jug, c1940, 7in (18cm) high.
$40–50 CSA

A charger, designed by Charlotte Rhead, design No. TL 40, c1940, 12in (30.5cm) diam.
$200–240 YY

A Burleigh Ware Avon bowl, designed by Charlotte Rhead, decorated with Garland pattern, No. 4101/A, c1928, 10in (25.5cm) diam.
$300–380 PC

A Royal Winton lustre jug, decorated with flowers on an orange ground, c1935, 12in (30.5cm) high.
$260–300 WTA

A Shorter Anemone pattern dish and preserve jar, c1935, dish 5in (12.5cm) wide.
$25–30 CSA

A Shelley tea set, marked 'Shelley, Lawley's, Regent Street', c1930, saucer 4in (10cm) diam.
$300–330 PSA

A Shorter dish, c1940, 13½in (34.5cm) wide.
$25–30 CSA

Clarice Cliff

A Clarice Cliff conical jug, decorated with House and Bridge pattern, c1931, 7in (18cm) high.
$1,300–1,600 *RIC*

A Clarice Cliff wall mask, Monique, the floral headband picked out in colours on a matt ground, printed mark in blue, late 1930s, 7in (18cm) high.
$600–680 *DN*

A Clarice Cliff Eton jug, decorated with Swirls pattern, c1930, 5in (12.5cm) high.
$750–900 *BKK*

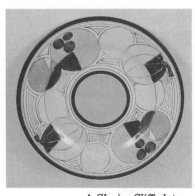

A Clarice Cliff plate, decorated with Melon pattern, c1930, 10in (25.5cm) diam.
$1,000–1,200 *BKK*

A Clarice Cliff Bizarre faceted baluster-shaped vase, decorated with Latona pattern, printed and painted marks in black, c1931, 8in (20.5cm) high.
$825–975 *DN*

A Clarice Cliff 'tea for two', decorated with Gibraltar pattern, plate 6in (15cm) diam.
$4,500–5,250 *BKK*

A Clarice Cliff Bonjour tea set, designed by Eva Crofts, decorated with Bizarre pattern in bright colours on a yellow ground, printed mark, c1933.
$3,200–4,000 *RBB*

Doulton

A Doulton Burslem brown stoneware Disraeli in Memoriam vase, the body moulded with a white head in profile on a green oval surrounded by white primroses above a green ribbon impressed '1804, His Favourite Flower 1881', impressed mark, 4in (10cm) high.
$100–110 SAS

MILLER'S COMPARES . . .

I A Royal Doulton character jug, Pearly Boy, blue version, designed by H. Fenton, printed mark in green, 1947–50, 6½in (16.5cm) high.
$2,250–2,700 DN

II A Royal Doulton character jug, Pearly Boy, brown version, designed by H. Fenton, printed mark in green, 1947–50, 6¼in (16cm) high.
$900–1,000 DN

Collectors are often very keen to acquire examples of pieces in all the variations in which they appeared. *Item I* realised considerably more than *Item II* when they were sold at auction simply because the coat collar and cap peak were painted blue, and the buttons had a white pearly glaze. The coat, peak and buttons of *Item II* were all painted brown which is far more common and therefore explains the lower price. DN

A pair of Royal Doulton candlesticks, decorated with Night Watchman scenes, 1905, 13in (33cm) high.
$300–380 TP

r. A Royal Doulton earthenware cheese dish and cover, printed with flowers and foliage within green borders with gilt highlights, printed mark, c1905, 10in (25.5cm) wide.
$110–130 Hal

l. A Royal Doulton character jug, designed M. Henk, printed mark in brown, 1930s, 7in (18cm) high.
$720–820 DN

A pair of Doulton Lambeth stoneware vases, by Hannah B. Barlow and Florence E. Barlow, incised with a scene of ponies and trees, incised monogram, numbered '406' and '481', c1890, 27in (68.5cm) high.
$2,400–2,700 Bon

A Royal Doulton Bunnykins teapot and cover, the ovoid body in the shape of a rabbit, the cover as its head, coloured in tones of brown, green and black, printed marks, c1940, 7¾in (20cm) wide.
$1,350–1,500 N

A Royal Doulton Lambeth vase, with applied decoration, initialled 'BH', No. 2/58, 1910, 3in (7.5cm) high.
$150–180 TP

A Royal Doulton bowl, by Florrie Jones, 1905, 7in (18cm) diam.
$270–300 PSA

Figures
Ceramic, Terracotta & Spelter

A Royal Dux classical figure with a vase, c1890, 27in (68.5cm) high.
$1,500–1,800 *VSt*

An Art Deco spelter figure lamp, 19¾in (50cm) high.
$600–680 *DAF*

A Goldscheider pottery figure of a female dancer, hand-decorated with a floral grey dress on a domed black base, 1930s, 18in (45.5cm) high.
$1,000–1,200 *AH*

An Art Deco spelter figure of a dancer, by Carlier, c1930, 16in (41cm) high.
$680–750 *DAF*

A Goldscheider porcelain figure, c1920, 15in (38cm) high.
$1,150–1,350 *ASA*

A Crown Devon figure of a lady in a yellow dress, c1935, 7in (18cm) high.
$600–680 *WTA*

A French Art Deco spelter figure of a ballet dancer, 18½in (47cm) high.
$520–600 *DAF*

A terracotta polychrome bust of a girl, by René Buthaud, c1930, 10¾in (27.5cm) high.
$3,750–4,500 *SUC*

A Royal Dux figural centrepiece, c1900, 15in (38cm) high.
$1,200–1,500 *ASA*

A Goldscheider terracotta group of 3 boys, seated on a brick wall, c1890, 22½in (57cm) high.
$3,200–4,000 *N*

Bronze & Ivory

A Symbolist table lamp, in gilt and silvered bronze, by Georg Flamond, c1895, 6in (15cm) high.
$4,200–4,800 *SUC*

An Art Deco bronze group, by M. Debut, entitled 'Girl with Deer', incised with artist's name, 16¼in (41.5cm) wide.
$750–830 *P*

An Art Nouveau bronze figural bell push, cast as a girl reclining with a pen in her hand, on a shaped oval base, 5in (12.5cm) wide.
$600–680 *P*

A parcel gilt-bronze figure of a dancer, by Affortunato Gori, c1930, 24½in (62cm) high.
$2,700–3,000 *S(NY)*

A bronze figure of a dancer, by Demêtre Chiparus, on a marble base, c1930, 11⅝in (30cm) high.
$2,700–3,000 *WTA*

A carved ivory, silvered and patinated bronze group, of a cowboy roping, by Marcel-André Bouraine, c1930, 44in (112cm) long.
$4,500–5,250 *S(NY)*

A patinated bronze figure of a kneeling nude girl, by J. D. Cormier (Joë Descomps), inscribed and impressed marks, c1930, 17in (43cm) high.
$4,500–5,250 *S(NY)*

A parcel gilt bronze group, entitled 'Country Dance', by Claire Jeane Roberte Colinet, inscribed, surrounding jardinière missing, c1930, 20½in (52cm) high.
$6,000–6,750 *S(NY)*

A bronze figure, by Maurice Guiraud-Rivière, entitled 'La Comète', impressed, c1930, 20¼in (51.5cm) high.
$20,250–23,250 *S(NY)*

A patinated bronze figure of a naked dancing girl, cast from a model by F. Preiss, in a silver grey patination, on a stepped black and green marble base, signed, c1930, 15in (38cm) high.
$4,200–5,000 *P*

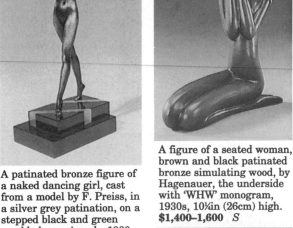

A figure of a seated woman, brown and black patinated bronze simulating wood, by Hagenauer, the underside with 'WHW' monogram, 1930s, 10¼in (26cm) high.
$1,400–1,600 *S*

A brown patinated bronze figural vase, by Antonin Larroux, inscribed and impressed 'CA 2', c1900, 11½in (29cm) high.
$4,500–5,250 *S(NY)*

r. A cold painted bronze and ivory figure, entitled 'Girl with Parrot', by Paul Philippe, marked, 1920s, 20in (50.5cm) high.
$12,750–14,250 *S*

An Art Deco patinated bronze bust of a young girl, entitled 'Saida', by E. Villanis, inscribed, incised signature, 18¾in (47.5cm) high.
$1,200–1,400 *Bon*

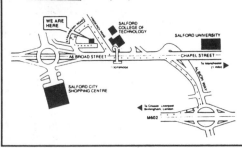

A bronze and ivory figure, Tambourine Dancer, by Philippe, 14in (35.5cm) high.
$9,000–10,500 *ASA*

An Art Deco patinated bronze figure, entitled 'Golden Apples', by Jean Verschneider, inscribed, 22½in (57cm) high.
$2,000–2,250 *S(NY)*

19TH & 20TH CENTURY SCULPTURE & BRITISH STUDIO CERAMICS AT PHILLIPS

An Ernst Wahliss figural vase, 62cm.
A Royal Dux model of a bathing beauty, 47.5cm
An amusing Rosenthal porcelain group by
Ferdinand. Leibermann, 46cm.

A group of Martinware, including a "Barrister"
double jug, 17cm, a pair of highly unusual
Martinware sculptures of reptilian creatures, 24cm
high, 27cm long, a globular vase, decorated with
comical fish and marine life, 18cm, an amusing
stoneware model of a baby owl with mouth agape,
27.5cm high and a rare and unusual grotesque bird,
modelled as a likeness of Benjamin Disraeli.

At Phillips we hold eight specialised auctions of Applied Arts a year, which not only include items of sculpture and British art pottery as illustrated here, but also the full range of disciplines, from glass, ceramics, silver, metalwares and jewellery to furniture, books, graphics, textiles and carpets.

Items for inclusion in these sales are accepted thoughout the year. For a free valuation either call into our London salerooms or send an adequate photograph with a brief description. Home visits can also be arranged by appointment.

For further information on buying or selling at auction please contact Keith Baker on (0171) 468 8381 or (0171) 629 6602.

http://www.phillips-auctions.com

LONDON

Phillips
INTERNATIONAL
AUCTIONEERS & VALUERS

101 New Bond Street, London W1Y 0AS

A centre table, by Eugène Gaillard, the frieze carved with stylised plants, c1900, 46in (117cm) wide.
$11,000–12,500 *S*

A 'Lyre' pattern MT 286 walnut stool, designed by Pierre Chareau, stained to simulate rosewood, c1923, 23⅝in (60cm) high.
$17,250–19,500 *C*

An Art Nouveau inlaid mahogany display cabinet, 53in (134.5cm) wide.
$3,500–4,000 *JNic*

A fruitwood inlaid vitrine, with corn and butterflies, the legs with bronze sabots cast as leaves, marked 'Gallé', c1900, 26½in (67.5cm) wide.
$33,000–39,000 *S*

A fruitwood two-tiered table, by Eugène Gaillard, the top with gilt bronze handles, on shaped incurved legs, c1900, 27in (69cm) wide.
$4,500–5,250 *S*

A pair of upholstered mahogany hall chairs, c1920.
$600–675 *APO*

An Art Nouveau oak purdonium, 15in (38cm) wide.
$525–600 *APO*

An Art Nouveau mahogany high-backed chair, by J. S. Henry, c1898, 49in (124cm) high.
$1,500–1,800 *SUC*

An Art Nouveau walnut fireplace surround, inlaid with satinwood, inset with needlework panel of roses, 68in (173cm) wide.
$1,800–2,000 *MAT*

An oak and ebonised sideboard, labelled 'Lamb Manchester', c1870, 90in (228.5cm) wide.
$6,500–7,500 *S*

A sideboard, by Ambrose Heal, designed by Christine Angus, of fumigated oak with ebony and pewter inlay depicting orange blossom dend fruit, c1901, 72in (183cm) wide.
$11,250–12,750 *ZAR*

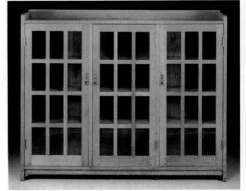

An oak bookcase, by L. & J. G. Stickley, the 3 doors eacg with 12 panes, opening to shelves, the side panels shaped to form front and rear feet, c1910, 69½in (176.5cm) wide.
$8,000–9,000 *S(NY)*

An Arts and Crafts oak smoker's cabinet, with painted decoration, 13¾in (35cm) wide.
$120–150 *APO*

An Arts and Crafts oak table, 18in (45.5cm) diam.
$150–185 *APO*

An Arts and Crafts oak table stand, with a tiled top, c1895, 36in (91.5cm) high.
$90–120 *GOO*

An Arts and Crafts carved oak umbrella stand, 26in (66cm) wide.
$450–500 *APO*

A Victorian inlaid oak leather-topped occasional table, 25in (63.5cm) square.
$1,400–1,800 *MSW*

An Arts and Crafts oak umbrella stand, 36½in (93cm) wide.
$525–600 *APO*

A rosewood cabinet, by Collinson & Lock, designed by T. E. Collcutt, c1870, 62in (157cm) wide.
$4,500–5,250 *C*

An inlaid cabinet, by Carlo Bugatti and Ricardo Pellegrini, with copper roundels and dentil friezes, vellum Oriental scenes, c1896, 33in (84cm) wide.
$12,000–13,500 *S*

A side table and pair of chairs, by Carlo Bugatti, decorated with ebonised wood and grey and yellow metal inlaid with geometric designs, c1900, table 43in (109cm) wide.
$50,000–55,000 *S*

A pair of Scottish Art Nouveau mahogany chairs, c1900, 43½in (110cm) high.
$300–375 *SUC*

An oak chair, with semi-circular back, made for Liberty & Co, c1895.
$300–450 *GOO*

A bedroom set, by Jacques Adnet, comprising wardrobe and cabinet incorporating a bed, c1935.
$22,500–25,500 *S*

A French Art Deco *ébène de Macassar* desk, one end with a brass-mounted columnar support, with inset leather writing surface, c1930, 70in (178cm) wide.
$11,500–13,000 *S(NY)*

An Art Deco walnut coffee table, with bent plywood legs supporting a shelf, 21in (53.5cm) wide.
$270–300 *DAF*

An Art Deco oak desk, with inlaid decoration, 29in (73.5cm) wide.
$375–425 *APO*

A *table éventail*, designed by Pierre Chareau, the 4 fan-shaped leaves rotating from a central joint, c1924, 32in (81.5cm) high.
$67,500–75,000 *C*

An Art Deco dining table, with central revolving section, on an ebonised pedestal base, 59in (150cm) diam.
$1,500–2,250 *AAV*

A sofa and 2 armchairs, by Pierre Chareau, with arched backs and scrolled arms, on bun feet, reupholstered, c1925, sofa 41in (104cm) wide.
$50,000–60,000 *S*

A brass and black marble side cabinet, probably French, with 2 doors flanking a square panel cast with the god Mercury, c1930, 100in (254cm) wide.
$17,250–19,250 *S(NY)*

A pair of X-frame stools, by Jacques-Emile Ruhlmann, the feet with silvered bronze sabots, c1928, 28½in (72.5cm) wide.
$55,000–65,000 *S*

An *ébène de Macassar* sideboard, by Jacques-Emile Ruhlmann, the top set with silvered bronze stringing, on tapering fluted front legs, marked and labelled, c1925, 71in (180.5cm) wide.
$100,000–120,000 *S(NY)*

An Art Nouveau Royal Dux maiden and cherub, modelled by Hampel, c1900, 13in (33cm) wide.
$1,250–1,275 *VSt*

A Gouda pottery jug, designed by Rembrandt, c1920, 9¼in (23.5cm) high.
$225–300 *OO*

An iridescent ceramic jug, by Zsolnay, the handle modelled as a naked girl, c1900, 12½in (32cm) high.
$1,350–1,500 *SUC*

A coffee pot, in the form of a bird, by Haviland, Limoges, France, designed by Edouard Sandoz, c1915, 12in (30.5cm) high.
$750–900 *SUC*

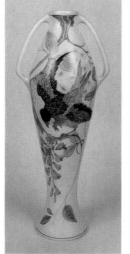

A Gouda Pottery Zuid factory vase, decorated with a bird and flowers, c1910, 17in (43cm) high.
$900–1,000 *OO*

An eggshell porcelain vase, by Rozenburg, designed by Sam Schellink, c1902, 16¼in (41.5cm) high.
$4,500–5,250 *OO*

A Gouda Pottery vase, made for Liberty & Co, c1903, 11½in (29cm) high.
$450–525 *OO*

A Carter & Co semi-stoneware tin glazed pot pourri, impressed 'Poole', c1915, 10¼in (26cm) high.
$600–675 *PP*

An enamelled pottery vase, by Villeroy & Boch, c1925, 13in (33cm) high.
$450–525 *SUC*

A Bretby majolica vase, with moulded Chinese dragon design, c1910, 12½in (32cm) high.
$75–90 *CSA*

A pair of Royal Doulton vases, decorated with butterflies, c1925, 6¾in (17cm) high.
$225–265 *PSA*

A Moorcroft MacIntyre jardinière, rim restored, c1900, 7in (18cm) high.
$550–675 *IW*

A Moorcroft MacIntyre vase, Rose Garland pattern, c1907, 8in (20cm) high.
$1,200–1,500 *HEA*

A Moorcroft Flamminian Ware vase, for Liberty & Co, c1910, 5in (12.5cm) high.
$225–275 *YY*

A Moorcroft Pomegranate pattern vase, c1910, 6½in (16.5cm) high.
$525–600 *WN*

A Moorcroft Leaf and Berry Flambé vase, c1930, 9½in (24cm) high.
$1,000–1,200 *HEA*

A Moorcroft vase, Pomegranate pattern, c1910, 16¼in (41.5cm) high.
$375–450 *GOO*

A Moorcroft Flamminian Ware vase, 1906–30, 8½in (21.5cm) high.
$525–600 *YY*

A Moorcroft vase, Orchid pattern, c1940, 6in (15cm) high.
$185–225 *WN*

A Moorcroft bowl and cover, c1914, 8in (20.5cm) high.
$1,125–1,350 *HEA*

A Moorcroft vase, Clematis pattern, c1950, 5in (12.5cm) high.
$180–210 *YY*

A William Moorcroft Wisteria pattern vase, c1920, 7in (18cm) high.
$400–500 *HEA*

A William Moorcroft Pomegranate pattern bowl, c1916, 8in (20.5cm) diam.
$300–360 *HEA*

A Moorcroft Leaf and Berry pattern jug, c1928, 5in (12.5cm) high.
$600–675 *HEA*

A Moorcroft Fruit and Leaves pattern vase, c1930, 6½in (16.5cm) high.
$400–450 *WN*

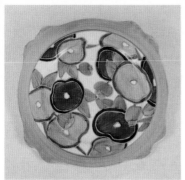

A Clarice Cliff Chintz
pattern plate, 1930s,
10½in (26.5cm) diam.
$525–600 *RIC*

A Clarice Cliff Inspiration Lily
design, c1929, 10in (25.5cm) diam.
$1,275–1,500 *BKK*

A Clarice Cliff Coral Firs
pattern charger, c1930,
13in (33cm) diam.
$750–900 *YY*

A Clarice Cliff Circle Tree pattern
jug, 1930s, 4in (10cm) high.
$675–700 *RIC*

A Clarice Cliff Orange
House pattern lamp
base, c1930,
14in (35.5cm) high.
$1,200–1,350 *RIC*

A Clarice Cliff Coronet jug,
c1930, 3½in 9cm) high.
$675–750 *PC*

A Clarice Cliff Castelated Circle pattern
Conical shape coffee service, cups and
saucers from Tankard shape range,
c1929, coffee pot 7¼in (18.5cm) high.
$2,550–3,000 *BKK*

Three Clarice Cliff Bizarre jugs, Coral
Firs pattern, Crown shape, 1930s, largest
4¼in (11cm) high.
$850–1,000 *TMA*

A Clarice Cliff Gay Day
pattern candlestick, 1930s,
3½in (9cm) square.
$375–450 *RIC*

A Clarice Cliff
Sunrise pattern
candlestick, 1930s,
7in (18cm) high.
$1,000–1,200 *RIC*

A wall plate, painted by Clarice Cliff
to a design by Frank Brangwyn,
c1925, 17in (43cm) diam.
$5,000–6,000 *Bon*

A Clarice Cliff Applique
biscuit barrel and cover,
Red Tree pattern, c1930,
6½in (16.5cm) high.
$3,000–3,500 *BKK*

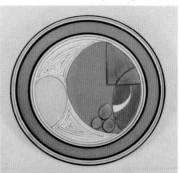

A Clarice Cliff wall plate,
Orange Melon pattern,
c1929, 10in (25.5cm) diam.
$1,350–1,500 *BKK*

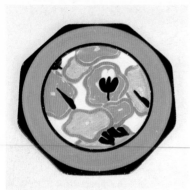

A Clarice Cliff Orange Chintz pattern plate, 1930s, 8in (20.5cm) diam.
$525–600 *RIC*

A Clarice Cliff Applique Lugano vase, c1930, 8in (20.5cm) high.
$8,250–9,000 *BKK*

A Clarice Cliff Clouvre pattern vase, Inspiration range, c1930, 6in (15cm) high.
$5,250–6,000 *BKK*

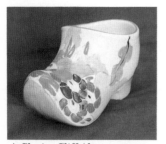

A Clarice Cliff Alton pattern sabot, printed factory marks, c1933, 5¾in (14.5cm) long.
$375–420 *WTA*

A Clarice Cliff Athens jug, brown Café-au-Lait pattern, 1930s, 8in (20.5cm) high.
$600–675 *RIC*

A Clarice Cliff Bizarre plate, Orange Roof Cottage design, c1932, 9in (223cm) diam.
$750–825 *WTA*

A Clarice Cliff Conical sugar sifter, Poplar pattern, 1930s, 5½in (14cm) high.
$1,125–1,275 *RIC*

A Clarice Cliff Conical jug, Delecia pattern, c1930, 9½in (24cm) high.
$375–450 *BKK*

A Clarice Cliff Red Autumn pattern tea-for-two, c1931, teapot 5in (12.5cm) high.
$5,250–6,000 *BKK*

A Clarice Cliff Applique plate, Caravan pattern, c1934, 9in (23cm) diam.
$4,500–5,250 *BKK*

A Clarice Cliff Orange Chintz sugar sifter, c1932, 6in (15cm) high.
$450–525 *WTA*

A Clarice Cliff Lotus jug, Applique Lucerne pattern, c1932, 11¾in (30cm) high.
$10,500–12,000 *BKK*

A Clarice Cliff vase, shape No. 370, Marigold pattern, c1931, 6in (15cm) high. **$4,000–5,000** *BKK*

A Clarice Cliff Tankard shape coffee pot, Geometric pattern, 7¾in (19.5cm) high. **$600–750** *RIC*

A Clarice Cliff wall plaque, 1930s, 13in (33cm) wide. **$1,200–1,500** *SUC*

A Clarice Cliff Conical sugar sifter, Orange Roof Cottage pattern, printed factory marks, c1932, 5½in (14cm) high. **$1,500–1,800** *WTA*

A Clarice Cliff Athens shape jug, Blue W pattern, c1929, 6¼in (16cm) high. **$600–750** *BKK*

A Clarice Cliff vase, shape No. 14, Coral Firs pattern, 1930s, 18in (45.5cm) high. **$4,500–5,250** *RIC*

A Clarice Cliff Stamford tea set for one, Swirls pattern, c1930, pot 6in (15cm) high. **$3,250–3,750** *BKK*

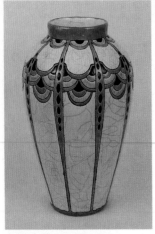

A Boch Frères Keramis vase, decorated in orange and black on an ivory ground, c1920, 14in (35.5cm) high.
$150–180 *GOO*

A Boch Frères Keramis vase, decorated in orange and black on a grey ground, c1920, 9in (23cm) high.
$150–180 *GOO*

A Winchcombe pottery bowl, with finger-combed decoration, probably by Michael Cardew, 6¼in (16cm) diam.
$90–110 *IW*

A female head, designed by Lotte Calm for the Wiener Werkstatte, with black hair, and blue, yellow and green decoration, c1930, 9in (23cm) high.
$3,750–4,500 *SUC*

A Myott jug, c1930, 9¾in (25cm) high.
$60–70 *CSA*

A Carter, Stabler & Adams Ltd dish, No. 528, The Ship Plate, made and painted at Poole Pottery, 1939, 15in (38cm) diam.
$900–1,000 *PP*

A Winchcombe pottery vase, by Raymond Finch, with yellow/green ground, c1939, 9½in (24cm) high.
$300–330 *IW*

A Crown Devon charger, c1930, 18in (46cm) diam.
$600–675 *WTA*

A Boch Frères Keramis vase, decorated in blue and yellow, c1920, 13⅝in (34.5cm) high.
$150–180 *GOO*

A pair of ceramic book-ends, formed as Pierrot and Pierrette, possibly Limoges, c1930, 7⅜in (19cm) high.
$185–225 *WTA*

A Crown Ducal charger, designed by Charlotte Rhead, pattern No. 6016, c1939, 12in (30.5cm) diam.
$330–400 *PC*

A brooch, with rhinestone and enamelled flowers, on a gilt setting, unsigned, c1930, 2½in (65mm) long.
$120–135 *BaH*

Three chrome and Bakelite sailing ship brooches, with amber, red and green sails, c1930, 1¼in (30mm) high.
$15–30 each *GOO*

A peacock pendant, set with diamonds and opal, incised mark 'Vever Paris', c1900, 4in (100mm) long.
$100,000–115,000 *S(G)*

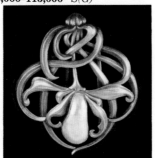

An Art Nouveau buckle, by Kolona, for Bing shoes, 2½in (65mm) wide.
$8,250–9,750 *SHa*

A riverscape pendant, with shaped circular frame set with rose diamonds, stamped 'G. Fouquet', c1908, 2½in (65mm) wide.
$80,000–95,000 *S(G)*

An Arts and Crafts fire opal and silver brooch, c1900, 2in (50mm) wide.
$140–180 *GOO*

A silver necklace, set with turquoise, opal and pearl, by Arthur and George Gaskin, c1910.
$1,500–1,800 *JES*

A pin brooch, with coloured rhinestones, glass stones and rhodium leaf setting, signed 'Art', c1930, 3in (75mm) wide.
$120–150 *PGH*

An Ophelia pendant, by Eugène Feuillâtre, with *plique à jour* enamel background, stamped, 3¼in (85mm) long.
$130,000–150,000 *S(G)*

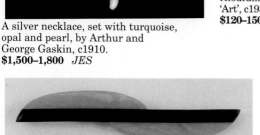

A black and amber Bakelite pin brooch, c1930, 5in (125mm) long.
$45–60 *GOO*

An Art Deco belt buckle, with turquoise enamel decoration, c1920, 3¼in (85mm) wide.
$30–50 *OD*

An iridescent glass bowl, by Tiffany, marked, c1890, 7in (18cm) diam.
$975–1,125 *SHa*

A glass vase, signed 'Gallé, Nancy, France', c1890, 6¼in (16cm) high.
$1,500–1,800 *SHa*

A glass vase, signed in cameo 'Gallé', c1900, 23½in (59.5cm) high.
$1,800–2,000 *Bon*

l. A glass vase, decorated with carved poppies, marked 'Daum Nancy', c1900, 11in (28cm) high.
$8,500–9,500 *S*

A Loetz glass vase, c1900, 7½in (19cm) high.
$975–1,200 *SUC*

A Loetz wood-mounted glass vase, designed by Josef Hoffmann, c1899, 18⅛in (46.5cm) high.
$16,000–18,000 *C*

A Loetz iridescent glass vase, inscribed, c1900, 8¼in (21cm) high.
$14,000–15,500 *S(NY)*

A Loetz iridescent glass vase, inscribed, c1900, 9½in (24cm) high.
$21,000–22,500 *S(NY)*

A cameo glass bottle, marked 'Daum/Nancy', c1900, 7½in (19cm) high.
$22,000–24,000 *S(NY)*

A glass vase, incised mark 'Daum, Nancy', c1900, 10in (25.5cm) high.
$7,000–8,250 *Bon*

A Tiffany Favrile mosaic glass and gilt-bronze stamp box, the lid set with 2 scarabs, with fitted interior, impressed, c1900, 4½in (11.5cm) wide.
$27,500–33,000 *S(NY)*

A Tiffany Studios glass inkwell, with 4 flying fish at the corners, the sides set with mosaic glass tiles, clear glass liner, impressed, c1900, 7in (18cm) wide.
$55,000–65,000 *S(NY)*

A Loetz iridescent glass vase, decorated with silver-blue feathers between swirled borders, inscribed, c1900, 9in (23cm) high.
$21,750–24,000 *S(NY)*

A Gallé mushroom and web vase, c1900, 12¼in (31cm) high.
$9,750–10,500 *S*

An iridescent ceramic vase, by Delphin Massier, c1900, 7in (18cm) high.
$750–900 *SUC*

A Gallé vase, of clear glass, decorated in *marquetrie-sur-verre* technique with crocus, engraved mark, c1900, 15in (38cm) high.
$17,250–19,500 *S*

A Gallé narcissus vase, decorated in *marquetrie-sur-verre* technique, engraved mark, c1900, 8¼in (21cm) high.
$27,750–30,000 *S*

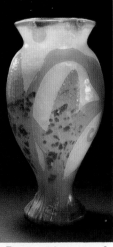

An iridescent pink ceramic vase with handles, by Delphin Massier, c1900, 10¾in (27.5cm) high.
$750–900 *SUC*

A Loetz vase, of pressed leaf design, in rainbow colours, 1910, 9in (23cm) high.
$375–450 *SUC*

A Tiffany Favrile reactive paperweight glass vase, inscribed, 'L.C.T. Y3030', c1905, 7¼in (18.5cm) high.
$14,250–15,000 *S(NY)*

A Daum maize vase, of opalescent dichroic glass, overlaid and etched, engraved mark, c1900, 11½in (29cm) high.
$5,000–5,500 *S*

A Daum wisteria vase, in opalescent glass, overlaid and etched, engraved mark, c1905, 20in (51cm) high.
$5,500–6,500 *S*

A Tiffany Favrile lava glass vase, in amber coated with blue, dripping golden-amber around the rim, inscribed, c1921, 4½in (11.5cm) high.
$23,250–26,250 *S(NY)*

A blue with black swirls cloud glass vase, with frog, 1930s, 13½in (34.5cm) diam.
$150–180 *BEV*

A *pâte-de-verre* vase, by Gabriel Argy-Rousseau, moulded marks, c1926, 8¾in (22cm) high.
$26,500–31,500 *S(NY)*

A *pâte-de-verre* glass vase, entitled 'Le Jardin des Hesperides', by Gabriel Argy-Rousseau, impressed mark, 1926, 9½in (24cm) high.
$28,000–33,000 *S*

An Art Deco vase, with a flecked base, 1930s, 7in (18cm) high.
$225–275 *PSA*

A Fenton's carnival glass lemonade set, 1930, jug 9in (23cm) high.
$450–525 *BEV*

An acid and wheel cut glass vase, by Daum, c1925, 5in (12.5cm) diam.
$550–675 *SUC*

A moulded opalescent and black enamel glass bowl, by Sabino, c1925, 7¾in (19.5cm) diam.
$900–1,000 *SUC*

A *pâte-de-verre* vase, entitled 'Les Loups dans la Neige', by Gabriel Argy-Rousseau, c1926, 9½in (24cm) high.
$9,500–10,500 *CNY*

A Jobling glass bowl, decorated with birds, 1930s, 7½in (19cm) diam.
$120–140 *BEV*

A Jobling glass jardinière, decorated with birds, 1930s, 15½in (39.5cm) wide.
$300–375 *BEV*

A pair of opalescent glass book ends, modelled as stylised doves, marked 'Model, Paris', c1930, 6¾in (17cm) high.
$525–600 *WTA*

A Duchess of Sutherland Cripple Guild Arts and Crafts copper and silver box, c1890, 5½in (14cm) wide.
$450–525 *SHa*

An Aesthetic Movement tea set, c1872, teapot 4½in (11.5cm) high.
$1,800–2,000, a letter tray, c1882.
$300–375, a smoker's set, c1882.
$1,500–1,800 *S*

An Art Nouveau bronze door knocker, formed as a face, the hair leaf-shaped, 7in (18cm) high.
$60–75 *OD*

An Arts and Crafts copper and brass inkwell, by W. A. S. Benson, signed, c1890, 5½in (14cm) diam.
$525–575 *SHa*

An Art Nouveau copper and steel firescreen, embossed and chased with an eagle, in a wrought iron frame, 24in (61cm) high.
$75–90 *TMA*

A Loetz green glass and pewter two-handled bowl, c1900, 4½in (11.5cm) high.
$180–220 *GOO*

A silver-mounted vase, with green ground, by Dalpayrat, c1895, 8in (20.5cm) high.
$1,500–1,800 *SUC*

A Gorham Co silver-coloured coffee pot in the Japanese style, maker's mark and 'C18', 1882, 11½in (29cm) high.
$8,500–9,750 *S*

An Arts and Crafts two-handled copper bowl, by Keswick School of Industrial Art, Cumbria, c1900, 9in (23cm) high.
$750–825 *SHa*

A silver three-piece tea set, by Hukin & Heath, after a design by Christopher Dresser, all pieces fit inside the teapot, London 1883, teapot 3½in (9cm) high.
$1,500–1,800 *SHa*

A WMF pewter inkwell, with the figure of girl, c1904, 8in (20.5cm) high.
$1,000–1,200 *SHa*

A pewter dish, with enamel centre, by Archibald Knox, for Liberty & Co, 1903, 9in (23cm) diam.
$180–220 *GOO*

An Edwardian enamelled bowl, by Archibald Knox, fc Liberty & Co, Birmingham 1907, 7in (18cm) wide.
$3,800–5,000 *MSW*

A Wiener Werkstätte alpaca desk set, designed by Josef Hoffmann, blotter stamped 'WW', c1905, pen tray 14¼in (36cm) wide.
$13,000–15,000 *C*

An Art Nouveau Loetz glass vase, with pewter mounts, c1900, 12in (30.5cm) high.
$450–600 *GOO*

A Powell vase, designed by Archibald Knox for Liberty & Co, in a pewter stand, c1905, 7in (18cm) high.
$150–225 *GOO*

An Austrian silver-gilt and *plique-à-jour* cigarette case, the catch set with a sapphire, stamped, 1924, 3in (8cm) high.
$1,500–1,800 *P*

An Art Deco silver plated tea set, by Walker & Hall, with Bakelite handles, 1930s, pot 8½in (21.5cm) high.
$375–450 *BEV*

A Ramsden & Carr glass vase, with silver mounts and handles, London 1916 17½in (44.5cm) high.
$12,750–10,000 *DN*

A pewter serving dish and cover, designed by Archibald Knox for Liberty & Co, c1905, 10½in (26.5cm) wide.
$150–180 *GOO*

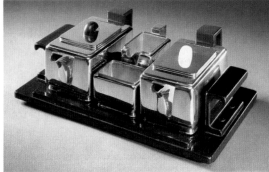

A silver tea service and tray, by Harold Stabler for Adie Brothers Ltd, with Bakelite handles, Birmingham 1936, tray 12½in (32cm) wide.
$15,000–18,000 *S*

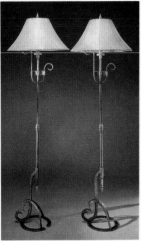

A pair of bronze and wrought iron lamps, by Oscar Bach, with modern parchment shades, c1925, 72in (183cm) high.
$7,000–8,250 *S(NY)*

A pair of wrought iron lamps, by Edgar Brandt, the mottled glass sconces by Daum, Nancy, inscribed and impressed, c1925, 21in (53.5cm) high.
$30,000–37,500 *S(NY)*

A Gallé glass lamp, overlaid with red and etched with autumn leaves, shade and base marked, c1900, 24½in (62cm) high.
$26,000–30,000 *S*

A pair of Arts and Crafts copper candlesticks, by Benham & Froud, c1890, 6½in (16.5cm) high.
$525–675 *SHa*

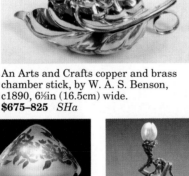

An Arts and Crafts copper and brass chamber stick, by W. A. S. Benson, c1890, 6½in (16.5cm) wide.
$675–825 *SHa*

A Gallé glass lamp, etched with flowering vines, c1900, 22in (56cm) high.
$10,500–12,000 *S*

A gilt and bronze lamp, by Gugny, c1900, 29in (74cm) high.
$13,000–15,000 *S*

A Handel reverse painted glass and metal parrot lamp, decorated by Henry Bedegie, c1923, 23½in (59.5cm) high.
$10,500–12,000 *S(NY)*

An Art Deco table lamp, with a chrome gazelle, 1930s, 19in (48.5cm) high.
$120–150 *BEV*

A French Art Deco bronze mermaid lamp, c1925, 43in (109cm) high.
$7,000–8,000 *S(NY)*

A pewter candelabra, designed by Archibald Knox for Liberty & Co, 1903, 11in (28cm) high.
$1,500–1,800 *GOO*

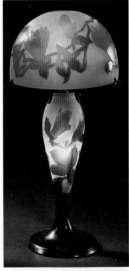

A Gallé glass lamp, byoverlaid and etched with magnolia branches, c1900, 20in (51cm) high.
$24,000–28,000 *S*

A Tiffany Favrile glass and
bronze blown-out lamp,
c1895, 19¾in (50cm) high.
$30,000–33,000 *S(NY)*

A Tiffany Favrile glass and
bronze filigree Poppy lamp,
c1910, 25in (63.5cm) high.
$43,000–48,000 *S(NY)*

A Tiffany Favrile glass and
bronze Hydrangea chandelier,
c1910, 29in (74cm) diam.
$36,000–39,000 *S(NY)*

A Tiffany Favrile glass and bronze Begonia
lamp, the shade impressed '350–6', the base
'7805', c1910, 16½in (42cm) high.
$50,000–60,000 *S(NY)*

A Tiffany Favrile glass
and gilt-bronze Lily lamp,
c1910, 21¼in (54cm) high.
$37,000–42,000 *S(NY)*

A Tiffany Favrile glass and
bronze Woodbine lamp,
c1910, 19in (48.5cm) high.
$18,000–21,000 *S(NY)*

A Tiffany Favrile glass and bronze Grape Trellis
chandelier, replaced ceiling cap and fittings,
impressed, c1920, 26½in (67.5cm) diam.
$25,500–28,500 *S(NY)*

A Tiffany Favrile glass and bronze Grape
Trellis chandelier, the crown pierced with
geometric devices, c1910, 31in (79cm) diam.
$112,000–128,000 *S(NY)*

A Tiffany Favrile glass and bronze
miniature Wisteria lamp, base
impressed, c1910, 17in (43cm) high.
$55,000–60,000 *S(NY)*

A Tiffany Favrile glass
and bronze Dogwood
ball lamp, c1910,
33in (84cm) high.
$17,500–19,500 *S(NY)*

A Tiffany Favrile
glass 'Gooseneck'
vase, 1912,
12¼in (31cm) high.
$7,500–9,000 *S*

A Tiffany Favrile
yellow glass 'Jack-in-
the-Pulpit' vase, 1905,
18¼in (46.5cm) high.
$8,000–9,000 *S*

A Royal Dux model, of
Diana the Huntress,
c1900, 13in (33cm) high.
$825–975 *VSt*

A bronze and carved ivory group,
entitled 'Friends Forever', by Demêtre
H. Chiparus, inscribed, early 20thC,
25½in (65cm) high.
$24,000–28,000 *S(NY)*

A Carter Stabler & Adams
glazed stoneware figure,
entitled 'The Bull', by Harold
and Phoebe Stabler, 1914,
13in (33cm) high.
$3,000–3,500 *PP*

A porcelain bust, by Ernst
Wahliss, depicting a girl
with a wreath on her head,
1898, 26in (66cm) high.
$2,700–3,500 *SUC*

A French gilt and brown
patinated bronze Yo Ho
girl, by Grevin and Beer,
c1895, 20in (51cm) high.
$1,500–1,800 *SUC*

A cold painted bronze and
tinted ivory figure, by Paul
Philippe, on an onyx base,
1920s, 25¼in (64cm) high.
$13,000–15,000 *S*

A bronze and gilt
figure, signed 'Sorenson
Ringi, Paris, 1899',
26in (66cm) high.
$4,500–5,000 *JES*

A cold painted bronze and carved ivory
group depicting Russian dancers, by
Demêtre H. Chiparus, inscribed, early
20thC, 15½in (39.5cm) high.
$31,500–34,500 *S(NY)*

A bronze and carved ivory figure,
entitled 'Simplicity', by Demêtre
H. Chiparus, inscribed, early
20thC, 20¾in (52.5cm) high.
$14,000–15,750 *S(NY)*

A patinated, silvered
bronze and carved ivory
figure, entitled 'Starfish', by
Demêtre H. Chiparus, early
20thC, 29½in (75cm) high.
$46,000–54,000 *S(NY)*

An Art Deco spelter figure group, depicting a male and female dancer, 15in (38cm) wide.
$375–400 *DAF*

A cold painted bronze and ivory figure, entitled 'Balancing', by F. Preiss, 1930s, 14¾in (37.5cm) high.
$10,500–12,000 *S*

A French cold painted spelter figure, on a marble base, c1935, 7in (18cm) high.
$450–525 *WTA*

A silvered and gilt bronze figure entitled 'Modern Venus', marked 'Cl. J. R. Colinet', on a marble base, 1921, 18½in (47cm) high.
$5,250–6,000 *S*

A patinated bronze and ivory figure, by F. Preiss, signed, c1925, 13½in (34cm) high.
$7,500–9,000 *DN*

A *pâte-de-cristal* figure, entitled 'Baigneuse', by Marcel Bouraine and Gabriel Argy-Rousseau, 1928, 10in (25.5cm) high.
$15,000–16,500 *S*

A Katzhütte porcelain figure, c1930, 17in (43cm) high.
$750–900 *ASA*

A pair of Art Deco spelter and marble book ends, by Vivian, 8¾in (22cm) high.
$375–450 *DAF*

A gilt bronze and ivory figure, by F. Preiss, 1920s, 13¼in (33.5cm) high.
$6,500–7,000 *S*

A patinated bronze and ivory figure, by J. Lormier, 1920s, 14¼in (36cm) high.
$3,000–3,500 *S*

An Art Deco spelter figure, depicting a seated lady, 6in (15cm) high.
$225–300 *DAF*

An Art Deco spelter figure, 14¼in (36cm) high.
$375–450 *DAF*

A Paul Richard silver gilt and carved mahogany clock, by Lepine, c1900, 7¼in (18.5cm) high.
$9,750–11,250 *S(NY)*

An Arts and Crafts clock, with porcelain painted panels, c1880, 12in (30.5cm) high.
$2,000–2,500 *ROD*

A slate and scagliola clock, with gilt bronze decoration, c1880, 14½in (37cm) high.
$750–900 *SUC*

An Art Nouveau mahogany clock, c1890, 11½in (29cm) high.
$675–825 *ROD*

A tortoiseshell and silver desk clock, Birmingham 1912, 7¾in (19.5cm) high.
$750–825 *SHa*

An Art Nouveau timepiece, with engraved dial, c1910, 4½in (11.5cm) high.
$980–1,200 *ROD*

An Art Nouveau clock, with silver front, Birmingham 1910, 12in (30.5cm) high.
$1,100–1,300 *SHa*

An Art Deco clock, with enamelled and gilt dial, 8-day movement, 1930s, 4in (10cm) square.
$450–525 *BWC*

An ebonised wood, alabaster and mother-of-pearl inlaid mantel clock, c1910, 18in (46cm) high.
$5,500–6,500 *C*

A Finnish carved walnut clock by Johann Friedl, signed, 1904, 27¼in (69cm) high.
$5,250–6,000 *SUC*

A French clock garniture set in onyx, with bronze figure group, by Davroff, 1930s, clock 20in (51cm) wide.
$2,700–3,000 *DAF*

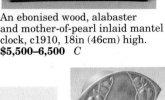

An Art Nouveau timepiece, the pewter case by Liberty & Co, No. 0370, c1910, 8in (20.5cm) high.
$2,200–2,700 *DN*

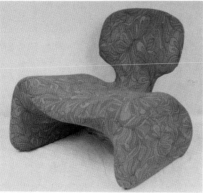

A Djinn chair, by Oliver Morgue, France, for Airborne, with a psychedelic stretch cover over polyfoam, on metal rails, 1965. **$900–1,000** *Bon*

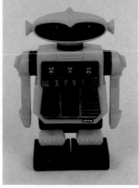

A plastic robot radio, which moves in time with the sound, 1970s, 8in (20.5cm) high. **$25–35** *RCh*

An American carved walnut and cherry single music stand, by Wharton Esherick, dated '1960', 44in (112cm) high. **$11,000–12,500** *S(NY)*

A Royal Winton lustre dish, c1950, 9¼in (23.5cm) wide. **$50–60** *PBi*

An American Philco Predicta television, 1959, 55in (1140cm) high. **$825–975** *ET*

Three vases, designed by Nils Landberg for Orrefors, c1954, largest 9in (23cm) high. **$150–180** *RCh*

A button-back upholstered sofa, designed by Finn Juhl, Denmark, made by Niels Vodder, on turned teak legs, 1946. **$1,125–1,425** *Bon*

A rhinestone and Bakelite brooch, gilt brass setting, 1950s, 2⅓in (65mm) high. **$75–90** *PGH*

A Norwegian silver and enamel brooch, 1950s, 3in (75mm) wide. **$75–90** *RCh*

A yellow and black plastic clock, c1965, 7in (18cm) high. **$30–40** *RCh*

A coffee set, by Cmielon, Poland, with sgraffito decoration, 1950s, pot 11½in (29cm) high. **$50–60** *RCh*

A Poole Pottery Delphis bowl, outlined in black wax, painted by Angela Wyburgh, 1968, 14in (35.5cm) diam. **$340–420** *PP*

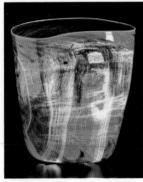

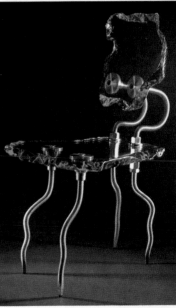

A glass cylinder, with a yellow lip wrap, by Dale Chihuly, c1940, 22in (56cm) high.
$7,000–8,000 *S(NY)*

A Poole Pottery Ltd Ionian plaque, shape No. 6, designed by Carole Holden, c1974, 12⅛in (32cm) wide.
$340–400 *PP*

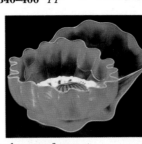

An Etruscan chair, glass and forged stainless steel studding, the seat signed 'Danny Lane 1900 4-42'.
$3,500–4,000 *Bon*

A glass sea form set, by Dale Chihuly, dated '89', 22in (56cm) wide.
$5,250–6,000 *S(NY)*

A dressing table and stool, by Wendell Castle, signed in gold leaf and dated '1983', 52in (132cm) wide.
$16,500–19,500 *S(NY)*

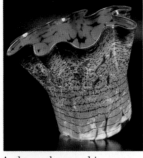

A Poole Pottery Ltd stoneware sculpture, entitled 'The Canada Goose', by Barbara Linley Adams, shape No. 704, made in a limited edition of 500 pieces, c1974.
$375–450 *PP*

A glass ruby macchia vase, with blue lip wrap, by Dale Chihuly, mid-20thC, 21¾in (55.5cm) wide.
$6,000–6,500 *S(NY)*

A Poole Pottery Aegean vase, shape No. 93, c1975, 12⅛in (32cm) high.
$150–200 *PP*

A Charles Eames lounge chair and ottoman, by Herman Miller, with rosewood moulded veneer and leather cushions, dated 'December 17, 1976'.
$2,000–2,500 *JL*

An American violet gold Venetian blown glass vase with five stems, by Dale Chihuly, unsigned, mid-20thC, 40in (101.5cm) high overall.
$17,250–18,750 *S(NY)*

TWENTIETH CENTURY FURNITURE – FOCUS ON WOOD

Fortune has favoured the brave and where collectors have led, auctioneers have followed. Many 20th century pieces are now valued as highly as pieces from earlier times and so age is not the defining characteristic it once was. The time is fast approaching when many of these items will pass into the properly defined realm of the antique. How then, are we to make sense of these things?

That wooden furniture continues to be made is in itself quite remarkable. The 20th century has seen the most enormous advances in materials technology, so that wood is now just one of many materials available to the furniture maker. Throughout the century there have been experiments with tubular steel, aluminium, perspex, plywoods, laminates and plastics. These new materials are often associated with periods of reconstruction and cultural experimentation.

Tubular steel in Germany, for example, became fashionable in the period after WWI when post-war reconstruction required cheap, mass-produced furniture. The same collusion between excess materials and cultural need occurred after WWII with the emergence of a whole range of plastic and steel furniture. Notwithstanding these experiments wood has been the preferred material for furniture makers and many examples have all the utopian associations that characterise the best of 20th century design.

The timber furniture from the beginning of the century shows a clear stylistic debt to the Art and Crafts Movement founded in the 19th century by William Morris. This is evident in the use of hand-crafted metalware and cabinet work.

The Arts and Crafts Movement and its successors have left relatively few pieces of furniture. The workshops tended to be small-scale with an emphasis on craft and handwork. The resulting pieces, although very fine, were beyond the reach of all but the wealthiest families. Luckily there are quantities of unattributable pieces whose style derives from this tradition. Commercial firms were quick to borrow the look and style of the tradition without the time-consuming emphasis on handwork and craft.

Gordon Russell started his workshop at Broadway, Gloucestershire, in the 1920s. It was based on those of Gimson and the Barnsleys, founders of the The Cotswold School, and the furniture from the first years of this workshop is as fine as anything produced this century or last.

Russell was from a commercial background and perhaps it was this that made him more of a realist than his Cotswold predecessors. By about 1930 he had realised that, if the workshop was to continue, it required a much higher volume of work. Accordingly, he began to provide walnut and inlaid cabinets for wireless sets. The firm prospered throughout the 1930s with a mixture of bread and butter work and the production of simple modernist designs suitable for the new domestic interiors of that decade.

Russell was appointed advisor to the utility range of furniture produced during WWII. This was created to establish minimum standards of quality and workmanship in various industries, so that the public would be protected during the difficult years of the war. Russell's legacy has been devalued by the perception that the designs were thin and old-fashioned. Perhaps they were, from a 1960s view, but any small auction or house clearance will reveal these products to be no thinner than many 1930s pieces and to be a good deal more robust.

Russell was a member of the Design and Industries Association as were Frank Pick and Ambrose Heal, and was committed to improving the quality of design in manufacturing. This utilitarian principle would, it was hoped, create a world fit for heroes in the aftermath of WWI. Ambrose Heal's background was uncompromisingly commercial; his family had founded and managed the shop in Tottenham Court Road, then the centre for furniture making in London. Heal organised workshops for maximum efficiency and accommodating machine tools into the processes of manufacture. His own furniture designs, from the 1890s onward, are characterised by a simplicity of design and construction. Heal's made its furniture with the suburban home or metropolitan flat in mind.

The new homes, whether within or without the city, were often smaller than those built at the end of the 19th century. The scale of their furniture reflects this, as does the fact that many pieces, tables especially, often combine storage space with their more usual function.

A new and avant-garde development in the 1930s was the production of plywood and bentwood furniture. This was based on the 19th century designs of Thonet and the bent-metal experiments of the 1920s. These ideas were launched in England by the firm of Isokon, founded by Jack Pritchard. He was influential in modernist circles and knew many of the European émigrés personally. Isokon furniture was available at Heal's and other forward-looking shops. Gerald Summers and Ernest Race were also English designers who experimented with new materials.

The pages that follow show some of the diverse forms that wooden and other furniture has adopted over the past ninety years. Many of these pieces and styles will be familiar and that is the great virtue of this furniture, which is contemporary without being too modernist. The furniture is plain, will age well, and is robust enough to cope with the demands of family life. A look at the prices will indicate that many pieces are still good value.

Paul Rennie

Furniture

An oak pedestal desk, by Maples, c1900, 54in (137cm) wide.
$1,500–1,800 *SPa*

An oak cottage sideboard, designed by Ambrose Heal, made by Heal & Son, c1910, 48in (122cm) wide.
$1,200–1,500 *REN*

A walnut sideboard, by Gordon Russell, with yew crossbanding, line inlay and ebony handles, c1925, 69in (175cm) wide.
$11,250–13,500 *REN*

A walnut and copper-topped table, attributed to Simpson's of Kendal, c1920, 25in (63.5cm) high.
$480–600 *REN*

An oak sideboard, designed by C. A. Richter and made by Bath Cabinet Makers, c1928, 49½in (126cm) wide.
$1,200–1,500 *REN*

Two black lacquered plywood and laminated birch armchairs, No. 31, made by Alvar Aalto for Finmar, labelled 'Made in Finland', c1931.
$1,650–2,000 each *Bon*

An aluminium side chair, model No. 307, by Marcel Breuer for Wohnbedart, 1932.
$3,300–3,750 *Bon*

A bent plywood side chair, by Gerald Summers, with drop-in upholstered seat, stamped '63'.
$5,000–6,750 *Bon*

A Danish Ax armchair, c1950.
$225–270 *GOO*

r. A 'cowhorn' teak chair, designed by Hans Wegner, plaque to frame 'Johannes Hansen Cabinet Maker, Copenhagen, Denmark', c1955.
$1,200–1,425 *Bon*

l. A bunk bed, by Carlo Mollino, with coat hangers on different levels, and white laminated plastic bedside folding table to one level, oak frames and brass fittings, c1954, 33¾in (85.5cm) wide.
$2,700–3,000 *Bon*

A chair No. 670, and ottoman, designed by Charles Eames, with rosewood veneer on laminated wood shell, original black upholstery, worn, 1956.
$600–675 *SK*

A Neptune stacking and folding deck chair, by Ernest Race Ltd, with white horse logo in green circle and 'Patent and Reg D Design applied for', 1953.
$1,200–1,425 *Bon*

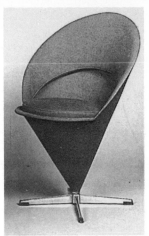

A 'cone' chair, by Verner Panton for Fritz Hansen, with red upholstery, on a four-prong swivel base, 1959.
$900–1,000 *Bon*

A cherry and ash rocking chair, by George Nakashima, c1966.
$3,000–3,600 *S(NY)*

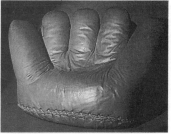

A 'Joe' Sofa, by Paolo Lomazzi, Donato d'Urbino and Jonathan de Pas for Poltronova, in the form of a baseball glove, the seat made of polyurethane foam and covered in olive-green leather, embossed 'Mod P100 Joe Made in Italy', 1970.
$4,800–5,700 *Bon*

This giant baseball glove, named after baseball star Joe DiMaggio, was inspired by the over-sized and surreal sculptures of Claes Oldenburg.

A Chauffeuse 1500 chair, by Etienne-Henri Martin for C.S.T.N. Mangan Atal France, the single piece free flowing, nylon stretch purple jersey-covered easy chair with foam upholstery and tubular metal frame, c1970.
$600–720 *Bon*

l. A rocking chair, with green upholstered seat raised on 2 U-shaped legs, damaged, c1958.
$300–375 *Bon*

A pair of 'swan' chairs, designed by Arne Jacobsen, reupholstered grey vinyl with original brown fabric beneath, paper label 'Fritz Hansen', 1957.
$1,800–2,000 *Bon*

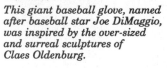

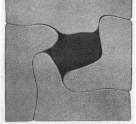

A Malitte Cushion System, by Sebastiano Matta for Gavina, with 4 combinable seats and ottoman linking to form a wall, the polyurethane units upholstered in lavender blue, the ottoman in dark blue, 1966.
$3,600–4,200 *Bon*

A 'tongue' chair, by Verner Panton for Fritz Hansen, manufacturer's label, 1974.
$375–450 *SK*

A 'First Chair', by Michèle de
Lucchi for Memphis, the metal
frame with painted lacquered
wood in turquoise and black,
first edition 1983.
$750–900 *Bon*

A 'bachelor' table, by Verner
Panton, labelled 'FH Made in
Denmark 1064 By Fritz Hansen'
and 'Furniture Makers Danish
Control', 1955, 28in (70cm) square.
$225–270 *Bon*

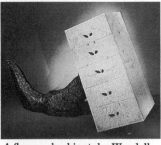

A 'banana' cabinet, by Wendell
Castle, the cherry and oak with
madrone and mahogany veneer,
signed and dated '1991',
68in (172.5cm) wide.
$13,800–16,500 *S(NY)*

An oak and steel compass desk,
by Jean Prouve, 1952,
55¼in (140.5cm) wide.
$4,200–4,800 *SK*

An occasional table, No. 536, by
Finn Juhl, labelled 'France
and Sons' and stamped 'FD
made in Denmark', 1958,
84in (213.5cm) wide.
$450–525 *Bon*

An E.S.U. 400 Series storage
unit, designed by Charles and
Ray Eames, manufactured by
Herman Miller, the angle iron
construction with birch plywood
shelves and coloured masonite
panels, with 2 pairs of 'dimple
doors', on metal doll legs with
angle supports, c1956,
47in (119.5cm) wide.
$450–525 *LHA*

A card table, by Isamu Noguchi
for Knoll, with green baize top
on a white painted steel wire
central frame and cast iron
hoop-shaped foot, c1954,
43¼in (110cm) diam.
$2,000–2,500 *Bon*

An Arco desk, by Studio B.B.P.R.
for Olivetti, moulded marks to
drawer front 'Olivetti, Anedamenti
Vetallici', 1963, 55in (140cm) wide.
$1,275–1,500 *Bon*

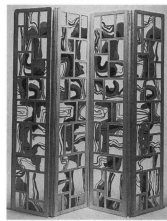

A Venini glass and painted iron
four-panel screen, the clear glass
panels streaked with blue and
black, c1955, 60in (152.5cm) high.
$8,000–9,600 *S(NY)*

A sycamore coffee table, the top and side with
pastel coloured decoration in shades of green and
peach, on sweeping legs, signed 'Rupert Williamson
1986', 27½in 70cm) wide.
$600–720 *Bon*

A burr ash table, by George Nakashima, signed and
dated '1966', 105in (266.5cm) long.
$21,750–24,750 *S(NY)*

Lighting

A white painted steel 'artichoke' hanging lamp, by Poul Henningson for Louis Poulsen, 1958, 28¼in (72cm) diam.
$1,000–1,200 *Bon*

An Eclisse table/wall lamp, by Vico Magistretti for Artemide, 1965, 7in (18cm) high.
$100–120 *Bon*

A '604 "Moon" 69' lamp, by Gino Sarfatti, for Arteluce, the yellow perspex shade over a metal base with small bulbs into a 'lunar surface', dimmer switch to side, 1969, 20½in (52cm) diam.
$2,000–2,500 *Bon*

A 'pencil' light, c1970, 19in (48cm) long.
$45–60 *RCh*

A Fantasma lamp, on a metal frame, designed by Tobia Scarpa for Flos, 1961, 72in (183cm) high.
$900–1,000 *CSK*

A pair of hand-made steel wall sconces, by André Dubreuil, first edition c1987, 24¾in (63cm) high.
$2,250–2,700 *Bon*

Miller's is a price GUIDE not a price LIST

r. An Eclisee table lamp, by Vico Magistretti for Artemide, c1965, 15½in (39.5cm) high.
$60–65 *RCh*

A desk lamp, the arched light raised on 4 adjustable red arms ending on black cube base, moulded mark 'Stilnova', c1968, 25in (63.5cm) high.
$100–120 *Bon*

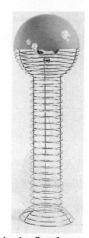

A wire floor lamp, by Verner Panton for Lüber, with 3 interchangeable semi-spherical shades in yellow, white and orange, 1969, 47¼in (120cm) high.
$480–570 *Bon*

A 'bubble' table lamp, by Crayonne for Conran Associates, c1970, 8in (20.5cm) high.
$30–45 *RCh*

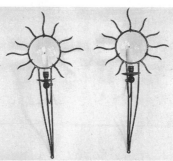

A set of 3 graduated white metal candlesticks, designed by Alessandro Mendini, made by Rossi & Arcandi for Cleto Munari, engraved signature, stamped marks, 1989.
$1,350–1,500 *Bon*

Ceramics

A Maling ware basket, decorated in green Peony Rose pattern, c1953, 10in (25.5cm) wide.
$90–100 *CSA*

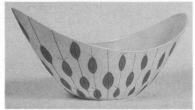

A Poole Pottery (Carter Stabler & Adams Ltd) bowl, shape No. 304, designed by Alfred Read and Guy Sydenham, decorated in Totem pattern, stamped, c1956, 14in (35.5cm) wide.
$210–240 *PP*

A Poole Pottery vase, c1950, 11¾in (30cm) high.
$225–270 *IW*

A Poole Pottery Delphis vase, shape No. 84, by Linda Garwood, painted with copper/iron oxide, red and yellow glazes on an orange base glaze, c1975, 9in (23cm) high.
$100–125 *PP*

A sculptural vase, by Frans Heindrich for Rosenthal, c1950, 11in (28cm) high.
$50–60 *RCh*

A Meissen white porcelain vase, c1955, 8in (20.5cm) high.
$30–40 *RCh*

A Poole Pottery Atlantis red earthenware vase, shape No. A20/5, by Guy Sydenham, decorated with black manganese dioxide, olive-green and magnolia white glazes, c1974, 8in (20.5cm) high.
$330–400 *PP*

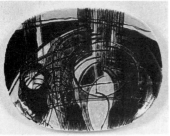

A Poole Pottery studio dish, by Robert Jefferson, painted with orange, yellow, greens and midnight-blue glazes on a magnolia white glazed ground, c1962, 16in (40.5cm) long.
$1,000–1,200 *PP*

A Polish organic coffee set, designed by Lubimor Tomaweski for Cmieløw, c1961, coffee pot 9½in (24cm) long.
$180–200 *RCh*

A Polish black sgraffito plate, by Chrodziez, 1950s, 12in (30.5cm) diam.
$60–75 *RCh*

A Poole Pottery (Carter Stabler & Adams Ltd) thrown vase, designed by Alfred Read and Guy Sydenham, shape No. 717, c1956, 10in (25.5cm) high.
$300–375 *PP*

A stoneware vase, by Janet Leach, c1960, 17in (43cm) high.
$750–900 *IW*

Glass

A Fucina Degli Angeli Guggenheim glass vase, the polished black glass sphere decorated with acid-etched names, chipped, c1954, 13⅜in (34cm) diam.
$1,800–2,000 *SK*

A Belgian glass vase, by Val Saint Lambert, c1950, 17in (43cm) long.
$90–100 *RCh*

A Cedenese and glass figure of a woman, designed by Fulvio Bianconi, with blue, black and white trail decoration, and drop-in head, c1950, 17¼in (43.5cm) high.
$2,250–2,700 *Bon*

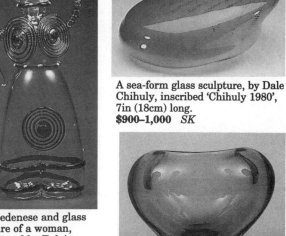

A sea-form glass sculpture, by Dale Chihuly, inscribed 'Chihuly 1980', 7in (18cm) long.
$900–1,000 *SK*

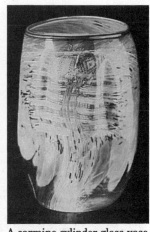

A Holmguaard glass vase, designed by Per Lutken, c1960, 4in (10cm) high.
$60–75 *RCh*

An Italian red glass vase, c1950, 22½in (57cm) high.
$75–90 *RCh*

A glass vase, by Vicke Linstrand for Kosta, c1955, 10½in (26.5cm) high.
$75–90 *RCh*

A Murano Geltrude glass vase, No. 5299, designed by Dino Martens, in the *orrente* technique, 1954, 12in (30.5cm) high.
$8,250–9,750 *Bon*

A carmine cylinder glass vase with cerulean lip wrap, by Dale Chihuly, signed and dated '88', 24⅜in (62cm) high.
$9,000–10,500 *S(NY)*

r. An Avem Anses Volantes glass vase, designed by Giorgio Ferro, with 2 loop handles and peacock lustre finish on red body, c1952, 10⅛in (26.5cm) high.
$1,800–2,000 *Bon*

A grey basket set with cobalt lip wraps, by Dale Chihuly, signed and dated '89', 42in (106.5cm) long.
$15,000–16,500 *S(NY)*

A Dutch freeform glass bowl, designed by Max Verboket for Maastricht Glass, mid-1950s, 19in (48cm) long.
$75–90 *RCh*

Jewellery

A Scandinavian silver brooch, signed 'Ayse', 1950s, 4½in (11.5cm) long.
$75–80 *RCh*

A Danish silver plated bracelet, by Jacob Hill, c1960, 6in (15cm) long.
$75–90 *RCh*

An acrylic and silver plated bangle, c1966, 1¾in (45mm) diam.
$40–50 *RCh*

An American brooch, with green rhinestones and Bakelite petals, in floral gilt setting, unsigned, 1950s, 2in (50mm) wide.
$90–100 *PGH*

An American pin brooch, by Trifari, with white rhinestones on gilt-brass setting, c1950, 2in (50mm) wide.
$120–150 *BaH*

A brooch, with large blue crystal stones and blue rhinestones, on gilt setting, unsigned, 1950s, 2in (50mm) long.
$75–110 *PGH*

A brooch and earring set, with amber rhinestones and Bakelite on floral gilt mount, unsigned, 1950s, brooch 3in (76mm) wide.
$90–110 *PGH*

A pewter brooch, by R. Tenn, 1950s, 2in (50mm) wide.
$30–45 *RCh*

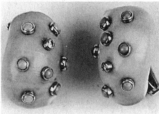

A pair of Andrew Grima clip earrings, each set with a colet-mounted diamond and 7 turquoises, the 18ct gold mounts with applied nameplate, c1970.
$825–975 *CSK*

A silver and blue enamel brooch, c1976, 2in (50mm) wide.
$75–90 *RCh*

A diamond and porcelain flower brooch, by Webb, chipped, signed, c1960, 2¾in (70mm) wide.
$6,750–7,500 *C*

A sapphire and diamond brooch, with a pair of matching earrings, c1960, brooch 2½in (60mm) wide, in Garrard & Co Ltd case.
$18,000–20,250 *C*

A pair of American clip earrings, by Lisner, with pink and green rhinestones on gilt brass settings, 1950s, 1in (25mm) wide.
$90–110 *BaH*

Radios & Televisions

A Marconi model 706 television and radio, with 5in (12.5cm) screen and LW/MW/SW radio, in figured walnut cabinet, 1936, 23in (58.5cm) wide.
$3,000–3,600 *P*

A yellow plastic 'Swinging' pool radio, c1970, 9in (23cm) diam.
$15–25 *RCh*

A Grundig transparent plastic television, by Zarach, pivoting on a chromed-metal flared pedestal, with 18in (45.5cm) screen, c1970.
$2,500–2,700 *CSK*

l. A Keracolour television, with 20in (51cm) screen, in a white acrylic cabinet, 1970, 27in (68.5cm) diam.
$225–270 *P*

A General Electric model 950 colour wheel projection television, with 21in (53.5cm) screen, in mahogany and maple cabinet, complete with original blueprints, instruction booklet and guarantee, 1946, 34in (86.5cm) wide.
$150,000+ *ET*

This is understood to be the earliest known colour television and dates from 1946. Known as a colour wheel set, it worked on the same principle as that demonstrated by the inventor of the television, John Logie Baird, in 1928. A normal black and white electronic camera was used, which incorporated a spinning wheel with coloured filters in the sequence red, blue and green, arranged so that sequential frames were transmitted through each filter in turn. As this was done at

great speed (25 frames per second), the effect of vision persistence resulted in the black and white film being seen in colour.

CBS began making regular broadcasts in the United States using this system in June 1951. However, within 4 months the service was suspended due to lack of sponsors, and the sets were recalled and ordered to be destroyed. It is thought that only 3 of these sets escaped destruction, and they are now in museum collections in the United States and Canada. In 1995, however, another 2 sets were discovered in a cellar in New York, in the possession of a retired television engineer who was involved in the earliest field tests of this particular system. These were the General Electric set pictured above left, and a colour wheel set by Zenith dating from 1949. The General Electric model is unique in that it is a projection set, the other 4 being direct view models. It had been illustrated in the May 1946 edition of the American magazine Radio News, which wrongly attributed manufacture to CBS. This may account for the fact that until this set came to light it was apparently unknown that General Electric had produced a world first in this field.

See colour advertisement on pp414–415

A Radio in the Bag, by Daniel Weil, for Parenthesis, the flexible PVC bag with printed designs, with the radio separated into simple component parts, 1981, 21in (53.5cm) wide.
$375–450 *Bon*

This radio was Weil's first important object, designed as part of a Royal College of Art degree. The model is now in permanent collections at the Museum of Modern Art, New York and the Victoria & Albert Museum, London.

A metallic orange television set, with torpedo-shaped base on a black cart with wheels, paint chipped, c1960, 43in (109cm) high.
$1,500–1,800 *SK*

A McMichael radiogram, in an Art Deco walnut cabinet, c1948, 48in (122cm) wide.
$720–900 *ET*

RUGS & CARPETS

A Napoleon III Aubusson carpet, 215 x 186in (546 x 472cm).
$13,500–15,000 *S*

A Napoleon III Aubusson carpet, the silver-grey field with ivory scrolling acanthus enclosed within rose garlands around a central ivory panel with floral bouquet, the inner frame bounded by strapwork, slight damage, 161 x 210in (409 x 509cm).
$26,250–30,000 *C*

A Koum Kapi silk and metal thread prayer rug, the blackcurrant-red field with overall floral, vine, occasional palmettes and cloudbands, an indigo floral cartouche panel above, the grey *mihrab* arch with yellow inscription band enclosing 2 baluster vases issuing floral, leafy vine and perching birds, in yellow split palmette, floral and leafy vine border between pink floral meander and grey and red reciprocal trefoil stripes, dry and split, Turkey, c1910, 53 x 37in (135 x 94cm).
$6,300–7,500 *C*

An Axminster carpet, small breaks, rewoven areas, overcast, late 18thC, 222in (564cm) long.
$112,500–127,500 *S(NY)*

A Koum Kapi silk and metal thread prayer rug, with 2 flowerhead cartouche columns issuing from zigzag and metal thread column bases, on a floral lattice panel, flanked by 2 part columns on a field of scrolling palmette, flowerheads and leafy vine panels, the columns supporting 3 arches depicting on either side 3 arched doors and in the centre a stylised plan of the mosque and Kaaba at Mecca, a panel of smaller arches above, in an interlocking floral panelled border, Turkey, c1920, 80 x 49in (203 x 124cm).
$30,000–36,000 *C*

Glossary

Abrash: Tone differences within a colour, normally due to variations in the dyes.
Arabesque: Leaf and vine scrollwork.
Boteh: A stylised floral bush similar to a Paisley design.
Div: A small devil.
Gul: From the Persian word for flower – usually used to describe a geometric flowerhead.
Herati: An overall repeating design of a flowerhead within a lozenge issuing small leaves.
Kufic: Arabic angular script – in rugs used to refer to stylised geometric calligraphy.
Mihrab: An arch representing the prayer niche in a mosque.
Palmette: A cross-section through a stylised flowerhead or fruit.
Spandrel: Decoration in the corner of the field.

A Spanish savonnerie carpet, the chocolate brown field with a central roundel enclosing a pale indigo acanthus rosette medallion, within a pale rose border of floral pendants and acanthus, signed 'G. Stuyek', Madrid, 1952, 382 x 162in (970 x 411cm).
$9,000–10,500 *S*

l. A Spanish savonnerie carpet, the rose-pink and ivory field with large slate-coloured panel enclosing a roundel monogrammed 'BS', supported by swans and acanthus, reduced in length and rewoven end border, Madrid, c1950, 154 x 140in (391 x 355cm).
$8,500–9,750 *S*

A Konya prayer rug, central Anatolia, late 19thC, 60 x 40in (152 x 101cm).
$14,250–15,750 *SK*

A Bergama rug, the mid-blue field with red re-entrant reserves, overall *guls,* within a saffron border of vines and curled leaves, west Anatolia, early 19thC, 81 x 62in (206 x 157cm).
$3,000–3,600 *S*

A Ushak Transylvanian rug, the plain red double-niche field with a red and yellow flowerhead medallion, abrashed blue spandrels with leaves and diced rosettes, within a yellow border of red and ivory stepped cartouches enclosing palmettes and floral vines, yellow kelim ends, west Anatolia, late 17thC, 67 x 47in (170 x 119cm).
$19,500–22,500 *S*

A Caucasian rug, the central red field woven with blues, yellow, red and ivory, narrow borders of blue and ivory, inscribed with mirror-imaged script comparing the carpet to a garden, Azerbaijan, c1800, 86 x 67in (218 x 170cm).
$30,000–36,000 *S*

An Azerbaijan rug, the red field with central ivory medallion enclosing red, blue, yellow and brown motifs, late 18thC, 70 x 57in (178 x 145cm).
$50,000–54,000 *S*

A Melas rug, with narrow brick-red panel enclosing a powder blue stem issuing polychrome flowerheads, within a green inner border of leafy vines and flowers, brick-red outer border of feathered vines and carnation sprays, south west Anatolia, c1840, 79 x 52in (201 x 132cm).
$5,250–6,300 *S*

A Kazak rug, the plain orange-red field with 3 lozenge medallions in pale green, ivory, blue and yellow, within a powder blue flowerhead border and 'running dog' guard stripes, south west Caucasus, dated '1338' (1920), 74 x 60in (188 x 152cm).
$2,550–3,000 *P*

r. A Yastik rug, with 6 *guls* in red, ivory, navy blue, gold and blue-green on a red field, gold border, worn, re-overcast, central Anatolia, late 19thC, 31 x 21in (79 x 53cm).
$2,550–3,000 *SK*

A Garabagh Kelleh, the dark blue field with 3 coral-red lobed flowerhead medallions linked by angular floral cartouches, pale pistachio stepped spandrels, all with cabbage roses and stylised birds, within a pale salmon pink border of turtle palmettes and angular vines, south Caucasus, c1900, 217 x 79in (551 x 200cm).
$300–360 *S*

A Garabagh floral carpet, the tomato red field with overall polychromatic large flaming palmettes and rosettes, within a green and tomato red surround, cut and rejoined, borders partially rewoven, south Caucasus, 18thC, 256 x 95in (650 x 241cm).
$9,750–11,250 *S*

A Garabagh Kelleh carpet, with blue field and unusual broad palmette and serrated leaf design border, south east Caucasus, 18thC, 257 x 103in (653 x 261cm).
$18,000–21,000 *S*

r. A Kuba long rug, worn, north east Caucasus, late 19thC, 112 x 36in (284 x 91cm).
$9,000–10,500 *SK*

A 'Dragon' Kelleh carpet, the russet red field with a 2 plane trellis of ochre and blue-green feathered leaves with flame palmettes, stylised dragons and animals in combat, within an ochre border of angular plants, south Caucasus or Balkans, c1900, 288 x 169in (731 x 429cm).
$19,000–22,500 *S*

> **Did you know?**
> *MILLER'S* Antiques Price Guide *builds up year-by-year to form the most comprehensive antiques photo-reference library available.*

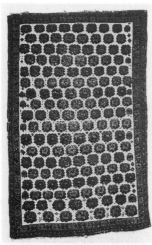

A Seichour rug, the ivory field with rows of carnations in navy and royal blue, dark red, rose and blue-green, red rosette and vine border, worn, north east Caucasus, late 19thC, 62 x 41in (157 x 104cm).
$1,800–2,000 *SK*

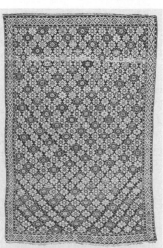

A Kuba carpet, the royal blue field with dense overall polychrome star *guls*, all within a blue-green and soft red stepped *gul* and star border, north east Caucasus, c1890, 181 x 128in (457 x 325cm).
$38,250–45,000 *S*

Large carpets from the Caucasus are rare. The use of diagonal rows of polychrome star flowerheads is a device often seen in rugs and, more particularly, in runners from this district.

A Shirvan rug, woven in many colours with geometric designs, moth damage and repair, east Caucasus, late 19thC, 76 x 58in (193 x 147cm).
$4,500–5,250 *SK*

A Daghestan prayer rug, the ivory field with diamond lattice and blossoming plants in midnight and royal blue, red, gold, maroon and blue-green, with red 'interrupted' vine border, repaired, north east Caucasus, late 19thC, 58 x 46in (147 x 117cm).
$5,250–6,000 *SK*

A Bidjar Kelim rug, dated 'AH 1288' (1871), west Persia, 66 x 36in (167 x 91cm).
$10,800–12,000 *S*

A Sarouk rug, the ivory field with quatrefoil medallion and pendants in cochineal, apricot and blue, midnight blue spandrels, and ivory 'turtle' variant border, worn, west Persia, late 19thC, 76 x 58in (193 x 147cm).
$3,750–4,500 *SK*

A Kashan carpet, the navy blue field with rosettes, vases of flowers and 2 cypress trees in red, rose, sky-blue, tan and blue-green, gold spandrels and red cartouche border, west central Persia, c1900, 182 x 122in (462 x 310cm).
$10,000–11,000 *SK*

r. A Tabriz silk carpet, the rust-red field with a stylised pond with swimming fish in foreground, a large central shaded blue tree with figures and animals, large serrated leaves, flowerheads and perching birds, in a broad shaded blue 'turtle' palmette and scrolling floral and leafy vine border between ice-blue flowerhead vine and flowerhead narrow stripes, plain broad outer rust-red stripe, worn and repaired, north west Persia, c1854, 152 x 108in (386 x 274cm).
$20,250–24,000 *C*

A Kurdistan Kellei carpet, the indigo field decorated with large palmettes and interlocking vines around an ivory, rose and powder-blue medallion, within terracotta floral borders, north west Persia 18thC, 234 x 82in (594 x 208cm).
$1,275–1,500 *P*

An Afshar rug, the sky-blue field with shaped medallions, bird and geometric motifs in midnight blue, ivory, red, gold and aubergine-brown, narrow ivory vine border, slight moth damage, south Persia, early 20thC, 76 x 56in (193 x 142cm).
$1,500–1,800 *SK*

A Heriz silk rug, with an inscription panel and cartouche dated 'AH 1238' (1822-3 AD), north west Persia, 65 x 38in (165 x 96cm).
$27,750–30,000 *S*

A Serapi carpet, the terracotta red field with quatrefoil navy blue and rose medallion, ice-blue and camel spandrels, within an ivory 'turtle' border, worn, north west Persia, late 19thC, 136 x 112in (345 x 284cm).
$9,750–11,250 *SK*

A Heriz silk rug, the terracotta field with large split arabesques enclosing pale-blue palmettes linked by vine tendrils and palmette sprays, within a terracotta border of stylised urns, palmettes and vines, north west Persia, c1870, 71 x 50in (180 x 127cm).
$9,750–11,250 *S*

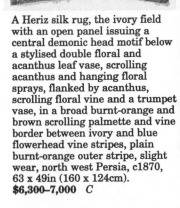

A Heriz silk rug, the ivory field with an open panel issuing a central demonic head motif below a stylised double floral and acanthus leaf vase, scrolling acanthus and hanging floral sprays, flanked by acanthus, scrolling floral vine and a trumpet vase, in a broad burnt-orange and brown scrolling palmette and vine border between ivory and blue flowerhead vine stripes, plain burnt-orange outer stripe, slight wear, north west Persia, c1870, 63 x 49in (160 x 124cm).
$6,300–7,000 *C*

Care of Carpets

Carpets should not be dry cleaned. However, they may be cleaned by a professional carpet cleaner, or washed with plain warm or cold water and a mild detergent. Snow is effective for removing dust: the dust can be brushed off with the snow! Alternatively, dust should be beaten out regularly unless the carpet is very frail.

l. A Tabriz silk prayer rug, the brown field with a central ivory arabesque and floral baluster vase issuing delicate floral and palmette leafy vine, an ivory *mihrab* arch above, in an indigo palmette, floral and leafy vine border, between ice-blue and steel-blue floral meandering vine stripes, ivory floral and multiple plain outer stripes, slight wear, north west Persia, c1880, 78 x 53in (198 x 134cm).
$15,000–18,000 *C*

A Tabriz silk prayer rug, the deep-blue field with a triple arched *mihrab*, the central arch with a large urn below and chandelier above, the 2 narrow outer arches with vases of daffodils and mosque lamps above, ivory shield palmette spandrels, within a narrow copper border of floral cartouches, north west Persia, c1890, 83 x 55in (211 x 140cm).
$9,750–11,250 *S*

A Tabriz silk rug, the royal blue field with dense overall arabesque interlace, a red quatrefoil medallion and similar pale-blue spandrels, within a very pale-blue border of palmettes and leaves, north west Persia, c1880, 59 x 52in (150 x 132cm).
$14,250–16,500 *S*

A Tabriz rug, the tan-gold field with rosette medallion and pendants in midnight blue, rust, ivory and light-blue-green rust spandrels and floral meander border, worn, north west Persia, late 19thC, 39 x 32in (99 x 81cm).
$870–1,000 *SK*

An Indo-Tabriz carpet, of Safavid Polonaise design, the field with a counterposed design of shaded red, grey, yellow and light-blue cartouches, shaded green and yellow minor lozenges containing angular palmettes, flowerheads and serrated leafy vines, within a yellow and grey border, between bottle green and light-blue angular floral vine stripes, c1930, 188 x 98in (477 x 249cm). **$7,800–9,000** *C*

An Afshar rug, the ivory field with a central flowering branch flanked by displaying peacocks, men on horseback, animals, birds and *guls*, within a walnut border of *kojanak guls,* south west Persia, c1870, 103 x 66in (261 x 167cm). **$5,250–6,000** *S*

A Beshir Kelleh, the walnut field with overall *herati* and a central roundel enclosing a star, 10 small symmetrically disposed moon medallions, charcoal inner border of polychrome rosettes, with brick red outer border of palmettes, central Turkestan, c1880, 367 x 128in (932 x 325cm). **$9,000–10,500** *S*

A Bakhtiari carpet, the indigo field with angular flowering sprays issuing from 4 red gabled medallions flanking a central similar aubergine and ivory medallion, each with central cruciform motif, in a red border of polychrome quartered lozenge medallions divided by angular floral sprays, with inscription cartouche, between ivory angular vine and minor zigzag stripes, slight wear, Persia, c1890, 153 x 83in (388 x 211cm). **$3,000–3,600** *C*

An Agra carpet, the crimson field with angular vine tendrils, large palmettes and cloud bands, within an indigo border of large palmettes linked by vines and small palmette sprays, north India, c1870, 177 x 122in (449 x 310cm). **$105,000–120,000** *S*

An Agra carpet, the crimson field with dense overall angular vine tracery bearing palmettes and feathery leaves, within an indigo border of large palmettes and vinery, cut and reduced on one side, north India, late 19thC, 170 x 160in (432 x 406cm). **$30,000–36,000** *S*

r. An Agra rug, the soft-blue field with 8 polychrome palmettes, feathered leaves, floral sprays and clouds, within an ivory border of crimson arabesques, north India, c1890, 55 x 87in (140 x 221cm). **$22,500–27,000** *S*

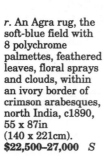

TEXTILES
Quilts & Covers

A Friendship quilt of printed cottons, of many colours, plain and with small patterns, arranged in squares and quilted to follow designs, late 19thC, 92 x 74in (234 x 188cm).
$550–630 *CSK*

A quilt, with white ground and cactus or grape baskets of apple-green cotton filled with triangles of yellow and pink prints, framed in apple-green, edged in pink print, quilted to follow design and with diamonds, late 19thC, 70 x 86in (178 x 218cm).
$300–360 *CSK*

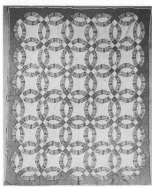

A quilt of brightly coloured printed cottons, in ring design against a white ground within a pink border, quilted to follow design with stellar and other infill patterns, 1930s, 90 x 76in (228 x 193cm).
$675–750 *CSK*

An appliqué quilt, the white ground sewn with 12 tulip stems of beige, red and yellow, with a similar border, closely quilted with feather designs including roundels with cross-hatching and diagonals, c1860, 72 x 86in (183 x 218cm).
$1,800–2,000 *CSK*

An Azerbaijan needlework coverlet, 17thC, 77 x 59in (195 x 150cm).
$66,000–72,000 *S*

A printed cotton cover, the tea ground with a design in deep red, brown and black with a central crown surmounted motif with horn, surrounded by scenes of a man wrestling a bull, within a floral frame, 19thC, 82 x 66in (208 x 167cm).
$330–375 *CSK*

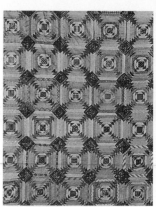

A log cabin coverlet, of printed cottons with many shades of browns, yellow, pink and blue, bound in a small print brown cotton, backed with a brown checked design, 1860s, 88 x 78in (223 x 198cm).
$2,250–2,700 *CSK*

A patchwork quilt, the centre with 9 diamonds of printed cotton with red centres and points, within frames of mainly small print squares, triangles and oblongs, reversing to a strip design, with diamond quilting, 19thC, 92 x 80in (234 x 203cm).
$630–750 *CSK*

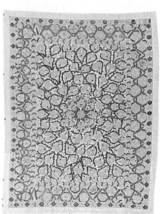

A Bokhara *susani*, the natural linen ground with a star flowerhead medallion radiating dense leaf encircled palmette sprays overall, within a border of zigzag feathery leaves and stylised flowers, central Turkestan, c1870, 91 x 71in (231 x 180cm).
$4,500–5,250 *S*

An appliqué coverlet, of coloured wools taken from soldiers' uniforms, arranged in roundels depicting the Life of Christ, with the Last Supper in the centre and 32 smaller ones, within a cable border and crowns at each corner, possibly Portuguese, 19thC, 46 x 48in (117 x 122cm). **$1,125–1,275** *CSK*

An American quilt, the cream ground with 8 roses in reds, plain yellow and red and yellow small print cottons, the side borders with striped tubs with meandering flower stems, quilted with an Ohio Rose and diamond design, late 19thC, 92 x 76in (234 x 193cm). **$525–600** *CSK*

A Nurata *susani*, the laid and couched gilt-metal ground worked in polychrome silks with a central floral medallion and floral sprays, within a running vine and carnation border, central Turkestan, c1880, 84 x 55in (213 x 140cm). **$7,200–8,250** *S*

An American cotton quilt, of navy blue, orange and terracotta patches arranged in an oak leaf and floral spray pattern, the white cotton field heightened with feather and cube quilting, Pennsylvania, 1878, 92in (234cm) square. **$2,250–2,700** *SNY*

A patchwork coverlet, of printed cottons in predominantly pink and light colours, the centre rows of small triangles, within a triple diamond frame, the corners of floral design, bordered by wide oblongs of flower prints, 19thC, 92 x 96in (234 x 244cm). **$450–525** *CSK*

An American quilt, of red, white and green cotton patches in a flower basket with blossoms pattern, the white cotton field heightened with feather, wreath and diagonal line quilting, stained, probably Pennsylvania, mid-19thC, 92in (234cm) square. **$825–975** *SNY*

An American quilt, of blue, brown, pink, orange and white printed and solid calico patches arranged in a star pattern, mounted on a white ground heightened with wreath feather and line quilting, stained, probably Pennsylvania, mid-19thC, 80 x 88in (203 x 223cm). **$675–750** *SNY*

An American quilt, of navy blue and white printed and solid calico patches mounted on a white cotton field, heightened with a diagonal line and feather wreath quilting, slightly faded, probably Pennsylvania, mid-19thC, 76 x 78in (193 x 198cm). **$975–1,125** *SNY*

An Indo-Portuguese embroidered coverlet, worked in crimson, saffron and ivory silk backstitch, with a central roundel of a pelican feeding her young, within a ring of birds, animals and scrolling vines, mermaid end panels, all within a border of huntsmen, west India, 17thC, 113 x 85in (287 x 216cm). **$12,750–14,250** *S*

Embroidery & Needlework

A needlework panel of 'The Banishment of Hagar and Ishmael', worked in a variety of stitches, the main figures in rococo stitch, a central fruiting tree highlighted with raised work pears, mid-17thC, 16 x 21in (40.5 x 53.5cm).
$4,000–4,800 *Bon*

A tent stitch embroidery, portraying a lady and gentleman with small boy, in a garden with a variety of animals, a butterfly, acorns and fruit, c1660, 12 x 18in (30 x 46.5cm), framed and glazed.
$3,750–4,500 *P*

A silk embroidered picture, portraying Hope, Logic and Rhetoric, in a garden within an oval cartouche, worked in long and short stitch on ivory satin, the surrounding embroidery including an applied tent stitch flower to each corner, c1660, 11 x 14½in (28 x 37cm), glazed in later beaded and scrolling gesso frame.
$4,200–5,000 *P*

An embroidered panel, the black silk ground worked in coloured silks with naturalistic stems of honeysuckle, lily-of-the-valley, tulips, snowdrops, briar and other flowers, mid-18thC, 18½ x 14in (47 x 35.5cm), framed and glazed.
$2,550–3,000 *CSK*

A stumpwork embroidery, worked in silks, coiled metal threads and chenille on an ivory satin ground, portraying Jeptha being greeted by his daughter, with a castle, animals and plants, repaired, c1670, 10 x 14½in (25.5 x 37cm), glazed in *verre eglomisé* frame.
$1,425–1,650 *P*

A needlework picture, of coloured wools with silk thread details, depicting a couple in a rural landscape, with a cottage in the background, 18thC, 16½ x 15½in (42 x 39.5cm), framed and glazed.
$2,000–2,250 *CSK*

A woolwork picture of a dog, with black, grey and white long hair, standing vigilantly on a rock, in a landscape with trees, c1800, 21 x 26½in (53 x 67cm), mounted and framed.
$675–750 *CSK*

A raised work picture, the ivory satin ground worked in coloured silks in different stitches and coloured purl, showing King Charles and his Queen, mid-17thC, 9¾in x 13½in (25 x 34.5cm), framed and glazed.
$5,700–6,750 *CSK*

An oval embroidered picture, the dark cream satin ground worked in coloured silks with a posy of roses, auricula, convulvulus and sweet peas, c1800, 8½ x 7in (21.5 x 18cm), mounted, framed and glazed.
$225–270 *CSK*

A Manya Luka appliqué saph, the field with 7 pale blue *mihrab* panels, each with decorated columns supporting an arch and enclosing a baroque urn issuing a flowering plant, floral spray spandrels, saffron divisional bands of floral cartouches, pale blue upper and lower borders, Bosnia, 19thC, 234 x 63in (594 x 160cm).
$6,300–7,500 *S*

An embroidered miniature casket with silver mount, holding a pin-cushion, mid-17thC, 3 x 2in (7.5 x 5cm). **$2,700–3,000** *RA*

A Victorian needlepoint picture of a King Charles spaniel, the dog grasping a glove, with foliage in the background, 21½ x 24in (54.5 x 61cm). **$7,500–8,250** *S(NY)*

A Continental embroidered picture of a saint, the ground worked in coloured silks, with painted details, the saint with arms outstretched and angels appearing through the clouds, 18thC, 9 x 7in (23 x 18cm). **$225–270** *CSK*

A South American Inca fragment, of stars and geometric motifs in red, black, gold, ivory and green, backed with fabric, slight wear, 14 x 19in (35.5 x 48cm). **$1,500–1,800** *SK*

A Lakai silk embroidered bagface, with 2 hooked floral motifs in ivory, green, black, purple, gold and sky blue on a red field, worn, central Asia, c1900, 20 x 15in (51 x 38cm). **$600–720** *SK*

An Italian embroidered Orphrey panel, the linen ground woven in yellow, lime-green, blue, cream, gold and silver threads, with velvet plush, depicting 5 saints, re-embroidered in places, c1425, in oak crucifix-shaped frame, 44½in (113cm) high. **$3,750–4,500** *S*

An embroidered silk picture, depicting a shepherd with crook and horn, standing on a hillock with his flock and hound, amidst birds, trailing foliage and flowers, early 19thC, 18½ x 21¼in (47 x 54cm), framed and glazed. **$4,500–5,250** *CSK*

l. A woolwork picture, with a basket of flowers and birds, inscribed 'M Morley's Work 1838' slightly discoloured, 15½ x 16½in (39.5 x 42cm). **$2,000–2,250** *DN*

A floral embroidered and appliqué cream wool panel, worked with coloured wools, with a basket filled with lily-of-the-valley, cornflowers, daffodils, carnations and other flowers, within a trailing ivy stem medallion, the field with bunches of flowers, fruit and nuts, the border with flowers and berries, c1830, 66 x 32in (167.5 x 81.5cm). **$1,650–2,000** *CSK*

A Berlin wool and beadwork panel, depicting a ruined archway and balustrade with deer and gushing fountain, surrounded by flowers and foliage, within a Gothic style border, on a brown field, mid-19thC, 39 x 67in (99 x 170cm). **$1,000–1,200** *DN*

Lace

A Brussels muslin appliqué stole, worked with a dense floral pattern, late 19thC, 108 x 23in (274.5 x 58.5cm).
$375–450 *CSK*

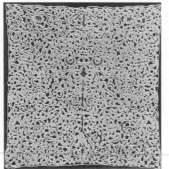

An apron of Flemish bobbin lace, worked in 2 halves with formal devices, late 17thC, 32 x 30in (81.5 x 76cm).
$1,200–1,350 *CSK*

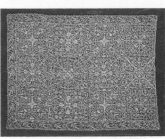

An Italian panel of needlelace, *punto in aria*, of chequered design with two-headed eagles, small deer, hares, boars and other animals, alterations and later additions, early 17thC, 28¼ x 38½in (72 x 98cm).
$1,300–1,400 *P*

A bridal veil of applied Brussels bobbin and needlelace, designed with swags of blossom and trailing foliage to the scalloped border, and scattered blooms to the spotted ground, late 19thC, 78¾ x 78in (200 x 198cm).
$900–1,000 *P*

A bridal mantle of applied Brussels bobbin needlelace, designed with a display of exotic blooms and foliage to the wide curved hem, ribbon garlands to the border and sprigs to the ground, c1860, 94½ x 197in (240 x 500cm).
$4,800–5,500 *P*

A pair of whitework lappets, worked with asymmetric undulating floral ribbons, mid-18thC, each 23in (58.5cm) long.
$240–270 *CSK*

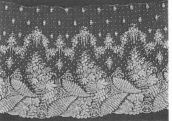

A flounce of Brussels appliqué lace, 19thC, 25in (63.5cm) deep.
$850–1,000 *CSK*

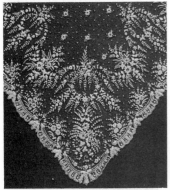

A bridal veil of applied Brussels bobbin and needlelace, designed with flower sprays above a formal border of twisted ribbon and scrolling leaves, a bouquet to each corner and scattered sprigs to the spotted ground, late 19thC, 78¾ x 74in (200 x 188cm).
$900–1,000 *P*

A Brussels tamboured bridal veil, designed with a formal repeat pattern of bouquets and swags of blossom to the scalloped border and scattered posies, c1880, 75 x 71in (190 x 180cm).
$600–675 *P*

A wide stole of Brussels Duchesse bobbin lace, designed with large lilies, roses, blossom, scrolls and foliage with needlemade detail, late 19thC, 112 x 39½in (285 x 100cm).
$2,000–2,500 *P*

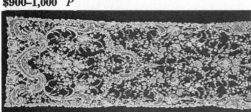

A stole of *point de gaze* lace, worked with raised petalled flowers, 19thC, 88 x 15in (223.5 x 38cm).
$825–975 *CSK*

A flounce of Brussels needlelace appliqué, worked with an angular guilloche border, c1870, 160 x 19in (406 x 48.5cm), and 2 matching pieces.
$850–1,000 *CSK*

Samplers

A sampler, by Elizabeth
Vincent, mid-18thC,
14 x 10in (35.5 x 25.5cm).
$1,500–1,800 *RA*

A sampler, finely worked in
coloured silks with a short
verse and a house, by
Margaret McLean, dated '1797',
16 x 12½in (40.5 x 32cm),
framed and glazed.
$2,550–3,000 *CSK*

A map of Scotland sampler, the
cream silk ground worked with
applied chenille, the border
embroidered with coloured silks
and designed with roses and leaves,
a ribbon bow bearing initials
'J.M.', late 18thC, 23 x 15¾in
(58 x 40cm), framed and glazed.
$450–525 *P(Sc)*

A sampler, finely worked in coloured
silks by Ellen Jackson, dated '1794',
with a verse 'Honest Labour', flanked
by white flower stems, perched
birds and flower urns, within a
stylised floral border, 16½ x 12in
(42 x 30.5cm) framed and glazed.
$375–450 *CSK*

An American needlework
sampler, by Elizabeth Horton,
1784, 13¾ x 10½in (35 x 26.5cm).
$2,250–2,700 *SK(B)*

A needlework sampler, by
Barbara Simpson, dated '1759',
with rows of alphabets above
rows of small birds, sprays of
flowers, and a religious verse
worked in black silk cross-
stitch, 13¾ x 8¾in (35 x 22cm).
$1,500–1,800 *Bon*

An American needlework
sampler, signed 'Joanna Tilden,
her Sampler', dated 'March the
17 Anno Domini 1762', worked
in green, blue, red and cream
wool on a linen ground,
13½ x 8½in (34.5 x 21.5cm).
$10,500–12,000 *S(NY)*

A sampler, by Mary Harmer, worked
in pink, yellow and other coloured
silks, with a verse at the base, dated
'1802', 17 x 12in (43 x 30.5cm).
$1,500–1,800 *CSK*

A Scottish sampler, by Helen Boyd,
worked in coloured silks in cross,
tent and satin stitches, dated
'1812', 16½ x 12½in (42 x 32cm).
$3,300–3,750 *P(Sc)*

A sampler, by Jane Staggs, finely worked in green and brown silks with details in white, blue and yellow, dated '1816', 16½ x 12½in (42 x 32cm), framed and glazed.
$4,200–4,800 *CSK*

A sampler, by Louisa Edwards, entitled 'Peace', worked in brightly coloured silks on wool in a variety of stitches, framed by a strawberry border, dated '1820', 15½in x 12in (39.5 x 30.5cm), framed and glazed.
$2,500–3,000 *MMo*

A sampler, by Catharine Aitchison, dated '1822', finely embroidered in coloured silk threads on wool, with initials of members of her family, slight damage, 14½ x 12½in (37 x 32cm), framed and glazed.
$1,800–2,000 *MMo*

A sampler, by Rachel Jacob, dated '1828', worked in green and shades of brown and cream silks with a verse in black silk, a church and floral spot motifs, within a stylised flower border, 16½ x 12½in (42 x 32cm), framed and glazed.
$1,000–1,200 *CSK*

A sampler, by Agnes Ogilvie, dated 'Nov 1824', the wool ground worked with red and brown wools and silks in cross stitch, 12½ x 10¼in (32 x 26cm), framed and glazed.
$680–780 *P(Sc)*

A sampler, by Alice Tuson, dated '1827', worked in brightly coloured silks with a poem, flanked by butterflies and flowers, with a parrot, a cat and a dog, within a stylised floral border, 16 x 12in (40.5 x 30.5cm), framed and glazed.
$700–820 *CSK*

A sampler, by Catharine Scott Allen, dated '1827', embroidered in silks on wool with a sailing ship, cliffs, a castle, a house flanked by trees, butterflies and animals, 15½ x 13in (39.5 x 33cm), framed and glazed.
$2,700–3,300 *MMo*

A George IV silk sampler, by Lucy Beeb, dated 'December 8, 1829', worked with a verse, alphabet, numbers, flowers, bird and animal motifs, within a meandering flower border, slight moth damage, 12 x 11½in (30.5 x 29cm).
$300–360 *DN*

A woolwork sampler, by Hannah Groves, dated 'November 28th, 1828', with a central panel of a figure feeding birds in a doorway, on a ground decorated with birds, flowers, urns, trees and cherubs within a meandering floral border, 18 x 19¼in (46 x 49cm), framed and glazed.
$1,275–1,425 *P(B)*

A sampler, dated '1829', worked in coloured silks with a verse, a house with trees and garden, figures, birds and dogs, within a stylised floral border, 12½in (32cm) square, framed and glazed.
$600–675 CSK

A sampler, by Elizabeth Anderson, dated '1831', worked in silk with her house and garden surrounded by flowers and trees, 13½ x 13in (34.5 x 33cm), framed and glazed.
$1,800–2,250 BHa

A sampler, by Eliza Brown, dated '1838', worked in silk cross-stitch with a verse, a house, figures, animals, flowers and birds, the alphabet and numbers, within a border of meandering roses, 17 x 13in (43 x 33cm).
$700–825 DN

A sampler, by 'E. W.' of the Birmingham Free Grammar School, dated '1847', worked in wool and silk with a large building, 2 rose sprays, birds and a verse within a border of carnations, slight moth damage, 24⅜in (62cm) square.
$525–600 DN

A sampler, worked in silk, metallic, wool and chenille threads, decorated with beads and sequins, with initials 'L.H.', dated '1842', slight damage, 21¼ x 20⅜in (54 x 53cm), framed.
$1,800–2,000 SK

A sampler, by Ann Tritton, dated '1834', worked in silk cross-stitch on linen with a verse, spot motifs, trees, plants and birds within a border, 11 x 11⅞in (28 x 30cm), framed and glazed.
$600–675 P

A sampler, by C. Cullum, with the number '384', dated '1874', worked in red silk cross-stitch with alphabets, numerals, stylised flowers and lozenges, above birds, a cow, a coat-of-arms and a Bible, 17½ x 13in (44.5 x 33cm), framed.
$1,800–2,000 Bon

The code number '384' on this sampler could possibly mean that it came from the Bristol Orphanage.

A sampler, by Eliza Matilda Excell, dated '1839', worked in green, crimson, cream and brown silks with a verse, a house, soldiers and bushes, topiary trees, fencing and spot motifs, within a stylised bud border and outer decoration of crimson silks, 16 x 12in (40.5 x 30.5cm), framed and glazed.
$1,000–1,100 CSK

r. A sampler, by Mary Catherine Greaves, dated '1843', worked in blue, green, cream and brown silks with a verse, alphabets and numerals, floral spot motifs and birds, within a stylised flower border, 10 x 12½in (25.5 x 32cm), framed and glazed.
$1,200–1,350 CSK

A sampler, by Emma Dodd, dated 'July 10, 1861', worked in cross-and chain stitches on canvas, with a house, figures, animals and birds, alphabets and a verse, within a border of trees, plants and birds, 17¼ x 13⅜in (44 x 35cm), framed.
$750–900 P

Tapestries

An Aubusson *verdure* tapestry, with 2 cranes before a castle and moat, surrounded by a foliate border, late 17thC, 96 x 129in (244 x 328cm). **$21,000–24,000** *S(NY)*

A Flemish tapestry fragment, depicting a queen enthroned in a tent among a gathering of admirers, 17thC, 88½ x 67in (225 x 170cm). **$6,000–6,750** *P*

An Aubusson tapestry fragment, woven in wools and silks, depicting a man in armour, probably Jupiter, embracing a lady, probably Venus, with a town being struck by lightning in the background, repaired, late 17thC, 93 x 54in (236 x 137cm). **$4,800–5,700** *C*

A Flemish *verdure* tapestry, depicting a forest landscape, fruit and foliate border, damaged, 17thC, 120 x 108in (305 x 275cm). **$12,000–13,500** *SK*

A Brussels historical tapestry fragment, woven in wools and silks depicting the siege of Tyre from the series of Alexander the Great, repaired, reduced in size, borders lacking, with later blue and white outer slip, c1600, 107½ x 74in (273 x 188cm). **$14,250–15,750** *C*

This tapestry is the 9th panel of a series of 11 tapestries depicting the life of Alexander the Great. It shows how the Ambassador of Tyre offered his city to Alexander to avoid a siege and raid of the city. The original series, woven in the late 16thC, is preserved in the Royal Spanish collection.

r. An Oudenaarde tapestry, woven in wools with wild animals and 2 shepherds in a wooded landscape with a town beyond, repaired, mid-16thC, 98 x 91in (249 x 231cm). **$25,500–30,000** *C*

A Flemish *verdure* tapestry, depicting flora and fauna in a landscape with a town beyond, within a fruit and flower-filled border, slight damage, c1700, 112 x 78in (284 x 198cm). **$7,500–9,000** *SK(B)*

A wool and linen tapestry, depicting a lady and a unicorn in a garden, parts associated and repaired, inscribed and indistinctly dated '1501', probably upper Rhine, 26½in (67.5cm) high. **$33,000–37,500** *C*

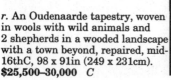

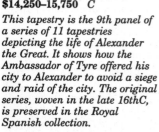

A Flemish tapestry, depicting men and dogs in a river landscape, with figures and a building behind, 17thC, 20 x 14in (51 x 35.5cm). **$1,200–1,300** *RA*

r. An Aubusson tapestry, after Charles Antoine Coypel, attributed to Pierre Mage, entitled 'The Memorable Judgment of Sancho Panza', from the Story of Don Quixote, c1750, 106½ x 124in (270 x 315cm).
$26,250–30,000 *S*

A post-Mortlake tapestry, depicting Vertumnus and Pomona from Ovid's *Metamorphoses,* in an egg-and-tongue pattern border, early 18thC, 78¾ x 115½in (200 x 293cm).
$17,250–19,500 *S*

A French or Flemish *verdure* chinoiserie tapestry panel, depicting birds in a landscape with a pagoda, slight damage, 18thC, 81 x 71in (206 x 180cm).
$7,500–9,000 *SK(B)*

A floral tapestry panel, woven in wools of reds, blue, greens and creams and silks of yellow, pink and cream, against a brown ground, c1800, 18½ x 15in (47 x 38cm), framed and glazed.
$420–480 *CSK*

A Brussels pastorale tapestry, after Teniers, depicting 2 male and 2 female figures, a shepherd with animals and a small farm amid trees and fields, early 18thC, 116½ x 74½in (296 x 189cm).
$8,250–9,750 *P*

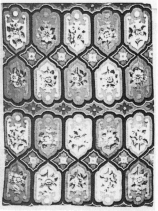

An Aubusson wool tapestry, entitled 'L'Homme avec Chiens', designed by Jean Lurçat, depicting a male figure surrounded by hounds beneath falling leaves and snow, in rich shades of red, white, gold, chartreuse and black, on a grey ground, woven signature and factory mark, c1945, 118in (300cm) square.
$11,250–12,750 *S(NY)*

A French tapestry, woven with arched panels of flowers with leaf motifs between, in black, scarlet, ivory, pinks, greens, blue and silver metallic threads, part of a larger hanging, c1875, 124 x 46in (315 x 117cm).
$2,550–3,000 *DN*

r. A Flemish tapestry, depicting 2 horsemen and hounds pursuing a boar in a forest, within a floral meander border, 19thC, 68 x 74in (173 x 188cm).
$2,000–2,500 *N*

l. A French tapestry, woven in coloured wools and silks with young children in classical costume dancing, in a wooded landscape, within a floral border and outer slip border, 18thC, 92 x 126in (234 x 320cm).
$16,500–19,500 *CSK*

A French landscape tapestry, woven in coloured wools and silks depicting 3 boys, one flying a kite, trees, a bridge and buildings, within a floral frame and outer blue slip border, 18thC, 90in (229cm) square.
$9,750–11,250 *CSK*

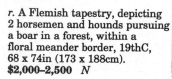

COSTUME

A pair of ivory brocaded lady's shoes, woven in lime green and yellow silk depicting wheat and other blooms, with dark green border edging, damaged, c1760, heels 2½in (6.5cm) high.
$3,000–3,750 *S*

A pair of soft tan leather ankle boots, with embossed linear decoration inset with metal eyelets for lacing, slight damage, probably 16thC.
$300–360 *S*

A pair of peacock blue brocaded lady's shoes, the heels and pointed toes brocaded with gold metal thread stylised poppies, worn, c1760, heels 2½in (6.5cm) high.
$1,500–1,800 *S*

A coat, waistcoat and breeches of powder blue ciselé velvet, embroidered with borders and pockets of ribbonwork pansies and roses, late 18thC.
$18,750–22,500 *CSK*

A pale blue silk damask sleeved waistcoat, worn by King George III, lined with cotton, c1820, and 3 autographed letters with references to the waistcoat.
$8,500–9,750 *CSK*

A striped mustard silk brocade French style dress, probably Spanish, altered, late 18thC.
$16,500–19,500 *S*

A scarlet wool greatcoat, with a green wool collar, large lapels, buttonholes embroidered in silver thread, and cast steel buttons, c1790.
$2,000–2,250 *S*

Did you know?
MILLER'S Antiques Price Guide *builds up year-by-year to form the most comprehensive antiques photo-reference library available.*

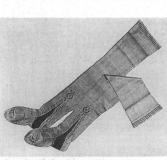

A pair of sky-blue silk stockings, with black instep, 18thC.
$3,750–4,500 *CSK*

An embroidered tailcoat, with a black wool stand-up collar, silver plated buttons, the front panels embroidered in raised silver thread with leaves and tassels, pockets to tail flaps, c1790.
$2,000–2,250 *S*

A lady's rattan sun bonnet, bound and lined in yellow silk, embroidered in silks with flowers and butterflies, probably Manila, Chinese workmanship for the European market, early 19thC.
$750–900 *CSK*

A gentleman's brown velvet jacket, with deep notched lapels, lined with brown linen, c1830.
$600–720 CSK

This jacket was discovered in the chimney of a cottage in north Yorkshire.

A lavender foulard lady's dress, with a bonnet veil of embroidered net, and a gentleman's waistcoat of ivory floral brocaded silk, c1850.
$525–600 P

An mid-18thC style ivory satin waistcoat, embroidered in gilt thread and tinsel with leafy curlicues, 19thC.
$225–270 CSK

An ivory and pale-blue moiré silk dress, woven with chiné flowers, embroidered with gilt thread borders, made in Turkey probably for a European lady, 1860s.
$480–570 CSK

A child's tulle overdress, with lace insertions and trimming, 1830s.
$160–190 CSK

An Indian starched muslin dress, the skirt and matching stole trimmed with beetle wing decoration in the form of arching floral sprays, the plain bodice trimmed with a band of tinsel and beetle wing at the low neckline, made for the European market, mid-19thC.
$1,800–2,000 CSK

A purple satin lady's jacket, woven with ivory velvet Bizarre motifs, labelled in the waistband 'Worth, 7 rue de la Paix, Paris', c1880.
$2,000–2,500 CSK

An ivory grosgrain wedding dress, with chiffon trimmed bodice, with ivory damask covered trousseau box monogrammed 'EH 14 June, 1900', containing orange blossom garlands for dress skirts, dried floral bouquets, ivory satin shoes, in a box from Hook Knowles & Co, inscribed 'Mrs Henderson', a lawn nightgown, camisole and open drawers, and a handkerchief.
$600–675 CSK

A girl's liberty bodice, of natural wool, laced at the rear, buttoned at the front, labelled 'Jaeger, Pure Wool', and 'Flora', early 20thC.
$210–250 CSK

A pair of Queen Victoria's leather kid gloves, embroidered with silk and purl wire thread, with the royal initials entwined below a crown and encased by a garland of leaves below, worn, c1890.
$900–1,000 S

These gloves were given by Queen Victoria as a present to a member of her staff upon their departure from the royal household.

A parasol, the fringed satin canopy elaborately decorated with gold thread and beadwork on a carved ivory 'chain link' handle, and a beadwork banner, late 19thC, 16½ x 18in (42 x 45cm).
$350–400 *P(B)*

A coral pink crêpe beaded evening gown, applied overall with a shimmer of silver pearlised turquoise, red and yellow beads in the form of passion flowers and leaf scrolls, probably French, early 1920s.
$300–360 *S*

A Fortuny full length coat, the olive green velvet ground stencilled in gold with early 17thC style pattern, lined in claret ottoman wool, moth damaged, early 1920s.
$4,500–5,250 *S*

A purple silk and black gown, designed by José Varona, made by Barbara Matera, worn by Joan Sutherland in Donizetti's *Lucrezia Borgia*, Act III, at the Vancouver Opera, 1972.
$1,000–1,200 *S*

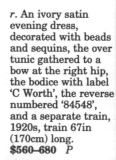

A black chiffon cocktail dress, embroidered with clear and opalescent bugle beads, with belt, 1920s.
$260–300 *CSK*

r. An ivory satin evening dress, decorated with beads and sequins, the over tunic gathered to a bow at the right hip, the bodice with label 'C Worth', the reverse numbered '84548', and a separate train, 1920s, train 67in (170cm) long.
$560–680 *P*

The gown worn by Joan Sutherland in the Mad Scene in Donizetti's *Lucia di Lammermoor*, Act III, designed by Franco Zeffirelli, at the Royal Opera House, Covent Garden, labelled with an inked name tag 'Miss Sutherland, Lucia di Lammermoor', and 'Zef. Mad Sc. 1' in ink, 1959.
$8,700–10,000 *S*

A gipsy costume, designed by José Varona, made by Barbara Matera, worn by Joan Sutherland in Donizetti's *Lucrezia Borgia*, Act I, at the Vancouver Opera, 1972.
$2,600–3,000 *S*

An ivory silk desert robe, worn by T. E. Lawrence, 'Lawrence of Arabia', together with a quantity of photocopies of correspondence.
$20,250–22,500 *S*

FANS

A printed fan, the leaf with an etching of vignettes of Queen Charlotte and the Prince of Wales, a ship, a sheep, a sheaf of corn, the reverse with inscription and Prince of Wales' feathers, decorated with cut paper work, with wooden sticks, c1760, 11in (28cm) wide.
$1,500–1,800 *CSK*

A fan with mother-of-pearl sticks, the paper panel decorated by the Hon Hugh Rowley, with a river landscape on one side, a spray of roses on the other, the sticks carved with a baronet's coronet and bellflower and swag ornament, 19thC, 12¾in (32.5cm) wide.
$2,000–2,250 *CAG*

A Chinese fan, the leaf painted with a cockerel by a flowering tree, inscribed, the reverse with sprays of flowers, the ivory sticks carved and pierced, late 18thC, 12in (30.5cm) wide.
$420–480 *CSK*

A fan, the ivory sticks carved, pierced and painted with figures and naval battle scenes, the leaf painted with a classical scene, the reverse with chinoiserie, the sticks carved with a face visible when closed, c1750, 10in (25.5cm) wide.
$525–600 *CSK*

A painted topographical fan, with a manor house within a river landscape, with figures and animals, the ivory sticks carved and pierced with figures, repaired, c1770, 11in (28cm) wide, in case, lid missing.
$2,250–2,700 *CSK*

A fan, the chicken skin leaf painted with a courting couple in woodland flanked by putti, the mother-of-pearl sticks pierced and gilded with musical trophies, 19thC, 11¼in (28.5cm) wide, with Duvelleroy case.
$850–930 *S(S)*

A wooden brisé fan, painted with 15 copies of Spy and Ape cartoons from *Vanity Fair* of Disraeli, Palmeston, the Marquess of Hartington, the Marquess of Lorne and others, the guardsticks with monogram 'AI' with crest above, c1865, 9in (23cm) wide.
$420–480 *CSK*

A fan, the silk leaf painted with a cat wearing a pink ribbon, signed 'A. Thomasse', the reverse signed 'Duvelleroy' and inscribed with a variety programme for 9 June, 1907, with wooden sticks studded with gilt sequins, 8in (20cm) wide.
$2,000–2,250 *CSK*

An Italian fan leaf, the paper ground painted in gouache depicting the Feast of Bacchus after the Carracci School, c1700, mounted in a giltwood and *verre eglomisé* frame, 12 x 20½in (30 x 52cm) wide.
$3,450–3,750 *P*

A fan of Flemish lace, worked with the arms of the King and Queen of the Belgians, the mother-of-pearl sticks carved and pierced with trophies of love, 1853, 11in (28cm) wide.
$6,750–7,500 *CSK*

A fan, painted with a pastiche of a *fête champêtre*, signed 'Vanier', the reverse with figures, the mother-of-pearl sticks carved, pierced and gilt with a lady, a hero and putti, c1850, 11in (28cm) wide.
$2,250–2,700 *CSK*

JEWELLERY
Bangles & Bracelets

A gold, blue enamel and diamond bracelet, designed as 3 lozenge-shaped panels, each decorated with floral motifs, set with a central diamond, monograms 'M' and 'IM' surmounted by coronets, inscribed, enamel imperfect, c1830.
$1,300–1,500 S

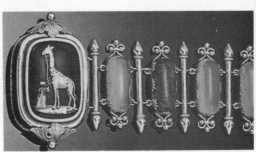

A gold, enamel and gem-set bracelet, designed as a row of baton-shaped links alternating with hardstones including stained chalcedony, agate and malachite, the clasp set with a malachite plaque applied with a later enamel giraffe within a foliate gold border, enamel imperfect, c1840.
$1,300–1,500 S

A gold and micro-mosaic bracelet, by Castellani, designed as a chain of 13 gold lentil-shaped links, both sides of the central micro-mosaics forming mottos, maker's mark, c1870.
$10,500–12,000 S

A Victorian gem-set gold and enamel bangle, by Carlo Giuliano, the band finely pierced with black and white trelliswork between lavender blue dots edged in black and white, the front with 3 cabochon garnets, signed 'C.G.', c1880, 2¼in (60mm) wide, in original tooled red leather case.
$10,500–12,000 C

A Victorian ruby and diamond half-hoop bangle, the front section set with alternate rubies and diamonds, with rose-cut diamond points and carved gallery to the hinged hoop, c1880, 2¼in (60mm) wide, in fitted Collingwood case.
$9,000–10,500 C

A Victorian turquoise and diamond bracelet, the central cluster with similar smaller shoulders, on a two-row Brazilian link bracelet with ribbon bow detail of 3 turquoise and diamond sections, c1870, 6½in (16.5cm) long, in later fitted case.
$3,000–3,750 C

A Victorian sapphire and diamond half-hoop bangle, set with 9 graduated sapphires with diamond spacers to the reeded hinged bangle, c1890, 2½in (65mm) wide.
$7,200–7,800 C

A diamond bracelet, designed as a row of old-mine diamonds supporting fringes styled as grapevines set with similarly cut stones, mounted in silver and gold, formerly part of a necklace, 19thC, 6½in (16.5cm) long.
$10,500–12,000 S(NY)

A pair of Victorian gold and Swiss enamel bracelets, each central panel painted as a floral spray, with enamelled openwork scroll surround to uniform openwork panel links.
$1,500–1,800 CSK

A gold and garnet bracelet, the central panel mounted with a porcelain plaque depicting a young girl, the surround with half-pearls, to a garnet and seed pearl cluster panel bracelet, repaired, 19thC.
$750–900 CSK

A gold and enamel hinged bangle, designed as a wide gold band set at the front with a Swiss enamel plaque depicting Raphael's *Madonna della Seggiola* within a gold beaded border, late 19thC.
$2,700–3,000 S

A late Victorian gem-set and gold fancy curb-link bracelet, each larger curb link alternately collet set with old brilliant-cut diamonds and mixed-cut sapphires, clasp stamped '15'.
$2,700–3,000 Bon

A Victorian medieval revivalist style gold bracelet, with foiled garnet and chain link panels.
$720–750 CSK

Brooches

An Edwardian diamond and untested pearl brooch, the trelliswork panel set with diamond, rose diamond and pearl decoration, with later brooch fittings.
$6,400–7,200 *CSK*

A Victorian aquamarine and diamond brooch, the pear-shaped drop suspended from an open scroll and foliate frame, mounted in silver and gold.
$3,000–3,750 *CSK*

A late Victorian emerald and diamond garland brooch/pendant, the square emerald within a border of old brilliant-cut diamonds, surrounded by diamond and pearl foliate swags beneath a bow, c1880, in fitted case.
$6,000–6,750 *Bon*

r. An enamel, pearl, emerald and diamond Renaissance revival brooch/pendant, with a pearl drop, and a silver chain set with step-cut emeralds and pearls, late 19thC.
$8,250–9,750 *S*

An early Victorian gold and aquamarine brooch, of Algerian knot and pendant design, interlaced with textured gold and aquamarine stylised buds, in a case.
$1,400–1,500 *CSK*

l. A diamond brooch/pendant, designed as a spray of eglantine set with cushion-shaped stones, with a detachable similarly set spray of leaves, late 19thC.
$26,250–30,000 *S*

r. A Victorian diamond flowerhead brooch, the centre mounted with an old mine cushion-shaped stone in a diamond cluster frame, with graduated diamonds set to the petals, c1865.
$8,250–9,750 *P*

A gold, aquamarine and diamond bar brooch, the central aquamarine framed by rose-cut diamonds, the corners with chased gold daisies, within a gold tapering bar with additional blossoms, c1900.
$3,400–4,000 *S(NY)*

Cameos

A shell cameo, depicting a classical scholar or wise man with a child, in a gold brooch mount with scrolling leaf decoration, 18thC.
$600–680 *CSK*

A hardstone cameo, within a granulated rope-twist border and matching frame, joined at the cardinal points, c1860.
$2,200–2,700 *Bon*

A Victorian shell landscape cameo, in a scrolled gold mount.
$825–975 *WL*

A shell cameo brooch, finely carved to depict a gentleman, within a fine gold ornate frame of scrolls and acanthus leaves, 19thC.
$600–680 *Bon*

An agate cameo, by Giuseppe Girometti, depicting the winged bust of Cupid, signed, in a Renaissance revival frame of polychrome enamel scroll motifs decorated with diamonds, pearls, rubies and emeralds, cameo mid-19thC, frame later.
$8,700–9,700 *S*

A gold and sardonyx cameo, set within a gold border of corded wire and foliate motifs, and a pair of matching pendant earrings, c1870.
$2,400–2,700 *S*

A cameo, depicting a scene from the Festival of Flora, with 2 classical female figures draping garlands on a statue, in a gold brooch mount with Etruscan wire and beadwork decoration, 19thC, in a fitted case.
$1,900–2,000 *CSK*

r. A French gold, hardstone cameo and split pearl brooch, the taupe and white agate carved with a classical head within a gold frame decorated with split pearls and rose-cut diamonds, a pendant hook at the top, 19thC.
$3,000–3,750 *S(NY)*

A gold, enamel, half-pearl and sardonyx cameo, by Castellani, depicting Medusa within a border of black and white enamel decorated with gold corded wire and mounted with 4 half-pearls at the cardinal points, maker's mark, c1860.
$9,750–11,250 *S*

A hardstone cameo, mounted as a brooch in a plain and wire-work silver surround, 19thC.
$1,500–1,800 *CSK*

A shell cameo, depicting a kneeling muse holding a cross beside a skull, in a gold brooch mount with engraved decoration, 19thC.
$300–360 *CSK*

Earrings

A pair of gold drop earrings, decorated with coronets, 19thC.
$380–450 *WL*

A pair of Victorian gold earrings, set with cabochon garnets.
$750–900 *WL*

A pair of Victorian gold earrings, with central blue enamel and half-pearl star drop, bead and wirework and applied foliate decoration, with later screw fittings.
$680–750 *CSK*

A pair of emerald and diamond earrings, each emerald drop with diamond-set cupola mount to a knife-edge and diamond collet line, mounted in silver and gold, c1890.
$6,750–7,500 *C*

A pair of Victorian gold drop earrings, in the Etruscan taste, the baluster-shaped drops suspended from an inverted horseshoe-shaped top and with applied bead and wirework decoration, some damage.
$680–750 *CSK*

A pair of Victorian pendant gold earrings, with original wires.
$630–730 *WL*

A pair of Victorian gold drop earrings, of openwork baluster design with wirework decoration and bead drop terminal.
$780–880 *CSK*

A pair of Victorian gold drop earrings, each modelled as an urn with applied bead and wirework decoration.
$720–840 *CSK*

Necklaces

A diamond rivière necklace, with collet two-stone spacers and larger collet clasp, mounted in silver, in closed back settings, c1810, 16in (41cm) long, in Collingwood case.
$24,400–27,000 *C*

A snake necklace, the gold graduated articulated links to a cabochon garnet head with cabochon garnet heart drop suspended from the mouth, 19thC.
$1,500–1,800 *CSK*

A ruby and chrysoprase fringe necklace, by Carlo Giuliano, in the Indian style, with openwork ruby foliate panels suspending cabochon chrysoprase drops with seed pearl surmounts, c1875, unsigned, clasp and safety chains adapted, 1 small stone missing, 15¾in (40cm) long, in original case.
$14,250–15,750 *C*

A Victorian opal and diamond necklace, the 7 graduated opal flowers set with heart-shaped opals, with central diamonds, diamond trefoil, collet and scroll spacers with opal detail to a knife edge and collet backchain, mounted in silver and gold, c1880, 14½in (37cm) long.
$10,750–12,750 *C*

A Victorian rock crystal and gem-set necklace, the 5 drops with applied ruby, sapphire or emerald and diamond flies with rock crystal and gem-set collet surmounts to a woven gold necklace with garland detail, and a pair of pendant earrings, c1880, 15¾in (40cm) long, in fitted case.
$9,500–10,500 *C*

A gold necklace, decorated with a row of pink topazes, with a fringe of pear-shaped pink topazes, spaced by links inset with split pearls, gold chain at the back, 19thC, 16in (40.5cm) long, and matching earrings with later screw-backs.
$4,500–5,250 *S(NY)*

r. A diamond pendant necklace, with a central cultured pearl drop within an openwork foliate frame to a diamond bow surmount, with diamond collet lines suspending a flexible diamond tassel with ribbon bow detail, to a link neckchain, c1905, pendant 3¼in (8.5cm) long.
$8,250–9,750 *C*

A Bohemian garnet necklace, the central cluster panel with twin cluster drops suspended from a cluster link necklet, 19thC.
$1,500–1,800 *CSK*

A Victorian diamond necklace/tiara, the fringe of openwork collet and scroll motifs with trefoil spacers to a knife edge and collet neckchain, mounted in silver and gold, c1880, 15½in (39cm) long, in fitted case.
$8,000–9,500 *C*

Pendants

A diamond pendant, decorated with sprays of cushion-shaped diamond foliate motifs, c1830. $68,250–75,000 *S*

A garnet and diamond pendant, the central garnet cabochon within a surround of 12 old brilliant-cut diamonds to pierced box settings, and rose-cut diamonds points, c1870. $4,500–5,250 *Bon*

A Victorian diamond and pearl pendant, the rose diamond capped untested pearl suspended within a diamond pear-shaped border, to a diamond collet two-stone surmount. $1,500–1,800 *CSK*

A ruby and diamond pendant, the central ruby and openwork diamond cluster with alternative ruby and diamond frame with pearl spacers to a pendant loop, mounted in gold, c1870, 2in (50mm) high. $3,300–3,700 *C*

A locket pendant, the locket with diamond and rose diamond star centre motif with rose diamond surround on pale blue enamel ground, the reverse with locket compartment containing a photograph, 19thC. $860–1,000 *CSK*

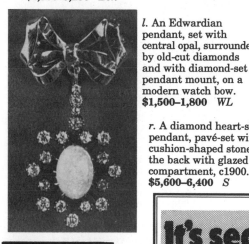

l. An Edwardian pendant, set with central opal, surrounded by old-cut diamonds and with diamond-set pendant mount, on a modern watch bow. $1,500–1,800 *WL*

r. A diamond heart-shaped pendant, pavé-set with cushion-shaped stones, the back with glazed compartment, c1900. $5,600–6,400 *S*

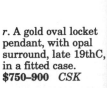

r. A gold oval locket pendant, with opal surround, late 19thC, in a fitted case. $750–900 *CSK*

A gold and triptych pendant, by Castellani, designed as 3 gold medallions decorated with micromosaics, the central medallion with a Greek cross within a Greek key and chequered border and with a gold acorn drop, the left with a portrait of the Virgin, the right with Christ, the rims decorated with corded wire, maker's monogram, c1865, in fitted wooden case. $33,000–39,000 *S*

Princess Salimah Aga Khan

The sale of jewellery belonging to the Princess Salimah Aga Khan achieved the highest total for a single owner sale of jewellery in Geneva since the Duchess of Windsor's jewels were sold in 1987. The jewels from the Princess's collection comprised a number of exceptional pieces, which were designed especially for her by the most celebrated jewellers, such as Boucheron, Cartier, Van Cleef & Arpels, Bulgari and Harry Winston. Each of the 238 lots found buyers, and the highlight of the sale – The Begum Blue, pictured here – set a new record for the highest price per carat for a blue diamond, whilst another blue diamond, mounted as a ring by Boucheron, set a new world record price. The attendance was so large that two additional salerooms were occupied, with bids being relayed by video link to the main auctioneer.

A pink coral, sapphire and diamond necklace, by Boivin, mounted in 18ct gold, French assay marks, 13¼in (33.5cm) long.
$22,500–27,000   *C(G)*

A clip brooch, by Van Cleef & Arpels, the pavé-set yellow diamond cartouche with diamond cluster centre and old European-cut diamond borders suspending a diamond briolette fringe, mounted in 18ct gold, signed, No. 26002, French assay marks.
$132,000–150,000   *C(G)*

A ruby and diamond brooch, by Harry Winston, designed as a calibré-cut ruby and circular-cut diamond cruciform, signed.
$19,000–21,000   *C(G)*

A sapphire, diamond and 18ct gold brooch, the white and yellow gold bouquet with diamond and sapphire detail gathered by a pavé-set diamond bow, English assay marks.
$5,600–6,400   *C(G)*

The Begum Blue, a deep blue diamond, weighing 13.78ct, and diamond, weighing 16.03ct, pendant necklace, by Poiray, the graduated heart-shaped diamond line with 2 detachable pendants, each in a collet mount with detachable heart-shaped diamond surmount, 13¾in (35cm) long.
$7,500,000+   *C(G)*

A pendant necklace, by Van Cleef & Arpels, designed as a pavé-set diamond and fluted emerald bead flower pendant suspending a series of ruby bead tassels with similar flower terminals to the ruby bead necklace with pavé-set diamond and fluted emerald bead spacers, each applied to the centre with a diamond collet, 16in (40.5cm) long, and a pair of ear pendants, mounted in 18ct gold, Nos. 11849 CS and 11921 CS, French assay marks.
$217,500–255,000   *C(G)*

A pair of coral and diamond earclips, each set with a cabochon coral drop in a circular and marquise-cut diamond three-quarter surround.
$9,000–10,500   *C(G)*

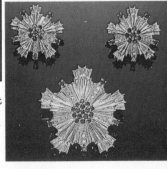

r. A sapphire and diamond clip brooch, designed as a circular-cut diamond and sapphire snowflake with sapphire cluster centre, and a pair of earclips, by Tiffany & Co, signed, No. AT2423905.
$11,250–13,500   *C(G)*

JACQUELINE KENNEDY ONASSIS
The Estate of Jacqueline Kennedy Onassis

This four-day sale attracted such enthusiastic bidding that the total realised for the first session alone was not far short of the estimate of $6.9 million for the entire sale. Comprising fine and decorative art, furniture, jewellery, antiquities and books, which came predominantly from the New York apartment where Jackie Onassis lived from 1964–94, the sale was a monument to her wide-ranging tastes, and was remarkable in that it took 19 specialists from Sotheby's to catalogue it.

Highlights of the sale included a Louis XVI ormolu-mounted bureau plat, a walnut humidor given to the President by Milton Berle, with an inscription which read 'To J.F.K. Good Health – Good Smoking', and an oak rocking chair which had belonged to the President. However, it was the charming, more personal objects in the sale which attracted the most bidding, such as the rocking horse which had been among the furnishings in Caroline Kennedy's nursery at the White House.

Jacqueline Kennedy Onassis was without doubt a most extraordinary woman, and this was reflected in the final prices realised for her possessions, so anxious were people to acquire a keepsake of the Kennedy's fascinating lives.

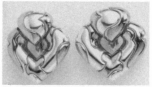

A pair of 18ct yellow and white gold earclips, signed 'MB' and 'Marina B'.
$37,500–45,000 *S(NY)*

A watercolour on paper, by Jacqueline Duhéme, *Jackie and Lee on a Camel*, signed, 6¼ x 7in (16 x 18cm).
$30,250–32,250 *S(NY)*

A French pair of diamond and enamel earclips, 2 diamonds missing, signed 'made in France' maker's mark, numbered '30760'.
$37,500–45,000 *S(NY)*

A Classical parcel gilt brass-mounted and ebonised mahogany swivel-top card table, by school of Charles Honore Lannuier, New York, restored, c1815, 36in (91.5cm) wide.
$107,250–127,500 *S(NY)*

An ebonised baby grand piano, by Henry F. Miller, together with a piano bench.
$167,250–182,250 *S(NY)*

An American child's rocking horse, covered with hide, fitted with leather saddle and bridle, on a brass-mounted maple platform, 50in (127cm) long.
$84,750–93,750 *S(NY)*

A Louis XVI ormolu-mounted mahogany bureau plat and cartonnier, with a gilt-tooled brown leather writing surface, signed 'E. Levasseur, JME', restored, 62½in (159cm) wide.
$477,500+ *S(NY)*
This is the desk on which the Nuclear Test Ban Treaty was signed by President Kennedy on October 7th, 1963.

A cabochon garnet and diamond flower brooch, mounted in gold, with fitted box stamped 'A La Vieille Russie, 781 Fifth Avenue, New York', 19thC.
$145,500–174,000 *S(NY)*

An oak rocking chair, with caned backrest and seat, together with loose cushions, stamped 'Manufacturer of the original Carolina Rocker P & P Chair Company Asheboro, North Carolina'.
$442,500+ *S(NY)*

r. Three framed prints of John Fitzgerald Kennedy, largest 15½ x 20in (39.5 x 51cm). **$22,800–24,750** *S(NY)*

l. A walnut humidor, with presentation plaque 'To J.F.K. Good Health – Good Smoking, Milton Berle – 1/20/61', 13in (33cm) wide. **$577,500+** *S(NY)*

A set of Ben Hogan power thrust golf irons, comprising irons 2–9, a wedge and a sand wedge, together with a black leather MacGregor bag, inscribed 'JFK Washington D.C.' **$390,000+** *S(NY)*

A bronze patinated plaster bust on a black composition base, by Robert Berk, John F.Kennedy: A Portrait Bust, inscribed '© Berk' and dated '68', 10in (25.5cm) high. **$40,500–45,000** *S(NY)*

The completed bronze portrait of John F. Kennedy, of which this bust is a patinated plaster version, was installed in time for the opening of the Kennedy Centre, Washington, DC, in September 1971. Berk's full-sized bronze is 96in (244cm) high and weighs 3,000 lbs.

John F. Kennedy, *Profiles in Courage*, published by Harper & Row, New York, 1964, photographic plates, blue morocco, covers gilt-panelled, 9 x 5¾in (23 x 14.5cm). **$68,250–75,000** *S(NY)*

This was one of two copies presented by the publisher to Mrs. John F. Kennedy and Robert F. Kennedy.

John F. Kennedy, *Memorial Addresses Delivered in Congress*, published by Government Printing Office, Washington 1964, photographic frontispiece portrait of J. F. Kennedy, blue morocco, front cover with gilt title, federal eagle and inscription 'Mrs. John F. Kennedy', 10¼ x 7in (26 x 18cm). **$34,500–37,500** *S(NY)*

This is Mrs. Kennedy's copy of the compilation of addresses and tributes given in the Senate and House of Representatives on the life and service of President Kennedy.

A charcoal on paper, by Elaine de Kooning, *Portrait of John F. Kennedy*, signed with initials and dated '63', 35 x 26in (89 x 66cm). **$102,000–111,000** *S(NY)*

r. A brown leather stetson hatbox, bearing a tag stating 'The President', 15in (38cm) wide. **$31,500–34,500** *S(NY)*

A gouache and watercolour, by Peter Paillon, *Study of a Snow Owl*, signed and dated '1755', 19½ x 14¾in (49.5 x 37.5cm). **$30,250–33,000** *S(NY)*

This painting was among the furnishings in Mrs Kennedy's bedroom at the White House.

ANTIQUITIES

A Mesopotamian alabaster unguent jar, in the form of a vulture, late Uruk, circa 3300 BC, 1¼in (3.5cm) high.
$7,200–8,200 *C*

An Egyptian bronze figure of the Goddess Isis, from an Isis and Horus group, Late period, 550–350 BC, 12½in (32cm) high.
$24,750–29,250 *S*

A Cypriot twin-handled bichrome amphora, the body and neck decorated in umber with parallel and wavy patterns, restored, Iron Age, circa 9th–7th century BC, 22in (56cm) high.
$1,200–1,400 *Bon*

An Egyptian mummy face mask, composed of multi-coloured beads, Ptolemaic period, after 300 BC, 6¾in (17cm) high, mounted, glazed and framed.
$1,500–1,800 *Bon*

An Egyptian cartonnage mummy mask, with gilded face and polychrome painted headdress, Roman period, BC 30–450 AD, 15in (38cm) high.
$5,700–6,700 *P*

A Corinthian black figure panel amphora, with cylindrical handles, each side painted with a cockerel, a rosette and spherical objects in the field, details added in red and white, circa mid-6th century BC, 13½in (34cm) high.
$15,000–18,000 *S(NY)*

A Romano-Egyptian stucco portrait head of a female, 1st century AD, 6in (15cm) high.
$3,000–3,600 *P*

A Laconian black figure kylix, attributed to the Hunt Painter, the tondo decorated with a komast scene, with radiate design on the underside, circa 6th century BC, 8¼in (21cm) diam.
$52,500–60,000 *C*

Three bronze ladles, each bowl decorated in relief, each with a long handle looped back and terminating in the head of an animal, all pierced for suspension, circa 5th–4th century BC, 6¾in (17cm) high.
$3,300–3,900 *C*

A Scythian silver-gilt appliqué, of square openwork form, with a stylised dragon's head and neck at each corner, circa 5th century BC, 1½in (4cm) square.
$15,750–18,750 *S*

A Greek Corinthian type bronze helmet, formed in one piece and fitted with a bronze split-peg for attaching a crest, retaining original mottled dark brown/green patina, damaged, circa 500–400 BC, 8¾in (22cm) high, including peg. **$21,000–24,000** *S(S)*

An Apulian red figure volute krater, decorated with figures and details in added yellow and white, on plugged foot, repaired, late 4th century BC, 30¾in (78cm) high. **$7,800–9,400** *C*

An Apulian red figure kernos, composed of 4 conjoined jars on pedestal feet, circa 4th–3rd century BC. **$2,700–3,000** *Bon*

An Etruscan pottery hydria, the front panel decorated with 2 human-headed sphinxes, with 2 sirens on the neck and white painted details, late 6th century BC, 16¾in (42.5cm) high. **$21,000–24,000** *S*

An Etruscan polychrome terracotta antefix, in the form of the head of a goddess, late 6th century BC, 10¾in (27cm) high. **£16,000–19,000** *S(NY)*

A Palmyran ribbed pottery amphora, in the shape of a bag, with 2 handles at the neck, body mishapen, circa 1st century BC/AD, 20in (51cm) high. **$380–450** *Bon*

r. A Persian dark-on-buff pottery storage jar, rim chipped, late 3rd millennium BC, 14in (35.5cm) high. **$4,500–6,300** *C*

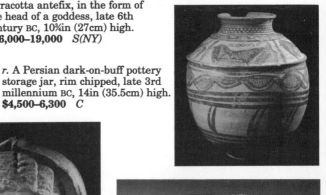

A Celtic sandstone moustached male head, with stylised features and engraved detail, circa 3rd–1st century BC, 2¼in (5.5cm) high. **$600–750** *Bon*

A Roman marble head of a woman, circa 1st century BC/AD, 14in (35.5cm) high. **$5,200–5,400** *S*

A Roman silver skyphos, with ovoid body, the twin flat winged thumb plates supported on foliate rings terminating in an ivy leaf, on stemmed foot, circa 1st century BC/AD, 4¼in (11cm) diam. **$5,700–6,300** *S*

An Anglo-Saxon gilded-bronze dress fastener, inlaid with niello and silver, circa 10th century AD, 1¼in (3cm) long.
$60–80 *ANG*

A Roman gold bracelet, of plain tubular form, the terminals twisted around each other forming spirals, 2nd–3rd century AD, 2¾in (7cm) wide.
$3,000–3,600 *S*

A Roman marble head of Apollo, after a Greek original of 4th century BC, 2nd century AD, 5in (12.5cm) high, mounted.
$7,500–9,000 *C*

An Anglo-Saxon gilded-bronze disc brooch, with chipped carved ornament incorporating central roundel containing angular face mask, 5th–6th century AD, 48mm diam.
$900–980 *ANG*

A Roman marble head of a veiled woman, repaired and restored, circa 160–180 AD, 10½in (26.5cm) high, mounted.
$24,250–27,000 *C*

A Hellenistic polychrome terracotta figure of a mourning woman, Magna Graecia, of attenuated form, circa 3rd century BC, 35½in (90cm) high.
$10,800–13,000

A Romano/British red and blue enamelled umbonate disc brooch, 2nd century AD, 22mm diam.
$60–80 *ANG*

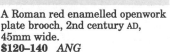

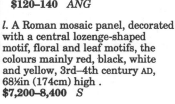

A Roman red enamelled openwork plate brooch, 2nd century AD, 45mm wide.
$120–140 *ANG*

l. A Roman mosaic panel, decorated with a central lozenge-shaped motif, floral and leaf motifs, the colours mainly red, black, white and yellow, 3rd–4th century AD, 68½in (174cm) high .
$7,200–8,400 *S*

PRE-COLUMBIAN ART OF CENTRAL & SOUTH AMERICA

A Nayarit seated couple, painted overall in reddish-brown and cream, the female holding a bowl, Ixtlán del Rio style, Protoclassic, circa 100 BC–AD 250, tallest 17in (43cm) high.
$14,250–15,750 *S(NY)*

A figure of mother and child, in greyish-white punctate ware, with incised decoration, damage to head, La Tolita Culture, Ecuador, circa 200 BC–AD 300, 3½in (9cm) high, with wooden stand.
$75–100 *ANG*

A Chinesco female figure, painted in red-brown, black and cream, type C, Protoclassic, circa 100 BC–AD 250, 11¼in (28.5cm) high.
$7,200–8,200 *S(NY)*

A Maya snarling jaguar head, one ear missing, Mexico, AD 600, 2in (5cm) high, with wooden stand.
$75–90 *ANG*

A figure of a shark, in greyish-white ware, slight damage, La Tolita Culture, Ecuador, circa 200 BC–AD 300, 4½in (11.5cm) long.
$180–210 *ANG*

A Mayan lidded tripod vessel, with cormorant's head handle to lid, decorated in brown and orange, Early Classic, circa AD 250–450, 10in (25.5cm) high.
$60,000–65,000 *S(NY)*

A Mayan polychrome vessel, painted in brown, black, white and dark orange, with 2 vertical glyph panels relating to death and the afterlife, Chamá region, Late Classic, circa AD 550–950, 6¾in (17cm) high.
$24,750–27,750 *S(NY)*

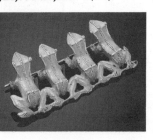

A Tiahuanaco gold mask, of hammered sheet repoussé with the physiognomy of the 'Face of the Sun', with distinctive streaming teardrops, pierced with 4 holes, circa AD 700–1100, 5½in (14cm) wide.
$24,750–27,000 *S(NY)*

r. A Veraguas gold pendant of frogs, consisting of 4 crouching frogs, circa AD 800–1500, 5in (12.5cm) wide.
$23,250–27,750 *S(NY)*

A Middle Chimu gold beaker, the stepped bands with rows of inlaid turquoise, pierced plaques and mother-of-pearl, Sicán, circa AD 1000–1250, mother-of-pearl possibly later, 7¼in (18.5cm) high.
$23,250–26,250 *S(NY)*

ETHNOGRAPHICA

A Bambara door lock, Mali, Africa, 20thC, 20in (51cm) high.
$100–120 *GOO*

A stone head, carved with incised cross-hatched coiffure, bulging eyes and distorted mouth and jaw line, Sierra Leone, 9½in (24cm) high.
$1,600–1,900 *P*

A Bambara N'tomo mask, Mali, Africa, 20thC, 21in (53cm) high.
$100–120 *GOO*

An Idoma currency blade, Nigeria, 20thC, 35in (89cm) high.
$100–120 *GOO*

A Bambara Tyiwara headdress, Mali, Africa, early 20thC, 36in (91.5cm) high.
$135–150 *GOO*

An Urhobo mask, with encrusted ochre, brown and white pigment, the broad forehead with vertical scarification, Nigeria, 17½in (44.5cm) high.
$5,250–6,000 *S(NY)*

A north west Edo processional or display image, with incised ornament and carved loincloth, possibly from Ishua, Nigeria, 35¾in (91cm) high.
$525–600 *CSK*

A Yoruba male twin figure, the coiffure with traces of blue pigment, the body with glossy red-brown patina, Oyo, west Africa, 10½in (27cm) high.
$675–825 *Bon*

A Keaka figure, Cameroons, 20thC, 24in (61cm) high.
$100–120 *GOO*

An Ashanti fertility doll, Ivory Coast, 20thC, 12¾in (32.5cm) high.
$150–180 *GOO*

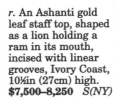

l. A beaded elephant mask, made from burlap and navy and crimson cloth, decorated with white, light blue, violet and lavender beads, Cameroons, 42½in (108cm) high.
$1,500–1,800 *S(NY)*

r. An Ashanti gold leaf staff top, shaped as a lion holding a ram in its mouth, incised with linear grooves, Ivory Coast, 10½in (27cm) high.
$7,500–8,250 *S(NY)*

A Songo carving representing a European trader riding an ox, standing on 2 birds, a male and female figure to each side within frames, on domed base, central Africa, 8½in (21.5cm) high.
$600–750 *Bon*

An Idoma dance headdress, with strongly carved features, keloid scarification to the forehead and temples, heightened in black on a kaolin pigmented face, west Africa, 14½in (37cm) high.
$2,500–2,700 *Bon*

A Sherbro stone figure, with large bulging eyes, standing on a circular base, head with recess, west Africa, 9¼in (23.5cm) high.
$525–400 *Bon*

A Tshokwe chair, with skin seat, both front legs carved with a female figure, the rungs decorated with scenes of daily life, with matt brown patina, Angola/Zaire, 42in (107cm) high.
$12,750–14,240 *S(NY)*

l. A Bakota Reliquary guardian figure, with 4 sections of striated copper on the face, embossed linear decoration, metal sheets attached with old nails, aged patina, Ivory Coast, 24½in (62cm) high.
$11,500–12,750 *S(NY)*

r. A Kongo fetish figure, the face with glass eyes and vertical cheek scarification, the top of the head with fetish cavity, nutty-brown patina, central Africa, 10½in (27cm) high.
$1,000–1,200 *Bon*

A Lobi terracotta head, with stippled coiffure, Africa, 9¼in (23.5cm) high.
$200–225 *CSK*

Two Senufo bas-relief granary doors, carved with figures, animals, birds, reptiles and masks, west Africa, 48½in (123cm) high.
$850–950 *Bon*

A Punu mask, the whitened face with pierced crescent eyes, the coiffure in 3 grooved lobes, Africa, 11½in (29cm) high.
$1,100–1,300 *CSK*

r. A Baule mask, with notched border to face, the eyes and mouth with traces of red and white pigments, black patina, Africa, 12½in (32cm) high.
$1,900–2,200 *CSK*

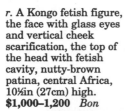

A Chokwe mask, with raised keloids to cheeks and temples and fibre hair sewn to the woven fibre headcovering, Africa, 7in (18cm) high. $750–900   CSK

A Chokwe mask, with keloids to cheeks, temples and forehead, the grooved coiffure in 3 lobes, whitened teeth, Africa, 8¾in (22cm) high. $450–525   CSK

A Lega mask, with dots on the forehead, fibre beard knotted at the chin and extensive kaolin encrustations, Africa, 5¾in (14.5cm) high. $2,200–2,700   CSK

An Aboriginal Melingimbi bird, with incised beak, decorated on the surface with an openwork cross-hatched motif of white and ochre on the breast and striated lines of black and white on an ochre field on the wings, Australia, 13in (33cm) high. $4,000–4,500   S(NY)

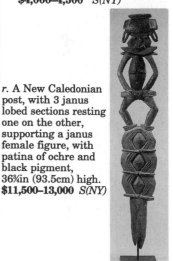

r. A New Caledonian post, with 3 janus lobed sections resting one on the other, supporting a janus female figure, with patina of ochre and black pigment, 36¾in (93.5cm) high. $11,500–13,000   S(NY)

A New Britain headdress, made from woven fibrous material sewn together over an open frame, a wooden nose, painted mouth and eyes, with a band of black feathers around the crown, 57in (145cm) high. $2,500–3,000   S(NY)

An important Cook Islands Raratonga head of a staff god, carved on the lower end with 5 miniature figures, 24in (61cm) high. $525,000+   S(NY)

A Bambara mask, carved as a hyena, with black patina, Africa, 18in (46cm) high. $700–750   CSK

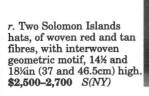

r. Two Solomon Islands hats, of woven red and tan fibres, with interwoven geometric motif, 14½ and 18¼in (37 and 46.5cm) high. $2,500–2,700   S(NY)

A pair of figures, probably Thonga, carved as an officer and his wife, east Africa, 18 and 19¼in (46 and 49cm) high. $975–1,125   CSK

BOOKS & BOOK ILLUSTRATIONS

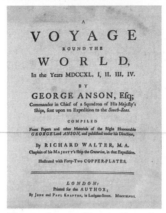

Eleazar Albin, (died c1741), *A Natural History of Birds . . . by . . . Albin . . . carefully colour'd by his Daughter and Self*, published in London, printed for the author, sold by John Clarke (vols I and II), William Innys and John Brindley, 1731–38, first edition, 3 vols, 4°, 306 fine hand-coloured etched plates after Eleazar, Elizabeth and Fortinalus Albin, by Henry Fletcher and others, coloured by Eleazar and Elizabeth Albin, with 3 hand-coloured impressions of a plate, titled 'Mites', by J. Scotin, mounted as frontispieces in each volume.
$14,500–16,500 *C*

George Anson, *Voyage Round the World*, published in London, 1748, illustrated, first edition, 4°, contemporary calf.
$980–1,200 *AG*

William Blake, illustrations of the 'Book of Job', engraved pictorial title page, 21 plates designed and engraved by William Blake, George Richmond's copy, 1825, largest plates 8¼ x 6½in (21 x 16.5cm).
$54,000–62,000 *S*

Samuel Curtis (1779–1860), *Monograph on the Genus Camellia . . . the whole from original drawings by Clara Maria Pope*, published in London by J. & J. Arch, 1819, large 2°, plates 28¼ x 23¼in (71.5 x 59cm), 5 fine grained aquatint plates, hand-coloured, by Weddell after Clara Maria Pope, in felt-lined purple morocco box.
$63,000–68,000 *C*

John James Audubon, *The Birds of America from Original Drawings*, reissued by J. W. Audubon, published in New York, by Roe Lockwood and Son, 1860, in sheets, second edition, 39¾ x 26½in (101 x 67.5cm).
$75,000–82,000 *S(NY)*

Frank L. Baum, *The Wonderful Wizard of Oz*, published in Chicago and New York, Geo. M. Hill Co, 1900, 24 colour plates and other illustratons by W. W. Denslow, first edition, square 8°, original pictorial cloth, slight damage.
$6,000–7,200 *CNY*

Book Sizes

The size or format of a book is expressed by the number of times a single sheet of paper is folded into the sections which, when gathered and sewn, make up the finished volume.
Shown below are some of the usual descriptions of sizes:

Folio:	1 fold	2 leaves	Fo or 2°
Quarto:	2 folds	4 leaves	4to or 4°
Octavo:	3 folds	8 leaves	8vo or 8°
Duodecimo:	4 folds	12 leaves	12mo or 12°
Sextodecimo:	5 folds	16 leaves	16mo or 16°
Vicesimo-quarto:	6 folds	24 leaves	24mo or 24°
Tricesimo-secundo:	7 folds	32 leaves	32mo or 32°

Guillaume Apollinaire, and André Derain, illustrator, *L'Enchanteur pourrissant*, published in Paris, by Henry Kahnweiler, 1909, limited edition, 4°, one of 75 copies signed by Apollinaire and Derain, half title, title printed in red and black, woodcut vignette to title, 12 woodcut plates after Derain, illustrations, some full page, inscribed, contemporary cloth, contrasting morocco.
$6,000–6,800 *CSK*

Geoffrey Chaucer, The Works, Kelmscott Press, *Hammersmith: William Morris at the Kelmscott Press, 1896*, 87 woodcut illustrations after Sir Edward Burne-Jones redrawn by Robert Catterson-Smith, cut by W. H. Hooper, designed by William Morris and cut by C. E. Keates, Hooper and W. Spielmeyer, printed in Chaucer type in black and red, in red morocco slipcase, damaged, 16¾ x 11½in (42.5 x 29cm).
$25,000–30,000 *S(NY)*

r. Charles Lutwidge Dodgson, (Lewis Carroll), and Marie Laurencin, *Alice in Wonderland*, published in Paris, by The Black Sun Press, 1930, oblong 8°, limited to 790 copies, this one of 350 of the American edition on Rives paper, 6 coloured lithographed plates by Laurencin, original wrappers, slipcase, worn.
$3,000–3,600 *CSK*

Warwick Goble, illustrator, *The Fairy Book, The Best Popular Fairy Stories Selected and Rendered Anew*, by Dinah Maria Mulock, later Mrs Craik, 1913, first edition, 4°, 32 colour plates, original gilt decorated cloth, slight damage.
$260–300 *DW*

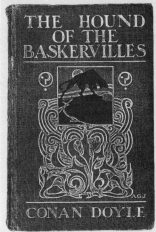

Arthur Conan Doyle, *The Hound of the Baskervilles*, 1902, first edition, first issue, 8°, half title present, 16 black and white illustrations after drawings by Sidney Paget, minor damage, original red cloth blocked in gilt, rubbed and slightly worn.
$320–400 *DW*

The Book of Hours, for the use of Rome, in Latin, illuminated manuscript on vellum, published probably in Paris, late 15thC, 97 leaves, 24 calendar miniatures, one small and 11 large miniatures, 6¾ x 4¾in (17 x 12cm).
$16,500–19,500 *P*

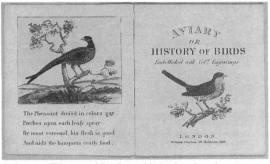

Aviary or History of Birds, published in London, by William Darton, 24°, hand-coloured vignette title and 11 hand-coloured engravings each depicting a bird above 4 lines of poetry, stitched as issued in original pink pictorial printed wrappers, rubbed.
$600–680 *P*

George du Maurier, a pair of ink drawings for cartoons, both entitled *A Contrast*, the second depicting Mr Punch, each signed with initials, framed and glazed, 7½ x 11½in (19 x 29cm).
$520–600 *S*

These drawings were published in Punch *in November 1873, and have labels for a Punch Exhibition and a Japan-British Exhibition, 1910.*

John Keats, *A Poetic Romance*, with engravings by John Buckland-Wright, printed in Great Britain at The Golden Cockerel Press, 1947, No. 359 of 500.
$380–450 *DW*

John Gould, *The Birds of Australia*, printed in London by Richard and John E. Taylor, published by the author, 1840–69, first edition, 8 vols. including supplement, 681 hand coloured lithographed plates, green half morocco, worn, 21¾ x 14¾in (54.5 x 37.5cm).
$96,000–100,000 *S(NY)*

Charles and Mary Lamb, *Tales from Shakespeare Designed for the Use of Young Persons*, published in London, by Thomas Hodgkins, 1807, first edition, first issue, 2 vols, 12°, engraved frontispieces and 18 plates after William Mulready.
$2,500–3,000 *CNY*

Antonio Locatelli, *Il Perfetto Cavaliere*, published in Milan, by Fratelli Sonzogno, c1825, 4°, 2 vols., with 76 lithographed and aquatint plates.
$1,200–1,400 *P*

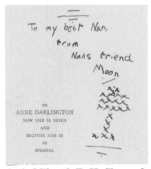

Jessie M. King, illustrator, *Mummy's Bedtime Story Book*, by 'Marion', published in London, by Cecil Palmer, 1929, 4°, bound in cloth.
$1,000–1,200 *DW*

A. A. Milne & E. H. Shepard, illustrator, *Now We Are Six*, published in New York, by E. P. Dutton, 1927, 8°, presentation copy from A. A. Milne and Christopher Robin to Olive Brockwell, signed and inscribed, original orange pictorial cloth gilt.
$5,600–6,000 *CSK*

Condition and Price of Books

Providing a guide to book prices is notoriously difficult. There are the purely bibliographical points of edition, issue, binding variants, etc, to take into account, but overall condition is a major determining factor. Some books are just so rare that almost anything is acceptable. The book should ideally be complete – advertisement leaves, half titles, etc, can be lost in re-binding and sometimes maps, even illustrations go missing – and most of today's collectors prefer to have their books as close as possible to the state in which they were first issued, untouched, in the original binding.

In the modern first editions market, a dust jacket is a must. Here, as in other book collecting fields, an author's signature or inscription, even an association can make a great difference to the price.

James Thomson & Adolphe Smith, *Street Life in London*, c1880, small 4°, including 36 mounted photographic plates.
$3,800–4,500 *HAM*

Edgar Allan Poe and Arthur Rackham, illustrator, *Tales of Mystery and Imagination*, 1935, 4°, one of 460 copies signed by the artist, including 12 mounted and coloured plates, pictorial endpapers, original decorative vellum, gilt, slight damage.
$900–1,000 *P*

l. William Upton, *The School Boy; a poem with coloured engravings*, 6 pages engraved throughout and hand-coloured at the pubisher's, the second leaf with the title, stitched as issued in original cerise stiff paper wrappers with a letterpress label in upper cover, 5¼ x 4in (13.5 x 10.5cm), imprint William Darton, 1820.
$680–750 *P*

Laurence Housman, illustrator, *Goblin Market*, by Christina Rossetti, published in London, by MacMillan & Co, 1893, 8°, black and white plates and illustrations, original gilt decoration to cloth designed by Housman, in dust jacket, frayed with loss to spine.
$560–640 *DW*

FURTHER READING

Catherine Porter, *Miller's Collecting Books*, Miller's Publications, London, 1995.

r. Ronald William Fordham Searle, 'Molesworth', signed and dated '1954', pen and brown ink and wash, unframed, from *How to be Topp*, published by Max Parris, London, 13 x 9in (33 x 23cm).
$1,200–1,400 *CSK*

l. Walt Whitman, *Leaves of Grass*, published in Brooklyn, New York, 1855, 4°, original dark green cloth gilt and blind stamped, first edition, first issue, with letter from Ralph Waldo Emerson to the author.
$50,000–54,000 *SK*

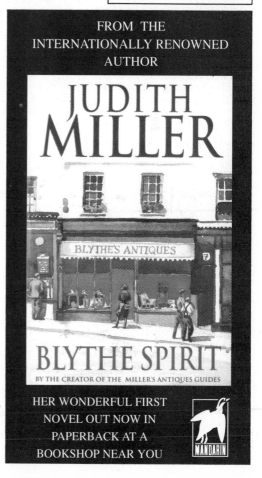

DOLLS
Wooden

A French carved and painted wooden doll, with blue eyes, cloth arms and wooden legs, in a silver thread embroidered bodice, brocaded skirt and train, green bonnet and yellow painted stockings and blue shoes, c1825, 24in (61cm) high.
$2,000–2,200 *S*

Wooden Dolls

Most very early wooden dolls were made in the traditional wood-carving areas of Germany and Austria from turned or carved wood. In Britain they were mainly made from about 1700, and shaped in the form of a skittle. The head and torso were carved from one piece and the hands were usually fork-like.

Wax

A wax-headed pedlar doll, the peg-jointed wooden body with kid-leather hands, in original clothing, the basket containing her wares, damaged, c1840, 9½in (24cm) high.
$720–820 *S*

A painted wooden doll, with painted features, rounded torso tapering to squared hips, jointed at hips and knees, and with painted orange heeled boots, arms missing, late 18thC, 24in (61cm) high.
$1,500–1,800 *S(S)*

Papier Mâché

A German papier mâché shoulder-headed doll, with painted features, the wooden body with tapered waist, square hips and peg-jointed limbs, yellow painted shoes, in original silk paper taffeta shot mauve and green tartan dress, damaged, c1830, 21¼in (54cm) high.
$1,400–1,600 *S*

A carved wooden doll, with blue enamel eyes, gessoed and painted features, with leather arms, jointed wooden legs, wearing original underpants, stockings, black silk shoes, 3 undergarments, a pocket and a dress with blue ribbons, with a matching necklace, damaged, c1828, 22½in (57cm) high.
$2,300–2,700 *Bon*

A papier mâché shoulder-headed doll, with kid body, carved wood arms and lower legs, in a cream dress with blue and brown stripes, damaged, c1825, 20in (51cm) high.
$5,300–6,300 *CSK*

---

l. A poured wax doll, with blue glass eyes, painted features, inserted blonde mohair wig, on a cloth body with poured wax lower limbs, dressed in lace trimmed red jacket and skirt, underwear and shoes, repaired, c1880, 20in (51cm) high.
$420–480 *Bon*

A poured wax shoulder-headed doll, with fixed blue glass eyes, inserted blonde real hair, cloth body, with poured wax lower limbs, in original pale blue silk dress, repaired, c1870, 21½in (54.5cm) high.
$1,300–1,500 *S*

A German wax-over-composition black and white two-faced doll, wearing a red dress and bonnet, damaged, c1890, 15in (38cm) high.
$980–1,200 *Bon*

A wax-over-composition shoulder-headed doll, with painted features, stuffed body, dressed in contemporary blue wool frock trimmed with black lace, fawn cape, silk hat and leather shoes, damaged, 19thC, 31in (79cm) high.
$1,000–1,200 *CSK*

Miscellaneous

A poured wax doll's house doll, dressed in original clothing, c1850, 6in (15cm) high, under a glass dome.
$1,000–1,200 *CSK*

A china shoulder-headed doll, with painted features, stuffed body, china limbs and green and white cotton striped gauze frock, c1850, 17½in (44.5cm) high.
$360–420 *CSK*

A French solid pate shoulder-headed doll, with painted features, blonde wig, kid-over-wood jointed arms with bisque forearms and a kid gusseted body, c1870, 10½in (27cm) high.
$3,800–4,500 *CSK*

A German group of composition shoulder-headed dolls, with painted features, dressed in contemporary clothing, c1910, 13½in (34cm) high.
$1,300–1,500 *CSK*

A German bisque shoulder-headed parian doll, with stuffed cloth body, in original clothing, unmarked, c1860, 13in (33cm) high.
$600–720 *YC*

r. A pair of German linen dolls, with embroidered faces, the gentleman with shirt and breeches in cream, the woman with dress and shawl in dark brown, late 17thC, 3¾in (9.5cm) high, and another with a wimple and habit in brown and cream.
$2,400–2,700 *P*

Bisque

A bisque doll, re-dressed, possibly French, c1910, 9½in (24cm) high.
$120–150 *PSA*

A bisque-headed doll, with fixed blue eyes, kid covered limbs, dressed as a pedlar, 19thC, 19in (48cm) high.
$1,300–1,500 *AH*

A bisque shoulder-head, with painted features, c1860, 5in (13cm) high.
$675–825 *CSK*

An all-bisque doll, with sleeping eyes and blonde wig, c1900, 5½in (14cm) high.
$270–320 *PSA*

A bisque black baby doll, No. AM351, repaired, c1920, 8½in (21.5cm) high.
$280–330 *PSA*

A French bisque swivel-head doll, with painted features, blonde wig and gusseted kid body, in original underclothes but later navy dress, c1865, 14½in (36.5cm) high, together with a quantity of clothes.
$1,500–1,800 *S(S)*

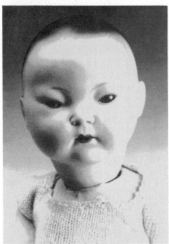

An Oriental bisque-headed baby doll, with weighted brown glass eyes, composition body, arms and legs, incised 'Germany 4', c1920, 18in (46cm) high.
$1,300–1,400 *Bon*

A French bisque jester doll, with open/closed mouth, fixed blue eyes, blonde wig, wooden body with squeeze box in chest causing hands to come together to play the cymbals, dressed in original costume, damaged, c1910, 14¾in (37cm) high.
$980–1,200 *S(S)*

A French bisque-headed doll, with jointed composition body, Limoges, wig and outfit replaced, c1920, 17in (43cm) high.
$450–530 *YC*

Selected Makers

An Alt, Beck & Gottschalck bisque socket-head doll, with mohair wig, closing blue glass eyes, painted features, the composition body with moving bent limbs, wearing a gold satin dress with pantaloons, head stamped monogram 'ABG 1361/45 Made in Germany', c1907, 20in (51cm) high.
$420–480 *P(HSS)*

r. A Bähr & Pröschild shoulder plate doll, with kid body and bisque lower arms, in original clothing, c1880, 14½in (36.5cm) high.
$600–680 *PSA*

l. A Bähr & Pröschild shoulder-headed doll, with brown sleeping eyes, blonde wig, jointed kid body with bisque arms and fairy dress, with wired wings and wand, impressed '309 2', c1890, 13in (33cm) high.
$520–600 *CSK*

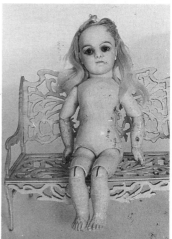

r. A Bru bisque-headed doll, with open/closed mouth, fixed brown eyes, blonde wig on cork pate, composition body with jointed wooden arms and legs, impressed 'Bru.Jne 2', c1880, 10in (25.5cm) high.
$3,800–4,500 *WW*

l. A Chad Valley doll, by Mabel Lucie Attwell, with felt face, brown mohair wig and velvet covered body, dressed in original clothing, c1920, 14in (35.5cm) high, in original box marked with labels 'Bye Bye Box' and 'Mabel Lucie Attwell'.
$1,800–2,200 *CSK*

MILLER'S COMPARES . . .

I A Chad Valley pressed felt Snow White and the Seven Dwarfs, Snow White with painted face and black mohair wig, her cloth body jointed at neck, shoulders and hips, wearing original blue and pink dress and pink shoes, each dwarf with spray-dyed and painted face, all wearing original costumes, each dwarf with textile label, c1938, Snow White 16in (40.5cm), dwarfs 6¼in (16cm) high, with original boxes.
$4,800–6,800 *S*

II A Chad Valley Snow White and the Seven Dwarfs, Snow White with painted face and black mohair wig, her cloth body jointed at neck, shoulders and hips, wearing original yellow, blue and pink dress, with 'Chad Valley' label to foot, each dwarf with spray-dyed and painted face, all wearing original costumes, Snow White shoes and her hair ribbon missing, 2 dwarfs' belts missing, c1938, Snow White 16in (40.5cm), dwarfs 10in (25.5cm) high.
$1,200–1,300 *S*

These two sets of Snow White and the Seven Dwarfs were sold in the same auction but one fetched four times the price of the other. The condition of an item is a major factor when establishing its value, and it can be seen from the photograph of *item II* and its accompanying caption that Snow White has lost her hair ribbon and shoes and some of the dwarfs are missing their belts. All the figures in *item I* are in immaculate condition, the colours being very fresh and with excellent detail on their faces, no doubt partly because they are still in their original boxes, an important factor with collectors. The dwarfs in *item I* are also smaller in relation to Snow White than those in *item II* which makes them more desirable, and quite unusual. *S*

A Cuno & Otto Dressel shoulder plate doll, in original dress, mould No. 1896, c1890, 16½in (42cm) high.
$450–530 *PSA*

A Max Handwerck Bébé Elite bisque-headed doll, mould No. 286, with sleeping eyes, original mohair wig, jointed composition body, c1910, 25in (63.5cm) high.
$720–780 *YC*

A Gebrüder Heubach bisque-headed doll, mould No. 7977, with intaglio painted eyes, jointed composition body, original clothing, c1910, 15in (38cm) high.
$3,000–3,300 *YC*

A Gebrüder Heubach Einco bisque character googly doll, with blue glass eyes, the eye movement activated by a lever to the rear of the head, blonde real hair wig, bent limb composition body, in green woollen army uniform, damaged, impressed, c1912, 17in (43cm) high, together with 3 other garments.
$6,600–7,600 *S*

A Farnell musical movement character doll, the brown velvet head with painted features, dressed in blue and white striped cotton frock and turban, marked with the Farnell Alpha Toys label, c1930, 14in (35.5cm) high.
$720–780 *CSK*

A Tête Jumeau bisque-headed doll, with brown paperweight eyes, blonde mohair wig, on a jointed wooden and composition body, wearing a whitework dress and cream cape, slight damage, red mark 'Deposé Tête Jumeau 13', c1880, 29½in (75cm) high.
$1,800–2,200
A Jumeau bisque-head doll, with brown paperweight eyes, auburn mohair wig, on a jointed wood and composition body, in a blue sailor suit, blue mark 'Jumeau Medaille d'or, Paris, red mark 'Deposé, Tête Jumeau, 7', c1880, 17in (43cm) high.
$2,400–2,700 *Bon*

A Heubach Koppelsdorf bisque-headed doll, with blue eyes, open mouth, 2 teeth and moving tongue, brown hair, and a composition body, early 20thC, 20in (51cm) high.
$300–360 *P(F)*

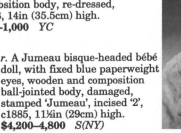

l. An Ernst Heubach Oriental bisque-headed baby doll, with composition body, re-dressed, c1918, 14in (35.5cm) high.
$900–1,000 *YC*

r. A Jumeau bisque-headed bébé doll, with fixed blue paperweight eyes, wooden and composition ball-jointed body, damaged, stamped 'Jumeau', incised '2', c1885, 11½in (29cm) high.
$4,200–4,800 *S(NY)*

A Kämmer & Reinhardt doll, with original wig, and underclothes, c1900, 9½in (24cm) high.
$380–420 *PSA*

A Kämmer & Reinhardt bisque character doll, with blonde real hair wig, weighted brown glass eyes, jointed bent limb composition body, wearing a white cotton christening robe, firing line on neck, impressed 'K•R 116/A 28', c1911, 12in (30.5cm) high.
$2,000–2,250 *S*

A German bisque doll, probably Kestner, with weighted brown eyes, open mouth and ball-jointed wood and composition body, wig replaced, pate missing, impressed '264 4', c1916, 23in (59cm) high.
$750–900 *S(S)*

A Kestner bisque-headed character baby doll, with brown brush-stroke hair, brown paperweight eyes, open/closed mouth and a composition body, wearing a gown and underwear, incised 'JDK', c1900, 12½in (32cm) high.
$560–660 *Bon*

A Kestner bisque character doll, with blonde mohair wig, weighted brown glass eyes, open mouth with upper teeth and ball-jointed wood and composition body, wearing a cream woollen dress, slight damage, impressed '192 6', c1910, 16in (40.5cm) high, together with her trunk and accessories.
$1,500–2,000 *S*

A Kestner bisque-headed doll, with wig, sleeping eyes and bent limb baby body, c1915, 18in (45.5cm) high.
$980–1,200 *YC*

A Kestner bisque character doll, with brown intaglio eyes, open/closed mouth, domed head and bent limb composition body, impressed '152', c1897, 9in (23cm) high.
$530–600 *S(S)*

A Kämmer & Reinhardt 'Flirty-Eye' doll, mould No. 126, c1920, 17in (43cm) high.
$750–900 *PSA*

A Kestner bisque-headed character doll, with brown mohair wig, blue-lashed sleeping eyes and jointed wood and composition toddler body, wearing original white tucked and lace trimmed dress, bonnet, underwear and shoes, impressed 'J.D.K. 260 27', c1920, 12½in (32cm) high.
$1,300–1,500 *CSK*

A Kestner bisque-headed character doll, with blonde mohair wig, blue sleeping eyes and bent limb composition body with voice box, wearing a cream silk, swansdown trimmed jacket, bonnet and dress, underwear, shoes and socks, one eye loose, impressed 'J.D.K. 257', c1914, 22in (56cm) high, together with extra clothing.
$1,000–1,200 *CSK*

A Käthe Kruse *Du Mein* cloth doll, with brush-stroke hair, floppy neck, painted features and cloth and sand-filled body damaged and repaired, signature and faded number on left foot, c1930, 18½in (47cm) high.
$3,000–3,600 *S(S)*

A Kling bisque shoulder-headed 'Scot's Boy' doll, with bisque arms and legs and cloth body, c1890, 10in (25.5cm) high.
$180–230 *YC*

A Kling shoulder-headed doll, with domed head, blonde mohair wig, blue eyes, bisque arms and cloth body, wearing original Swiss Regional costume, c1890, 10in (25.5cm) high.
$480–580 *CSK*

An all bisque miniature doll, possibly by Kling, clothes replaced, c1890, 5½in (14cm) high.
$300–380 *PSA*

r. A Lenci felt doll, with auburn wig, 5-piece body, painted features, the brown eyes looking to the left, the 2 middle fingers stitched together, dressed as an Italian officer, slight damage, c1930, 16in (41cm) high.
$2,300–2,700 *S(S)*

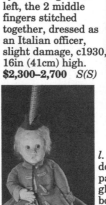

l. A Lenci pressed felt doll, with blonde wig, painted features, brown glass 'flirty-eyes', the body jointed at the hip and stitched at the shoulder, separately stitched fingers, wearing original costume, stains to face, c1930, 20in (50cm) high.
$1,800–2,000 *S(S)*

An Armand Marseille bisque-headed character doll, with brown mohair wig, blue sleeping eyes and bent limb composition body, wearing original spotted muslin dress and underwear, arms need re-stringing, impressed '700', c1920, 11in (28cm) high.
$1,800–2,000 *CSK*

An Armand Marseille bisque-headed doll, with original mohair wig, sleeping eyes and jointed composition body, wearing clothes made from old material, c1894, 16in (40.5cm) high.
$380–450 *YC*

An Armand Marseille bisque-headed doll, with original mohair wig, sleeping eyes and composition toddler body, c1925, 18in (45.5cm) high.
$330–420 *YC*

A Montanari poured wax shoulder doll, with inserted blonde hair, fixed blue glass eyes, cloth body and poured wax lower arms, wearing original costume, slight damage, with ink inscription 'Montanari, Counter 180, Soho Bazaar', c1860, 23in (59cm) high.
$2,000–2,600 *S(S)*

A pair of Ichimatza Ningyo dolls, the boy with painted hair, the girl with black wig, both with inset eyes and pierced nostrils, wearing original clothing, on black stands, c1950, 20in (51cm) high.
$1,800–2,000 *CSK*

A Revalo coquette doll, with moulded blonde hair, grey intaglio eyes, open/closed mouth with painted teeth, jointed cotton body, wood and composition arms, wearing original clothing, c1925, 13in (33cm) high.
$520–600 *CSK*

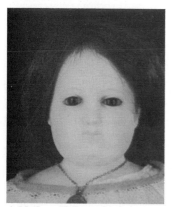

A Madame Rohmer bisque shoulder doll, with brown real hair wig over cork pate, fixed blue glass eyes, gussetted kid body and wood and bisque forearms, 6 fingers missing, impressed '5', c1870, 19in (49cm) high.
$1,000–1,200 *S(S)*

A Schmidt wax-over-composition girl doll, with blonde real hair wig, set blue glass eyes, moulded and painted features, wearing lace-inserted dress, underwear, shoes, socks, coat and bonnet and cream cape trimmed in duck down, c1880, 20in (51cm) high.
$1,500–1,800 *Bon*

A Simon & Halbig doll, made for Swaine & Co, with sleeping eyes and jointed body, clothing replaced, c1900, 19in (48.5cm) high.
$750–830 *PSA*

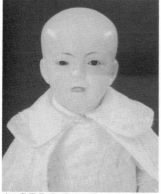

An S.F.B.J. character boy doll, with domed brush-stroke head, fixed blue glass eyes, open/closed mouth and jointed wood and composition body, wearing original costume, impressed '226 4', c1910, 13in (33cm) high.
$1,200–1,400 *S(S)*

l. An S.F.B.J. character boy doll, with brown brush-stroke hair, grey paperweight eyes, open/closed mouth with 6 painted moulded teeth and jointed wood and composition body, with paper label, incised '227', c1910, 15½in (39.5cm) high.
$980–1,200 *Bon*

A girl doll with Simon & Halbig head and Jumeau body, wig and clothing replaced, c1890, 23in (58.5cm) high.
$750–900 *YC*

A Simon & Halbig bisque-headed lady doll, with blonde mohair wig, blue glass sleeping eyes, jointed composition body, wearing fur-trimmed coat and hat, impressed '1159', c1910, 13in (33cm) high.
$500–680 *SK*

A Jules Steiner pressed bisque doll, with brown real hair wig, fixed blue glass paperweight eyes, open/closed mouth, jointed papier mâché body with sticker, wearing peach dress, slight damage, impressed 'J. Steiner Bte S.G.D.G. Fire A9', c1885, 16½in (42cm) high.
$8,500–9,800 *S*

A Jules Steiner walking doll, with bisque socket head, blonde mohair wig, fixed blue glass eyes, painted eyebrows and lashes, open mouth with moulded teeth, shoulders and moving arms, with pressed cardboard skirt enclosing inoperative clockwork mechanism, with winding key, the doll wearing a lace-trimmed cotton skirt and petticoat, c1880, 14½in (37cm) high.
$1,800–2,000 *P(HSS)*

This doll is accompanied by a letter addressed to the original owner, Miss Mary Ann Storey of Creswell, Mansfield, dated 1894, from her friend Princess Marguerite, Windsor Castle.

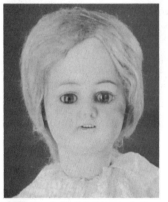

A Simon & Halbig bisque doll, with weighted brown eyes and ball-jointed wood and composition body, wearing cream silk jacket, chipped to back of head, impressed '1078', c1890, 24in (61cm) high.
$780–900 *S(S)*

A Jules Steiner crying doll, with original blonde mohair wig, blue paperweight eyes, open mouth with teeth, composition arms and legs, legs need connecting to working mechanism, late 19thC, 17½in (44.5cm) high.
$1,500–1,800 *SK(B)*

Jules Steiner

Jules Steiner was a clockmaker by trade, hence the number of mechanical walking and talking dolls produced at his factory in Paris in the latter part of the 19th century. The company is also particularly famous for their production of bébés, a term used to describe French dolls representing a child from infancy to about 7 years old.

Dolls' Accessories

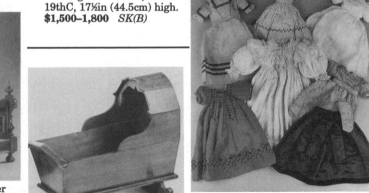

A doll's mahogany half tester bed, with moulded canopy, curtain rail with wooden rings, slatted wooden base, curved bed end with turned supports and finials, with mattress, late 19thC, 26in (66cm) long.
$750–900 *S(S)*

A doll's mahogany and pine cradle, with hooded canopy, 19thC, 19in (48.5cm) long.
$230–270 *Oli*

A selection of dolls' clothes, including a striped printed cotton dress trimmed with braid, a grey challis dress trimmed with bright blue velvet, a tucked cotton and a red wool dress, mid-19thC.
$1,200–1,300 *CSK*

DOLLS' HOUSES

A painted wooden model of Combe Hall in the 18thC, furnished and decorated by Mrs Haskell, c1920, 26in (66cm) wide, late 18thC, and an album of other houses.
$5,250–6,000 *CSK*

A painted and carved dolls' house, named 'Brigg House', with contents, façade cracked, late 19thC, 39¼in (100cm) wide.
$4,500–5,300 *S*

A painted and carved dolls' house, named 'Christie', wired for electricity, façade split, c1900, 38in (96.5cm) wide.
$1,500–1,800 *S*

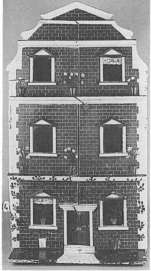

An Edwardian style town house dolls' house, the two-section front opening to reveal 5 rooms, damaged and restored, early 20thC, 20½in (52cm) wide.
$560–660 *Bon*

A Triangtois mock Tudor dolls' house, fitted for electricity, with contents, including a Dol-Toi bedroom suite, Art Deco furniture, a grand piano, an H & S metal vacuum cleaner, on a plinth base, 1930s, 47in (120cm) wide.
$680–750 *Gam*

A Moritz Gottschalk dolls' house, model No. 166/11, with a blue roof, lithographed paper on wood façade, with contents, stamped, c1900, 6in (15cm) wide.
$1,100–1,300 *CSK*

A Bliss dolls' house, yellow and blue lithographed, with 'Mrs Crackerjack', a paper doll and miniature furniture, slight damage, American, c1910, 11in (28cm) high.
$450–530 *Bon*

A painted and carved dolls' house, named 'Annabelle House', with electrical fittings, 20thC, 31in (79cm) wide.
$1,200–1,400 *S*

r. A painted and carved dolls' house, named 'Ivy Cottage', damaged, 20thC, 36in (91.5cm) wide.
$3,000–3,800 *S*

A Bliss dolls' house, paper lithographed, multi-coloured, American, marked 'R. Bliss' on the door, c1910, 14in (35.5cm) high.
$980–1,200 *Bon*

Dolls' House Accessories

A French panelled oak room setting, the contents on a 1:12 scale, with bronze stags' head trophies, candle arms and an ormolu mirror on the walls, a large quantity of 18thC style furniture including an apprentice piece by Denis Weigel of a cylinder bureau, other furniture by Patricia Herbillon, Viennese bronzes, an ivorine mantel clock, pair of porcelain vases and candlesticks, and a composition doll, c1900, 51½in (131cm) wide.
$31,500–37,500 *S*

A collection of German dolls' house furniture and accessories, including a Walterhausen piano, a sewing table with lift-off lid, a purple silk settee and 5 chairs, marble-top bureaux, dressers, a chest of drawers, beds, kitchen furniture and accessories, and 2 metal fireplaces, c1870.
$2,400–3,000 *Bon*

A collection of German dolls' house furniture and birdcages, including an R. Bliss dresser, and a clockwork clock birdcage, c1900.
$1,200–1,400 *Bon*

A collection of dolls' garden accessories, by Britains and others, including a No. 053 Span Roof Greenhouse, in original box, some damage, 20thC.
$1,300–1,500 *S(S)*

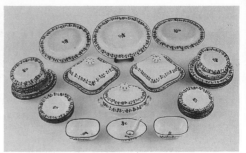

A Victorian Wedgwood creamware dolls' 54-piece dinner service, each piece with painted green leaf borders and puce rims, impressed factory marks, c1840.
$760–980 *WL*

A collection of dolls' fashion accessories and dolls' house glass, comprising a leather and brass button-covered picnic bag, with contents, 2 pairs of scissors, a set of pen and watercolour playing cards, a carved bone and seed box with silver spoons, hand-painted flowered dishes and gilt blown glass decanters and glasses, c1880.
$1,200–1,400 *Bon*

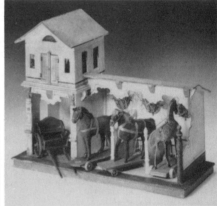

A German painted and carved dolls' stable, the façade painted yellow, green and red, the ground floor entrance flanked by painted Corinthian columns, original papered tiled floor, together with 3 horses, and a wooden cart, slight damage, c1900, 28½in (72.5cm) wide.
$1,300–1,500 *S*

A dolls' conservatory, with Perspex windows, black and white tiled floor and door, a painted wall surround on 3 sides of a garden, named 'Secret Garden', containing items including trees, flower borders, statues, ponds and a dovecote, and 3 modern dolls, 20thC, 69in (175.5cm) wide.
$1,200–1,400 *S*

TEDDY BEARS

A French journalist, when asked to cover the tourist potential of a certain English town, wrote 'all shops in the town have teddy bears in their windows and one particular shop, obviously the house of bears, has 700 of them in every shape, colour and size. The proprietor of this shop boasts of a customer list, male and female, ranging in age from one day old to 86 years!' The popularity of teddy bears extends to a large number of countries worldwide, not just Britain, and so much so that a new word, 'Arctophile' (from the Greek *arctos* – bear and *philos* – love), entered the language some years ago to describe collectors of teddy bears.

It is not difficult to understand the ever-increasing demand for teddy bears as collectables and whilst there are now more collectors of new bears there is still a very exciting market for bears made prior to 1914, as well as those dating from the 1920s and 1950s. When a 1926 Steiff bear called 'Happy' fetched a record-breaking $82,500 at Sotheby's in 1989, it was felt that circumstances had perhaps led to an unrealistic figure. A few years later at Christie's, the late Colonel Henderson's 1904

Steiff bear 'Teddy Girl' literally ridiculed the previous figure with a new record of $165,000.

The history of the teddy bear began in 1902 with a hunting expedition in the United States led by President Theodore (Teddy) Roosevelt who refused to shoot a defenceless bear cub. A cartoonist called Berryman drew the incident for the national press and Teddy's bear was born. By coincidence King Edward VII, known as Teddy to his friends, ascended the English throne in 1902 so there was a Teddy on each side of the Atlantic. The famous German company, Steiff, founded in 1877 by Margarete Steiff, was able to take full advantage of the sudden extreme popularity of the teddy bear and a new jointed bear which could be dressed, cuddled and loved was created by Richard Steiff, her nephew, in 1902. Steiff's records show that they made 12,000 bears in 1904 and an astounding 974,000 in 1907. Since then many other manufacturers of toys have produced teddy bears, such as Farnell, Dean's, Chad Valley, Merrythought and Chiltern.

Richard Tatham

A Chad Valley teddy bear, with long mohair, labelled, 1950s, 16in (40.5cm) high.
$525–560 *CMF*

Chad Valley

Chad Valley, one of England's major toy manufacturers, was established in Birmingham but later moved to Wellington in Shropshire. The firm produced teddy bears, as well as other soft toys, from the 1920s. Production of bears continued throughout World War II, although they were made with shorter mohair and less refined stuffing than usual. The company went public in 1950, took over the Chiltern Toy Works (another important producer of bears) in 1967, and was itself bought by Palitoy in 1978. At this time all the company's records and previous catalogues were destroyed and its bears can, therefore, be difficult to date.

A Chad Valley teddy bear, with pink mohair, brown glass eyes, black embroidered nose and mouth, fully jointed, kapok filled, cream velvet pads, worn, 1950s, 16in (40.5cm) high.
$374–420
A Merrythought teddy bear, with gold mohair, brown glass eyes, black embroidered nose and mouth, small ears, fully jointed, kapok and excelsior filled, gold felt pads, 4 claws, small hump on back, 1930s, 19in (48.5cm) high.
$575–625 *Bon*

A Chad Valley teddy bear, with golden curly mohair, deep amber and black glass eyes, black stitched button nose and mouth, centre face seam, swivel head, long jointed limbs, Rexine pads, label stitched to chest seam and right foot pad, slight damage, 1950s, 30in (76cm) high.
$600–700
A Chad Valley teddy bear, named 'Peter', with golden mohair, amber and black plastic eyes, black stitched button nose, mouth and claws, swivel head, jointed limbs, Rexine pads, cardboard-lined feet and label stitched to right side seam, c1950, 11in (28cm) high.
$330–400 *CSK*

l. A Chiltern teddy bear, with golden mohair, deep amber and black glass eyes, pronounced clipped snout, black stitched nose, mouth and claws, swivel head, jointed shaped limbs, velvet pads and cardboard-lined feet, slight wear, 1930s, 12in (30.5cm) high.
$420–500 *CSK*

A Dean's teddy bear, designed by Silvia Willgoss, with black mohair, black rubber nose, lips and eyelids, white mohair snout, brown plastic eyes, large ears, in sitting position, labelled, slight wear, 1950s, 18in (45.5cm) high.
$1,125–1,275 *Bon*

A Dean's Gwentoy teddy bear, with label, 1970s, 18in (45.5cm) high.
$100–130 *CMF*

A Farnell teddy bear, with golden mohair, clear and black glass eyes painted on reverse, pronounced clipped snout, black stitched nose, mouth and claws, swivel head, jointed shaped limbs, felt pads, webbed paw claws and cardboard lined feet, one ear missing, small repair, 1920s, 17in (43cm) high.
$1,500–1,800 *CSK*

A Farnell teddy bear, with golden mohair, deep amber and black glass eyes, pronounced clipped snout, black stitched nose, mouth and claws, swivel head, jointed shaped limbs, felt pads, webbed paw claws, cardboard lined feet, hump and squeaker, eyes replaced, 1920s, 16in (40.5cm) high.
$1,300–1,500 *CSK*

A Farnell teddy bear, with golden mohair, large brown and black glass eyes, pronounced clipped snout, black stitched nose and claws, swivel head, long jointed shaped limbs, felt pads, webbed paw claws, large shaped feet and hump, damaged, c1920, 25in (63.5cm) high.
$1,200–1,400 *CSK*

A German S.A.F. teddy bear, with long cream mohair, brown glass eyes, cream mohair trimmed snout, brown embroidered nose, open mouth, red felt tongue, small ears, fully jointed, excelsior filled, cream felt pads, begging arms, pink checked ribbon, labelled on right ear, 1930s, 20in (51cm) high.
$675–750 *Bon*

A Merrythought teddy bear, with curly pink/lilac mohair, clear and black glass eyes, pronounced clipped snout, large ears, black stitched nose and claws, swivel head, jointed shaped limbs, webbed paw claws and linen pads, damaged, 1930s, 35in (89cm) high.
$300–360 *CSK*

A Steiff teddy bear, with honey mohair, black button eyes, embroidered nose, mouth and claws, excelsior stuffing, fully jointed, ear button missing, some damage, c1906, 27in (68.5cm) high.
$10,500–12,000 *SK*

l. A Schuco black and white teddy bear, fully jointed, 1930s, 3½in (9cm) high.
$300–350
r. A Schuco cinnamon teddy bear, fully jointed, 1940s, 4½in (11.5cm) high.
$270–300 *CMF*

A Steiff centre seam teddy bear, with golden mohair, black boot button eyes, pronounced clipped snout, black stitched nose, mouth and claws, swivel head, elongated jointed shaped limbs, felt pads and hump, growler broken, worn, c1908, 16in (40.5cm) high.
$1,500–1,800 *CSK*

A Steiff teddy bear, with long gold plush fur, cup-shaped ears, black boot button eyes, pointed snout with 3 seams, stitched nose over black felt, long moving limbs with later felt pads, humped back, excelsior filled, with growl box, button to ear, some wear, c1905, 25in (63.5cm) high.
$6,000–6,750 *P(HSS)*

A Steiff centre seam teddy bear, covered in dark blonde mohair plush, black boot button eyes, pronounced clipped snout, black stitched nose, mouth and claws, swivel head, elongated limbs, large paws, slight hump, damaged and worn, c1908, 15½in (39.5cm) high.
$2,400–2,700 *DN*

A Steiff cinnamon centre seam teddy bear, with curly mohair, black boot button eyes, pronounced clipped snout, remains of black stitched nose, mouth and claws, swivel head, elongated jointed shaped limbs, felt pads, large card reinforced feet, hump and button in ear, worn, c1908, 24in (61cm) high.
$5,000–5,500 *CSK*

A Steiff centre seam teddy bear, white plush, with beige stitched snout, black boot button eyes, wide apart pricked ears, hump back, swivel joints, excelsior stuffed, growler, button removed, damaged, c1908, 24in (61cm) high.
$5,000–5,500 *S*

Steiff

Steiff is arguably the most famous of all teddy bear makers. The company was founded in Germany in 1877 by Margarete Steiff who, having been crippled with polio as a child, had occupied herself by making felt toys with remnants from a local felt factory. Her nephew Richard, who had studied art in Stuttgart, was the company's designer, and the animal sketches he made at Stuttgart zoo served as inspiration for many of his toy designs. By 1899 Steiff catalogues offered polar bears, dancing bears and bears on rockets; jointed bears were made from 1902. All Steiff animals have a characteristic metal button in the ear, which from 1905 bore the word 'Steiff', underscored from the E–F of the name. Prior to that date, the button bore an elephant logo, and in 1904 it was blank.

A Steiff centre seam teddy bear, gold plush, with black stitched snout, black boot button eyes, wide apart pricked ears, swivel joints, hump back, excelsior stuffed, growler, button in ear, worn, c1910, 28in (71cm) high.
$7,500–8,250 *S*

A Steiff centre seam teddy bear, blonde mohair, with black boot button eyes, black stitched embroidered nose and mouth, small ears, fully jointed, small hump on back, excelsior filled, cream felt pads, 4 claws, c1909, 21in (53cm) high.
$3,500–4,000 *Bon*

A Steiff cinnamon plush teddy bear, black stitched snout, black boot button eyes, wide apart pricked ears, hump back, excelsior stuffed, growler, button in ear, c1910, 15in (38cm) high, with a smaller teddy bear, and a photograph of the owner.
$6,750–7,500 *S*

A Steiff cinnamon teddy bear, named 'Sam', with black boot button eyes, pronounced clipped snout, brown stitched nose and claws, humped back, elongated jointed limbs, curly mohair and cream pads, c1910, 21in (53.5cm) high, together with a 1985 Teddy Bear Calendar featuring 'Sam', a ceramic mug, a plate and figure group.
$8,250–9,750 *CNY*

A Steiff teddy bear, with curly mohair, black boot button eyes, swivel head, elongated nose with clipped mohair, jointed and elongated limbs, hump back, stitched claws and felt pads, button in ear, c1910, 28in (71cm) high.
$16,000–18,000 *CNY*

A Steiff teddy bear, with golden mohair, black boot button eyes, pronounced clipped snout, black stitched nose, remains of mouth and claws, swivel head, elongated jointed shaped limbs, felt pads, hump and button in ear, damaged, c1910, 16in (40.5cm) high.
$3,000–3,750 *CSK*

A Steiff white teddy bear, dressed in a girl's sailor suit, with black boot button eyes, pronounced clipped snout, brown stitched nose and claws, swivel head, elongated jointed shaped limbs and hump, pads recovered, slight wear, c1910, 13in (33cm) high.
$1,500–1,800 *CSK*

A Steiff pocket bear, with golden mohair, fully jointed, 3¼in (8.5cm) high.
$300–340 *CMF*

A Steiff teddy bear, named 'Edward', with golden mohair, black boot button eyes, black stitched nose, mouth and claws, swivel head, elongated jointed shaped limbs, felt pads and hump, growler broken, worn, c1910, 17in (43cm) high.
$2,500–2,700 *CSK*

A Steiff cinnamon teddy bear, with black boot button eyes, pronounced clipped snout, black stitched nose, mouth and claws, swivel head, elongated jointed shaped limbs, hump and button in ear, worn, c1910, 16in (40.5cm) high.
$2,250–2,750 *CSK*

A Steiff centre seam teddy bear, with golden mohair, black boot button eyes, pronounced clipped snout, black stitched nose, mouth and claws, swivel head, elongated jointed shaped limbs, felt pads and hump, worn, c1908, 16in (40.5cm) high.
$6,000–8,000

A Steiff white teddy bear, with black boot button eyes, pronounced clipped snout, beige stitched nose, mouth and claws, swivel head, elongated jointed shaped limbs, cream felt pads and hump, wear, c1910, 10in (25.5cm) high.
$1,300–1,500 *CSK*

A Steiff teddy bear, with golden mohair, brown and black glass eyes, pronounced snout, remains of black stitched nose, mouth and claws, swivel head, jointed shaped limbs, felt pads, hump and button in ear, slight wear, c1920, 20in (51cm) high.
$3,000–3,750 *CSK*

A Greek icon, of the Archangel
Michael, 17thC, 10 x 7½in (25 x 19cm).
$4,500–5,250 *S*

An icon, by Afanasiy Portnov,
Yaroslavl, of the Tolga Mother of
God, 18thC, 12½ x 10¼in (32 x 26cm).
$1,400–1,500 *P*

An icon, depicting the
Descent into Hell, 18thC,
15 x 12¾in (38 x 32.5cm).
$1,400–1,500 *CSK*

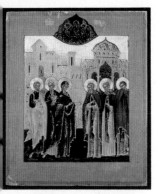

An icon, depicting the Appearance
of the Mother of God, 19thC,
12¼ x 10¼in (31 x 26cm).
$1,200–1,350 *P*

An icon, the Vladimir Mother of God,
18thC, 12½ x 10½in (31.5 x 27cm).
$1,900–2,200 *P*

A double-sided icon, with Christ
Pantocrator and Archangel Michael,
19thC, 9¾ x 7in (24.5 x 18cm).
$1,000–1,200 *P*

An icon, painted in 3 registers,
foliate borders, Moscow, 1853.
$1,800–2,000 *P*

An icon, the Mother of God, Refuge
for Sinners with Saints, 19thC,
14 x 12in (35.5 x 30.5cm).
$600–750 *CSK*

An icon, the All-Seeing Eye,
God the Father in nimbus,
19thC, 17¾ x 15¾in (45 x 40cm).
$1,300–1,500 *P*

A double-sided icon, with the
Mother of God of Smolensk,
18thC, 25½ x 17in (65 x 43cm).
$1,800–2,000 *P*

An icon, the Crucifixion, with
Nicholas, Feodor and Luke,
19thC, 17¼ x 15in (44 x 38cm).
$900–1,000 *CSK*

An icon, the Entry into Jerusalem,
painted on a green ground, 19thC,
12¼ x 10½in (31 x 26.5cm).
$1,500–1,800 *P*

A portrait miniature of a nobleman, by Nicholas Hilliard, c1610, 2in (50mm) high, in a gold frame.
$54,000–66,000 *S*

A silkwork portrait of Charles I, in a glazed silver-gilt frame, inscribed and dated '1648 Jan 30th', 6½in (16.5cm) high.
$15,000–18,000 *HAM*

A portrait miniature, by John Brewster, watercolour on ivory, early 19thC, 2 x 2½in (50 x 65mm).
$5,200–6,000 *S(NY)*

A portrait miniature, by Charles Buncombe, depicting a junior officer of the Light Company of the Royal Fusiliers, painted on card, inscribed on reverse, c1802, in a gilt-mounted papier mâché frame, 5¼in (13.5cm) high.
$3,750–4,500 *Bon*

A portrait miniature, by Cornelius Durham, signed 'C. D.', c1830, 2¾in (70mm) high.
$2,300–2,700 *BHa*

A portrait miniature, by G. G. Jannasch, depicting a lady wearing the sash of the Order of St Catherine, signed and dated '1780', 2¾in (70mm) diam.
$2,700–3,000 *S*

A portrait miniature, by Anson Dickinson, depicting Henry Seymour, in a gold frame, the reverse containing hair, c1810, 2½in (65mm) high.
$2,300–2,700 *Bon*

A portrait miniature, English School, depicting Lord Vere of Tilbury, from an original painting on vellum by Peter Oliver, c1800, 2¾in (70mm) high, in a *verre églomisé* frame.
$1,000–1,300 *BHa*

A pair of portrait miniatures, by Richard Cosway, depicting Mr and Mrs Johnson Wilkinson, c1790, 2in (50mm) high.
$9,250–10,500 *Bon*

A silver and wood lamp base, by Fabergé, workmaster J. Armfeldt, c1900, 12½in (32cm) high.
$14,250–16,500 *S(G)*

A silver-mounted wood photograph frame, by Fabergé, c1908, 11¾in (30cm) high.
$8,500–9,750 *S*

A jewelled gold and enamel cigarette case, by Fabergé, c1908, 3¾in (9.5cm) wide.
$15,000–18,000 *S(G)*

A silver and nephrite lamp base, by Fabergé, c1900, 12¾in (32.5cm) high, with a silver and *plique-à-jour* shade.
$45,000–52,500 *S(G)*

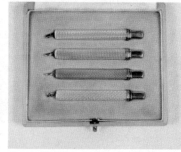

A set of bridge pencils, by Fabergé, workmaster August Höllming, St Petersburg, c1896, in a fitted case, 4in (10cm) wide.
$11,250–12,750 *SHa*

An enamelled photograph frame, by Fabergé, c1908, 10½in (27cm) high.
$33,000–39,000 *S*

A white metal table lighter, hinged at the neck and with hollow tail, marked 'Fabergé' with Imperial Warrant, c1908, 4¼in (11cm) high.
$21,250–24,750 *C*

An enamel and nephrite photograph frame, by Fabergé, c1896, 6in (15cm) high.
$22,500–25,500 *S*

A carved chalcedony pig, by Fabergé, the eyes set with diamonds, c1900, 2¾in (70mm) long.
$9,750–11,250 *S(NY)*

An enamelled yellow and white metal paper knife, marked 'Fabergé', workmaster August Höllming, c1908, the handle imitating the claw of a bird of prey, c1908, 7¾in (19.5cm) long.
$11,250–12,750 *C*

A silver, enamel and nephrite barometer, by Fabergé, workmaster H. Wigström, the hardstone drum supported by dolphins, on a stepped nephrite base applied with anthemion motif and leafy banding, on 4 lobed bun feet, c1896, 9¼in (23.5cm) high.
$215,000–245,000 *S(G)*

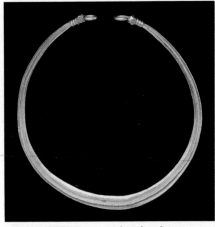

A painted limestone relief, depicting 3 male offering bearers, carrying food, drink and floral offerings, part of a ladder style border, traces of red paint on the bodies, mounted, Dynasty VI, 2323–2150 BC, 18 x 26½in (45.5 x 67.5cm).
$8,500–9,750 *C*

A Celtic gold torque, with 6 deeply cut channels, the terminals each in the form of a polyhedron with ribbed collar, circa 1st–4th century AD, 5¾in (14.5cm) wide.
$27,000–30,000 *S(NY)*

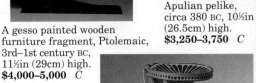

An early red figure Apulian pelike, circa 380 BC, 10½in (26.5cm) high.
$3,250–3,750 *C*

A gesso painted wooden furniture fragment, Ptolemaic, 3rd–1st century BC, 11½in (29cm) high.
$4,000–5,000 *C*

A limestone figure of a striding man, 11th Dynasty, 2081–1938 BC, 10in (25.5cm) high.
$12,000–14,000 *S(NY)*

A Roman marble figure of the god Sozon, inscribed, 2nd/3rd century AD, 12½in (32cm) high.
$23,250–26,250 *S(NY)*

A Roman bronze figure of a Zebu bull, circa 1st century AD, 2in (50mm) high.
$5,500–6,500 *C*

A Corinthian pottery Aryballos, a serpentine motif on the handle, circa late 7th century BC, 6½in (16.5cm) high.
$9,500–10,500 *S(NY)*

A pair of Roman gold rings, with ribs on one side, inset with an onyx cameo Medusa mask, circa 1st–2nd century AD, 2½in (65mm) diam.
$60,000–67,500 *S*

An Attic black figure cup, the interior with a reserved medallion with a concentric circle and dot, decorated on both sides with a pair of cockerels, the decoration on the exterior enriched with white and red-painted details, 6th century BC, 5¼in (13.5cm) diam
$15,750–18,000 *S*

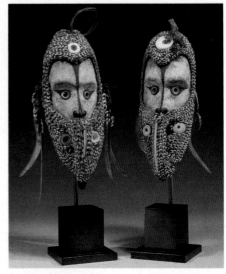

A pair of Iatmul Mwai masks, the flat backs showing numerous adzed marks, decorated with mother-of-pearl and cowrie shells, kaolin and blackening on faces, 11in (28cm) high. **$75,000–90,000** *S(NY)*

A Bakota Reliquary Guardian figure, covered with brass and copper, 22¼in (56.5cm) high. **$21,000–24,000** *S(NY)*

A Yoruba Epa mask, with areas of white kaolin and indigo pigment, 43½in (110.5cm) high. **$9,500–10,500** *S(NY)*

A Songye Kifwebe wood initiation mask, early 20thC, 20in (51cm) high. **$120–180** *GOO*

A Tshokwe mask, of hollowed form, triangular pointed teeth, honey brown patina with areas of blackening, 8½in (21.5cm) high. **$3,000–3,800** *S(NY)*

A Bwa female figure, with heavily encrusted patina, 35in (89cm) high. **$16,500–19,500** *S(NY)*

A Lega Kahimka Mpitu figure, 14in (35.5cm) high. **$30,000–36,000** *S(NY)*

A Bateke discoid mask, from the Congo, early 20thC, 14in (35.5cm) high. **$150–230** *GOO*

A Baule face mask, of hollowed form, black-red pigment on face, 9½in (24cm) high. **$10,500–12,000** *S(NY)*

An Eastern Pende wooden mask, from the Congo, early 20thC, 12in (30.5cm) high. **$80–120** *GOO*

A New Ireland Malangan figure, matte patina with black, ochre and white pigment, 33¾in 85.5cm) high. **$15,000–18,000** *S(NY)*

A Mexican Teotihuacan head, excellent condition, Classic, AD 250–450, 3½in (9cm) wide. **$75–95** *ANG*

A Colombian anthropomorphic mask, Tierradentro region, 500 BC–AD 500, 3in (7.5cm) wide. **$11,000–12,000** *S(NY)*

A Veraguas zoomorphic pendant, cast in criss-crossed openwork design, AD 800–1500, 4¾in (12cm) wide. **$19,500–22,500** *S(NY)*

A Veracruz warrior, covered in a shiny black *chapapote*, Remojadas, early Classic, AD 250–450, 26in (66cm) high. **$12,750–14,200** *S(NY)*

A Mayan polychrome tripod vessel, AD 250–450, 10½in (26.5cm), high. **$11,000–12,000** *S(NY)*

A Chinesco seated musician, 100 BC–AD 250, 8¾in (22cm) high. **$11,000–12,200** *S(NY)*

A middle Chimu beaker, with repoussé and 2 friezes, AD 1000–1250, 7½in (19cm) high. **$16,000–18,000** *S(NY)*

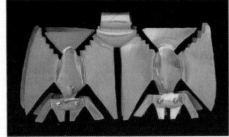

A Panama pedestal dish/plate, Veraguas, circa AD 800. **$180–200** *ANG*

An early Mochica ornament, in the form of 2 stylised birds, possibly Salinar, 400–100 BC, 6½in (16cm) wide. **$15,000–16,500** *S(NY)*

A Mayan seated noblewoman, in a *huipil,* necklace, earrings and a turban, Jaina, late Classic, AD 550–950, 6½in (16cm) high. **$7,500–8,300** *S(NY)*

A Mayan polychrome vessel, depicting a scene from the Underworld, late Classic, AD 550–950, 11½in (29cm) high. **$10,500–11,300** *S(NY)*

A Mochica effigy stirrup-spout vessel, the modelled diamond-shaped serpent, painted in cream and brown, AD 300–600, 8in (20.5cm) high. **$7,500–8,300** *S(NY)*

A Charles X Aubusson carpet, with acanthus, rosettes, vases and floral sprays, slight repair, backed, 265 x 254in (673 x 644cm).
$52,000–60,000 *C*

A Morris & Co Hammersmith hand-knotted carpet, with scrolling stem design, c1890, 195 x 187in (495 x 475cm).
$210,000–240,000 *S*

A Shirvan rug, with stylised shrubs and birds, 1856, 114½ x 41in (291 x 104cm).
$4,800–5,800 *P*

A Caucasian Dragon carpet, with stylised pheasants, ducks, lions, deer and cranes, late 17thC, 154 x 71in (391 x 180.5cm).
$34,500–37,500 *S*

A Heriz carpet, partial end guard borders, minor moth damage, slight damage, late 19thC, north west Persia, 150 x 122in (381 x 310cm).
$21,500–25,500 *S(NY)*

A corridor carpet, worn and repaired, north west Persia, early–mid-19thC, 210 x 78in (533.5 x 198cm).
$18,500–21,000 *SK*

An Agra carpet, the crimson field with an overall design of palmettes, cloud bands and leafy vine tendrils, within a walnut border, north India, c1870, 235 x 211in (595 x 535cm).
$185,000–210,000 *S*

A Star Ushak rug, with central medallion, west Anatolia, c1600, 101 x 57in (255 x 145cm).
$24,000–27,000 *S*

An Esfahan carpet, with scrolling vines, palmettes and leaves, central Persia, 17thC, 111 x 58in (282 x 147cm).
$13,000–15,000 *S*

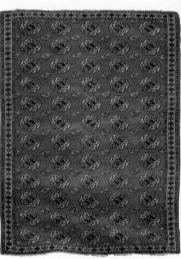

An Axminster carpet, with
an overall floral decoration,
early 19thC, 219 x 147in
(555 x 343cm).
$200,000–225,000 *S*

A Hereke carpet, the ivory and
pale blue cloud collar pole
medallion enclosing a flowerhead,
north west Turkey, c1890,
371 x 207in (940 x 525cm).
$12,000–14,250 *S*

A part silk carpet, the red field with
5 columns of Salor *guls*, slight wear,
east Turkmenistan, early 19thC,
116 x 88in (295 x 224cm).
$26,000–30,000 *C*

A Garabagh rug, south east
Caucasus, 18thC, 63 x 55in
(160 x 140cm).
$26,000–30,000 *S*

A Kirman pictorial carpet, the
field depicting animal groups
and figures, a stylised village
above, in a pictorial border,
south east Persia, c1890,
148 x 100in (376 x 254cm).
$10,500–12,000 *C*

A pinwheel Kazak rug,
south west Caucasus, slight
wear, repaired, early 19thC,
108 x 72in (274 x 183cm).
$9,000–10,500 *SK*

A silk Fereghan rug, the ivory field
with an overal design of flowerheads
and leafy vines, small repairs, Persia,
c1875, 75 x 57in (190.5 x 145cm).
$17,250–19,500 *C*

A 'vase' carpet, repaired,
central Persia, c1700,
106 x 71in (270 x 180cm).
$10,500–12,000 *S(NY)*

A Sultanabad carpet, slight
damage, central Persia,
late 19thC, 202 x 143in
(513 x 363cm).
$34,500–39,000 *S(NY)*

A Berlin woolwork picture, depicting figures and animals in a landscape, c1850, 48 x 36in (122 x 91.5cm).
$450–530 *RA*

A silkwork picture, depicting a shepherdess and lamb in a landscape, c1830, 14 x 12in (35.5 x 30.5cm).
$530–600 *RA*

An Ottoman embroidered quilt cover, Yorgan Yüzü, worked in laid and couched silk on a linen ground, 17th/18thC, 80 x 49in (203 x 124.5cm).
$21,750–25,000 *S*

An Azerbaijan embroidered panel, silk on cotton, with a central star and hexagons with birds and flowers, early 18thC, 37in (94cm) square.
$12,000–14,000 *S*

A silkwork picture, depicting a child running in a landscape, c1800, 14 x 10in (35.5 x 25.5cm).
$759–830 *RA*

A silkwork picture, depicting the five senses, buildings and flowers, worked in panels in a variety of stitches, c1670, 11 x 14½in (28 x 37cm).
$3,750–4,500 *BHa*

A needlework picture, worked in cross stitch, depicting the meeting of Rebecca and Elijah, in a landscape with a shepherd and his flock, a fountain, camels, and a town in the distance, mid-17thC, 14 x 22½in (35.5 x 57cm).
$3,000–3,500 *RA*

An Azerbaijan embroidery, densely worked in 2 strand S-ply silk in cross stitch in 11 colours, on a linen ground, late 17thC, 45 x 28in (114 x 71cm).
$19,000–22,500 *S*

A Cretan embroidered bolster cover, decorated with vases of flowers, in a floral border, 17th/18thC, 87 x 25in (221 x 63.5cm).
$5,250–6,000 *S*

A sampler, by Mary Minshull, worked in coloured silks with alphabets, numerals, a verse and 2 figures, inscription, c1694, 19 x 7½in (48 x 19cm).
$12,750–15,000 *CSK*

A sampler, by Elizabeth Palfrey, aged 6, worked in coloured silks with a verse, flowers, foliage, a bird and a house, c1811, 16 x 13in (40.5 x 33cm), in original frame.
$3,000–3,300 *HIS*

A sampler, by Elizabeth Staines, worked in coloured threads with a verse, flowers, a male and female figure, dated '1805', 17 x 13in (43 x 33cm).
$1,300–1,400 *RA*

A needlework sampler, by Margaret Elizabeth Nuttman, decorated with birds, animals, trees, flowers, a house and 2 figures, dated '1826', 17 x 13in (43 x 33cm).
$1,100–1,300 *RA*

A needlework sampler, by Jerusha Lyman, aged 8 years, worked in coloured silks, with alphabet, trees, a basket of fruit, birds and dogs, probably Hampshire or Hampden County, Massachusetts, dated '1792', 16 x 13in (40.5 x 33cm).
$28,500–33,000 *S(NY)*

A needlework sampler, by Phebe Giles, aged 7 years, worked in silks on a linen ground, with the alphabet, a verse, trees, birds and a cottage, dated 'June 23, 1826', 18 x 12¾in (45.5 x 32.5cm).
$2,500–3,000 *S(NY)*

A late Victorian wool sampler, worked with alphabets and 2 deer, 1860, in a modern frame, 13½ x 12in (34.5 x 30.5cm).
$160–200 *PSA*

A sampler, depicting Blickling Hall, Norfolk, c1900, 14¾ x 11in (37 x 28cm).
$230–250 *PSA*

A woolwork sampler, by Maria Edwards, with a verse, church, flowers, trees, birds, dogs and figures, 1846, 24½ x 20½in (62 x 52cm).
$1,000–1,200 *BHa*

An Aubusson tapestry, 17thC, 116 x 70in (295 x 178cm). **$7,500–9,000** *P*

A Franco-Flemish wool and silk tapestry fragment, mostly 16thC, 113½ x 95in (287 x 241cm). **$28,500–31,500** *C*

A Gobelins tapestry, 'Les Deux Taureaux', dated '1753', 194 x 168 (493 x 427cm). **$322,000–375,000** *S(NY)*

A Brussels Biblical tapestry, by Peter van der Borght, mid-18thC, 145½ x 166in (370 x 422cm). **$100,000–120,000** *C*

A Brussels tapestry fragment, 17thC, 187 x 83in (478 x 211cm). **$10,000–12,000** *P*

A Franco-Flemish *mille-fleurs* pastoral tapestry fragment, woven in wools and silks, c1500, 57 x 75in (145 x 190.5cm). **$49,000–59,000** *C*

A Marche Feuilles d'Aristoloche tapestry, woven in wools, late 16thC, 121 x 251½in (307 x 693cm). **$45,000–52,500** *C*

A Flemish mythological tapestry fragment, woven in wools and silks, extensively rewoven, reduced in size, 16thC, 100½ x 107½in (255 x 273cm). **$15,000–18,000** *C*

A Beauvais tapestry panel, the centre with 2 wolves, 18thC, in a 19thC giltwood frame, 67 x 62in (170 x 157cm). **$8,400–9,600** *P*

A Flemish mythological tapestry fragment, woven in wools, depicting soldiers and a burning town, possibly Troy, 16thC, 87 x 62in (221 x 157.5cm). **$11,250–12,750** *C*

A display of ammunition, by G. Kynoch & Co Ltd, Birmingham, 19thC, 38½ x 26½in (98 x 67cm). **$1,800–2,200** *ND*

An Edwardian Imperial German Garde du Corps trooper's helmet, with silvered eagle crest, leather lined, 10in (25.5cm) high. **$2,700–3,000** *WAL*

A late Victorian officer's gilt helmet of The 6th Dragoon Guards (Carabiniers), with padded silk lining, 13in (33cm) high. **$1,500–1,800** *WAL*

An Edwardian brass Merryweather pattern fireman's helmet, leather lined, 12in (30.5cm) high. **$630–730** *MR*

A close helmet, Innsbruck Court Workshop, in the manner of Hans Seusenhofer, c1515, 11in (28cm) high. **$40,500–48,000** *S(S)*

An Edwardian Ordinary Ranks helmet, of The 5th Dragoon Guards, 16in (40.5cm) high. **$750–850** *MR*

The Royal Order of Victoria and Albert, 3rd class breast badge, by J. Ronca, with pearl and diamond border, c1870, 1½in (38mm) high. **$12,000–14,250** *S(S)*

A Persian Qjar matching Khula Khud and Bazu Band, 19thC, 14in (35.5cm) long. **$1,200–1,400** *WAL*

A group of orders, decorations and medals, including the Unique Quadruple Second War and Korea DSO to Major Gen Sir D. A. Kendrew, late Royal Leicestershire Regiment, Brigade Commander and Governor of Western Australia. **$15,750–18,000** *Sp*

An archer's pavise, Austrian or south German, slight damage and wear, c1480, 49½in (125.5cm) high. **$52,000–62,000** *S(S)*

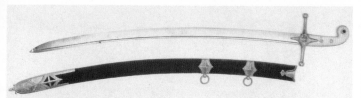

A Georgian Light Cavalry officer's Mameluke sword, with curved single-edged piped back 30¾in (78cm) blade, etched with crowned 'GR' cipher, a copper gilt hilt, 2 piece ivory grips, in velvet covered steel scabbard with copper gilt mounts, good condition.
$2,000–2,500 *WAL*

A Naval officer's dress sword, c1970, 33in (84cm) long.
$525–600 *Tem*

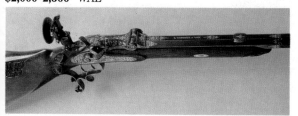

An Austrian Wänzl system breech-loading target rifle, No. 343, by L. Wurzinger, Wien, with blued octagonal barrel inlaid with gold scrollwork, signed in gold, repaired, c1867, barrel 29in (74cm) long.
$5,500–6,750 *S(S)*

Four flintlock pistols, by Staudenmayer, c1800, longest 15in (38cm), cased.
$7,500–9,000 *GV*

A set of flintlock duelling pistols, by Ketland & Co, with browned octagonal barrels, cased with three-way flask, bullet mould and cleaning rod, c1820, 15in (38cm) long.
$6,750–7,500 *GV*

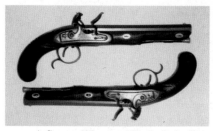

A George III pair of flintlock duelling pistols, by Manton, with browned octagonal barrels, 12in (30cm).
$2,200–2,700 *MR*

A south German wheel-lock pistol, with octagonal barrel etched with scrollwork, the flat lock with maker's mark, damaged, c1550, 17¼in (44cm) long.
$37,000–39,000 *S(S)*

A German wheel-lock holster pistol, with slender octagonal barrel, marks to breech 'Neuer Støckel 5816 and 5226', damaged, c1640, 24¾in (63cm) long.
$8,500–9,500 *S(S)*

A pair of French flintlock officer's pistols, by Boutet, Directeur Artiste à Versailles, with twist octagonal barrels, signed flat border engraved locks with roller and gilt pan, repaired, c1810, 14½in (37cm) long.
$9,000–10,500 *S(S)*

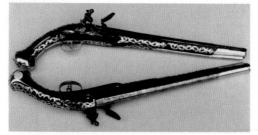

A pair of flintlock holster pistols, made in Europe for the Turkish market, the stocks overlaid with silver-gilt and seaweed decoration, the steel locks chiselled with scrolls, c1820, 18½in (47cm) long.
$3,000–3,750 *GV*

An Ernst Heubach doll, with blue paperweight eyes, wearing a purple dress and gold apron, c1890, 16½in (42cm) high.
$450–530 *PSA*

A Jumeau doll, with brown paperweight eyes, wearing a sailor suit and beret, c1890, 14in (35.5cm) high.
$2,300–2,600 *DOL*

A Bähr & Pröeschild doll, mould No. 244, with closed mouth, c1890, 14in (35.5cm) high.
$1,800–2,200 *DOL*

A 'Mein Leibling' Kämmer and Reinhardt bisque-headed character doll, No. 117A, with weighted blue glass eyes, 24½in (62cm) high.
$2,600–3,000 *Bon*

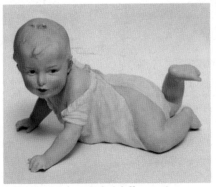

A Heubach 'piano baby' doll, wearing a white shift, c1903, 12in (30.5cm) long.
$600–680 *DOL*

These figures were intended for display on pianos, hence the name.

A Kämmer and Reinhardt bisque character 'Marie' doll, impressed mark, c1909, 19in (48cm) high.
$5,000–5,500 *S*

A Kämmer and Reinhardt doll, with sleeping eyes, mould No. 117, 1915, not original clothing, 18in (45.5cm) high.
$1,500–1,800 *PSA*

A Bähr & Pröeschild bisque-headed doll, with kid body, new clothing, 1890, 20in (51cm) high.
$520–600 *PSA*

A Walküre (Kley & Hahn) bisque-headed doll, with sleeping brown eyes, c1912, 28in (71cm) high.
$1,000–1,200 *BaN*

A Schmitt et Fils pressed bisque doll, marked, c1880, 24in (61cm) high.
$10,000–11,250 *S*

An Oriental doll, unmarked, c1910, 14½in (37cm) high.
$1,000–1,200 *PSA*

An S.F.B.J. bébé jointed doll, 1905, 24in (61cm) high.
$1,000–1,200 *PSA*

A Simon & Halbig Jutta doll, No. 1349, fixed eyes, original clothes, 1900, 27in (68.5cm) high.
$1,200–1,300 *PSA*

A wax flirty-eyed doll, c1880, with new clothes, 14½in (37cm) high.
$330–390 *PSA*

A Kling jointed doll, 1900, 17½in (44.5cm) high.
$480–600 *PSA*

A Leopold Lambert musical automaton doll, with Jumeau head, c1880, 19in (48.5cm) high.
$10,000–12,000 *S*

A Simon & Halbig key-wind walking doll, No. 1078, re-dressed, 1900, 13½in (34.5cm) high.
$1,200–1,400 *PSA*

A blonde haired parian ware doll, 'Alice', wearing original clothes, c1885, 21in (53.5cm) high.
$900–1,000 *DOL*

A wax two-faced doll, wearing all original clothes, c1890, 12in (30.5cm) high.
$1,000–1,200 *DOL*

A Margarete Steiff diagonal seam gypsy character doll, with 16 Steiff shirt buttons, a Steiff button in each ear, c1908, 12in (30.5cm) high.
$2,400–2,700 *CNY*

A Steiff cinnamon centre seam teddy bear, with wide apart pricked up ears and button in ear, faded, c1907, 16in (40.5cm) high. **$4,500–5,300** *TED*

A Steiff cinnamon teddy bear, with black boot button eyes, stitched nose and claws, swivel head, jointed elongated limbs, hump back and blank button, c1905, 21in (53.5cm) high. **$7,500–8,300** *CNY*

A Hermann Zotty teddy bear, with long shaggy mohair, an open felt mouth, stiched nose, felt paw pads, growler, c1945, 16½in (42cm) high. **$250–300** *PSA*

A Steiff cinnamon plush teddy bear, with button eyes, wide apart ears, hump back, swivel joints, button in ear, and growler, c1908, 28in (71cm) high. **$4,200–4,800** *S*

A Farnell mohair teddy bear, with long shaved muzzle, wide apart pricked up ears, webbed claw stitching, c1925, 19in (48cm) high. **$1,200–1,500** *TED*

A Steiff white plush teddy bear, with a peach stitched snout, black boot button eyes, wide apart ears, hump back, swivel joints, button in ear and growler, c1908, 17in (43cm) high. **$7,200–7,800** *S*

A Steiff white plush teddy bear, with stitched nose, black boot button eyes, wide apart ears and hump back, c1910, 20in (51cm) high. **$8,500–9,500** *S*

A Steiff gold plush centre seam teddy bear, with stitched snout, black boot button eyes, wide apart ears, hump back, swivel joints, c1908, 28in (71cm) high. **$4,000–4,800** *S*

A Joy Toys yellow mohair teddy bear, with fixed neck, jointed arms and legs, pointed paws, label on foot, c1930, 23in (58.5cm) high. **$330–400** *TED*

A Bing teddy bear, with long muzzle, hump back, swivel joints, fair condition, c1920, 23in (58.5cm) high. **$1,500–1,800** *DOL*

A Roosevelt laughing teddy bear, by Columbia Teddy Bear Manufacturing, NY, c1907, 14in (35.5cm) high.
$3,750–4,500 *TED*

A white Steiff teddy bear, black boot button eyes, and curly mohair, c1907, 20in (51cm) high.
$5,500–6,750 *CNY*

A Steiff teddy bear, with arms that wind to make him turn somersaults, button and remnant of white tag in ear, c1909, 12in (30.5cm) high.
$2,300–3,000 *TED*

A Steiff mohair teddy bear, fully jointed, with label and button, 1960, 6in (15cm) high.
$375–450 *CMF*

A Merrythought Cheeky teddy bear, with label and bell in ears, 1950s, 15in (38cm) high.
$375–450 *CMF*

A Schuco rose teddy bear, in a three-wheeled vehicle, marked on side of car, c1935, 3in (7.5cm) high.
$2,000–2,300 *TED*

A Hornby Dublo three-rail Southern tank locomotive, No. '2594', c1940, 5½in (14cm) long.
$270–300 *RAR*

A Hornby Dublo three-rail motor coach and trailer, c1962, with original boxes.
$450–500 *RAR*

A Hornby O gauge clockwork LMS 4-4-4 tank locomotive, c1930.
$270–300 *RAR*

A Dinky Toys 25h streamlined fire engine, with a ladder and bell on the roof, some metal fatigue, pre-1939.
$120–150 *TMA*

A spirit-fired traction engine, with a canopy, by Fareham Engineering Co, c1970, 20in (51cm) long.
$1,000–1,200 *RAR*

A Hornby tinplate clockwork train set, with 6 pieces of track, c1930, coaches 5in (12.5cm) long.
$120–150 *PSA*

A German painted tinplate carpet toy train, with locomotive 'Gotha', tender, 2 carriages and wagons, 19thC. **$3,750–4,200** *HOLL*

A G.W.R. Bulldog No. 3407 'Madras' engine and tender, built by J. S. Beeson to exhibition standard, c1950, 15½in (39.5cm) long. **$4,800–5,500** *CSK*

A clockwork four-seater open tourer, with ratchet operated steering, brake and reversing levers, in a Märklin box, c1912. **$9,500–10,500** *CSK*

A clockwork lithographed tinplate limousine, by Greppert & Kelch, with handbrake, chauffeur, opening doors, marked 'G&K', '515', and 'Made in Germany', c1930, 7in (18cm) long.
$400–450 *WW*

A painted wooden dolls' house, opening in 3 sections, together with the contents including 15 dolls, damaged, c1850, 50in (127cm) wide.
$7,200–8,200 *S*

A German painted wooden Noah's ark, the roof with hinged lid, containing 8 figures and 40 pairs of carved painted animals and birds, c1840, 26in (66cm) long.
$21,800–23,200 *S*

An American Gottschalk two-storey dolls' house, with hinged front opening, c1910, 15in (38cm) high.
$450–530 *Bon*

A Shönhut painted wooden 'Humpty Dumpty Circus', all the animals with glass eyes, the figures wearing cloth costumes, c1925, with box, base 36in (91.5cm) long.
$7,500–8,300 *CNY*

A painted Regency style dolls' house, c1910, 21¾in (55cm) wide.
$2,200–2,700 *P(B)*

An American George Brown clockwork tinplate jockey with horses and tinplate driver, c1860, 14in (35.5cm) long.
$13,500–15,000 *CNY*

A Britains ambulance, doctor, nurses, orderlies and wounded, from Set 1897, without box, c1950.
$600–680 *RAR*

A Lines Bros mock Tudor dolls' house, the facade opening in 4 sections, slight damage, label to base, c1930, 44in (112cm) long.
$560–680 *S(S)*

A 'Mechanical Yacht Race' game, in good condition, 1897, box 8 x 9½in (20.5 x 24cm).
$120–140 *Bon*

A clockwork tinplate model of Buckingham Palace, with marching guardsmen, one missing, c1920, 8in (20.5cm) high.
$680–750 *RAR*

A German mechanical tinplate Mickey Mouse bank, possibly by Sehulmer and Strauss, c1930, 6in (15cm) high.
$21,800–23,200 *S*

A giant Steiff tiger, reclining, without button or tags, c1950.
$260–300 *CNY*

Four Steiff Disney characters, Peri, Bambi and Baloo with buttons, and Tramp, c1955.
$860–980 *CNY*

An Aegean enamelled gold ship pendant, probably Venetian dependencies, c1700, 4in (10cm) high.
$17,500–19,500 *S*

A Victorian gold and enamel pendant cross, by Carlo Giuliano, c1865, 3in (8cm) high.
$3,500–4,000 *C*

A German diamond mounted gold pomander pendant, modelled as a seated lion with flowing mane, detachable diamond studded collar, inscribed, c1575, 2¾in (70mm) high.
$142,000–165,000 *S*

A diamond bracelet, designed as a series of 5 graduated cushion-cut diamond clusters with single-stone collet connections, c1860, with later chain link bracelet and clasp, 6¾in (17cm) long.
$13,000–15,000 *C*

An Italian enamelled gold and pearl eagle pendant, 17thC, 4in (10cm) high.
$11,000–12,000 *S*

A French onyx cameo of a blackamoor, with diamond and ruby detail, in a gold brooch mount, c1860, 2¼in (60mm) high.
$8,500–9,750 *C*

A ruby and diamond butterfly brooch, mounted in silver and gold, c1880, 2¼in (60mm) high.
$9,500–11,000 *C*

An amethyst and diamond suite of jewellery, mounted in silver and gold, c1850, brooch 2¼in (60mm) wide.
$5,250–6,000 *C*

A Victorian emerald and diamond lozenge brooch, c1870, 1½in (38mm) wide.
$3,800–4,500 *C*

A diamond and peridot flowerhead brooch, mounted in silver and gold, c1890, 2in (50mm) wide.
$15,500–17,250 *C*

An enamelled brooch, set in gold with diamond scrolls, probably Swiss, c1870, 1¼in (33mm) high.
$750–825 *DN*

A Victorian emerald and diamond brooch, mounted in silver and gold, c1870, 1½in (38mm) wide.
$7,500–8,250 *C*

A George III diamond necklace, forming a tiara of graduated garland and scrollwork design, set with foliate motifs, mounted in silver and gold, later rhodium plated, c1800, 15½in (39.5cm) long, with tiara frame and 7 brooch fitments.
$19,000–22,500 *C*

An A. Calderoni Gioielliere lithograph poster, by Adolfo Hohenstein, on two sheets, some damage, 1898, 63 x 38in (160 x 97cm).
$10,000–11,250 *CSK*

A Will's Embassy cigarettes 3-D stand-up advertising show card, with cut-out front section, c1930, 29 x 19in (74 x 48cm).
$180–200 *P(B)*

A Robinson's Patent 'Barley & Groats' advertising show card, with printed slogans, c1930, 18 x 12in (45.5 x 30.5cm).
$130–150 *P(B)*

A paper-backed film poster, *The Searchers*, Warner Bros, 1956, 30 x 40in (76 x 101.5cm).
$1,125–1,275 *CSK*

A one sheet film poster, *Sleeping Beauty*, Walt Disney, 1959, 41 x 27in (104 x 68.5cm).
$1,125–1,275 *CSK*

New York World's Fair, 1940 comic book, good condition.
$1,200–1,500 *CNY*

Donald Duck Finds Pirate Gold 4 colour comics, No. 9, Dell Publishing, by Carl Barks, 1942, good condition.
$2,000–2,500 *CNY*

A paper-backed film poster, *The African Queen,* with Humphrey Bogart and Katharine Hepburn, Romulus, 1951, 30 x 40in (76 x 101.5cm).
$7,000–8,000 *CSK*

A German film poster, *Dr No,* with Sean Connery as James Bond, United Artists, 1962, 33 x 47in (84 x 119.5cm).
$1,200–1,400 *CSK*

A La Bodiniere lithograph poster, by Theophile Alexandre Steinlen, printed by Charles Verneau, Paris, restored, c1894, 23½in x 32in (60 x 81cm).
$4,500–5,250 *CSK*

Batman No. 2 comic book, National Periodical Publications, good condition, 1940.
$3,000–3,750 *CNY*

A robe, worn by boxer
Roberto Duran,
on 9 August 1981.
$330–400 *CNY*

An American League
baseball, hit by Babe
Ruth in the 1933 All Star
game, signed by Ruth and
12 other American
League All Stars.
$45,000–52,500 *CNY*

A 3in Blacker brass
multiplying reel, with
curved crank arm and
ivory knob, marked, c1842.
$1,400–1,600 *ND*

A German hand made
No. 3 silver bait casting
reel, by F. Meel & Sons,
Louisville, Kentucky,
engraved, c1910.
$575–675 *ND*

Twelve Slazenger tennis
balls, in original box
and wrapping, c1922.
$450–525 *DA*

A bowfronted case, made by W. F. Homer, with label,
containing a chub, inscribed 'Chub 3lb 6oz caught by
W. Shail at Inglesham, on 5th March 1932'.
$700–825 *ND*

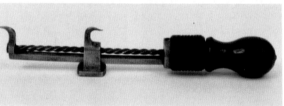

A Jardine's pike gag, c1898, 9½in (24cm) long.
$900–1,000 *PC*

A Hazell Streamline
'Blue Star' lawn tennis
racket, c1930,
27in (68.5cm) long.
$200–240 *MSh*

A lob-sided lawn tennis
racket, stamped
'Cassiobury', c1870,
26½in (67.5cm) long.
$1,150–1,350 *MSh*

A smooth-face iron golf
club, by Tom Morris, c1895.
$200–225 *MSh*

An Ornum putter golf club,
with steel face, c1920.
$300–375 *MSh*

A full size billiard table, by Thurston & Co, London, the figured mahogany frame with scroll decoration, on 8 octagonal legs, c1856. $4,500–5,300 *BRA*

A mahogany billiard marker, with brass fittings, c1915, 27in (68.5cm) high. $450–530 *BRA*

A mahogany billiard and life pool scoreboard-on-cupboard, by Burroughes & Watts, c1900, 62¾in (159.5cm) high. $900–1,200 *MSh*

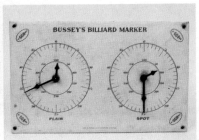

A full size billiard table, by George Wright & Co, London, with mahogany frame, the 8 carved legs capped with lions' masks, the cushion friezes with 'Rose' buttons, c1870. $6,000–6,800 *BRA*

A Bussey & Co, London, billiard marker, c1910, 10½in (27cm) long. $60–90 *MSh*

A mahogany revolving cue stand, c1910, 45in (114.5cm) high. $1,000–1,200 *BRA*

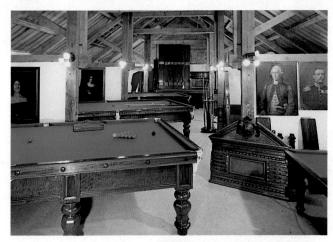

A polychrome carved wood tea merchant's sign, English, mid-19thC, 21½in (54cm) high.
$2,200–2,700 *CSK*

A Regency shellwork, wood and silk figure within a gazebo, 1817, 13½in (34cm) high.
$1,125–1,275 *CSK*

A polychrome pine double-sided inn sign, mid-18thC, 32½in (82.5cm) high.
$5,000–6,000 *CSK*

A sheet tin and rough hewn wood chimney sweep's sign, c1900, 46in (117cm) high.
$16,500–19,500 *CSK*

A Victorian stuffed fabric and card group, in a painted and glazed shadow box, c1865, 25in (63.5cm) wide.
$2,700–3,500 *CSK*

A red painted tin cookie box, with hinged lid, Pennsylvania, c1825, 10in (25.5cm) wide.
$23,250–27,750 *S(NY)*

A root carved cherry-wood walking stick, early 19thC, 34½in (87.5cm) long.
$1,275–1,425 *S(NY)*

A turned and painted saffron cup, c1880, 5in (12.5cm) high.
$2,000–2,500 *S(NY)*

An American carved and painted pine and mahogany fire box, 1861, 3½in (9cm) high.
$1,800–2,000 *S(NY)*

A painted and moulded zinc cigar store sign, late 19thC, 67in (170cm) high.
$7,500–9,000 *S(NY)*

A polychrome wood and wrought iron whirligig, modelled as Uncle Sam, c1920, 34½in (87.5cm) high.
$6,000–7,000 *CSK*

A pair of hand-carved and painted mallard duck decoys, retaining original decoration, late 19thC, 14in (36cm) long.
$550–650 *RYA*

A moulded and gilded copper horse weather-vane, by A. L. Jewell & Co, Waltham, Massachusetts, late 19thC, 19¼in (49cm) high.
$6,750–7,500 *S(NY)*

A Steiff gold centre seam teddy bear, with black stitched snout, black and brown glass eyes, wide apart pricked ears, hump back, swivel joints, excelsior and kapok stuffed, press growler, button missing, c1927, 13in (33cm) high.
$1,900–2,200 S

A Steiff miniature teddy bear, 'Theodore', with golden mohair, black bead eyes, remains of black stitched nose and mouth, swivel head and jointed padless limbs, 1948, 3½in (9cm) high, and other related accessories.
$22,500–25,500 CSK

A Steiff Zotty teddy bear, c1950, 9in (23cm) high.
$100–130 CMF

Teddy Bears

In the past few years there has been a dramatic increase in the number of collectors of old bears and prices have risen steeply as a result. Unfortunately this has also given rise to an increase in the number of artificially 'aged' bears, which can easily deceive new collectors. Many genuine old bears are unmarked and a novice collector will need to gain experience, both by handling as many bears as possible and seeking advice from specialist dealers or museums, before they can attribute a bear with any confidence. Prices depend on the age, colour, condition, rarity and above all, the maker.

A Steiff teddy bear, with brown mohair, brown and black glass eyes, pronounced snout, black stitched nose, mouth and claws, swivel head, long jointed shaped limbs, felt pads, hump, growler, button in ear with remains of white label, 1920s, 18in (45.5cm) high.
$4,000–4,500 CSK

A Steiff Jackie teddy bear, made to commemorate the 50th anniversary of the Steiff teddy bear, button in ear, 1953, 10in (25.5cm) high, with original booklet.
$2,000–2,500 TED

A German pull-along teddy bear, the wire frame go-kart with wooden wheels, with painted black glass eyes, brown embroidered nose and mouth, small ears, fully jointed, straw-filled, cream felt pads, blue bow, worn, c1910, 10½in (26.5cm) high.
$900–1,000 Bon

Miscellaneous

A miniature teddy bear, possibly by Schuco, c1940, 5in (12.5cm) high.
$100–120 PSA

A miniature teddy bear, c1945, 6in (15cm) high.
$35–45 PSA

r. A German teddy bear, with blonde mohair plush, glass eyes, protruding black stitched snout, excelsior filled body with centre squeak, swivel joints, damaged, 1920s, 12½in (32cm) high.
$450–525 P(Ba)

SOFT TOYS

l. A Steiff plush pig, with canvas snout, black shoe button eyes, excelsior stuffed, with press growler, button in ear, damaged, 15in (38cm) long.
$1,000–1,200 *S*

r. A brown and white plush-covered kangaroo, Kanga, with clear and black glass eyes painted on reverse, black stitched nose and mouth, with a pouch holding Roo, slightly worn, c1920, 12in (30.5cm) high, and an autographed letter from Christopher Robin Milne to Mrs Darlington, and a collection of photographs.
$4,000–5,000 *CSK*

Felix the Cat, with short black mohair, white mohair muzzle, large black velvet button eyes backed on white velvet, black velvet button nose, black cloth mouth with white stitched teeth, swivel head, wired framed limbs and tail, standing in traditional 'keep on walking' pose, 1920s, 17in (43cm) high.
$600–675 *CSK*

Four Steiff *Jungle Book* characters, Baloo the bear, Baby Hathi the elephant, King Louie, and Shere Khan, after Walt Disney, c1968, largest 15in (38cm) high.
$3,750–4,500 *CSK*

A Steiff 'Bully' on wheels, with black and white mohair, clear and black glass eyes painted on reverse, black stitched nose and claws, velvet cut muzzle, swivel head, original collar and bell, on 4 wheels joined by rods, worn, c1930, 19in (48.5cm) long.
$1,000–1,200 *CSK*

A model of Winnie the Pooh, made in flannel, 1950s, 13in (33cm) high.
$300–360 *CSK*

A Steiff tiger head plaque, with button and tag, mounted on wood, on placard suitable for engraving, c1950, 24in (61cm) high.
$450–525 *CNY*

l. A white plush-covered pull-along sheep, with clear and black glass eyes painted yellow on reverse, white felt ears, face and legs, red stitched nose and mouth, original bell and ribbon, on metal wheels joined by rods, c1920, 17in (43cm) long.
$600–675 *CSK*

A Bing 'Tripple-Trappel' walking dog, white felt, black patch on head, black boot button eyes, black stitched nose and mouth, collar and lead missing, 1920s, 6in (15cm) high.
$220–270 *CSK*

TOYS
Mechanical Toys

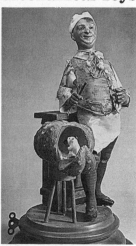

A Gustave Vichy musical automaton of a pumpkin eater, with a keywind stop/start mechanism within the circular base, worn, c1880, 20½in (52cm) high.
$18,000–21,000 *Bon*

An automaton of a girl magician, Renou, by Ferdinand Gaultier, with a keywind stop/start mechanism within the red velvet covered base, impressed 'F.G.', clothing replaced, c1900, 17½in (44.5cm) high.
$750–900 *Bon*

A Portrait Jumeau automaton of a woman watching horse racing, possibly by Phalibois, with keywind stop/start musical mechanism within the green velvet base, clothing replaced, c1890, 22in (56cm) high.
$4,000–4,500 *Bon*

A Roullet & Decamps somersaulting acrobat toy, with composition head, wood and metal body containing keywind mechanism, c1900, 10in (25.5cm) high.
$800–950 *S(S)*

Roullet & Decamps (c1832–1972)

One of the most prominent makers of automata, this firm was founded by Jean Roullet in partnership with his son-in-law, Ernest Decamps. The company is famous for the exceptional quality and variety of its products, which included simple furry animals suitable for children, as well as acrobats, conjurers, Orientals, musical figures, idealised peasants and smoking and drinking figures more suitable for adult amusement.

In the production of their automata Roullet & Decamps used heads made from bisque, papier mâché, composition and even celluloid. These were supplied by both French and German makers, including Simon & Halbig. Roullet & Decamps figures are typically clad in colourful satin costumes, embellished with braid and lace.

The company also produced a wide variety of less elaborate automata suitable for children. These included dolls and animals mounted on a wheeled platform which activated when pulled along, as well as simple key-wound toys.

A Britains mechanical Equestrienne, the fly-wheel drive circulates the horse while the acrobat jumps the hurdle, in good condition, in original box, c1890.
$800–900 *CSK*

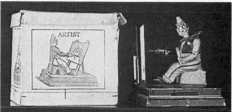

A Vielmetter hand-cranked lithographed tinplate clown artist, the mechanism with interchangeable cams contained in the base, in good condition, c1900, 5in (13cm) high, in original box with 5 cams and instructions.
$3,500–4,000 *CSK*

Two Günthermann hand-painted tin automaton clown musicians, with wind-up animated violin and bell players, good condition, c1890.
$1,400–1,500 *SK*

A Lehmann tinplate clockwork toy, New Century Cycle, marked 'AM POL', 'D.R. Patent' and bearing the 1911 Lehmann trademark, parasol missing, 5in (13cm) long.
$450–525 *WW*

An automaton picture of a cat playing a fiddle, with a rear box containing clockwork and musical mechanism, in good condition, probably German, c1900, 9in (23cm) high.
$750–850 *Bon*

Trains

A Bassett-Lowke clockwork 4-6-2 'Flying Scotsman' locomotive, No. 4472, with matching eight-wheeled tender, finished in LNER livery, good condition, c1930.
$1,100–1,350 *Bon*

A Bassett-Lowke clockwork 4-4-0 'Prince Charles' locomotive, No. 62078, with matching six-wheeled tender, finished in blue BR livery with white and black lining, good condition, 1951.
$270–300 *Bon*

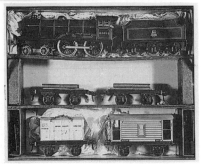

A Bassett-Lowke clockwork 'Prince Charles' locomotive, No. 62453, with tender, finished in BR green, a 20 ton brake goods van and flat truck with BR container, and 2 flat trucks with metal sheeting, together with instruction sheet and running notes, excellent condition, in original box, c1950.
$580–620 *Bon*

A Wrenn 00 gauge West Country Class 4-6-2 'Tavistock' locomotive, a special limited edition, c1985, 11in (28cm) long.
$675–750 *RAR*

r. A Hornby Dublo two-rail LMR 2-8-0 locomotive and tender, c1962, 10in (25.5cm) long.
$300–375 *RAR*

A Hornby No. 2 special 'County of Bedford' locomotive, No. 3821, with matching six-wheeled tender, finished in GWR green livery, some repainting, motor converted, good condition, c1930.
$400–525 *Bon*

A Hornby clockwork 4-4-0 'Eton' locomotive, No. 900, with matching six-wheeled tender, locomotive with brass pipes and clack boxes, finished in green Southern livery, with smoke deflectors, good condition, c1938.
$800–920 *Bon*

A Hornby LMS clockwork 4-4-0 compound locomotive, No. 1185, with matching six-wheeled tender, finished in maroon livery with gold lining, some repainting, good condition, c1936.
$375–450 *Bon*

A Hornby clockwork 4-4-2 'Flying Scotsman' locomotive, No. 4472, with matching six-wheeled tender, finished in green LNER livery, with smoke deflectors, some repainting, fair condition, c1936.
$200–270 *Bon*

A GWR 4-6-0 'County of Devon' locomotive, No. 1005, built by J.P. Richards, with Read Maxwell electric motor, with tender, 2-rail pick-up and external details, finished in GWR livery and lining, 1950, 17½in (44.5cm) long.
$2,700–3,000 *CSK*

A Bing clockwork 4-6-0 'Royal Scot' locomotive, No. 6508, with matching six-wheeled tender, finished in maroon LMS livery, with yellow and black lining, brass nameplate, good condition, c1920.
$525–600 *Bon*

A Hornby 0 gauge 20 volt electric 4-4-2T locomotive,
No. 2091, finished in green Southern livery, c1938.
$450–525 *RAR*

A Radiguet and Massiot 3in gauge
steam brass 2-2-0 locomotive, with
externally fired boiler, twin double-
acting cylinders, solid wood buffer
beams, on open cast-brass chassis,
overpainted and chipped, fair
condition, c1885, 14¾in (37.5cm) long.
$1,800–2,000 *CSK*

A Bing gauge 1 clockwork 0-4-0 locomotive, with matching
four-wheeled tender, finished in green livery with red and
yellow lining, together with 2 coaches, finished in brown and
cream livery with red and gold lining, fair condition, c1910.
$600–675 *Bon*

A French tinplate clockwork
carpet train, probably by
Dessin, comprising a 2½in
gauge 2-2-0 locomotive,
with matching four-wheeled
tender, finished in gold, green
and black with red lining, one
blue and one red passenger
coach, both with yellow lining,
and a luggage van finished
in green, defective, some
rust, restored, label 'Brevete,
D.S. S.G.D.G.', c1890.
$1,000–1,200 *S(S)*

A German lead miniature floor train, comprising an 0-6-0 'Vulcan'
locomotive, a four-wheeled tender finished in green, tuscan red and
black, an open coal wagon, cattle truck, passenger coaches and a
guard's luggage van, finished in red, blue and yellow, good condition,
in original box with sliding lid, fair condition, mid-19thC.
$4,500–5,250 *CSK*

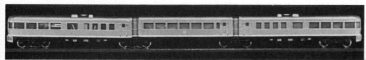

A 3-unit diesel-electric railcar, No. 3025, finished in red, good condition,
c1959, in original dark orange box with original packing, tested tag and
instructions, fair condition.
$2,700–3,000 *CSK*

**Miller's is a price GUIDE
not a price LIST**

A Bing Pullman coach, 'Plato', finished in brown
and cream with gold lining, the hinged roof opens
to reveal chairs and tables, good condition, c1920.
$120–140 *Bon*

A Märklin hand-painted tin freight station,
with 4 sliding doors and 2 booms, good
condition, c1904, 16in (40.5cm) wide.
$3,500–4,500 *SK*

A Bing for Bassett-Lowke, clockwork 4-4-0
'George The Fifth' locomotive, No. 5320, with
matching six-wheeled tender, finished in red
LMS livery with yellow and black lining, good
condition, c1924.
$360–420 *Bon*

A pair of 0 gauge railway carriages, by Karl Bub
of Nuremberg, c1912.
$90–110 *AH*

Vehicles

A Dinky Supertoys Guy 4 ton lorry, No. 511, finished in brown and black, in original box, good condition, c1947.
$525–600 *WAL*

A Günthermann clockwork tinplate 49 Ford saloon, finished in maroon, in original box, good condition, c1940, 11in (28cm) long.
$475–575 *CSK*

A Dinky Supertoys Pullmore Car Transporter gift set, No. 990, c1956.
$825–975 *RAR*

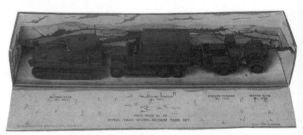

A Dinky No.151 Royal Tank Corps – Medium Tank Set, comprising a tank, six-wheeled wagon, cooker trailer, water tank trailer, driver and 2 figures, fair condition, pre-WWII, in original box.
$450–525 *TMA*

A Dinky Toys Sports Cars Gift Set, No. 149, comprising a 107 Sunbeam Alpine, 108 M.G. Midget, 109 Austin Healey, 110 Aston Martin and a Triumph TR2, in original box, fair condition, c1959.
$825–975 *Bon*

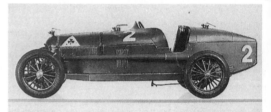

A CIJ clockwork tinplate Alfa Romeo P2 racing car, finished in red, Michelin tyres, black spoked-wheels with drum brakes, Excelsior adjustable shock absorbers and key, some damage, c1928, 21in (53cm) long.
$2,200–2,700 *CSK*

A Dinky Supertoys Foden diesel 8-wheel wagon, No. 501, finished in blue, black and silver, in original early style box, good condition, c1950.
$75–90
A Dinky Supertoys Foden diesel 8-wheel wagon, finished in red, fawn and silver, in original box, good condition, c1952.
$150–180 *WAL*

A Chad Valley lithographed London Transport double-decker bus biscuit tin, finished in red and cream LT livery, with dark grey removable roof, good condition, in an original box for the mechancial version, c1950.
$475–575 *WAL*

A Dinky Toys Triumph 2000, No. 135, finished in white and grey, c1965, 4in (10cm) long. $1,800–2,000 *RAR*

A Movosprint 52 Ferrari racing car, with red diecast metal body, with gas powered Super Tigre engine, good condition, c1952, 12in (30.5cm) long. $2,700–3,000 *CSK*

A Yonezawa friction-driven tinplate Cadillac, No. 10798, finished in black, with white trim, blue tinted windows, in original box, good condition, 1960, 18in (46cm) long. $2,000–2,500 *CSK*

A Schuco 6080 Electro Construction battery-operated remote control tinplate fire engine, finished in red, with 3 composition figures, fair condition, c1968, 10in (25.5cm) long. $1,800–2,000 *CSK*

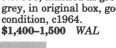

A Dinky Supertoys Leyland Octopus flat truck with chains, No. 935, finished in green and grey, in original box, good condition, c1964. $1,400–1,500 *WAL*

A Bing hand painted tinplate clockwork rear-entry tonneau, finished in dark blue with light blue and gilt lining, with red-buttoned upholstery, and composition chauffeur, in original labelled box, good condition, c1910, 8½in (21.5cm) long. $11,250–13,500 *CSK*

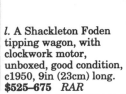

l. A Shackleton Foden tipping wagon, with clockwork motor, unboxed, good condition, c1950, 9in (23cm) long. $525–675 *RAR*

Dinky, Corgi, Matchbox, Britains, Schuco, Bing, Bassett Lowke
Hornby, Jouef, Wrenn, Meccano, Mettoy, Triang, Spot On, Chad Valley
Distler, Benbros, Trix, Graham Farrish, Elastolin, Fleischmann, Marklin
All these famous Toy manufacturers are likely to be found
in our auctions sales

A rare Gift Set No 38 'Rallye Monte Carlo' made £575
in our Febuary 1996 sale

Auction Dates for your Diary

Thursday 29th August 1996
Monday 7th October 1996
Monday 18th November 1996
Monday 6th January 1997
Monday 10th February 1997
Monday 17th March 1997
Monday 28th April 1997
Monday 9th June 1997
Monday 14th July 1997

Last entries 9am to 1pm on the
Saturday following the previous sale

*Illustrated Catalogue £4.50
inclusive of postage*

INTERNATIONALLY YOURS

WALLIS & WALLIS

Britain's Specialist Auctioneers of Die-Cast, Tinplate Toys & Models
WEST ST. AUCTION GALLERIES, LEWES, SUSSEX, BN7 2NJ, England
Telephone 01273-480208   Fax 01273-476562

Boats

A painted wooden-hulled model pond yacht, with weighted keel below simulated planked deck, with linen cloth sails, c1910, 36in (91.5cm) long, in original felt cover.
$1,200–1,275 *BWe*

MILLER'S COMPARES . . .

I A Märklin clockwork tinplate steam yacht, 'Jolanda', finished in cream, with 2 masts and single funnel, planked effect superstructure, with 4 lifeboats, anchor on chain, adjustable rudder and 4 figures, on wheeled wave base, slight damage, c1910, 29in (73.5cm) long.
$24,000–25,500 *S*

II A Märklin clockwork tinplate steam yacht, 'Jolanda', finished in green and white, with 2 masts and single funnel, planked effect superstructure, with 4 lifeboats, anchor on chain, adjustable rudder, on wheeled wave base, paintwork crazed, super-structure has been restored, c1920, 29in (73.5cm) long.
$10,000–11,000 *S*

An item which is fresh to the market often attracts enthusiastic bidding, and *item I* achieved a very good price because it had not been offered at auction before. It had the added advantage of being in extremely good condition with very little restoration. Items in their original condition always command a premium, however good the restoration of a similar piece might be. The superstructure above the hull of *Item II* had been repainted, which rendered it less desirable to buyers. *S*

A Bing clockwork tinplate torpedo boat, Cat. No. 13957/2, the hull finished in grey above scarlet, with 3 funnels and key wind, damaged, c1906, painted 'No. 121', 39½in (100.5cm) long, original box.
$6,200–6,800 *S*

A wood and tinplate model of a flotilla leader, probably Bassett-Lowke, the wooden-hull finished in grey with red beneath water line, painted tinplate deck with 4 guns, torpedo tubes and 2 funnels, fitted with later motor, together with its original single cylinder steam engine, minor damage, c1930, 39½in (100.5cm) long, wooden storage box.
$525–600 *S(S)*

Bing Boats

As part of the fascination in the early 20th century with the latest modes of transport, Bing produced a wide range of toy boats to suit all pockets, and to rival their competitor's, Märklin's, products. Characteristics typical of Bing boats are a lightness of touch – which contrasted with the thickly painted and sturdy style of Märklin – transfer portholes, a distinctive streamlined shape and attention to realistic details, as designs were often closely based on real vessels.

r. A Bing tinplate and clockwork gunboat, finished in grey and black, with twin-rotating turrets and side-mounted guns, twin funnels and flags, damaged, c1910, 19in (49cm) long.
$1,000–1,200 *S(S)*

Soldiers

A Britains 1st Version Set 81 trumpeter of 17th Lancers, a Set 8 trumpeter of 12th Lancers, and a Set 12 mounted officer of the 11th Hussars, good condition, c1895.
$240–270 *CSK*

r. A Company of British Line Infantry on the march, by Heyde or similar German maker, with mounted captain, 2 lieutenants and ensign with flag, dog mascot, musical director and band, 2-horse supply wagon and driver, damaged, good condition, 1895.
$975–1,000 *P*

A Heyde No. 2 size set of British Volunteer Corps Bicyclists, comprising 20 pieces, good condition, c1895.
$1,200–1,275 *P*

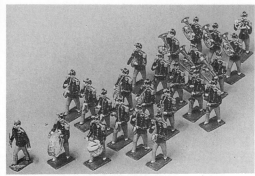

A Band of the French Infanterie à Grande Tenue, with musical director and 23 bandsmen, 50mm scale, good condition, 1895.
$1,250–1,350 P(Ba)

A Britains group, previously unknown, of 13 Barbary Coast corsairs, each with one movable arm, good condition, 1922.
$6,000–6,750 P

A Britains Set 9435 Black Watch Highland Pipers, comprising 20 soldiers, post WWII, in original box.
$1,125–1,275 DN

A Britains Set 1904 Officers and Men of the US Army Air Corps, excellent condition,1940, in original green box with typeset label, fair condition.
$1,400–1,700 P

A Britains Set 1339 Royal Horse Artillery, 4th Version, with 6-horse team and 2 mounted gunners, in service dress with steel helmets, some missing, good condition, 1940.
$1,800–2,000 P

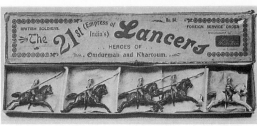

A Britains Set 94, 21st Lancers, 1st Version, wearing foreign service dress, 1899, very good condition, in original printer's decorated 'Heroes of Omdurman & Khartoum' box.
$975–1,125 P

A Britains Set 1622 Band of the Royal Marine Light Infantry, excellent condition, 1938, in original box.
$14,250–15,750 P(Ba)

A Britains Set 316 Royal Horse Artillery, in full dress, with officer and 6-horse team, 2nd Version limber and gun 1201, in khaki finish, very good condition, 1933.
$1,800–2,000 P

Miscellaneous Toys & Games

A Victorian rocking horse, in original condition, 32in (81.5cm) high.
$675–750 *DaD*

A dapple grey rocking horse, with glass eyes, the remains of a leather bridle, velvet saddle, stirrup leathers, horse hair mane and tail, on trestle base with metal rockers, damaged, early 20thC, 44in (112cm) long.
$800–900 *S*

A rocking horse, with original paint, 19thC, 41in (104cm) long.
$350–375 *FOX*

A 1935 Steelcraft Pontiac pedal car, yellow with maroon wheel arches and running boards, chromed steering wheel, windscreen, radiator grille, headlights, horn and mascot, completely restored, 36in (91.5cm) long.
$1,800–2,000 *S(NY)*

A 1932 Steelcraft Lincoln pedal car, in two-tone brown, with leatherette interior, chromed mascot, bumpers, steering wheel, head and tail lights, spotlamp, lined in maroon and silver, completely restored, 46in (117cm) long.
$2,000–2,500 *S(NY)*

A novelty painted cast iron mechanical money bank, with green and red base, the boy dressed in yellow and red, paint loss and damage, c1890, 10in (25.5cm) long, together with a John Harper & Co Ltd, 'Little Joe Bank'.
$2,200–2,700 *CSK*

When a coin is placed on the boy's tray and the lever in front of the goat is pushed, the goat butts the boy forward and the frog moves upwards as the coin slides from the tray into the frog's mouth.

An J & E Stevens 'Bad Accident' cast iron money bank, designed by Charles A. Bailey, damaged, c1887, 10¼in (26cm) long.
$1,125–1,275 *S*

When a coin is placed in between the feet of the water melon eating driver and is deposited in the cart, the boy appears from his hiding place scaring the mule to jolt the cart back as the lever is pushed.

An Elastolin composition and wood Noah's Ark, with hinged ramp and removable roof, on 4 wooden wheels, with a collection of animals, with label, early 20thC, the ark 17in (43cm) long.
$1,800–2,000 *CSK*

A German painted wood Noah's Ark, with a collection of composition, papier mâché and metal animals and figures, 19thC, the ark 24in (61cm) long.
$525–600 *AH*

l. A French pull-along bird, covered in real feathers of yellow, with orange wings and tail, red plume, wooden beak and painted eyes, on papier mâché 4-wheeled moulded base painted green, with fabric flowers, c1890, 13in (33cm) long.
$1,800–2,000 *Bon*

An J & E Stevens Dark Town battery money bank, the pitcher with articulated arm and head, the catcher with articulated head and coin flap, damaged, c1900, 9¾in (25cm) long.
$975–1,125 *S(S)*

A Bing pull-along fire pump, finished in green and orange, with wood effect seats and rear hinged compartment flap, brass-topped pump section and lamp, lever bars each side, brass bell, 2 reproduction wooden firemen, slight damage and hose missing, c1910, 19in (48cm) long.
$2,700–3,200 S

An American construction set, The New Pretty Boat House Set, containing cardboard houses and a variety of cut-out people, in original box, good condition, c1897, box 12 x 8½in (30.5 x 21.5cm).
$60–75 Bon

A Märklin cast iron and tinplate hand-drawn live steam fire pump, with piston pump, brass and copper steam dome, finished in red, black and gold, with original hose, c1890, 19in (48cm) long.
$21,000–22,500 CNY

A Bell Toys & Games Ltd board game based on the TV show *Highway Patrol*, 1960s, 14½in (36.5cm) square.
$45–60 CTO

A Britains archery set, with 3½in (9cm) high archer with wire bow and 2 lead and wire target frames, enclosing paper targets, very good condition, c1880.
$1,900–2,200 WAL

A Spanish embossed cardboard toy theatre, with scene of Roman people and ruins, wood and paper stage, paper curtains, 19 slots for scenery and 6 variable height slots, together with coloured paper printed scenery for 8 plays, a quantity of figures and some play books, in original box, good condition, early 20thC.
$1,500–1,800 Bon

l. A Chad Valley TV game of *Hancock's Half Hour*, 1960s, box 13½ x 15¼in (34.5 x 39cm).
$75–90 CTO

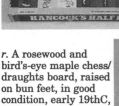

r. A rosewood and bird's-eye maple chess/draughts board, raised on bun feet, in good condition, early 19thC, 14½in (37cm) square.
$450–550 JC

A late Victorian games compendium, in burr walnut box, by Bagshaw & Sons, Church Street, Liverpool, 18in (45.5cm) wide.
$1,000–1,125 McC

EPHEMERA
Annuals, Comics & Magazines

New York World's Fair Comics, National Periodical Publications, comic book, 1940.
$1,200–1,350 *CNY*

Donald Duck finds Pirate Gold, by Carl Barks, Dell Publishing, Four Colour Comics, No. 9, 1942.
$1,900–2,200 *CNY*

Batman No. 1, National Periodical Publications, comic book, origin of *Batman* retold by Bob Kane, as well as the first appearance of the Joker and Catwoman, 1940.
$10,500–12,000 *CNY*

Superman No. 2, National Periodical Publications, 2nd issue of Superman's own title, 1939.
$5,000–6,000 *CNY*

Captain Marvel Adventures No. 3, Fawcett Publications, comic book, 1941.
$975–1,125 *CNY*

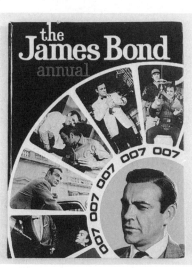

The James Bond Annual, 1968, 10½ x 8¼in (28 x 21cm).
$10–15 *CTO*

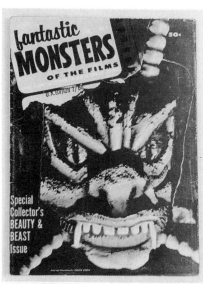

Fantastic Monsters of the Films, Vol. 1, No. 5, 1963, 8¼ x 11in (21 x 28cm).
$10–15 *CTO*

Captain America No 2, by Joe Simon, Timely (Marvel) Comics, original art, full colour cover re-creation, acrylic on board, 1995, 22 x 16in (56 x 40.5cm).
$6,000–6,750 *CNY*

Fantastic Four No. 1, Marvel Comics Group, origin of *Fantastic Four*, 1961.
$8,500–10,500 *CNY*

Autographs

A signed photograph of Enrico Caruso, framed and glazed, c1910, 5¼ x 4¼in (13.5 x 10.5cm).
$750–825 *S*

A signed and inscribed photograph of James Cagney, 10 x 8in (25.5 x 20.5cm).
$90–110 *VS*

A signed and inscribed photograph of Peter Tchaikovsky, by Konarsky of Moscow, glazed, in a satinwood cabinet frame, 1885, 9½ x 7¼in (24 x 18.5cm).
$5,500–6,500 *S*

An autographed photograph of Sir Winston Churchill, supporting Randolph Churchill as Parliamentary Candidate, Devonport, 1950, 9½ x 7½in (24 x 19cm).
$600–675 *RBB*

A signed sepia photograph of Spencer Tracy, 7 x 5in (18 x 12.5cm).
$135–175 *VS*

A signed photograph of Stan Laurel and Oliver Hardy, 5 x 7in (12.5 x 18cm).
$560–600 *VS*

r. A signed photograph of Audrey Hepburn, from *Breakfast at Tiffany's*, 7 x 5in (18 x 12.5cm).
$250–275 *VS*

A menu from a dinner given by the Guild of Air Pilots, signed by Charles Lindbergh, Amy Johnson, and Captain the Rt Hon F. E. Guest, and another, mounted with 2 photographs of the flyers, 1930s, framed and glazed.
$1,400–1,500 *S(S)*

Cigarette & Trade Cards

Pascall, Tricks and
Puzzles, set of 40,
very good to
excellent condition.
$160–180 *VS*

Maynard, Girl Guide
Series, set of 6, good to
very good condition.
$65–75 *VS*

Liebig, Military
Uniforms, set of 6,
one with damaged
corner, fair to very
good condition.
$270–300 *VS*

R. & J. Hill Ltd,
Battleships and
Crests, set of 25, good
to excellent condition.
$375–450 *VS*

Postcards

A German album of Hallowe'en postcards,
by Raphael Tuck and other makes,
all in bright colours, 1905–20.
$675–750 *Bon*

An album of cigarette cards, including 119
Churchman's Boy Scouts, John Player &
Sons Cricketers, 1934, 49 of 50 Cricketers
Caricatures by RIP, 1926, 80 of 100
Gallagher's Association Footballer Club
Colours, 1910, Churchman's Footballers,
1914, Player's Footballers, Caricatures
by RIP, 1926, Churchman's Boxing
Personalities, 23 of 25 Ogdens Boxing,
1914, and Taddy & Co Sports and
Pastimes, 1912.
$675–750 *DN*

Britain's first postcard, with
advertisement on reverse,
Tavistock, October 1st 1870,
good to very good condition.
$630–700 *VS*

Lancashire, sepia, J. Coupe ice
cream seller, horse drawn vehicle,
Leyland, slight creasing,
good condition.
$45–50 *VS*

Louis Wain, The
Merry Mascot,
Raphael Tuck, 3553,
excellent condition.
$90–100 *VS*

A hand-drawn postcard, showing a
gamekeeper standing by a signpost
entitled 'Eleven A.M. The X Roads
Dec. 22nd 1887', very good condition.
$240–270 *VS*

*This type of card was not allowed by
postal regulations until 1894.*

l. Berkshire, International
Stores Shopfront, with a staff
of 6, by May of Reading, good
to very good condition.
$50–60 *VS*

Posters

A lithograph poster in colours, for Almanacco Italiano, by C. Casaltoli, printed by Angiolo Gambi, Firenze, on 2 sheets, slight damage, 1900, 84 x 31in (213.5 x 78.5cm).
$5,250–6,500 *CSK*

A poster for Bitter Campari, by Adolfo Hohenstein, linen-backed, worn and repaired, c1900, 78¼ x 37in (199 x 94cm), framed.
$3,500–4,000 *SK*

A lithograph poster, entitled 'Flirt', by Alphonse Mucha, printed in colours by F. Champenois, signed, 1899, 23 x 10¼in (58.5 x 26cm), framed.
$3,750–4,500 *S(NY)*

A poster depicting Humphrey Bogart, in *To Have and Have Not*, Warner Bros, Australian day bill, 1945, 29 x 13in (73 x 33cm).
$750–825 *CSK*

A one-sheet poster for *Superman and the Mole Men*, Lippert Pictures, linen-backed, 1951.
$600–675 *Bon*

A chromolithograph poster, for the New York World's Fair, 1939, by Grinnel Litho Co, 29½ x 19¼in (75 x 49cm).
$550–630 *P*

A one-sheet movie poster, depicting Elvis Presley in a blue shirt, singing and playing the guitar, as well as scenes from the film *Love Me Tender*, signed in black ink, 1956, 41 x 28in (104 x 71cm).
$3,250–4,000 *B&B*

r. A French cinema poster, entitled 'Napoléon Bonaparte', Gaumont, 1927, linen-backed, 94 x 63in (239 x 160cm).
$17,250–20,000 *CSK*

A poster for the Kunsthaus Maskenfest, Zurich, linen backed, slight damage, 1926, 50½ x 35⅞in (128 x 91cm), framed.
$975–1,125 *SK*

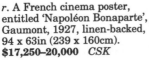

ROCK & POP

An American long playing stereophonic record of The Beatles, on the Vee Jay label, 1963.
$1,300–1,500 *ED*

A copy of *Mad Magazine*, UK edition No. 81, featuring The Beatles with Maharishi on the front cover, 1967, 11 x 8in (28 x 21cm).
$20–25 *CTO*

A Coral Records publicity postcard, signed on the front in black and blue biro by Buddy Holly and The Crickets, creased and torn, 1958, 5 x 3½in (12.5 x 9cm).
$825–975 *CSK*

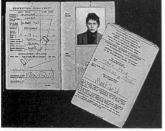

A Remo black Weather King drumskin, inscribed and signed in gold felt pen by The Beach Boys, 1994.
$800–975 *CNY*

Sheet music, entitled 'Shake' by Sam Cooke, by Kags Music Corp, c1965, 11 x 8½in (28 x 21.5cm).
$10–15 *CTO*

The Apple Song Book, by Apple Publishing, USA, early 1970s, 11 x 9in (28 x 23cm).
$120–150 *CTO*

A cancelled British Passport for Marc Bolan, valid for 5 years, signed 'Mark Feld', issued on March 31st 1967.
$1,800–2,000 *CSK*

Six turquoise set panels from a fringe necklace, an arrowhead, and a leather choker with gilt metal beads, worn by Jimi Hendrix, with a letter of authenticity, c1967.
$2,500–2,700 *CSK*

Bob Dylan's harmonica, the Hohner 'Marine Band', signed in black marker pen, in a plastic case, with a statement of authenticity from César Diaz, Dylan's equipment technician.
$3,500–4,000 *S*

An Australian presentation platinum sales award, for 'The Best of The Doors', presented to Elektra International, 1991, 16¼ x 24in (40.5 x 61cm), framed.
$1,200–1,500 *CSK*

r. An American Express credit card, signed by Elvis Presley, expiry date April 30, 1959, 2¼ x 3½in (5.5 x 9cm).
$65,000–70,000 *B&B*

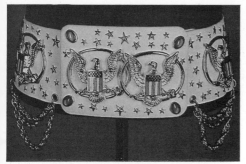

A white leather belt, designed by Bill Belew, with faux gold stars, red stones and 7 gold American eagles with stars and stripes in the centre, gold coloured metal rope chains suspended from the bottom.
$9,750–11,250 *B&B*

This is believed to be one of 2 belts made, which were later to be known as the American Eagle belt. This was worn by Elvis at the rehearsal of Aloha From Hawaii, when he threw it into the audience.

A copy of the magazine *Record Mail*, the cover commemorating Cliff Richard's 21st birthday, 1961, 13½ x 10¼in (34 x 26cm).
$10–15 *CTO*

A cream jumpsuit, with floral pattern, worn by Brian Connolly of Sweet, and a letter and cheque signed by Connolly, 1970s.
$1,500–1,800 *S*

A United States $1,000 bill, signed by Elvis Presley in red ink, 2¼ x 6in (5.5 x 15cm).
$6,800–8,200 *B&B*

Elvis was known to sometimes give joke gifts as Christmas presents. One year he is reported to have given his close friends 50 cent book coupons for MacDonalds, but then later gave someone a $1,000 bill.

l. A two-piece suit of soft black leather, worn by Annie Lennox, labelled 'Yelena, Melbourne', and a cropped jacket, labelled 'Zack Carr Collection', c1994.
$1,300–1,500 *CSK*

A Fender 200SX acoustic guitar, serial No. 9051644, with natural finish, spruce top, 20 fret fingerboard with dot inlays, pin bridge and tortoiseshell pickguard, signed on the body by all 5 members of INXS.
$950–1,000 *CSK*

A flesh-coloured nylon gauze sequinned pant suit, designed by Jeff Banks, made by Jimmy Parker, embroidered by Freda Fairway, worn by Sandie Shaw at the Montreux Film Festival, late 1960s.
$270–300 *S*

ARMS & ARMOUR
Armour

A cabasset, formed in one-piece, with pear stalk finial, brass rosette rivets around the base, good condition, c1600.
$300–350 *WAL*

A trooper's cuirass, the breastplate with a low medial ridge and narrow flange at the base, together with its original backplate, shoulder straps missing, c1640.
$1,400–1,600 *S(S)*

A trooper's pot helmet, the two-piece skull joined by a low comb, with three-bar face guard, a neck guard and ear pieces, chipped and repaired, c1640, 11½in (29cm) high.
$1,500–1,800 *S(S)*

A Georgian universal pattern copper gorget, engraved with crowned 'GR' cipher, retaining traces of gilding, together with another Georgian brass gorget, engraved with Royal Arms, slight damage.
$475–575 *S(S)*

A Georgian officer's silver-coloured gorget of The 62nd (The Wiltshire) Regiment, engraved with pre-1801 Royal Arms and trophies, good condition.
$675–750 *WAL*

A German composite infantry part armour, breastplate with light wear and pitting, late 16thC.
$3,250–3,750 *S(S)*

A French or Italian falling buffe for a burgonet, with a chin piece slotted for turning pins, the upper plate embossed and pierced with diagonal slots, light wear, late 16thC, 8⅝in (22cm) high.
$1,800–2,000 *S(S)*

A heavy bullet-proof breastplate, with distinctive medial ridge, studs for securing shoulder straps and side clips for aligning waist belt, good condition, 17thC.
$450–575 *WAL*

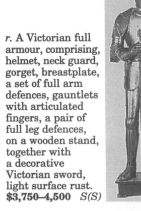

A German composite full armour, comprising a helmet, neck guard, gorget, fluted breastplate, articulated waistplate, a pair of full arm defences, mitten gauntlets, and a pair of full leg defences, on a tailor's partially articulated torso dummy adapted to stand, with wooden base, c1530.
$50,000–60,000 *S(S)*

Armour
Many fine quality copies of suits of armour were made in the late 18th and early 19thC. The fluted designs of 16thC Maximilian armours make them one of the most attractive styles, and one of the most often reproduced, especially by armour enthusiasts in the Georgian period. Good reproductions are well articulated, properly proportioned and heavy. Early 20thC reproductions are inferior, the metal is thin, the anatomy is inaccurate and the articulation often faulty.

r. A Victorian full armour, comprising, helmet, neck guard, gorget, breastplate, a set of full arm defences, gauntlets with articulated fingers, a pair of full leg defences, on a wooden stand, together with a decorative Victorian sword, light surface rust.
$3,750–4,500 *S(S)*

A close helmet, with one-piece skull, the visor with double sight aperture above ventilation slots, 2 gorget plates, chin piece associated, probably German, c1580.
$9,000–10,000 *Gle*

Helmets

A helmet consists of a 'skull' to protect the top of the head, usually made from one piece of metal. 'Close' helmets have a variety of additional parts which are hinged or riveted to the skull, including a visor to protect the face, with breathing holes or 'breaths', ear flaps and a nose guard, often adjustable. Helmets with articulated neck guards, known as 'lobster tails', appeared in the early 17th century in several European countries. They were made famous in England by Cromwell's cavalry.

A German composite fluted close helmet, the skull formed in one piece, embossed with tapering bands of broad flutes over the sides, c1530, later plume holder, visor, chin piece and neck guard, 11¾in (30cm) high.
$2,000–2,500 *S(S)*

A German or Dutch closed burgonet, with two-piece skull, a plume holder, pointed fall, chin piece and neck guard, with crack, early 17thC, 12in (30.5cm) high.
$2,200–2,700 *S(S)*

A German or Dutch trooper's zischägge, with one-piece skull, pointed peak, adjustable nasal bar, neck guard and pierced ear pieces, one rivet missing, c1640, 9¾in (25cm) high.
$1,500–1,800 *S(S)*

An Italian composite infantry part armour, comprising comb morion, breastplate, associated skirt carrying a pair of tassets extending to the knee, associated backplate and articulated skirt, on a wooden stand, late 16thC, with some 19thC additions.
$4,000–5,000 *S(S)*

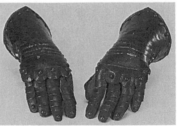

A pair of Swedish or Danish copper gauntlets, originally gilt, each with short pointed cuff in two parts, articulated fingers, knuckle plate with articulated finger defences, damaged, c1700.
$1,125–1,275 *S(S)*

An Italian or Flemish composite close helmet, with two-piece skull, plume holder, associated visor, bevor and chin piece, neck guard with 2 plates, worn and pitted, c1580, 12½in (32cm) high.
$2,300–2,700 *S(NY)*

> **Miller's is a price GUIDE not a price LIST**

r. An animé breastplate, from a Polish Hussar's armour, formed of 5 plates of shot-proof weight, 4 articulated lower plates, and slotted for straps at the shoulders and sides, slight damage, c1640, 17¼in (44cm) high.
$8,000–9,000 *S(S)*

Breastplates of this form were worn by the so-called 'Winged' Hussars. Similar examples are preserved in the State Collection of Art at Wawel Castle in Cracow. Examples of this type rarely appear on the market.

Bows

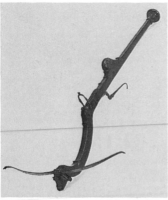

r. A German sporting crossbow, with steel bow, fitted with string of cord, fruitwood stock, the top veneered in engraved bone, the bottom inlaid at the front with a bone plaque carved with scrollwork, the top and bottom pierced for rods to set the mechanism, with iron lugs, small stirrup, back sight, safety catch, trigger and pivot trigger, dated '1667', together with a crossbow bolt, worn, small repairs, 19thC, 21¾in (55cm) long.
$3,750–4,500 *S(S)*

An Italian stonebow, with steel bow retained by iron loops, walnut carved stock, back sight, string release and trigger, fore sight missing, stock slightly chipped, early 17thC, 33½in (85cm) long.
$1,800–2,000 *S(S)*

Daggers

A Scottish officer's dirk, of The Cameronians, with 11¼in (28.5cm) blade, with faceted back edge etched with thistles, regimental number '79' and battle honours to Lucknow, carved wood basketweave hilt with gilt studs, reverse carved, embossed gilt mounts, pommel set with a stone, in its black leather scabbard, with gilt mounts applied with regimental number and thistles, complete with companion knife and fork, in its matching skean dhu, 4½in (11cm) etched blade, carved wood hilt, gilt-mounted leather scabbard, and plaid brooch and battle honours, 1870s.
$3,750–4,500 *Gle*

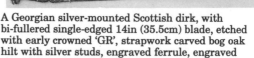

An English or Dutch dagger, so-called Buckingham type, with tapering blade with serrated back edge and reinforced point, etched on one side with the date, small iron guard decorated on both sides, fluted rosewood grip capped by an engraved brass flowerhead washer, small brass collar missing, worn and cracked, dated '1630', 13½in (34.5cm) long.
$2,500–3,000 *S(S)*

A European dagger, with single-edged 12in (30.5cm) blade, gold decoration to spine, the bone hilt carved with Adam, Eve and the serpent, early 17thC, 16in (40.5cm) overall.
$1,200–1,400 *GV*

Guns

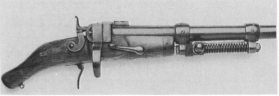

A Georgian silver-mounted Scottish dirk, with bi-fullered single-edged 14in (35.5cm) blade, etched with early crowned 'GR', strapwork carved bog oak hilt with silver studs, engraved ferrule, engraved shoulders and silver pommel with square button, probably cut down from a sword blade, good condition.
$1,100–1,200 *WAL*

A George II Brown Bess flintlock musket, with brass trigger guard and butt plate, the lock engraved with Royal cipher and maker's name 'Farmer 1748', proof marks and rack number '15', 42in (106.5cm) barrel.
$1,500–1,800 *AG*

The maker Joseph Farmer held Royal government contracts for the manufacture of flintlock muskets. He worked in Birmingham and London 1718–62.

l. An Italian Snaphaunce mechanism, the flat plate struck inside with the maker's initials 'IPK', the pan formed with an integral buffer engaging the breast of the cock, fitted with sliding pancover, c1640, plate 6½in (16.5cm) long.
$325–375 *S(S)*

A 3 bore hammer punt gun, by Tolley, serial No. 1006, 59in (150cm) steel barrel, fitted beneath with swivel mounts and recoil spring, oak stock, black powder proof, in its wooden box, complete with 8 steel re-loadable cartridge cases, late 19thC.
$2,200–2,700 *Gle*

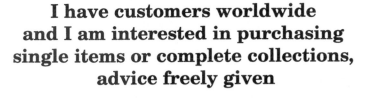

Pistols

An east Scottish all-steel flintlock belt pistol, with sighted barrel formed in 6 stages, octagonal breech and swamped muzzle, plain bevelled lock with dog safety catch, incised stock, heart-shaped pommel, pierced button trigger, long belt hook cusped bevelled finial, engraved ramrod pipe, claw-topped iron ramrod, top jaw associated, pricker and fore-end screw missing, light pitting, c1700, 20in (51cm) long.
$8,500–9,750 *S(S)*

Antique Firearms

The two main types of antique firearms that collectors will encounter today are the flintlock and the percussion. Flintlocks, which first appeared in the mid-17th century, use a flint to strike sparks from a steel plate in order to ignite the powder charge. Percussion firearms, invented in the early 19th century, use a disposable metal cap containing a minute amount of solid explosive. The percussion method, although relatively unsophisticated, dominated firearms development until the widespread adoption of the modern metallic cartridge.

A set of full stocked duelling pistols, by H. W. Mortimer, the browned octagonal barrels with gold touch holes, swan necked cocks, set triggers and sliding safety, c1800, 15½in (39.5cm) long, cased.
$8,500–9,750 *GV*

A pair of half-stocked duelling pistols, by John Probin, with 10in (25.5cm) octagonal Damascus steel barrels, French style cocks and roller frizzens, c1810, 16in (40.5cm) long overall.
$6,750–8,250 *GV*

A 28 bore flintlock pistol, by Green, octagonal 6½in (16.5cm) barrel, stepped bolted lock, swan-neck cock and roller to frizzen spring, full stocked with flat panelled butt, silver mounts, damaged, Birmingham silver hallmarks for 1818.
$1,400–1,700 *S(S)*

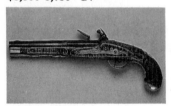

An American engraved and inlaid brass wrought iron and curly maple flintlock pistol, with two-stage sighted barrel, brass line inlaid stock, decorated trigger plate, trigger guard and wooden ramrod, Valley of Virginia, Rockingham, Augusta or Rockbridge Counties, 18thC, 14¾in (37.5cm) long.
$36,000–42,000 *S(NY)*

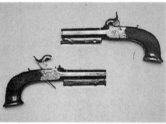

A pair of boxlock pistols, signed on the 3½in (9cm) octagonal barrels 'Southall', with swivel ramrods, foliate engraved frames, sliding top thumb safety catches, concealed triggers, chequered walnut butts with oval terminals, slight damage, 19thC, 8¼in (21cm) long overall.
$975–1,125 *DN*

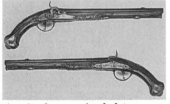

A pair of percussion holster pistols, by Daniel Theirmay, Paris or Liège, converted from flintlock, with browned sighted barrels signed on the sighting rib, the breech with maker's mark 'DT', bevelled flat decorated locks, carved figured Grenoble walnut full stocks, full steel mounts, barrels and stocks chiselled and gilt, spurred faceted pommels with domed cap, faceted ramrod pipes, chiselled and gilt escutcheons, iron-capped wooden ramrods, minor damage, c1730, 20½in (52cm) long.
$3,250–3,750 *S(S)*

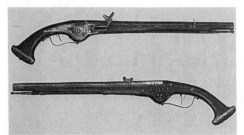

A pair of German wheel lock holster pistols, with three-stage barrels, each struck with Zella control marks, and the barrelsmith 'NCM' in shield, with rounded locks, with external wheel, sliding pan cover, wooden full stocks, the slender butts bound with an iron band and fitted with a carved domed wooden cap, iron trigger guards, ramrod pipes and fore-end bands, and original iron-tipped wooden ramrods, damaged, some parts missing and some replaced, c1650, 25in (63.5cm) long.
$7,500–9,000 *S(S)*

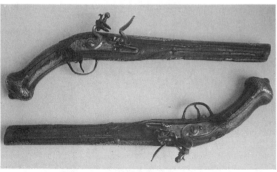

A pair of Continental flintlock holster pistols, with chased steel barrels, engraved steel locks and carved walnut stocks, c1780, 13in (33cm) long.
$1,000–1,200 *MR*

Powder Flasks & Horns

An American powder horn, engraved with the British coat-of-arms, a sailing vessel, a map of Boston, the harbour, ships with many named hills, waterways and other landscape features, retains what appears to be the original turned wood spout, stopper and base, old repairs, signed 'John Hill', probably Boston, dated '1775', 15in (38cm) long.
$3,000–3,750 *S(NY)*

Revolvers

A 5 shot 80 bore Tranter's patent double-action percussion revolver No. 21121T, 4½in (11.5cm) barrel, Birmingham proved, top engraved 'Griffiths & Worsley (Late) J W Edge Manchester', foliate engraved frame, swivel ramrod, one-piece chequered walnut grip, good working condition, 10in (25.5cm) long, in green felt-lined mahogany case, with twin cavity bronze mould stamped 'Tranter's Patent', Dixon oil bottle and flask, nipple key and tins, good condition, c1860.
$1,800–2,200 *WAL*

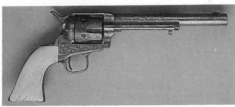

A .44 Rimfire single-action army model revolver No. 484, the 7½in (19cm) barrel stamped 'Colt's Pt. F.A. Mfg. Co. Hartford, Ct. U.S.A.', engraved ejector rod housing, the frame with patent markings '1871' and '1872', gripstraps engraved, patinated ivory grips, c1875.
$7,000–8,250 *S(NY)*

An American hunter's leather carrying pouch with powder horn, together with a wrought iron-mounted powder horn with sawtooth edge, probably Pennsylvania or Southern, c1780, pouch 18½in (47cm) long including strap.
$600–675 *S(NY)*

l. A Colt .36 calibre model 1851 Navy percussion revolver No. 1643 for 1854, with blued 7½in (19cm) barrels, stamped, cylinder engraved with a continuous scene of men o' war, walnut grips, brass trigger guard, in its oak baize-lined case with bullet mould and nipple key.
$2,300–2,700 *HAL*

A commemorative powder horn, engraved with a city scene with churches, a fort scene and allegorical dogs of war, slight damage, signed 'Zelemus Williams', dated '1775', 14½in (37cm) long.
$5,250–6,000 *S(NY)*

A copper and brass powder flask, by Hawksley, with horses' heads relief decoration, mid-19thC, 7in (18cm) long.
$225–275 *MR*

A copper and brass powder flask, by Hawksley, with scroll decoration, mid-19thC, 7in (18cm) long.
$120–150 *MR*

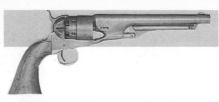

A 6 shot .44 Colt army single-action percussion revolver, No. 72477, with 8in (20.5cm) barrel, stamped 'Col Saml Colt New York US America', underlever rammer, cylinder roll engraved with naval engagement scene, frame stamped, brass trigger guard, frame slotted for detachable shoulder stock, good working condition, c1860, 13¾in (35cm) long.
$2,000–2,500 *WAL*

A 5 shot .451 percussion double-action revolver, octagonal 6¾in (17cm) sighted barrel, engraved 'Deane Adams & Deane, 30 King William St, London Bridge', spring hammer safety, one-piece chequered walnut grip, No. 8681R, with ball mould, c1880.
$675–825 *EP*

A transitional revolver, stamped 'Registered Baker's patent 24th April 1852', with German silver frame, steel trigger guard, original trade label, 8in (20.5cm) long, cased.
$1,500–1,800 *GV*

A 5 shot 54 bore Beaumont Adams double action percussion revolver No. 36,456R, London proved, top strap engraved 'Robert Adams, 76 King William Street, London, barrel stamped, swivel rammer, frame engraved, one-piece chequered walnut grip, sliding catch locks cylinder as safety catch, repaired, good working condition, c1865, 11⅛in (29cm) long, in its green felt-lined oak case with Dixon flask, Adams twin cavity bronze mould and nipple key, good condition.
$2,000–2,700 *WAL*

A 5 shot 54 bore double-action percussion revolver No. 5022L, octagonal 6in (15cm) barrel, London proved, top strap engraved 'Deane & Son, London Bridge', polished underlever rammer, frame engraved, one-piece chequered walnut grip, good working condition, c1865, 12in (30.5cm) long, in its green felt-lined oak case with trade label, containing twin cavity Adams bronze mould, copper flask, Dixon oil bottle and ebony-handled nipple key, good condition.
$1,800–2,000 *WAL*

Firearms

Each country has its own laws affecting the collecting and owning of guns. It is the responsibility of the collector to make absolutely certain that he or she is conforming with these laws.

Rifles

A flintlock smooth bore experimental cavalry carbine built on the Crespi breech loading system, by Durs Egg, London proof marks, with re-browned twist sighted barrel, twist tip-up breech chamber, signed, locked by a two-part pivot lever engaging lugged projections, hinged folding arm locked by a spring-catch, figured walnut full stock, plain brass butt plate, side plate and trigger guard, c1785.
$5,250–6,000 *S(S)*

A .700 military flintlock rifle of Baker type, by Richards, sighted barrel, stepped lock, full stocked with brass furniture including patchbox and escutcheon engraved 'Walworth Yeomanry', steel ramrod, damaged and repaired, c1820, 30½in (77.5cm) long.
$1,400–1,600 *S(S)*

A .577 three-band Enfield percussion rifle, with 39in (99cm) barrel, border engraved lock struck with crowned 'VR Tower', and '1853', full stocked with solid barrel bands, damaged and part refinished.
$325–375 *S(S)*

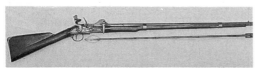

A breech loading needle fire military rifle, rotating 33½in (85cm) barrel to sprung breech, engraved 'Royal Letters Patent' with crowned 'VR' within garter motto, barrel tang engraved 'Alexr Melville & Edwd Callow London Row', full stocked, brass mounts hammer with needle-shaped nose for igniting paper cartridge containing explosive compounds, chequered trigger guard spur, patchbox, steel sling swivels, good working condition, 1850, 53½in (136cm) long.
$1,300–1,500 *WAL*

A .577 1858 pattern percussion short rifle, with 33in (84cm) barrel, Tower proved, ladder rear sight to 1100 yards, full stocked, lock stamped '1859 Tower' with crowned 'VR', stock with Birmingham storekeeper's stamp for 1859, good working condition, 49in (124.5cm) long.
$1,500–1,800 *WAL*

Swords

A German processional two-hand sword, with broad double-edged blade, iron quillons, pommel and original leather-covered wooden grip, slight wear, early 17thC, blade 49½in (125.5cm) long.
$5,000–5,500 *S(S)*

A broadsword, with German double-edged blade formed with a short fullered ricasso and shallow fuller at the forte, both sides cut with a running wolf mark and struck with a series of decorative marks framing the inscription 'Andrea' on one side and 'Ferara' on the other, iron basket-guard in relief, some wear, c1645, blade 35in (89cm) long.
$2,800–3,500 *CSK*

A rapier, the 38½in (98cm) blade with shallow double fullers, steel hilt with upturned pierced shells, recurved quillons and pierced pommel, all retaining traces of silver inlaid decoration, mid-16thC.
$2,000–2,500 *Gle*

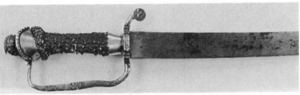

A silver-hilted hunting hanger, the 18½in (47cm) blade stamped with half-moon mark, the hilt with embossed knuckle-guard and quillons, the cleft pommel surmounted by a Negroid head, natural staghorn grip, Britannia hallmark London 1697.
$1,600–2,000 *Gle*

A Victorian 1845 pattern infantry officer's sword, slightly curved blade 35in (89cm) by Henry Wilkinson, copper gilt-hilt, gilt wire bound fishskin covered grip, in steel scabbard, good condition.
$225–300 *WAL*

A Georgian 1796 pattern infantry officer's sword, with blue and gilt blade, 38in (96.5cm) long.
$270–300 *MR*

A gold-hilted presentation sword, of two hundred guineas value, to His Excellency Major-General Ainslie, Governor of The Dominica, London hallmarks for 1814, maker's mark 'TP', signed 'Rundell Bridge & Rundell, London', blade 31½in (80cm) long.
$35,000–40,000 *S(NY)*

MILITARIA
Badges

A Victorian officer's silver Maltese cross pouch belt badge of The King's Royal Rifle Corps, good condition, hallmarked Birmingham 1898.
$75–90 *WAL*

A Victorian officer's gilt fur cap grenade badge of The Royal Fusiliers, very good condition.
$375–450 *WAL*

Helmets

An officer's black cloth spiked helmet of the 2nd ER Yorks Royal Garrison Artillery (V), with gilt fittings, chin chain, helmet plate with Royal Artillery cipher, in a lacquered hat box from Hobson & Sons, Military Outfitters, London, bearing owner's plate of 'Capt. H. Hall', c1900.
$500–600 *DN*

A brass 1871 pattern other ranks helmet of the 2nd Dragoon Guards, with brass fittings, bi-metal helmet plate, some restoration.
$825–900 *S(S)*

An officer's blue cloth helmet of the Welsh Regiment, by H. Lehmann, Aldershot, with gilt fittings, spike, chin chain and King's Crown plate, bearing badge and scroll, in a metal tin, named to a different owner, pre-1920.
$675–750 *Sp*

A Prussian infantry officer's pickelhaube, with gilt helmet plate, leather-backed chinscales, spike and mounts, both cockades, leather and silk lining, very good condition, c1900.
$950–1,150 *WAL*

A Victorian officer's blue cloth helmet of the Royal Sussex Regiment 2nd Volunteer Batallion, with nickel helmet plate, nickel fittings, with chin chain and leather headband, worn.
$675–750 *S(S)*

l. An Imperial German other rank's Hessian pickelhaube, with white metal badge mounts and trim, leather chinstrap, both cockades, leather lining, good condition, rear peak marked '1911 B.A. XVIII'.
$420–500 *WAL*

An Imperial German Saxon artillery non-commissioned officer's kugelhelm, with gilt star badge, leather-backed chinscales, both cockades, leather and cloth lining, good condition, gilt rubbed, c1900.
$850–1,000 *WAL*

r. An Imperial German Saxony general officer's pickelhaube, the gilt star helmet plate with silvered-star and enamelled centre of the Order of St Henry, gilt spike, leather-backed chinscales, both cockades, leather and silk lining, very good condition, c1900.
$1,800–2,200 *WAL*

Helmet Plates

A Victorian officer's helmet plate of the 2nd Regiment Sussex Rifle Volunteers.
$375–450 *S(S)*

A Victorian other ranks Cinque Ports Artillery Volunteer's helmet plate, gun part detached.
$200–240 *S(S)*

A Victorian other ranks 1st Sussex Royal Engineer Volunteer's helmet plate.
$300–330 *S(S)*

A Victorian other ranks 1st Sussex Royal Artillery Volunteer's helmet plate.
$225–275 *S(S)*

Medals

A Naval General Service one bar medal 1793, inscribed 'Pelagosa 29th Novr 1811', very fine.
$570–630 *WAL*

A Queen's South African medal, 2 bars Defence of Mafeking, Transvaal, awarded to 2588 Tpr A H Jones, B.S.A. Police, very fine.
$1,100–1,200 *WAL*

A South African medal 1877–79, bar 1879, awarded to Qr Mr Sgt W. Currie, Natal Horse, very fine.
$420–450 *WAL*

A Cabul medal 1842, un-named as issued, very fine.
$300–360 *WAL*

A group of 4 medals, awarded to Sergeant T. Stone, Royal Canadian Regiment of Rifles, late 13th and 55th Regiments, comprising: Crimea three clasps, Turkish Crimea with silver clip, Canada General Service one clasp 1866, Long Service and Good Conduct, V.R, the group with some contact marks, very fine, with silver riband bar and copied service papers.
$1,000–1,200 *Sp*

A group of 6 medals awarded to Lt John Henry Vere Barr, 9th Bombay (109,120) Infantry, comprising: Indian General Service medal with bar, the 1914–15 Star, British War medal 1914–18, Victory medal with oak leaf clasp 1914–19, Indian General Service medal with bars 1908–35, and the General Service medal with bar 1918, and the medals in miniature.
$525–600 *MCA*

r. A DSO group of 7 medals, for China 1900 to Captain C. Mackenzie, Royal Navy, being one of five awarded to the Royal Navy for the attack and capture of Taku Forts, comprising: Order of the Indian Empire (CIE) Commander's neck badge (not shown), Distinguished Service Order VR, China 1900 one bar, 1914-15 Star, British War and Victory medal with MID oak leaf, Coronation 1911, mounted as worn, good very fine.
$10,500–12,000 *Gle*

Pouches

A late Victorian officer's full dress pouch of the Royal Artillery, with gilt bullion wire decoration.
$150–180 *MR*

An Indian Volunteer officer's full dress embroidered blue cloth pouch of the Cossipore Volunteer Artillery, damage, good condition, post-1902.
$270–300 *WAL*

A Victorian officer's full dress embroidered blue cloth pouch of the 2nd Sutherland Artillery Volunteers, very good condition.
$250–300 *WAL*

Uniforms

A Victorian officer's full dress embroidered blue cloth sabretache of the Edinburgh Artillery (Militia), bearing embroidered Royal Arms over black scroll and wreath, in its foul weather cover, some wear and 4 small moth holes to lower edge, good condition.
$620–700 *WAL*

A military tailcoat, of scarlet wool with yellow stand collar, facings and cuffs, with double row of gilded brass buttons, and pockets to each tail and chest lining, c1790.
$1,200–1,300 *S*

A herald's scarlet, yellow and aubergine silk tabard dorsal, with the arms of Great Britain, France and Ireland in raised work and couched metallic thread, now in 2 separate halves, one mounted, in fragile condition and lacking sleeves, 18thC.
$650–750 *DN*

Miscellaneous

A bed plate, inscribed 'Grenadier Guards 22213676 Eggington D', c1920, 4½in (11.5cm) wide.
$20–30 *OD*

A Georgian other rank's oval brass shoulder belt plate of the Letterkenny Corps (Irish Militia), engraved with a crowned harp and title scrolls, very good condition, un-issued.
$500–600 *WAL*

A Royal Sussex Regiment side drum, by George Potter & Co, nickel-plated and painted brass body with Battle Honours to Afghanistan 1919 and bearing Royal Arms with GR and 1st Bn. The Royal Sussex Regiment, wooden hoops, finished in blue and orange, buckskin tensioners, restored, 17¼in (44cm) diam.
$720–800 *S(S)*

l. An autograph of W. Cdr. Guy Gibson, VC, DSO, DFC, in blue ink, dated '12/1/44' and annotated 'W/C', mounted with a black and white photograph of the legendary wartime pilot, framed and glazed.
$2,200–2,700 *S(S)*

A French regimental silk Colour, inscribed with gold lettering on one side, c1812, 38in (96.5cm) wide.
$5,000–5,750 *Sp*

An important trophy of the Napoleonic Wars of the Garde Nationale.

SPORT
Baseball

A scrapbook with newspaper clippings and handwritten notes about the 1903 World Series between Boston and Pittsburgh, including two ticket stubs.
$11,500–13,500 *CNY*

OFFICIAL SOUVENIR
TRANS-CONTINENTAL TOUR

STARS
AMERICAN AND NATIONAL LEAGUE
BASE BALL TEAMS

A programme for the 1913–14 World Tour of the National and American League Baseball teams, featuring photographs of the New York Giants and Chicago White Sox teams that toured Europe, Australia and Egypt, good condition.
$450–530 *CNY*

An official National League ball, signed by Babe Ruth, Tris Speaker, Bob Shawkey and another, and inscribed 'World Series – Pittsburgh v. New York, Oct. 1927', excellent condition.
$2,000–2,400 *CNY*

An official American League baseball, signed by 18 members of the 1936 New York Yankees, including Joe DiMaggio, Lou Gehrig, Tony Lazzeri, Frank Crosetti, Bill Dickey, Red Ruffing and Lefty Gomez, very good condition.
$1,800–2,000 *CNY*

An official National League ball, signed by members of the 1944 team, including Mel Ott, Joe Medwick, Vince DiMaggio, Stan Musial, Mickey Owen, Marty Marion, Rip Sewell and Honus Wagner, excellent condition.
$1,000–1,200 *CNY*

A New York Yankee's uniform worn by Mickey Mantle, in the 1951 World Series.
$75,000–82,000 *CNY*

r. A 9 page letter, written in green ink by Ty Cobb on May 5, 1955, in which he discussed his feelings about early baseball and the players of the day.
$5,500–6,300 *CNY*

Basketball

A 14ct gold championship ring, by Diamond Cutters International of Houston, Texas, presented to Hakeem Olajuwon, engraved, 1994, and other related items.
$18,000–20,000 *CNY*

Olajuwon did not accept this ring, owing to his religious belief which forbids the wearing of yellow gold.

A Certificate of the International Young Men's Christian Association Training School in Springfield, Massachusetts, signed by the faculty including Luther Gulick and James Naismith, dated 'June 20, 1894'.
$14,250–15,750 *CNY*

A yearbook for the 1973–74 New York Knicks, with each player's autograph on the page bearing his picture and statistics, excellent condition.
$900–1,000 *CNY*

Billiards

A full size walnut billiard table, by J. Taylor, 1875.
$9,500–10,500 *HAB*

A full size mahogany billiard table, by George Wright, with carved scrolls, c1885.
$8,300–9,000 *HAB*

A full size Cuban mahogany billiard table, by George Wright, with tulip style legs, c1875, 144 x 72in (366 x 183cm).
$2,700–3,000 *BRA*

A Victorian billiard table, by Frères, c1880, 108 x 54in (275 x 137cm).
$4,500–5,000 *HAB*

l. A full size mahogany billiard table, by Burroughes & Watts, with carved tulip legs, domed insert panels beneath a figured frame, and Patent Eureka steel block cushions, c1887, 144 x 72in (366 x 183cm).
$7,500–8,300 *BRA*

A full size mahogany billiard table, by Thurston & Co, with octagonal legs and carved scrolls, c1856, 144 x 72in (366 x 183cm).
$4,200–4,800 *BRA*

A Victorian bagatelle table, with 4 pockets, c1870, 126in (320cm) long.
$3,800–4,500 *HAB*

A mahogany billiard table, by Burroughes & Watts, c1890, 120 x 60in (305 x 152.5cm).
$5,200–6,000 *HAB*

A walnut billiard table, by J. Taylor, c1895, 120 x 60in (305 x 152.5cm).
$6,000–6,800 *HAB*

A full size oak refectory style billiard table, by Burroughes & Watts, c1910.
$9,000–9,800 *HAB*

A full size walnut billiard table, by Thurston, c1905.
$10,500–11,300 *HAB*

l. A billiard/dining table, by E. J. Riley, c1915, 84 x 42in (213.5 x 106.5cm).
$5,000–5,400 *HAB*

A full size burr walnut billiard table, by J. Ashcroft, with reeded decorative cushion friezes, ornately carved bowed side frame, on 8 scroll topped turned and gadrooned legs, c1900, 144 x 72in (366 x 183cm).
$9,000–10,000 *BRA*

A full size mahogany billiard table, by Burroughes & Watts, with steel vacuum cushions, c1920.
$7,500–8,300 *HAB*

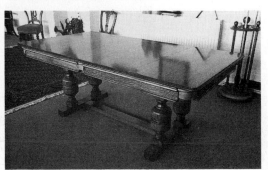

An oak refectory style billiard/dining table, c1920, 72 x 36in (183 x 91.5cm).
$2,700–3,000 *HAB*

An Italian pool table, in kingwood, mahogany and walnut, with pewter hinged ball receptacles, c1925, 120 x 60in (305 x 152.5cm).
$6,000–6,800 *BRA*

A full size mahogany billiard table, by George Wright, with reeded legs and heavily carved lion's mask knee plates, c1875, 144 x 72in (366 x 183cm).
$6,000–6,800 *BRA*

l. An oak revolving billiard cue rack, to hold 12 cues, on a ball bearing mechanism, c1920, 48in (122cm) high.
$530–600 *BRA*

A mahogany revolving billiard cue stand, c1880, 46in (117cm) high.
$1,200–1,500 *BRA*

A carved oak revolving billiard cue stand, c1895, 58in (147cm) high.
$1,800–2,200 *BRA*

A mahogany billiard accessories cabinet and scoreboard, c1885, 72in (183cm) wide.
$5,400–6,000 *HAB*

A walnut revolving scoreboard, by John Taylor & Son, c1885, 42in (106.5cm) wide.
$450–550 *BRA*

r. A life pool board, by Thurston, c1890, 46in (117cm) wide.
$3,000–3,600 *HAB*

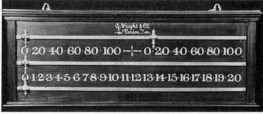

A billiard marker board, by G. Wright & Co, c1880, 34in (86.5cm) wide.
$280–340 *HAB*

A walnut life pool scoreboard, by George Wright & Co, c1900, 14in (35.5cm) wide. $450–550 *BRA*

A mahogany revolving scoreboard, by Ashcroft & Sons, with life pool sliders, revolving billiard and snooker scorer, penny box and ball storage, c1895, 44in (112cm) wide. $1,200–1,500 *BRA*

An oak scoreboard, by J. & T. Scott, with mother-of-pearl inlay, revolving billiard scorer and slate board, c1890, 46in (117cm) wide. $1,200–1,500 *BRA*

A Victorian brass electrolier, for a full size billiard table, with Art Nouveau style decoration, c1895, 110in (279.5cm) long. $2,700–3,000 *BRA*

l. A life pool board, by Cox & Yeman, c1875, 36in (91.5cm) wide. $2,700–3,000 *HAB*

A billiard trophy shield, inscribed 'The Felix Redelien Shield', made by the Alexander Clark Co, c1928, 28in (71cm) high. $380–450 *MSh*

l. An oak scoreboard, by Burroughes & Watts, with sliding markers and slate blackboard, c1920, 26in (66cm) wide. $300–380 *BRA*

A mahogany slider style scoreboard, by T. Padmore & Sons, c1915, 31in (78.5cm) wide. $200–230 *BRA*

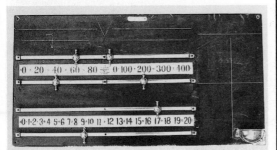

An Art Deco style slate scoreboard, by Thurston & Co, c1930, 34in (86.5cm) wide. $450–550 *BRA*

Boxing

A bound copy of *Bob Fitzsimmons, His Life and Battles*, published by Richard J. Fox, 1895, with a card signed and inscribed 'Compliments of Robert Fitzsimmons'.
$1,500–1,800 *CNY*

A Dana photograph of J. Johnson and S. Ketchel in the ring for their bout on October 16, 1909, 17 x 22in (43 x 56cm).
$1,300–1,500 *CNY*

A spelter figure depicting a boxer, on a marble base, c1920, 8in (20cm) high.
$180–220 *MSh*

A watercolour painting of Randolph Turpin, by Bob Kingshott, with a signed inscription from the artist, dated '1951', mounted, framed and glazed, 21½ x 17¾in (55 x 45cm).
$330–380 *P*

A pair of red leather boxing gloves, worn by Henry Cooper in his fight with Cassius Clay in 1963, inscribed 'These are the gloves which did not split', in a wood and glass display case, 15¾ x 14in (40 x 36cm).
$7,500–8,500 *P*

A bronze desk inkwell, with a figure of a boxer in the centre, inscribed 'Presented to Bob Olin, World Lightweight Champion by the New York Golden Glovers of 1927 to 1934–Dec. 20th, 1934', cracked, 14in (35.5cm) wide.
$480–560 *CNY*

Miller's is a price GUIDE not a price LIST

l. A ring, with 25 diamonds, presented by Evander Holyfield to commemorate his victory over Buster Douglass, given to Perry Waldrip, inscribed and dated 'October 25, 1990'.
$2,200–2,700 *CNY*

r. A silk Japanese robe, presented to and worn by Muhammed Ali in 1972 while in Japan for the Foster fight, with a gold and red thread dragon, autographed 'Muhammed Ali, Tokyo 1972', with letter of authenticity.
$1,500–1,800 *CNY*

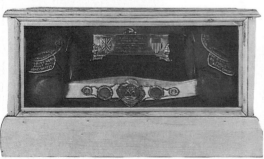

A silver belt awarded to Freddie Mills by *Boxing News*, inscribed, 1948, 30½in (77cm) long, a pair of gloves worn by Mills in 1942, and a silver cigarette box, inscribed and dated '26.7.48'.
$2,000–2,400 *P*

Two point-of-sale box inserts for Topps Ringside Cards, each containing an advertisement on one side and 8 cards on the other, one with Rocky Marciano, 1951.
$600–680 *CNY*

Cricket

A full size Jack Hobbs Ltd 'Val' cricket bat, 51 signatures in ink by Surrey, Warwickshire, Lancashire, Kent and Worcestershire, 1930s.
$270–300 *P*

Cricket Bats

The earliest known cricket bat is dated 1729 and is housed at the Oval in south London. In those days, bats were very large and heavy, weighing as much as 5lbs (2.3kg). There has never been a weight limit, but nowadays the average is approximately 2lbs 5oz (1.05kg). From the mid-1830s the design was modified so that the cane handle extended from the shoulders of the bat into the heart of the blade. This projection is known as the 'splice'. The first sprung bats appear in the 1860s. A comprehensive collection showing the evolution of the cricket bat can be seen in the Memorial Gallery at Lord's Cricket Ground, also in London.

l. A chromolithographed plate of W. G. Grace, by Spy, for *Vanity Fair*, folio, 1877, framed and glazed.
$180–220 *P*

A photograph of the touring side on the MCC Australian tour 1928–29, signed in ink on the mount by all 18 members, framed and glazed, 18 x 22in (46 x 56.5cm).
$560–680 *P*

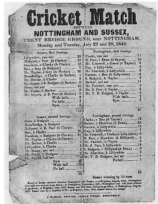

A scoresheet, printed by J. Hicklin, Nottingham, for the cricket match between Nottingham and Sussex, Trent Bridge Ground, July 27 and 28, 1840, slight damage, 10 x 7½in (25.5 x 19cm).
$750–850 *CSK*

Four full size cricket bats, signed by Compton, Hammond, Wisden, and others, c1945.
$30–50 each
Two miniature cricket bats, signed, 1960s, 12in (30.5cm) long.
$80–90 each *MR*

l. A full size Percy Holmes autographed cricket bat, by Farnell & Sons, signed in ink by 25 team members of the England v. Australia 5th Test at the Oval, slight fading, 1921.
$520–600 *P*

A cloth-covered autograph album, with over 200 ink signatures of County and Test cricketers, collected by Shelton 1905–07, the later pages with signatures from Australia, 1948 and Notts 1936.
$3,000–3,600 *P*

A dark green Australian test cricket cap, by Farmer's of Sydney, worn by Colin McDonald, with embroidered badge and name label '1959–60'.
$1,300–1,600 *P*

A print, entitled 'Play', depicting a game of cricket, monogram 'HS', published by the Fitzroy Library, the border with a design of cricket bales, framed, c1900, 28 x 38in (71 x 96.5cm).
$380–450 *MSh*

A Panama hat, by Christy's of London, signed by Geoff Boycott, with maroon and cream hat band.
$220–270 *P*

A black and white photograph of the MCC team in the West Indies, 1925–26, signed by all the tour party, mounted, 13 x 11in (33 x 28cm).
$900–1,000 *P*

A silver plated toast rack, with crossed cricket bats, stumps and a cricket belt, c1870, 7¼in (18.5cm) wide.
$220–270 *MSh*

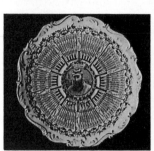

A Coalport porcelain plate, commemorating W. G. Grace's century of centuries, the centre printed in light blue with a portrait and dates within a semi-gadrooned rim, gold lined decoration, c1875.
$900–1,000 *P*

A Doulton Lambeth cricket mug, decorated with a batsman, bowler and wicket keeper, c1900, 5in (12.5cm) high.
$680–750 *MSh*

F. Neville Piggott, editor, *M.C.C. Tour in Australia, Warner's Team! 1911–12*, published by The Cricket Press, London, slim 8°.
$120–150 *DW*

Charles Box, *The English Game of Cricket*, first edition, 4°, 1877.
$220–270 *DW*

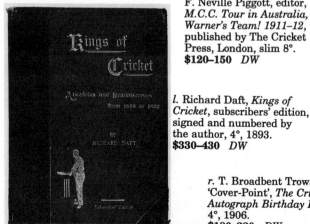

l. Richard Daft, *Kings of Cricket*, subscribers' edition, signed and numbered by the author, 4°, 1893.
$330–430 *DW*

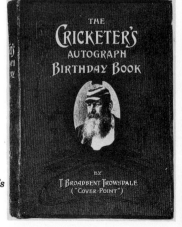

r. T. Broadbent Trowsdale, 'Cover-Point', *The Cricketer's Autograph Birthday Book*, 4°, 1906.
$180–220 *DW*

Fishing

An Edward vom Hofe ebonite and German silver 6/0 multiplier, with patent dates 'July 14-96' and 'January 23 1883', and on/off check button.
$220–270 *ND*

A 2½in Hardy Birmingham platewind reel, with oval logo, horn handle, bent foot, and a similar 4in reel, engraved with owner's name, c1890.
$630–720 *C(S)*

A 2¾in Hardy Original Perfect reel, c1890.
$7,500–9,000 *PC*

A 4in Hardy Silex reel, 3 rim control, 1896–1911.
$270–300 *PC*

An Edward vom Hofe ebonite and German silver 6/0 multiplier, No. 321 patent July 14, 1896, with one rim control, on/off check button with line.
$240–270 *ND*

A 5in Hardy alloy combined fly/spinning reel, with twin ivorine handles on fluted brass cups, brass pillars, the backplate with enclosed oval logo and 'Hardy's Pat', brass check button and central bearing adjuster, waisted brass foot with 2 perforations, c1894.
$1,000–1,200 *EP*

r. A 2⅝in Hardy Perfect brass-faced trout fly reel, with Rod-in-Hand trademark, enclosed oval straightline logos, strapped tension screw, early check, ivorine handle and brass foot, c1904, in Hardy leather case.
$720–820 *EP*

l. A 3¾in Malloch brass and ebonite salmon fly reel, retailed by J. Bernard & Son, 5 Church Place, Piccadilly, with sun and planet gearing, faceted wooden handle and nickel silver rims, c1900.
$240–270 *EP*

A 3½in Hardy Silex multiplier, c1924–39.
$600–680 *PC*

A 2¼in Hardy Silex No. 2 reel, 1911–22.
$300–380 *PC*

A 4¼in Hardy Perfect salmon fly reel, with strapped tension screw with turk's head locking nut, circular revolving nickel line guide in brass frame, ivorine handle with brass foot, c1905.
$480–560 *EP*

A Walter Stanley cast aluminium pre-production reel, and other related items.
$420–480 *ND*

A Hardy Triumph reel, c1923.
$300–380 *PC*

A 5in Slater (Newark) casting reel, the drum with 6 perforations, twin handles and Slater latch, the backplate with brass check button, brass pillars and foot, c1915.
$680–750 *EP*

r. A 5in Hardy Silex No. 2 reel, c1920–22.
$380–450 *PC*

r. A 6in Milward Overseas walnut sea reel, with perforated plate with twin 'Through Pin' handles, solid brass drum which runs in brass cupped lining, brass frog back-optional check, line guide, drum fitted with 'Tension Brakenut', with line, c1926.
$420–480 *ND*

A 3½in Milward The Brownie casting reel, with wooden drum, alloy frame and foot, c1921, cased.
$420–480 *EP*

A 4in Hardy Super Silex reel, 1928–53.
$270–300 *PC*

A 3in Coxon Aerial improved model centrepin reel, with ventilated aluminium flange, twin xylenite handles, wooden backplate with starback and optional check, 1925–29.
$1,500–1,800 *EP*

A 6in Hardy Zane Grey sea fishing reel, made from Monel metal, c1930.
$3,000–3,750 *PC*

A 3in Allcock Aerial centrepin reel, retailed by A. Carter & Co, 11 South Molton Street, London, with ventilated drum flange, twin ivorine handles, brass foot and optional check, 1930s.
$600–680 *EP*

A 9in Hardy Fortune aluminium sea fishing reel, 1934–56.
$3,000–3,800 *PC*

A 3½in Hardy Super Silex Multiplier reel, with tapered ebonite handle, ivorine rim lever, rim regulator screw, white indicator dial and grooved brass foot, 1930–39.
$480–560 *EP*

r. A Howell & Co The Howban side casting reel, with instructions and cardboard box, c1950.
$300–360 *ND*

l. A Hardy The Exalta fixed spool reel, in a leather case, c1960.
$300–360 *ND*

A J. A. Coxe nickel silver and Bakelite level wind reel, model No. 25, in original fitted case, c1935.
$240–300 *ND*

A Victorian set of wooden drawers, with 24 compartments containing a large collection of metal and wooden Devons.
$850–950 *ND*

A brass artificial bait, The Clipper, with glass eyes and curved tails, stamped 'C. Farlow & Co, 191 Strand', 5in (12.5cm) long.
$220–270 *ND*

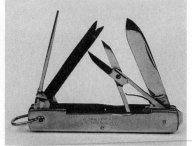

A Farlow's angler's knife, c1920, 4in (10cm) wide.
$600–680 *PC*

A bowfronted case, containing a grayling, gold lined and inscribed 'Grayling 2lb 4½ozs, Caught by J. Higgs, River Test, December 6th 1901', 21in (53.5cm) wide.
$920–1,000 *ND*

A French spelter figure of a boy fishing, by G. Omerth, c1890, 20½in (52cm) high.
$220–270 *MSh*

r. A display of artificial baits, by Guillaume of Redditch, comprising 50 lures, 50 insects and 13 spoons, the mount inscribed, framed and glazed, c1900, 45 x 37in (114 x 94cm).
$3,000–3,800 *S(S)*

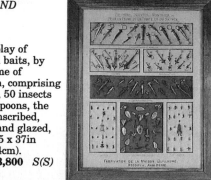

A glass-fronted case, containing a pike, with a note stating that the fish was caught in 1913 by Mr Samuel Smith on the Great Ouse between St Neots and Eaton Socon Locks, Bedford, pike 34in (86cm) long.
$560–640 *P(HSS)*

A bowfronted case, containing a pike, by J. Cooper & Sons, inscribed 'Pike, 28lbs, Caught by James Hall, Lough Corrib, Ireland, 1929', 53in (134.5cm) long.
$1,800–2,000 *S(S)*

Football

A 15ct gold medal, by F&S, the front with a blue enamel central mounted shield with a moon and star, the outer green enamel border inscribed 'In Commemoration of Season 1911–12', the reverse with monogram 'RB' in relief, with link, Birmingham 1912, 1in (25mm) diam.
$270–300 *P*

Golf

An electrotype footballing figure, on a marble base, c1890, 13¾in (35cm) high.
$680–750 *MSh*

r. A 9ct gold medal, in the form of a shield, the front enclosing central mounted shield with blue and white enamel flag, outer laurel leaf borders, the reverse inscribed 'Northern Football Alliance, Diamond Jubilee Year, 1896–7, Hebburn Argyle, R.B.', Chester 1897, 1in (25mm) wide, and a gold plated medal, monogrammed 'SFL', for Sheffield Football League, boxed.
$270–300 *P*

An ink and watercolour drawing of a football match, by H. M. Bateman, signed, c1937, 12½ x 13½in (32 x 34cm), framed and glazed.
$1,500–1,800 *P*

This picture was commissioned by the Imperial Tobacco Co for the advertising of Turf cigarettes.

A long nosed spoon golf club, by McEwan, c1875, 43in (109cm) long.
$1,800–2,000 *MSh*

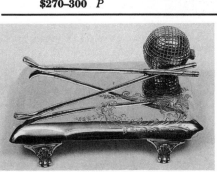

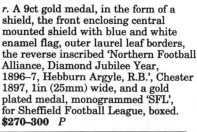

A silver plated inkwell, with 2 crossed clubs as a pen rest, and a mesh pattern ball as the well, c1890, 6¾in (17cm) wide.
$270–330 *MSh*

A Copeland Spode jug, with figures of golfers in white on a blue ground, c1890, 4in (10cm) high.
$520–600 *MSh*

A feather golf ball, by Gourlay, c1840, 1½in (38mm) diam.
$3,800–4,500 *MSh*

A bronze figure of Harry Vardon, by Henry Pegram, the base inscribed, c1908, 12in (30.5cm) high.
$9,500–10,500 *CNY*

A hand-hammered gutta ball, in the manner of Robert Forgan of St Andrews, c1860.
$2,600–3,000 *CNY*

Sporting Guns

A breech-loading flintlock sporting gun, by Robert Rowland, London, with four-stage tip-up barrel for ball or shot moulded at the muzzle, signed and engraved, repaired, barrel 26in (66cm) long.
$4,200–4,800 *S(S)*

A 12 bore flintlock sporting gun, by Sykes of Oxford, gold inlaid and engraved, c1790, barrel 32in (81.5cm) long, in green felt-lined mahogany case with copper powder flask.
$4,200–5,000 *WAL*

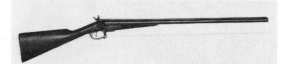

A double-barrelled underlever hammer gun, by Purdey, No. 7372, damascene barrels, engraved, 1875, barrel 30in (76cm).
$1,200–1,400 *WAL*

A 14 bore double-barrelled back action percussion sporting gun, by James Wilkinson & Son, No. 4110, engraved, barrel 30in (76cm) long, in a blue velvet-lined mahogany case, with Hawksley powder flask, Dixon brass double shot container, and other accessories.
$2,000–2,500 *WAL*

A .577 hammer rifle, No. 4209, 9 groove 'Henry' rifling, engraved platinum lined folding leaf sights to 250 yards, 1877, Damascus barrels 28in (71cm) long, in oak and leather case with accessories.
$13,000–15,000 *S(S)*

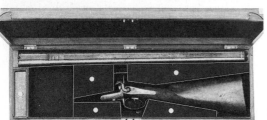

A double-barrelled .577 underlever sporting rifle, by H. Snowie, Inverness, engraved, c1890, barrels 29¾in (75.5cm) long, in a lined and fitted brass-bound mahogany case, in leather travelling case.
$1,500–1,800 *WAL*

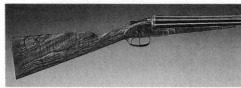

A pair of 12 bore self-opening sidelock ejector guns, by J. Purdey & Sons, Nos. 28063/4, engraved, 1975, chopper-lump barrels 28in (71cm) long, in lightweight leather case.
$42,000–48,000 *S(S)*

Tennis

A lawn tennis racket, with tilted head, original coarse gut strings, walnut convex wedge and round walnut handle, worn, mid-1870s.
$2,000–2,400 *CSK*

A Birmal tennis racket, by the Birmingham Aluminium Co, all-metal with piano wire strings, c1920, 27in (68.5cm) long.
$180–220 *MSh*

A flat-topped lawn tennis racket, by Thomas J. Tate, 64 Portland Street, London, c1885.
$560–600 *MSh*

A lawn tennis tape measure, in leather case with label showing the correct layout and measurements of a court, c1910, 4½in (11.5cm) diam.
$60–80 *MSh*

FOLK ART

Folk art reflects both the creative talents of individual artists and the traditions and values held by their communities. It is generally accepted that objects not only have a functional purpose, such as serving bowls, store signs, weather vanes, textiles, etc, but also an aesthetic appeal far beyond their intended purpose. Most were unsigned and undated, as a result many older examples of folk art have lost much of their original decoration due to wear and tear of daily use. Good examples of surviving folk art in America and the UK date from the mid-18th century.

Unlike other artists and craftsmen who learned their skill through formal often classical training, folk artists were mainly self-taught, often carrying on a tradition by incorporating design and techniques learned from their parents and their parents before them, and their work lacked the technical expertise of trained artists.

Folk art items were generally created in poorer households as a means of brightening up dreary surroundings or for ceremonial or festive occasions. Having said this, many middle-class women, with idle time on their hands, would create elaborate embroidered and cross-stitch designs for their garments, furniture or wall decorations.

As a collecting area the American antiques market thrives on folk art, from painted furniture to metalware, but in the UK this field is not so clearly defined as yet. A good example of the difference between the British and American markets was provided by an auction of folk art from the Judkyn/Pratt collections. Significantly, the collection was formed by two Anglophile Americans in Britain, as an adjunct to the American Museum in Britain, near Bath, a celebration of American antiques. The fate of one of the most striking pieces in the collection, a late 18th century chimney sweep's sign, made from sheet tin and rough hewn wood, showed the different values of such things.

In London it was valued by Christie's South Kensington at $2,250–3,000, sold for $15,800,

and within weeks was being offered at the prestigious Winter Antiques Show in New York at $45,000. It sold!

Folk art in the UK may be found scattered around country auctions, at fairs and in shops, but as yet there are few specialist dealers in folk art alone. Sotheby's tried marketing folk art as a separate entity in the mid-1980s and still feature it occasionally, but sales devoted to the subject are almost exclusively held by Christie's South Kensington. Across the country, folk art is more likely to be tucked away in sales of general antique, country furniture or bygones rather than presented as a distinct category, but some collections do turn up.

A pair of Charles I elm and leather bellows, with concentric ring mouldings and punched with bands of foliate motifs, with simple cylindrical tapering handles, one restored with a wrought iron sleeve, nozzle missing, 11½in (29cm) diam, from the John Fardon collection.
$1,800–2,000 *CSK*

l. A pair of brass lever action nutcrackers, incised with foliate scrolls and the initials 'R.L.', the part wrythen handles terminating in knops, c1700, 4in (10cm) long, from the John Fardon collection.
$675–750 *CSK*

A lead/bronze mortar, cast with the maker's name and date 'Samuell Stringer 1696', within a band of fleur-de-lys motifs, above a conforming band to the centre, the base with triple ribbed ornament, on an inverted foot, late 17thC, 14in (35.5cm) high, from the John Fardon collection.
$5,250–6,000 *CSK*

A Charles I embroidered silk patch box, depicting the King and Queen to the obverse, within metal thread borders, the sides with flowers and foliage, with a white metal hinge, 2½in (6.5cm) high, from the John Fardon collection.
$675–750 *CSK*

FURTHER READING

Hilton, Alison, *Russian Folk Art* Indiana University Press, Bloomington and Indianapolis, 1995

Bearden, Romare, and Henderson, Harry, *A History of African-American Artists*, Pantheon Books, New York, 1993

Kardon, Janet, ed, *Revivals! Diverse Traditions: The History of Twentieth Century American Craft, 1920–45*, Harry N. Abrams, Inc, New York, 1994

A pair of miniature silver-mounted leather blackjacks, with looped handles, the mounts to the rims incised with crests, depicting rampant lions and griffins within a shield, with maker's mark 'H', the bodies stamped with foliate motifs, 18thC, 3in (7.5cm) high, ex-John Fardon collection.
$8,500–9,500 *CSK*

A pencil, pen, black ink, watercolour and bodycolour panorama of Portsmouth Harbour, depicting numerous vessels, and children playing on the foreshore, English Naive School, 19thC, 15 x 22in (38 x 56cm).
$1,200–1,500 *CSK*

A high-relief carved pine sign modelled as a standing bull, painted as a black and white Friesian, traces of gilt, 19thC, 29½in (75cm) long.
$7,000–7,800 *CSK*

An American fine leather key basket, the tapering oval form with sides incised with stars, diamonds, hearts and running vines along with the initials 'J.R. McK', 'G' and 'F', flanking a star on bottom inside diamond, the handle with appliquéd leather hearts, with red leather interior, probably Richmond, Virginia, c1830, 5½in (14cm) wide.
$42,000–48,000 *S(NY)*

Folk Art

Folk Art is a very broad term encompassing many collecting areas. For other examples in our price guide please refer to the sections on Kitchenware, Marine, Metalware, Wood, Treen, Boxes and Textiles.

A German papier mâché Santa pulling a wooden sled, in good original condition, early 20thC, 17in (43cm) long.
$1,200–1,500 *SK(B)*

An American black cloth doll, with embroidered eyes, eyebrows, nose and mouth, looped hair, with blue silk bow, the fabric body clothed in a blue, red ochre and cream wool flannel dress, over a white lace petticoat, red stockings and high button leather boots, early 20thC, hair possibly later, 37in (94cm) high.
$2,400–2,700 *S(NY)*

An American stamped leather key basket, the rigid black leather embossed with stylised flowers, diamonds and interlacing chain devices, mounted with a silvered metal plaque inscribed 'L. C. Brooks 1883', probably Richmond, Virginia, 4¼in (11cm) wide.
$7,000–7,800 *S(NY)*

An American gilded cast iron 'Jenny Lind' mirror, the oval plate outlined with a leaf-form filigree pivoting between profile figures of Jenny Lind perched on willow branches, on a base flanked by the American flag and shield, on scrolling leaf-form feet, 19thC, 21½in (54.5cm) high.
$1,000–1,200 *S(NY)*

r. An American finely carved walking stick, attributed to Alanson Porter Dean, the angular handle carved with a crocodile attacking a tiger, a young girl riding a large dog and a lion attacking a scrolled serpent, inscribed and dated 'Henry L. Sabin . . . 1875', continuing to a shaft with an eagle clutching an arrow, a falcon and hands in various signing positions, inscribed, the lower section with a cross and a corona, an eagle with a shield and arrow, a squirrel, ram, horse, grasshopper and a fish, the base encased in brass, 35in (89cm) long.
$11,800–13,000 *S(NY)*

An American fabric bird mobile, the circular wrought iron ring suspended with a group of variously coloured stuffed fabric birds with applied silk wings and tails, damaged, probably Pennsylvania, 19thC, 27in (68.5cm) high when suspended.
$5,200–6,000 *S(NY)*

An American painted, composition and plaster squeak toy, moulded as a peafowl with blue and white polka dot body, mounted on wire spring legs continuing to an accordion base, probably Pennsylvania, late 19thC, 8in (20.5cm) high.
$1,500–1,800 *S(NY)*

An American carved and painted pine group of a man pushing a cat in a wheelbarrow, the man bearded and wearing a brown shirt and black trousers, on a black pine base, slight damage, late 19thC, 5in (12.5cm) high.
$600–680 *S(NY)*

A Santa in a sleigh pulled by a reindeer, with papier mâché and cloth figure, wicker and wood sleigh, flannel-covered papier mâché deer with clockwork nodding head, damaged, early 20thC, 36in (91.5cm) long.
$2,500–3,000 *SK(B)*

An American pictorial hooked rug, worked in brown, beige, cream and peach with a running horse, on a beige and cream striped ground, the sides with scrolled leafage, 19thC, 29 x 58in (74 x 147.5cm), now framed.
$4,500–5,500 *S(NY)*

An American School Indian Medicine Man, of carved and painted pine with horsehair and painted fabric, with a carved wood bow and quiver, late 19thC, 66½in (169cm) high.
$90,000–100,000 *S(NY)*

An American moulded and gilded copper centaur weathervane, attributed to A. L. Jewell & Co, Waltham, Massachusetts, the figure aiming its bow and arrow, with applied ridged sheet metal tail, mounted on a rod and a black metal base, restored, late 19thC.
$11,250–12,250 *S(NY)*

An American moulded copper and cast zinc eagle weathervane, by A. L. Jewell & Co, Waltham, Massachusetts, the stylised figure with upraised sheet copper wings and cast zinc head, perched on an orb, now mounted on a black steel base, mid-19thC, 25in (63.5cm) high.
$9,000–10,000 *S(NY)*

r. An American moulded and silvered zinc prancing horse weathervane, the figure with sheet metal ears, ridged mane and stylised leaf fitted between its ears, mounted on a rod, minor repairs, tail loose, late 19thC, 40½in (103cm) long.
$9,200–10,000 *S(NY)*

GLOSSARY

We have attempted here to define some of the terms that you will come across in this book. If there are any terms or technicalities you would like explained or you feel should be included in future, please let us know.

Aalto, Alvar (1898-1976): A Finnish Art Deco architect and furniture designer, noted for his bentwood chairs, made from the 1930s onwards.

acid engraving: Technique of decorating glass by coating it in resin, incising a design and exposing the revealed areas to hydrochloric acid fumes.

acid-gilding: 19thC technique for decorating pottery whereby the surface is etched with hydrofluoric acid and the low-relief pattern gilded.

acorn knop: Wine glass stem moulding in the shape of an upturned acorn – the cup uppermost.

Adam, Robert (1728-1792): A Scottish born architect who created a neo-classical architectural and decorative style of furniture.

agate ware: 18thC pottery, veined or marbled to resemble the mineral agate.

air-beaded: Glass containing bubbles of air, like strings of beads.

air-twist: Helical decoration in the stem of wine glasses, developed 1740-70, in which an air bubble in the glass is drawn out and twisted to form complex spirals, e.g. lace twist, multiple spiral, spiral gauze, corkscrew multi-ply, cable, etc.

albarello: Pottery vessel of hour-glass shape, used for storing pharmaceutical ingredients.

ale glass: Drinking glass with tall stem and tall narrow bowl, capacity 3-4 fluid ounces, used for strong beer, sometimes decorated with barley ears and hops, 18thC.

all-bisque doll: One with body and limbs as well as head of biscuit-fired ceramic.

amboyna: Yellowish-brown burred wood imported from the West Indies and used as a veneer.

American Victorian: The period between 1830-1900 that incorporates several styles of furniture; Victorian, Gothic, Victorian rococo, Victorian renaissance and Eastlake.

Americana: Antiques and collectables that reflect the growth, culture and character of American culture.

antefix: Carved ornament at the eaves of a roof to hide the joint between the tiles.

antiquities: Generally accepted to mean objects made before AD600 in Europe, and of ancient Egyptian, Greek or Roman origin. Also used to cover the pre-Columbian era in the Americas and the products of civilisations now extinct.

architect's table: Table or desk, the top of which rises at the back to provide an angled working area.

Arita (1): Blue and white Japanese pottery imported from the mid-17thC and much imitated by European makers.

Arita (2): Japanese 18thC porcelain, typically with flower-basket pattern in blue, red and gold, also called Imari ware after the port from which it was exported.

armoire: A large French cupboard or wardrobe, usually of monumental character.

associated (1): Term used of a set of silverware in which one part is of the same design but not originally made for it – e.g. of a teapot and associated stand.

associated (2): Of weapons, any part which is not original.

Aubusson: French town producing tapestries, and tapestry-weave carpets, since 17thC although formal workshops were not established until c1743.

automata: Any moving toy or decorative object, usually powered by a clockwork mechanism.

ball-jointed doll: One with ball-jointed limbs, able to swivel in all directions, as opposed to stiff jointed.

baluster stem: Glass with a swelling stem, like an architectural baluster: 'true' if the thicker swelling is beneath, 'inverted' if above. From late 17thC.

barley-twist: Form of turning popular in late 17thC which resembles a spiral of rope.

basaltes: Black porcelain invented by Josiah Wedgwood with a polished, stone-like finish; modern reproductions are called basalt wares.

Bauhaus: Influential German artistic style which was inspired by new industrial materials, such as stainless steel, with the emphasis on cubic, unadorned shapes. The term was coined by the architect Gropius who became director of the Weimar School of Arts and Crafts in 1919, and renamed it the Bauhaus.

bébé: French dolls made by Bru and others in the latter half 19thC, modelled on actual children of 8-12 years of age.

bellarmine: Bottle with a spout in the form of a grotesque human face, named after Cardinal Bellarmio (1542–1621), who sought to outlaw alcoholic beverages. Usually of salt-glazed stoneware from the early 17thC, but still being produced in the mid-19thC in many forms.

Belleek: Very thin and iridescent parian ware, originally made at Belleek, in Ireland, late 19thC.

bisque: French term for biscuit ware, or unglazed porcelain.

Bizarre: Name of a highly-colourful range of Art Deco tableware designed by Clarice Cliff and manufactured by the Staffordshire potter, A. J. Wilkinson Ltd, in the 1930s.

bombé: Outswelling, curving or bulging. Term used to describe a chest with a bulging front. In fashion from Louis XV period.

bonheur du jour: Small French writing table of delicate proportions with a raised back comprising a cabinet or shelves.

Bow: Important London porcelain factory producing blue and white wares 1749-76, and polychrome wares 1754 onwards; early work shows Chinese influence (peony and chrysanthemum flower decorations), later work in Meissen style.

bowfront: An outwardly curving front.

boxwood: A closely grained yellow coloured wood.

bracket clock: Originally a 17thC clock which had to be set high up on a bracket because of the length of the weights; now generally applied to any small mantel or table clock.

bracket foot: A type of foot for case pieces which appears somewhat shaped as a right-angled bracket below the front edge.

Breakfast table: A small table with hinged side leaves, suitable for one or two people.

Bristol: Important porcelain factory established c1749, producing delftware, and (c1770) enamelled and gilded wares decorated with flowers and swags. Also, 17th and 18thC delftwares (bowls, figure groups, jugs) produced by several factories in the area.

Bru & Cie: Leading French doll maker 1866-99; noted for dolls in elaborate contemporary costumes.

buffet: Open structures, of more than one tier.

bureau: Writing desk with either a fall, a cylinder or a tambour front.

bureau bookcase: Bureau with a glazed-fronted bookcase fitted above it.

bureau cabinet: Bureau with a solid-doored or mirrored cabinet fitted above it, often containing further fitted cupboards and drawers.

bureau de dame: Writing desk of delicate appearance and designed for use by ladies. Usually raised above slender cabriole legs and with one or two external drawers.

bureau-plat: French writing table with a flat top and drawers in the frieze.

cabaret set: Tea set for 3 or more people.

cabriole leg: Tail curving leg subject to many designs and produced with club, pad, paw, claw-and-ball, and scroll feet.

caddy: Usually silver (but also of ceramic, wood or enamel) container for tea with a lead-lined compartment; often two compartments with a spoon and glass bowl for blending two types of leaf.

camaieu: Porcelain decoration using different tones of the one colour.

cameo glass: A sandwich of coloured glass which is then cut or etched away to create a multi-colour design in relief. An ancient technique rediscovered by Emile Gallé and popular with Art Nouveau and Art Deco glassmakers in the early 20thC.

Canton: The general term for blue and white porcelains imported to the west in the 18thC when Canton was the chief trading port.

Carlton House desk: A distinct type of writing desk which has a raised back with drawers which extend forward at the sides to create an 'enclosed' central writing area.

Carlton Ware: Brand name of Art Nouveau pottery made by Wiltshaw and Robinson, a Stoke-on-Trent pottery founded in 1897.

carousel figures: Horses and other animals from fairground carousels or roundabouts, usually classified as either 'jumpers' or 'standers'.

carriage clock: Originally one fitted with a device to ensure that the jolts common in the days of coach travel would not interfere with the oscillations of the balance spring. Now any small portable oblong clock of rectangular form, popular from the 19thC to the present day.

cartel clock: An 18thC French wall clock in the shape of a shield, often with a gilded bronze case and elaborately ornamented in rococo style.

cartouche: An ornate tablet or shield surrounded by scrollwork and foliage, often bearing a maker's name, inscription or coat-of-arms.

castelli: Maiolica from the Abruzzi region of Italy, noted for delicate landscapes painted by members of the Grue family.

Caughley: Shropshire factory, established c1750, producing porcelain very like that of Worcester, including early willow-pattern, often embellished by gilding.

celadon: Chinese stonewares with an opaque grey-green glaze, first made in the Sung dynasty and still made today, principally in Korea.

cellaret: Lidded container on legs designed to hold wine. The interior is often divided into sections for individual bottles.

centrepiece: Silver ornament, usually decorative rather than functional, designed to occupy the centre of a dining table.

Chaffers, Richard & Partners: Liverpool pottery manufacturer, operating around 1754-65, producing earthenwares resembling china and modelled on Worcester forms.

chaise longue: An elongated chair, the seat long enough to support the sitter's legs.

champlevé: Enamelling on copper or bronze, similar to cloisonné, in which a glass paste is applied to the hollowed-out design, fired and ground smooth.

character doll: One with a naturalistic face, especially laughing, crying, pouting, etc.

character jug: Earthenware jugs and sometimes mugs, widely made in 18th and 19thC, depicting a popular character, such as a politician, general, jockey or actor.

chest-on-chest: A chest of drawers supported on another chest of drawers, also known as a tallboy.

chesterfield: Type of large over-stuffed sofa introduced in late 19thC.

cheval mirror: Large toilet mirror in a frame with four legs, the mirror being pivoted and adjustable within the frame. Also known as a horse dressing glass and a psyche. Made c1750 onwards.

chiffonier: Generally a twin door cupboard with one or two drawers above and surmounted by shelves.

Chin dynasty: period in Chinese history AD1115-1260.

Chinese export porcelain: 16th to 18thC wares made in China specifically for export and often to European designs.

Chinese Imari: Chinese imitations of Japanese blue, red and gold painted Imari wares, made from the early 18thC.

Ch'ing dynasty: From 1644 to 1912, the period during which much decorated Chinese porcelain was exported to Europe.

chinoiserie: The fashion, prevailing in the late 18thC, for Chinese-style ornamentation on porcelain, wallpapers and fabrics, furniture and garden architecture.

chryselephantine: Originally made of gold and ivory, but now used for Art Deco statues made of ivory and another metal, typically bronze and very desirable.

claw-and-ball foot: A carved foot, shaped like a ball held in a talon, or claw.

Cliff, Clarice (1899-1972): Employed by A. J. Wilkinson Ltd, the pottery at Newport, Staffordshire, as artistic director in the 1930s. Designer of the colourful 'Bizarre' and 'Fantasque' ranges of mass-produced china.

clock garniture: A matching group of clock and vases or candelabra made for the mantel shelf. Often highly ornate.

cloisonné: Enamelling on metal with divisions in the design separated by lines of fine brass wire. A speciality of the Limoges region of France in the Middle Ages, and of Chinese craftsmen to the present day.

Coalport china: Porcelain manufactured at Coalbrookdale, Shropshire, from the 1790s, noted for the translucent felspathic wares produced from 1820 and the delicate colours of the figure groups.

coffer: In strict definition a coffer is a travelling trunk which is banded with metalwork and covered with leather or other material. However, the word tends to be used quite freely to describe chests of various kinds.

Colonial: An American object made during the period when the country consisted of 13 Colonies.

Commedia dell'Arte: Figures from traditional Italian theatre (Harlequin, Columbine, Scaramouche, Pantaloon) often depicted in porcelain groups in 18thC.

compound twist: In a wine glass stem, any air-twist made of multiple spirals; e.g. lace twist, gauze and multi-ply.

console table: Decorative side table with no back legs, being supported against the wall by brackets.

cordial glass: Smaller version of a wine glass, with a thick stem, heavy foot and small bowl; evolved 17thC for strong drink.

country furniture: General term for furniture made by provincial craftsmen; cottage furniture and especially that made of pine, oak, elm and the fruitwoods.

credenza: Used today to describe a type of side cabinet which is highly decorated and shaped. Originally it was an Italian sideboard used as a serving table.

crested china: Pottery decorated with colourful heraldic crests, first made by Goss but, by 1880, being produced in quantity by manufacturers throughout the UK and in Germany.

cup and cover: Carved decoration found on the bulbous turned legs of some Elizabethan furniture.

curule chair: A folding seat with curved legs.

cut glass: Glass carved with revolving wheels and abrasive to create sharp-edged facets that reflect and refract light so as to sparkle and achieve a prismatic (rainbow) effect. Revived Bohemia 17thC, and common until superseded by pressed glass for utilitarian objects.

Cymric: The trade-name used by Liberty & Company for a mass produced range of silverware, inspired by Celtic art, introduced in 1899, and often incorporating enamelled pictorial plaques.

cypher: An impressed or painted mark on porcelain which gives the year of manufacture; each factory had its own set of codes; used principally mid-to late 19thC.

davenport (1): Small writing desk with a sloping top and a series of real and false drawers below. Some have a writing surface which slides forward and rising compartments at the rear.

davenport (2): American term for a day-bed or reclining sofa with headrest.

Davenport (3): Important factory at Longport, Staffordshire, founded 1793 by John Davenport; originally manufactured earthenware, but noted from 1820 for very fine botanical wares and Imari style decoration.

day-bed: Couch with one sloped end to support the head and back whilst reclined. Either upholstered or caned. Made from 16thC until the mid-18thC. Also known in the US as a davenport.

Delft: Dutch tin glazed earthenwares named after the town of Delft, the principal production centre. 16thC Delft shows Chinese influence but by 17thC the designs are based on Dutch landscapes. Similar pottery made in England from the late 16thC is usually termed 'delftware'.

Della Robbia: Florentine Renaissance sculptor who invented technique of applying vitreous glaze to terracotta; English art pottery made at Birkenhead, late 19thC, in imitation of his work.

Denby: Stoneware made by Bourne & Son, at Denby, 19thC; also known as Bourne pottery.

Derby: Important porcelain factory founded 1756, producing very fine figure groups - often called English Meissen - as well as painted wares decorated with landscapes and botanical scenes.

diaper: Surface decoration composed of repeated diamonds or squares, often carved in low relief.

die-stamping: Method of mass producing a design on metal by machine which passes sheet metal between a steel die and a drop hammer. Used for forming toys as well as stamping cutlery, etc.

Ding Yao: Northern Chinese pottery of the Sung Yuan dynasties.

Dresser, Christopher (1835-1904): Influential English pottery and glass designer who was inspired by Japanese art and worked for Tiffany as well as the pottery firms of Ault, Linthorpe and Pilkington.

drop-in seat: Upholstered chair seat which is supported on the seat rails but which can be lifted out independently.

ducai: Chinese for contrasting colour.

Du Paquier: Porcelain from Vienna, especially chinoiserie wares produced early 18thC.

écuelle: 17thC vessel, usually of silver, but also of ceramic for serving soup. Has a shallow, circular bowl with two handles and a domed cover. It often comes complete with a stand.

eglomisé: Painting on glass, associated with clock faces: often the reverse side of the glass is covered in gold or silver leaf through which a pattern is engraved and then painted black.

electroplate: The process of using electrical current to coat a base metal or alloy with silver, invented 1830s and gradually superseding Sheffield plate.

enamel (1): In ceramics, a second coloured but translucent glaze laid over the first glaze.

enamel (2): Coloured glass, applied to metal, ceramic or glass in paste form and then fired for decorative effect.

EPNS: Electroplated nickel silver; i.e. nickel alloy covered with a layer of silver using the electroplate process.

etched glass: Technique of cutting layers of glass away, using acid, much favoured by Art Nouveau and Art Deco glassmakers. Such sculpture in high relief is known as deep etched, and layers of multi-coloured glass were often treated in this way to make cameo glass.

faïence: Tin glazed earthenwares named after the town of Faenza in Italy, but actually used to describe products made anywhere but Italy, where the same wares are called 'maiolica'.

fairings: Mould-made figure groups in cheap porcelain, produced in great quantity in the 19th and 20thC, especially in Germany; often humorous or sentimental. So called because they were sold, or given as prizes, at fairs.

famille jaune: 'Yellow family'; Chinese porcelain vessels in which yellow is the predominant ground colour.

famille noire: 'Black family'; Chinese porcelain in which black is the predominant ground colour.

famille rose: 'Pink family'; Chinese porcelain vessels with an enamel (overglaze) of pink to purple tones.

famille verte: 'Green family'; Chinese porcelain with a green enamel (overglaze), laid over yellows, blues, purples and iron red.

Fantasque: Name of a colourful range of household china designed by Clarice Cliff and manufactured in the 1930s by the Staffordshire pottery, A.J. Wilkinson Ltd.

fauteuil: French open-armed drawing room chair.

filigree: Lacy openwork of silver or gold thread, produced in large quantities since end 19thC.

flag bottom chair: Chair made with a rush seat.

flow blue: A process used principally after 1840, in which flowing powder is added to the dye used in blue and white transferware so that the blue flows beyond the edges of the transfer, rendering the pattern less sharply defined. Items using this process were made primarily for the American market.

flatware: Collective name for flat pottery, such as plates, trenchers and trays, as opposed to cups, vases and bowls.

fluted: A border that resembles a scalloped edge, used as a decoration on furniture, glass, silver and porcelain items.

foulard: A soft light fabric of plain weave or twill weave silk or rayon, usually with a printed design.

frosted glass: Glass with a surface made to resemble frost patterns or snow-crystals; common on pressed glass vessels for serving cold confections.

Fulda: Factory at Hessen that produced some of Germany's best faience in the mid-18thC; in the late 18thC turned to producing Meissen-style porcelain.

fusee: 18thC clockwork invention; a cone shaped drum, linked to the spring barrel by a length of gut or chain. The shape compensates for the declining strength of the mainspring thus ensuring constant timekeeping.

Gallé, Emile (1846-1904): Father of the French Art Nouveau movement and founder of a talented circle of designers based around Nancy. Simultaneously, in the 1880s, he designed delicate furniture embellished with marquetry and began experimenting with new glass techniques. In 1889, he developed cameo glass; in 1897 'marquetry in glass', or 'marquetrie de verre'. After his death, factories continued to produce his wares, signed Gallé but marked with a star, until the 1930s.

gilding: Process of applying thin gold foil to a surface. There are two methods. Oil gilding involves the use of linseed oil and is applied directly onto the woodwork. Water gilding requires the wood to be painted with gesso.

Glasgow School: Originally the name of the Glasgow School of Art at which Charles Rennie Mackintosh studied in the 1880s, and whose new buildings he designed in the 1890s. Now used to describe the style developed by Mackintosh and his followers, a simplified linear form of Art Nouveau highly influential on Continental work of the period.

Granite ware: A durable and inexpensive white earthenware, sold in the USA during the mid-1800s.

grisaille: Type of monochrome used to decorate furniture during the 18thC.

hall chair: Strongly constructed chair lacking intricate ornament and upholstery, being designed to stand in a hall to accommodate messengers and other callers in outdoor clothing. At the same time it had to be attractive enough to impress more important callers and was often carved with a crest or coat-of-arms for this purpose.

hallmark: Collective term for all the marks found on silver or gold consisting of an assay office, quality, date and maker's marks; sometimes the term is used only of the assay office mark.

hand pressed: Any glass object made in a hand operated press instead of a machine press.

hard paste: True porcelain made of china stone (petuntse) and kaolin; the formula was long known to, and kept secret by, Chinese potters but only discovered in the 1750s in England, from where it spread to the rest of Europe and the Americas.

harewood: Sycamore which has been stained a greenish colour is known as harewood. It is used mainly as an inlay wood and was known as silverwood in the 18thC.

Hirado: Japanese porcelain with figure and landscape painting in blue on a white body, often depicting boys at play, made exclusively for the Lords of Hirado, near Arita, mid-18th to mid-19thC.

hiramakie: Flat decoration in Japanese lacquerware, as opposed to carving or relief.

Hornby: manufacturers of clockwork and electric locomotives from c1910, best known today for the 'Dublo' range, introduced mid-1940s.

hydria: A large water jar.

indianische Blumen: Indian flowers; painting on porcelain in the Oriental style, especially on mid-18thC Meissen and Höchst.

intaglio: Incised gem-stone, often set in a ring, used in antiquity and during the Renaissance as a seal. Any incised decoration; the opposite of carving in relief.

ironstone: Stoneware, patented 1813 by Charles James Mason, containing ground glassy slag, a by-product of iron smelting, for extra strength.

ivory porcelain: Development of 19thC, similar to parian but ivory coloured in biscuit form.

Jacobite: Wine glasses engraved with symbols of the Jacobites (supporters of Prince Charles Edward Stuart's claim to the English throne). Genuine examples date from 1746 to 1788. Countless later copies and forgeries exist.

Jumeau, Pierre François: Important French doll maker noted for 'Parisiennes', active 1842-99.

Kakiemon: Family of 17thC Japanese potters who produced wares decorated with flowers and figures on a white ground in distinctive colours: azure, yellow, turquoise and soft red. Widely imitated in Europe.

kelim: Flat woven rugs lacking a pile; also the flat woven fringe used to finish off the ends of a pile carpet.

kernos: A jar bearing small cups around its lip.

kneehole desk: Writing desk with a space between the drawer pedestals for the user's legs.

knop (1): Knob, protuberance or swelling in the stem of a wine glass, of various forms which can be used as an aid to dating and provenance.

knop (2): In furniture, a swelling on an upright member.

Knox, Archibald (1864-1931): English designer of the Cymric range of silverware and Tudric pewter for Liberty's store in London, responsible for some 400 different designs.

Kylix: A shallow two-handled drinking vessel.

Lalique, René (1860-1945): French designer of Art Nouveau jewellery in gold, silver and enamel, who founded his own workshop in Paris in 1885. After 1900 he turned to making figures in crystal and opalescent glass. From 1920 he emerged as the leading Art Deco glass maker, and his factory produced a huge range of designs.

Leach, Bernard (1887-1979): Father of English craft pottery who studied in China and Japan in order to master Oriental glazing techniques.

Lenci: Italian company manufacturing dolls with pressed felt faces in Turin in the 1920s, noted for the sideways glance of the painted eyes.

lianzi: Chinese name for a lotus bowl.

Liberty & Co.: Principal outlet for Art Nouveau designs in England. Arthur Lasenby Liberty (1843-1917) founded his furniture and drapery shop in 1875. Later he commissioned designs exclusive to his store, including Cymric silver and Tudric pewter, which gave rise to a distinctive 'Liberty style'.

linenfold: Carved decoration which resembles folded linen.

Liverpool: Important pottery production centre from the mid-18thC, noted for blue painted delftware punch bowls, and early porcelain produced by several different factories, now eagerly collected.

longcase clock: First made c1660 in England, a tall clock consisting of a case which houses the weights or pendulum and a hood housing the movement and dial. In U.S.A. also known as a tallcase clock.

lorgnette: A pair of opera glasses, or spectacles, mounted on a handle.

lowboy: A small dressing table, usually with a single frieze drawer or a small central shallow drawer flanked on either side by a deep drawer.

lyre clock: Early 19thC American pendulum clock, its shape resembling that of a lyre.

majolica: Often used, in error, as an alternative spelling for maiolica; correctly, a richly-enamelled stoneware with high relief decoration developed by Minton, mid-19thC.

mandorla: An almond-shaped area of light, usually surrounding the resurrected Christ or the Virgin at the Assumption.

mantel clock: Clock provided with feet to stand on the mantelpiece.

martele: Form of faceted glass, made to resemble hammered metal, invented by the Daum Brothers and used for their Art Nouveau glass.

Martinware: Art pottery made by the Martin brothers between 1873 and 1914, characterised by grotesque human and animal figures in stoneware.

medicine chest: Used by itinerant medics from 17thC, usually with compartments, labelled bottles, spoons and balances.

Meiji: Period in Japanese history 1868 to 1912, when the nation's art was much influenced by contact with the West, and much was made specifically for export.

Mei ping: Chinese for cherry blossom, used to describe a tall vase, with high shoulders, small neck and narrow mouth, used to display flowering branches.

mihrab: Prayer niche with a pointed arch; the motif which distinguishes a prayer rug from other types.

millefiori: Multi-coloured, or mosaic, glass, made since antiquity by fusing a number of coloured glass rods into a cane, and cutting off thin sections; much used to ornament paperweights.

Minton: Pottery established by Thomas Minton, at Stoke-on-Trent, in late 18thC. Originally produced earthenwares and creamware; then, most famously, bone china. After 1850 the company produced fine copies of Renaissance maiolica and, in 1870, set up the Minton Art Pottery Studio in London as a training academy for young designers, producing fine Art Nouveau work.

Moorcroft, William (1872-1946): Staffordshire art potter, who worked for MacIntyre & Co. from 1898, and set up independently in 1913. Known for colourful vases with floral designs and his 'Florian' and 'Aurelian' wares.

Moore, Bernard: Founder of art pottery based in Longton, Staffordshire, c1900 specialising in unusual glaze effects.

Morris, William (1834-96): Regarded as the progenitor of the Art Nouveau style. The company Morris, Marshall and Faulkner (later simply Morris & Co.) was founded in 1861 to produce wallpaper, stained glass, chintz carpets and tapestries. The origins of his style can be traced to medieval Gothic, but his organic flowers and bird motifs encouraged later artists to seek inspiration for their designs in nature.

Mortlake: Factory founded in 1619 with royal patronage and financial backing of Charles I.

netsuke: Japanese carved toggles made to secure sagemono ('hanging things') to the obi (waist belt) from a cord; usually of ivory, lacquer, silver or wood, from the 16thC.

New Hall: Late 18thC potters' co-operative in Staffordshire making porcelain and bone china wares.

ormolu: Strictly, gilded bronze or brass but sometimes used loosely of any yellow metal. Originally used for furniture handles and mounts but, from the 18thC, for ink stands, candlesticks, clock cases, etc.

overlay: In cased glass, the top layer, usually engraved to reveal a different coloured layer beneath.

overmantel: Area above the shelf on a mantelpiece, often consisting of a mirror in an ornate frame, or some architectural feature in wood or stone.

over-stuffed: Descriptive of upholstered furniture where the covering extends over the frame of the seat.

ovolo: Moulding of convex quarter-circle section. Sometimes found around the edges of drawers to form a small overlap onto the carcase.

paperweight glass: Glass of which the design is embedded and manipulated within layers of clear glass, a process loosely akin to that used for paperweights.

papier mâché: moulded paper pulp, suitable for japanning and polishing, used for small articles such as trays, boxes, tea-caddies, and coasters.

Parisienne doll: French bisque head doll with a stuffed kid leather body, made by various manufacturers 1860s to 1880s.

pate: Crown of a doll's head into which the hair is stitched, usually of cork in the better quality dolls.

pâte-sur-pâte: 19thC Sèvres porcelain technique, much copied, of applying slip decoration to the body before firing.

Pembroke table: Small table with two short drop leaves along its length. Named after the Countess of Pembroke who is said to have been the first to order one. Also once known as a breakfast table.

percussion lock: Early 19thC firearm, one of the first to be fired by the impact of a sharp-nosed hammer on the cartridge cap.

pier glass: Mirror designed to be fixed to the pier, or wall, between two tall window openings, often partnered by a matching pier table. Made from mid-17thC.

Pilkington: Associated with the Lancashire glass factory, this pottery produced Art Nouveau ceramics in the early 20thC, remarkable for its iridescent and colourful glazes.

Pinxton: Soft-paste porcelain imitating Derby, made in Nottingham by William Billingsley, from c1800.

plate: Old fashioned term, still occasionally used, to describe gold and silver vessels; not to be confused with 'Sheffield plate', or plated vessels generally, in which silver is fused to a base metal alloy.

pole screen: Small adjustable screen mounted on a pole and designed to stand in front of an open fire to shield a lady's face from the heat.

portrait doll: One modelled on a well known figure.

poupard: Doll without legs, often mounted on a stick; popular in 19thC.

poured wax doll: One made by pouring molten wax on to a mould.

powder flask: Device for measuring out a precise quantity of priming powder made to be suspended from a musketeer's belt or bandolier and often ornately decorated. Sporting flasks are often made of antler and carved with hunting scenes.

powder horn: Cow horn hollowed out, blocked at the wide end with a wooden plug and fitted with a measuring device at the narrow end, used by musketeers for dispensing a precise quantity of priming powder.

pressed glass: Early 19thC invention, exploited rapidly in America, whereby mechanical pressure was used to form glassware in a mould, instead of using compressed air.

purfling: A ruffled or curved ornamental band.

puzzle jug: Delftware form made from the 17thC, with several spouts and a syphon system, none of which will pour unless the others are blocked.

quarter clock: One which strikes the quarter and half hours as well as the full hours.

Quimper faience: From the factory in Brittany, France, established late 17thC and closely modelled on Rouen wares.

rack: Tall superstructure above a dresser.

refectory table: Modern term for the long dining tables of the 17thC and later.

regulator: Clock of great accuracy, thus sometimes used for controlling or checking other time pieces.

rosette: A round floral design ornament.

rummer/roemer: Originally 16th/17thC German wide bowled wine glass on a thick stem, decorated with prunts, on a base of concentric glass coils, often in green glass (waldglas). Widely copied throughout Europe in many forms.

sabre leg: Elegant curving leg associated with furniture of the Regency period but first appearing near the end of the 18thC. Also known as Trafalgar leg.

St Cloud: Factory near Paris, famous for soft-paste porcelain in the first half of the 18thC, decorated in Kakiemon style and imitation blanc-de-chine.

salon chair: General term to describe a French or French style armchair.

satinwood: A moderately hard, yellow or light brown wood, with a very close grain, found in central and southern India, Coromandel, Ceylon and in the West Indies.

scent bottle: Small, portable flask of flattened pear shape, made of silver, rock crystal, porcelain or glass.

seal bottle: Wine bottles with an applied glass medallion or seal personalised with the owner's name, initials, coat-of-arms or a date. Produced from the early 17th to the mid-19thC when bottles were relatively expensive.

secrétaire bookcase: Secrétaire with a bookcase fitted above it.

SFBJ: Société de Fabrication de Bébés et Jouets; doll maker founded 1899 by merging the businesses of Jumeau, Bru and others. Products regarded as inferior to those of the original makers.

Sheraton revival: Descriptive of furniture produced in the style of Sheraton when his designs gained revived interest during the Edwardian period.

silver table: Small rectangular table designed for use in the dining room. They usually have a fretwork gallery.

Six Dynasties: Period in Chinese history AD265–589.

six-hour dial: One with only six divisions instead of twelve, often with the hours 1 – 6 in Roman numerals and 7 – 12 superimposed in Arabic numerals.

snuff box: Box made to contain snuff in silver, or any other material: early examples have an integral rasp and spoon, from 17thC.

sofa table: Type of drop leaf table which developed from the Pembroke table. It was designed to stand behind a sofa, so is long and thin with two short drop leaves at the ends and two drawers in the frieze.

softwood: One of two basic categories in which all timbers are classified. The softwoods are conifers which generally have leaves in the form of evergreen needles.

spelter: Zinc treated to look like bronze and much used as an inexpensive substitute in Art Nouveau appliqué ornament and Art Deco figures.

Steiff, Margarete: Maker of dolls and highly prized teddy bears, she first exhibited at Leipzig, 1903, but died 1909. The company she founded continued to mass produce toys, dolls and bears for export. Products can be identified by the 'Steiff' button trademark, usually in the ear.

stirrup cup: Silver cup, without handles, so-called because it was served, containing a suitable beverage, to huntsmen in the saddle, prior to their moving off. Often made in the shape of an animal's head.

Sung dynasty: Ruling Chinese dynasty from AD960–1279.

susani: A Middle Eastern embroidered cover for the bridal bed.

table clock: Early type of domestic clock, some say the predecessor of the watch, in which the dial is set vertically: often of drum shape.

tallboy: Chest of drawers raised upon another chest of drawers. Also known as a chest-on-chest.

tazza: Wide but shallow bowl on a stem with a foot; ceramic and metal tazzas were made in antiquity and the form was revived by Venetian glassmakers in 15thC. Also made in silver from 16thC.

tea kettle: Silver, or other metal, vessel intended for boiling water at the table. Designed to sit over a spirit lamp, it sometimes had a rounded base instead of flat.

teapoy: Piece of furniture in the form of a tea caddy on legs, with a hinged lid opening to reveal caddies, mixing bowl and other tea drinking accessories.

tear: Tear-drop shaped air bubble in the stem of an early 18thC wine glass, from which the air-twist evolved.

tester: Wooden canopy over a bedstead which is supported on either two or four posts. It may extend fully over the bed and be known as a full tester, or only over the bedhead half and be known as a half tester.

tête à tête: Tea set for 2 people.

thuyawood: Reddish-brown wood imported from Africa and used as a veneer.

tin glaze: Glassy white glaze of tin oxide; re-introduced to Europe in 14thC by Moorish potters; the characteristic glaze of delftware, faience and maiolica.

Toby jug: Originally a jug in the form of a man in a tricorn hat, first made by Ralph Wood of Burslem, mid-18thC; since produced in great quantity in many different forms.

tondo: A circular relief carving.

transfer printed: Ceramic decoration technique perfected mid-18thC and used widely thereafter for mass produced wares. An engraved design is printed on to paper (the bat) using the ink consisting of glaze mixed with oil; the paper is then laid over the body of the vessel and burns off in firing, leaving an outline, usually in blue. Sometimes the outline was coloured in by hand.

trefoil: Three-cusped figure which resembles a symmetrical three-lobed leaf or flower.

tripod table: Descriptive of any table with a three-legged base but generally used to describe only small tables of this kind.

tsuba: Guard of a Japanese sword, usually consisting of an ornamented plate.

Tudric: Range of Celtic inspired Art Nouveau pewter of high quality, designed for mass production by Archibald Knox and retailed through Liberty & Co.

tulipwood: Yellow brown wood with reddish stripe imported from Central and South America and used as a veneer and for inlay and crossbanding. It is related to rosewood and kingwood.

veilleuse: Night light.

Venetian glass: Fine soda glass and coloured glass blown and pinched into highly ornamented vessels of intricate form, made in Venice, and widely copied from 15thC.

verge escapement: Oldest form of escapement, found on clocks as early as AD1300 and still in use 1900. Consisting of a bar (the verge) with two flag shaped pallets that rock in and out of the teeth of the crown or escape wheel to regulate the movement.

vesta case: Ornate flat case of silver or other metal for carrying vestas, an early form of match. From mid-19thC.

vitrine: French display cabinet which is often of bombé or serpentine outline and ornately decorated with marquetry and ormolu.

volute: A carved ornament in the form of a spiral scroll.

voyeuse: A chair with a padded top to the back, on which one could sit astride to watch card games, etc.

washstand: Stand designed to hold a basin for washing in the bedroom. Generally of two types. Either three or four uprights supporting a circular top to hold the basin and with a triangular shelf with a drawer. Or as a cupboard raised on four legs with a basin let into the top, sometimes with enclosing flaps. Also known as a basin stand.

Wedgwood: Pottery founded by Josiah Wedgwood (1730-95) at Stoke-on-Trent and noted for numerous innovations; especially creamware, basaltes, and pearlware; perhaps best known for jasperware, the blue stonewares decorated with white relief scenes from late 18thC.

Wellington chest: Distinct type of tall, narrow chest of drawers. They usually have either six or seven thin drawers one above the other and a hinged and lockable flap over one side to prevent them from opening. Made in the 19thC.

whatnot: Tall stand of four or five shelves and some-times a drawer in addition. Some were made to stand in a corner. Used for the display of ornaments and known in Victorian times as an omnium.

wucai: Chinese for five colours.

yew: Hard, deep reddish brown wood used both as a veneer and solid. It is very resistant to woodworm and turns well.

Yuan dynasty: Period in Chinese history AD1280-1368 during which the art of underglaze painting was developed.

Yuhuchun: Chinese name for a bottle vase in the shape of a pear. The form first appeared in the T'ang dynasty and was popular thereafter.

DIRECTORY OF SPECIALISTS

If you wish to be included in next year's directory, or if you have a change of address or telephone number, please advise Miller's Advertising Department by April 1997. We would advise readers to make contact by telephone before a visit, therefore avoiding a wasted journey.

ANTIQUITIES

Dorset

Ancient & Gothic,
PO Box 356,
Christchurch
BH23 2YD
Tel: 01202 478592

ARCHITECTURAL ANTIQUES

Cheshire

Nostalgia,
61 Shaw Heath,
Stockport
SK3 8BH
Tel: 0161 477 7706

Devon

Ashburton Marbles,
Grate Hall,
North Street,
Ashburton
TQ13 7QD
Tel: 01364 653189

Dorset

Dorset Reclamation,
Cow Drove,
Bere Regis,
Wareham
BH20 7JZ
Tel: 01929 472200
Fax: 01929 472292

Lincolnshire

Britannia Brass Fittings,
Hemswell Antiques Centre,
Caenby Corner Estate,
Hemswell Cliff,
Gainsborough
DN21 5TJ
Tel: 01482 227300

Surrey

Drummonds of Bramley,
Birtley Farm,
Horsham Road,
Bramley,
Guildford
GU5 0LA
Tel: 01483 898766
Fax: 01483 894393

Sussex

Brighton Architectural
Salvage,
33 Gloucester Road,
Brighton
BN1 4AQ
Tel: 01273 681656

ARMS & MILITARIA

Lincolnshire

Garth Vincent,
The Old Manor House,
Allington,
Nr Grantham
NG32 2HD
Tel: 01400 281358

Surrey

West Street Antiques,
63 West Street,
Dorking
RH4 1BS
Tel: 01306 883487

Sussex

Wallis & Wallis,
West Street Auction
Galleries,
Lewes
BN7 2NJ
Tel: 01273 480208

West Midlands

Weller & Dufty Ltd,
141 Bromsgrove Street,
Birmingham
B5 6RQ
Tel: 0121 692 1414
Fax: 0121 622 5605

Yorkshire

Andrew Spencer Bottomley,
The Coach House,
Thongs Bridge,
Holmfirth
HD7 2TT
Tel: 01484 685234
Fax: 01484 681551

BAROMETERS

Berkshire

Walker & Walker,
Halfway Manor, Halfway,
Nr Newbury
RG16 8NR
Tel: 01488 658693

Cheshire

Rayment Antiques,
Derek & Tina, Orchard House,
Barton Road, Barton,
Nr Farndon
SY14 7HT
Tel: 01829 270429
Also repair & restoration

Wiltshire

P A Oxley,
The Old Rectory, Cherhill,
Nr Calne SN11 8UX
Tel: 01249 816227

BEDS

Hereford & Worcester

S. W. Antiques,
Abbey Showrooms, Newlands,
Pershore WR10 1BP
Tel: 01386 555580
Fax: 01386 556205

Sussex

Sleeping Beauty Antique Beds,
212 Church Road,
Hove
BN3 2DJ
Tel: 01273 205115

Wales

Seventh Heaven,
Chirk Mill, Chirk,
Wrexham,
Clwyd LL14 5BU
Tel: 01691 772622/773563
Fax: 01691 777313

BOOKS

Middlesex

John Ives,
5 Normanhurst Drive,
Twickenham TW1 1NA
Tel: 0181 892 6265
Fax: 0181 744 3944
Reference books

BOXES & TREEN

London

Coromandel,
16 Clivedon Road,
Wimbledon SW19 3RB
Tel: 0181 543 9115

Somerset

Boxwood Antique Restorers,
Alan Stacey,
67 High Street,
Wincanton BA9 9JZ
Tel: 01963 33988
Cabinet making, polishing, carving and specialists in tortoiseshell, ivory and mother-of-pearl on boxes, caddies and furniture. See our main advertisement in Boxes (Colour) section.

BRITISH ANTIQUE FURNITURE RESTORERS' ASSOCIATION

BAFRA (Main Office),
The Old Rectory,
Warmwell,
Dorchester DT2 8HQ
Tel: 01305 852104

Avon

Stuart Bradbury,
M & S Bradbury,
The Barn, Hanham Lane,
Paulton,
Bristol BS18 5PF
Tel: 01761 418910

Robert P Tandy,
Unit 5 Manor Workshops,
Manor Park,
West End,
Nailsea,
Bristol BS19 2DD
Tel: 01275 856378

Bedfordshire

DME Restorations Ltd,
11 Church Street,
Ampthill MK45 2PL
Tel: 01525 405819
Fax: 01525 405819

Berkshire

Alpha (Antique) Restorations,
High Street,
Compton,
Newbury RG20 6NL
Tel: 01635 578245

Ben R.W. Norris,
Knowl Hill Farm,
Knowl Hill, Kingsclere,
Newbury RG20 4NY
Tel: 01635 297950
Fax: 01635 299851
Gilding, carving & architectural woodwork (ie panelling)

Cambridgeshire

Ludovic Potts Restorations,
Unit 1 Haddenham Business
Park, Station Road,
Haddenham, Ely CB6 3XD
Tel: 01353 741537
Fax: 01353 741537
Cane and rushwork, gilding

Robert Williams,
Osborn's Farm,
32 Church Street,
Willingham
CB4 5HT
Tel: 01954 260972

Cheshire/Derbyshire

Anthony Allen,
Antique Restorers &
Conservators,
The Old Wharf Works,
Redmoor Lane,
Newtown,
New Mills via Stockport
SK12 3JL
Tel: 01663 745274
Boule, marquetry, walnut, oak, veneering, upholstery

Cornwall

Graham Usher,
5 Rose Terrace,
Mitchell,
Nr Newquay
TR8 5AU
Tel: 01872 510551
Furniture restoration, french polishing, veneering, marquetry - Tunbridge work

Cumbria

Peter Hall, & Son,
Danes Road,
Staveley,
Nr Kendal LA8 9PL
Tel: 01539 821633
Fax: 01539 821905

Devon

Tony Vernon,
15 Follett Road,
Topsham EX3 0JP
Tel: 01392 874635

Dorset

Michael Barrington
The Old Rectory,
Warmwell,
Dorchester DT2 8HQ
Tel: 01305 852104
Fax: 01305 852104
"18th & 19th" century furniture, gilding, upholstery, antique metalwork. organ case work and pipe decoration, mechanical models, automatons and toys.

Richard Bolton,
Meadow Court,
Athelhampton House,
Dorchester DT2 7LG
Tel: 01305 848346
All aspects of furniture restoration.

Philip Hawkins,
Glebe Barn, Semley,
Nr Shaftesbury SP7 9AP
Tel: 01747 830830
Specialising in oak & country furniture

Tolpuddle Antique
Restorers,
Raymond Robertson,
West Dean/BADA Dip,
The Stables,
Southover House, Tolpuddle,
Dorchester DT2 7HF
Tel: 01305 848739

Essex

Clive Beardall,
104B High Street
Maldon CM9 7ET
Tel: 01621 857890

Dick Patterson,
Forge Studio Workshop,
Stour Street,
Manningtree CO11 1BE
Tel: 01206 396222

Gloucestershire

Keith Bawden
Mews Workshops,
Montpelier Retreat,
Cheltenham GL50 2XG
Tel: 01242 230320

Alan Hessel,
The Old Town Workshop,
St George's Close,
Moreton-in-Marsh
GL56 0LP
Tel: 01608 650026
Fax: 01608 650026

Stephen Hill,
5 Cirencester Workshops,
Brewery Court,
Cirencester GL7 1JH
Tel: 01285 658817
Fax: 01285 652554

Hunt & Lomas,
Christian Macduff Hunt,
Village Farm Workshops,
Preston Village,
Cirencester GL7 5PR
Tel: 01285 640111

Andrew Lelliott,
6 Tetbury Hill,
Avening,
Tetbury GL8 8LT
Tel: 01453 835783
*Furniture and clock cases,
included on the Conservation
Unit Register of the
Museums and Galleries
Commission.
Control and monitoring of
furniture environment and
insect pests.*

Hampshire

Guy Bagshaw,
The Old Dairy,
Plain Farm,
East Tisted,
Nr Alton
GU34 3RT
Tel: 01420 588362
*Eclectic items, tutored
weekends*

John Hartley
The Old Forge,
Village Street,
Sheet,
Petersfield
GU32 2AQ
Tel: 01730 233792
Fax: 01730 233922

David C. E. Lewry,
Wychelms,
66 Gorran Avenue,
Rowner,
Gosport
PO13 0NF
Tel: 01329 286901
Fax: 01329 289964
Furniture

Hertfordshire

Charles Perry
Restorations Ltd,
John R. Carr,
Praewood Farm,
Hemel Hempstead Road,
St Albans
AL3 6AA
Tel: 01727 853487
Fax: 01727 846668

Kent

Timothy Akers,
The Forge,
39 Chancery Lane,
Beckenham BR3 6NR
Tel: 0181 650 9179
*Longcase and bracket clocks,
cabinet making, french
polishing.*

Benedict Clegg,
Rear of 20 Camden Road,
Tunbridge Wells TN1 2PT
Tel: 01892 548095

Timothy Long Restoration,
St John's Church,
London Road,
Dunton Green,
Sevenoaks TN13 2TE
Tel: 01732 743368
Fax: 01732 742206
*Cabinet restoration,
polishing, upholstery, brass
and steel cabinet fittings.*

Bruce Luckhurst,
Little Surrenden Workshops,
Ashford Road,
Bethersden,
Ashford TN26 3BG
Tel: 01233 820589
1 year course available

Raymond Konyn,
Antique Restorations,
The Old Wheelwright's Shop,
Brasted Forge,
Brasted,
Westerham TN16 1JL
Tel: 01959 563863
Fax: 01959 561262

Lancashire

Eric Smith,
Antique Restorations
The Old Church,
Park Road,
Darwen BB3 2LD
Tel: 01254 776222
*Furniture, vernacular
furniture, longcase clocks.
Registered with Museums
& Galleries Commission -
London*

Lincolnshire

E Czajkowski & Son,
96 Tor-o-Moor Road,
Woodhall Spa LN10 6SB
Tel: 01526 352895
*Restoration antique
furniture, clocks and
barometers. U.K.I.C.
Registered with Museums
and Galleries Commission.*

London

Tracy Clifford,
6–40 Durnford Street,
Seven Sisters Road
N15 5NQ
Tel: 0181 800 4773

Lucinda Compton,
Compton Hall Restoration,
Unit A, 133 Riverside
Business Centre,
Haldane Place SW18 4UQ
Tel: 0181 874 0762
*Lacquer, gilding, painted
furniture*

William Cook,
167 Battersea High Street
SW11 3JS
Tel: 0171 736 5329

Marie Louise Crawley,
39 Wood Vale SE23 3DS
Tel: 0181 299 4121
Fax: 0181 299 0756
*Painted furniture, papier
mâché, tôle ware, lacquer
and gilding.*

Robert H. Crawley,
Aberdeen House
75 St Mary's Road,
Ealing W5 5RH
Tel: 0181 566 5074

Sebastian Giles Furniture,
Sebastian Giles,
11 Junction Mews W2 1PN
Tel: 0171 258 3721
Comprehensive

Hope & Paiget,
Brian Duffy,
1K Leroy House,
436 Essex Road,
Islington N1 3QP
Tel: 0171 359 1400
Fax: 0181 208 3140

Phoenix Antique Furniture
Restoration Ltd,
David Battle,
96 Webber Street SE1 0QN
Tel: 0171 928 3624

Titian Studio,
Rodrigo Titian, Unit 4
318 Kensal Road
W10 5BN
Tel: 0181 960 6247
Fax: 0181 969 6126
*Carving, gilding, lacquer,
painted furniture and french
polishing.*

Norfolk

David Bartram,
The Raveningham Centre
Beccles Road,
Raveningham
NR14 6NU
Tel: 01508 548721

Roderick Nigel Larwood,
The Oaks, Station Road,
Larling,
Norwich
NR16 2QS
Tel: 01953 717937

Oxfordshire

Alistair Frayling-Cork,
2 Mill Lane,
Wallingford
OX10 0DH
Tel: 01491 826221
*Furniture restoration,
stringed instruments, clock
cases and brass fittings
repaired.*

Scotland

Gow Antique Restoration
Jeremy Gow,
Pitscandly Farm
Forfar,
Angus
DD8 3NZ
Tel: 01307 465342
*17th & 18thC marquetry
English & Continental*

Trist & McBain,
135 St Leonards Street
Newington,
Edinburgh
EH8 9RB
Tel: 0131 667 7775
Fax: 0131 667 4333
*Furniture, clocks, barometers,
cane & rush seating*

Shropshire

Richard Higgins,
The Old School, Longnor,
Nr Shrewsbury
SY5 7PP
Tel: 01743 718162
Fax: 01743 718022
*All fine furniture, clocks,
movements, dials and cases,
casting, plating, boulle,
gilding, lacquer work,
carving, period upholstery.*

Somerset

Boxwood Antique Restorers,
Alan Stacey,
67 High Street,
Wincanton
BA9 9JZ
Tel: 01963 33988
*Cabinet making, polishing,
carving and specialists in
tortoiseshell, ivory and
mother-of-pearl on boxes,
caddies and furniture. See
our main advertisement in
Boxes (Colour) section.*

Nicholas Bridges,
20 Newchester Cross,
Merriott TA16 5QJ
Tel: 01460 74672

Michael Durkee,
Castle House, Units 1 & 3,
Bennetts Field Estate,
Wincanton
BA9 9DT
Tel: 01963 33884
Fax: 01963 33884
Antique furniture

Surrey

A. E. Booth & Son,
9 High Street
Ewell,
Epsom KT17 1SG
Tel: 0181 393 5245
Fax: 0181 393 5245
*Comprehensive restoration &
large showrooms*

Courtlands Restoration
David A. Sayer,
Courtlands,
Park Road,
Banstead SM7 3EF
Tel: 01737 352429
Fax: 01737 373255

G & R Fraser-Sinclair & Co,
11 Orchard Works,
Streeters Lane,
Beddington SM6 7ND
Tel: 0181 669 5343
Mobile: 0589 193453

Michael Hedgecoe,
21 Burrow Hill Green,
Chobham,
Woking GU24 8Q
Tel: 01276 858206
Fax: 01276 858206

Stuart Dudley Hobbs,
Meath Paddock,
Meath Green Lane,
Horley RH6 8HZ
Tel: 01293 782349
Furniture, clocks, barometers

Simon Marsh,
The Old Butchers Shop,
High Street,
Bletchingley RH1 4PA
Tel: 01883 743350
Fax: 01883 744844

Timothy Morris,
Unit 4A,
19 St Peter's Street,
South Croydon CR2 7DG
Tel: 0181 681 2992
Furniture & marquetry

Timothy Naylor,
The Workshop,
2 Chertsey Road,
Chobham,
Woking GU24 8NB
Tel: 01276 855122

Sussex

William Maxwell Black,
Brookhouse Studios,
Novington Lane,
East Chiltington,
Lewes BN7 3AX
Tel: 01273 890175

Peter G. Casebow,
Pilgrims,
Mill Lane,
Worthing
BN13 3DE
Tel: 01903 264045
*Marquetry, parquetry,
metalwork*

Noel Pepperall,
Dairy Lane Cottage,
Walberton,
Arundel
BN18 0PT
Tel: 01243 551282
Gilding, painted furniture

Albert Plumb,
31 Whyke Lane,
Chichester
PO19 2JS
Tel: 01243 789100/771212
Fax: 01243 788468
Cabinet making, upholstery

Thakeham Furniture,
Timothy Chavasse,
Marehill Road,
Pulborough
RH20 2DY
Tel: 01798 872006

Worcestershire

Jeffrey Hall,
Malvern Studios,
56 Cowleigh Road,
Malvern
WR14 1QD
Tel: 01684 574913
Fax: 01684 569475

Phillip Slater,
93 Hewell Road,
Barnt Green,
Nr Birmingham
B45 8NL
Tel: 0121 445 4942
Inlay work, marquetry

Yorkshire

Lucinda Compton,
Compton Hall Restoration,
Manor House,
Marton-Le-Moor,
Ripon
HG4 5AT
Tel: 01423 324290
*Lacquer, gilding, painted
furniture*

Fine Furniture Restoration
T. L. Phelps,
8 Mornington Terrace,
Harrogate
HG1 5DH
Tel: 01423 524 604
*Special restoration &
conservation*

Rodney F. Kemble,
16 Crag Vale Terrace,
Glusburn,
Nr Keighley
BD20 8QU
Tel: 01535 636954/633702
*Furniture and small
decorative items*

CLOCKS & WATCHES

Bedfordshire

House of Clocks,
11 Church Street,
Ampthill
MK45 2PJ
Tel: 01525 403136

Cheshire

Coppelia Antiques,
Holford Lodge,
Plumley Moor Road,
Plumley
WA16 9RS
Tel: 01565 722197

Essex

It's About Time,
863 London Road,
Westcliff on Sea
SS0 9SZ
Tel: 01702 72574

Gloucestershire

Jonathan Beech,
Nurses Cottage,
Ampney Crucis,
Nr Cirencester
GL7 5RY
Tel: 01285 851495

Gerard Campbell,
Maple House,
Market Place,
Lechlade
GL7 3AB
Tel: 01367 252267

Grandfather Clock Shop,
Styles of Stow,
The Little House,
Sheep Street,
Stow-on-the-Wold,
GL54 1AA
Tel: 01451 830455
Fax: 01451 830455

Humberside

Bell Antiques,
68A Harold Street,
Grimsby
DN35 0HH
Tel: 01472 695110

Kent

Gem Antiques,
28 London Road,
Sevenoaks
TN13 1AP
Tel: 01732 743540

Gaby Gunst,
Antique Clocks &
Barometers,
140 High Street,
Tenterden
TN30 6HT
Tel: 01580 765818

Old Clock Shop,
63 High Street,
West Malling
ME19 6NA
Tel: 01732 843246

Derek Roberts,
24-25 Shipbourne Road,
Tonbridge TN10 3DN
Tel: 01732 358986

Lincolnshire

Pinfold Antiques,
3 Pinfold Lane,
Ruskington,
NG34 9EU
Tel: 01526 832057
Fax: 01526 834550

London

The Clock Clinic Ltd,
85 Lower Richmond Road,
SW5 1EU
Tel: 0181 788 1407

Newcombe & Son,
89 Maple Road,
Penge SE20 8UL
Tel: 0181 778 0816

Pendulum,
51 Maddox Street W1
Tel: 0171 629 6606

Pieces of Time,
1-7 Davies Mews
W1Y 1AR
Tel: 0171 629 2422

Raffety,
34 Kensington Church
Street W8 4HA
Tel: 0171 938 1100

Roderick Antiques Clocks,
23 Vicarage Gate
W8 4AA
Tel: 0171 937 8517

Norfolk

Keith Lawson,
Scratby Garden Centre,
Beach Road, Scratby,
Great Yarmouth
NR29 3AJ
Tel: 01493 730950

Oxfordshire

Rosemary & Time,
42 Park Street,
Thame
OX9 3HR
Tel: 01844 216923

Scotland

John R. Mann,
Canonbie Village,
Next to Cross Keys Hotel,
Dumfriesshire
DG14 0RY
Tel: 0850 606147

Staffordshire

The Essence of Time,
Tudor of Lichfield Antique
Centre, Bore Street,
Lichfield
WS13 6LL
Tel: 01543 263951

James A. Jordan,
7 The Corn Exchange,
Lichfield
WS13 6JR
Tel: 01543 416221

Suffolk

Antique Clocks by Simon
Charles,
Little St Mary's Court,
Hall Street,
Long Melford
CO10 6LT
Tel: 01787 880040/375931

Surrey

Bryan Clisby,
86B Tilford Road,
Farnham
GU9 8DS
Tel: 01252 716436

The Clock Shop,
64 Church Street,
Weybridge
KT13 8DL
Tel: 01932 840407

Horological Workshops,
204 Worplesdon Road,
Guildford
GU2 6UY
Tel: 01483 576496

Sussex

Antique Clocks,
36 High Street,
Hurstpierpoint,
Nr Brighton
BN6 9RG
Tel: 01273 832081

Wiltshire

P A Oxley,
The Old Rectory,
Cherhill,
Nr Calne
SN11 8UX
Tel: 01249 816227

Allan Smith Clocks,
Amity Cottage,
162 Beechcroft Road,
Upper Stratton,
Swindon
SN2 6QE
Tel: 01793 822977

Yorkshire

Brian Loomes,
Calf Haugh Farm,
Pateley Bridge
HG3 5HW
Tel: 01423 711163

Time & Motion,
1 Beckside,
Beverley
HU17 0PB
Tel: 01482 881574

**COUNTRY
FURNITURE**

Shropshire

No 7 Antiques,
7 Nantwich Road,
Woore
CW3 9SA
Tel: 01630 647118

DECORATIVE ARTS

Gloucestershire

Arts Decoratifs,
18-20 Suffolk Parade,
Cheltenham
GL50 2AE
Tel: 01242 512774/227753
Fax: 01242 227753

Greater Manchester

A. S. Antiques,
26 Broad Street,
Pendleton,
Salford
M6 5BY
Tel: 0161 737 5938

Hampshire

Bona Arts Decorative Ltd,
19 Princes Mead
Shopping Centre,
Farnborough
GU14 7TJ
Tel: 01252 372188

London

The Collector,
9 Church Street,
Marylebone
NW8 8EE
Tel: 0171 706 4586
Royal Doulton

Pieter Oosthuizen,
1st Floor,
Georgian Village,
Camden Passage
N1 8DU
Tel: 0171 359 3322/376 3852

Shapiro & Co,
Stand 380,
Gray's Antique Market,
58 Davies Street
W1Y 1LB
Tel: 0171 491 2710

Surrey

Gooday Gallery,
20 Richmond Hill,
Richmond
TW10 6QX
Tel: 0181 940 8652

Succession,
18 Richmond Hill,
Richmond
TW10 6QX
Tel: 0181 940 6774

Sussex

Witney and Airault,
Prinny's Gallery,
3 Meeting House Lane,
The Lanes,
Brighton
BN1 1HB
Tel: 01273 735479

Warwickshire

Rich Designs,
1 Shakespeare Street,
Stratford-upon-Avon
CV37 6RN
Tel: 01789 261612/772111

Yorkshire

Muir Hewitt,
Halifax Antiques Centre,
Queens Road,
Gibbet Street,
Halifax HX1 4LR
Tel: 01422 347377

EXHIBITION & FAIR ORGANISERS

Surrey

Cultural Exhibitions Ltd,
8 Meadrow,
Godalming GU7 3HN
Tel: 01483 422562

EXPORTERS

Devon

McBains of Exeter,
Exeter Airport,
Clyst Honiton
Exeter EX5 2BA
Tel: 01392 366261
Fax: 01392 365572

Essex

F. G. Bruschweiler,
(Antiques) Ltd,
41-67 Lower Lambricks,
Rayleigh SS6 7EN
Tel: 01268 773761

Somerset

MGR Exports,
Station Road,
Bruton BA10 0EH
Tel: 01749 812460
Fax: 01749 812882

Sussex

Bexhill Antique Exporters,
Bexhill Antique Centre,
Quakers Mill,
Old Town,
Bexhill-on-Sea TN40 2HA
Tel: 01424 210182
Fax: 01424 731430

Lloyd Williams Antiques,
Anglo Am Warehouse,
2A Beach Road,
Eastbourne BN22 7EX
Tel: 01323 648661
Fax: 01323 648658

FURNITURE

Cumbria

Anthemion Antiques,
Bridge Street, Cartmel,
Grange Over Sands
LA11 7SH
Tel: 015395 36295/36362

Hertfordshire

Collins Antiques,
Corner House,
Wheathampstead AL4 8AP
Tel: 01582 833111

Kent

Flower House Antiques,
90 High Street,
Tenterden TN30 6JB
Tel: 01580 763764

Old Bakery Antiques,
St Davids Bridge,
Cranbrook TN17 3HN
Tel: 01580 713103
Fax: 01580 712407
Oak & country

The Old Mill,
High Street,
Lamberhurst TN3 8EQ
Tel: 01892 891400/784315

Pantiles Spa Antiques,
4,5,6 Union House,
The Pantiles,
Tunbridge Wells
TN4 8HE
Tel: 01892 541377

Sparks Antiques,
106 High Street,
Tenterden TN30 6HT
Tel: 01580 762939

Lincolnshire

Seaview Antiques,
Stanhope Road,
Horncastle LN9 5DG
Tel: 01507 524524

Mitchell Simmons
Antiques Ltd,
Hopton Ironworks,
The Wong,
Horncastle LN9 6EB
Tel: 01507 523854

London

Adams Rooms Antiques
& Interiors,
18-20 The Ridgeway,
Wimbledon Village
SW19 4QN
Tel: 0181 946 7047

Butchoff Antiques,
233 Westbourne Grove
W11 2SE
Tel: 0171 221 8174

Furniture Cave,
533 King's Road SW10 0TZ
Tel: 0171 352 4229

Oola Boola,
166 Tower Bridge Road
SE1 3LS
Tel: 0171 403 0794

Middlesex

Robert Phelps Ltd,
133-135 St Margaret's Road,
East Twickenham
TW1 1RG
Tel: 0181 892 1778

Northamptonshire

Paul Hopwell Antiques,
30 High Street,
West Haddon NN6 7AP
Tel: 01788 510636
Oak & country

Nottinghamshire

Meadow Lane Antiques,
Meadow Lane,
Nottingham NG2 3HQ
Tel: 0115 986 7374
Fax: 0115 986 7375

Oxfordshire

Key Antiques,
11 Horse Fair,
Chipping Norton
OX7 5AL
Tel: 01608 643777

Somerset

The Granary Galleries,
Court House,
Ash Priors,
Nr Bishops Lydeard,
Taunton TA4 3NQ
Tel: 01823 432402

Suffolk

Hubbard Antiques,
16 St Margaret's Green,
Ipswich
IP4 2BS
Tel: 01473 226033
Fax: 01473 233034

Oswald Simpson,
Hall Street,
Long Melford CO10 9JL
Tel: 01787 377523
Oak & country

Wrentham Antiques,
40-44 High Street,
Wrentham,
Nr Beccles NR34 7HB
Tel: 01502 675583

Surrey

Albany Antiques,
8-10 London Road,
Hindhead GU26 6AF
Tel: 01428 605528

The Chair Set Antiques,
84 Hill Rise,
Richmond TW10 6UB
Tel: 0181 332 6454
Fax: 0181 332 6454

Dorking Desk Shop,
41 West Street,
Dorking RH4 1BU
Tel: 01306 883327
Desks

J. Hartley Antiques Ltd,
186 High Street
Ripley GU23 6BB
Tel: 01483 224318

Ripley Antiques,
67 High Street,
Ripley GU23 6AN
Tel: 01483 224981

The Refectory,
38 West Street,
Dorking RH4 1BU
Tel: 01306 742111/01483
729646
*Oak & country - refectory
table specialist*

Anthony Welling,
Broadway Barn,
High Street,
Ripley GU23 6AL
Tel: 01483 225384
Oak & country

Sussex

British Antique Replicas,
School Close,
Queen Elizabeth Avenue,
Burgess Hill RH15 9RX
Tel: 01444 245577

Chichester House Antiques,
High Street,
Ditchling BN6 8SY
Tel: 01273 846615
Oak & country

Dycheling Antiques,
34 High Street,
Ditchling,
Hassocks BN6 8TA
Tel: 01273 842929
Chairs

International Furniture
Exporters,
The Old Cement Works,
South Heighton,
Newhaven BN9 0HS
Tel: 01273 611251

Selecta International,
Paul Harland,
Trading Estate,
Bexhill Rd,
Woodingdean,
Brighton
BN2 6QT
Tel: 01273 300628

Wales

Country Antiques (Wales),
Castle Mill,
Kidwelly,
Dyfed SA17 4UU
Tel: 01554 890534
Oak & country

Warwickshire

Apollo Antiques Ltd,
The Saltisford,
Birmingham Road,
Warwick CV34 4TD
Tel: 01926 494746

Don Spencer Antiques,
36A Market Place ,
Warwick CV34 4SH
Tel: 01926 499857
Desks

West Midlands

Pierre L.P. Furniture,
Short Acre Street,
Walsall WS2 8HW
Tel: 01922 746764

Martin Taylor Antiques,
140B Tettenhall Road
Wolverhampton WV6 0BQ
Tel: 01902 751166
Fax: 01902 746502

Wiltshire

Cross Hayes Antiques,
19 Bristol Street,
Malmesbury SN16 0AY
Tel: 01666 824260

Chris Watts Antiques,
The Salisbury
Antiques Warehouse,
94 Wilton Road,
Salisbury SP2 7JJ
Tel: 01722 410634

FURNITURE AND EXPORTERS

Sussex

The Old Mint House,
High Street, Pevensey,
Nr Eastbourne
BN24 5FE
Tel: 01323 762337
Fax: 01323 762337

GLASS

Avon

Somervale Antiques,
6 Radstock Road,
Midsommer Norton,
Bath BA3 2AJ
Tel: 01761 412686

West Midlands

David Hill,
96 Commonside, Pensnett,
Brierly Hill DY5 4AJ
Tel: 01384 70523
*Reference books on glass -
mail order only*

MARINE

Devon

Great Western Antiques,
Torre Station,
Newton Road,
Torquay TQ2 5DD
Tel: 01803 200551
Fax: 01803 295115

MARKETS & CENTRES

Hampshire

Folly Antiques Centre,
Folly Market,
College Street,
Petersfield GU31 4AD
Tel: 01730 265937

Kent

Heirloom Antiques,
68 High Street,
Tenterden
TN30 6AU
Tel: 01580 765535

Lincolnshire

Hemswell Antique Centre,
Caenby Corner Estate,
Hemswell Cliff,
Gainsborough DN21 5TJ
Tel: 01427 668389
Fax: 01427 668935

London

The Old Cinema,
160 Chiswick High Road
W4 1PR
Tel: 0181 995 4166

Sussex

Church Hill Antiques Centre,
6 Station Road,
Lewes BN7 2UP
Tel: 01273 474842

Yorkshire

Thorne Antique Centre,
5-7 King Street, Thorne,
Nr Doncaster DN8 5BD
Tel: 01405 741494
*Open 10-5pm Mon - Sat,
11-5pm Sundays*

MONEY BOXES

Yorkshire

John & Simon Haley,
89 Northgate,
Halifax HX6 4NG
Tel: 01422 822148

ORIENTAL PORCELAIN

Devon

Mere Antiques,
13 Fore Street, Topsham,
Exeter EX3 0HF
Tel: 01392 874224

PACKERS & SHIPPERS

Avon

A. J. Williams,
607 Sixth Avenue,
Central Business Park,
Petherton Road, Hengrove,
Bristol BS14 9BZ
Tel: 01275 892166
Fax: 01275 891333

Dorset

Alan Franklin Transport,
26 Blackmoor Road,
Verwood BH31 6BB
Tel: 01202 826539
Fax: 01202 827337

London

Featherston Shipping Ltd,
7 Ingate Place SW8 3NS
Tel: 0171 720 0422
Fax: 0171 720 6330
*Fine Art: 0171 720 0422
Moving: 0171 720 8041
Fax: 0171 720 6330*

Stephen Morris Shipping,
Barpart House,
Kings Cross Freight Depot,
York Way N1 0UZ
Tel: 0171 713 0080
Fax: 0171 713 0151

PAPERWEIGHTS

Cheshire

Sweetbriar Gallery,
Robin Hood Lane,
Helsby WA6 9NH
Tel: 01928 723851

PIANOS

Avon

Piano Export,
Bridge Road, Kingswood,
Bristol BS15 4PW
Tel: 0117 956 8300
Fax: 0117 956 8776

Kent

Period Piano Company,
Park Farm Oast,
Hareplain Road, Biddenden,
Nr Ashford TN27 8LJ
Tel: 01580 291393
Fax: 01580 291393
*Specialist dealer and restorer
of period pianos*

Sussex

Sound Instruments,
Worth Farm,
Little Horsted,
Nr Uckfield TN22 5TT
Tel: 01825 750567
Fax: 01825 750566

West Midlands

Birmingham Piano
Warehouse,
Unit L, 68 Wirley Road,
Witton, Birmingham
B6 7BN
Tel: 0121 327 2701

PINE

Berkshire

Hungerford Pine Company,
14-15 Charnham Street,
Hungerford RG17 0EF
Tel: 01488 686935
Fax: 01488 686936

Buckinghamshire

Jack Harness Antiques,
Westfield Farm,
Medmenham,
Nr Marlow SL7 2HE
Tel: 01491 410691

Cheshire

Richmond Galleries,
Watergate Building,
New Crane Street,
Chester CH1 4JE
Tel: 01244 317602
*Pine, country and Spanish
furniture*

Mellor Country Pine,
219 Longhurst Lane,
Mellor,
Stockport SK6 5PN
Tel: 0161 426 0333
Fax: 0161 426 0149

Cleveland

European Pine Imports,
Riverside Park
Industrial Estate,
Middlesborough TS21 1QW
Tel: 01642 584 351
Fax: 01642 584351

Cumbria

Ben Eggleston,Antiques,
The Dovecote,
Long Marton,
Appleby CA16 6BJ
Tel: 01768 361849
Trade only

Dorset

Overhill Antiques,
20 Wareham Road,
Holton Heath,
Poole B16 6JW
Tel: 01202 621818

Eire

Delvin Farm Antiques,
Gormonston, Co Meath
Tel: 00 353 1 8412285

Honans Antiques,
Crowe Street, Gort,
County Galway
Tel: 00 353 91 31407

Old Court Pine ,
Old Court, Collon, Co Louth
Tel: 00 353 41 26270

Gloucestershire

Campden Country
Pine Antiques,
High Street,
Chipping Campden
GL55 6HN
Tel: 01386 840315
Fax: 01385 841740

Europa Antiques
Unit 5 The Old Dairy,
Fosseway Industrial Estate,
Moreton-in-the-Marsh
GL56 9NQ
Tel: 01608 652241
Fax: 01606 652250

Amanda House,
The Barns,
Twigworth Court,
Twigworth GL2 9PG
Tel: 01452 731296

Hampshire

Pine Cellars,
39 Jewry Street,
Winchester
SO23 8RY
Tel: 01962 777546

Kent

Clive Cowell,
Glassenbury Timber Yard,
Iden Green, Goudhurst,
Cranbrook TN17 2PA
Tel: 01580 212022

Old English Pine,
100 Sandgate High Street,
Sandgate,
Folkestone CT20 3BY
Tel: 01303 248560

The Old Mill,
High Street,
Lamberhurst TN3 8EQ
Tel: 01892 891196

Up Country,
The Old Corn Stores,
68 St John's Road,
Tunbridge Wells
TN4 9PE
Tel: 01892 523341

Lancashire

Enloc Antiques,
Birchenlee Mill,
Lenches Road,
Colne BB8 8ET
Tel: 01282 867101

Leicestershire

Hartwell Antiques,
Unit 30 Long Furrow,
East Goscote,
Leicester LE7 3XJ
Tel: 0116 260 3203
Fax: 0116 260 3202

London

Antique Warehouse,
9-14 Deptford Broadway
SE8 4PA
Tel: 0181 691 3062

Northamptonshire

Country Pine Shop,
Northampton Road,
West Haddon NN6 7AS
Tel: 01788 510430

Northern Ireland

Albert Forsythe,
Mill House,
66 Carsontown Road,
Saintfield,
Co Down BT24 7EB
Tel: 01238 510398

Nottinghamshire

Harlequin Antiques,
79 Mansfield Road,
Daybrook,
Nottingham NG5 6BH
Tel: 0115 967 4590

Somerset

Gilbert & Dale,
The Old Chapel,
Church Street, Ilchester,
Nr Yeovil BA22 8LA
Tel: 01935 840464
Fax: 01935 841599
Painted pine

Westville House Antiques,
Littleton,
Somerton TA11 6NP
Tel: 01458 273376

Sussex

Bob Hoare,
Pine Antiques,
Unit Q, Phoenix Place,
North Street,
Lewes BN7 2DQ
Tel: 01273 480557

Ann Lingard,
Ropewalk Antiques,
Ropewalk, Rye TN31 7NA
Tel: 01797 223486

Graham Price Antiques Ltd,
Unit 4, Chaucer Industrial
Estate, Dittons Road,
Polegate BN26 6JD
Tel: 01323 487167

The Netherlands

Van Der Tol, Jacques,
Antiek & Curiosa,
Antennestraat 34,
1322 A E Almere-Stad,
Tel: 00 31 3653 62050

Wales

Heritage Restorations,
Maes Y Glydfa, Llanfair
Caereinion, Welshpool,
Powys SY21 0HD
Tel: 01938 810384

Pot Board,
30 King Street, Carmarthen,
Dyfed SA31 1BS
Tel: 01267 236623

Warwickshire

Cottage Pine Antiques,
19 Broad Street,
Brinklow,
Nr Rugby CV23 0LS
Tel: 01788 832673

Old Pine House,
16 Warwick Street,
Royal Leamington Spa
CV32 5LL
Tel: 01926 470477

Wiltshire

North Wilts Exporters,
Farm Hill House,
Brinkworth SN15 5AJ
Tel: 01666 510876

PORCELAIN

Hampshire

Goss & Crested China Ltd,
62 Murray Road,
Horndean PO8 9JL
Tel: 01705 597440
Goss & Crested

London

Marion Langham,
Tel: 0171 730 1002
Fax: 0171 259 9266
Belleek

Shropshire

Teme Valley Antiques,
1 The Bull Ring,
Ludlow SY8 1AD
Tel: 01584 874686

Yorkshire

Crested China Co ,
The Station House,
Driffield YO25 7PY
Tel: 01377 257042
Goss & Crested

POTTERY

Berkshire

Special Auction Services,
The Coach House,
Midgham Park,
Reading RG7 5UG
Tel: 01734 712949

Buckinghamshire

Gillian Neale Antiques,
PO Box 247,
Aylesbury HP20 1JZ
Tel: 01296 23754
Blue & white transferware

Kent

Serendipity,
168 High Street,
Deal CT14 6BQ
Tel: 01304 369165
Staffordshire Pottery

Lancashire

Roy W. Bunn Antiques,
34/36 Church Street,
Barnoldswick,
Colne
BB8 5UT
Tel: 01282 813703
Staffordshire Pottery

London

Antiques Arcadia,
22 Richmond Hill,
Richmond Hill TW10 6QX
Tel: 0181 940 2035
Staffordshire Pottery

Jonathan Horne
(Antiques) Ltd,
66C Kensington Church
Street W8 4BY
Tel: 0171 221 5658

Valerie Howard,
2 Campden Street W8 7EP
Tel: 0171 792 9702
Masons & Quimper

M. S. Antiques,
25a Holland Street,
Kensington
W8 4NA
Tel: 0171 937 0793
Staffordshire Pottery

Sue Norman,
L4 Antiquarius,
135 King's Road
SW3 5ST
Tel: 0171 352 7217
Blue & white transferware

Jacqueline Oosthuizen,
23 Cale Street,
Chelsea
SW3 3QR
Tel: 0171 352 6071
Staffordshire Pottery

Rogers de Rin,
76 Royal Hospital Road
SW3 4HN
Tel: 0171 352 9007
Wemyss

Wales

Islwyn Watkins,
1 High Street, Knighton,
Powys LD7 1AT
Tel: 01547 520145

POTTERY AND PORCELAIN

Oxfordshire

Joanna C. Glyn,
The Swan at Tetsworth
Antiques Centre, High Street,
Tetsworth OX9 7AB
Tel: 01844 281777/351375
*British pottery & porcelain
1740 - 1820*

PUBLICATION

Australia

CGC Gold Pty Ltd,
PO Box 322, Roseville,
NSW 2069, Australia
Tel: (02) 560 6022
Fax: (02) 416 7143
*Jewellery, gold & silver
makers & marks*

France

Guide Emer,
Paris
Tel: (1) 427 42715
Fax: (1) 427 40799
Directory

London

Antiques Trade Gazette,
17 Whitcomb Street
WC2H 7PL
Tel: 0171 930 9958

West Midlands

Antiques Bulletin,
2 Hampton Court Road,
Harborne,
Birmingham B17 9AE
Tel: 0121 681 8000
Fax: 0121 681 8005

RESTORATION

Hertfordshire

Workshop Interiors,
6 Stanley Avenue,
Chiswell Green,
St Albans AL2 3AB
Tel: 01727 840456,
Fax: 01727 841705
*Furniture, restoration,
polishing, carving, turning,
gilding and upholstery.*

ROCK & POP

Cheshire

Collectors Corner,
(Tudor House)
29-31 Lower Bridge Street,
Chester CH1 1RS
Tel: 01244 346736/01260
270429
Fax: 01260 279113

SCIENTIFIC INSTRUMENTS

London

Thomas
Mercer,(Chronometers) Ltd,
32 Bury Street,
St James's SW1Y 6AU
Tel: 0171 930 9300
Fax: 0171 321 0350

Scotland

Early Technology,
84 West Bow,
Edinburgh EH1 2HH
Tel: 0131 226 1132
Fax: 0131 665 2839

SERVICES

Hampshire

Securikey Ltd,
P O Box 18,
Aldershot
GU12 4SL
Tel: 01252 311888/9
Fax: 01252 343950
Security

Isle of Wight

Thesaurus Group Ltd,
Mill Court,
Furrlongs,
Newport PO30 2AA
Tel: 01983 826000

London

Just Brothers & Co,
Unit 3 Roeder House,
Vale Road N4 1NG
Tel: 0181 880 2505
Fax: 0181 802 0062
Jewellery boxes

West Midlands

Retro Products,
The Yard, Star Street,
Lye, Nr Stourbridge
DY8 2RR
Tel: 01384 894042
Fax: 01384 442065
Fittings & accessories

SILVER

Oxfordshire

Thames Gallery,
Thameside,
Henley-on-Thames RG9 2LT
Tel: 01491 572449

Shropshire

Teme Valley Antiques,
1 The Bull Ring,
Ludlow SY8 1AD
Tel: 01584 874686

SPORTS & GAMES - BILLIARD TABLES

Berkshire

William Bentley Billiards,
Standen Manor Farm,
Hungerford
RG17 0RB
Tel: 01488 681711
Fax: 01488 685197

Hertfordshire

Hamilton Games Co,
Park Lane,
Knebworth
SG3 6PJ
Tel: 01438 811995
Fax: 01438 814939

London

Mallard Billiard Co,
Unit 1
134 Liverpool Road N1 1LA
Tel: 0171 700 5600

Somerset

Billiard Room Antiques,
The Old School,
Church Lane,
Chilcompton,
Bath BA3 4HP
Tel: 01761 232839

Surrey

Academy Antiques,
5 Camp Hill
Industrial Estate,
West Byfleet
KT14 6EW
Tel: 01932 352067
Fax: 01932 353904

Sports & Games - Fishing

Hampshire

Evans & Partridge,
Agriculture House,
High Street,
Stockbridge SO20 6HF
Tel: 01264 810702

Kent

Old Tackle Box,
PO Box 55,
Cranbrook
TN17 3ZU
Tel: & Fax: 01580 713979

Pembrokeshire

John Brindley Ayers,
8 Bay View Drive,
Hakin,
Milford Haven
SA73 3LJ
Tel: 01646 698359
Fax: 01646 690733

Scotland

Rob Maxtone-Graham,
Timeless Tackle,
1 Blackwood Crescent,
Edinburgh EH9 1QZ
Tel: 0131 667 1407
Fax: 0131 662 4215

Shropshire

Nock Deighton,
Livestock & Auction Centre,
Tasley,
Bridgnorth WV16 4QR
Tel: 01746 762666
Fax: 01746 767475
*Vintage & modern fishing
tackle & sporting
memorabilia*

TEDDY BEARS

Oxfordshire

Teddy Bears of Witney,
99 High Street,
Witney OX8 6LY
Tel: 01993 702616

TOYS

Sussex

Wallis & Wallis,
West Street
Auction Galleries,
Lewes BN7 2NJ
Tel: 01273 480208
Fax: 01273 476562

Yorkshire

John & Simon Haley,
89 Northgate,
Halifax HX6 4NG
Tel: 01422 822148/360434

Yorkshire

G. M. Haley,
Hippins Farm
Blackshawhead,
Hebden Bridge HX7 7JG
Tel: 01422 842484

WINE ANTIQUES

Buckinghamshire

Christopher Sykes Antiques,
The Old Parsonage,
Woburn MK17 9QM
Tel: 01525 290259

Scotland

Chris Barge Antiques,
5 Southside Place,
Inverness IV2 3JF
Tel: 01463 230128
Fax: 01463 716268

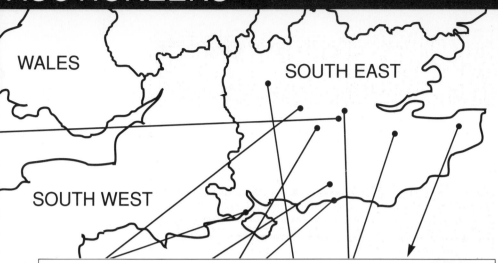

WALES

SOUTH EAST

SOUTH WEST

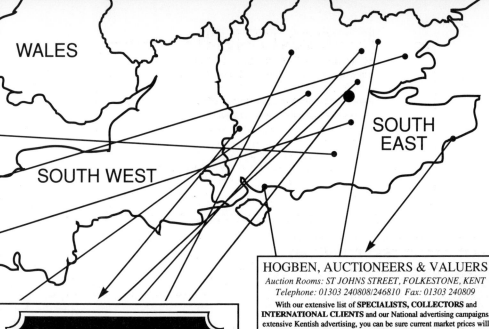

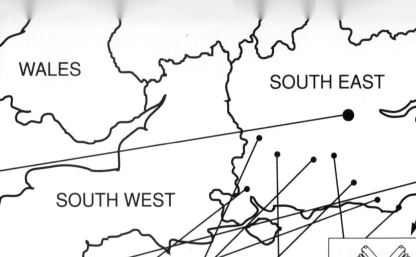

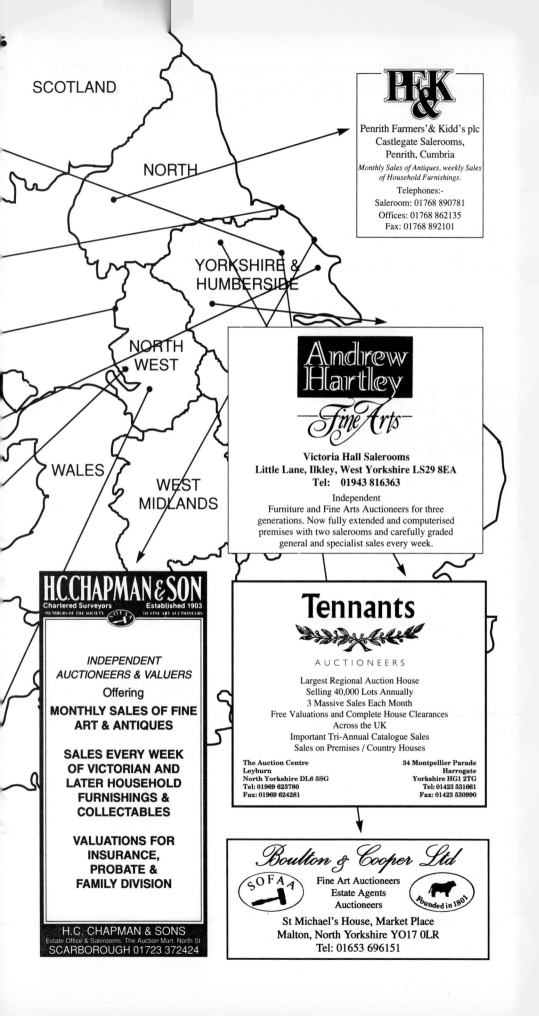

DIRECTORY OF AUCTIONEERS

Auctioneers who hold frequent sales should contact us for inclusion in the next Edition. Entries must be received by April 1997. Entries will be repeated in subsequent editions unless we are requested otherwise.

London

Academy Auctioneers &
Valuers,
Northcote House,
Northcote Avenue,
Ealing
W5 3UR
Tel: 0181 579 7466

Bloomsbury Book Auctions,
3/4 Hardwick Street,
Off Rosebery Avenue,
EC1R 4RY
Tel: 0171 833 2636

Bonhams,
Montpelier Street,
Knightsbridge,
SW7 1HH
Tel: 0171 584 9161

Bonhams,
Lots Road,
Chelsea
SW10 0RN
Tel: 0171 351 7111

Christie, Manson &
Woods Ltd,
8 King Street,
St James's,
SW1Y 6QT
Tel: 0171 839 9060

Christie's South
Kensington Ltd,
85 Old Brompton Road,
SW7 3LD
Tel: 0171 581 7611

Criterion Salerooms,
53 Essex Road,
Islington
N1 2BN
Tel: 0171 359 5707

Emerald Auctions,
212 High Road N2 9AY
Tel: 0181 883 0234

Forrest & Co,
Stratford E15 2HU
Tel: 0181 534 2931

Stanley Gibbons
Auctions Ltd,
399 Strand WC2R 0LX
Tel: 0171 836 8444

Glendinings & Co,
101 New Bond Street,
W1Y 9LG
Tel: 0171 493 2445

Hamptons Fine Art
Auctioneers and Valuers
6 Arlington Street,
SW1A 1RB
Tel: 0171 493 8222

Harmers of London,
91 New Bond Street,
W1Y 9LA
Tel: 0171 629 0218

Hornsey Auctions Ltd,
54/56 High Street,
Hornsey N8 7NX
Tel: 0181 340 5334

Lloyds International
Auction Galleries,
118 Putney Bridge Road,
SW15 2NQ
Tel: 0181 788 7777

Lots Road Chelsea
Auction Galleries,
71 Lots Road,
Worldsend,
Chelsea SW10 0RN
Tel: 0171 351 7771

MacGregor Nash & Co,
Lodge House,
9-17 Lodge Lane,
North Finchley N12 8JH
Tel: 0181 445 9000

Thomas Moore,
217-219 Greenwich
High Road, SE10 8NB
Tel: 0181 858 7848

Onslows,
Metrostore,
Townmead Road
SW6 2RZ
Tel: 0171 793 0240

Phillips,
101 New Bond Street,
W1Y 0AS
Tel: 0171 629 6602

Phillips Bayswater,
10 Salem Road, W2 4DL
Tel: 0171 229 9090

Rippon Boswell & Co,
The Arcade,
South Kensington Station,
SW7 2NA
Tel: 0171 589 4242

Rosebery's Fine Art Ltd,
Old Railway Booking Hall,
Crystal Palace Station Road,
SE19 2AZ
Tel: 0181 778 4024

Sotheby's,
34-35 New Bond Street,
W1A 2AA
Tel: 0171 493 8080

Southgate Auction Rooms,
55 High Street,
Southgate N14 6LD
Tel: 0181 886 7888

Spink & Son Ltd,
5 Kings Street,
St James's,
SW1Y 6QS
Tel: 0171 930 7888

Town & Country House
Auctions,
42A Nightingale Grove,
SE13 6DY
Tel: 0181 852 3145

Avon

Aldridges, Bath,
The Auction Galleries,
130-132 Walcot Street,
Bath BA1 5BG
Tel: 01225 462830 & 462839

Auction Centres Bristol,
Prewett Street, Redcliffe,
Bristol BS1 6TB
Tel: 0117 926 5996

Bristol Auction Rooms,
St John's Place, Apsley Road,
Clifton, Bristol BS8 2ST
Tel: 0117 973 7201

Clevedon Salerooms,
Herbert Road,
Clevedon BS21 7ND
Tel: 01275 876699

Gardiner Houlgate,
The Old Malthouse,
Comfortable Place,
Upper Bristol Road,
Bath BA1 3AJ
Tel: 01225 447933

Phillips,
1 Old King Street,
Bath BA1 2JT
Tel: 01225 310609

Phillips Fine Art
Auctioneers,
71 Oakfield Road,
Clifton,
Bristol BS8 2BE
Tel: 0117 973 4052

Woodspring Auction Rooms,
Churchill Road,
Weston-super-Mare
BS23 3HD
Tel: 01934 628419

Bedfordshire

Wilson Peacock,
The Auction Centre,
26 Newnham Street,
Bedford MK40 3JR
Tel: 01234 266366

Berkshire

Edwards & Chancellors,
32 High Street,
Ascot SL5 7HG
Tel: 01344 872588

Dreweatt Neate,
Donnington Priory,
Donnington,
Newbury RG13 2JE
Tel: 01635 31234

Martin & Pole,
12 Milton Road,
Wokingham RG40 1DB
Tel: 01734 790460

Shiplake Fine Art,
31 Great Knollys Street,
Reading RG1 7HU
Tel: 01734 594748

Buckinghamshire

Amersham Auction Rooms,
125 Station Road,
Amersham HP7 0AH
Tel: 01494 729292

Bourne End Auction Rooms,
Station Approach,
Bourne End SL8 5QH
Tel: 01628 531500

Hamptons,
10 Burkes Parade,
Beaconsfield HP9 1PD
Tel: 01494 672969

Wigley's,
Winslow Sale Room,
Market Square,
Winslow MK18 3AP
Tel: 01296 713011

Cambridgeshire

Cheffins Grain & Comins,
2 Clifton Road,
Cambridge CB2 4BW
Tel: 01223 358721/213343

Goldsmiths,
15 Market Place,
Oundle PE8 4BA
Tel: 01832 272349

Grounds & Co,
2 Nene Quay,
Wisbech PE13 1AG
Tel: 01945 585041

Maxey & Son,
1-3 South Brink,
Wisbech PE13 1RD
Tel: 01945 584609

Phillips Auctioneers,
The Golden Rose,
17 Emmanuel Road,
Cambridge CB1 1JW
Tel: 01223 66523

Cheshire

F W Allen & Son,
15/15a Station Road,
Cheadle Hulme
SK8 5AF
Tel: 0161 485 6069

David Dockree,
224 Moss Lane,
Bramhall,
Stockport SK7 1BD
Tel: 0161 485 1258

Highams Auctions,
Waterloo House,
Waterloo Road,
Stalybridge
SK15 2AU
Tel: 0161 338 8698/303 2924

Andrew Hilditch & Son,
Hanover House,
1A The Square,
Sandbach
CW11 0AP
Tel: 01270 762048/767246

Frank R Marshall & Co,
Marshall House,
Church Hill,
Knutsford WA16 6DH
Tel: 01565 653284

John Maxwell of Wilmslow,
133A Woodford Road,
Woodford SK7 1QD
Tel: 0161 439 5182

Phillips North West,
New House,
150 Christleton Road,
Chester CH3 5TD
Tel: 01244 313936

Peter Wilson,
Victoria Gallery,
Market Street,
Nantwich CW5 5DG
Tel: 01270 623878

Wright Manley,
Beeston Castle Salerooms,
Tarporley CW6 0DR
Tel: 01829 260318

Co. Durham

Denis Edkins,
Auckland Auction Room,
58 Kingsway,
Bishop Auckland DL14 7JF
Tel: 01388 603095

Thomas Watson & Son,
Northumberland Street,
Darlington DL3 7HJ
Tel: 01325 462559/463485

Wingate Auction Co,
Station Lane,
Station Town,
Wingate TS28 5DG
Tel: 01429 837245

Cornwall

Jeffery's,
5 Fore Street,
Lostwithiel PL22 0BP
Tel: 01208 872245

Lambrays incorporating
R J Hamm ASVA,
Polmorla Walk,
The Platt,
Wadebridge PL27 7AE
Tel: 0120 881 3593

W H Lane & Son,
65 Morrab Road,
Penzance TR18 2QT
Tel: 01736 61447

David Lay ASVA,
Auction House,
Alverton,
Penzance TR18 4RE
Tel: 01736 61414

Phillips Cornwall,
Cornubia Hall,
Par PL24 2AQ
Tel: 0172 681 4047

Pooley and Rogers,
Regent Auction Rooms,
Abbey Street,
Penzance TR18 4AR
Tel: 01736 68814

Martyn Rowe,
Truro Auction Centre,
Calenick Street,
Truro TR1 2SG
Tel: 01872 260020

Cumbria

Cumbria Auction Rooms,
12 Lowther Street,
Carlisle CA3 8DA
Tel: 01228 25259

Hackney & Leigh,
Main Street,
The Auction Centre,
Grange-Over-Sands
LE11 6AB
Tel: 015395 33316/33466

Mitchells,
Fairfield House, Station Road,
Cockermouth CA13 9PY
Tel: 01900 827800

Alfred Mossops & Co,
Loughrigg Villa, Kelsick
Road, Ambleside LA22 0BY
Tel: 015394 33015

Penrith Farmers' & Kidd's plc,
Devonshire Chambers
Devonshire Street,
Penrith CA11 7SS
Tel: 01768 862135

James Thompson,
64 Main Street,
Kirkby Lonsdale LA6 2AJ
Tel: 015242 71555

Thomson, Roddick & Laurie,
24 Lowther Street,
Carlisle CA3 8DA
Tel: 01228 28939/39636

Derbyshire

Neales,
The Derby Saleroom,
Becket Street,
Derby DE1 1HW
Tel: 01332 343286

Richardson & Linnell Ltd,
The Auction Office,
Cattle Market,
Chequers Road,
Derby DE21 6EP
Tel: 01332 296369

Noel Wheatcroft,
The Matlock Auction
Gallery, Old English Road,
Matlock DE4 3LX
Tel: 01629 584591

Devon

Bearnes,
Avenue Road,
Torquay TQ2 5TG
Tel: 01803 296277

Bonhams West Country,
Devon Fine Art Auction
House, Dowell Street,
Honiton EX14 8LX
Tel: 01404 41872

Michael J Bowman,
6 Haccombe House,
Netherton,
Newton Abbot TQ12 4SJ
Tel: 01626 872890

Eric Distin,
Chartered Surveyors,
2 Bretonside,
Plymouth PL4 0BY
Tel: 01752 663046 or 664841

Robin A Fenner & Co, Fine
Art & Antique Auctioneers,
The Stannary Gallery,
Drake Road,
Tavistock PL19 0AX
Tel: 01822 617799/617800

Kings Auctioneers,
Pinnbrook Units,
Venny Bridge,
Pinhoe,
Exeter EX4 8JX
Tel: 01392 460644

Kingsbridge Auction Sales,
113 Fore Street,
Kingsbridge TQ7 1BG
Tel: 01548 856829

Phillips,
Alphin Brook Road,
Alphington,
Exeter EX2 8TH
Tel: 01392 439025

Potbury's,
High Street,
Sidmouth EX10 8LN
Tel: 01395 515555

Rendells,
Stone Park,
Ashburton TQ13 7RH
Tel: 01364 653017

G S Shobrook & Co,
20 Western Approach,
Plymouth PL1 1TG
Tel: 01752 663341

John Smale & Co,
11 High Street,
Barnstaple EX31 1BG
Tel: 01271 42000/42916

Southwest Auctions,
South Street,
Newport,
Barnstaple EX32 9DT
Tel: 01837 810756

Martin Spencer-Thomas,
Bicton Street,
Exmouth EX8 2RT
Tel: 01395 267403

Taylors,
Honiton Galleries,
205 High Street,
Honiton EX14 8LF
Tel: 01404 42404

Ward & Chowen,
Tavistock Auction Rooms
Market Road,
Tavistock PL19 0BW
Tel: 01822 612603

Whitton & Laing,
32 Okehampton Street,
Exeter EX4 1DY
Tel: 01392 52621

Dorset

Chapman, Moore
& Mugford,
9 High Street,
Shaftesbury
SP7 8JB
Tel: 01747 852400

Cottees of Wareham,
The Market,
East Street,
Wareham
BH20 4NR
Tel: 01929 552826

Dalkeith Auctions,
Dalkeith Hall,
Dalkeith Steps,
Rear of 81 Old
Christchurch Road,
Bournemouth BH1 1EW
Tel: 01202 292905

HY Duke & Son,
Dorchester Fine Art
Salerooms,
Dorchester DT1 1QS
Tel: 01305 265080

House & Son,
Lansdowne House,
Christchurch Road,
Bournemouth BH1 3JW
Tel: 01202 556232

William Morey & Sons,
The Saleroom,
St Michaels Lane,
Bridport DT6 3RB
Tel: 01308 422078

Riddetts of Bournemouth,
26 Richmond Hill,
The Square,
Bournemouth BH2 6EJ
Tel: 01202 555686

Semley Auctioneers,
Station Road
Semley,
Shaftesbury SP7 9AN
Tel: 01747 855122

Southern Counties
Auctioneers,
Shaftesbury Livestock
Market, Christy's Lane,
Shaftesbury SP7 8PH
Tel: 01747 851735

Michael Stainer Ltd,
St Andrew's Hall,
Wolverton Road,
Boscombe,
Bournemouth BH7 6HT
Tel: 01202 309999

Essex

Baytree Auctions,
23 Broomhills
Industrial Estate,
Braintree CM7 7RW
Tel: 01376 328228

Black Horse Agencies
Ambrose,
149 High Road,
Loughton
IG10 4LZ
Tel: 0181 502 3951

William H Brown,
Paskell's Rooms,
11-14 East Hill,
Colchester
CO1 2QX
Tel: 01206 868070

Cooper Hirst Auctions,
The Granary Saleroom,
Victoria Road,
Chelmsford
CM2 6LH
Tel: 01245 260535

Grays Auction Rooms,
Ye Old Bake House,
Alfred Street,
Grays RM17 6DZ
Tel: 01375 381181

Leigh Auction Rooms,
John Stacey & Sons,
88-90 Pall Mall,
Leigh-on-Sea SS9 1RG
Tel: 01702 77051

Saffron Walden Saleroom,
1 Market Street,
Saffron Walden
CB10 1JB
Tel: 01799 513281

G E Sworder & Sons,
14 Cambridge Road,
Stansted Mountfitchet
CM24 8BZ
Tel: 01279 817778

Trembath Welch,
The Old Town Hall,
Great Dunmow CM6 1AU
Tel: 01371 873014

Gloucestershire

Bruton, Knowles & Co,
111 Eastgate Street,
Gloucester GL1 1PZ
Tel: 01452 521267

Fraser Glennie & Partners,
The Old Rectory,
Siddington,
Nr Cirencester GL7 6HL
Tel: 01285 659677

Hobbs & Chambers,
Market Place,
Cirencester GL7 1QQ
Tel: 01285 654736

Hobbs & Chambers,
15 Royal Crescent,
Cheltenham GL50 3DA
Tel: 01242 513722

Mallams,
26 Grosvenor Street,
Cheltenham GL52 2SG
Tel: 01242 235712

Moore, Allen & Innocent,
33 Castle Street,
Cirencester GL7 1QD
Tel: 01285 651831

Specialised Postcard
Auctions,
25 Gloucester Street,
Cirencester GL7 2DJ
Tel: 01285 659057

Wotton Auction Rooms,
Tabernacle Road,
Wotton-under-Edge
GL12 7EB
Tel: 01453 844733

Greater
Manchester

Capes Dunn & Co,
The Auction Galleries,
38 Charles Street,
Off Princess Street,
M1 7DB
Tel: 0161 273 6060/1911

Phillips,
Trinity House,
114 Washway Road,
Sale M33 1RF
Tel: 0161 962 9237

Hampshire

Andover Saleroom,
41A London Street,
Andover SP10 2NY
Tel: 01264 364820

Basingstoke Auction Rooms,
82-84 Sarum Hill,
Basingstoke RG21 1ST
Tel: 01256 840707

Evans & Partridge,
Agriculture House,
High Street,
Stockbridge SO20 6HF
Tel: 01264 810702

Fox & Sons,
5 & 7 Salisbury Street,
Fordingbridge
SP6 1AD
Tel: 01425 652121

Jacobs & Hunt,
Lavant Street,
Petersfield
GU32 3EF
Tel: 01730 262744/5

George Kidner,
The Old School,
The Square,
Pennington,
Lymington SO41 8GN
Tel: 01590 670070

May & Son,
18 Bridge Street,
Andover SP10 1BH
Tel: 01264 323417

D M Nesbit & Co,
7 Clarendon Road,
Southsea
PO5 2ED
Tel: 01705 864321

Odiham Auction Sales,
The Eagle Works, Rear of
Hartley Wintney Garages,
High Street,
Hartley Wintney
RG27 8PU
Tel: 01252 844410

Phillips Fine Art
Auctioneers,
54 Southampton Road,
Ringwood BH24 1JD
Tel: 01425 473333

Phillips of Winchester,
The Red House,
Hyde Street,
Winchester SO23 7DX
Tel: 01962 862515

Romsey Auction Rooms,
86 The Hundred,
Romsey SO51 8BX
Tel: 01794 513331

Hereford & Worcester

Carless & Co,
58 Lowesmoor,
Worcester WR1 2SE
Tel: 01905 612449

Andrew Grant,
St Mark's House,
St Mark's Close,
Worcester WR5 3DJ
Tel: 01905 357547

Griffiths & Co,
57 Foregate Street,
Worcester WR1 1DZ
Tel: 01905 26464

Philip Laney,
The Portland Room,
Portland Road,
Malvern WR14 2TA
Tel: 01684 893933

Morris Bricknell,
Stuart House,
18 Gloucester Road,
Ross-on-Wye
HR9 5BU
Tel: 01989 768320

Phipps & Pritchard,
Bank Buildings,
Kidderminster DY10 1BU
Tel: 01562 822244/6

Russell, Baldwin & Bright,
Ryelands Road,
Leominster HR6 8NZ
Tel: 01568 611166

Philip Serrell,
The Malvern Saleroom
Barnards Green Road,
Malvern WR14 2AE
Tel: 01684 892314

Village Auctions,
Sychampton Community
Centre,
Ombersley WR2 4BH
Tel: 01905 421007

Nigel Ward & Co,
The Border Property Centre,
Pontrilas HR2 0EH
Tel: 01981 240140

Richard Williams,
2 High Street,
Pershore WR10 1BG
Tel: 01386 554031

Hertfordshire

Brown & Merry
Tring Market Auctions,
Brook Street,
Tring HP23 5EF
Tel: 01442 826446

Hitchin Auctions Ltd,
The Corn Exchange,
Market Place,
Hitchin SG5 1DY
Tel: 01462 442151

Andrew Pickford,
The Hertford Saleroom,
42 St Andrew Street,
Hertford SG14 1JA
Tel: 01992 583508

Humberside

Gilbert Baitson FSVA,
The Edwardian Auction
Galleries, Wiltshire Road,
Hull HU4 6PG
Tel: 01482 500500

Dickinson Davy &
Markham,
Wrawby Street,
Brigg DN20 8JJ
Tel: 01652 653666

H Evans & Sons,
1 St James's Street,
Hessle Road,
Hull HU3 3DH
Tel: 01482 23033

Kent

Albert Andrews,
Auctions & Sales,
Maiden Lane,
Crayford DA1 4LX
Tel: 01322 528868

Bracketts,
27-29 High Street,
Tunbridge Wells
TN1 1UU
Tel: 01892 533733

Canterbury Auction
Galleries,
40 Station Road West,
Canterbury CT2 8AN
Tel: 01227 763337

Mervyn Carey,
Twysden Cottage,
Benenden,
Cranbrook TN17 4LD
Tel: 01580 240283

Halifax Property Services,
Fine Art Department,
53 High Street,
Tenterden TN30 6BG
Tel: 01580 763200

Halifax Property Services,
15 Cattle Market,
Sandwich CT13 9AW
Tel: 01304 614369

Edwin Hall,
Valley Antiques,
Lyminge,
Folkestone CT18 8EJ
Tel: 01303 862134

Hobbs Parker,
Romney House,
Ashford Market,
Elwick Road,
Ashford TN23 1PG
Tel: 01233 622222

Hogben Auctioneers,
St John's Street,
Folkestone CT20 1JB
Tel: 01303 240808

Hythe Auction Rooms,
35 Dymchurch Road,
Hythe CT21 6JE
Tel: 01303 237444/264155

Ibbett Mosely,
125 High Street,
Sevenoaks TN13 1UT
Tel: 01732 452246

Kent Sales,
Giffords,
Holmesdale Road,
South Darenth DA4 9AF
Tel: 01322 864919

Lambert & Foster,
77 Commercial Road,
Paddock Wood
TN12 6DR
Tel: 01892 832325

Lambert & Foster,
102 High Street,
Tenterden
TN30 6HT
Tel: 01580 762083/763233

B J Norris,
The Quest,
West Street,
Harrietsham, Maidstone
ME17 1JD
Tel: 01622 859515

Phillips Fine Art
Auctioneers,
49 London Road,
Sevenoaks TN13 1AR
Tel: 01732 740310

Phillips Folkestone,
11 Bayle Parade,
Folkestone CT20 1SG
Tel: 01303 245555

Town & Country House
Auctions,
North House,
Oakley Road,
Bromley Common
BR2 8HG
Tel: 0181 462 1735

Walter & Randall,
7-13 New Road,
Chatham ME4 4QL
Tel: 01634 841233

Wealden Auction Galleries
Desmond Judd,
23 Hendly Drive,
Cranbrook TN17 3DY
Tel: 01580 714522

Peter S Williams FSVA,
Orchard End,
Sutton Valence,
Maidstone ME17 3LS
Tel: 01622 842350

Lancashire

Charles Edwards & Co Ltd,
4-8 Lynwood Road,
Blackburn BB2 6HP
Tel: 01254 691748

Entwistle Green,
The Galleries,
Kingsway Ansdell,
Lytham St Annes FY8 1AB
Tel: 01253 735442

Robert Fairhurst & Son,
39 Mawdsley Street,
Bolton BL1 1LR
Tel: 01204 528452/528453

Mills & Radcliffe Inc
D Murgatroyd & Son,
101 Union Street,
Oldham 0L1 1QH
Tel: 0161 624 1072

David Palamountain,
1-3 Osborne Grove,
Morecambe LA4 4LP
Tel: 01524 423941

J R Parkinson Son &
Hamer Auctions,
The Auction Rooms,
Rochdale Road,
Bury BL9 7HH
Tel: 0161 761 1612/7372

Smythe's Son & Walker,
174 Victoria Road West,
Thornton Cleveleys
FY5 3NE
Tel: 01253 852184

Warren & Wignall Ltd,
The Mill, Earnshaw Bridge,
Leyland Lane,
Leyland PR5 3PH
Tel: 01772 453252/451430

Leicestershire

William H Brown,
Warner Auction Rooms,
16-18 Halford Street,
Leicester
LE1 6AS
Tel: 0116 255 9900

Churchgate Auctions,
The Churchgate Saleroom,
66 Churchgate,
Leicester
LE1 4AL
Tel: 0116 262 1416

Gildings,
64 Roman Way,
Market Harborough
LE16 7PQ
Tel: 01858 410414

Heathcote Ball & Co,
Castle Auction Rooms
78 St Nicholas Circle,
Leicester
LE1 5NW
Tel: 0116 253 6789

David Stanley Auctions,
Stordon Grange,
Osgathorpe,
Loughborough
LE12 9SR
Tel: 01530 222320

Lincolnshire

A E Dowse & Son,
Forresters Galleries,
Faulkland Way,
Barton-upon-Humber
DN18 5RL
Tel: 01652 632335

Escritt & Barrell,
24 St Peter's Hill,
Grantham NG31 6QF
Tel: 01476 65371

Goldings,
The Grantham Auction
Rooms, Old Wharf Road,
Grantham NG31 7AA
Tel: 01476 65118

Richardsons,
Bourne Auction Rooms,
Spalding Road,
Bourne PE10 9LE
Tel: 01778 422686

Henry Spencer & Sons
(Phillips),
42 Silver Street,
Lincoln LN2 1TA
Tel: 01522 536666

Marilyn Swain Auctions,
The Old Barracks,
Sandon Road,
Grantham NG31 9AS
Tel: 01476 568861

John Taylor,
Cornmarket Chambers,
Louth LN11 9PY
Tel: 01507 603648

Walter's,
No 1 Mint Lane,
Lincoln LN1 1UD
Tel: 01522 525454

Merseyside

Cato Crane & Co,
Liverpool Auction Rooms,
6 Stanhope Street,
Liverpool L8 5RF
Tel: 0151 709 5559

Hartley & Co,
12 & 14 Moss Street,
Liverpool L6 1HF
Tel: 0151 263 6472/1865

Kingsley & Co,
3-5 The Quadrant,
Hoylake,
Wirral L47 2EE
Tel: 0151 632 5821

Outhwaite & Litherland,
Kingsway Galleries,
Fontenoy Street,
Liverpool
L3 2BE
Tel: 0151 236 6561

Worralls,
13-15 Seel Street,
Liverpool
L1 4AU
Tel: 0151 709 2950

Norfolk

Ewings,
Market Place,
Reepham,
Norwich
NR10 4JJ
Tel: 01603 870473

Thomas W M Gaze & Son,
Diss Auction Rooms,
Roydon Road,
Diss IP22 3LN
Tel: 01379 650306

Nigel F Hedge,
28B Market Place,
North Walsham
NR28 9BS
Tel: 01692 402881

G A Key,
Aylsham Salerooms,
8 Market Place,
Aylsham NR11 6EH
Tel: 01263 733195

Northamptonshire

Corby & Co,
30-32 Brook Street,
Raunds NN9 6LR
Tel: 01933 623722

Lowery's,
24 Bridge Street,
Northampton NN1 1NT
Tel: 01604 21561

Merry's Auctioneers,
The Old Corn Exchange,
Cattle Market,
14 Bridge Street,
Northampton NN1 1NJ
Tel: 01604 32266

Nationwide Surveyors,
28 High Street,
Daventry NN11 4HU
Tel: 01327 312022

Southam & Sons,
Corn Exchange,
Thrapston,
Kettering NN14 4JJ
Tel: 01832 734486

H Wilford Ltd,
Midland Road,
Wellingborough NN8 1NB
Tel: 01933 222760

Northumberland

Louis Johnson Auctioneers,
63 Bridge Street,
Morpeth NE61 1PQ
Tel: 01670 513025

Nottinghamshire

Arthur Johnson & Sons Ltd,
The Nottingham Auction
Rooms, The Cattle Market,
Meadow Lane,
Nottingham NG2 3GY
Tel: 0115 986 9128

Neales,
192-194 Mansfield Road,
Nottingham NG1 3HU
Tel: 0115 962 4141

John Pye & Sons,
Corn Exchange,
Cattle Market,
London Road,
Nottingham NG2 3GY
Tel: 0115 986 6261

C B Sheppard & Son,
The Auction Galleries,
Chatsworth Street,
Sutton-in-Ashfield
NG17 4GG
Tel: 01773 872419

Henry Spencer and Sons
(Phillips),
20 The Square,
Retford DN22 6BX
Tel: 01777 708633

T Vennett-Smith,
11 Nottingham Road,
Gotham NG11 0HE
Tel: 0115 983 0541

Oxfordshire

Dreweatt Neate Holloways,
49 Parsons Street,
Banbury OX16 8PF
Tel: 01295 253197

Green & Co,
33 Market Place,
Wantage OX12 8AH
Tel: 01235 763561/2

Mallams,
24 St Michael's Street,
Oxford OX1 2EB
Tel: 01865 241358

Oxfordshire County
Auctions,
Pinnocks Farm Estates
Northmoor OX8 1AY
Tel: 01865 300626

Phillips,
39 Park End Street,
Oxford OX1 1JD
Tel: 01865 723524

Simmons & Sons,
32 Bell Street,
Henley-on-Thames
RG9 2BH
Tel: 01491 571111

Shropshire

Halls Fine Art Auctions,
Welsh Bridge,
Shrewsbury SY3 8LA
Tel: 01743 231212

Livestock & Auction Centre,
Tasley,
Bridgnorth WV16 4QR
Tel: 01746 762666

Ludlow Antique
Auctions Ltd,
29 Corve Street,
Ludlow SY8 1DA
Tel: 01584 875157

McCartneys,
Ox Pasture, Overture Road,
Ludlow SY8 4AA
Tel: 01584 872251

Timothy Mear & Co,
Temeside Salerooms,
Ludford Bridge,
Ludlow SY8 1PE
Tel: 01584 876081

Perry & Phillips,
Newmarket Salerooms,
Newmarket Buildings,
Listley Street,
Bridgnorth WV16 4AW
Tel: 01746 762248

Somerset

Black Horse Agencies,
Alder King,
25 Market Place,
Wells BA5 2RG
Tel: 01749 673002

Cooper & Tanner,
Frome Auction Rooms,
Frome Market,
Standerwick,
Nr Frome BA11 2PY
Tel: 01373 831010

Dores & Rees,
The Auction Mart,
Vicarage Street,
Frome BA11 1PU
Tel: 01373 462257

John Fleming,
4 & 8 Fore Street,
Dulverton TA22 9EX
Tel: 01398 323597

Gribble Booth & Taylor,
13 The Parade,
Minehead TA24 5NL
Tel: 01643 702281

Lawrence Fine Art
Auctioneers, South Street,
Crewkerne TA18 8AB
Tel: 01460 73041

Richards,
The Town Hall,
The Square,
Axbridge BS26 2AR
Tel: 01934 732969

Wellington Salerooms,
Mantle Street,
Wellington TA21 8AR
Tel: 01823 664815

Wells Auction Rooms,
66/68 Southover,
Wells BA5 1UH
Tel: 01749 678094

Staffordshire

Bagshaws,
17 High Street,
Uttoxeter ST14 7HP
Tel: 01889 562811

Hall & Lloyd,
South Street Auction Rooms,
Stafford ST16 2DZ
Tel: 01785 258176

Louis Taylor Auctioneers
& Valuers,
Britannia House,
10 Town Road, Hanley,
Stoke on Trent ST1 2QG
Tel: 01782 214111

Wintertons Ltd,
Lichfield Auction Centre,
Wood End Lane,
Fradley,
Lichfield WS13 8NF
Tel: 01543 263256

Suffolk

Abbotts Auction Rooms,
Campsea Ashe,
Woodbridge IP13 0PS
Tel: 01728 746323

Boardman Fine Art
Auctioneers,
Station Road Corner,
Haverhill CB9 0EY
Tel: 01440 730414

William H Brown,
Ashford House,
Saxmundham IP17 1AB
Tel: 01728 603232

Diamond Mills & Co,
117 Hamilton Road,
Felixstowe IP11 7BL
Tel: 01394 282281

Lacy Scott,
Fine Art Department,
The Auction Centre,
10 Risbygate Street,
Bury St Edmunds IP33 3AA
Tel: 01284 763531

Neal Sons & Fletcher,
26 Church Street,
Woodbridge IP12 1DP
Tel: 01394 382263

Olivers,
Olivers Rooms,
Burkitts Lane,
Sudbury CO10 6HB
Tel: 01787 880305

Phillips,
Dover House, Wolsey Street,
Ipswich IP1 1UD
Tel: 01473 255137

Suffolk Sales,
Half Moon House,
High Street,
Clare CO10 8NY
Tel: 01787 277993

Surrey

Barbers Ltd,
Mayford Centre
Smarts Heath Road,
Woking GU22 0PP
Tel: 01483 728939

Chancellors,
74 London Road,
Kingston-upon-Thames
KT2 6PX
Tel: 0181 541 4139

Clarke & Gammon,
The Guildford Auction
Rooms, Bedford Road,
Guildford GU1 4SJ
Tel: 01483 566458

Crows Auction Gallery,
Rear of Dorking Halls,
Reigate Road,
Dorking RH4 1SG
Tel: 01306 740382

Ewbank Auctioneers,
Burnt Common Auction
Rooms, London Road,
Send, Woking GU23 7LN
Tel: 01483 223101

Hamptons Antique & Fine
Art Auctioneers,
93 High Street,
Godalming GU7 1AL
Tel: 01483 423567

Lawrences Auctioneers,
Norfolk House,
80 High Street,
Bletchingley RH1 4PA
Tel: 01883 743323

John Nicholson,
The Auction Rooms,
Longfield,
Midhurst Road,
Fernhurst GU27 3HA
Tel: 01428 653727

Parkins,
18 Malden Road,
Cheam SM3 8SD
Tel: 0181 644 6633 & 6127

Phillips Fine Art
Auctioneers,
Millmead,
Guildford GU2 5BE
Tel: 01483 504030

Richmond & Surrey
Auctions,
Richmond Station,
Kew Road,
Old Railway Parcels Depot
Richmond TW9 2NA
Tel: 0181 948 6677

Wentworth Auction
Galleries,
21 Station Approach,
Virginia Water
GU25 4DW
Tel: 01344 843711

P F Windibank,
Auction Hall, Rear of The
Dorking Hall,
Reigate Road,
Dorking RH4 1SG
Tel: 01306 884556/876280

Sussex

Ascent Auction Galleries,
11-12 East Ascent,
St Leonards-on-Sea
TN38 0DS
Tel: 01424 420275

John Bellman Auctioneers,
New Pound Business Park,
Wisborough Green,
Billingshurst RH14 0AY
Tel: 01403 700858

Burstow & Hewett,
Abbey Auction Galleries and
Granary Salerooms,
Lower Lake,
Battle TN33 0AT
Tel: 01424 772374

Peter Cheney,
Western Road Auction
Rooms, Western Road,
Littlehampton
BN17 5NP
Tel: 01903 722264/713418

Clifford Dann Auction
Galleries,
20-21 High Street,
Lewes BN7 2LN
Tel: 01273 480111

Denham's
Horsham Auction Galleries,
Warnham,
Horsham RH12 3RZ
Tel: 01403 255699/253837

Eastbourne Auction Rooms,
182-184 Seaside,
Eastbourne
BN22 7QR
Tel: 01323 431444

R H Ellis & Sons,
44-46 High Street,
Worthing BN11 1LL
Tel: 01903 238999

Gorringes Auction Galleries,
Terminus Road,
Bexhill-on-Sea
TN30 3LR
Tel: 01424 212994

Gorringes Auction Galleries,
15 North Street,
Lewes BN7 2PD
Tel: 01273 472503

Graves, Son & Pilcher,
Hove Auction Rooms
Hove Street,
Hove BN3 2GL
Tel: 01273 735266

Edgar Horn,
Fine Art Auctioneers,
46-50 South Street,
Eastbourne
BN21 4XB
Tel: 01323 410419

Raymond P Inman,
The Auction Galleries,
35 & 40 Temple Street,
Brighton BN1 3BH
Tel: 01273 774777

Lewes Auction Rooms
(Julian Dawson),
56 High Street,
Lewes BN7 1XE
Tel: 01273 478221

Nationwide,
Midhurst Auction Rooms,
West Street,
Midhurst
GU29 9NG
Tel: 01730 812456

Phillips Fine Art
Auctioneers,
Baffins Hall,
Baffins Lane,
Chichester PO19 1UA
Tel: 01243 78754

Rye Auction Galleries,
Rock Channel,
Rye TN31 7HL
Tel: 01797 222124

Sotheby's Sussex,
Summers Place,
Billingshurst RH14 9AD
Tel: 01403 783933

Stride & Son,
Southdown House,
St John's Street,
Chichester PO19 1XQ
Tel: 01243 780207

Sussex Auction Galleries,
59 Perrymount Road,
Haywards Heath
RH16 3DR
Tel: 01444 414935

Rupert Toovey
Auctioneers,
Star Road,
Partridge Green
RH13 8RJ
Tel: 01403 711744

Wallis & Wallis,
West Street
Auction Galleries,
Lewes BN7 2NJ
Tel: 01273 480208

Watsons,
Heathfield Furniture
Salerooms, The Market,
Burwash Road,
Heathfield TN21 8RA
Tel: 01435 862132

Worthing Auction
Galleries Ltd,
31 Chatsworth Road,
Worthing BN11 1LY
Tel: 01903 205565

Tyne & Wear

Anderson & Garland
(Auctioneers),
Marlborough House,
Marlborough Crescent,
Newcastle-upon-Tyne
NE1 4EE
Tel: 0191 232 6278

Boldon Auction Galleries,
24a Front Street,
East Boldon NE36 0SJ
Tel: 0191 537 2630

Thomas N Miller,
18-22 Gallowgate,
Newcastle-upon-Tyne
NE1 4SN
Tel: 0191 232 5617

Phillips North East,
St Mary's, Oakwellgate
Gateshead NE8 2AX
Tel: 0191 477 6688

Sneddons,
Sunderland Auction Rooms,
30 Villiers Street,
Sunderland SR1 1EJ
Tel: 0191 514 5931

Warwickshire

Bigwood Auctioneers Ltd,
The Old School, Tiddington,
Stratford-upon-Avon
CV37 7AW
Tel: 01789 269415

Locke & England,
Black Horse Agencies,
18 Guy Street,
Leamington Spa CV32 4RT
Tel: 01926 889100

West Midlands

Biddle and Webb Ltd,
Ladywood Middleway,
Birmingham B16 0PP
Tel: 0121 455 8042

Cariss Residential,
20 High Street,
Kings Heath,
Birmingham B14 7JU
Tel: 0121 444 0088

Ronald E Clare,
Clare's Auction Rooms,
70 Park Street,
Birmingham B5 5HZ
Tel: 0121 643 0226

Frank H Fellows & Sons,
Augusta House,
19 Augusta Street,
Hockley,
Birmingham B18 6JA
Tel: 0121 212 2131

Giles Haywood,
The Auction House,
St John's Road,
Stourbridge DY8 1EW
Tel: 01384 370891

James & Lister Lea,
1741 Warwick Road,
Knowle,
Birmingham B93 0LX
Tel: 01564 779187

Phillips,
The Old House,
Station Road,
Knowle,
Solihull B93 0HT
Tel: 01564 776151

K Stuart Swash FSVA,
Stamford House,
2 Waterloo Road,
Wolverhampton WV1 4DJ
Tel: 01902 710626

Walker, Barnett & Hill,
Waterloo Road Salerooms,
Clarence Street,
Wolverhampton WV1 4JE
Tel: 01902 773531

Weller & Dufty Ltd,
141 Bromsgrove Street,
Birmingham B5 6RQ
Tel: 0121 692 1414

Wiltshire

Henry Aldridge & Son,
Devizes Auction Rooms,
1 Wine Street,
Devizes SN10 1AP
Tel: 01380 729199

Hamptons,
20 High Street,
Marlborough SN8 1AA
Tel: 01672 516161

Kidson Trigg,
Friars Farm,
Sevenhampton,
Highworth,
Swindon SN6 7PZ
Tel: 01793 861000/861072

Swindon Auction Rooms,
The Planks (off The Square),
Old Town,
Swindon SN3 1QP
Tel: 01793 615915

Dominic Winter
Book Auctions,
The Old School,
Maxwell Street,
Swindon SN1 5DR
Tel: 01793 611340

Woolley & Wallis,
Salisbury Salerooms,
51-61 Castle Street,
Salisbury SP1 3SU
Tel: 01722 411422

Yorkshire

Audsley's Auctions
(C R Kemp BSc),
11 Morris Lane,
Kirkstall,
Leeds 5 LS5 3JT
Tel: 0113 275 8787

Bairstow Eves,
West End Saleroom,
The Paddock,
Whitby YO21 3AX
Tel: 01947 603433

Boulton & Cooper,
St Michaels House,
Market Place,
Malton YO17 0LR
Tel: 01653 696151

H C Chapman & Son,
The Auction Mart,
North Street,
Scarborough YO11 1DL
Tel: 01723 372424

Cundalls,
15 Market Place,
Malton YO17 0LP
Tel: 01653 697820

M W Darwin & Sons,
The Dales Furniture Hall,
Bedale DL8 2AH
Tel: 01677 422846

De Rome,
12 New John Street,
Westgate,
Bradford BD1 2QY
Tel: 01274 734116

Dee, Atkinson & Harrison,
The Exchange Saleroom,
Driffield YO25 7LJ
Tel: 01377 253151

Eadon Lockwood & Riddle,
411 Petre Street,
Sheffield S4 8LL
Tel: 0114 261 8000

Eddisons,
Auction Rooms,
4-6 High Street,
Huddersfield HD1 2LS
Tel: 01484 533151

Andrew Hartley,
Victoria Salerooms,
Little Lane,
Ilkley LS29 8EA
Tel: 01943 816363

Hutchinson Scott,
The Grange,
Marton-Le-Moor,
Ripon HG4 5AT
Tel: 01423 324264

Lithgow Sons & Partners,
The Antique House,
Station Road, Stokesley,
Middlesbrough TS9 7AB
Tel: 01642 710158/710326

Malcolms No1 Auctioneers
& Valuers,
The Chestnuts,
16 Park Avenue,
Sherburn-in-Elmet,
Nr Leeds LS25 6EF
Tel: 01977 684971

Christopher Matthews,
23 Mount Street,
Harrogate HG2 8DQ
Tel: 01423 871756

Morphets of Harrogate,
4-6 Albert Street,
Harrogate HG1 1JL
Tel: 01423 502282

Nationwide Fine Arts
& Furniture,
27 Flowergate,
Whitby YO21 3BB
Tel: 01947 603433

Phillips,
1 Princes Square,
Harrogate HG1 1ND
Tel: 01423 500566

Phillips Leeds,
17a East Parade,
Leeds LS1 2BH
Tel: 0113 2448011

John H Raby & Son,
The Sale Rooms,
21 St Mary's Road,
Bradford
8 BD8 7QL
Tel: 01274 491121

Henry Spencer & Sons Ltd
(Phillips),
1 St James' Row,
Sheffield S1 1WZ
Tel: 0114 272 8728

Geoffrey Summersgill ASVA,
8 Front Street,
Acomb,
York YO2 3BZ
Tel: 01904 791131

Marilyn Swain,
Stanilands Auction Room,
28 Nether Hall Road,
Doncaster
NG31 9AS
Tel: 01302 367766

Tennants,
The Auction Centre,
Harmby Road,
Leyburn DL8 5SG
Tel: 01969 623780

Tennants,
34 Montpellier Parade,
Harrogate
HG1 2TG
Tel: 01423 531661

Thompson's Auctioneers,
Dales Saleroom,
The Dale Hall,
Hampsthwaite,
Harrogate
HG3 2EG
Tel: 01423 770741

Ward Price,
Royal Auction Rooms,
Queen Street,
Scarborough
YO11 1HA
Tel: 01723 353581

Wilby's,
6a Eastgate,
Barnsley S70 2EP
Tel: 01226 299221

Wilkinson & Beighton
Auctioneers,
Woodhouse Green,
Thurcroft,
Rotherham SY3 8LA
Tel: 01709 700005

Windle & Co,
The Four Ashes,
541 Great Horton Road,
Bradford BD7 4EG
Tel: 01274 57299

Isle of Wight

Phillips Fine Art
Auctioneers,
Cross Street Salerooms,
Newport PO19 1UA
Tel: 01983 822031

Watson Bull & Porter,
Isle of Wight Auction Rooms,
79 Regent Street,
Shanklin PO37 7AP
Tel: 01983 863441

Ways Auction House,
Garfield Road,
Ryde PO33 2PT
Tel: 01983 562255

Northern Ireland

Morgans Auctions Ltd,
Duncrue Crescent,
Duncrue Road,
Belfast BT3 9BW
Tel: 01232 771552

Temple Auctions Limited,
133 Carryduff Road,
Temple, Lisburn,
Co. Antrim BT27 6YL
Tel: 01846 638777

Scotland

Lindsay Burns & Co Ltd,
6 King Street,
Perth PH2 8JA
Tel: 01738 633888

Christie's Scotland Ltd,
164-166 Bath Street,
Glasgow G2 4TG
Tel: 0141 332 8134

Frasers Auctioneers,
8A Harbour Road,
Inverness
IV1 1SY
Tel: 01463 232395

William Hardie Ltd,
15a Blythswood Square,
Glasgow G2 4EW
Tel: 0141 221 6780

J & J Howe,
24 Commercial Street,
Alyth,
Perthshire
PH12 8UA
Tel: 01828 632594

Loves Auction Rooms,
The Auction Galleries,
52-54 Canal Street,
Perth PH2 8LF
Tel: 01738 633337

Robert McTear & Co,
(Auctioneers & Valuers) Ltd,
Clydeway Business Centre,
8 Elliot Place,
Glasgow G3 8EP
Tel: 0141 221 4456

M.D.'s Auction Co,
Unit 15-17 Smeaton
Industrial Estate
Hayfield Road,
Kirkcaldy,
Fife KY1 2HE
Tel: 01592 640969

John Milne,
9 North Silver Street,
Aberdeen
AB1 1RJ
Tel: 01224 639336

Robert Paterson & Son,
8 Orchard Street,
Paisley,
Renfrewshire
PA1 1UZ
Tel: 0141 889 2435

Phillips Scotland,
65 George Street,
Edinburgh EH2 2JL
Tel: 0131 225 2266

Phillips Scotland,
207 Bath Street,
Glasgow G2 4HD
Tel: 0141 221 8377

L S Smellie & Sons Ltd,
Within the Furniture
Market, Lower
Auchingramont Road,
Hamilton ML10 6BE
Tel: 01698 282007

Sotheby's,
112 George Street,
Edinburgh EH2 4LH
Tel: 0131 226 7201

Thomson, Roddick & Laurie,
20 Murray Street,
Annan DG12 6EG
Tel: 01461 202575

West Perthshire Auctions,
Dundas Street,
Comrie,
Perthshire
PH6 2LN
Tel: 01764 670613

Wales

Dodds Property World,
Victoria Auction Galleries,
9 Chester Street,
Mold,
Clwyd CH7 1EB
Tel: 01352 752552

E H Evans & Co,
Auction Sales Centre,
The Market Place,
Kilgetty,
Dyfed SA68 0UG
Tel: 01834 812793 & 811151

Peter Francis,
The Curiosity Saleroom,
19 King Street,
Carmarthen,
Dyfed SA31 1BH
Tel: 01267 233456

Morgan Evans & Co Ltd,
28-30 Church Street,
Llangefni,
Anglesey,
Gwynedd
LL77 7DU
Tel: 01248 723303/421582

Morris Marshall & Poole,
10 Broad Street,
Newtown,
Powys SY16 2LZ
Tel: 01686 625900

Phillips in Wales
Fine Art Auctioneers,
9-10 Westgate Street,
Cardiff,
Glamorgan CF1 1DA
Tel: 01222 396453

Players Auction Mart,
Players Industrial Estate,
Clydach,
Swansea SA6 5BQ
Tel: 01792 846241

Rennies,
87 Monnow Street,
Monmouth NP5 3EW
Tel: 01600 712916

Rogers Jones & Co,
33 Abergele Road,
Colwyn Bay,
Clwyd LL29 7RU
Tel: 01492 532176

Wingett's Auction Gallery,
29 Holt Street, Wrexham,
Clwyd LL13 8DH
Tel: 01978 353553

Channel Islands

Hamptons, Martel,
Maides Ltd,
The Old Bank,
29 High Street,
St Peter Port,
Guernsey GY1 4NY
Tel: 01481 713463

Langlois,
Westaway Chambers,
Don Street,
St Helier JE2 4TR
Tel: 01534 22441

Eire

James Adam & Sons,
26 St Stephen's Green,
Dublin 2
Tel: 00 3531 676 0261/661
3655

Christie's Dublin,
52 Waterloo Road,
Dublin 4
Tel: 00 3531 668 0585

Mealy's,
Chatsworth Street,
Castle Comer,
Co Kilkenny
Tel: 00 3535 641229

Germany

Sotheby's Berlin,
Palais amFestungsgraben,
Unter den Linden,
Neue Wache D–10117
Tel: 49 (30) 394 3060

Italy

Christie's Rome,
Palazzo Massimo,
Lancellotti,
Piazza Navona 114,
Rome 00186
Tel: 00 396 687 2787

Sotheby's Rome,
Piazza d'Espana 90,
Rome 00186
Tel: 396 6841791/6781798

Monaco

Sotheby's Monaco
BP 45-98001
Tel: 93 30 8880

Christie's (Monaco),
S.A.M., Park Palace,
98000
Tel: 00 339 325 1933

Netherlands

Sotheby's Amsterdam,
Rokin 102,
Amsterdam 1012 KZ
Tel: 31 (20) 627 5656

Switzerland

Christie's (International)
S.A.,
8 Place de la Taconnerie,
1204 Geneva
Tel: 00 41 22 311 1766

Sotheby's,
13 Quai du Mont Blanc,
Geneva CH-1201
Tel: 00 41 22 732 8585

Canada

D & J Ritchie Inc,
Auctioneers & Appraisers of
Antiques & Fine Arts,
288 King Street East,
Toronto
M5A 1K4
Tel: 001 416 364 1864

Waddingtons,
189 Queen Street East,
Toronto,
Ontario
M5A 1SZ
Tel: 001 416 362 1678

Hong Kong

Christie's Hong Kong,
2804-6 Alexandra House,
16-20 Chater Road,
Tel: 00 852 2521 5396

Sotheby's,
502-503 Exchange Square
Two, 8 Connaught
Place Central,
Hong Kong
Tel: 852 524 8121

Singapore

Bonhams Singapore,
319A Orchard Road,
Ngee Ann City Tower A
238873
Tel: (65) 3388925

Christie's,
501 Orchard Road,
15-02 Lane
Crawford Place 0923
Tel: (65) 737 3884

U.S.A.

Frank H Boos Gallery,
420 Enterprise Court,
Bloomfield Hills
Michigan
48302

Butterfield & Butterfield,
220 San Bruno Avenue,
San Francisco
CA 94103
Tel: 415 861 7500

Christie, Manson & Woods
International Inc,
502 Park Avenue, (including
Christie's East),
New York
NY 10022
Tel: 001 212 546 1000

Christie's East,
219 East 67th Street,
New York NY10021
Tel: 001 212 546 1184

William Doyle Galleries,
175 East 87th Street,
New York NY 10128
Tel: 001 212 427 2730

Du Mouchelle Art Gallery,
409 East Jefferson Avenue,
Detroit MI 48226
Tel: 001 313 963 6255

Dunning's,
755 Church Road,
Elgin IL 60123
Tel: 001 708 741 3483

Eldred's,
Robert C Eldred Co Inc,
1475 Route 6A,
East Dennis,
Massachusetts
0796 02641
Tel: 001 508 385 3116

Freeman Fine Art Of
Philadelphia Inc,
1808 Chestnut Street
Philadelphia
PA 19103
Tel: 001 215 563 9275

Morton M Goldberg,
547 Baronne Street,
New Orleans
LA 70113
Tel: 001 504 592 2300

Grogan & Co,
890 Commonwealth Avenue,
Boston MA 2215
Tel: 001 617 566 4100

Hanzel Galleries,
1120 S Michigan Avenue,
Chicago
IL 60605
Tel: 001 312 922 6234

Gene Harris Antiques,
203 S 18th Avenue,
Marshalltown IA 50158
Tel: 001 515 752 0600

Hart Galleries,
2301 South Voss Road,
Houston TX 77057
Tel: 001 713 266 3500

Lesley Hindman
Auctioneers,
215 West Ohio Street,
Chicago,
Illinois
IL 60610
Tel: 001 312 670 0010

Louisiana Auction
Exchange,
2031 Government Street,
Baton Rouge LA 70806
Tel: 001 504 387 9777

Lubin Galleries,
30 West 26th Street,
New York NY10010
Tel: 001 212 929 0909

John Moran Auctioneers,
3202 E Foothill Boulevard,
Pasadena CA 91107
Tel: 001 818 793 1833

Mystic Fine Arts,
47 Holmes Street,
Mystic CT6355
Tel: 001 203 572 8873

Neal Auction Co,
4038 Magazine Street,
New Orleans LA 70115
Tel: 001 504 899 5329

Northeast Auctions,
694 Lafayette Road,
Hampton NH 3842
Tel: 001 603 926 9800

Selkirk's,
4166 Olive Street,
St Louis MO 63108
Tel: 001 314 533 1700

Skinner Inc,
357 Main Street,
Bolton MA 01740
Tel: 001 508 779 6241

Skinner Inc,
The Heritage on the Garden,
63 Park Plaza,
Boston MA 02116
Tel: 001 617 350 5400

Sloan's,
4920 Wyaconda Road, North
Bethesda MD 20852
Tel: 001 301 468 4911

Sotheby's,
1334 York Avenue,
New York NY 10021
Tel: 001 212 606 7000

Don Treadway Gallery,
2128 Madison Road,
Cincinnati OH 45208
Tel: 001 513 321 6742

Adam A Weschler & Son,
909 E Street NW,
Washington DC 20004
Tel: 001 202 628 1281

Wolfs Gallery,
1239 W 6th Street,
Cleveland OH 44113
Tel: 216 575 9653

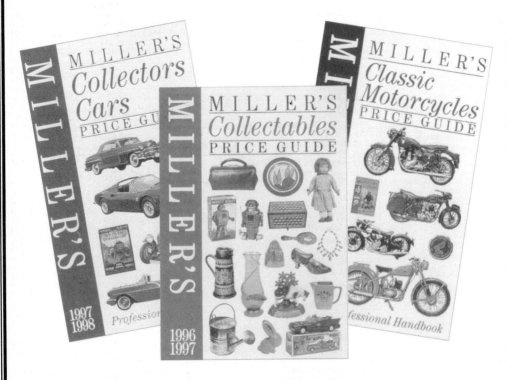

INDEX TO DISPLAY ADVERTISEMENTS

INDEX

Italic page numbers denote colour pages; **bold** numbers refer to information and pointer boxes